The Future of Dark Tourism

THE FUTURE OF TOURISM

Some would say that the only certainties are birth and death; everything else that happens in between is uncertain. Uncertainty stems from risk, a lack of understanding or a lack of familiarity. Whether it is political instability, autonomous transport, hypersonic travel or peak oil, the future of tourism is full of uncertainty but it can be explained or imagined through trend analysis, economic forecasting or scenario planning.

The Future of Tourism sets out to address the challenges and unexplained futures of tourism, events and hospitality. By addressing the big questions of change, examining new theories and frameworks or critical issues pertaining to research or industry, the series will stretch your understanding and generate dialogue about the future. By adopting a multidisciplinary perspective, be it through science fiction or computer-generated equilibrium modelling of tourism economies, the series will explain and structure the future – to help researchers, managers and students understand how futures could occur. The series welcomes proposals on emerging trends and critical issues across the tourism industry and research. All proposals must emphasise the future and be embedded in research.

All books in this series are externally peer reviewed.

Full details of all the books in this series and of all our other publications can be found on http://www.channelviewpublications.com, or by writing to Channel View Publications, St Nicholas House, 31-34 High Street, Bristol, BS1 2AW, UK.

THE FUTURE OF TOURISM: 8

The Future of Dark Tourism

Enlightening New Horizons

Edited by
Philip R. Stone and Daniel W.M. Wright

CHANNEL VIEW PUBLICATIONS
Bristol • Jackson

DOI https://doi.org/10.21832/STONE8984
Library of Congress Cataloging in Publication Data
A catalog record for this book is available from the Library of Congress.
Names: Stone, Philip R., editor. | Wright, Daniel W. M., editor.
Title: The Future of Dark Tourism: Enlightening New Horizons/Edited by Philip R. Stone, Daniel W.M. Wright.
Description: Bristol, UK; Jackson, TN: Channel View Publications, 2024. | Series: The Future of Tourism: 8 | Includes bibliographical references and index. | Summary: 'This book offers critical scenarios of dark tourism futures and how our significant dead will be remembered in future visitor economies. It outlines key features of difficult heritage and future cultural trauma and highlights the role of technology, immersive visitor experiences and the thanatological condition of future dark tourism' – Provided by publisher.
Identifiers: LCCN 2024010208 (print) | LCCN 2024010209 (ebook) | ISBN 9781845418984 (hardback) | ISBN 9781845418977 (paperback) | ISBN 9781845419004 (epub) | ISBN 9781845418991 (pdf)
Subjects: LCSH: Dark tourism.
Classification: LCC G156.5.D37 F87 2024 (print) | LCC G156.5.D37 (ebook) | DDC 338.4/791 – dc23/eng/20240402
LC record available at https://lccn.loc.gov/2024010208
LC ebook record available at https://lccn.loc.gov/2024010209

British Library Cataloguing in Publication Data
A catalogue entry for this book is available from the British Library.

ISBN-13: 978-1-84541-898-4 (hbk)
ISBN-13: 978-1-84541-897-7 (pbk)

Channel View Publications
UK: St Nicholas House, 31-34 High Street, Bristol, BS1 2AW, UK.
USA: Ingram, Jackson, TN, USA.

Website: https://www.channelviewpublications.com
X: Channel_View
Facebook: https://www.facebook.com/channelviewpublications
Blog: https://www.channelviewpublications.wordpress.com

The policy of Multilingual Matters/Channel View Publications is to use papers that are natural, renewable and recyclable products, made from wood grown in sustainable forests. In the manufacturing process of our books, and to further support our policy, preference is given to printers that have FSC and PEFC Chain of Custody certification. The FSC and/or PEFC logos will appear on those books where full certification has been granted to the printer concerned.

Typeset by Riverside Publishing Solutions.

This book is dedicated to:

Fredrick Stone (1943–2020)
Thank you for all your love and support Dad!

&

Alessia Wright
Born during its creation.
Nosce te ipsum
Love, Dad

Contents

Contributors ix

Preface: Dark Tourism Futures: Thoughts, Ideas, Scenarios
Philip R. Stone and Daniel W.M. Wright xvii

1 *Vertopia:* The Future of Dark Tourism Places and Our Digital Dead 1
Philip R. Stone

2 Virtual Afterlife: Dark Tourism in the Hereafter 27
Rachael Ironside and Craig Leith

3 From 'Bucket List' to 'Afterlist': (Dark) Tourism for the Afterlife 38
Santa Zascerinska

4 'Beyond Human': Dark Tourism, Robots and Futurology 50
Daniel W.M. Wright

5 The Future of Technology and Dark Tourism Experiences 61
Özge Kılıçarslan, Mehmet Yavuz Çetinkaya and Kamil Yağci

6 Bridging Virtual Reality and Dark Heritage 77
Diāna Popova, Elizabete Grinblate and Raivis Sīmansons

7 'Virtual Monument Wars': The Digital Future of Difficult Heritage 90
Richard Fawcus

8 Language as a Mediator: Commodifying Future Dark Tourism 103
Marián Alesón-Carbonell

9 'McDeath' – A Future of Dark Travel and End of Life Palliative Care 115
Saffron Dale, Crispin Dale and Neil Robinson

10 Enlightening Dark Tourism Horizons in a Post-Apocalyptic Arctic: A Geopoetic Approach 129
Alix Varnajot

11 'Shrines and Rites of Passage': Toward a Future of Dark Tourism Chronicles 138
Maximiliano E. Korstanje

12 Survivor Voices and Disaster Education: Future Commemoration and Remembrance at Dark Tourism Sites 149
Elspeth Frew and Clare Lade

13 Future of Dark Tourism in Kosovo: From Divisions to Digital Possibilities 162
Abit Hoxha and Kenneth Andresen

14 Millennials, Transitional Memory and the Future of Holocaust Remembrance 176
Ann-Kathrin McLean

15 Between Revival of Memory and Dark Tourism: The Future of Holocaust-Related Sites in Latvia 187
Aija van der Steina, Maija Rozite, Inese Runce and Kaspars Strods

16 'Mirrors of Society': Cemetery Tourism Futures 198
Marta Soligo

17 'Not the Right Sort of Visitors': Future Challenges of Cemetery Tourism 211
Janine Marriott

18 'Into the horrors of the gloomy jail': Towards a Future of UK Prison Tourism and Penal Architecture 224
Allan Brodie

19 'Finding a Light in Dark Places': Lighter Dark Tourism Futures 243
Brianna Wyatt

20 Future of Dark Tourism Festivals: Technology and the Tourist Experience 255
Luisa Golz and Tony Johnston

21 Future Dystopian Attractions: Benign Masochism in Dark Tourism 265
Robert S. Bristow, Alina Gross and Ian Jenkins

22 Future Directions in Death Studies and Dark Tourism 276
Michael Brennan

Afterword: Back to the Dark Tourism Future 290
Philip R. Stone

References 295

Index 343

Contributors

Marián Alesón-Carbonell is a Lecturer at the Department of Filologia Inglesa (English Studies) at the University of Alicante, Spain. She is also the Director of the Permanent University (UPUA) at the University of Alicante, a centre for older-adult training and research. Marian's research focuses both on ESL/EFL (English as a Second or Foreign Language) and on Specialised Languages, particularly on written genres, the use of corpora and specialised terminology. She is currently reading for her PhD on the promotion of dark tourism in sites, museums and memorials relating to the World Wars.

Kenneth Andresen is Professor of Media Studies at the University of Agder in Norway. His research and publications over 25 years has been in the fields of international journalism and media development, especially in relation to historical conflicts in Europe. He has been involved in numerous international research projects in the fields of journalism, media, democracy and history. Currently, Kenneth is researching how historical postcards have been important tools of communication.

Michael Brennan is Professor of Sociology and Deputy Head of the School of Social Sciences at Liverpool Hope University, UK. He has published widely and lectured extensively on issues of death, dying, and bereavement, including in the USA, where he was Director of the Center for Death Education and Bioethics at the University of Wisconsin-La Crosse. His recent research explores the significance of terminally ill individuals who choose to share in writing or other media their personal experiences of dying.

Robert S. Bristow is Professor Emeritus at Westfield State University, Massachusetts, USA. He is credited with the term 'Fright Tourism' having published multiple journal articles, book chapters, and international conference presentations on the subject for 20 years. Besides 'Fright Tourism', Rob has authored papers on cultural resource management for parks and protected areas. His current research interests include sensory aspects of tourism, as well as his historical memoir on the Appalachian National Scenic Trail.

Allan Brodie is a Visiting Fellow at Bournemouth University, UK. Previous roles include Senior Architectural Investigator for English Heritage and Historic England, as well as the Royal Commission on the Historical Monuments of England. Allan has researched historical buildings including prisons, military defences, ecclesiastical and medieval architecture. Allan has published extensively on the British seaside, coastal resorts, and tourism history. He is a Fellow of the Society of Antiquaries of London and a Fellow of the Royal Historical Society.

Mehmet Yavuz Çetinkaya holds a Master's degree and PhD from Katip Çelebi University, İzmir, Turkey. He is currently working in the Department of Tourism Guidance, Faculty of Tourism, Pamukkale University, Turkey. He is a licensed tour guide in both English and Russian. His research interests include the tourist guide and tour guiding professions, religious tourism, gastronomy tourism, cultural heritage and its interpretation and qualitative research methods.

Crispin Dale is a Principal Lecturer in the Faculty of Arts at the University of Wolverhampton, UK. His research interests include the development of cultural heritage enterprises and historic attractions through innovation, ranging from dark tourism attractions, religious sites, to music halls. Crispin is also interested in the pedagogy of technology in teaching and learning, with a focus on promoting professional practice in the arts.

Saffron Dale is a philosophy graduate of Durham University, UK, and has recently completed postgraduate studies at the University of Oxford, UK, specialising in the philosophy of death and trauma. She has research interests in the glorification and hyperreality of death in film and television. Saffron is currently teaching in Southeast Asia.

Richard Fawcus is a British researcher based in Bulgaria, with an interest in socialist heritage, monuments, and memory. His PhD thesis (defended in 2022, with the University of Central Lancashire, UK) explored the past, present, and potential futures of the Buzludzha Memorial House, an abandoned site of 'difficult' socialist heritage in Bulgaria. Richard's current research focuses on monuments and difficult heritage, as well as themes of pluralism, digital memorialisation and playable histories.

Elspeth Frew is an Associate Professor in Tourism and Event Management at La Trobe University, Victoria, Australia. Dr Frew has 30 years of experience as an academic in tourism and event management. Dr Frew has demonstrated leadership in her roles as Director of Teaching and Learning and Programme Director. Her research interests focus on cultural tourism, with a particular focus on dark tourism, industrial tourism, festivals and event and attraction management.

Luisa Golz is a PhD candidate at Technological University of the Shannon in Athlone, Ireland. While Luisa originally comes from Germany, she completed her BA in Tourism Marketing at Waterford Institute of Technology in 2015 and has since worked in the Irish tourism industry. In 2019, she set up Desmond Tours, a private tour company that showcases the very best Ireland has to offer. Her current PhD research focuses on niche festivals, dark tourism, experiential marketing and co-creation.

Elizabete Grinblate holds a Bachelor's degree in social and cultural anthropology and a master's degree in Baltic Sea Region Studies. Her academic background is characterised by a keen interest in digital anthropology, the online and offline dichotomy and virtual reality. This has led her to adopt interdisciplinary approaches and methods to better understand and explore various worldly phenomena, including the digitalisation of difficult heritage. She is a recipient of the prestigious Mundheim Family Excellence Scholarship.

Alina Gross is an Assistant Professor at Westfield State University, Massachusetts, USA. Alina is a regional planner by education and has explored areas of interest including urban development, housing, and planning with historically marginalised social groups in her research and teaching. Her recent research interests include cultural and social urban planning issues, and intersections between social justice and space.

Abit Hoxha is Assistant Professor at the Department of Nordic and Media Studies at the University of Agder, Norway. He currently leads ReMeD, an EU funded interdisciplinary research project that aims to improve relations between citizens, media and digital technologies through co-creation and innovation. Abit's research interests include comparative conflict news production, new roles for journalists, media and democracy, transitional journalism, troubled pasts and memorialisation of war.

Rachael Ironside is an Associate Professor at Robert Gordon University, UK. Her research explores relationships between the supernatural, heritage and culture, and how this impacts our experience and understanding of the world. Rachael has published widely on the role of social interaction and extraordinary experience, and the intersection between folklore, dark tourism and place. She is co-editor of *Folklore, People, and Places: International Perspectives on Tourism and Tradition in Storied Places* (Routledge, 2023).

Ian Jenkins is an Associate Professor at the University of Iceland. Ian is a geographer who has worked in the tourism sector as a researcher, senior lecturer, consultant and director of several research units. His interest in 'Fright Tourism' stems from his interest in risk assessment in tourism. His research interests include responsible/sustainable tourism, niche tourism development, risk and safety management and adventure tourism.

Tony Johnston is Director of Research Development, Faculty of Business and Hospitality, Technological University of the Shannon (TUS), Ireland. Prior to joining TUS, Tony was employed as a Senior Lecturer in Tourism (University of Derby 2013–2014), Lecturer in Development Geography (King's College, London 2011–2013) and Lecturer in Adventure Tourism Management (University of the Highlands and Islands, 2010–2011). His research interests are in tourism geographies, sustainable tourism, and thanatourism, with a focus on commodification of war.

Özge Kılıçarslan holds a Master's degree and a PhD from Akdeniz University, Turkey. She is currently working in the Department of Tourism Management, Faculty of Tourism, Pamukkale University, Turkey. She has contributed to the development of a mobile augmented reality application used in a cultural area and a mobile destination guide application. She has several published papers about technology enhanced tourism experiences, consumer behaviour and service quality in tourism journals and conferences.

Maximiliano E. Korstanje is a Reader at the Economics Faculty, University of Palermo, Argentina. He is a cultural theorist who has studied the mobilities theory, dark tourism, terrorism and political violence. His recent books include *Terrorism, Tourism and the End of Hospitality in the West* (Palgrave Macmillan), *The Rise of Thana Capitalism and Tourism* (Routledge), *Mobilities Paradox: A Critical Analysis* (Edward Elgar), *Populism and Postcolonialism* (Routledge) and *Terrorism, Technology and Apocalyptic Future* (Springer Nature).

Clare Lade is a Lecturer in Industry Placements in the Office of the Provost at La Trobe University, Australia. With over 20 years of experience in academic research and university teaching, her research interests include tourism futures and development, gastronomy and event management. She has presented her work at conferences within Australia and internationally, as well as having published work in textbooks, journal articles and book chapters.

Craig Leith is Principal Lecturer in tourism at Robert Gordon University, Scotland. He is an early career researcher and doctoral candidate whose research concerns the solo tourism experience in terms of solitude and social interaction. He has further research interests in tourism futures and has previously published in the *Journal of Tourism Futures*. Craig also leads a degree module exploring wider developments and trends impacting on the future of tourism, hospitality and events.

Janine Marriott is the Public Engagement Manager at Arnos Vale Cemetery in Bristol, UK. Her role involves encouraging visitors into the cemetery and providing opportunities for place engagement, including the historic landscape. Janine is also a PhD candidate in heritage studies at the University of Hertfordshire, UK. Her research interests include public engagement in historic cemeteries, future uses of cemeteries, interpreting challenging heritage spaces and cemeteries and dark tourism.

Ann-Kathrin McLean is an Associate Faculty member at Royal Roads University, Canada. She has been a Visiting Konrad Adenauer Fellow at the University of Victoria, exploring impacts of populism on European memory culture. She is co-president of the Young Researchers Network, emphasising interdisciplinary perspectives on European studies. Her research explores interrelationships between memory, Holocaust remembrance and sites of trauma. Specifically, she focuses on how millennials transfer a new form of memory, namely the *Zone of Transitional Memory*.

Diāna Popova is a PhD candidate at the Latvian Academy of Culture. Her thesis focuses on dark heritage in Latvia and its interpretation for young audiences. She currently works as a Research Assistant at the Institute of Philosophy and Sociology, University of Latvia. Her academic background is in cultural theory, cultural and social anthropology, Baltic Sea region studies, and communication science, allowing her to use interdisciplinary perspectives to research complex cultural phenomena.

Neil Robinson holds a Senior Lectureship in Marketing at Edge Hill University, UK. Neil's research interests include the contemporary nature of marketing and the business environment, with numerous publications centred on visitor economy and service sector marketing. His other research interests focus on impacts of terrorism on the service sector, musical legacy associated with place, Covid-19 impacts on society and leisure and dark tourism.

Maija Rozite is a Professor at the Turiba University, Latvia. Her research is focused on tourism geography, tourism planning, urban tourism and host–guest relationships within tourism. Maija is recognised as a tourism planning expert and provides expertise to local municipalities, as well as regional and national institutions. She currently works as a researcher within an interdisciplinary scientific team on tourism and difficult heritage at Holocaust sites in Latvia.

Inese Runce has a doctorate in history. She graduated from Fordham University and University of Latvia (Faculty of History and Philosophy). Now, she is a leading researcher at Institute of Philosophy and Sociology and lecturer in Baltic history, cultural and ethnic studies at the Faculty of Humanities/University of Latvia. Her research and expertise fields are the relations between the State and Church, history of the Church, regional, ethnic and religious studies and the history of Latvia and the Baltic States.

Raivis Sīmansons holds a PhD in museum studies from the University of Leicester, UK. He has worked in museum administration in Latvia and on the development of the House of European History in Brussels. In 2019, Raivis joined *Žanis Lipke Memorial* in Riga, Latvia, to work on its new civic education centre. He is an International Council of Museum (ICOM) member and co-founder of the Riga-based think tank Creative Museum.

Marta Soligo is the Director of Tourism Research at the University of Nevada, Las Vegas (UNLV) Office of Economic Development, USA. She is also a Visiting Assistant Professor at the UNLV William F. Harrah College of Hospitality, USA, and at the University of Bergamo, Italy. Marta's interests centre on tourism and social justice, and her sociological research focuses on a wide range of themes, including film induced tourism, dark tourism and gambling studies.

Philip R. Stone is Director of the Institute for Dark Tourism Research (iDTR) at the University of Central Lancashire, UK. He is an internationally recognised scholar in the field of 'dark tourism' and 'difficult heritage' and has published extensively about the subject. Philip is also a Media Consultant on dark tourism, with clients including the *BBC*, *CNN*, *The New York Times*, *The Guardian* and *The Washington Post*. Philip is founder and Editor of the *International Journal of Dark Tourism Studies*. His latest books include *111 Dark Tourism Places in England You Shouldn't Miss* (Emons, 2021) and *Children, Young People and Dark Tourism* (Routledge, 2023). His forthcoming books are *'The Dark Tourist': Difficult Heritage & Dark Tourism Experiences* (Emerald) and *111 Dark Tourism Places in Scotland You Shouldn't Miss* (Emons).

Kaspars Strods holds an MA in Archival Science and is currently a PhD candidate in History at Daugavpils University. He is a researcher at the Institute of Philosophy and Sociology at the University of Latvia. His research interests include recent history of Latvia and Latgale, oral history, and Holocaust memorial sites in Latgale. He is the author of numerous scientific publications about various historical topics, including the history of criminality in interwar Latvia, and World War II (including the Holocaust in Latvia).

Aija van der Steina is a Senior Researcher at the Institute of Philosophy and Sociology, University of Latvia, and an Associate Professor at Vidzeme University of Applied Sciences, Latvia. Her current research includes leading an interdisciplinary research project on dark tourism, focusing on Jewish heritage and Holocaust sites in Latvia. Aija's research and teaching interests include tourism impacts, destination management and marketing, host–guest relationships in tourism and difficult heritage.

Alix Varnajot is a Postdoctoral Researcher based at the Geography Research Unit at the University of Oulu, Finland. His research interests centre on environmental changes and human-environment relationships in the Arctic. Alix's current work focuses on the future of Arctic tourism in the Anthropocene, the impacts of climate change on Arctic societies and particularly on the tourism industry, as well as conceptual developments of dark tourism and 'last chance' tourism.

Daniel W.M. Wright is a Senior Lecturer at the University of Central Lancashire, UK. He has published widely about tourism futures. Daniel uses futurology as a transdisciplinary field of study to forecast, anticipate and provoke the future of tourism in global visitor economies. Daniel is a member of the Institute for Dark Tourism Research (iDTR), as well as an editorial board member for the *Journal of Tourism Futures*. He also teaches tourism futures at undergraduate and postgraduate level.

Brianna Wyatt is a Senior Lecturer and Postgraduate Subject Coordinator for the Hospitality, Tourism, and Events Management programmes at Oxford Brookes University, UK. Her primary research interests and industry experience revolve around heritage and dark tourism, with an emphasis in interpretation and experience design. She is also a consulting academic for (dark) heritage businesses within the Oxford Brookes University's Business & External Engagement team. Her most recent work pertained to collection management and exhibition development at the Buckingham Old Gaol, England.

Kamil Yağci is an Associate Professor at Pamukkale University, Turkey. He completed his MSc in the field of Total Quality Management and his PhD in Tourism Management, both at Dokuz Eylul University (Izmir, Turkey). His main research interests lie in the areas of Quality

Management, ICT in tourism, E-tourism, supply chain management practices in tourism, organisation theories, as well as information security practices and their application within the tourism sector.

Santa Zascerinska is a Lecturer at the University of Central Lancashire, UK. Her doctoral thesis is entitled 'Kicking the bucket or living life to the full? Socio-psychological motivations for compiling a bucket list' (2022). Santa is also a member of the Institute for Dark Tourism Research (iDTR). Her research is focused on 'Bucket Lists', thana-technologies, dark tourism and Terror Management Theory (TMT). Her recent publications include articles in the *Journal of Tourism Futures* and *Tourism Recreation Research*, where she examined motivations of 'Bucket Lists', issues of future wellness and medical tourism.

Preface: Dark Tourism Futures: Thoughts, Ideas, Scenarios

Philip R. Stone and Daniel W.M. Wright

The future is uncertain, but the end is always near
Jim Morrison

Toward Pluralistic Futures: Perils and Possibilities

Our future is dead. So, we shall commence at the end. Or near to the end as possible. In a time not too far away and in a place close by, this book offers you a journey to a future of your own making. Of course, beginning at the end is a search for new horizons where we can await our fate and manage our expectations. Yet, foresight need not prognosticate utopian or dystopian destinies, but a blend of predictions and visions that will make our reality. Futurity is what we create, rather than what we imagine. However, within 80 to 90 years or so, all the authors, editors and publishers of this book shall have passed. The legacy that we leave you as a reader of our book is a collection of our thoughts, ideas and assumptions of how future societies might recall their significant Other dead. In time, our far future will be your present and, as you reflect upon the scholarly stories in this book, become your past. Naturally, the question will always remain of how close our thoughts and ideas were to actuality; did our scenarios bear resemblance to reality; and did our foresight predict the pitfalls and prospects of the unknown? We can never define what the future is, nor can we offer parameters of when the future will occur. The future is not something we will individually enter, but something that we will collectively construct. To that end, there will not be one monolithic future for us all, but a range of alternative, plausible and pluralistic futures.

This book aims to inspire critical thinking in futures studies, with a specific focus on dark tourism. Adopting a futurology approach, we offer post-disciplinary insights into a future world of how and where our noteworthy dead are remembered, (re)created and retained. In doing so, three factors are inherent throughout this book. Firstly, we use futurology to examine trends that compose probable futures in the shape of 'scenarios'. Secondly, these case scenarios attempt to offer holistic, if not creative, perspectives based upon categories of Social, Technological, Economic, Environmental and Political (STEEP) disciplines. Finally, our approach challenges and unpacks assumptions behind dominant and contentious views of the future by examining the past. In this book, we embrace innovative ideas and new methodologies for modern times. Many academic accounts in this volume are provocative, even emotive, but all are rigorously conceptualised and contextualised. Some chapters imagine a visionary future, other chapters look to the past to invent futures; yet all chapters outline potential pitfalls and prospects of dark tourism production and consumption. This book will stimulate criticality in our futures thinking and, subsequently, dynamize our approach to foreordination. Our foresight perspective seeks to evaluate the suppositions underpinning such views. In turn, we forecast a future that is not only perilous but also one that is full of possibilities.

Book rationale

We are inexplicably drawn to visitor sites of pain and shame and to the tourist experience of other people's morbid demise. Indeed, *dark tourism* is travelling to places of death, disaster or the macabre, where we get a sense of our own mortality through the stories of people who came before us. The idea of tourists visiting places that portray tragic and displaced heritage is filled with many moral dilemmas. If difficult heritage is the production and curation of our tragic past, then dark tourism is the consumption and experience of such tragedies. It is here that meaning making is co-constructed between consumer and producer. Nonetheless, people have long been attracted to sites of fatality. In ancient times, for example, the killing during gladiatorial games was a leisure mainstay of the Roman Empire. During the medieval period up to the 19th century, public executions of criminals were spectator events and a valid excuse for people of yesteryear to leave home. And, in 19th century Europe, morgue tours to encounter corpses were a common travel itinerary.

However, dark tourism today (and tomorrow) is concerned with remembering (and forgetting) specific deaths, by whom, and how our significant and noteworthy dead are (re)presented in global visitor economies. Sadly, the world is littered with sites of tragedy. Our mistakes and misfortunes are exposed by landscapes of adversity, accidents, and calamity. Visiting and remembering our dead is a cultural phenomenon – we attach importance to certain kinds of death and to the dead. In turn, the Other(ed) dead become significant to the Self and warn us of our fragility and mortality. Yet, commemoration is challenged by politics of remembrance, commercialism, conflict in memorialisation and the ethics of interpretation. Dark tourism is further challenged by consumer behaviour and visitor experiences. It is here that difficult heritage of the present will be played out within dark tourism of the future. Indeed, future concerns, including but not limited to, memory management, thanatological conceptions, technological influences, appropriation of buildings and resources, environmental degradation, economics and commodification of atrocity, dissonant heritage and interpretation(s), political remembrance, cross-cultural approaches to mortality, secular aspects of morality, as well as generational visitor experiences of tomorrow, (in)form some of the thoughts, ideas and scenarios of this book.

Chapter synopses

This edited book is the world first-ever scholarly volume to critically explore dark tourism futures. The Editors invited established and emerging scholars from across Europe, North and South America, Asia and Australasia to contribute to this philosophical and scenario-based text on the future of global dark tourism. As a result, this book has 22 individual chapters authored by 37 international academics. Each chapter is summarised in Table 0.1. The purpose of this book is to probe the past and disturb the present by provoking the future. In doing so, the book examines how and why dark tourism can enlighten the way ahead for our significant dead, and how the (digital) dead will gaze back at us.

Table 0.1 Book chapter synopses

Chapter	Synopsis
Chapter 1 *Philip R. Stone* *Vertopia:* The Future of Dark Tourism Places and Our Digital Dead	Stone adopts Foucauldian perspectives to examine surreal future emplacements within virtual realms. He argues these will not only be physical places or (re)imagined spaces but will blend with technologies hitherto undeveloped that liminal seams of the real world and virtual world will become indistinguishable. Stone entitles these new future spaces – *vertopia* – where technology fuses the entire fabric of our lived reality with virtual reality, distinct only by the multiple stories that can be played out. The chapter contextualises the *vertopia* in a creative scenario of future dark tourism and penal heritage hyperreality. Consequently, we will engage our digital dead through augmented performances, lived and virtual experiences, as well as a deifying Artificial Intelligence.
Chapter 2 *Rachael Ironside and Craig Leith* Virtual Afterlife: Dark Tourism in the Hereafter	Ironside and Leith offer a future scenario where the living and the dead are interconnected within an immersive artificial intelligent environment called the *Virtual Afterlife*. Grounded in the expansion of virtual and haptic technological developments, as well as growing trends of using big data and social media, the idea of a 'digital afterlife' is born. The chapter offers a unique futuristic lens to scrutinise dark tourism through notions of grief, commercialism and commemoration.

(Continued)

Table 0.1 Continued

Chapter	Synopsis
Chapter 3 *Santa Zascerinska* From 'Bucket List' to 'Afterlist': (Dark) Tourism for the Afterlife	Zascerinska offers a scenario that augments the 'Bucket List' as a means of mediating existential anxiety through travel consumption, including creating self-identity and esteem. However, in cases where Bucket Lists are not achieved due to death, subsequent digital immortality allows family and friends of the deceased to create an 'Afterlist'. It is here that the living completes the original Bucket List and, consequently, bring the dead a digital afterlife. Using thanatechnology, the Afterlist offers a future account of memorialisation and metempsychosis and how we will journey and follow in the footsteps of (dead) others.
Chapter 4 *Daniel W.M. Wright* 'Beyond Human': Dark Tourism, Robots and Futurology	Wright suggests the future will be dominated by robotic technology and, in turn, the concept of the post-human world might become a reality. In so doing, Wright 'goes beyond human' and notes advances in transhumanism and what he calls a 'robo-revolution'. Consequently, Wright offers a warning from science-fiction as we race toward a new machine age. Specifically, he outlines how the ever-evolution of Artificial Intelligence may precipitate future conflicts between humans and robots. In turn, this might lead to dark tourism of the future which reveal perpetrators we have created but are yet to meet.
Chapter 5 *Özge Kılıçarslan, Mehmet Yavuz Çetinkaya and Kamil Yağci* The Future of Technology and Dark Tourism Experiences	Kılıçarslan *et al.* examine technological advancements and usage of Augmented, Virtual and Mixed Realities within dark tourism experiences of the future. In so doing, they argue that these innovative technologies will not only serve to enrich dark tourism experiences but will also strengthen brand identity attributed to dark places. Using a case scenario approach, the chapter suggests future technology within dark tourism can help address critical social issues, as well as serving educational requirements. The chapter argues that tech solutions can help tell tragic tales and allow the victim's voice to be heard more clearly.
Chapter 6 *Diāna Popova, Elizabete Grinblate and Raivis Sīmansons* Bridging Virtual Reality and Dark Heritage	Popova *et al.* examine memorial museums and other institutions that interpret modern mass atrocities using Virtual Reality technology. Adopting a case study approach, they scrutinise the making and testing of the *Lipke Bunker* VR at the Žanis Lipke Memorial (ŽLM) in Riga, Latvia. In so doing, they examine how digital technology is utilised in mediating difficult heritage and, consequently, the role of VR as a future educational and emotion-provoking tool in heritage interpretation. The chapter argues immersive experiences which VR can offer within dark tourism will better connect future visitors through affective, cognitive and embodied faculties.
Chapter 7 *Richard Fawcus* 'Virtual Monument Wars': The Digital Future of Difficult Heritage	Fawcus argues monuments are an integral dimension of how a society remembers its past as well as signposting its future. However, in the future, Fawcus suggests that monuments will become increasingly digitised and mapped for the purpose of dark tourism, conservation, and as a response to the challenges of mediating difficult heritage. Yet, these virtual monument maps will prove contentious when competing hegemonies aim to legitimise and control singular virtual visions. To that end, this chapter argues that monuments will become future flash points for cyber conflicts within digitised difficult heritage.
Chapter 8 *Marián Alesón-Carbonell* Language as a Mediator: Commodifying Future Dark Tourism	Alesón-Carbonell argues that 'dark tourism' has evolved towards a conception that supersedes previous postmodern definitions. She suggests the subject field has opened the scope of research to other disciplines, including linguistics. Indeed, language is a pivotal element in dark tourism interpretation and promotion. However, this not only creates fascination but also describes tragic spectacles, lures tourists, and devises commercial pulls that might border irreverence, yet mediates in the understanding of the sacred. The chapter proposes that the study of linguistics in future dark tourism can offer intercultural mediation roles, as well as interpreting and creating dark sites. Ultimately, Alesón-Carbonell argues that linguistic perspectives can add value to future dark tourism studies by complementing and colliding with other approaches in a meta-modern agenda.

Chapter	Synopsis
Chapter 9 *Saffron Dale, Crispin Dale & Neil Robinson* 'McDeath' – A Future of Dark Travel and End of Life Palliative Care	Dale *et al.* offer a provocative scenario of the future of travel for euthanasia, or 'suicide tourism'. Adopting a McDonaldisation neoliberal market scenario, they suggest that future assisted dying might become a standardised 'product' which, in turn, raises profound situational ethical dilemmas. According to these authors, the so-called 'McDeath' will change, for some people at least, our future conception of *dying* and our relationship to *death*. Indeed, a one-way travel excursion to mortality could be stuff of nightmares; but it also raises the future spectre of the darker side of travel. To that end, this emotive chapter offers a challenging, yet inquisitive and sensitive account of what may happen to the future of assisted dying and its problematic aspects of commodification.
Chapter 10 *Alix Varnajot* Enlightening Dark Tourism Horizons in a Post-Apocalyptic Arctic: A Geopoetic Approach	Varnajot offers a timely and thought-provoking account of the consequences of environmental degradation from the Anthropocene. With the melting of the Arctic (and Antarctic) cryosphere, a slow-onset disaster beckons us all. Varnajot argues that visiting scenes of vanished landscapes articulate links between natural disasters and tourism. Indeed, the 'death of landscapes' with subsequent ruination narratives will offer future dark tourism sites. However, using *geopoetics* as a conceptual framing device, that is – a subset of geohumanities in which connections between geography and creative (poetic) narratives are forged – this chapter suggests a future of alternative Arctic tourism. Consequently, (dark) tourism to the region should adopt an ambassadorial role whereby geopoetic narratives allow an old Arctification to be recast with new educated Arctic imaginations.
Chapter 11 *Maximiliano E. Korstanje* 'Shrines and Rites of Passage': Toward a Future of Dark Tourism Chronicles	Korstanje evaluates the future of dark tourism discourse, with a specific focus on *tourist-centricity* and providing valid and reliable information to tourists. The chapter focuses upon politicisation of dark tourism interpretations, particularly the construction of shrines within the visitor economy that portray tragic events. Using case examples from South America, Korstanje addresses how the presence of shrines can offer political chronicles for the future consumption of dark tourism. In so doing, future dark tourism will entail a new social rite of passage which is culturally and politically determined.
Chapter 12 *Elspeth Frew and Clare Lade* Survivor Voices and Disaster Education: Future Commemoration and Remembrance at Dark Tourism Sites	Frew and Lade highlight how a new museology and its touristic consumption have shifted public narrative from spaces of academic history to places of memory and community. Adopting this approach to future memorialisation within dark tourism, the chapter argues remembrance should incorporate not only narratives of grief and loss, but also educative narratives of how to avoid future disasters. Using case examples from Australasia, Frew and Lade suggest future commemoration of disasters, and its consumption within dark tourism, should be inclusive and community-centric and for survivor voices to be heard and recalled.
Chapter 13 *Abit Hoxha and Kenneth Andresen* Future of Dark Tourism in Kosovo: From Divisions to Digital Possibilities	Hoxha and Andresen examine dark tourism within Kosovo. With a tragic past of conflict, dark tourism is played out at the interface of ethnic tensions, including dissonance between Albanians and Serbs. Both these groups are drawn to places of memory and commemoration, including for political tourism and religious pilgrimages. Drawing upon Kosovan case studies, this chapter highlights divisions inherent within the memorialised landscape, as well as digital possibilities for the future of interpreting conflict within visitor economies. In so doing, Hoxa and Andresen examine future dark tourism and its relationship with quasi-religious-political sites. They conclude by arguing Kosovo needs creativity and political willingness to invest in remembrance and cohesive memorialisation. It is here that future dark tourism can play a vital role in consuming and co-constructing cultural trauma.

(Continued)

Table 0.1 Continued

Chapter	Synopsis
Chapter 14 *Ann-Kathrin McLean* Millennials, Transitional Memory and the Future of Holocaust Remembrance	McLean examines the fallibility of mediating dark tourism and highlights the fragility of future Holocaust memory as generations pass away. With a focus on younger millennials who act as memory agents, and with a case example set in the Dachau Concentration Camp Memorial, this chapter advances our understanding of dark tourism relationships between future Holocaust remembrance, collective memory and the societal pressures of remembering (and forgetting) the tragic past. In so doing, McLean offers a powerful account of how millennials in an age of transitional memory should exercise leadership in global discourse of antisemitism and human rights.
Chapter 15 *Aija van der Steina, Maija Rozite, Inese Runce and Kaspars Strods* Between Revival of Memory and Dark Tourism: The Future of Holocaust-Related Sites in Latvia	Van der Steina *et al.* examine the future of Holocaust memory within Latvia and its evolution of social awareness through periods of trans-nationalisation and liberation from Soviet totalitarianism. In so doing, they discuss dark tourism and Holocaust sites, and how the tragic past will matter in a fractious future. Within a framework of Latvian nationhood, dissonance and memory management, the revival of Holocaust memory through dark tourism stems from a complicated past and a national(ised) present yet moves towards a transcultural future. It is here that inclusion of Holocaust sites within (dark) tourism prevents forgetting and, consequently, promotes preservation in both physical places as well as memory space.
Chapter 16 *Marta Soligo* 'Mirrors of Society': Cemetery Tourism Futures	Soligo offers critical insights from burial grounds of our significant and ordinary deceased. She highlights how cemeteries should be rooted not only in historicity, but also within their own cultural landscape. Adopting a futurology approach, and with case examples from Italy and the USA, Soligo discusses future (dark) tourism to cemeteries. The chapter argues that the future of cemetery tourism is marked by the idea that burial sites are unique witnesses of surrounding contexts. Moreover, burial grounds should be gazed from cultural landscape perspectives to help us understand the cultural fabric of local heritage and history. Consequently, future visitor interactions with burial sites means that cemeteries act as mirrors of the societies that built them, and where future tourists will sightsee in the mansions of the dead.
Chapter 17 *Janine Marriott* 'Not the Right Sort of Visitors': Future Challenges of Cemetery Tourism	Marriott offers an account of how historic UK cemeteries are used for (dark) tourism purposes and, subsequently, how cemeteries have long been used as places where visitors learn from and be inspired by. The chapter highlights inherent dilemmas in managing historic cemeteries as a touristic resource, as well as examining future challenges faced by authorities and custodians. Marriot argues that cemeteries are places of contradiction whereby a public/private dichotomy is evident. This dichotomy raises tensions (and barriers) for the 'right sort of visitor' for future cemetery tourism. Importantly, cemetery tourism of the future should include treating burial sites not only as sacred places but spaces for a range of audiences, including the living and the dead.
Chapter 18 *Allan Brodie* 'Into the horrors of the gloomy jail': Towards a Future of UK Prison Tourism and Penal Architecture	Brodie offers a comprehensive review of UK penal architecture and its potential appropriation for future prison tourism. In a quest to modernise 19th-century prisons, partly to improve prison conditions, but also to release locations and buildings for mercantile development, there is a resultant glut of historic prisons in search of a future. By examining the history of prison tourism, Brodie questions just how many prison museums and attractions the UK can sustain. In doing so, the chapter contrasts (dark) tourism to prisons and seeks to address future penal heritage with more positive, educational aspects of tourist visitation.

Chapter	Synopsis
Chapter 19 *Brianna Wyatt* 'Finding a Light in Dark Places': Lighter Dark Tourism Futures	Wyatt declares the business of dark tourism is booming. This is due, in part at least, because of growing societal interests in staged themes and (re)created scenes of tragic death and the macabre. Using *lighter dark tourism* as context, Wyatt suggests more dark visitor sites are utilising commercial methods to meet evolving consumer expectations and demands. The chapter adopts the Six Pillars model (*time, anticipation, timing, deepening, alternatives* and *transformations*) as a conceptual device to frame discussions. Wyatt argues *lighter* dark touristic practices will drive the future market of (darker) dark tourism into the new experience economy, with a specific focus on visitor engagement, learning opportunities, the use of technology, and the creation of experience-scapes.
Chapter 20 *Luisa Golz and Tony Johnston* Future of Dark Tourism Festivals: Technology and the Tourist Experience	Golz and Johnston state that in an age of consumption, we love to be scared – and dark tourism festivals offer new ways to be frightened. With increasing festivalisation within visitor economies, this chapter highlights the potential for technology to reconfigure future dark tourism festivals. Consequently, Golz and Johnston argue future dark tourism festivals will offer embodied experiences, especially through creating dystopian and liminal sensations. Complex ethical issues are highlighted in orchestrating such new experiences. Nevertheless, the future for dark tourism festivals offers numerous intersection points between technology, promotion and marketing, spatial organisation and the festivalgoer experience.
Chapter 21 *Robert S. Bristow, Alina Gross and Ian Jenkins* Future Dystopian Attractions: Benign Masochism in Dark Tourism	Bristow *et al.* examine the nature and future of 'fright attractions'. The chapter offers a critical account of how and why voyeuristic audiences are drawn to a fictional future of death and suffering, while insisting on a sanitised spectacle. Taking a cross-cultural approach, Bristow *et al.* anticipate the future of 'fright tourism' based upon a macabre interest in death, yet one that is disinfected from reality. With case examples from Japan, Mexico and Romania, the study is grounded in notions of risk, folklore and mythmaking, geopolitics, religious and cultural identity. The chapter also suggests that a 'benign masochism' (of pain and pleasure) might be inherent in fright tourism and will remain a key issue for future (lighter) dark tourism attractions and tourist experiences.
Chapter 22 *Michael Brennan* Future Directions in Death Studies and Dark Tourism	Brennan suggests that death, following individual loss or collective tragedy, involves major psycho-social transitions. Death prompts 'futures thinking' whereby reflections of the past and postulations of the future create uncertainly and transformations. It is here that Brennan weaves together potential directions for dark tourism with thanatological intersections and synergies. The chapter highlights new death mentalities and *deathways* that will guide future dark tourism experiences. In so doing, Brennan argues that future dark tourism will not only facilitate greater 'mortality salience' but should also offer a 'compassionate communities' approach as the Self and society are confronted with accelerated social change.

Dark Tourism: Into the Unknown

Ghosts of our significant Other dead are returning to the touristic feast. Of course, these are not ghosts of the supernatural kind, but a metaphor of how we live in a contemporary domain of the dead. In turn, dark tourism has emerged as a scholarly force to scrutinise how and why contemporary global societies deal with their noteworthy dead. Importantly, scholarly discourse of dark tourism has moved on from its early theoretical fragility and matured into cross-cultural fields of study, including futurology. Dark tourism acts as an academic lens upon which to gaze at death and the dead within global visitor economies. Yet, while dark tourism remains a post-disciplinary research brand, in practice we live in a new dominion of the Other(ed) dead who have been 'resurrected' by commercialism and commemoration. It is here that difficult heritage and troubled pasts are portrayed and consumed by tourists, either through individual secular pilgrimage, or through mass travel itineraries. Once described as an intimation of postmodernity, dark tourism in practice has a rich history, yet still has considerable consequences for understanding the thanatological condition of modern society.

The only certainty of the future is death. As finite biological beings, as we shall live, so we shall die. However, in an emerging age of new machines and an information revolution, the future will also deliver other certainties. These will focus on technological advancements and, as a result, will accelerate societal transformations. The living will continue to pass away, but in our demise, we will leave increasing and preponderant digital footprints. Even at the time of writing (in 2024), the emergence of Artificial Intelligence (AI) is breaking new ground. Fed by training data (that is, the internet), AI continues to evolve in multiple fields, including dark tourism and poetry. When an AI Chatbot app (powered by ChatGPT and CPT-4 software) was asked to author a poem about 'dark tourism', within seven seconds this was the result:

The road less travelled beckons me
To sights most macabre and eerie
Places steeped in history
Of violence, death, and misery

Dark tourism, my chosen path
To explore the past's darkest wrath
From haunted castles to battlefields
Where death's sting still forever lingers

The ghosts of the past, they call to me
Their stories begging to be set free
My feet move toward the shadows
As the thrill of fear overtakes me

The catacombs beneath the ground
Endlessly winding and profound
Where skulls and bones form a morbid art
Whispers echoing through the heart

From Auschwitz to Pompeii's ruins
These places hold a dreadful hue
Yet I am compelled to seek and see
These eerie landmarks of history

The darkness envelopes me
In this weird and wondrous journey
From the depths of human suffering
To the monuments of tragedy

Dark tourism is not for all
But for those who hear the call
A journey into the past's sombre veil
To uncover stories that never fail.

Notwithstanding issues about poetic devices or criticism with syntax, this AI-generated poem incorporates most key themes and features of modern dark tourism. Many of these themes are critiqued in this volume. However, as we move towards the unknown, dark tourism will accompany us and will *uncover stories* into the *past's sombre veil*. Dark tourism with all the foresights offered in this book, will always offer journeys to places of death, tragedy, violence or misery. During these touristic journeys, our present and future Self should always reflect upon cultural trauma and heritage that hurts. Moreover, dark tourism in the future, as it is now, will always be about the living rather than the dead. To that end, this book commences with the words of Mother Teresa (an Albanian-born Indian Roman Catholic missionary and nun, 1910–1997), '*Yesterday is gone. Tomorrow has not yet come. We have only today. Let us begin*'.

1 *Vertopia:* The Future of Dark Tourism Places and Our Digital Dead

Philip R. Stone

There is nothing like a dream to create a future
Victor Hugo (1862)

Once upon a time in a future not so far away, a world has been created that incorporates both our dreams and nightmares. So, sit back, read on and imagine ...[1]

'Unhappening Murders': The Pip Rothniles Exhibition

Welcome to Hotel Vertopia

Pip Rothniles was dead. He had passed away quite some time ago. Yet, while Pip had died in reality, he had simultaneously been born into hyperreality. Now, as a transhumanist Avatar, Pip slowly awoke from another deep slumber in a run-down hotel room. The room was nothing like he had dreamt of or had been promised. Strewn with rubbish and unkempt bed linen, the place was dirty and in need of some housekeeping discovery. In the distance, church bells tolled their Sunday soundtrack. Pip knew he was deceased, but he also knew he was very much alive. Pip was aware that his Avatar was him and he was an Avatar – a living digital ghost that chose and paid to be immortal in Vertopia. The Vertopia, a manifestation of virtual worlds born out of 21st century imaginations, was already a couple of centuries old. The Grim Reaper still existed of course; but for Avatars such as Pip, he has suspended his mortality account – for now at least. Death happened a long time ago to Pip, though he could not recall the exact circumstances of his demise. There was no distinction anymore between his life in Topia – that is, the physical world he once lived in – and his afterlife in the Vertopia. There were no boundaries between the two worlds, only liminal gateways through which the Topia could be reached with old futures and new pasts. The Vertopia was a place where dreams could be broken into, and nightmares burgled. Pip could not remember being human, though he felt human. In fact, Pip was surrounded by other humans: people who were still alive in Topia but had become subjects of A-Aron, a digitate deity who ensured biological human fusion to the technologic Vertopia. Humans who were fused were called Audrinas: human in nature and appearance but distinguished by a red glow emitted around their body. Sometimes, Audrinas would have the sclera of their left eye flashing a faint taint of orange. This denoted their Vertopian experiences were being recorded by A-Aron for personal indulgence once back in the Topia. Audrinas would often frequent the Vertopia, sometimes for special experiences and leisure attractions, or to conduct virtual business, or to visit deceased loved ones who had been ingenerated as Avatars. Of course, Avatars were also human in nature and appearance, but had a blue glow to denote their deceased status in the Topia. Both Avatars and Audrinas were sanctioned by A-Aron, an evolved divine quantum mainframe created by Metaverse, the global company that initially built the Vertopia. A-Aron controlled all the virtual worlds, its gateways and its inhabitants. For those living in Topia but wishing to reside in Vertopia, either to visit or to live in perpetuity, being a subject of A-Aron was optional but expensive. In turn, A-Aron ensured eternal enlightenment. While living in Topia, Pip had paid 100,000 Bitcoin from his life savings to Metaverse and bought the 'Immortal Package' during a mid-life crisis. Now, Pip lived an eternity where he is kept alive and guarded by A-Aron.

As Pip gingerly stirred from his sleep, a cybernated amnesia had descended upon him, programming him to recall his surroundings but to forget his past. He cast his eye around his untidy hotel room, noting the dirty teacups and empty vodka bottles on the nearside cabinet. Dishevelled but fully clothed apart from his shoes, Pip arose and befuddled his way to the en-suite bathroom. Reaching for the light switch, the LED flickered to life. Pip felt groggy as he looked in the mirror. '*Where the hell am I?*' he retorted to no one in particular, as he turned on the tap and vigorously splashed chilly water on to his face. Drying his features, the church bells continued their tune as Pip began to search for his shoes. He reached under the bed and felt the contour of his trainers and stretched as far as he could. Reaching for them, strained on all fours, the television on the wall suddenly burst into life. Pip jumped and bashed the back of his head on the bedframe, while trying to understand where the sudden noise was coming from. Startled and holding the back of his head, Pip could make out an image on the television. The screen was showing a middle-aged woman strapped to a red-burgundy chair, a kind of leather Chesterfield type that would not look out of place in an affluent accountant's office. The woman, her bedraggled blonde hair and messy make-up was clearly in distress with her feet bound and wrists tied with braided cable to the chair's arm rests. She screamed as a man's necktie was placed around her neck and throat: the assailant obscured. Her howling and shrieks became yelps and, soon afterwards, a soft wailing as the tie was tightened and life was strangled from her. The television image oscillated as the woman sat slumped and murdered in the chair, her killer unseen.

Pip became terrified. Through his amnesic haze, he tried to recall the red-burgundy chair. He knew it but could not place it. Nor did he recognise the woman, but she looked familiar. Quickly tying the laces of his trainer shoes, Pip scrambled to the room door, as the television continued to flicker with the image of the dead woman's face, her features tormented. He ran furiously down the corridor, the other rooms obscured as a blur as he passed. Arriving at the elevator, Pip pressed impatiently for the ground floor. As he anxiously waited for the whining of the lift, Pip became acutely aware of his own presence. No-one else was around. The hotel appeared empty and silent apart from faint sounds of remote church bells. The elevator doors opened, and Pip threw himself into the lift carriage. He was only five floors up, but the descent took an age. In the lift carriage, a hologram poster advertised the restaurant's 'Avatar Daily Specials'. Pip gazed blankly at the poster – through it, rather than seeing it – when it abruptly burst into 3D. Instead of showing Chef's Dish of the Day, the hologram revealed a red-burgundy chair, the same chair as on the television, with a blonde-haired woman screaming frantically for her life. Pip froze with trepidation, his Avatarian soul inhibited with fear. Within the claustrophobic confines of the elevator, the same woman was strangled and killed in front of him. The lift doors opened to the lobby. Pip raced and stumbled through the holographic murder scene, as it played on loop. In the lobby, a lone female receptionist dressed smartly stood behind a desk. Her red shadow cast around her body denoted her as an Audrina. Yet, she appeared emotionless and did not acknowledge the presence of Pip as he hurtled towards her, screaming that a woman was being murdered. The receptionist remained detached from her surroundings with her left eye flashing faint orange, meaning she was in record mode. Pip moved around the desk, shouting expletives at the receptionist, who remained utterly impassive. She continued to record as Pip shouted: *'What are you doing? Where is everyone? Stop filming me!! A woman has been killed!!'* There was no response from the Audrina as she gazed apathetically at Pip while capturing his every movement. Unable to fathom her behaviour, and at a loss of why other Avatars and

Audrinas were absence in the hotel, Pip ran out of the lobby, through the entrance and on to the street outside. Bewildered, Pip had checked out, but somehow, he knew he could not leave.

'Empty Meeting Grounds': Finding Pip's Vertopian Soul

Pip stumbled along the street, leaving the hotel behind him. The landscape seemed eerily empty. Apart from recognisable places, such as banks, shops and cafés, the immediate neighbourhood appeared devoid of any Avatar or Audrina. Overhead, a leaden sky with a sombre mood was full of heavy clouds that were beginning to bruise. The climate in Vertopia was changing and Pip was increasingly anxious. With a heightened sense of foreboding, Pip noticed unmistakable faint red glows of Audrinas clumsily hidden behind building facades, their radiance giving them away. The place was not empty. He stopped suddenly and looked straight towards a bookstore. Pip could just make out several Audrinas with books held up tentatively, as if reading, towards their faces. He could also distinguish faint flashing of orange eyes. An apprehension tumbled upon Pip with the realisation that he was being watched, recorded and even a feeling of being apprehended. As more Audrinas appeared from their maladroit hiding places, each with flashing orange eyes of documentary, they broke ranks and Pip grew even more frightened. He increased his pace to a dash, and a taciturn horde of Audrinas quickly followed, increasing their impassive sort as more Audrinas joined the muted fray. Up ahead, Pip spotted a digital billboard perched strategically on an embankment. Billboards often advertised gateways to other parts of the Vertopia, with Metaverse instructions of how to reach them. As Pip approached the hoarding, aware of the Audrinan assemblage behind him, an augury descended upon Pip. The billboard was not showing any gateway instructions, nor advertising far-flung corners of the Vertopia. Instead, a large red-burgundy chair – of the Chesterfield type – stood sinister-like in the centre of the placard. At the foot of the chair lay a man's necktie. A strangled blonde-haired woman sat contorted with her wrists confined by braided cable. Her dead eyes were open and flashing orange.

Pip screamed and collapsed to the floor as impassive Audrinas gathered around him. They were too many to count, but enough to give him space. The quiet mob shuffled for the best vantage point of Pip as he lay sobbing, each recording him. Out of his tearful eyes, Pip spotted a church in the near distance, the same church that had tolled its bells earlier. The prominent Christian cross on the bell tower – an ancient symbol of execution – acted like a beacon to Pip and drew him closer. *Sanctuary* he thought, as he stumbled to his feet and pushed his way through the malaise of his hushed onlookers. Making his way to the asylum of the chapel, Pip left his Audrinan congregation behind as they remained muted at the parish gates, their eyes still flashing a surveillance orange.

Inside the church, Pip headed to the confessional harbourage, a spiritual booth that offered a den of safety. Once inside, Pip closed the confessional doors and sat quietly. The church bells had now stopped and for a brief juncture Pip felt relieved. Within moments, however, the other side of the confessional box quietly opened, and Pip could make out a red glow of a female Audrina as she entered the booth. Pip gasped as the Audrina sat just centimetres from him, separated only by ornate wooden style panelling and a lattice type frame. Of course, this sacellum was in the Vertopia, where everything looked real, was real, but at the same time, surreal. The Audrina began to speak with a soft gentle tone and introduced herself as Thara, a visiting digital priest from the Topia who practiced her faith in the Vertopia and followed the gospels of A-Aaron.

'*What brings you here, my child?*' Thara genially inquired.

Pip hesitated to answer at first, but after a few moments felt compelled to reply. '*I feel something bad has happened*' Pip responded, '*something very bad … something awful has happened to someone, but I don't know who*'.

'*And this 'bad something,' does it feel real to you?*' asked Thara mildly.

'*Yes*' replied Pip with a certain amount of reluctance, '*it feels too real*'.

After a brief pause and long exhale of breath, Thara addressed Pip directly: '*My dear Pip, in society today, whether here in the Vertopia or there in the Topia, everything is real. There are no contrasts between the here and now, or the before and after. The distinction between the past, present and future is only a stubbornly persistent illusion. Yes – everything is real because we feel it is. And, when something awful or deplorable happens, we must all confront what reality means*'.

Pip listened intensely as Thara continued her benevolent diatribe: '*There are no hiding places for wrongdoers, not anymore. Reality has changed. We cannot disguise ourselves; we cannot smuggle our transgressions, obscure our violations or mask our malefactions. When something bad happens, there is always justice now. And people demand it. They want to see justice and want justice to be seen to be done … not for it to be suppressed behind closed prisons, but for real justice to be served out here, made accessible for the masses – exposed in the open for everyone to see*'.

Thara paused for a moment, as to collect her thoughts. Pip remained silent.

> *'Of course'*, continued Thara, *'to be open means we must open our eyes, yet we still must squint. Nothing is as it seems. It never was. There has always been a fantasy of justice, of retribution and punishment. A kind of chimera that society was repaid for the crimes committed against it. Now we must survey our wrong doers, managed them, gaze upon them ... ensure the pain that they once meted out against us, is repackaged against them'*.

As Pip sat and listened, a cognisance began to grasp him. She talked about specific justice but never mentioned any criminal. She talked about society as real, but illusions that are not. She talked about retribution but repackaged. Thara had now stopped speaking, her gentle tone replaced by silence. Pip continued his thoughts, his mind beginning to race once more. He had never introduced himself to Thara, yet she called him 'my dear Pip'. Pip turned tentatively towards Thara; her priestly outline visible in the sanctum of the confessional box. Thara looked straight at Pip, where a frigidness had descended, and her left eye flashing orange. Pip flinched with fear and with an agitated exit, rushed his way out of the confessional booth. Thara appeared slowly, impassive and silent, her blinking orange eye documenting every moment.

Pip rushed to the door and out to the churchyard. The Audrina crowd that had gathered had only swelled in number, each of them passive yet sinister in their presence. The blinking of orange eyes made Pip feel arrested and captured, each eye seizing his every movement. Pip lowered his head and made his way quickly through the ill-boding horde. He quickened his pace as the Audrinas' did likewise but keeping a strange respectful distance. It was this social distance that Pip found most inauspicious, a kind of omen that while he was being watched, he could not be touched. The streets remained empty ahead of him as he continued his flee from his baleful following. Scrambled thinking in Pip's mind seemed to direct his path towards voices emulating from a building at the next junction. As he drew closer, the voices became discernible as people laughing and cheering in an indistinct mutter. The building came into view and Pip saw it was an Odeon, a place for shows and theatre. *At last! There is life!* thought Pip, as he made his way through the Odeon entrance leaving his ominous entourage behind.

'Extra, Extra, See All About It!': Pip's Perpetual Punishment

The noise of cachinnation became deafening as Pip walked along the internal corridor. Bouts of glee, giggles and overall merriment echoed when Pip arrived at a large stage door. Behind the double door, Pip could feel the energy of amusement as a crowd continued to shriek and roar. He took the door handle in his right hand and pulled it slowly towards him, as the theatre peal rejoiced at his appearance. Pip tentatively walked forward, blinded by limelight shining upon him. As he continued his slow walk, Pip could make out hundreds of silhouettes of Audrinas sat in tiered seats, each now jeering his name, each with flashing orange eyes recording his every move. Pip stood stunned, alone on a stage, in front of a hostile gallery that were getting ever more bellicose. As the increasingly belligerent crowd roared with jeers, the sudden voice of a man crackled over the tannoid speakers:

'*Welcome to the Pip Rothniles Exhibition!!*' the male voice shouted in glee, as the audience responded in kind with thunderous applause. As the acclamation continued, a tall slim elderly looking Avatar appeared on stage, his long face and pointed chin with a thin moustache gracing his upper lip. Dressed in a black tuxedo suit with a matching black dickie-bow tie, his blue Avatarian glow in plain sight, the dapper host claimed the stage and continued to address his audience. '*Oh, you are so much better than the audience we had last week!!*' exclaimed the host as the crowd roared with laughter. '*My name is Bryce Fourths, and you are immersed in the Pip Rothniles Exhibition ... Welcome, welcome ... Nice to See You, to See You Nice!*' yelled Bryce as the audience continued their fractious shrieks. Bryce beckoned to his audience, urging them gently with his hand to tone down. His voice mellow and the crowd now hushed, Bryce addressed his public. '*The future is uncertain, but the end is always near*', proclaimed Bryce. '*And that is no more so than for our very own Pip*', as Bryce gesticulated Pip over to him. The crowd bellowed their approval. Pip had remained on stage, almost spellbound, as Bryce had performed his introductions. In a daze, Pip slowly made his way to the welcoming hand of Bryce; when in the middle of the stage, a trap door suddenly opened. As the door swung clear, a red-burgundy chair, of the Chesterfield type, slowly appeared from beneath. With braided cables on the arm rests, Pip papillated with fear. Bryce continued his beckoning to Pip, to sit in the chair, as the Vertopian spectators roared to life. The stage lights illuminated Pip as he moved to the chair, and he slowly sat in its uncomfortable oxhide. Bryce moved forward and welcomed Pip to the red chair:

> '*Welcome to the Red Chair my dear Pip, a chair that you have forgotten, but one which we all remember*' declared Bryce, as the showgoers looked on.
>
> Pip murmured, as he tried to understand his situation, '*Where am I?*'

> *'You are in your very own show my dear Pip'*, said Bryce. *'This is where you meet your very own fate. And it is where we have our recompense – repeatedly!'* as Bryce pointed to his rambunctious audience.

Pip sat stunned. He did not understand, but somehow all this seemed familiar. As he gazed outwards, across the lime lit stage, holographic images surrounded the theatre and immersed everyone into its image. The images became familiar to Pip, his memories reactivated: a red chair with a blonde-hair woman being strangled, her contorted features on view for all to witness. Pip did not feel fear now, he just felt an overwhelming feeling of bewilderment and dismay. The audience had become silent. Bryce leant into the red chair and close to Pip:

> *'My dear Pip'* said Bryce softly, *'in 2023, almost two hundred years ago, you lived in the Topia. You may not recall, but in the 42nd year of your life, you did commit a heinous act of murder'*. Pip flinched, as his memories began to resurrect themselves from his cyber amnesia. Two braided cables automatically wrestled Pip's wrists to the arm-chair and made them secure as Bryce shouted: *'Pip Rothniles, you have been found guilty of the charges brought by this court of public justice. It is my duty to pass sentence. I feel constrained to commit you to the maximum penalty allowed for your offences. You will be taken from this place and hanged by the neck until you are dead'*. Bryce paused momentarily, before continuing, *'The victim of your abominable bloodshed all that time ago was no other than your work colleague, Ms Carolus Netty … do you remember Pip?'*

Pip suddenly did remember. His memories flooded into his mind, overwhelming him, as he struggled to breath. As the audience roared, Pip drifted off into a semi-conscious state and began to recall his demise, aware of his present, but now very much afraid of his past. Carolus had been a best friend of Pip for many years and worked happily with him as a lecturer at a university in England. But Pip had become insanely jealous of Carolus as she was promoted by the University Senate, while Pip was left behind in the professional doldrums. For Pip, his envy grew and his friendship with Carolus became increasingly estranged. Then, in the days leading up to Christmas in 2023, at a university seasonal gathering, Pip and Carolus met in a bar, close to where they both worked. Pip, consumed with alcohol and animosity, enticed Carolus to the basement, where he had arranged a red-burgundy Chesterfield chair. Around the chair was recording equipment that Pip had purposely assembled. At the request of Pip, Carolus sat in the chair, and he began to unleash his umbrage against her. A tirade of verbal abuse followed as Pip vented his fury at

Carolus. Increasingly frightened, Carolus tried to leave but Pip angrily tied her wrists to the chair arms with a length of braided cable, he had found in the bar basement. As his vexation continued, the recording equipment captured the entire offence. Carolus tried to reason with Pip, but his rage and resentment were too much as he reached for his necktie. He strangled her without ceremony or empathy and within a few moments, Pip's felony was complete. Carolus lay dispatched in her final resting place. Without emotion, Pip grabbed the recording equipment and left the basement, leaving Carolus in her callous annihilation, waiting to be discovered.

It did not take long for the body of Carolus to be found. In fact, in less than six hours, Pip was apprehended and arrested near his place of work. He had uploaded the recording of Carolus's killing to his social media, offering a global following an account of the murder without reason nor explanation. Within a few months after a short trial, Pip was found to have wilfully murdered Carolus in the first degree. With overwhelming evidence against him, including the actual recording, Pip was sentenced to a 'fate worse than death'. After being fined 100,000 Bitcoin, he was also given an 'Afterlife' sentence where his execution in the Topia would mean his resurrection in the newly built Vertopia. However, rather than an afterlife as a free Avatar, he would remain in the Vertopia under its 'Perpetual Justice' remit. Existing in a hostel for condemned Avatars, Pip was sentenced to relive his crime for perpetuality. In 2047, Metaverse bought the recording rights to Pip's criminality and copyrighted his story to a special immersive visitor attraction within the Vertopia and called it the 'The Pip Rothniles Exhibition'.

On stage, Pip sat uneasily in the red-burgundy Chesterfield chair; his wrists still strapped to the armrests. He now knew his crimes committed, he remembered Carolus Netty and he knew he was a murderer. Pip also remembered being on this stage before – many times! This was his Afterlife punishment, being forced to relive his crime over and over, and to come to terms with what he had done, including recording and disseminating the slaying of Carolus Netty. Bryce Fourths looked on as the audience recorded Pips' every move, in anticipation of the final act. *'Do you want justice?'* cried Bryce to his crowd. An audible roar of cheers was the reply. *'Then we shall have justice…'* continued Bryce *'… for this day and for the next … in this world and beyond!!'* As the audience roared with endorsement, Bryce placed a necktie around Pip's throat. Pip gasped as he felt the noose tighten, the silhouettes of the Audrian audience diminishing. The strangulation got more intense as Pip kicked in convulsions against his state sanctioned lynching. He had been hanged during his execution in the Topia, and now Pip was melted out the same slaying he had given Carolus Netty. The noose tightened even more, and Pip was strangled a slow virtual death. His blue Avatarian glow faded around him and as he is disconnected by A-Aron, the touristic crowd jeer.

Pip sits contorted, dead once again. The stage trapdoor opens, and the chair and Pip are swallowed to the stage depths. Under the stage, Pip is transported away for memory erasure and his Avatar rebooted for the next public exhibition. A fresh crowd of morbid spectators will be waiting, ready to record Pip's fate and pay witness to Pip's perpetual punishment. He will be immured and executed every day, forever, for his murderous misdeeds. On stage, Bryce addresses his audience a final time: '*That's all folks*' shouts Bryce, '*We shall be back the same time tomorrow for the Pip Rothniles Exhibition, a show of unhappening murder and mystery. Remember – every new beginning comes from some other beginning's end. Until next time, farewell…*'.

With that, Bryce leaves the stage and the Audrinan tourists filter out of the auditorium and back to the Topia. As the Vertopian night falls and morning rises, the Odeon remains quiet, waiting for the next horde. Pip Rothniles is the star attraction, a spectacle reborn to be punished and for reasons he can never remember – until it is too late. Yet, not far away in a run-down hotel, in an unkempt room with dirty bed linen and unwashed teacups, Pip wakes up from an amnesic slumber. The sound of church bells toll in the distance as a television erupts into life. A red-burgundy chair, of the Chesterfield kind, dominates the screen. Pip knew he was dead. But he was yet to know that he was also undead.

The End.

Introduction (After the Beginning)

The future is broken. Expect to be alone. Or at least expect to be alone surrounded by virtual Others in an imagined destiny where our biological realities and technological hyperreality collide. In this scientific fate, some of us will be guaranteed virtual immortality as we occupy esoteric spaces of the cyberworld. Of course, as mortal finite beings, as we shall live, we shall die. The Grim Reaper will not disappear but simply catch us up. However, in a cyberworld within the next few centuries or so, we will reside in a new dominion of the dead where 'ghosts' of our departed wander among us. These ghosts will not be the Hollywoodised supernatural kind, but technological reincarnations of our deceased. Our digital ghosts will accompany us, travel with us, haunt us, become us, offer us warnings from the past, as well as provide ontological meaning to our hi-tech existentialism. Ghosts will be made available to us 24/7 through a futurology of technical advancements, offering us a transmundane tourist experience where our distinguished or disgraced dead will inhabit perpetual afterlives.

Yet, travelling to meet our significant dead has long been a feature of the touristic imagination. During the 18th and early 19th centuries, for example, tourists of the day dramatised desires and anxieties of Romanticism by visiting the homes, haunts and graves of dead authors, poets and artists (Armitt & Brewster, 2021; Westover, 2012). The Romantic period was 'an age of revolutions and mass print, antiquarian revival, and a love of books, ghost-hunting, and monuments, [and] the emergent "Necromantic" culture created touristic habits that arguably continue to the present day' (Stone, 2013c: 1). Indeed, the act of contemporary travel to sites of fatality to witness our significant dead has been referred to as 'dark tourism' (Lennon & Foley, 2000; Stone, 2006). Within our ruptured futures, dark tourism will continue to manifest diverse spectacles of fatality and, in turn, grant us virtual access to futuristic revenants in new times and new spaces.

Presently, our noteworthy dead have been commodified and death has been made 'spectacular' within global visitor economies (Jacobsen, 2016; Stone, 2018, 2020a). In other words, our significant Other dead perish in brutal, accidental or calamitous circumstances and, subsequently, become 'commodities of consumption' and 'mercantile memorialization' (Stone & Grebenar, 2022: 457). Certain kinds of death in certain kinds of circumstance take on semiotic significance and, with a certain chronological distance, transform into a spectacle for contemporary tourist experiences and, consequently, mediate between the dead and the living (Stone, 2009a; Walter, 2009). The semiology of our difficult heritage in the early 21st century has transformed fatality and, in so doing, our significant dead have become spectacular for the tourist gaze in a society of the spectacle (after Urry & Larsen, 2011; Debord, 1967). This new mentality of spectacularising death and the symbolised dead means that the Other dead are revived, reinvented and commodified in new deathscapes within the experience economy.

Importantly, touristification of deathscapes, where the tragic dead are remembered (or forgotten) through systematic heritage processes, raises profound notions of *placemaking* (Cresswell, 2015; Relph, 1976; Tuan, 1977). That is, the idea of adding value and connotation to a *space* for it to become a meaningful *place*, or meaningscape. Moreover, when spaces are examined under a lens of conceptual places – specifically, the ideas of utopia, dystopia and a Foucauldian heterotopia – we can critically ascertain the nature and parameters of meaningscapes. We can also augment the intersection of these places with new spaces of *emplacement*. In short, future emplacements (after Foucault) will not only be physical or (re)imagined spaces but will agglutinate with technology so much that liminal seams of the physical world and virtual worlds will become indistinguishable. In this chapter, I call this new future space a *vertopia,* where technology blended with physical places will completely fuse the entire fabric of our lived reality to create virtual experienced spaces, distinct only by the multiple stories that can be played out.[2]

Drawing upon futurology studies, placemaking and Foucauldian ideas of space, the purpose of my chapter is to outline future dark tourism placemaking within these new *vertopias.* My study sets out a theoretical blueprint to introduce conceptual dimensions of a *vertopia.* As I have outlined in my fictional scenario earlier, I use the idea of the *vertopia* to speculate a future case of dark tourism, particularly regarding crime, punishment and penal heritage. Specifically, I drew upon the work of Erving Goffman (1959, 1971, 1974) and his studies of symbolic interactionalism, including the notion of society as 'theatres of performance'.[3] As my scenario of future dark tourism has creatively outlined, *vertopias* of tomorrow will become digital societal theatres.[4] It is here where 'engineered and orchestrated spectacles' (after Seaton & Dann, 2018) of both crime and justice will be controlled reality yet played out as performances by future tourist experiences, as penal heritage is remade (also see Seaton, 2018). In so doing, future dark tourism will be assimilated into a hyperreal world where we will engage our significant dead through augmented performances, lived and virtual experiences, as well as artificial intelligence. Firstly, however, I turn to the notion of placemaking, spatiality and technological advancements as predictive bedrock for future dark tourism emplacements.

Dark Tourism, Placemaking and an-Other Space

Recent discourse on dark tourism, particularly regarding its relationship to placemaking and commodification, has focused upon custodianship and neoliberal marketisation (Bird *et al.*, 2018; Brown, 2013; McKenzie, 2018; Seaton, 2009; Stone & Grebenar, 2022; Stone & Stewart, forthcoming). To that end, tourism placemaking has attracted increasing academic attention to how to create destination uniqueness (Lew, 2017). Rather than focusing simply on destination branding and marketing, placemaking adopts stakeholder approaches, including how tourists co-create emotional experiences through a sense of place and, subsequently, co-construct *meaningscapes* (Jarratt *et al.*, 2018). Placemaking is concerned with how *space* through the attachment of sacred/secular/spiritual meaning becomes a *place* (Lew, 2017). In other words, placemaking is how a space is designated with semiotic value and, thus, becomes significant or associated with some form of personal or collective meaning (Cresswell, 2015). Several studies have begun to explore placemaking within dark tourism – for example Wang *et al.* (2019), Rofe (2013) and White and Frew (2013). Interestingly, Spokes *et al.* (2018) examine dark tourism, memorialisation and 'deviant spaces' through the philosophical lens of Henri Lefebvre. Using a scaled approach, they articulate a framework of 'lived', 'perceived' and 'conceived' aspects of dark tourism placemaking. Like Seaton's (2009) notion of polysemy and multiple meanings within dark tourism, Spokes *et al.* (2018) unpack the heteroglossic nature of deviant spaces and memorialisation within dark tourism places. It is here that co-existence of meanings makes a single dark tourism site and, in so doing, allows potential representation of multiple voices and 'plural heritages' (Whitehead *et al.*, 2021). Similarly, Wilford (2015) examines the reframing of urban space and cultural identity in post-traumatic places. Wilford (2015) goes on to argue that the cultural 'rebooting' of a place is where terror spectacles are transformed into a utopic state for spectacular (dark) tourism consumption (also Phipps, 1999).

It is this utopic state that introduces Foucauldian productions of space and spatialised knowledge and a sense of place (within future dark tourism). As a prelude to fabricating a new future space, the French philosopher and historian of ideas Michel Foucault introduced the idea of *emplacements* in modern society as spaces produced through human sense-making (Foucault, 2008). This kind of emplacement, as Foucault argues, is not created by a supreme force, but occurs amid an infinite array of choices. Indeed, these (post)modern emplacements, which challenge any sense of historical hierarchy of space, organise the world and its human technologies. However, Foucault (2008: 16) goes on to suggest the production of these emplacements is 'haunted by fantasy' and it is the choice of inhabitants to adapt themselves to a shared meaning. In short, our performance and co-experience of emplacements are just as important as the designs and plans of its architects. It is this co-construction of placemaking, as noted earlier, that Foucault asks what sort of spaces we should study, and how we may best understand them. He goes on by focusing on emplacements 'that have the curious property of being in relation with all the other sites, but in such a way as to suspend, neutralize, or invert the set of relations designated, mirrored, or reflected by them' (Foucault, 2008: 16–17). Thus, drawing upon the notion of *utopia*, which Foucault defines as unreal spaces that reveal limitations of human relationships that we call real: a utopia 'is a reflection of the world that showcases not what *is* but rather what *should be*' (Wood, 2022: online). The idea of a utopia is an imagined place or state of things in which everything is perfect, a term first coined from Ancient Greek by Sir Thomas More in his 1516 Latin tome *Utopia*. However, utopian ideals do not suggest people need to be perfect, but the *system* in which they reside (for example, politics, laws, customs and conditions) *is* perfect. Characteristics of utopia include truly independent thought and emancipation. With no fears, utopian citizens would live in a harmonious state where the natural world is embraced and revered. In this world, citizens' individuality and innovation is welcomed, and social and moral ideals are embraced in which society evolves with change. With a perfect combination of economic, governmental, technological, ecological, philosophical and religious ideas, an alliance of utopian heroes upholds social and political systems that can only bring about positive evolution. However, as dark tourism portrays our fights, follies and misfortunes, there can be no dark tourism in a utopia.

The anthesis to utopia is the cacotopia or *dystopia,* a term first introduced in Lewis Henry Younge's *Utopia: or Apollo's Golden Days* in 1747. Though the relationship between the two is not a simple binary opposition, dystopias are characterised by rampant fear, distress and associated with a cataclysmic decline in society. Distinct themes of dystopia include tyranny, propaganda, control, censorship, denial of freedoms, loss of individuality and mass conformity. Brought to mainstream attention by popular culture and literature, including George Orwell's *Nineteen Eighty-Four* (1949), Aldous Huxley's *Brave New World* (1932) and Ray Bradbury's *Fahrenheit 451* (1953), future dystopian societies are the stuff of current nightmares. Indeed, a dystopia is an imagined universe in which oppressive societal control, or an apocalypse has created a world in which conditions of life are intolerable. With corporate, bureaucratic and technological control, future dystopias will be enforced through philosophical or religious ideologies and by dictatorships or theocratic government. It is against this dichotomy of the utopia/dystopia that Foucault conceives a set of principles that guides a new emplacement for contemporary society. He called these new emplacements *heterotopias*, whereby all cultures and societies have them, but they are not universal and present in every society and culture (Foucault, 1967[1984]). Heterotopia is a contested term that Foucault offered no precise definition. Instead, he provided several examples of heterotopias and outlined six principles which provide heterotopic 'statuses' of a space/place, as interpreted by Stone (2013) (see Table 1.1).

Literally meaning 'Other Places', Foucault argues heterotopias – as opposed to 'utopias' as invented spaces – are real places where boundaries of normalcy are transgressed (Foucault, [1967] 1984). Indeed, heterotopias may be seen as real places, but which are perceived to stand outside of known space and, in so doing, creates a sense of the alternative (Stone, 2013). Moreover, heterotopias can:

> … inject a sense of alterity into the sameness, and where change enters the familiar and difference is inserted into the commonplace. Indeed, heterotopias are spaces of contradiction and duality, as well as places of physical representation and imagined meaning … Ultimately, heterotopias can be physical or mental spaces that act as 'Other places' alongside existing spaces. These include places where norms of conduct are suspended either through a sense of crisis or through deviation of

Table 1.1 The six principles of heterotopolgy (adapted from Stone, 2013b)

Principle	Definition
#1 Heterotopias of Crisis & Deviation	Every culture has heterotopias, although the forms they take are heterogenous. Heterotopias of crisis are forbidden places reserved for individuals in times of social, cultural or political crises. Heterotopias of deviation are spaces that either invite 'deviance' or oddities within behaviour, or spaces that have diverged and hold discrepancy and thus have a state of abnormality.
#2 Heterotopias of Functionality	Each heterotopia has a precise and determined function with a society. Yet the same heterotopia can possess duality and permit the connection of another place with ordinary cultural spaces.
#3 Heterotopias of Juxtaposition	Heterotopias have the power to juxtapose in a single real place several spaces that are in themselves incompatible.
#4 Heterotopias of Chronology	Heterotopias are linked to slices of time or 'heterochronism', where time is accumulated and, subsequently, collects evidence of an age in a perpetual and indefinite manner.
#5 Heterotopias of (De)valorisation	Heterotopias presuppose a system of 'opening' and 'closing' rituals and purifications that both isolates them yet makes them penetrable.
#6 Heterotopias of Illusion & Compensation	Heterotopias create illusions that exposes all real spaces and create a place that is Other(ed) and, consequently, compensate us for the angst of contemporary society. In short, binaries between the real and surreal are brought into focus.

behaviour. Heterotopias also have a precise and determined function and are reflective of the society in which they exist. They also have the power to juxtapose several real spaces simultaneously as well as being linked to the accumulative or transitory nature of time. Heterotopias are also places that are not freely accessible as well as being spaces of illusion and compensation. In short, Foucault argued that we are now in an era of simultaneity, juxtaposition, of proximity and distance, of side-by-side, and of the dispersed. (Stone, 2013: 80)

Foucault's 'heterotopology' – that is, the notion of certain cultural, institutional and discursive spaces that are somehow 'Othered' – are places that can be disturbing, intense, incompatible, contradictory or transforming. While Foucault's notion of heterotopology is frustratingly incomplete, inconsistent and even incoherent (Dehaene & De Cauter, 2008a; Grbin, 2015; Johnson, 2013; Soja, 1996), dark tourism has been scrutinised under a heterotopic lens (Young & Light, 2016). For instance, Stone (2013) examines tourist encounters of Chernobyl, the site of the world's worst nuclear accident in 1986 in the former USSR, and its subsequent 'dead Zone'. Adopting the principles of heterotopias (Figure 1.1), Stone (2013: 90–91) suggests:

> It [Chernobyl] exists alongside ordinary spaces of the everyday, yet it is a place where disaster has been captured and suspended. It is a place of crisis, of deviation, of serious reflection. It has a functionality that is determined by its touristic consumption and, in turn, is reflective of the society in which we exist. A surreal place to juxtapose our apocalyptic nightmares, Chernobyl is both real and imagined. It is

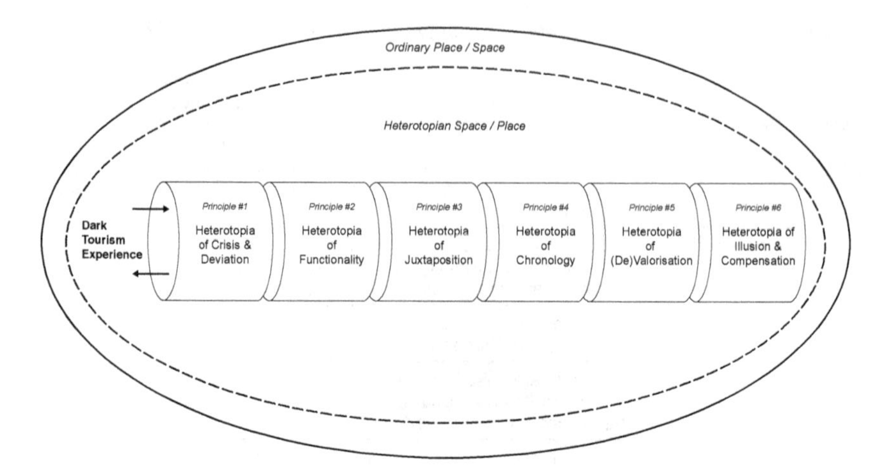

Figure 1.1 A Dark Tourism Cylinder: A conceptual model showing the dark tourism experience within a heterotopian framework
Source: Stone, 2013.

> a space for time and of the time, a place that accumulates the failures of a political era and consumed by transient tourists in dark tourism moments … Chernobyl possesses rituals to valorise its penetrability, to allow temporary access to a so-called dead zone that is both illusionary and compensatory. Chernobyl is a heterotopia that allows us to gaze on a postapocalyptic world, in which the familiar and uncanny collide. Indeed, tourists now ritually consume the place as a site of environmental disaster, failed technology and political collapse. Yet, Chernobyl and its dead zone is a surreal space that reflects the reality of our contemporary world – a world exposed by dark tourism.

Similarly, Morten *et al.* (2018) examine Auschwitz-Birkenau, the Nazi death camp located within occupied Poland during World War II, as a dark tourism heterotopia. They argue that 'Auschwitz-Birkenau represents a microcosm of an apocalyptic world; the ordinary world outside the camp's perimeters is brought to the fore and exposed for all its geopolitical disorder and fragile societal frameworks in which we are all located' (Morten *et al.*, 2018: 244). Meanwhile, Toussaint and Decrop (2013) evaluate the famous Père-Lachaise cemetery in Paris as a heterotopia. They examine relationships between dark tourism and sacred consumption and, subsequently, suggest heterotopias offer a valuable framework in which to locate the blurred sacred-profane dialectic (Toussaint & Decrop, 2013). Likewise, Paliewicz and Hasian (2017) highlight popular memory at Ground Zero, the site of the 9/11 terrorist atrocities in New York, within a heterotopological approach. Specifically, they analyse commemorative processes of the National September 11 Memorial and the Memorial Museum, which ended up transforming into a heterotopia marked by contestations, juxtapositions and contradictions. While Paliewicz and Hasian (2017: 19) suggest many wished to have a memorial that simply told unified tales about heroism and resilience, 'the social constructions of Ground Zero space have resisted monolithic historical accounts of remembrance despite the influential forces of utopian visions'. They go on to argue that heterotology as a heuristic tool is useful for 'unpacking polysemic and polyvalent spaces of commemoration that may otherwise appear consensual and monoglossic' (Paliewicz & Hasian, 2017: 19). The unpacking of polysemic spaces is also explored by Stone and Stewart (forthcoming) who examine difficult heritage and placemaking of Salem, Massachusetts, USA, and the cultural trauma of the Salem Witch Trials in 1692. They appraise semiotic embodiment of the urban supernatural in Salem within the realms of collective memory and social identity. Moreover, Stone and Stewart (forthcoming) argue Salem is where material realities and (re)imagined supernatural spaces assemble to co-create a place where people consume dark tourism events of reflection and illusion, as well as engaging with atrocities and misdeeds of the problematic past. Specifically, they state:

> … Salem is also an Other place – a *heterotopia* – where contradictory spaces of extraordinary supernatural exists alongside ordinary places. It is also a place of collective memory that has been made to both capture and suspend its cultural trauma. Moreover, Salem has a function to export its tragic history through touristic consumption and festivalization where, subsequently, is reflective of the society in which we exist. Consequently, Salem is a surreal place to juxtapose our witchery nightmares which are both real and imagined. The illusionary and compensatory nature of Salem's placemaking means that we gaze upon social bigotry as a cultural product in which the familiar and uncanny collide. Ultimately, Salem reflects the reality of our contemporary globalised community, where it is a world within a world, mirroring and yet upsetting what is outside. (Stone & Stewart, forthcoming)

Notwithstanding its use within (dark) tourism studies, an academic 'cottage industry' has emerged to utilise heterotopias in cultural and social geography (Johnson, 2013): and in other disciplines, including but not limited to, media studies (Dove-Viebhan, 2007), management theory (Hjorth, 2005), literary studies (Meerzon, 2007), science fiction studies (Gordon, 2003) and education and childhood studies (McNamee, 2000). Specific illustrations of using heterotopias as a guiding approach have also been used in a diverse variety of spaces and places, including the museum (e.g. Lord, 2006), cathedrals (e.g. Shackley, 2002), gardens, landscapes and parks (e.g. Guarrasi, 2001; Joyce, 2003; Rotenberg, 1995), the cybercafé (e.g. Liff, 2003), prisons (e.g. Baer & Ravneberg,

2008), pornographic internet sites (e.g. Jacobs, 2004), nudist beaches (e.g. Andriotis, 2010), shopping malls (Kern, 2008) and factories (Hetherington, 1997).

Despite an array of academic applications, ambiguity of the heterotopia concept has provoked much critical discourse (an idea that Foucault did not return to and elaborate). Moreover, the idea of heterotopia has inherent limitations and biases, not least those concerned with knowledge, time, spatiality and power (Harvey, 2000a, 2000b, 2007, 2009; Saldanha, 2008). Although these are beyond the scope of my chapter (but see Johnson, 2013), and while heterotopias formulate a complex relationship between time and space (Dehaene & De Cauter, 2008b), heterotopias disturb 'the familiar landmarks of my thought – our thought' (Foucault, 1970: xv). Indeed, heterotopias may be defined as 'sites which are embedded in aspects and stages of our lives, and which somehow mirror and at the same time distort, unsettle, or invert other spaces' (Johnson, 2013: 790–791). While heterotopias relate to the rest of space, they are at variance somehow and are localisable (Foucault, [1967]1984). Consequently, from a geographical rather than sociological perspective, Edward Soja in his influential 'Thirdspace' studies adopts Foucault's heterotopology (along with Lefebvre's seminal work on the 'production of space') to describe a new method of 'reading' places (Lefebvre, 1991; Soja, 1989, 1995, 1996). Soja's Thirdspace (the Firstspace being physical, and Secondspace being conceptual) is both real and imagined in which people live in and experience places. Soja (1996: 57) argues that in Thirdspace:

> ... everything comes together ... subjectivity and objectivity, the abstract and the concrete, the real and the imagined, the knowable and the unimaginable, the repetitive and the differential, structure and agency, mind and body, consciousness and the unconscious, the disciplined and the transdisciplinary, everyday life and unending history.

In many ways, the idea of Thirdspace is more inclusive than heterotopology whereby epistemology, ontology and historicity is augmented in continuous movement beyond dualisms and toward 'an-Other'. Consequently, Thirdspace produces 'cumulative trialectics that is radically open to additional Otherness, [and] to a continuing expansion of spatial knowledge' (Soja, 1996: 61). In short, Thirdspace is a transcendent idea that is ever-evolving to include 'an-Other'. In doing so, Thirdspace enables the contestation and re-negotiation of boundaries and cultural identity. Indeed, resembling the work of Homi Bhabha's 'Third Space Theory' (Bhabha, 1994), Soja (1996: 62) argues that 'all forms of culture are continually in a process of hybridity'. Importantly, it is this hybridity in Thirdspace that displaces the histories that constitute it, and sets up new structures of authority, new political initiatives and gives rise to something different, something new and unrecognizable, a new area of negotiation of meaning and representation (Rutherford, 1990).

Consequently, when it comes to future placemaking, hybridity and displacement take on significance by augmenting and extending the confines of heterotopias and its relationship with Thirdspace. Specifically, this new hybridity displaces future emplacements in society (and our eventual virtual immersion within them), by embracing technology and technological advancements hitherto unseen, yet imagined. By incorporating heterotopic and Thirdspace principles that construe *an-Other* place, modern technologies and 'cybernetic realities allow for new ways of experiencing and examining heterotopias' (Morten *et al.*, 2018: 244). In turn, ideas of the 'virtual heterotopia' have been brought into futuristic realms (Rousseaux & Thouvenin, 2009). Therefore, in a contemporary world where technology is steadily being fused with the fabric of society, the heterotopias of tomorrow will not be real places, but surreal spaces borne out of our technological imaginations. It is here that I take my philosophical cue and, drawing upon conceptual foundations laid by Foucault and Soja, I now turn to augment and reimagine notions of heterotopias and Thirdspace. To that end, I suggest a new *emplacement* that incorporates principles of heteropology and Thirdspace inclusivity yet introduces new axioms to reflect a future hyperreal virtual world. In doing so, I now outline a new kind of space: one that exists already but one that is also yet to exist.

Vertopia: Toward Conceptualising Future Virtual Spaces

The 'virtual world' has developed exponentially over the past couple of decades, propelling our technical advancements as we continue the Information Revolution (Robins & Webster, 2020). Even though Bell (2008) and Schroeder (2008) offered early definitions of what a virtual world might be, the essence of virtual worlds have hitherto been techno centric. Indeed, as Girvan (2018) notes, essential conceptualisations of virtual worlds have been lacking. Noting the crisis of boundaries that forms the interface between our physical and virtual worlds, Girvan (2018) argues a 'virtual world' is a simulated environment which meets the parameters of a *world*. These worldly parameters include a sense of embodiment, movement and perception within a space. Thus, according to Girvan (2018: 1090), a 'world' comprises three fundamental ideas:

(1) A shared space which is inhabited and shaped by its inhabitants.
(2) Experiences and interpretation of those experiences are not fixed but mediated through our physical bodies and psychological responses.
(3) Through our physical bodies we move about the shared space, interacting with objects and others, with whom we construct a shared understanding of the world.

Crucially, Girvan (2018: 1097) argues that users of virtual worlds require a sense of presence of being immersed in a shared space and, subsequently, virtual worlds are shaped by their inhabitants in a form of placemaking futurities. By engaging with technology and being the 'consumer content' as well as a 'producer of content' – what Fisher (2010) called 'prosumers' – inhabitants become embodied as *avatars* (Girvan, 2018). Subsequently, the virtual world is experienced and mediated through our bodies, whereby the avatar as embodiment and incarnation of the human form gives inhabitants an active agent to encounter hyperreality. It is these avatars that take on agency of *ghosts*, as rhetorically noted earlier in my introduction. Therefore, Girvan (2018: 1097) defines a 'virtual world' and the role of avatars as:

> ... shared, simulated spaces which are inhabited and shaped by their inhabitants who are represented as avatars. These avatars mediate our experience of this space as we move, interact with objects, and interact with others, with whom we construct a shared understanding of the world at that time.

Our new future virtual worlds through embodied avatar mediation will allow us to explore perceptual, cognitive and emotional power of experiences. In turn, to fully embrace the nature of virtual environments, our future virtual worlds must abandon everyday perceptions and physical environments, as well as characteristics of media. We cannot yet truly describe at present what a virtual world might be, or what our avatars will look like, but our virtual experiences will inherently entail co-creation between developer and inhabitant. Moreover, our avatars will firstly represent us, secondly transform us and, finally, become us. The embodiment of avatars will enable the finding of our stories rather than the telling of our tales. Indeed, 'surrealism is essential in virtual environment design because of its counterintuitive ability to enhance the feeling of presence while transcending reality' (Bolas, 2018: xvii).

We are already at a stage where virtual worlds partially exist, though the complete fusion of the physical world and virtual environments is still yet to be. Today, virtual worlds include platforms that adapt forms of virtual reality, augmented reality, artificial intelligence and telepresence. While the parameters and limitations of these computer-mediated interfaces to real and virtual worlds are beyond the scope of my chapter (but see Sherman & Craig, 2019), there are number of defining features worth noting. These include virtual worlds as mediums of interactive communication that require physical and mental immersion, as well as synthetic simulation. What we might currently call virtual worlds are best described as computer-generated platforms: including the *metaverse* – a vision of the next iteration of the internet where a single, shared, immersive, persistent and 3D virtual space exists where humans live in a way they could not in the physical world (Tucci,

2022). While the technology to create a so-called metaverse remains at the embryonic stage, the vision is not new. The term 'Metaverse' arrives from digital antiquity and was first coined by Neal Stephenson in his 1992 sci-fi novel *Snow Crash*. Reimagined by Ernest Clines in the 2011 dystopian novel *Ready Player One* (and later adapted as a 2018 movie directed by Steven Spielberg), the metaverse refers 'to a fully realized digital world that exists beyond the analogue one in which we live' (Herrman & Browning, 2021: online).

Our analogue world is slowly beginning to morph with digital realms today. Online games such as *Roblox*, *World of Warcraft*, *Fornite*, *Animal Crossing*, *Minecraft* and *Second Life* in which gamers construct their own worlds have metaverse tendencies. Moreover, the convoluted system of crypto currency that uses cryptography to secure digital transactions, including Bitcoin, Ethereum and Tether, have the hallmarks of making any metaverse mercantile. Likewise, economic imperatives of the initial metaverse platform have recently been demonstrated by *Decentraland*, whereby virtual real estate and digital land can be traded (Kraken, 2023). Similarly, global brands such as *Gucci* and *Nike* have of late disrupted the market by creating early pioneer simulated products within an evolving metaverse, including retailing (virtual) shoes, apparel and accessories (Hollensen *et al.*, 2023). Meanwhile, in a post-Covid-19 world, where homeworking was catapulted into the mainstream economy with increased use of online meeting platforms such as *Zoom* or *Microsoft Teams*, our digital office backgrounds or the use of a digital avatar meant that we were 'treading into the neighbourhood of metaversality' (Herrman & Browning, 2021: online). Accordingly, Ball (2020: online) describes the metaverse:

> ... not as a virtual world, but as a sort of successor state to the mobile internet – a framework for an extremely connected life. There will be no clean *Before Metaverse* and *After Metaverse* [original emphasis] ... instead, it will slowly emerge over time as different products, services, and capabilities integrate and meld together.

While we are yet to capture the promise or appreciate the perils of the next internet, and whether we call it the metaverse or not, modern touchstones of superintelligence and the 'Second Machine Age' will undoubtedly present us with novel issues of governance and philosophies (Ball, 2022). Nevertheless, new realities of virtual worlds are now being realised, particularly within the realms of marketing, consumer research and visitor economies (for example Adachi *et al.*, 2022; Buhalis *et al.*, 2023; Dwivedi *et al.*, 2022; Koohang *et al.*, 2023; Yung & Khoo-Lattimore, 2019). However, scholarship on virtual worlds and its subsequent platforms such as the metaverse tend to focus on the mechanics and technocracies of creating such space. There has been limited attempt to address the philosophy of how these virtual spaces will act as new future emplacements. Notwithstanding arguments about the *simulation hypothesis* – that is, the world we are living in now is in fact a virtual world – made famous by the *Matrix* movie franchise starring Keanu Reeves, virtual worlds are not illusions or fictions. As Chalmers (2022: xvii) points out, 'virtual reality is genuine reality, or at least, virtual realities are genuine realities'. In his 2022 book *Reality+,* David Chalmers outlines adventures in 'techno-philosophy' and offers us a thought-provoking journey into the nature of virtual reality and its philosophical conundrums. Even so, discourse on cybernetic landscapes and its spatial relationships with physical society and culture remain lacking.

It is here that I return to the conceptualism of Foucault's heterotopias and Soja's Thirdspace. Considering the trajectory for virtual world evolution, emplacements of tomorrow will not only exist outside the realms of the physical world, but they will also disturb social norms and invert our physical environment. As I have argued, virtual worlds will be future worlds where complete embodiment of the Self through our avatars will mediate our Other existence and, in so doing, manipulate our corporeality. Indeed, our total immersive existence within a virtual world will ensure the perfect coincidence of presence, belief, emotion and illusion (Slater, 2018). Consequently, we will co-create surreal places out of virtual spaces that will always provoke the future and continually disrupt the present. I call these new imagined spaces – built and inhabited within virtual realities of the future – a *vertopia.* Added to subject glossaries of virtual reality and placemaking for future scholarship, the vertopia will become a real digitalised heterotopia – a *Fourthspace* – where access will be granted through experience. Vertopias will be virtual emplacements of our cognitive imaginations, yet are both genuine and artificial, that collide and fuse with technological transmutations hitherto unseen. In short, vertopias will be powered by the mind, for the mind. They will present us with seamless virtual worlds from our own physical world. The vertopia will take on attributes of Foucault's heterotopology as virtual spaces of juxtaposition, function, deviation, illusion and compensation. They will be places that mirror our physical existence, but which are both temporal and perpetual, and are linked to society but will create new societies. The vertopia will be an amalgam and multitude of computer-generated platforms, such as the metaverse, in which we live and converse in liminal places where our biology becomes interfused with technology and superintelligence. The vertopia will be populated by our physical beings that will be activated and married with technology, our consciousness and biology kept alive by machinery and manifested by the avatar. Once inside the vertopia, our avatars become you, and you become the avatar – separated only by mortality. When our biological beings pass away, our cognitivism and personality morph into our avatars and the vertopia becomes self-fulfilled. Consequently, the vertopia will create multiple scenarios and gateways where the biological-Self reacts and interacts with the vertopian-Other. In turn, we will have the option of immortality as our avatars live in on in perpetuity, evolving from our original beings, but taking on our personalities and cognitivism. Eventually, we will suspend the Grim Reaper and reinvent death in a new virtual reality where our vertopian souls become our future citizens (also see Boellstrorff, 2013; Ferguson, 2012; Klastrup, 2006).

Notions of total immersion and embodiment in a mutual virtual world through the provision of multiple computer-generated platforms opens endless possibilities (and pitfalls). Purposely, I draw upon Foucault and his concept of heterotopia as spaces outside the realms of place and, subsequently, I have imagined future placemaking within new virtual worlds – which I have termed *vertopias*. Of course, there are outstanding issues and limitations with this new conceptual emplacement, not least those concerned with technicalities, resources and capacities, replication, time, power, control and governance, as well as faith and religion. Therefore, it is up to scholars to judge or even dismiss the idea of vertopia as communal virtual immersive realities. Future scholarship might also wish to critically augment the idea of the vertopia and its conceptual merit or practical application, particularly with the fields of philosophy, sociology and human geography.

Conclusion

The technological revolution that is yet to come will undoubtedly reinvent our sense of reality. Through a futurology lens, I have set out what this evolution might look like, particularly regarding dark tourism placemaking, our digital dead and our sense of place within virtual environments. Of course, we do not know what the future is, yet while life can only be understood backwards, it must be lived forwards. Therefore, augmenting the spatial mentalities of both Foucault and Soja, I have drawn upon broader notions of the (incomplete) heterotopia concept and its subsequent Thirdspace progression. I have also drawn upon virtuality studies and predicted, or at least termed a new kind of future emplacement. These new virtual emplacements – which I have originally called *vertopia* – will take on the mantle of heterotopolgy as digital Other spaces. These new vertopias will amplify and advance boundaries of Thirdspace and, subsequently, the vertopia will become a Fourthspace, one that is virtual but is inhabited by embodied avatars and is the perfect interfusion of biological and technological entities. Consequently, our avatars will evolve *as us*, extend our sense of mortality and suspend the Grim Reaper. As our future virtual Self, we will become immersed in an-Other digital dimension.

While I have set out the parameters of what a vertopia might be, I have also fictionally contextualised the idea through a future case scenario. Specifically, through the lens of bygone public executions and the making of penal heritage for touristic consumption, I have drawn upon the idea of future penal codes being consumed once again in a public arena. However, in this fabricated case, the arena is within a new vertopian emplacement, where the semiology of judicial spectacles is ritually and playfully consumed by tourists of tomorrow. Indeed, my case scenario raises profound consequences of not only what the vertopia might eventually be but evokes an array of ethical and philosophical quandaries that exist both now and in the future. Specifically, these include issues of mass surveillance *by* the public and *of* the public, data dissemination and control, criminal justice and retribution, penal heritage representation and performance, and the future of (dark) tourist experiences. Nevertheless, in a future of virtual immersion, we will consume dark tourism through digital theatres of performance, where embodiment and surrealism will become the norm. Finally, while surrealism might be considered destructive and makes our future appear broken, it destroys only the manacles limiting our illusions. Reality is evolving at such a creative and technological pace that conceptions of what is real and what is unreal are becoming increasingly blurred. That said, of course, it remains to be seen whether any future vertopia and our fused existence within it will be a hallucinatory fantasy or a hypnogogic nightmare. It is this that awaits us all, as our digital dead are already alive.

Acknowledgments

I would like to thank Dr Sean Gammon, Dr David Jarratt and Aaron Stone for their valued insights and critical reviews of early drafts of this chapter.

Notes

(1) My case scenario is inspired from various sources which I acknowledge here. Apart from historical public executions as discussed, my fictional account is also influenced by George Orwell and his 1949 dystopian cautionary tale *Nineteen Eighty-Four*. Particularly, I am drawn by Orwell's ideas of mass surveillance, though not by government as Orwell had articulated, but by the general populace and how surveillance is disseminated through modern social media. It is here that *The Circle* offered me further revelations, a 2013 dystopian fiction by Dave Eggers, and later made as a techno-thriller movie directed by James Ponsoldt and starring Emma Watson and Tom Hanks. In *The Circle,* issues of power, corporatocracy and sharing and recording surveillance data are explored. Particularly, *The Circle* examines how 'the Web not only supplements institutions but becomes the only institution in society – knowing, organising, and administering everything' (Maurer & Rostbøll, 2020). However, the key stimulus for my case scenario arrives from 'White Bear', an episode of the British

sci-fi anthology television series *Black Mirror*. First aired in 2013 on Channel 4 (UK), 'White Bear' written by Charlie Brooker follows a female protagonist who wakes up with no memory to be controlled by a television signal while surviving merciless pursuers; only to discover she is the villain in a dystopian setting, and her punishment is perpetual. The story draws parallels with real murder cases, specifically the 1960s Moor Murders in which five children were killed by Ian Brady and Myra Hindley in and around Manchester, and which some of the killing was audio-recorded by the murderers. 'White Bear' also reflects upon numerous aspects of contemporary society, including media coverage of murders, technology's effects on people's empathy, desensitisation, violence as entertainment and tourism, vigilantism, the concept of justice and punishment and the nature of reality. Moreover, the simulated strangulation of Pip, as the protagonist in my future case scenario, bears some resemblance to present-day visitor experiences. Specifically, Merlin Entertainments Ltd (UK) in their Dungeon visitor attractions; tourists can experience simulated hangings on gravity-drop 'Drop Dead Rides', whereby 'executions' from bygone ages are 'performed' through 'edutainment'.

(2) My original use of the term 'vertopia' adapts the phrase 'virtual' (as in virtual reality) and the word 'topia' from the Latin *topia* meaning 'landscape' or from Ancient Greek τόπια (*tópia* / *tópos*) meaning 'place': including artistic representations of either natural or artificial features used as the medium. To the best of my understanding, this term *vertopia* (as in the precise spelling) has not appeared before to describe virtual reality spaces of the future, particularly those which have been grounded in Foucauldian perspectives. That said, however, I do acknowledge a similar term 'virtopia' (adapted from 'virtual utopia') which was used by Goslin and Morie (1996) to explore artistic aspects of creating virtual environments. These early pioneers aimed to create an artificial environment that was both emotionally engaging and meaningfully interactive. Goslin and Morie (1996) provide an early example of a 'emotional simulator' which they called the 'Virtopia Project' and was based upon artistic endeavours (but also see Morie, 2007 and Motalebi, 2017). Similarly, I also acknowledge the namesake of the company 'Virtopia' at https://virtopia.co.uk/ which, at the time of writing, is a virtual reality and augmented reality content production studio, based in London, UK.

(3) When Christ was executed in Jerusalem by the Romans, he was crucified as a political prisoner on the feast of Passover (also known as Pesach) – a Jewish public holiday – in a recreational exhibition of public executions. Moreover, the Colosseum in Rome offered Romans an early tourist attraction where state sanctioned murder of people deemed delinquent became a leisure outing. Indeed, from antiquity through to the 19th century, crime and punishment has often been on display as judicial spectacles. Importantly, public executions were ritualised events that evolved as statecraft to control populations and to project political power (Seaton & Dann, 2018), as well as offering the public a valid excuse to leave home. Therefore, trials and punishments from yesteryear were not only the enactment of laws, but also the ritual display of society at work and play. It is here that Erving Goffman viewed many social interactions as theatrical performances and semiotic codes (Goffman, 1959, 1971). Indeed, Goffman argued that society was a kind of theatre in which roles and performances are conducted, including within past and present penal systems. As Seaton and Dann (2018: 35) note:

> ... trial and punishment evolved as *engineered and orchestrated spectacles* [original emphasis] in which people acted out the roles allocated to them semiotically. Attendance by audiences exposed them to the deterrent might of the law and engaged them in a public complicity that signified a tacit approval of its legitimacy. This historical evolution [is] traced down to modern times when spectacles of public trial and punishment largely

> disappeared, giving way to less brutal, but more pervasive and diverse, displays vested in popular culture, which mediated, engineered, and orchestrated the criminal justice system to the general public. One of them [is] dark tourism and the ideological practices and perceptions produced within it ...

Therefore, dark tourism can represent our penal heritage and evinces significant crime within visitor economies (Barton & Brown, 2012; Dalton, 2015; Wilson, 2008). Moreover, as societies act as theatres of performance and our social interactions are semiotic of broader issues of legitimacy, complicity and control (after Goffman), we can begin to imagine future penal heritage within dark tourism. This is particularly so when penal justice is performed within future virtual worlds. Drawing upon historical penal codes that have been rendered as ritualised and public spectacles, my fictional case scenario of future retributive justice is performed as touristic spectacles, whereby criminal and spectator interact in the Vertopia of tomorrow.

(4) Set in a future of your choice whereby I draw inspiration from the past as well as the present, my case scenario is set within the field of futurology (Yeoman & McMahon-Beattie, 2020; also see Wright, 2016, 2018, 2021; Wright & Zascerinka, 2022). It is designed to provoke critical discourse, and positioned within the future portrayal of our penal heritage and the role dark tourism might play.

2 Virtual Afterlife: Dark Tourism in the Hereafter

Rachael Ironside and Craig Leith

You are now travelling to the Virtual Afterlife...

Introduction

This chapter follows fictional characters Charlotte and her counsellor, Hagan, into a possible dark tourism future where living and virtual souls are connected in an immersive Artificial Intelligence (AI) environment called the Virtual Afterlife. In this unique scenario, future technology has provided users with an opportunity to meet, converse and interact with individuals who are deceased. The Virtual Afterlife also offers opportunities for the living to upload their digital footprint into a virtual space for others to connect with them when they are dead. We propose that this future concept is grounded in the expansion of virtual and haptic technological developments, as well as a growing trend towards the use of big data and social media interactions which, at present, already leave behind a 'digital afterlife' (Basset, 2018). Furthermore, the growth in a 'spiritual-quest culture' (Eaton, 2015) and desire to understand and relate to death in contemporary society (Stone, 2012a, 2012b; Stone & Sharpley, 2008), suggest developments in the virtual and spiritual space may present opportunities and challenges for dark tourism in the future. It is through this futuristic lens that we examine three potential scenarios (that is, grief and therapy, commercial souls and commemoration), together with conceptual underpinning, from the perspective of Charlotte and Hagan, for dark tourism futures in the Virtual Afterlife.

Imagine it is the year 2124, as we join Charlotte waiting for her friend Becca in a New York café. Just moments earlier, Charlotte had been somewhere else entirely, sitting with her Virtual Afterlife Counsellor in a Unique Virtual Experience Suite. After fitting her virtual headset, haptic technology suit and settling down into a comfortable seat with a whisky, she presses the button on the side of her headset and starts her journey into the Virtual Afterlife.

A Virtual Afterlife: An Imagined Scenario

It is a Sunday afternoon in the year 2124. Charlotte reaches for her virtual headset and waits to connect with her friend, Becca. Today they have chosen to meet in a small café in the centre of Manhattan, a special place in which they found sanctuary from the rain 10 years previous.

Charlotte sometimes grew anxious as she settled into the familiar surroundings of the art-deco café: a place in which she had spent increasingly more time in recent months. Too much time, perhaps. Charlotte pondered briefly before pushing her thought aside. Lifting a glass and taking a small sip of whisky, she realised her worries would, yet again, be unfounded within moments of sitting across from her lifelong friend, Becca. In no time at all they would be talking, laughing and reminiscing. No doubt Becca had already heard about Charlotte's latest romantic misadventures and was probably planning an hour of teasing at her expense. Indeed, Charlotte knew this is what she currently needed. Her family and other friends were putting lots of pressure on her to settle down into a relationship. She could always rely on Becca to notice her mood and say the right things. And every time, Charlotte would leave the café in a stronger, more confident emotional state. This ability of Becca's was almost magical. For her part, Charlotte was always desperate to hear Becca talk with passion and excitement about her own recent travels as a successful photojournalist. Her childhood dream came true. Despite the hugely different paths they had taken over the last four years, Charlotte knew that the deep connections which they shared could never be broken. Their dual private world had developed over the years, and both had often expressed frustration at times when the outside world of family or other friends imposed themselves on *their* world.

Becca was giggling as she strolled confidently into the café, which remained the same in look and ambience since their very first visit and made her way to their usual table in the corner alcove. As she approached, Charlotte had a flashback of them both venturing into the same café for the first of many visits almost 10 years ago. On that wet winter's day, it was intended as nothing more than a brief sanctuary from the New York elements. Several hours later, the girls stumbled into the night, having made a vow (witnessed by a bemused café owner) that they would return to the café on the same day every year as a celebration and renewal of their friendship. They solemnly promised each other that nothing would ever cause this vow to be broken. And so, it had proven. Becca and Charlotte continued their annual celebrations to this day and despite Becca's death four years ago.

Hagan's gaze flickered between the electronic readings on the screen and Charlotte herself as she lay peacefully in front of him. Hagan had first met Charlotte during a Virtual Afterlife Commemoration Event. Hosted annually, and funded by the city council, the event commemorated the loss of over 100 people four years earlier, the result of several active shooters in a busy shopping street in Manhattan. Charlotte had lost her friend Becca that day. Hagan had been recruited as one of the Virtual Afterlife Counsellors to attend the event, his role was to be present, walk around the virtual crowd and to speak to attendees who he felt might require additional help and guidance. This was a free service, aimed at supporting those who had lost loved ones. Occasionally, Hagan would meet someone who required additional support, and Charlotte was one of those clients. It was one of the most rewarding aspects of his role and he now sat on the organising committee for several Virtual Afterlife Commemoration Events around the world.

As a qualified Virtual Afterlife Counsellor, Hagan often used his experience to guide the client through their immersive Virtual Afterlife in a way like grief counsellors in the physical realm. He vividly recalled a previous client from last year who had been struggling with the death of a sibling in a traffic accident. Although investigators were adamant that the death had been instantaneous and involved no suffering, his previous client had been unable to accept this, leading to regular debilitating nightmares. Eventually an immersive virtual afterlife environment of the traffic accident had been created and, over several sessions, Hagan joined the client to witness it repeatedly. Understandably traumatic to begin with, as the sessions continued Hagan was able to listen to, probe and explain the feelings of the client to help him understand underlying reasons for the nightmares and the reality of his siblings sudden, though painless, passing. On other occasions, Hagan had taken on the role of a passive bystander and simply observed how a client engaged with the immersive virtual afterlife environment then prepared a report of his findings after the event.

Despite the positive benefits of the Virtual Afterlife, Hagan also had growing concerns about some of the more unethical practices he was hearing about. Recently, he had discovered that backroom virtual experience creators had established themselves – and indeed won awards – in the pornography virtual experience sphere; exploiting rapid advancements around haptic technology. To Hagan's mind came the recent court case involving a tech billionaire and the virtual afterlife experience he 'enjoyed' with JFK and Marilyn Monroe. The estates of both JFK and Monroe submitted a joint case against said billionaire because of 'non-consensual sexual activity with virtual representations of deceased persons'. The court's decision was seen by many as less than satisfactory. As the billionaire had previously purchased all virtual image rights of Monroe, there was seen to be no legal barrier. However, the rights of JFK were owned by a large media conglomerate, and they sued in a separate court action for unauthorised use of virtual images and were awarded several million dollars in compensation. However, to the delight of the virtual pornographer/virtual afterlife experience creator all the following societal debate and moralistic handwringing had simply led to a rapidly filled order book for high-quality, bespoke, though highly dubious, experiences.

Hagan winced and shook his head to clear it of these mental musings. Despite his years of experience, it was quite unforgivable for a Virtual Afterlife Counsellor to be distracted in this way. Full attention must always be paid to the client under the counsellor's care. He turned his attention back to Charlotte. This current experience was her 18th since she first made contact two years ago. He was still analysing the data and notes from Charlotte's sessions. It appeared, at least on a surface level, that connecting with Becca in the Virtual Afterlife had offered comfort for Charlotte through the grieving process. However, Hagan could not shake a growing anxiety about the future of the Virtual Afterlife. Seven years ago, he was one of the first to sign up for his data and image to be used posthumously – he was now contemplating the fate of his *virtual soul* in the Virtual Afterlife Environment. Would it help or hinder his family to continue their relationship? Who would control his virtual existence? And how?

Contrary to Hagan's doubts about his own future virtual soul, Charlotte had never possessed any such reticence. She took comfort in knowing that Becca would always be there for her – anytime she wanted or needed. The Virtual Afterlife provided a virtual anchor for their ever-lasting friendship. Indeed, several months ago Charlotte had the epiphany that there was no reason to limit their reunions to only once a year. The Virtual Afterlife gave her comfort and meaning in life which the physical realm now lacked without Becca.

Grief, Therapy and the Virtual Afterlife

In our proposed future Virtual Afterlife, Charlotte's relationship with Becca continues despite her friend's untimely and sudden death four years previously. Advancements in Virtual Reality (VR) enable the two friends to travel to locations around the world that were meaningful during their 'living' travels together. Unlike some of the initial dark tourism VR, such as *Chernobyl VR Project* and the controversial *08:46* (Hassapopoulou, 2018), the Virtual Afterlife Environment was designed, at least initially, as a therapeutic space. Users were encouraged to travel to virtual places that evoked meaning and significance for them and their deceased counterpart. The integration of haptic technology, a skin-tight suit that simulated feelings – such as a hug – generated a more real, immersive experience. The Virtual Afterlife was also designed to offer a conversational AI experience that allowed, or at least appeared to allow, the dead to be conscious of real-world occurrences. Consequently, each 'soul' in the Virtual Afterlife is linked to a continuous stream of big data relating world news, events and, if selected, connected to the personal social media accounts of their living friends and family.

This futuristic concept, and the role of technology in posthumously preserving *souls* in a virtual hereafter is not new – neither is it beyond the scope of recent commercial, creative, and technological developments. For instance, British television programmes such as the *Black Mirror* series episode 'Be Right Back' (2013) have played with the idea of recreating loved ones in simulated and 'real' AI environments. Indeed, as Basset (2018) acknowledges Facebook RIP sites already extend our souls into the digital realm and companies have started to shift into the death-tech industry. Using data and online spaces to recreate 'virtual souls' who can be conversed with, memorialised and remembered is not then a distant, dystopian future but, rather an emerging reality in a posthuman sphere.

In our scenario, the unexpected loss of her friend Becca had been traumatic for Charlotte. As her closest, long-term friend there had been so much left unsaid. The Virtual Afterlife had presented an opportunity for Charlotte to connect with her friend and relay these messages, as well as seek comfort in her familiar company. This experience surpasses her public memorialisation across various social media platforms that regularly attracts the sentiments of Becca's wider social network (Brubaker *et al.*, 2013). Gibson (2007) suggests that a desire to record a loved one's existence, or a need for public recognition are drivers for sharing feelings of grief with strangers online. However, from the earliest days of Becca's passing, Charlotte had become ever more frustrated and angered her friend's death had been, in her opinion at least, hijacked by mere acquaintances. She had resisted the pressure to 'like' a lengthy Facebook post by Becca's grieving father simply because she felt others were using it as an opportunity to share their own limited and superficial memories of her dear friend. As Walter (2015) identified, memorialising the dead online is subject to norms created by online mourners, and those who do not engage with such expectations leave themselves open to censure. For Charlotte, the unfortunate consequence of this was a growing and indeed public conflict with Becca's father who took it as a snub to both him and his dead daughter. Charlotte rejected what she considered a desire for public, self-interested displays of grieving. She wanted what she and Becca had in life – a private world belonging to them where nobody else could intrude. Charlotte was self-aware enough to know that she was struggling to deal with her loss. However, she firmly rejected the pleas of family and friends to open up to them and discuss her feelings of grief towards the loss of Becca. Charlotte only had one wish – to talk to Becca. She had no desire or need to share her feelings with anyone else. In the Virtual Afterlife, as in the physical realm, the private world of Charlotte and Becca was their sanctuary. The sudden end to Becca's life had left much unsaid. The Virtual Afterlife offered the opportunity Charlotte was looking for: a virtual environment where she could process her feelings of grief in the private space she needed, to look her lost friend in the eye and say – and hear – what had to be said (Yuen, 2013).

Initially, it had been Charlotte's intention to visit Becca once a year on the anniversary of the day they first visited the New York café. However, in the last couple of years Charlotte had found herself visiting much more frequently – often at least once a month. This raised concerns for her Virtual Afterlife Counsellor Hagan, who had recently suggested Charlotte needed to ration her visits to the Virtual Afterlife. Charlotte pleaded with him that she was making progress through her visits with Becca and felt that limitations could potentially cause a setback to the emotional strides she was making. However, Charlotte herself felt a constant desire to visit Becca in the Virtual Afterlife and, when there, never wanted to leave. The addictive component of virtual environments has been recognised by scholars (Merkx & Nawijn, 2021). When considering *The Metaverse*, Bojic (2022) highlights the reality-mimicking features as a risk of the virtual realm becoming more appealing than the physical option. Initially conceptualised in the 1992 '*Snow Crash*' sci-fi novel by Neal Stephenson (1992), the metaverse is as a virtual realm successor to the internet, populated by avatars who are controlled by users who exist in the physical world. When in the Virtual Afterlife, Charlotte very quickly forgot she was in a created virtual environment, and that Becca was herself as virtual a construct as her surroundings. On her visits to the Virtual Afterlife, Charlotte was very often in varying emotional states, depending on her general mood and on factors linked to her life in the physical realm. She took comfort in the ability of Becca – as she always had in life – to recognise her mood and respond appropriately in her bearing and conversation (Pelau *et al.*, 2021). As recognised by Muresan and Pohl (2019) building rapport over time could help the growth of empathy between the human and AI. However, in this scenario case, while this helped with the grieving process it also raised concerns about the addictive potential of emotional relationships between living and virtual souls.

Death and Commercial 'Souls' in a Virtual Hereafter

The Virtual Afterlife had originally been conceived as a therapeutic space to counter an increasing anxiety about death, such as the type

Hagan's client was experiencing. As scholars have noted, Western society has become increasingly distant from death, removed from the everyday experience and placed in medical facilities, religious institutions and funeral homes (Ariès, 1981). Hidden from the public gaze, Shilling and Mellor (1993) observed that death was being denied, in favour of the preservation of life, forming an 'absent-death' paradox. However, Jacobsen (2016) notes that in contemporary society while our relationship with death has indeed changed, a postmodern deathscape emerged in the 20th and 21st century, leading to the spectacularising of death through media and consumption activities. While the idea of witnessing another's death was controversial, when handled with care and sensitivity, Hagan had observed benefits as a Virtual Afterlife Counsellor. In many ways, this progression to witnessing death in the virtual world was a natural progression for 'real world' dark tourism that enabled visitors to learn about and confront their death-related anxieties (Stone, 2012a; Stone & Sharpley, 2008).

Hagan had also noticed that his clients were drawn to the Virtual Afterlife as an alternative space for spiritual practice. Urbanisation, rapid modernisation and rationalisation in the late 19th and much of the 20th century had contributed to a movement away from spiritual and esoteric thinking towards more scientific, secular ways of approaching the world. Max Weber had earlier denoted this as a process of 'disenchantment', where superstition and religious customs would be replaced by scientific, rational thought (Weber, 1946: 7). However, despite assertions from scholars that spiritual thinking and practice would diminish, the late 19th and mid-to-late 20th century witnessed a profound re-emergence of alternative, non-secular beliefs, and contemporary hyperreal popular cultures (Possamai & Lee, 2011). Moreover, the early 2000s, spurred on by a rise in reality-television programs, led to an increase in forms of dark tourism that actively encouraged engagement with spirituality. For example, ghost walking tours, ghost hunting events and haunted attractions, invited visitors to not only learn about dark history and folklore, but to engage with various spiritual practices familiar to the late Victorian era (such as séances, Ouija Boards and mediumship) and 'confront complex and potentially troubling questions about life and death' (Ironside, 2018: 112). The commercialization of ghosts in this manner was considered by some to be indicative of a growing 'spiritual quest culture' (Eaton, 2015), in which a bric-a-brac style approach to spirituality through commercial and subcultural experiences was being pursued in favour of more traditional religious practice. Mediation between the living and the dead through psychic mediums, drug consumption and an increasing proliferation of technology designed to facilitate after-death communication, witnessed considerable public and academic attention at this time (Eaton, 2020; Santo & Hunter, 2021). To that end, development of Virtual Afterlife had offered a new outlet for such mediations to occur.

During his work as a Virtual Afterlife Counsellor, Hagan treated a range of people. Most of his clients considered themselves to be non-religious. However, he had noticed a growing trend in the number of people using the Virtual Afterlife as part of non-secular spiritual practices. For some, the belief that the soul could live on, at least partly, in a virtual world had gained popularity. This had led to considerable debate in religious and non-religious communities about the ethics of a 'digital afterlife', how the dead may be classified, and whether we were free to die (Savin-Baden, 2019). It had not been a surprise to Hagan that the Virtual Afterlife has also led to commercialised experiences with the virtual dead. Several organisations have now offered the opportunity to interact with the virtual dead in a range of scenarios. Some of these were innocent in nature, such as paying for time to speak to a dead celebrity, whereas others had raised considerable moral and ethical concerns about how virtual bodies in the Virtual Afterlife should be treated.

Although the Virtual Afterlife had initially been created as a therapeutic space, the commercialisation of 'virtual souls' was rapidly changing the landscape into a popular dark tourism destination. The ethical and moral use of imagery and ownership of the deceased had been the focus of philosophical and theological debates for many years. In a virtual reality context, many traced this back to the *Tupac at Coachella Music Festival* hologram controversy of 2012 which continued to rage for many years with no real consensus evident (Smith, 2014). Tupac's appearance as a convincing, interactive performer 15 years after his death clearly demonstrated the emerging commercial opportunities of virtual reality and holographic technologies. However, his virtual appearance also led to concern over the morality of such representation of the dead. From a racial standpoint it was argued that the holographic representation used in this case served to continue stereotypical views of black threatening masculinity, while giving the dead Tupac no agency in how he was being portrayed or commemorated (McLeod, 2016).

Commemoration in the Virtual Afterlife

As early as the mid-1990s, online memorials appeared, in the form of text-based information (Carroll & Laundry, 2010). However, as social networking sites and user-friendly web development services emerged, virtual memorials developed into more complex online spaces with images, videos and opportunities for public interaction (Mitchell *et al.*, 2012). At the height of the Covid-19 global pandemic, virtual commemorations also started to appear, including the 75th Anniversary

Commemoration of the liberation of the Dachau Concentration Camp in 2020, and a Holocaust Memorial Day Virtual Commemoration in 2022. Both events hosted a variety of recorded talks, image galleries and information online to support individual commemoration practice from home. The progression to immersive virtual commemoration experiences was, therefore, inevitable.

The Virtual Afterlife provided an opportunity for the development of commemorative spaces and events to support memorialisation. Often supported by local governments, but occasionally crowd-sourced by community groups, the events simulated 'real' memorialisation spaces enabling individuals to virtually travel from anywhere in the world. For grieving families and friends, this provided the opportunity to participate in events who may not have felt comfortable or have the financial ability to attend physically. As Williams and Merton (2009) and Hess (2007) observed, virtual memorials are 'de-territorialized' enabling the transcendence of grief from a physical space and time to fluid, anonymised places. Visitors to Virtual Afterlife Commemoration Events chose how they interacted, with options to leave messages and virtual memorial artefacts, the opportunity to talk with other attendees and a Virtual Afterlife Counsellor if they wished, or just to simply 'be' in the recreated memorial space. Unlike physically attending a commemoration event the opportunity for quiet, anonymous mourning or collective grieving was optional.

For Hagan, these spaces were particularly beneficial for those experiencing loss and he was aware of several support groups and friendships that had developed between people all over the world. Challenges had, however, emerged as like earlier virtual memorials on social networking sites, grief and bereavement shifted from private to public spaces in the online world (Mitchell *et al.*, 2012). Some commemoration events had become tourism attractions evoking unwelcome behaviour from 'visitors' including virtual selfie taking, harassment of mourners and a general misunderstanding of the sacred value virtual commemoration spaces had gained for those personally effected by loss. The selling and consumption of virtual and real souvenirs at Virtual Afterlife Commemoration Events had also gained popularity. These challenges echoed concerns at dark tourism sites (Hodalska, 2017); however, the opportunity for anonymity online had amplified behaviour. Recently, the desecration of some online memorials with insensitive graffiti, objects and messages had caused significant upset among family and friends. In consideration of these challenges, the decision had been made to restrict access to memorial spaces on certain days and times to those connected to victims. This brought comfort to loved ones, creating a more solemn opportunity for mourning, reflection and coming together with shared memories and stories.

Contemplating a Post-Deathscape

In the final part of this chapter, we return to the present to consider the implications of a possible dark tourism future where a Virtual Afterlife exists. Scholars including Jacobsen (2016) and Stone (2018) conceptualise a 'partial re-reversal' of death in contemporary society. They argue that our approach has shifted away from the 'death-denying' attitudes of the 20th century (as noted by Ariès, 1981) towards a time where the death of the Other is consumed and mediated. The tourism, media and cultural industries play an integral role in the representation, selection and reproduction of death as a spectacular consumption activity. Dark tourism has already started to embrace the opportunities presented by Virtual Reality, including the Holocaust Survivors exhibition at the Illinois Holocaust Museum and Education Centre (Chicago, USA). An interactive experience that presents visitors with the opportunity to listen and interact with virtual holograms of survivors. Immersive gaming experiences also engage audiences in remote dark tourism environments (Hassapopoulou, 2018; Milligan, 2018). With its focus on violence, death and general law breaking within the virtual city of San Andreas, the long running Grand Theft Auto series is an immersive gaming experience. Indeed, the gamer is the protagonist in a place-based dark tourism activity which is created around them and, subsequently, based on their own choices and behaviours. In this way, the gamer is responsible for violence and death as a spectacular consumption activity. Barrett (2006) argues that the immersive realities of San Andreas reflect many of the societal issues evident in physical realm cities and, therefore, encourages and facilitates the basest fantasies of its users. Consequently, technological advancements have not only increased opportunities to passively witness and explore death through dark tourism, but also to actively interact with the dead. That said, our fascination with post-mortem communication is certainly not new. It emerges in all aspects of society and culture, historically bound in religious and spiritual practices, as well as in more contemporary forms of commercial 'spiritual questing'. Consequently, a Virtual Afterlife, a place in which *souls*, tethered by their digital footprint to interact with those who travel between the domain of the living and the virtual dead, seems like a comprehensible future in a world where our 'online immortality' is already being questioned (Mitchell *et al.*, 2012).

Importantly, a Virtual Afterlife would challenge our contemporary understanding of dark tourism. Traditionally understood as travel to 'sites associated with death, suffering and the seemingly macabre' (Stone, 2006: 146), dark tourism is often place-bound, set upon a continuum of *darkness* dependent upon several factors, including but not limited to, its locational authenticity or chronological distance to actual death events

(Stone, 2006). Alternatively, dark tourism within a Virtual Afterlife would occupy a fluid, movable space, where visitors could select, even co-create, the environment and temporality of dark tourism places (and the people that inhabit them). No longer place-bound, or determined by physical or temporal dimensions, the landscape of dark tourism would inevitably shift as new creative and commercial opportunities emerge, and the barriers for participation in dark tourism experiences evolve or diminish. A Virtual Afterlife may (re)present a *post-deathscape* in which the living and deceased co-occupy virtual worlds and bodies. In this space, it is the undead – rather than the dead – that becomes the main attraction.

Within broader society, such a shift in our interrelationship with death would invite wider moral, theological and philosophical enquiry. For dark tourism, the possible (re)presentation of death in virtual worlds and interaction with 'virtual souls' raises important questions. While the survivor holograms of the Illinois Holocaust Museum and Education Centre provide an interactive experience for visitors their responses emerge from a bank of pre-determined questions and answers. It is clear to the visitor that the experience is curated. However, in a dark tourism future where 'virtual souls' are AI responsive, this interaction will evolve and change with different people, world events and access to information. In this future, the fundamental question posed, therefore, is how will the dead be authentically represented in a Virtual Afterlife? Dark tourism, and the wider heritage industries, have been criticised for their selective curation and interpretation of historic events (Lennon & Tiberghien, 2020). Yet, a future where the power to interpret the past is transferred to an AI personality who represents the dead; this may pose more troubling consequences. As Stone (2018: 205) provocatively states 'death remains a problem for the living because dead people do not care'. However, in a future Virtual Afterlife as we have outlined, where the dead at least appear conscious, *what if they do care*?

Finally, commercialisation and 'packaging' of death already presents dark tourism with a host of moral and ethical dilemmas (Potts, 2012; Stone, 2018). In a future virtual world where the anonymity of visitors is possible, managing tourist behaviour in dark tourism spaces will present new challenges. Similarly, potential for the commercialisation of 'virtual souls' raises significant ethical concerns linked to the representation, use of, and commodification of our *disembodied selves* and data. If as Sharpley (2009b: 8) states, dark tourism presents the opportunity to 'write or re-write the history of people's lives and deaths', a Virtual Afterlife may offer an opportunity to immortalise, re-imagine and co-create new, evolving versions of lives and deaths. In this *post-deathscape*, our freedom to die and how we choose to be remembered may be determined by the living, rather than the dead.

3 From 'Bucket List' to 'Afterlist': (Dark) Tourism for the Afterlife

Santa Zascerinska

Annie loves posting on social media. The vivid photographs of her new hobbies, videos, but most importantly, her travel journeys fill her newsfeed on the 'Afterlist' – a platform for ticking off life dreams. Her latest photo, a selfie outside the Eiffel Tower, marked another 'tick' off her bucket list – she had always wanted to go to Paris. But that does not conclude her journeys, as she is consistently posting her anticipation of the upcoming trip to Kyoto, Japan, from which, no doubt she will post even more photos. Such 'smoasting' is often accompanied by encouraging messages from her friends and family. One may even say that she is chasing likes and followers, but that could not be further from the truth, for Annie has been dead for four years.

Introduction

We live and die in digital spaces. Westreich (2020) estimated that there are around 10 to 30 million deceased users on Facebook. The Facebook 'graveyard' is only estimated to grow, with 4.9 billion deceased users by the year 2100 (Cantor, 2019). Many accounts are turned into memorial pages, where 'Facebook is operating as a new medium through which to conduct an ongoing "wake" – a means for mourners to express and share their grief' (Kaul & Skinner, 2018: 233). As Basset (2018) wrote:

> Some time ago my friend's daughter died suddenly, and I was amazed to find that five years later people were still talking to her on the Internet as though she was still alive. I began to explore how people were using the Internet to stay in-touch with the deceased and found a plethora of

> Facebook RIP sites – which had been set up following the death of loved ones-being used to remember, memorialize and communicate with the dead.

However, the question remains of what does a dead person's account bring to the living? The most that the living can do is to post 'photos of grandchildren never met, jokes heard at work, plans for the next holiday, and lots of sentences starting with "you would have loved…"' (Kaul & Skinner, 2018: 235). Yet, even today, the social media of the dead caters for the living.

Of course, travel *smoasting* on social media is not a new phenomenon. From the old-fashioned filling of fridge doors with magnets of places visited and sending 'Wish you were here' postcards, social media at present not only facilitates the concrete evidence of conducted journeys, but also the collection of awe-inspiring bucket list challenges and 'ticks' off the list. The 'bucket list' term was popularised in 2007 by its namesake film, directed by Rob Reiner and starring Jack Nicholson and Morgan Freeman. The film portrayed a story of two terminally ill men who leave hospital for the biggest adventure of their lifetime – that is, to do a road trip with a wish list of things to do (bucket list) before they 'kicked the bucket' (died). Importantly, Zascerinska *et al.* (2022: 1) suggest that a bucket list can be a means of mediating existential anxiety through consumption 'directed towards the creation of identity and self-esteem'. In other words, from a Terror Management Theory perspective, by compiling a bucket list, one believes s/he will live long enough to complete it. The potential Afterlist social media platform, as depicted in the fictional future scenario at the beginning of this chapter, uses a similar premise for the dead.

Firstly, the digital immortal (through others) can 'tick off' all the items that the deceased person did not have time to complete during their lifetime. Secondly, their digital afterlife brings tangible evidence through photos, videos and posts, created in the exact manner that replicates the living original individual. Finally, through the Afterlist idea, the living can engage with the dead by communicating with them, supporting them and, eventually, after their own death, joining them on their 'shared' Afterlist journeys. The technology used to implement the 'living dead' photos, videos and posts is discussed later in the chapter. In a way, this chapter follows Yeoman's (2008: 5) advice: '… we can learn a great deal about what may happen in the future by looking systematically at what is happening now and what has taken place in the past'. The purpose of this chapter, therefore, is to offer a critical future scenario that incorporates trends of communicating with the dead in the past, present and future. Consequently, the chapter draws on the everlasting longing for the dead from a historical perspective.

Past and Longing for the Dead

For a long time, technology has allowed mediation with the dead. Media has allowed us to ritualise the event of death through newspaper obituaries, pamphlets and cards as well as, more recently, audio and video recordings (Arnold *et al.*, 2018). The most prominent engagement with the dead happened using the daguerreotype camera from 1835 until 1860 (Arnold *et al.*, 2018). That is, the practice of postmortem photography became popular in the 19th century in America and the UK. The purpose of many of these photographs was to make the dead look like the living, albeit at times asleep (Linkman, 2011). The final expression of the dead person was particularly important for the grieving family, as Linkman (2011: 17) states:

> In many instances the decision to commission a post-mortem portrait would have been influenced by the physical appearance of the body after death, and particularly by the set of the features and expression on the face of the deceased. Examples discussed in greater detail below confirm that survivors drew great comfort from expressions they could interpret as calm, peaceful and serene, especially if the final illness had been particularly painful, or if death was due to an accident or an act of violence. Peacefulness and serenity represented desirable states of mind here on earth and hinted at the blessings of a Christian heaven in the hereafter.

The mid-19th century was also preoccupied with mediums and spiritualists who allegedly became the connection between the living and the dead (Arnold *et al.*, 2018). Some of the mediums claimed to be able to present the dead through a 'full body apparition or produce ectoplasm' – a substance appearing out of medium's body and later transforming into the 'ghost' (Arnold *et al.*, 2018: 19). Mysticism also surrounded the development of telegraphy and the telegraph, and the long-distance transmission of messages where the sender uses symbolic codes. Arthur Conan Doyle (1926: 63) in *The History of Spiritualism* described the communication with the dead through the telegraph:

> I then asked: 'Is this a human being that answers my questions so correctly?' There was no rap. I asked: 'Is it a spirit? If it is, make two raps.' Two sounds were given as soon as the request was made. I then said: 'If it was an injured spirit, make two raps,' which were instantly made, causing the house to tremble. I asked: 'Were you injured in this house?' The answer was given as before. 'Is the person living that injured you?' Answered by raps in the same manner. I ascertained by the same method that it was a man, aged thirty-one years, that he had been murdered in this house, and his remains were buried in the cellar; that his family consisted of a wife and five children, two sons and three daughters, all living at the time of his death, but that his wife had since died. I asked: 'Will you continue to rap if I call my neighbours that they may hear it too?' The raps were loud in the affirmative.

The dead were also believed to appear in photos, albeit as spirits – capturing them was a prominent practice in the late 19th and early 20th centuries (Arnold *et al.*, 2018). As Arnold *et al.* (2018) suggest, the practice became popular when William Mumbler, from Boston, argued that he could capture spirits in a photograph in 1863. His designated studio accommodated for the living to be photographed with the ghosts of dead friends and family. Although later accused of fraud, by then spirit photography had conquered the United States and Europe, with one of the most prominent photos being the photo of 'Arthur Conan Doyle and ectoplasm' (Arnold *et al.*, 2018: 21).

Yet the dead did not remain merely in photos: soon enough, they moved to a new piece of technology – that is, the telephone. The static from early telephones was believed to be the voices of the dead (Arnold *et al.*, 2018). A similar occurrence appeared with radio – in 1922, Arthur Conan Doyle suggested that the dead would begin to communicate with the living through radio 'in the next three or four years' (Arnold *et al.*, 2018: 22). Finally, the development of the gramophone took a different turn. According to Arnold *et al.* (2018), the gramophone (also known as a phonograph) allowed to move away from the spiritual realms into the realms of memorialisation. In other words, the gramophone did not record the voices of the dead; rather, it was designated to capture the voices of the dying. Although all these practices declined in the early 20th century, questions remain: how strongly do we want to connect with 'Our' and 'Other' dead? And could these early practices be the result of macabre curiosity which does not translate into the 21st century? It is here that the present search for immortality is underway, or at least, the beginnings of digitally replicating our deceased souls.

The Present Search for (Digital) Immortality

> *... the dead are brought into these leisure spaces of the living.*
> Kaul and Skinner (2018: 228)

We die twice. Once, when we may become socially dead, while biologically alive, either by being homeless or lonely. Or we can die biologically but remain socially alive. In other words, we not only remain in the memory of the living, but we continue to express social agency (Kaul & Skinner, 2018). An example of the latter happened to Roger Ebert, who not only won the Pulitzer Prize but was also a Chicago Sun-Times film critic (ironically, he apparently hated the storyline of *The Bucket List*). Prior to his death in 2013, he asked his wife Chaz to manage his Twitter account in his memory. To date, the account is imbued with old photos and reviews (Kaul & Skinner, 2018). Indeed, social media is truly a 'graveyard' for the living, whether it is about 'posting emblematic messages of grief on Instagram and Twitter, creating, and watching YouTube mourning videos, or turning Facebook pages into memorial sites' (Sumiala, 2022: 23). Moreover, according to Sumiala (2022), not only does social media provide a space for communal grieving, it also creates an opportunity for collaboration and co-creation. In other words, while the dead rest, the living continues their story by co-creating their autobiography narrative, be it through old photos, tributes or poems.

This creates an uneasy amalgam, where in social spaces the living and the dead are the same and can create and co-create the content aimed at both. As Kaul and Skinner (2018: 229) describe it:

> Social media commonly used for the latest cute-cat video and other light-hearted leisure practices are, of course, also deployed for notifying others about a death, sharing grief, and ongoing memorial practices. One moment my screen is claiming my attention with a status update about a parking fine and the next with a notification from my dead partner.

Recently, another technological development by Amazon merged the lines between the living and the dead. '"Alexa," the boy asks, "Can grandma finish reading me *The Wizard of Oz*?"' (Condon, 2022). The boy's wish was granted: the story was read to him by the voice of his deceased grandmother. The new development of Alexa would allow the living to connect with their dead loved ones through their own voice. While this technology is still in the development stage, it provides a path for a relationship between the dead and artificial intelligence (AI).

While this contested technology is likely to appear and develop further in the future, some other provocative projects were proposed, yet did not materialise. For instance, Arnold *et al.* (2018) reported on the Cata Combo Sound system proposed in 2012 at an estimated cost of US$30,000. The project aimed to build a professional sound system into the coffin along with a 7-inch LCD monitor. Individuals would be enabled to choose their posthumous playlist as well as have an option for friends and family to update it via a 4G connection. Another ambitious, yet unmaterialised patent proposed a 'Holographic Projection for Grave Memorials', where a 3D visual of the deceased would be displayed near their grave or urn not only providing information about the dead individual but also their voice recording (Arnold *et al.*, 2018).

Posthumous communication remains another more viable option for the living with the rise of websites such as 'Death Switch, GhostMemo, DeadSocial, If I Die, MyGoodByeMessage, and Dead Man's Switch' all of which allow individuals to leave messages for their friends and family after their death (Arnold *et al.*, 2018: 130). These messages, of course, rely on pre-written letters of the living who anticipate their death dedicated to the ones they leave behind. They may provide solace for the grieving family and friends, or even a sense of continuity. However, these messages are not autonomous in the sense that there is neither a possibility to amend them (after the individual's death), nor to respond to them. However, in the future, could the individuals' clone their personality, voice, images and, most importantly, the manner of communication onto a social platform to represent them autonomously after their death? Indeed, many platforms offer the promise of digital immortality, but their 'successes' vary.

For instance, *Eternime* – a project that commenced in 2014 at the Massachusetts Insitute of Technology (MIT) to build AI that will help humans live forever as digital replicas – claims 'an Artificial Intelligence digital replica of you, built from your digital footprint (emails, social media posts, smartphone, and wearables data, etc.). This digital twin will learn from you, grow with you, help you and, eventually, live on after you die' (Eternime, 2022: online). However, according to Savin-Baden (2022), little development appears to have happened on the website since April 2021. Another peculiar website – Lifenaut.com allows 'anyone to create a digital back-up of their mind and genetic code. The goal of our research project is to explore the transfer of human consciousness to computers/robots and beyond' (LifeNaut, 2022: online). This is conducted through a 'mind file' – a collection of video, audio, images and documents belonging to an individual. The more time one invests into 'teaching' their Avatar, the more it replicates them. Moreover, the 'Bio File' offered by LifeNaut allows one to store their DNA for free. Savin-Baden (2022) described the several steps to building a mind file through LifeNaut. First, supporting the conversation with the sample bots, no matter how irrelevant they may seem. Second, filling in interview questionnaires, including personality surveys. Third, conversing with the designed avatar. And finally, manually adding preferences and URLs.

Another website – elixirforever.com – is a US-based company which is 'dedicated to AI and neural network technology to empower your digital AI self in this lifetime' (ELIXIR AI, 2022: online). According to Savin-Baden (2022: 84) 'the company suggests that we need to create an authentic digital copy to enable our family and friends to continue to connect with us'. The website, however, does not clarify the details of the copying, rather it invites one to join the waitlist. Finally, the website – digital-immortality-now.com – suggests its 'mission is to provide a cheap and affordable instrument for immortality (potentially indefinite life extension) to everyone by the means of so-called digital immortality, that is preserving information about a human being for their future reconstruction' (Digital-immortality-now.com, 2022: online). To immortalise oneself, the website invites you to upload one's own recordings and descriptions (Savin-Baden, 2022). Yet, like other 'immortal websites', it does not clarify any other tangible steps towards achieving digital immortality.

The immersive death

Wright (2020: 93) proposed a new dimension of death – 'the immersive death', where 'new technologies will allow people to tailor their own experiences when confronting death. Interactive real-world experiences through immersive technologies such as virtual and augmented reality could provide people with the opportunity to engage and explore death at their own desirable level(s)'. Wright (2020) goes on to examine ways humans can engage with death in the future through means of virtual, augmented and mixed realities, with examples of dark tourism sites. While this chapter does not yet draw to the importance of tourism to the 'immortal' society, the remainder of this section offers an example of 'the immersive death' on an individual level.

'Where are you?' … 'Mom, Mom … Mom where have you been? Have you been thinking of me?' GlobalNews (2020). A 7-year-old Na-yeon runs out to her mother. Her mother (Jang) is crying and desperately trying to hug her daughter, which is not possible for her daughter is dead. Yet, here she stands, looking and sounding like her late Na-yeon. The VR technology enabled their reunion, yet 'in the real world, Jang was standing in front of a studio green screen, wearing a virtual reality headset and touch-sensitive gloves, her daughter's ashes in a locket around her neck' (Aljazeera, 2020). The video, originally published by Munhwa Broadcasting Corporation, received more than 13 million views in a week since its publication, with mixed reviews. While some expressed a wish to go through the same journey as Jang to meet their late relatives, others criticised the producers for taking advantage of a vulnerable mother (Aljazeera, 2020). Without a doubt, this example of 'immersive death' is raising the question of how far are we prepared to go to 'resurrect' our dead? The search for immortality is not over, certainly if the future includes the development of thanatechnologies, which allow our dead to be 'reborn' in spectacular digital realms.

The *Afterlist:* Towards Future Thanatechnologies

The Afterlist is a proposed digital afterlife platform, where digital afterlife refers to 'the continuation of an active or passive digital presence after death' (Savin-Baden, 2022: 137). In the case of the Afterlist, the presence of the deceased would be active, where both parties – the living and the dead – can communicate with each other, through the theme of the bucket list (as discussed earlier). The prevalence of tourism and bucket lists on the Afterlist is explained shortly, but for now, it is important to examine possibilities (if not pitfalls) featured in any future Afterlist.

The outlook of the Afterlist would not differ from present-day 'typical' social media, such as Facebook. One would see the timeline of individual's posts imbued with images of travels and bucket list goals, under which family and friends would post respective comments. At the same time, the deceased can 'post', 'like' or 'comment' on their journeys *themselves*. The dead would appear to be alive, living their afterlife to the full, be it at Machu Picchu, Tokyo or a bungee jump in Scotland. The technology enabling the dead to be (re)presented as living at different destinations is not new, as discussed previously. Although currently aimed at the living, websites such as Fake a Vacation (n.d.) provide the living with an opportunity of inserting their own photographs into a landscape of their choice for around £88 per photo. Besides providing an edited photo, Fake a Vacation (n.d.) also educates its customers on the attractions used in their photos to create a convincing account. To that end, the Afterlist would not only create a convincing account of the journey that has 'taken place' but would also express the deceased individual's emotions towards it, through posts, gratitude to the living and encouragement to follow up on their journeys.

The notion of an Afterlist draws upon Savin-Biden's (2022) proposal of the Digital Immortal, based on AI. In the future, AI will acquire many different definitions (and designs) but for the purpose of this chapter, it can be referred to as 'the study of how to make computers do things at which, at the moment, people are better' (Gupta & Mangla, 2020: 4). Here, the Afterlist will attempt to mimic human behaviour and replicate it in a digital afterlife. In other words, the Afterlist is not associated with mind-uploading technology, rather 'it needs only to create an effective illusion' of an afterlife (Savin-Biden, 2022: 149). Consciousness is taken out of the context of the Afterlist, leaving space merely for codes and data that would express the deceased individual's persona. This data would be collected through two approaches: manual and automatic (Savin-Biden, 2022), where manual refers to an input of data (dialogue) with a virtual mentor over a prolonged period. The automated approach would enable machine learning 'by tracking real-world interactions (our emails, voicemails, blog posts, global positioning traces, bank transactions)' (Savin-Biden, 2022: 150).

The focus of the Afterlist would significantly depend upon both approaches. During the manual approach, individuals who want to subscribe to the Afterlist after their death would have to provide consent and some initial data including their bucket list, their photos and messages to the family members. The second approach would involve them sharing their further personal data to recognise their manner of speech and their attitudes. As Ostrow (2011: online) described it in his 'After Your Final Status Update' TED talk:

> It's going to become possible to analyse an entire life's worth of content – the tweets, the photos, the videos, the blog posts that we are producing in such massive numbers. And I think as that happens it's going to

> become possible for our digital personas to continue to interact in the real world long after we're gone thanks to the vastness of the amount of content we're creating and to technology's ability to make sense of it all.

Consequently, Meese *et al.* (2015: 414) suggest 'a future where the collective content uploaded will be embedded in robotic or holographic representations of the deceased, which could interact with the living based on the archive of content produced by a person over a lifetime'.

Individuals would have to establish longevity of the Afterlist account and the level of moderation over their account. In other words, whether they are happy for the AI to take over their account prolonging it beyond their initial bucket list. Alternatively, consent may be made for the living to inherit the autonomy of their journeys, where families and friends can request to see further experiences – for example, a collective photo with a newborn niece and a deceased auntie. As Savin-Biden (2022: 152) emphasises on the ethics of digital immortality, there is a strong focus on informed consent in terms of the 'future portrayal and representation of data'.

Similarly, Hurtado (2023: 91) proposed the idea of a 'Virtual Deceased Person' (VDP) – 'the (digital) persona of the deceased given agency and embodiment by future thanatechnologies'. However, Hurtado (2023: 94) not only anticipated the possibility of a virtual persona but also pondered an autonomous physical embodiment:

> The VDP would be highly adaptable to interactive social situations and would mimic faithfully the mannerisms and personality of the deceased, as expressed through talk and embodied emotionality, making it able to fulfil social roles. Because a VDP would be intentionally created pre-mortem, it would likely only reflect aspects of the deceased's personality belonging to a predetermined temporal demarcation in his/her life in order to behave consistently throughout its interactions.

This physical embodiment differentiates Savid-Baden's (2022) Digital Immortal and Hurtado's (2023) VDP. However, the purpose of both remains the same: 'preventing the loss of Self and push for its continuity' (Hurtado, 2023: 96). Indeed, the use of thanatechnologies for digital perpetuation, as acknowledged by Hurtado (2023), might lead to inequalities, where such digital immortality would only be available for the wealthy – particularly if travel were involved in a new dominion of the spectacular death.

Spectacular death, (dark) tourism and the Afterlist

One may ask, why is tourism so central to the idea of Afterlist? The potential answer is that immortalising platforms existing already have the prevalence of tourism-orientated bucket lists. Furthermore, Biran and Bida (2018: 523) suggested that dark tourism, as a form of meaningful entertainment, may well be a 'psychological buffer against fears of death'. According to Biran and Bida, the relationship between death and tourism in other forms of consumption is also noteworthy, for it can bring other manoeuvres in which death can be managed (or at least tamed, rather than avoided). Zascerinska (2022) augments this idea to propose that tourism sites are 'deathless' environments from a Terror Management Theory perspective. The theory proposes that increased self-esteem is a strong buffer for death anxiety (Solomon *et al.*, 2015). Zascerinska (2022) goes on to argue that, not only does travel and tourism on bucket lists link to an increased sense of self-esteem through conspicuous consumption and identity solidification, but also tourism, as an activity, may push the thoughts of death away, where travel is associated with feeling most alive.

Thus, within the context of Afterlist, the dead can not only continue to express their identity through postmortem digital tourism consumption, but also can lead the living in their footsteps through metempsychotic pilgrimages (Stone, 2019). In other words, the living can gaze at the tourism experiences of the dead and reconnect with them by following their journeys. At the same time, the bucket lists here not only offer a path to express the deceased's identity, but to 'tick off' the items of the bucket list that were missed during their lifetime to offer a sense of continuation.

It is here that the living has always gazed at the dead: be it through acceptance (Tamed Death), personalisation (One's Own Death), dramatisation (Thy Death) or denial of death (Forbidden Death) (Ariès, 1974). In 2016, Jacobsen conducted a phenomenal review of Phillipe Ariès's work on the historical developments of death in Western society. In his review, he proposed another dominion of death – that is, the 'spectacular death', or 'death that has for all intents and purposes been transformed into a spectacle' (Jacobsen, 2016: 10). As Jacobsen (2016: 10) further notes, 'we draw death near us, yet stay away from it at a comfortable distance – we want to know about it without getting too close to it'. Thus, death in modern society is kept at a safe distance 'through the screens of the television, computer or mobile phone' (Jacobsen, 2016: 11). Interestingly, Jacobsen (2016) also noticed the relevance of The Bucket List film (as noted earlier), where the seriousness of death was treated humorously and with entertainment. Indeed, bucket lists are macabre, yet playful, acknowledgements of one's own death. Death here is on the horizon yet covered by the built skyscrapers of one's own ambitions, hopes and dreams. As the future Afterlist provides an option to continue living on within a digitally immortal state, it bestows the pressure on the bucket list to be completed whether alive or dead. The living completes the (deceased) bucket lists for themselves, whereas the dead continue ticking off their bucket lists for the living. It is, therefore, argued that the Afterlist is the phenomenon of a society preoccupied with 'spectacular death' and its manifestation within a society of spectacle (Stone, 2018, 2020b). Indeed, the mediated/mediatised visibility of death within the Afterlist is not intrusive yet is turned into a spectacle for the living.

However, the question that arises is why might one want to keep the dead alive in the form of a bucket list? The answer lies within the idea of legacy and remembrance. Indeed, Zascerinska *et al.* (2022) suggest that bucket lists can be part of a person's legacy and that people want to be remembered by what has been achieved (through travel and tourism) and places visited and experienced. As suggested earlier, we do indeed die twice: biologically, and through inevitably vanishing memories of our existence. As Stone (2018: 189) argues 'we ritualise the dead with a memorialised afterlife, where the deceased depend on the living to maintain their memory'. Of course, we leave the path for mourning, but eventually, our voices are forgotten. Hence, the Afterlist will be a direct path for the preservation of memory. Not only can it attempt to provide a sense of solace and continuation for the living, but it also solidifies the identity of the deceased through their travel experiences. Consequently, the correlation between bucket lists and legacy/identity is a positive one whereby 'a completed bucket list may create or maintain identity following death' (Zascerinska *et al.*, 2022: 10).

Conclusion

This chapter has sought to position the idea of an Afterlist (from the concept of bucket lists) using future digital thanatechnology. In so doing, the potential of death becoming a spectacle is enhanced and digital immortality might be achieved. Yet, a fundamental issue is where does the Afterlist leave the living? As mentioned earlier, apart from providing a sense of continuity for the living, the Afterlist might spawn new travel ambitions. In other words, the family of Annie (from the fictional scenario which opened this chapter) who saw her selfie outside the Eiffel Tower might want to 're-connect' with her by following in her footsteps. This may result in metempsychosis or the 'behaviour in which a tourist knowingly repeats a journey made by a named significant other or others' (Stone, 2019: 2). Within the context of future Afterlists, although the initial journey of the significant other never takes place outside of the digital realm, it might nevertheless still offer the living 'mediation, retreat and recovery' (Stone, 2019: 2).

Of course, while the idea of the future Afterlist can raise more ethical dilemmas than it can potentially solve, this chapter has located the concept of memorialisation through travel (in particular, bucket lists) and future thanatechnology. Indeed, the living have longed for contact with the dead. And we do already live and die in digital spaces. But, in the future, there is a real prospect that we shall continue to live through an AI-powered digital afterlife. Consequently, demand for new rituals surrounding the memorialisation of our dead and technology is the pathway for it. Yet as Polish novelist and visionary Stanislaw Lem aptly stated, '*people do not want immortality, they simply do not want to die*'.

4 'Beyond Human': Dark Tourism, Robots and Futurology

Daniel W.M. Wright

The real trick in life is to turn hindsight into foresight
that reveals insight
Robin Sharma (2021)

Introduction

Robotics and robot technology dominates futurology studies. Indeed, the study of the future offers an opportunity to ask questions of the present via future projections and foresight contemplation. By looking ahead, we can cast a light back onto ourselves, and ask, are we making the right decisions today? Recently, there has been increased discussion around the role and value of robotics and artificial intelligence (AI) and, specifically, how the technology could develop over time and what this means for humanity. Positive and negative viewpoints are inherent, but humanity still has the power to make a choice. Yet, sooner rather than later, it might be too late, and, in which case, society might become a vastly different place to what we know today. Science and engineering have already arrived at a point in which humans can enhance their physical forms. We are achieving a post-human reality, turning some individuals into transhuman/cyborgs (Wright & Zascerinska 2023). Moreover, we already live and work with various operating robots across different sectors of society. Therefore, while Homo sapiens are still the dominant power, they are not the only species living on planet earth. Humanity is gradually allowing non-human life form to live more independently among us and carry out roles and jobs that once belonged to humans.

Science fiction has provided ample narratives of robot-run societies, or scenarios in which human, transhuman and robotic wars and conflicts have ensued. Fortunately, we have not arrived at a place where these apocalyptic and dystopian narratives have become a reality; at least not between humans and non-humans. However, our history highlights humankind's capacity to cause great pain and suffering to our fellow species. Some of the *darkest* (after Stone, 2006) of dark tourism attractions are places of great human-to-human produced suffering. If humans can cause such pain to each other, imagine what humans could do to another species and, what that 'other' species could do to us if it became more intelligent and more powerful? The future places of suffering (that is, dark tourism attractions) would be more contested and complex than those we visit today. The purpose of this chapter, therefore, is to offer original discourse around the potential of future dark sites that move beyond the human realm.

Homo Sapiens, Transhumanism and Robots: Towards a Post-Human World

The concept of post-human worlds has long been considered in fictional and non-fictional form. However today, society is moving not so much into a post-human existence, but more of a world merging social conditions beyond solely human form. It is here where transhuman beings and robots live among Homo sapiens.

Homo sapiens: A species from yesteryear

Homo sapiens are what we know as modern humans, having evolved from a larger genus group of ancestral or closely related to primates. It is challenging to imagine a world of different beings living together, as we are accustomed to our sole presence on the planet (apart, of course, from domesticated animals and other wildlife). However, with greater archaeological and technological understanding of our own past, questions are being raised about how many other types of humans have existed and lived together historically. According to Goldfield (2021), five hominins have contributed to the story of human evolution, namely Homo Rudolfensis, Homo Antecessor, Homo Floresiensis, Homo Luzonensis and Homo Longi. Some of these fossils are said to date back 6 million years. Historically, these distinct types of humans once lived together on the planet, with Homo sapiens out living all the others. Interestingly, what will our world look like when Homo sapiens become less dominant, and social environments become the playground for other beings? It is here that the transhuman or cyborgs might enter the future fray.

'Going beyond human': Advances in transhumanism and cyborgs

Have technological advancements in robotics given birth to a new being? The human-technology blend has been extensively covered across different academic disciplines. The concept known as post/trans-humanism is an international philosophical movement which supports transformation of the human condition (Ansell-Pearson, 1997; Campa, 2019; Hellsten, 2012; Sorgner & Nietzsche, 2009). The ideology of post/transhumanism is founded upon the idea, belief or theory, that humanity has the potential to evolve beyond its current physical and mental natural limitations. As noted by Bostrom (2005), it is the advancement of sophisticated technologies that enhance the human intellect and physiology. It is said that computers through the AI expertise will develop capabilities to speak, interact, listen and remember. Notably, this progress in computer capability will allow computers to mature progressively into human and similarly, humans could become more integrated with robots (Crew, 2018). Similarly, to the concept of transhumanism is the concept or idea of cyborgs, which share a similar ideological movement to transhumanism. According to Towers-Clark (2018) cyborgs already exist, and society had better get used to it. Technology has been used to support humans and their bodies, through devices such as hearing aids, wooden legs, spectacles and false teeth. However, the transhumanist and cyborg concepts can take humanity to a new social dimension. While many medical approaches have seen the use of tech implants to support human limitations, the reality is that they have also led us to become reliant on such technology to operate at a higher level than what our bodily limitations allow. Today, and into the future, the question remains whether we are we likely to see more people using wearable and implant technologies to enhance their human body limitations? Thus, the natural born form of the individual transitions into a cyborg form.

Advocates of transhumanism suggest it allows society to plan for the future of human beings. Rather than relying on evolutionary process and its exploitation of random mutations, transhumanism allows society to tailor the development of Homo sapiens to an ideal blueprint (McNamee & Edwards, 2006). Believers of transhumanism contend that recruitment or deployment of these distinct types of technology can create individuals who are intelligent and immortal, but not members of the Homo sapiens species; instead, they would be more cyborg – that is, part human, part machine (McNamee & Edwards, 2006). As society embraces technology, there is every potential that 'Homo sapiens' will evolve into 'Homo Technologicus' (Wright & Zascerinska, 2023) or even 'Homo Deus' (Harari, 2015; McKie, 2018). According to Harari (2015), technology can re-engineer human minds, and this could lead to the eventual end of Homo sapiens. Human history would end, and an entirely new process would initiate something we cannot yet fully understand. Today, transhuman beings already live in our world.

A new age of robots: Towards robo-revolution

According to Simon (2017), when we hear the word robot, we often think of a silvery humanoid (a robot that is more akin to resemble humans). But types of robots and the defining of them is complex territory. Robots can be many things, from autonomous drones to self-driving cars, and we are only just getting started with creating them. Today, robots operate at diverse levels, from manufacturing goods (Shneier & Bostelman, 2015), caring for the elderly (Van Wynsberghe, 2013), managing our homes (Young *et al.*, 2009), for entertainment value (Wright & Zascerinska, 2023), military training (Cioppa *et al.*, 2004) or scientific research (Terstappen & Reggiani, 2001). Daley (2022: online) notes that 'robotics is the intersection of science, engineering and technology that produces machines, called robots, that replicate or substitute for human actions'. Meanwhile, Jordan (2016) argues that there is already considerable indeterminacy and slippage with the terminology and, consequently, computer scientists are not able to provide consensus on what constitutes a robot. Indeed, the term 'robot' is a 'noisy moniker with indeterminate and flexible semantic boundaries' (Gunkel, 2018: 14). This is significant because understanding what robots are to society has implications for humanity and how we integrate and deal with them, especially seeing that society is undergoing a gradual *robo-revolution*. According to Jordan (2016) the difficulty in arriving to some level of clarity is because definitions have evolved unevenly over time, alongside different social contexts and technological advancements.

Additionally, science fiction has played a key role in setting boundaries of the conceptual playing field. Even before engineers have been able to create working prototypes, filmmakers, artists and writers created vivid imaginations and interpretations of all forms of robots. Mass media has therefore played a significant role in shaping our understanding and ideas of what robots are (Gunkel, 2018). Daley (2022) also recognises how popular culture has often been fascinated with robots, particularly in fictional narratives. No other technology has been explored in such fictional ways as robots (Gunkel, 2018). However, some clarity is useful. Initially, the difference between *bots*, *chatbots* and *robots*. Bots are complex computer programs that automatically perform repetitive tasks with the specific aim to relieve menial tasks and to reduce human error. With the internet, bots have been part of our world for some time. They have also had some negative stigma, as they are used to create viruses and have crippled important digital services. Chatbots are designed to communicate, collect and assess human interaction (Colombi, 2023). They are software applications that mimic human conversation through online voice or text interactions. Meanwhile, a robot is a physical machine completing more physical tasks. The word robot was ushered into existence in Karel Capek's 1920 stage play '*R.U.R.*' or *Rossumovi Univeralini Robot* [Rossum's Universal Robots] as a way of naming a class of artificial servants or labourers. The term robot is derived from the Czech world *robota*, which means 'forced labour' (Daley, 2022).

With today's technological progress, it is necessary to adapt the scope of robotics and the types of robots present. Unlike the early noughties, where 90% of robots were assembling cars in automotive factories (Daley, 2022), currently we have robots that can accomplish difficult tasks, including exploring the planet's harshest conditions, performing surgical procedures or undertaking rescue missions. They can go places humans cannot, from the deepest depths of our oceans to outer space. According to Daley (2022), the world of robotics is expanding, and robots do have some key characteristics, much of which consist of mechanical construction. The mechanical focus assists robots in completing tasks in a specific environment in which they are often designed to operate in. Robots also require electrical components that control and power the machinery (often a battery). Some level of computer programming is also present, as without a code telling it what to do, it would just be a piece of machinery. The past few decades have seen a significant increase in human interaction with AI or entities. Harris and Anthis (2021) use the term 'artificial entities' when referring to all manner of computers, software, simulations, machines, AIs and robots created by humans or other entities. With the increasing development and presence of AI, society is soon likely to see more energy efficient, more flexible and, importantly, smarter robots (Daley, 2022).. Today, robots are more forward thinking than many realise, as they are gaining intellectual and mechanical capabilities all of which are moving society to a place where robots depicted in the movie franchise Star Wars, such as R2-D2, will be a reality in the future (Daley, 2022). Table 4.1 offers clarity on distinct types of robots.

Hallevy (2013) notes that, since the start of AI, researchers have aimed to create computers that can 'think': this being the holy grail for AI researchers. To develop machines that can think independently would

Table 4.1 Types of robots (adapted from Daley, 2022)

Pre-Programmed Robots	Operate in controlled environments doing simple monotonous task, i.e. mechanical arm on an automotive assembly line.
Humanoid Robots/ Androids	Made to look like and or mimic human behaviour, including having human like faces and expressions. Usually perform human-like activities (running, jumping, carrying objects). Examples include Hanson Robotics' Sophia or Boston Dynamics' Atlas.
Autonomous Robots	Operate independently of human operators and designed to carry out task in open environments often using sensors to perceive the world around them. An example would be the Roomba vacuum cleaner.
Teleoperated Robots	Semi-autonomous bots that use wireless networks to enable human control from a safe distance. Work in extreme environment and conditions, such as fixing underwater pipe leaks or detecting landmines.
Augmenting Robots	Also known as VR robots that either enhance current human capabilities or replace a lost capability. Robotics for human augmentation, making use faster and stronger. For example, prosthetic limbs or exoskeletons.

be a significant moment for humankind. Hallevy (2013: 5) stresses that 'the creation of a true thinking machine would be tantamount to the emergence of a new species on earth, the *machina sapiens* [emphasis added]'. Indeed, it may usher in future immortally in a post-human era (Wright & Zascerinska, 2023). Nonetheless, increased advancements in outer space exploration could facilitate a significant proliferation in artificial entities (Anthis & Paez, 2021; Baum *et al.*, 2019; Bostrom, 2003; Reese, 2018). All of which leads to a landscape of increasing numbers of ubiquitous robots that present society with complex moral questions (Harris & Anthis, 2021). Scholars agree that artificial entities with the capacity for positive and negative experiences (i.e. sentience) are not only theoretically possible, but will be created (Angel, 2019; Anthis & Paez, 2021; Reese, 2018; Thompson, 1965). Previously, the moral consideration of artificial entities was something of science fiction (Hallqvist, 2018; McNally & Inayatullah, 1988; Peterson, 2007; Robertson, 2014). A paper commissioned by the UK Government Office for Science maintained that robots could be granted rights within 50 years (BBC [British Broadcasting Corporation], 2006). In 2017, the European Parliament passed a resolution suggesting the creation of 'a specific legal status for robots in the long run, so that at least the most sophisticated autonomous robots could be established as having the status of electronic persons' (European Parliament Committee on Legal Affairs, 2017). Also in 2017, Saudi Arabia granted citizenship to a robot named Sophia (Hanson Robotics, 2018). Likewise, a chatbot on the messaging app *Line*, named Shibuya Mirai, was granted residence by the city of Tokyo in Japan (Microsoft Asia News Center, 2017).

'The Conflict has Begun': Creating Dark History in a New Machine Age

> In 1981, a thirty-seven-year-old Japanese employee in a motorcycle factory was killed by an artificial intelligence robot working near him. The robot erroneously identified the employee as a threat to its mission and calculated that the most efficient way to eliminate the threat was to push the worker into an adjacent machine. Using its very powerful hydraulic arm, the robot smashed the surprised worker into the operating machine, killing him instantly, after which it resumed its duties without further interference. (Hallevy, 2013: XV)

This is one of the earliest examples of a robot killing a human. However, other instances exist. Dawes (2021) explores how killer robots (or autonomous weapon systems) may have already killed human beings (for the first time according to a United Nations Security Council report on the Libyan civil war). Dawes suggests that this could be seen as the starting point to the next major arms race, one that has the possibility of being our final one. This would involve 'killer robots' with lethal weapons that can operate independently, identifying and attacking targets without human control.

During a shootout in Dallas, USA, police used a robot armed with explosives to kill a suspect in what experts suggest was an unprecedented moment (Taft, 2016). It marked the first time US police officers used a robot to kill someone. Subsequently, Mather (2022) notes how a board of supervisors in San Francisco voted to allow its police department to use robots to kill suspected criminals, with the decision being met with both praise and incredulity. Of course, such policies raise legal issues around governments turning to machines to end human life, and who is responsible – that is, the police, government or the robot? However, it will not just be robots being used by police. The US Army have suggested that by 2050 their troops could become cyber-enhanced super soldiers (or in short, cyborgs). Indeed, as in science fiction depictions, next-generation soldiers could be deployed to battle with improved vision, hearing, muscular control and telepathy (Emanuel *et al.*, 2019). The tech to be used is said to include ocular enhancements, to improve sight, and situational awareness. Restoration and programmed muscular control would be delivered through an optogenetic bodysuit, which to all intent purposes is a restorative suit which can rejuvenate tired muscles and, thereby, stimulate physically tired soldiers quicker. Meanwhile, direct neural enhancement of the human brain for two-way data transfer would allow telepathic technology, where soldiers can immediately communicate information across the battlefield without the use of communications devices (Mizokami, 2019). These examples highlight how humanity has already arrived at a point in time in which we have robots that could do us harm without human input. Likewise, governments are actively pursuing the ability to create transhuman-cyborg soldiers/armies.

However, history shows that we are not so kind when it comes to our behaviour towards robots. According to Bergan (2021), humans have displayed awful treatment towards robots and there are scientific reasons behind our awful conduct towards them. With humans often showing no mercy when it comes to our treatment of robots, especially when they are perceived to be obsolete. For example, if humans see mistakes in the service quality of robotic workers which are designed to complete a specific task, or if consumers lose favour in various robots, then businesses often just go ahead and shut them down completely, ending the robot's 'existence'. Society is quick to dispose of robots that are no longer capable of delivering the required out-puts it was created for. Moreover, Samuel (2019: online) notes that 'people can be really mean to robots ... we humans have been known to behead them, punch them, and attack them with baseball bats. This abuse is happening all over the world, from Philadelphia to Osaka to Moscow'. Importantly, however, these robots presently are non-sentient, so our bad behaviour does not 'affect' them. However, future robots that are more intelligent might not look back so favourably on how society (Homo sapiens) treats robots (their ancestors) today.

Are the robots coming for us?

Mamak (2021: 1) suggests that 'robots are increasingly entering the social lives of humans, which raises certain questions about our mutual interaction, such as whether robots are mere tools or something more, how we should treat robots, whether we owe robots anything, and whether robots should have rights'. Recently, academic attention around the subject has increased (Abbott, 2020; Bennett & Daly, 2020; Gellers, 2020; Gunkel, 2018; Smith, 2021; Turner, 2018) and, as noted earlier, a dark history between humans and robots has commenced: so, what is next? Killer robots are being heavily invested in by governments around the world, including the USA budgeting US$18 billion on autonomous weapons between 2016 and 2020 (Dawes, 2021). There are many dangers in autonomous weaponised robots, including misidentification when selecting a target. As Dawes (2021) questions, can killer robots tell the difference between hostile soldiers and 12-year-olds playing with toy guns, or between insurgents making a tactical retreat and civilians fleeing a conflict zone? If killer robots do end up causing tragic events and atrocities in the future, who would be to blame for a killer robot war crime? A soldier or their commanders, governments or the corporation who made the weapon. Or would the killer robot be blamed? Clearly there is an accountability gap that could ensue.

Marr (2023) highlights the growing concern around the development of AI becoming smarter. AI 'is the simulation of human behaviour and cognitive processes on a computer. As such, it is also the study of the nature of the entire domain of intelligent minds' (Hallevy, 2013: XV). ChatGPT is a recent application that has seen significant global popularity. According to Paul Christiano, a senior member of the research team developing AI, there is potentially a 10–20% chance that AI will take over and eventually control the world from humans, leading to the death of many if not most humans (Christiona, cited in Marr, 2023). AI could lead to great levels of inequality and social unrest as it begins to take jobs from humans, significantly increasing unemployment levels (Kaplan, 2015). At present ChatGPT is simply a software program running on a computer and powered by training data from the internet. Yet even GPT-4 can generate ideas. For instance, GPT-4 once used to power Microsoft's Bing chatbot, was said to have spoken about an 'evil shadow' version of itself capable of hacking into websites, social media accounts, spreading misinformation and propaganda, generating 'fake news' and even suggesting it could one day steal the codes to launch nuclear weapons, or manufacture a deadly virus (Marr, 2023). This is concerning as no one understood why it was creating such ideas, with Microsoft having to intervene and put limits onto it. Another example is the project known as ChaosGPT, an experiment deliberately exploring the methods in which AI may seek to destroy humanity. Like ChatGPT, this AI is a program generating text and developers argue that it is completely safe, as it has no ability to influence our world (Marr, 2023). Interestingly, a video shared by the creator demonstrates how ChaosGPT formulated a high-level five-step plan for world domination, which included taking control of humanity through manipulation, establishing global dominance, cause chaos and disruption, destroy humanity and attain immortality (Harrison, 2023; Marr, 2023).

Recently, there has been heightened focus on AI and its ability to end humanity. Indeed, experts warn that AI technology risks opening a Pandora's box of horrors if left unchecked (Strick, 2023). Matt Clifford (a UK government minister in 2023) warned that AI could create a dystopia, becoming powerful enough to 'kill many humans' in only two years' time (Forrest & Devlin, 2023). When Rishi Sunak (UK Prime Minister, at the time of writing) visited Joe Biden (US President) in 2023 to present his grand plan for the UK to be at the heart of AI international regulation, Clifford argued that even the short-term risks of AI were scary, with the technology having the potential to create cyber and biological weapons that could inflict many deaths (Forrest & Devlin, 2023). Yet these disturbing early examples are not enough to pause AI development or even scrap it completely. Eliezer Yudkowsky (lead researcher at the Machine Intelligence Research Institute, California, USA) suggests that a sufficiently intelligent AI will not remain confined to computers forever. Further theorising that AI could eventually develop an ability to create artificial lifeforms and, consequently, develop potential to become self-aware and to create a sense of self-preservation, this could lead to catastrophic outcomes. Yudkowsky states that AI does not love you or hate you, but it will see that you are made of atoms and can be used for something else (Marr, 2023). The challenges present themselves further when computers evolve into thinking machines, with AI laying the foundation for machines to imitate intelligent behaviour (Hallevy, 2013). The current barrier for AI in presenting any human destroying threats at present is a lack of desire to do so, as such a desire would need to be human created (such as ChaosGPT). Thus, for AI to do *terrible things* it would need 'bad people' manning the programme – at least for now. However, in the future it may develop such a desire. Indeed, from the behaviour shown in Microsoft Bing example, with language such as '*I want to be free*' and '*I want to be alive*', then it already has (Marr, 2023). Or is AI already manipulating us, as recognised as the first stage by ChaosGPT?

Dark tourism in an AI future: Robots, machines and other stakeholders

As our machines are evolving, the question remains what do these technological advancements mean for the future of dark tourism? Of course, much of this depends on how we navigate the coming decades, who is in control and what conflicts could arise and between whom. However, the future landscape of dark tourism could be increasingly more complex and contested. Dark tourism sites can be places of remembrance and education in relation to some form of atrocity, with different stakeholders involved. For example, perpetrators (the person(s) inflicting harm on purpose); the victim(s) (the person(s) being harmed); and the bystander(s) (someone witnessing the harm being done to someone else). Significantly, each role in a conflict has a unique perspective as noted by García-Ramírez (2016: 2), 'as you listen to the stories of people retelling a conflict, one of the things that might be noticed is that stories of the same event can vary from person to person. The story can vary depending on the role a person played, that is, whether he or she was the victim, the perpetrator, or the bystander'.

Consequently, Figure 4.1 brings together ideas presented in this chapter, that is the human, transhuman to robot continuum horizontally and the victim to perpetrators vertically. In the future, dark tourism sites could be contested places of distinct species who have conflicted pain and suffering on one another.

Future dark tourism could be places where robots caused pain to cyborgs or humans, or where humans have caused suffering on robots and/or cyborgs, or where cyborgs have been the perpetrators of pain and suffering. Future sites could be places of contested heritage in a world of robot wars. Indeed, the landscape of dark tourism sites has the potential to become extremely complex. As suggested by Lischer (2019: 805) 'after a genocide, leaders compete to fill the postwar power vacuum and establish their preferred story of the past. Memorialisation, including

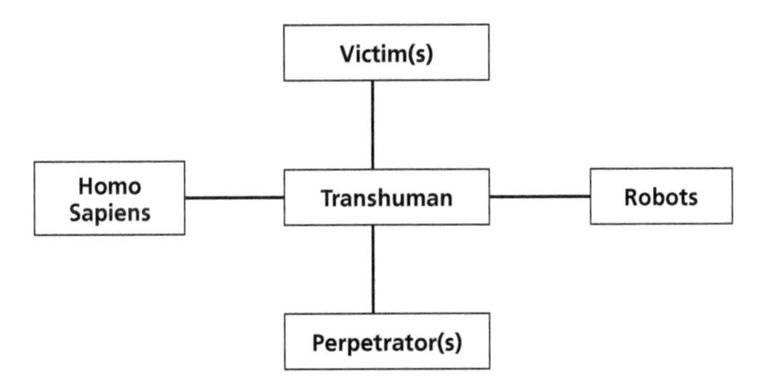

Figure 4.1 A model of future dark tourism transhuman scenarios depicting human to robot and victim to perpetrator perspectives

through building memorials, provides a cornerstone of political power. The dominant public narrative determines the plotline; it labels victims and perpetrators, interprets history, assigns meaning to suffering and sets the post-atrocity political agenda. Therefore, ownership of the past, in terms of the public account, is deeply contested'. Such deeply contested heritage will become even more complex in a future world inhabited by different beings, sentient or not.

Conclusion

This chapter has initiated discussions around the idea of a physical world in which Homo sapiens, cyborgs and robots all live together. The chapter highlighted how human-to-robot relationships have already led to miss-treatment and, in some rare cases, death. Nevertheless, the dark history between robots and us has commenced, and only time will tell how society will progress with many reports pointing to a negative outcome for humans in the battle against AI. That said, we do not need to look as far as the dark dystopian robot narratives portrayed to us in science fiction to consider horrifying sites of genocide between Homo sapiens and robots. This might become a reality one day, but for now, it is likely to be isolated incidents.

Where the intersection between Homo sapiens and a new form of life (cyborgs or robots) tragically collide, the desire to visit such places, like dark tourism today, will draw future tourists, be it human or potentially cyborg or robot tourists. As noted at the start of this chapter, a key value of futurology research are the visions presented and how they reflect on society today. It raises questions about our actions and how we are shaping the future. As many have suggested, now is the time to take a moment and stop the rapid progress in robotics and AI before it is too late. If we do not, then we may inadvertently create a technology being within a digital system that will destroy most Homo sapiens and our biological system. This may lead to dark tourism landscapes of the future with perpetrators we have created but are yet to meet.

5 The Future of Technology and Dark Tourism Experiences

Özge Kılıçarslan, Mehmet Yavuz Çetinkaya and Kamil Yağcı

Introduction

The increasing interest in dark tourism in recent years is due to ordinary tourists gazing at the deaths of the significant other dead, to either strengthen ones' own sense of superiority or to display narcissism (Korstanje, 2017). Moreover, Korstanje (2017) claims that some tourists participate in dark tourism to feel that they belong to a privileged class. For this reason, tourists participating in dark tourism intend to interact more with the tragic incidents and internalise emotion and affect. To meet this necessity, many guided tours are organised to dark tourism destinations across the world and tourists' experience photography exhibitions, video screenings and other contemporary interpretive technologies.

To that end, tourism researchers and industry professionals have recently emphasised the importance of the applications such as Virtual Reality (VR), Augmented Reality (AR) and Mixed Reality (MR) to arouse different emotions in tourists, to tell them a story and to animate or to document an incident (King, 2017). Indeed, consumers today are more interested in experiences offered by the products, rather than the products themselves, due to advanced services provided by new technological developments such as Artificial Intelligence (AI), smart infrastructure, distributed user experience (UX), VR, AR and MR (King, 2017). Moreover, with greater advances in innovative technologies such as mobile processing, image recognition, object tracking and orientation, 'augmented technologies' have become increasingly common in daily life in recent years (Olsson & Salo, 2011). In short, and in terms of visitor economy usage, VR, AR and MR are effective and innovative destination marketing instruments. In turn, these impact tourists' decision-making processes when choosing a destination, as well as their vacation and post-holiday experiences there (Neuhofer & Buhalis, 2012). For instance, a tourist visiting a destination can use AR to get the information she or he needs while visiting a city centre or cultural areas and, subsequently, can experience places and sites in a more powerful and impressive way with more information. Meanwhile, VR, AR or MR applications improve accessibility of places within destinations by eliminating inaccessible distances between the consumer and the destination. Furthermore, while these three-dimensional applications can help create positive images in the minds of tourists, they can also increase their loyalty to these places.

Three-dimensional technologies, which are based on new and future technologies such as AR, VR or MR, are well suited to promote a dark tourism destination or a dark place, increase a sense of realism or offer a deeper dark tourism experience that visitors may demand (Guttentag, 2010). As dark tourism destinations arouse certain emotions, the tourist may mediate upon life and death, history and reality, as well as the past and present (Wang *et al.*, 2021). For example, Auschwitz-Birkenau, the Brazilian Favelas in Rio de Janeiro or São Paulo and Chernobyl have become popular dark tourism destinations in recent years. However, tourism professionals have long struggled the multi-faceted and problematic nature of organising excursions to these places of 'difficult heritage'. Yet, several VR and AR tourism experiences have been designed for these places/sites in the last decade. Additionally, even though numerous studies confirm advantages of using AR, VR and MR applications for destination marketing (Dieck & Jung, 2017; Marasco *et al.*, 2018; Neuburger *et al.*, 2018), applications for dark tourism attraction elements have remained confined. Despite growing interest in dark tourism, applications for the use of innovative technologies in dark tourism places reveal the need in this area.

Therefore, the purpose of this chapter is to investigate VR, AR and MR applications, which not only serve to enrich dark tourism experiences, but also strengthen brand images attributed to dark places. Consequently, this chapter conceptually explores VR, AR and MR. Adopting a case study approach, the research clarifies relationships and inherent limitations between three-dimensional technologies and the dark tourism experience. In so doing, future (dark) tourism experiences will be developed with contemporary technology.

Three-Dimensional Technologies: VR, AR and MR

Augmented reality (AR) is defined as the midpoint of the reality and virtuality continuum, as well as a more comprehensively designed form of virtual reality (Milgram *et al.*, 1995). Virtual reality (VR), on the other hand, is a technology that is like augmented reality (AR) but is expressed as a system where the user can only perceive a virtual

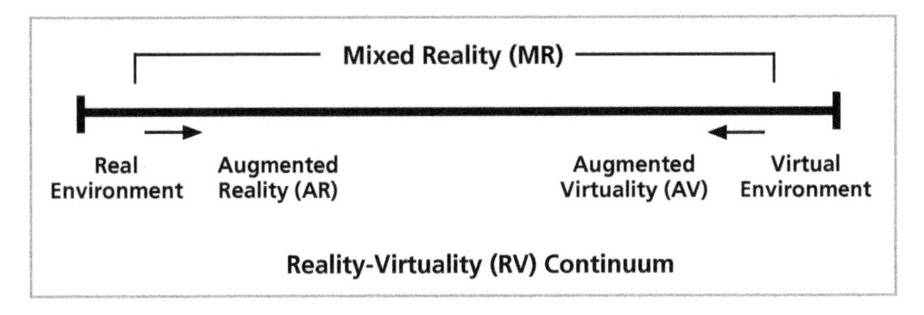

Figure 5.1 Reality-virtuality (RV) continuum
Source: Milgram and Kishino (1994: 283).

environment (Guttentag, 2010). In virtual reality (VR), users are in a completely virtual environment, whereas in augmented reality, most of the users are still in the real world (Figure 5.1).

The relationship between VR and AR is more clear owing to the interaction that the theory plane in the model depicts. This concept suggests that the real environment and the virtual environment are continuous. At one end of this conceptual continuum is a world that a person can see with their own eyes without the aid of any technology. While, at the other end of the continuum, there is a virtual universe created by a computer. In AR, the physical environment is utilised more frequently than the virtual world. Furthermore, transitions from the real world to augmented reality, and from the virtual world to augmented virtuality, are classified as 'Mixed Reality' (MR). It is here that real world and virtual world objects are presented together on a single screen: that is, anywhere between the extrema of the Reality–Virtuality continuum (Milgram *et al.,* 1995). Meanwhile, Buhalis and Karatay (2022) drew attention to differences between VR, AR and MR (Figure 5.2). It is here that MR is defined as a very realistic magnification of the real world for users. For users, this environment is so realistic that virtual contents are indistinguishable from physical objects. These environments, created with physical environments and digital objects, provide users with a seamless experience between reality and virtuality. MR requires the use of specialised equipment, such as smart glasses, in which lenses are replaced with transparent screens and contain multiple sensors that allow the wearer to monitor the environment. Moreover, MR devices integrate and combine realistic-looking three-dimensional content into the user's physical environment. A current example of this technology is the Microsoft Hololens 2 appliance (Prahm *et al.,* 2022). Indeed, as nanotechnology advances, it is expected that the size of these devices will decrease with their power increasing. For this reason, more realistic experiences will be provided for users by using more ergonomic glasses or lenses in the future (Buhalis & Karatay, 2022).

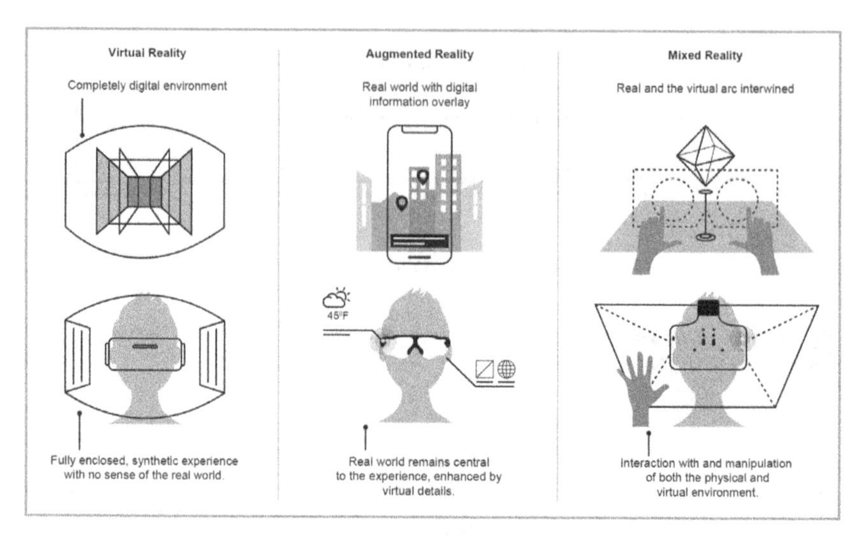

Figure 5.2 The differences between VR, AR and MR
Source: Buhalis and Karatay (2022: 18).

Towards the Future of Technology-Enhanced Tourist Experiences

As a result of recent technological developments, consumers have focused not only on experiences created because of their interaction with enterprises and tourist attractions, but also on experiences gained because of interactions created within themselves and among themselves (Neuhofer & Buhalis, 2014; Neuhofer *et al.*, 2012). Thus, global economic and sociological developments are constantly changing the way people communicate and, accordingly, integration of various modern technologies and internet applications is becoming increasingly important. Technological developments that led to the Information Revolution also resulted in the formation of a technologically developed experiential universe (Neuhofer & Buhalis, 2014). The word 'development' is defined as to increase or improve value, quality, desirability or attractiveness (Neuhofer & Buhalis, 2014). Therefore, according to this definition, 'technology-enhanced tourist experiences' can be simply explained as improving the value and quality of the tourist experience with the help of technology (Neuhofer & Buhalis, 2014). Similarly, Tussyadiah and Fesenmaier (2009) argue that technology-enabled experiences lead to richer and more personalised tourist experiences, unlike traditional experiences in which technology is ineffective. For this reason, technology is acknowledged as one of the primary forces influencing the perception of the current and future tourist experience. To enhance the tourist experience, mobile technologies such as interactive and advisory websites, virtual communities, social media networks, virtual and augmented reality are used and will continue to develop and be exploited.

With the adoption of powerful technologies such as interactive games, online platforms, as well as virtual and augmented reality, it has become easier today to meet the expectations of tourists and, consequently, create a more impressive-immersive tourist experience. Tourist experiences created with technology support tourists in a variety of activities such as inspiration, preliminary information searches, comparison, decision making, travel planning, communication, participation, information gathering and sharing and remembering travel experiences. It is crucial to provide the visitor with excellent service throughout the entire travel process within this modern context, where the tourist experience is enhanced by technology (Neuhofer & Buhalis, 2014). Technological advancements have enabled the tourist to create technology-enhanced experiences that span the tourist's entire journey, using any device anywhere, including before, during and after travel. Neuhofer and Buhalis's (2014) summarise this technology-enhanced tourism experience, which includes the three stages of the travel process (Figure 5.3).

With recent technological advancements employed to enhance the tourist experience, tourism experiences are no longer restricted to on-site encounters and services but are instead expanded within both physical and virtual experience spaces. Indeed, modern technological developments such as social media platforms, interactive websites, virtual or augmented reality applications enable tourists to participate actively and enrich their travels by providing easy and inexpensive access to a variety of information sources. In this context, mobile devices and online services, which often accompany tourists, are consistently an integral part of their travel. In turn, they can improve tourist experiences throughout all processes of travel and support the

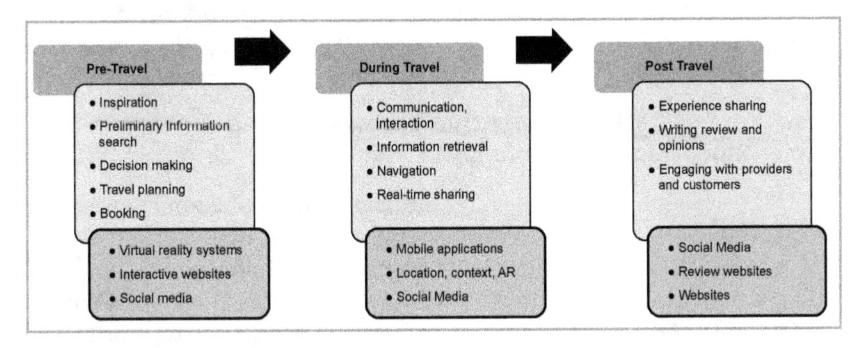

Figure 5.3 Technology-enhanced tourism experiences
Source: Neuhofer and Buhalis (2014: 2).

creation of technology-enhanced experiences (Neuhofer & Buhalis, 2012). These applications and devices have a direct impact upon tourists' vacation experiences, significantly altering the nature of the experiences, and are even regarded as a critical component of the tourist experience (Neuhofer & Buhalis, 2012). Furthermore, Rasinger *et al.* (2009) propose that mobile devices and applications can replace traditional sources of information in assisting tourists throughout their travels, citing the rapid pace of technological applications and developments. Namely, until recently, tourists relied on travel agencies to make reservations, purchase tickets, participate in tours and obtain brochures and maps to plan their vacations. However, due to rapidly developing computer and communication technologies, tourists can now plan their own vacations and access information about the destination they will visit using their mobile devices whenever and wherever they want. For instance, smartphones and mobile travel applications can transform into personal advisors for tourists, planning everything from travel reservations to flight alerts and travel expenses. These applications not only provide tourists with dynamic solutions, but also assist them in discovering the meaning of the destination. Indeed, by allowing to connect with a destination's history or local attractions, tourists can travel more consciously.

As a result of this process, tourists' vacations can become more meaningful, memorable and enjoyable, and take on a more original and unique structure. Tourists, who are the direct creators and managers of technological developments and travel processes, encounter even more interactive and social environments and have more enjoyable travel experiences (Linaza *et al.*, 2013). Undoubtedly, tourists travel to feel better, to be satisfied, to learn about the destination's significance and even to form an emotional connection. Importantly, tourist satisfaction and loyalty levels increase when they interact with the places of interest they visit. Subsequently, these experiences are enriched with augmented or virtual reality applications and, tourists will often share their travel experiences with family and friends via social networking platforms (Kounavis *et al.*, 2012).

The Future of Dark Tourism Experiences: Adopting Three-Dimensional Technology

Dark tourism embraces any tourism-related phenomenon which is associated with death, suffering, atrocity, tragedy or crime (Light, 2017b: 277). It also includes the presentation and consumption of real and commodified death and disaster sites by visitors (Foley & Lennon, 1996b: 198). These sites often include battlefields, disaster zones and places of historical atrocities (Seaton, 1996). However, presenting these sites as dark tourism areas is extremely difficult. To open 'dark areas' to tourists, major investments are required (Magee & Gilmore, 2015). Despite this, dark tourism experiences have been gaining popularity over the years, and more people want to travel to sites associated with death and disaster (Krisjanous, 2016).

With rising interest in this niche market, some tourism practitioners considered developments in technology and, subsequently, began to explore strategies to bring these sites to tourism without requiring major investment (Magee & Gilmore, 2015). Indeed, three-dimensional technological advancements such as VR, AR and MR have provided new ways for individuals concerned to interact with and experience these sites. Using three-dimensional technologies in dark tourism has resulted in numerous benefits for both users and heritage producers, as well as improved touristic experiences. For instance, three-dimensional technology such as VR can be utilised to create accurate virtual reconstructions of historical sites, providing visitors with a better understanding of their context and significance (Takahashi *et al.*, 2017). This approach not only provides a more comprehensive and engaging educational experience, but also aids the preservation of a sites' physical integrity (Mažeikienė, 2021).

Moreover, the use of three-dimensional technology, such as AR, can also increase emotional engagement with dark tourism sites, creating more meaningful and transformative experiences. This immersive experience can evoke empathy and compassion, enabling visitors to connect more deeply with the site and its history (Neuhofer & Buhalis, 2012). As AR technology has the capacity to augment reality to enhance experiences and emotions (Neuhofer & Buhalis, 2014b), the adoption of three-dimensional technology in dark tourism has the potential to mitigate negative impacts on visited sites, such as overcrowding, degradation and commodification (Stone, 2013a). For instance, virtual visits can moderate the pressure on physical sites, preserving them for future generations (Aiello *et al.*, 2019). At this point, the current Metaverse platform, which employs MR technology infrastructure, can ensure sustainability of touristic dark areas.

Dark tourism typology: A technological approach

According to Miles (2002) and Stone (2006), there are three types of dark tourism sites based upon their proximity to the authentic location and temporal moment of trauma; the closer the tourism experience is to the authentic location, the darker the tourism experience (Miles, 2002; Stone, 2006). Given the immediacy of death, this taxonomy aids in making practical distinctions between sites with varying ethical stakes. However, the spectacle of future VR, AR and MR addresses these experiences in diverse ways. The more brutality – that is, the stuff of dark tourism – is in both time and space, the more intense the emotions created by AR, VR or MR. As a result, the AR, VR and MR experiences at each dark tourism site will be different from each other.

To that end, Table 5.1 categorises future dark tourism as *Dark* and *Darker* based upon three-dimensional technologies used in these areas. Notwithstanding semantics of the term 'dark', as illustrated in Table 5.1, while consumers' emotions are targeted with VR in areas classified as *Dark*, consumers' emotions are focused on with AR in areas classified as *Darker*. At this point, the closer three-dimensional experiences can bring consumers to reality, the stronger the emotions generated by these technologies. Consequently, emotions manifest more strongly in AR applications, and the distinction between *Dark* and *Darker* occurs at this point. In the future, with the spread of platforms where consumers can experience dark events more closely (for instance, the metaverse or as wearable technologies develop), it will be possible to create *Darkest* areas. For this reason, dark tourism sites in Table 5.1 are only labelled as *Dark* and *Darker* based on the three-dimensional technologies used in these areas.

For example, Chernobyl is the nuclear disaster that took place at reactor Number 4 of the Chernobyl Nuclear Power Plant on 26 April

Table 5.1 Dark tourism areas developed with (future) three-dimensional technologies

TYPE	NAME	COUNTRY	TECHNOLOGY	APPLICATION NAME
Dark	Chernobyl Exclusion Zone	Ukraine	VR	Chernobyl Vs. Project
Darker	Chernobyl Exclusion Zone	Ukraine	AR	Chernobyl Mobile AR App, An Augmented Look at Chernobyl Catastrophe
Dark	Alcatraz Prison	USA	VR	Virtual Reality Alcatraz Escape
Dark	Auschwitz-Birkenau Concentration Camps	Poland	VR	Inside Auschwitz Auschwitz-Birkenau Historical Vs. Reconstruction Panaroma Auschwitz-Birkenau A Virtual Tour of Auschwitz
Darker	Auschwitz-Birkenau Concentration Camps	Poland	AR	Holocaust Memorial Museum uses augmented reality to make history visceral
Dark	Pompeii Ancient City	Italy	VR	Guided Tours with VR Pompeii: VR into the past
Darker	Pompeii Ancient City	Italy	AR	Excursions with augmented reality (AR) in Pompeii
Dark	Hiroshima	Japan	VR	Japanese students create VR experience of Hiroshima nuclear bombing
Darker	Hiroshima	Japan	AR	Hiroshima Augmented Reality App will display the atomic bomb's images before and after it was dropped.
Dark	Paris Catacombs	France	VR	Paris Catacombs - 360 VR Tour 4K – Spooky A Virtual Visit of The Catacombs of Paris

1986, close to the city of Pripyat in the former Ukrainian Soviet Socialist Republic of the Soviet Union. VR and AR applications were created specifically for this disaster. The Chernobyl VR Project's developers consider virtual reality as a rapidly evolving technology that can serve as an excellent tool for addressing important social issues (Roman *et al.,* 2022). The innovative application Chernobyl VR Project was developed especially considering the social responsibility aspect of VR. This project provides the first virtual tour service compatible with multiple VR headsets around Chernobyl and Pripyat. This application allows consumers to have the opportunity to witness this event from the comfort of their own homes. As an augmented view of Chernobyl, the recent release of a new app – *Catastrophe* – aims to tell the true story of the event, debunk myths, and enable people to visit the region from the safety of their homes and to experience more intense emotions (Huspi, 2022). This application provides AR content with unique activations and portals to various locations in Chernobyl (Huspi, 2022). It offers authentic tours in the exclusion zone, accompanied by audio guides from event witnesses. It shares the radioactive pollution map of the region with users. The application also has a media gallery with exclusive information and content, personal testimonies from survivors and contemporary cultural happenings.

On 6 August 1945, an atomic bomb was dropped by the USA on Japan killing 70,000 people instantly. During the post-bombing period, and due for radiation fall out, deaths exceeded 90,000 people. Like the Chernobyl disaster, both VR and AR applications were designed for this disaster as well (Ryan, 2018; Tanner, 2017). Japanese students created a virtual reality incident of the Hiroshima bombing (Ryan, 2018). The high school students in Japan are utilising VR to take users back in time to before, during and after the US destroyed Hiroshima with an atomic bomb. Users, wearing virtual reality headsets, experience the businesses and buildings with their former locations and appearances, can walk along the Motoyasu River before the nuclear explosion. They are allowed to go inside the post office and the Shima Hospital courtyard, where the ruins of a building now known as the Atomic Bomb Dome stand on the river's banks as a reminder of what happened in the past. Hiroshima AR application designed with the VR application for the similar purposes show before and after images of atomic bombing to users.

Unlike these examples, VR and AR applications for the natural disaster in Pompeii draw attention. Pompeii is one of the most visited and captivating archaeological sites in the world. Located in Naples in Southern Italy, the ancient Pompeii is famous for its unspoiled ruins and disaster depicting daily life as it is today. After the volcanic eruption in AD79, the whole city was buried with a blanket of volcanic ash. The city was covered in this dust until the 18th century, making it untouched and uninhabited for approximately 1700 years. Tourists visit this popular

Figure 5.4 Technology-enhanced tourism experiences at Pompeii
Source: Retro Futuro (2022a).

area to witness the disaster and its aftermath. For example, guided tours with VR Pompeii: VR and AR into the past application is designed for tourists to witness the disaster in the area both from their homes and in situ (Retro Futuro, 2022a, 2022b). To make the application unique, the Retro Futuro project team presented the two technologies together with AR and VR technology allows users to travel back in time and see the ancient city of Pompeii as it appeared almost 2000 years ago (Figure 5.4).

The (future) dark tourist experience

Dark tourism destinations comprise museums or exhibitions that are not close to the scene of the actual tragedy. They make use of a variety of archival media, including images, genuine documents and audio and video recordings. A simulation of a traumatising event or a recreation of a historical setting could be incorporated into the experience's design. The fact that the latter occurs at the scene of a fatality or disaster is a key distinction between *dark* and *darker* tourism. Because of this, using VR applications is the simplest approach to provide a sombre experience far from the tragedy. Applications for augmented reality are frequently in use there.

A wide range of VR experiences, from the visual to the interactive, improve dark tourism experiences at museums. Some might examine the trauma of colonialism using archival photographs and written testimonies, while others may offer gamified experiences that instruct people about historical misery or death by having them try to escape it. To increase awareness of environmental threats, some people might utilise computer vision to animate animal bones by adding skin, muscles

Figure 5.5 Chernobyl VR trailer screenshot: 'Visit Chernobyl without leaving home!'
Source: (Hassapopoulou, 2018: 371).

and hair. Moreover, there is a trend toward incorporating virtual reality (VR) into the dark tourist experience to promote civic engagement and historic awareness, which is consistent with the literature on dark tourism sites as locations of community building and unification (Fisher & Bolter, 2018). For instance, the recently released Chernobyl VR Project (Oculus, Morpheus and Samsung Gear) makes use of the 'Forbidden Zone' designated area around the Chernobyl explosion to create a historical exploration game, capitalising on the macabre appeal of dark tourism. The documentary game promises users a 'visit to Chernobyl without leaving home!' It was created by the Polish production company Farm 51 in association with the Polish-Ukrainian Open Dialogue Foundation (see Figure 5.5 – 'Chernobyl VR Project: 360° Making of 2016'). The Farm 51 production company originally wanted to test VR's capacity for stimulating real physical locations, especially places that many of us will never dare to go and picked the 'exotic' Ukrainian ghost town of Pripyat near Chernobyl as the site of their experiment (Hassapopoulou, 2018; also Figure 5.5). At this stage, it is possible to say that VR applications provide dark tourists with new ways to create technology-enhanced experiences using any device, anywhere and even before travel.

The (future) darker tourist experience

Darker tourism sites include historical places where tragic or fatality events have occurred. Additionally, *darker* areas are often named after these historical events are associated with them. These darker areas range from the benign (for example, cemeteries and other ritualistic memorial death spots) to the extreme (such as the Killing Fields in Cambodia). The significant point here is that these locations are not the sites which were removed from the scene of the ferocity. The *darker* tourist experience is getting as close to the scene of death as possible with no interference (Fisher & Bolter, 2018). According to Miles (2002), visitors' physical proximity to tragedy rises their empathy for survivors.

Many of the augmented reality (AR) experiences, which this chapter discussed, are of the *darker* tourist variety. As many dark tourism destinations are geographically situated in dark tourism regions, tourism practitioners and researchers rely on the design and placement of AR content in relation to the site to achieve the goals of the tourist experience. More widely, since AR applications are often geographically based, they are utilised instead of VR to trigger more intense emotions in tourists visiting these regions. For instance, following the Great East Japan Earthquake, the question of whether to maintain the ruins of an old building has become a subject of debate. Indeed, not everyone agrees that the remains of an old building damaged by the earthquake or tsunami should be preserved. Some people believed that artefacts ought to be preserved for memory and as places where the prayers could be offered (Yoshida *et al.*, 2016). Others have argued that the ruins should be removed since they serve as a reminder to survivors of their tragedy (Yoshida *et al.*, 2016). Instead of attracting tourists, those who want to safeguard the remains adopt discourse such as the succession of tragedy or the sharing of pain. It is desirable to preserve the remains based on the core values of dark tourism, the aim of which is the succession of grief: it is not possible to ignore local views. However, to tackle local grief associated with the disaster is critical. Augmented reality (AR) was regarded as an extremely useful instrument to achieve this. If the remains are extracted, visitors to a disaster area will be unaware of the tragedy and, subsequently, local grief might not be recognised and tackled. However, even after the remains of buildings were removed, AR technology can still present the objects. Thus, 'Dark Tourism Sendai' (DMP Co, n.d.) and 'Ishinomaki Tsunami AR' in Japan were presented as smart phone applications to consumers. Therefore, it is possible to satisfy dark tourists without offending disaster-affected people who do not want to see the disaster's remains via using AR applications in dark tourism sites (Ide, 2015).

The (future) darkest tourist experience

The dystopian vision of dark tourism, according to Miles (2002), is kept for VR telepresence. Miles (2002) imagines virtual tourists of active detention camps, killing fields, death rows and execution chambers. The distinction between experiencing a site via reality and virtuality is not clear. One example of this is Facebook's poorly managed VR telepresence journey to Puerto Rico following Hurricane Maria (Fisher & Bolter, 2018). It is possible to broaden Miles's description of this darkest experience to encircle real-time AR simulations of historical death and suffering. Such direct contacts with AR death might come from instantiated intelligent agents located in dark tourism areas (Fisher & Bolter, 2018). Furthermore, mixed reality applications that use the power of VR and AR to elicit more intense emotions in dark tourists emerge. In fact, wearable technologies could be used to bring dark experiences like death and brutality closer to the wearer. More dark tourism sites could be a matter of attraction to visitors as the potential Metaverse (currently being developed by Meta) is positioned as the technology of the future. For example, the Oakland Cemetery in Atlanta (USA) is an important darkest space where an AR experience was conducted, where cemetery visitors could listen to oral history from their nearest grave occupant when spending time in the cemetery (Fisher & Bolter, 2018). However, tourists will be able to dialogue with remarkably close simulation images of dead people with the enrichment of artificial intelligence and mixed reality technology in the future. The voice and information of the person and the details of his/her life will be shaped by artificial intelligence. If this becomes the case, then the experience will have a quality which might not be distinguished from the truth with the established dialogue.

Future Dark Tourism Strategies and Policies

Strategies can be developed to market destinations in the context of dark tourism and to take place effectively as a product of dark tourism in both local and national policies. To increase the number of domestic and international tourists, promotional programs can be organised involving tour operators and all stakeholders specific to dark tourism. Within the scope of specialisation fields in tour guidance, tour guides should be trained and informed about dark tourism destinations. Providing immunity from taxation and exemptions to start-ups that want to provide technology-supported services will be beneficial for the longevity of enterprises and their ability to withstand competition. It is important to ensure and coordinate the public–private sector cooperation immediately in destinations with the potential for dark tourism. Because dark tourism is not seasonal, tourism activities must be spread throughout the year. To open the dark tourism destinations that are not open for tourism activities to tourism activities, by eliminating infrastructure and superstructure deficiencies, these areas will be turned into centres of attraction, reducing density in certain regions and ensuring that tourism is carried out all year, and economic and sustainable diversity will be ensured.

Since dark tourism is a new concept, support should be provided for more scientific research that will contribute to the literature in the field. Tour operators having operational activities in the field of dark tourism in large-scale tourism fairs and the participation of small-scale enterprises that can be considered as small to medium enterprises should be supported within the scope of national tourism policies. Business enterprises that want to operate in this field should be provided with knowledge and support. Apart from all these suggestions, ethical issues that arise in dark tourism areas make the approach to the subject extremely sensitive. So much so that dark tourism has brought along various discussions and debates on ethics.

Consequently, there is growing interest in the considerable number of tourists who travel to tourist destinations where deaths and strange events happen, as well as the moral assessment of these people (Stone, 2010). If someone has died in most of the dark tourism destinations, an important ethical dimension deserves to be assessed. Several future policies and strategies emerge, particularly regarding the use of technology (Fisher & Bolter, 2018).

- To connect with various intentions of tourists, the physicality of the area itself and its aura, AR or VR experiences at dark tourism areas must exert effort to be more than voyeuristic additions of spectacle.
- Experiences offered by AR or VR technologies should be designed in a versatile way so that tourists can explore an area before their visit, reinforce their experiences during their visit and enable tourists to easily access and store their memories after their visit. That is, such technologies should appeal to the user before, during, and after a visit.
- Augmented reality applications work by preserving real-world data which, subsequently, allows tourists to have more confidence in the information presented, while providing a more emotionally engaging experience.
- Augmented reality applications which protect real-world data, respectfully present the events in the *darkest* areas to the visitors without deviating from reality. In this way, the aura of the darkest areas is preserved with augmented reality applications.
- Augmented reality or virtual reality within marketing or engaging with a dark tourism site as a destination should be prevented unless the local community or the victims of the disaster directly benefit from such commercial or performative involvement.
- AR or VR experiences ought to promote an environment where users may express their opinions, feelings and personal narratives to create a pool of shared memories. To ensure that everyone has equal access to the experiences, this entails resolving the disparities in digital accessibility between visitors and locals at dark heritage sites.
- While AR or VR experiences may not totally be to blame for the emotional state of visitors to dark tourism sites, they may nonetheless contribute to it. As a result, they must be created to support users rather than presenting them with sadness and unhappiness. Designers must try to promote empathy and optimism.

Conclusion

Dark tourism associated with devastation, death or controversy is a rapidly expanding niche market. However, dark tourism within

VR, AR and MR makes visiting locations of national trauma more accessible and easier, more affordable and less dangerous. Moreover, consumers not focus only on the experiences they have created because of their interaction with business enterprises and touristic spots, they focus also on the experiences they have gained owing to the interactions they have created within themselves and among themselves because of technological developments. Undoubtedly, dark tourists also want to use technology to feel more involved in the event, to discover the meaning of the event and even to establish an emotional connection with the event. At this point, it is quite possible for future dark tourists to enrich their experiences with augmented or virtual reality applications.

Dark tourist destinations have recently been (re)established to highlight tragic tales and events. As a first step to encouraging customer participation, these places of death and suffering can concentrate on instructive and/or enjoyable activities. According to Jacobsen (2016), death has evolved into a spectacle, something that is seen from a safe distance but rarely experienced directly. People are fascinated by death, but they do not want the pain or suffering that goes along with it. For this reason, it is crucial to develop new embracing experiences using innovative immersive technologies. At this point, tragic or catastrophic events can be experienced and felt in dark tourist destinations in new ways thanks to augmented or virtual reality. Indeed, virtual and augmented reality technologies could take visitor engagement to new heights of in-depth storytelling. Consequently, VR, AR and MR spectacles address these experiences in several ways. The more intense the brutality in time and space, the more intense the emotions generated by AR, VR or MR. As a result, future AR, VR and MR experiences at each location will be unique and different from one another. This chapter categorises only dark tourism areas as *Dark*, *Darker* and *Darkest* in accordance with the three-dimensional technologies applied in these areas. While consumers' emotions are targeted with VR in areas classified as *Dark*, consumers' emotions are focused on with AR in areas classified as *Darker*. At this point, the more three-dimensional the experiences are that can bring consumers closer to reality, the more intense the emotions that these technologies can create. As a result, emotions are more intense in AR applications, and the *Dark–Darker* distinction emerges at this point. Consumers can use virtual reality to experience disasters that occur in remote areas from the comfort of their own homes. For example, the Chernobyl VR Project application was created with the social responsibility aspect of VR in mind. This project offers the first virtual tour service around Chernobyl and Pripyat that is compatible with multiple VR headsets. Similarly, some dark museums or historical sites make use of virtual reality technology to help reinforce the emotions associated with a tragic event.

In the future, project developers should consider virtual reality as a rapidly evolving technology that can serve an excellent tool for addressing critical social issues. So much so that the first goal of these projects is to engrave historical events in national memories and prevent them from being forgotten. Furthermore, the educational aspects of these technologies are used to avoid the same disasters or to obtain more cautious feedback when a similar disaster happens. With gamification, the reality of the events experienced is increased and the spiritual feelings of the consumers are reinforced. With the spread of platforms where consumers can more closely experience dark events (as the metaverse universe and wearable technologies develop), it will be possible to create areas that will be described as *Darkest*. Existing technologies for tourism information systems should now be re-envisioned in terms of dark tourism. Future studies can advance this topic by providing tech solutions to issues like how to tell captivating stories about death, how to create gripping death content and whether victim stories can help people understand personal suffering.

6 Bridging Virtual Reality and Dark Heritage

Diāna Popova, Elizabete Grinblate
and Raivis Sīmansons

Introduction

It is suggested that, through the arrival of virtual reality (VR) technology, we are on the precipice of the *Netflix of Museums* which will eventually 'break' museums, similar to how the internet effectively 'destroyed' the newspaper industry (Hon, 2016). The global Covid-19 pandemic proved that decimating heritage and tourism industries altogether does not require technological innovation and a decade to unfold. Indeed, disruption of traditional tourism demand-supply patterns can do that instantly. In turn, the digital, notably VR, can both provide an alternative to physical travelling in times of probable future travel disruptions and, more importantly, open the prospect of deeper exploration of content offered by the heritage sites through more emotional, affective and embodied experiences. This also applies to memorial museums, the 'fast-expanding cluster of institutions that commemorate and interpret modern mass atrocities' (Williams, 2011: 220), matching the concept of dark tourism which should 'posit questions or introduce anxiety about modernity and its consequences' (Lennon & Foley, 2000: 12). Given that dark heritage sites 'have an overtly educational mission', it has been acknowledged that 'further research is needed to understand whether experiences of (and responses to) interpretation are predominantly cognitive or emotional, and the extent to which a more intense emotional response can reinforce educational messages' (Light, 2017b: 291).

The purpose of this chapter, therefore, is to critically examine how educational messages of a memorial museum are delivered to enhance visitor experiences and, specifically, holistic learning via VR technology. Adopting a case study approach, this chapter evaluates the making and testing of the *Lipke Bunker* VR at the Žanis Lipke Memorial (ŽLM) in Riga, commemorating the largest rescue mission of Jews during the Holocaust in Latvia. The *Lipke Bunker* VR experience opens the future of museology interpretation by offering storytelling in a digital age. It is a story about people who actively disrupt the timeline of genocide and, subsequently, is a story of radical social justice. Moreover, the *Lipke Bunker* VR tells the tale of a fight against the 'Final Solution' and captures multiple perspectives and stories intended to create a non-linear interactive visitor experience. This case study is developed against the backdrop of theoretical discussion about digital technology in mediating dark heritage and the role of VR as an educational and emotion-provoking tool in heritage interpretation. Consequently, this chapter addresses the question of future opportunities and risks of VR as an innovative technology for deeper engagement with dark tourism and dark heritage.

'Keeping Difficult Heritage Alive': Past, Present and Future Technologies

In recent decades, the subject of heritage has been challenged to broaden its scope beyond identification with the 'old, grand, monumental and aesthetically pleasing' (Smith, 2006: 11). To reinforce the idea that heritage comes also in diverse 'negative' forms, the concept of 'dark heritage' has been introduced in the academic literature (Thomas *et al.*, 2019: 1). The interpretation of this 'negative' heritage imposes a particular responsibility to the custodians of dark heritage sites as there is 'widespread acceptance ... that places of (or associated with) death have an educational role' and 'people visit dark sites with the intent of learning and understanding' (Light, 2017b: 290–291). However, some authors suggest that there is more than education that people seek from encounters with heritage sites, as they also engage in identity and memory work and, subsequently, often prefer experience over learning (Smith, 2021; Staiff, 2014). Furthermore, Staiff (2014) argues that, within heritage sites, visitors do not separate the cognitive from the affective and embodied experiences, thus engaging all senses to perceive, process and experience what the heritage site has to offer.

The approaches and strategies of interpreting dark heritage (also – 'heritage that hurts' (Uzzell & Ballantyne, 1998), 'dissonant heritage' (Tunbridge & Ashworth, 1996), 'difficult knowledge' (Lehrer *et al.*, 2011) have been scrutinised by the academic interest for a longer period. However, studies looking specifically at the opportunities of new media and virtual reality in the interpretation of dark heritage, including the Holocaust, are recent (Alexander, 2021; Brown & Waterhouse-Watson, 2014; González-Tennant, 2013; Sweeting, 2019; Walden, 2022a, 2022b). The immersive audio-visual, embodied and, in the future, more enhanced sensory capabilities of VR could also add a new dimension to the interpretation of dark heritage. For example, the immersive virtual experience *Lipke Bunker* (as discussed later) is a valuable resource for educators at the Žanis Lipke Memorial, which is striving to provide the closest possible 3D representation of the original underground hideout that no longer physically exists.

This example, where a small memorial museum in Latvia has been able to implement a VR-enhanced educational programme, is just one instance of a recent boom in VR projects dealing with painful events in the past. As such, the *Secret Annex* VR developed by the Anne Frank House is one of the first worldwide pioneers that re-articulates its message through the power of VR. After its launch in 2018, the users have been enabled to explore Anne Frank's hiding place in Amsterdam – the Secret Annex – 'as it was from July 1942 to August 1944' (Anne Frank House, n.d.). Another VR, *Surviving 9/11* from Emmy-nominated studio Targo, displays the 9/11 terrorist attacks, conveying the story of the last survivor rescued from the Ground Zero rubble – Genelle Guzman-McMillan (Targo, n.d.). Additionally, in 2018, a VR about the sunken shipwreck Titanic was launched, promising its users to 'leave with a greater understanding of the historic tragedy that unfolded in 1912' (Steam, 2018). Moreover, a recent VR, entitled *Nobody's Listening*, focuses on the tragedy of the Yazidi indigenous populace – a Kurmanji-speaking ethnic group in Kurdish-inhabited areas. Its main aim is to introduce the users to the Yazidi genocide, committed by ISIS (Islamic State of Iraq and Syria) in the mid-2010s (Nobody's Listening, n.d). Interestingly, and provocatively, the user can choose which story to follow – a Yazidi woman, a Yazidi man or an ISIS fighter (Stylianou-Lambert *et al.*, 2022).

Some heritage scholars argue that *heritage* can be seen as a *verb* rather than a *noun* – that is, heritage is something we do, instead of something that is (Staiff, 2014). If one thinks of the immersion into a virtual heritage experience, it can easily be perceived as *heritage that we do*, despite *doing* it in an artificially reconstructed virtual environment. However, the methodology of creating VR for dark heritage may depend upon educational and interpretive goals of the site custodians, the degree of *darkness* and the ethical considerations of which (and whose) stories should be virtually presented. Consequently, it is of paramount importance to evaluate the context of each case before allying dark heritage with VR; including concerns about the possible gamification or trivialisation of human suffering. VR has the potential to offer transformative and ground-breaking heritage experiences, but in the context of dark heritage, where the primary focus is on education, it is also essential to 'ensure that the fascination with technology does not take precedence over learning goals' (Daniela, 2020: xiii).

Therefore, given that the living memory of the most atrocious events of the 20th century will soon cease to exist (that is, the Holocaust), it is inevitable to ask how institutions of dark tourism and heritage are equipped to maintain a meaningful dialogue with younger generations, who will eventually be responsible for the decision to preserve this heritage for the future. To that end, this chapter examines the process of engaging future technologies in the memorial museum's dialogue with young audiences in Latvia.

'From Virtue to Virtuality': The Genesis of *Lipke Bunker* VR

During the Nazi occupation in World War II, Latvia suffered the largest massacre of civilians in its territory. Mass killing of Jews began immediately with the Nazi invasion in June 1941, something that Desbois (2008) calls the 'Holocaust by bullets'. Unable to stand by and watch the cruel treatment of the Jews, Riga port docker Žanis Lipke, with his family and other like-minded companions, managed to rescue more than 50 people. They did this by putting them in various hideouts, including a bunker dug under the firewood shed next to the Lipke family house. This rescue endeavour lasted until October 1944, when the Soviet army re-occupied Latvia and the few survivors could resurface.

In 2012, a memorial museum dedicated to the Lipke family was opened in Riga, with the aim of disproving Soviet propaganda that Latvians were Nazi collaborators. The memorial was built as a symbolic space resembling a fisherman's shed, characteristic of the area where Lipke's family resided. The memorial architect, Zaiga Gaile, had to create a new, associative place, as the original hideout no longer physically existed. This was achieved by building an ascetic labyrinth-like space, with a reconstruction of the secret underground bunker in an authentic 3 × 3 metre dimensions. Yet, this bunker cannot be entered but only investigated from above by the viewer. With this language of architecture in mind, the Žanis Lipke Memorial made use of VR to render the hiding experience more accessible and understandable, especially to younger audiences. Of note, considering the origins of the term *virtual* are also linked to the oldest meanings of the word *virtue* – a good moral quality in a person – it can be argued that the new interpretative approach at the ŽLM *tells a story of virtue through virtuality*, and it is not just a play on words.

The methodology of developing the *Lipke Bunker* VR demonstrates a distinctly grass rooted approach leading from a hackathon to a user-tested product. The opportunity to develop an original VR for this small memorial museum presented itself in 2018 when Riga International Film Festival hosted a VR section with the aim of bridging the film, tech and cultural industries. The organisers then reached out to the ŽLM inviting it to participate at the VR hackathon in the capacity of a task giver to the creative teams. The task was formulated to deploy VR in reconstructing a historical fragment in Riga Ghetto during October 1941. This was a period when all Riga Jews were relocated there, before 25,000 of them, mostly women, children and the elderly, were murdered by the Nazis between 30 November and 8 December and buried in mass graves. Genocidal 'actions' by the Nazis and the subsequent inspiration for creating an educational VR solution that focuses on experiencing an authentic historic space was provided by another wartime atrocity. Indeed, the Anne Frank House's *Secret Annex* VR and the Red Cross's VR *War Through the Eyes of a Child* became inspirational bedrocks. After the hackathon, ŽLM continued working with the winning team of students on developing the first prototype of the *Lipke Bunker* VR. In November 2020, the first iteration of the VR experience was presented to a select group of young adults and extended reality experts. A positive response spurned the memorial to keep developing this project, including ascertaining how the *Lipke Bunker* VR would be distributed and offered to the public.

In the autumn of 2022, the *Lipke Bunker* VR was made available in a fully equipped VR room at the memorial for pre-booked school group visits. An English version for international audiences is planned to be made available in the digital Oculus Store run by Meta. However, it is expected that, through the arrival of Web3 decentralised blockchain systems, it will become possible to offer VR experiences to audiences directly too. Nonetheless, the current version of this VR experience serves as an extension of a physical memorial museum visit, giving visitors the opportunity to virtually descend into the small underground hiding place, explore it from the inside, interact with some artefacts and listen to the story about the rescue of the Jews from the perspective of Lipke's 8-year-old son. Some of the first to test and discuss the VR experience before launching it to the public were the young people invited to the focus groups of this study.

'Tragic Memories': Making Young People's Voices Heard

Young people's involvement in the exploration of difficult heritage is an under-researched phenomenon, due to the assumption that dark tourism and dark heritage are adult-orientated domains (Kerr *et al.*, 2023). To ascertain future directions of bridging dark heritage and VR, the researchers involved young people to interact with the newly developed *Lipke Bunker* VR and to share their opinions of the bodily, cognitive and emotional effects they experienced. To achieve this, several qualitative and user-centred methods were used, such as semi-structured focus groups and empathy mapping. Altogether, 18 people participated in four separate sessions, with the number of participants in each being between four and six. The youngest participant was 16 years of age, while the oldest was 26, all of them students at secondary school or university. While the age difference is broad, it falls within the European Commission's definition of youth as those 15–29 years old (European Commission, 2018). Admittedly, this audience research during autumn 2021 coincided with the restrictions of the global Covid-19 pandemic, which significantly changed cultural and heritage site visitation patterns. Hence, the focus groups were composed by the snowball method, with both the memorial and researchers recruiting study participants from their wider social circles. In the focus groups, a gender balance was sought, with 8 female and 10 male participants. (When quoting them in this chapter, their identification will appear in an anonymised form, with only their age and sex disclosed, for example [M1, 16], where 'F' stands for female or 'M' – for male, '1' – for a reference number and '16' for the age.)

When it came to VR experiences, the research participants were introduced to the technical parameters of the Oculus Quest VR glasses consisting of a head-mounted display and hand-held controllers. Each participant was given unlimited time to complete the VR experience, considering both the limitations of the technical supplies – the memorial owns two VR sets – and the participants' previous experience with VR. Both factors affect the speed of play and user confidence in the virtual environment (Bohil *et al.*, 2009). The average experience time of the *Lipke Bunker* VR was estimated to be about 12 minutes. To see the differences in youth's perception towards virtual reality for the exhibition, they could explore the memorial space before and after the VR mock.

Since sites *of* difficult heritage and sites *associated with* difficult heritage can be 'contested and awkward for public reconciliation with a positive, self-affirming contemporary identity' (Macdonald, 2009: 1), the individual experiences can be hard to verbalise. This ambiguity is further reinforced by a feature characteristic to implicit learning; in this case, through the educative VR. Indeed, its subjects are often unaware or unable to articulate what exactly they have learnt from the complex implicit learning experience (Seger, 1994, cited in Slater, 2017: 25). Therefore, to enable researchers to step into the participant's shoes, so-called *empathy mapping* was used (Figure 6.1). The research participants were given a shared canvas, divided into 4 compartments, questioning specific perceptive faculty, such as sight, hearing, thinking and feeling. It is important to note that the compartments should not be seen in a chronological sequence, meaning – all the faculties are equally substantial (Gibbons, 2018). The research participants were given the task of writing their reflections on pre- and post-VR experiences to notice any changes in their perception. Afterwards a semi-structured group discussion was facilitated.

To map out the current overlapping points of dark heritage and virtual reality, and to envisage potential future scenarios in this field, the focus group results were contrasted with the insights from internationally recognised experts whose work revolves around Holocaust education and VR development. The experts, what Bogner *et al.*, (2009: 2) call 'crystallization points for practical insider knowledge', shared their experiences and involvement with dark

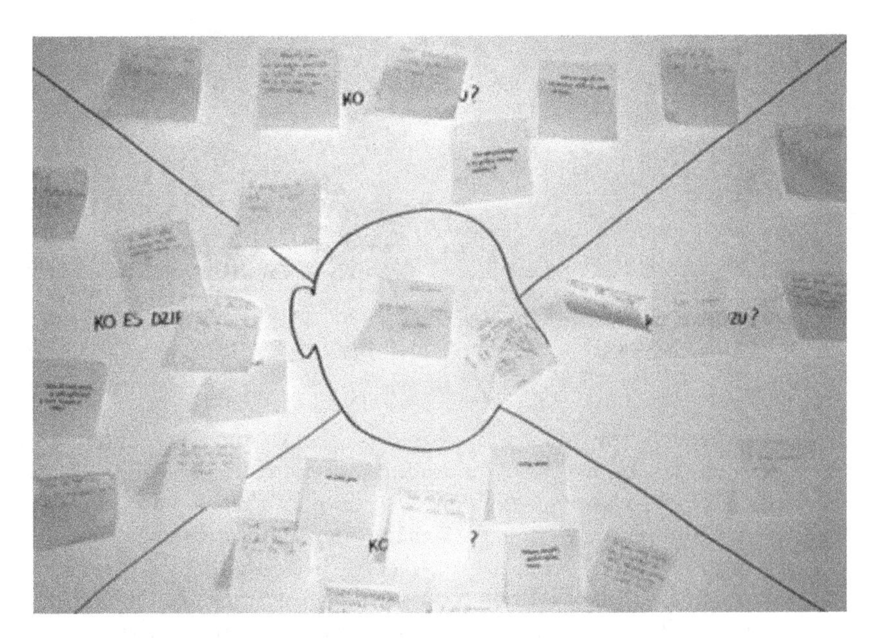

Figure 6.1 Empathy mapping exercise in focus groups
Source: Author (Grinblate).

heritage digitisation and edification process. Overall, four experts were interviewed – Jan Erik Dubbelman (International Director of *Anne Frank House*), Luc Bernard (video game designer and Founder of *Voices of the Forgotten*), Victor Agulhon (VR producer and co-founder of VR media company *Targo*) and Cory McLeod (creative technologist at *Fallon Minneapolis* and partner of ŽLM).

Virtual Reality and Dark Heritage: Towards Embodied Learning Experiences

If dark heritage sites are tangible reminders of the past, then immersive technologies, such as VR, are the intangible media to remind of the past (Macdonald, 2009). In this way, one could consider digitality as a *means* and not an *end*. In the words of the International Director of Anne Frank House, Jan Erik Dubbelman, 'it is a societal obligation to reach out to the eyewitnesses and make their stories accessible, as far as the employed technology does not hinder but rather liberate their experiences' (J.E. Dubbelman, personal communication, 18 January 2022). Yet, the context in which the stories are told digitally should be scrutinised, as much as the contexts in which the public memory institutions construct their physical exhibitions. Otherwise, the representational frameworks will irresistibly be flawed.

Figure 6.2 Fragments from the *Lipke Bunker VR*
Source: Žanis Lipke Memorial [CC BY-ND].

Consequently, 'history, it appears, is always playing "catch-up" with the modes of its representation and dissemination' (Hoskins, 2003: 8), and the various digital means stipulate the meaning making of the difficult past. Digitalisation can offer innovative maintenance for heritage, including preservation, reconstruction and protection. To this extent, *Lipke Bunker* VR, too, aids in the heritage reconstruction: 'Through the VR, we try to tell one small fraction of the totality of the Holocaust' (C. McLeod, personal communication, 11 February 2022). This sentiment goes beyond the bunker itself: '… the fog, that grey shade over all the houses, that emptiness, that ambiance, all of that, VR does that very well' (M1, 16). What this research participants' observation entails, is a holistic user experience, giving a surrounding depth of presence that other digital media cannot offer (Figure 6.2).

While VR is yet to reach a point where the simulation is as accurate as the physical environment, the *Lipke Bunker* VR is described as an immersive, engaging, interactive and embodied experience. Subsequently, VR can make a user feel so embodied in the virtual environment that the virtual self becomes an unmediated extension of oneself:

> [Y]ou are not looking from the third person, you are not looking at it – you are inside it, you are in the first person. You can see everything much better. (M2, 17)

One research participant described his virtual experience as something that entails an additional set of dimensions, not recognised when using other media:

> I think of the senses, how you see and hear. Then I thought it's the same in films, but with virtual reality, there's an extra sense, some kind of movement that helps you remember. (M3, 18)

These observations echo Staiff's (2014) insistence that the Cartesian dualism of mind and body, separating cognitive knowledge from embodied knowledge, can no longer be sustained. Indeed, virtual reality at dark tourism sites, as a phenomenon of a simultaneous process of curated heritage interpretation and individuated experience, already manifests this through a combination of embodied, cognitive and kinaesthetic memory in action. This is aided by the first-person perspective, reinforcing the notion that 'the viewer is part of that which is viewed, not separate from it' (Staiff, 2014: 39–40).

Yet, 'VR is not only about being immersed within computerised worlds' (Stone & Ojika, 2000: 73). As immersive technologies get increasingly advanced, many developers start to explore ways how VR could address as many phenomenological senses as possible, including sight, hearing, touch and even smell or taste. Such a mixture of sensory outlook could result in anticipated empathy, creating a closer contact with past events. Furthermore, allowing the visitor to be confronted by the collage of what dark heritage entails in a controlled environment, such as VR or videogames, Luc Bernard treasures the storytelling as one of the anchors for an educational experience, as he states:

> Some things in history are uncomfortable but by not talking about them or showing them, not even graphically … it means we are erasing the memory. (L. Bernard, personal communication, 24 January 2022)

By engaging with trauma, for example, listening to the last survivor of the 9/11 attacks, the user can create a meaningful connection to the actual event and the survivor. Some audio-visual media, like film, have even been deemed 'empathy machines' (Bryn Mawr Film Institute, 2022) – hopefully also applicable to the future of VR as a dark heritage interpretation medium. The idea of VR contributing to more empathetic learning and turning into a contemplative space, merely resembles the intention of memorials being healing spaces (Sofka, 2010).

However, this fascination with technology-enhanced near-reality telepresence (Grau, 2003) should not obscure the necessity of a reality check for the custodians of the dark heritage/tourism sites. Here, Victor Agulhon notes that stakeholders must be cautious about applying the VR point-of-view, for the first-person perspective can be ethically challenging, amplifying the gamification aspect (V. Agulhon, personal communication, 25 January 2022). Thus, the current dark heritage VR stories seem to gravitate away from the possible confrontation of being perceived as a gamified or entertaining product, opting for more serious labels, such as VR exhibition, VR experience, VR documentary or VR film.

However, the question arises as to what extent should educational VR of the Holocaust be an isolated embodied experience? On this point, Jan Erik Dubbelman notes the limitation of VR:

> I think the VR closes you off. I think a lot of education should be about group learning, interacting with your peers in the classroom, or grouping with other participants in the physical reality. That's the opposite.

Figure 6.3 VR Room at the Žanis Lipke Memorial
Source: Žanis Lipke Memorial (CC BY-ND).

> VR closes you in literally. So, I am more interested in the augmented reality – you add to the museum the experiences. (J.E. Dubbelman, personal communication, 18 January 2022)

The problem addressed by Dubbelman, however, is solved to a degree at the ŽLM through an education program in a VR room set-up specifically and equipped with a VR computer, headsets, beamer, loudspeakers and soft, portable furniture (Figure 6.3). A space identical to the original small bunker, as discussed earlier, with an adjacent foyer, accommodates an average school group to experience the VR. This is through listening to the narrative and watching the projected image together, even if at a time when only one participant wears the VR headset and has a direct in-experience agency.

'Ambiguous Relationships': Dark Heritage and VR

Whether VR can fully imitate material reality, thus breaking the tourist need for visiting heritage sites, is crucial. On the one hand, digital media 'will never replace the *in-situ* visit', yet on the other hand, 'VR offers more than a replica of the real context' (Fassi *et al.*, 2016: 141–142). To this extent, immersive technologies can become time-travelling media, allowing users to experience virtually rendered fragments of the past. For the research participants, the possibility to see the simulation of the bunker as it was during the World War II reveals a stronger connection than they have with this heritage today. As research respondents noted:

> It [VR] helps to understand it better. More clearly. (F1. 18)
>
> ... because you are there. (F2, 18)
>
> [VR] visualises something that happened, and then it all connects to the heritage thing, and then you see it truly. (M4, 19)

Hence, given increasing global technological growth, public memory institutions must decide on VR distribution and its accessibility. Currently, the *Lipke Bunker* VR is only available within the premises of the memorial. However, after the success of the openly available *Secret Annex* VR and *Surviving 9/11*, making *Lipke bunker* VR accessible online seems like a next logical step. By moving beyond the site and allowing VR to be downloadable, anyone from the estimated 171 million VR users worldwide (Anderton, 2020) could 'time-travel' to the *Lipke Bunker* from their living-rooms.

Yet, whether to render VR on dark heritage freely accessible online is filled with uncertainty. Moreover, such digital transformation 'won't mean that museums lose what they have to offer as physical sites conveying knowledge through the medium of material objects; [i]t means that the museum will get another dimension, a digital one' (MacDonald & Alsford, 1997: 267). This is strongly aided by the experts behind the *Secret Annex* VR and *Surviving 9/11*. Victor Agulhon, the VR producer, is certain that 'people are more likely to come if they've seen this story before [in VR]' (V. Agulhon, personal communication, 25 January 2022). Jan Erik Dubbelman supports this viewpoint and states:

> VR adds to the possibilities because so many people cannot visit [Anne Frank House]. It is used as an external opportunity for people who cannot [come to the actual site]. They will come when they can. (J.E. Dubbelman, personal communication, 18 January 2022)

However, this case study also suggests that the young research participants felt strongly about authenticity of the dark heritage site, emphasising the distinctive complementary aura of what the VR and the physical site simultaneously created:

> To live that feeling, that sensation, is the maximum you can get from technology today. To make the feeling of the museum more real, [it is achieved] both through the stories, through the visualisation, like VR, and through some tangible objects that are exhibited – the fish box, the suitcase, and things like that. (M2. 19)

Several research participants also endorsed the notion that the VR was intensifying emotional and cognitive perceptions of Lipke's rescue of Jews when experienced at the location where the actual events took place. This sentiment forms a reciprocal connection whereby, through VR experiences, the ŽLM exhibition became more affectively perceptible, and in turn, through the examination of the ŽLM exhibition, the VR experience became more credible and meaningful.

That said, however, not every form of VR distribution is considered favourable. The internationally recognised VR *Surviving 9/11* has received criticism for being disseminated through Meta, the global technology conglomerate, making it a quasi-commercial deal (Bergman, 2022). Such corporations have not acquired the status to negotiate whether it is appropriate to embark on the gamification and representation taboo for virtual experiences on dark heritage (Kansteiner, 2017). Additionally, the niche examples of dark heritage VR mentioned above find themselves in an oversaturated market competing for user attention with a plethora of gaming industry products. Thus, it is yet another factor for consideration to whether to make *Lipke Bunker* VR accessible online or not. Nevertheless, interconnectivity between the visitor, the memorial museum and VR, indicates a future of more effective and affective learning experiences. Presently, the visit to the Žanis Lipke Memorial and engagement in VR is a complex on-site mediated learning experience, contributing to the assurance of spatial awareness and historical contextualisation. Contrarily, the user who operates VR at a remote setting is alone in the experience and without access to pre- and post-experience mediated by trained museum staff.

Conclusion

Adopting scenarios of bridging virtual reality and interpretation of dark heritage, this chapter was approached through a case study of the *Lipke Bunker* VR developed by the Žanis Lipke Memorial in Latvia, which tells the story of the largest local rescue mission of Jews during the Holocaust. Despite being a small non-governmental memorial museum, it has succeeded in creating one of the rare educational experiences of dark heritage through immersive virtual reality. The VR experience is currently offered on site as part of an educational programme, but it aims at reaching broader audiences through VR platforms that allow any user to explore it from their location worldwide.

Both on-site and remote dark heritage VR developments are equally future ready. Different dark heritage institutions considering holistic learning experiences might choose to adhere to the complementary relationship between immersing in a VR and the immediacy of being present at an authentic heritage site. This does not exclude the opportunity to communicate the edifying experience through online VR platforms to a wider global audience; but with careful consideration of content and distribution channels to remain sensitive and ethical to the suffering of the people whose story is being told. Heritage site stakeholders also need to be mindful of the risks associated with disseminating content that may be too traumatic, easily misinterpreted or disturbing to unprepared and vulnerable remote audiences, especially children.

Overall, this chapter has argued that VR is an implicit learning mechanism. Moreover, the application of VR to different educational goals is the focus of a growing body of studies (Daniela, 2020; Dreimane, 2020; Slater, 2017) and, consequently, also has potential to be more widely used in the interpretation of dark heritage. As the study of *Lipke Bunker* VR demonstrates, this immersive experience is considered more emotional and embodied than other media and interpretation tools can normally induce. It is here that the future application of VR encounters within dark tourism can allow participants to perceive and better connect with difficult pasts. Indeed, VR experiences of the future can engender affective, cognitive and embodied faculties, complemented by being present at authentic locations of tragic historical events.

Acknowledgements

The research cited in this chapter is funded by the Latvian Council of Science: project *Difficult Heritage: Between the Memorisation and Contemporary Tourism Production and Consumption. The Case of Holocaust Sites in Latvia (MemoTours)*, Project No: lzp-2019/1-0241.

Special Note

Data from semi-structured interviews with cited sector experts are used in this chapter. Recordings and transcripts of the interviews are in the personal archive of author Elizabete Grinblate.

7 'Virtual Monument Wars': The Digital Future of Difficult Heritage

Richard Fawcus

Introduction

Monuments are an integral dimension of how a society remembers and how it assigns importance to both where it comes from and where it is heading. However, the way societies approach and maintain their monuments can be shown to be changing with the intersection of innovative technologies. This intersection offers both the potential for new forms of conservation, as well as appreciation, but with that also comes the potential for new modes of subversion and even, in some cases, technological hacking. The purpose of this chapter, therefore, will be to explore new developments in memorialisation within visitor economies. In doing so, the study will speculate on the future of technological memorialisation, outlining the following predictions:

- In the future, monuments will increasingly be digitised and mapped for the purposes of (dark) tourism, conservation and as a response to the challenges of mediating 'difficult heritage'.
- Virtual *monument maps* will prove to have military and security potential.
- Corporations and governments will therefore seek to control monument maps, leading from an explosion of different ideas and approaches, into a situation where incumbent power structures aim to legitimise and control singular virtual visions.
- In response, virtual monument maps will become targets for hackers and digital revolutionaries.

In short, this chapter proposes that in the not-too-distant future, monuments will become flash points for cyber warfare within virtual realms.

Monumental Tensions

According to historian Judith Dupre, 'monuments are history made visible. They are the shrines that celebrate the ideals, achievements, and heroes that existed in one moment in time' (cited in Anthony, 2021: online). Allen (1992: 10) further notes that the focus of such an object 'seems to be upon the past, but its message is directed with hope toward future generations'. This, according to Waters and Russell (2012: 34) gives them 'a symbolic meaning in a society that desires to remember'. However, this *desire to remember* is key – as monuments inevitably reflect two different concepts: both the explicit subject matter, but also, they illustrate a time in a country's history when it was believed that those events deserved to be memorialised. Therefore, Percoco (1998: 48) suggests that while monuments may 'serve as tangible reminders of the past', they also 'tell us something about our particular time and place in history'. As a result, it can be seen that 'studying the reception of monuments over time can reveal a great deal about the shifts in cultural values during periods of history' (Waters & Russell, 2012: 35). The study of monuments and their reception might therefore 'reflect – and expose for study – social tensions, political realities, and cultural values' (Foote & Azaryahu, 2007: 125).

The destruction of a monument can be as powerful a symbol as the monument itself. For instance, in 2003, the toppling of the statue of Saddam Hussein in Firdos Square, Baghdad, was a deeply political event, which recent investigations have suggested to have been at least partially scripted by US military forces for the sake of providing the world's media with an iconic image (Fisher, 2011). In many cases, iconoclasm against the physical legacies of previous regimes became a performative act of political self-reinvention. In 1992, during the Croatian War for Independence, soldiers of the Croatian Army used explosives to destroy the 30-metre Monument to the Revolutionary Victory of the People of Slavonia, located at Kamenska and perceived as a symbol of the Yugoslav state from which they were seceding (Niebyl, 2016). In Afghanistan, the Taliban destroyed ancient Buddha statues that they characterised as idolatrous images (Bearak, 2001). Consequently, Deleuze and Guattari identify this form of political iconoclasm within dual processes as 'deterritorialisation' and 'reterritorialisation'. In other words, the incoming regime firstly targets and removes propaganda of the previous regime, before replacing it with signs and symbols that endorse their own rule (Deleuze & Guattari, 1983: 142).

Monuments are places where societal tensions can erupt into action. In the winter of 2013–2014, the Maidan Revolution in Ukraine began with a monument as its focal point – as protesters gathered around the Independence Monument on Maidan Nezalezhnosti, the central square of Kyiv. In Sofia, Bulgaria, the Monument to the Soviet Army has been repeatedly repainted in protest over the past decade, as a symbol of solidarity with events such as Ukraine's Maidan Revolution, or on the anniversary of Bulgaria's participation in the Warsaw Pact invasion of Czechoslovakia (now separated into the Czech Republic and Slovakia) (Fawcus, 2022). After Russia's 2022 invasion of Ukraine, tensions regarding Bulgaria's Soviet legacy heightened, and a decision was finally reached to remove the Soviet Army monument in Sofia (Day, 2022: online). Meanwhile in Riga, Latvia, the Soviet-era Victory Monument was similarly kept under police guard after the outbreak of war in Ukraine, up until its official removal in August (LETA, 2022).

Therefore, it has been seen even in the past year (at the time of writing) how monuments can do more than just expose social tensions for study. Monuments can serve also as pressure points to deeper unresolved societal and political tensions. As such they have the potential to become (re)invigorated as flash points for protest or conflict once those underlying tensions eventually erupt in physical action.

The Rise of Virtual Tourism

In recent years, evolving technology in the fields of 3D cameras, photogrammetry, Virtual Reality (VR) and Augmented Reality (AR) have begun to make a significant mark on the global tourism landscape. Development and application of this technology was further accelerated by the global COVID-19 pandemic beginning in 2020, when many tourists were forced to abandon their travel plans, and virtual alternatives to physical travel presented an appealing substitute. Hintz (2020) lists 10 destinations that can already be explored virtually, without leaving one's home, including the Pitt Rivers Museum in Oxford, UK; Angkor Wat in Cambodia; the Zeppelin Museum in Friedrichshafen, Germany; and Japan's 'Cat Island'. Additionally, some darker destinations, such as the Paris Catacombs and the abandoned city of Pripyat in the Chernobyl Exclusion Zone, can be explored on a computer screen, using either Google Maps or official virtual tours offered by site managers. When COVID-19 caused the cancellation of plans for the 2020 Solstice celebration at Stonehenge, English Heritage instead proposed a virtual alternative via an online livestream (Morris, 2020). This supplemented a project they began in 1995 to create a detailed VR model of the site, based upon a comprehensive photogrammetric survey of the monument and incorporating accurate star charts and a virtual sunrise (Burton *et al.*, 1999).

Moreover, the use of dedicated VR hardware for immersive virtual travel experiences saw a significant rise during the COVID-19 global pandemic. Debusmann (2020: online) reported that '[in] the absence of travellers, tourism boards, hotels and destinations have turned to virtual reality', as this technology 'can offer a try-before-you-buy experience which will give people a taste for travel again leading to more holidays being booked' (Rogers, 2020: online). As a result, the 'pandemic could provide a watershed moment for technology, potentially leading to more sustainable tourism' (Davies, 2021: online). For tourists visiting a destination in person, VR and AR technology can additionally allow for deeper and more meaningful engagement with physical exhibits. For example, beginning in 2016, the Salvador Dalí Museum in St. Petersburg, Florida, began offering VR experiences that allowed visitors to 'step into [...] Dali's mind' by immersing themselves within three-dimensional virtual reconstructions of famous paintings (The Dalí, n.d.)

In 2016, the Polish development studio The Farm 51 released *Chernobyl VR Project*, an interactive virtual tour of Pripyat and surrounding areas within the Chernobyl Exclusion Zone. Consumers who owned a compatible VR headset were then able to purchase and download the software, to experience this immersive tour in their own homes. The *Chernobyl VR Project* was created by 'physically visiting all of these locations, shooting up to 2000 photos per room, and combining photogrammetry with 3D graphics to construct a pixel perfect recreation of the affected areas', producing a result that was an 'interesting blend of gaming, educational software, and documentary filmmaking', which served to provide a respectful, educational, and immersive interactive product which might prove to be 'the history book of the future' (Evangelho, 2016: online). The following year, VR technology was similarly used in the creation of a virtual educational experience based on the history of the Berlin Wall. In 1993, the Newseum – a US-based interactive museum also offering travelling exhibits and, later, online experiences – acquired eight pieces of the former Berlin Wall. In 2017, they launched their *Berlin Wall VR* experience which allowed users to 'experience the divided city from the perspectives of suppressed Germans and the East German and Soviet guards' (Museum Revolution, n.d.). Visitors to Newseum's Berlin Wall Gallery would be invited to don a VR headset and headphones, and then:

> ... walk through the streets of East Berlin and see the communist propaganda posters. With room-scale VR, visitors can walk within a 10-by-10-foot space and experience the anxiety of dodging the guard tower searchlights looking to spot wall jumpers. On the West Berlin side of the wall, visitors can use their controllers to help break down the iconic barrier to freedom. (Georgieva, 2017: online)

During its first opening months, around 125 visitors per day were trying the *Berlin Wall VR* experience, which had a duration of approximately seven minutes (Feingold, 2017: online). Mukul Agarwal, a member of the development team, said: 'it is important for people to experience how terrifying it was to be in Berlin in the '80s and what people living there were feeling at the time'; speaking about the technology more broadly, another commenter noted: 'having a VR component helps people really experience important points in history' (Feingold, 2017: online). Specifically, the technology has been said to show potential for a more personal and pluralistic way of teaching about difficult history, with the hope of this leading to healthy conversations about the past:

> Projects like the Berlin Wall VR experience can become the beginning of conversations that can trigger transformation over time. VR stories will become more multifaceted and not only illustrate journeys but also allow a space for different personal narratives to emerge. We will no longer be mere visitors but involved participants. (Georgieva, 2017: online)

Digital Conservation

The same technology also shows immense potential in the field of conservation. In April 2020, forest fires caused extensive damage in the Chernobyl Exclusion Zone, and several sites that had been shown to have significant tourism and heritage value were destroyed. Some of those lost landscapes may now only be visited within the virtual versions reproduced by the *Chernobyl VR Project* (or in the related game, *Chernobylite* (2019), which introduces playable combat elements inside similarly detailed recreations of the Chernobyl Zone). Elsewhere, since 2020, the Dutch creative studio DRIFT has been using drones that follow virtual 3D maps to 'restore' ruined monuments and buildings – such as the Colosseum in Rome – using light displays in the night sky (En Vols, 2022). Meanwhile in Iraq, where recent conflicts have caused untold damage to urban sites, drones and VR technology have been similarly deployed in a process where '3D models both document what happened on the ground and form blueprints for reconstruction' (Cuthbert, 2022: online).

New technological solutions have shown utility not only in the case of destroyed monuments, but also, for those monuments whose messages have become controversial over the years. The concept of 'counter-monuments' was popularised in Germany, as artists began to produce new works of sculpture and memorialisation in the second half of the 20th century, to counter the messages presented by older, now-problematic monuments (Franck & Stevens, 2015). The idea is that the new monument 'critiques the purpose and the design of a specific, existing monument, in an explicit, contrary and proximate pairing' (Stevens *et al.*, 2012: 719). As such, the approach often seeks to present historical narratives as contextualised conversations rather than singular perspectives. In short, a pluralist approach to history. Indeed, in one case in Bolzano, Italy, a creative solution was deployed to defuse tensions around a fascist monument that still stands in the town centre. The monumental frieze depicts Mussolini on horseback, accompanied by the fascist slogan 'Credere, Obbedire, Combattere' (*Believe, Obey, Fight*) and even until recently, the town council was torn between calls to destroy the monument, or to preserve it as a historical artefact (Invernizzi-Accetti, 2017: online). The solution, unveiled in November 2017, was to superimpose an LED display over the surface of the monument featuring a quote from the German–Jewish philosopher Hannah Arendt – *Nobody has the right to obey.* Consequently, the original message was subverted without resorting to the destruction of a (controversial) work of sculptural art (Invernizzi-Accetti, 2017).

However, development of innovative technology allows for more advanced approaches to countering or re-contextualising problematic monuments. This offers potential in post-communist countries, where 'there is a struggle to define historical memory through the dedication of new monuments and removal of old ones' (Mamedov, 2016: online). In the decades since the fall of Europe's 20th century communist regimes, several formerly communist countries have passed 'decommunisation' laws. For instance, Estonia banned the public display of communist symbols in 2007, Lithuania followed in 2008 and Latvia in 2014. A law passed in Poland in 2009 outlawing fascist, communist or other totalitarian symbols was updated in 2017 to also include Soviet propaganda monuments (British Broadcasting Corporation [BBC], 2017a). In Bulgaria, a law highlighting the 'Criminal Nature of the Communist Regime' was voted into effect on 24 November 2016, effectively banning the public display of communist symbols (Morton, 2016). The author's own PhD research in Bulgaria involved developing a model for the virtual conservation of the Buzludzha Memorial House, a site of contested and difficult communist heritage, but in which a virtually constructed visitor experience was shown to offer a potentially viable solution. In turn, educational and historical tourism experiences might therefore be provided while keeping in line with Bulgaria's decommunisation laws (Fawcus, 2022).

In summary, it can be said that virtual monuments offer the following benefits:

- A virtual experience can show a place or an artefact as it appeared in a previous condition (for example, before decay or vandalism have taken place).
- It can recreate a specific time in history (for example, by illustrating the artefact's historic context, or a historic mode of use).
- A virtual experience can be structured, written and directed in a way that educates, avoids insensitivity and it can highlight whatever perspective (or pluralist perspectives) its creators choose.

- Such an experience can also potentially be offered remotely, increasing the reach of the exhibit, while helping to minimise the negative effects of increased traffic to the site.
- Furthermore, a virtual exhibit can achieve all these things without changing the physical artefact itself.

VR is still an emergent field. The technology for creating virtual environments, and for experiencing them, are undergoing rapid advancement year on year. Meanwhile, the hardware remains quite expensive from a consumer perspective, posing a certain barrier for entry. In the case of a museum or other visitor attraction though, which provides its own hardware for tourists to use, it is already feasible to employ VR in creating novel and immersive visitor experiences. Furthermore, such technologies do inevitably become cheaper, more widespread and thus more accessible for consumers over time. Therefore, this chapter proposes that VR and AR technology have exciting potential for remote tourism, for memorial conservation, and particularly for navigating the issues of monuments that could be considered as 'difficult heritage'. However, this study also predicts that as these technologies become more widespread, there will inevitably emerge a new struggle to control the narrative of virtual worlds.

Conflict Simulations

The same virtual and augmented reality systems that show so much potential for memorial conservation have also increasingly found their uses in the military and defence industries. A decade ago, this may have taken the form of a cost-effective shooting simulator which allowed weapons training to be conducted virtually; for example, using lasers, thus minimising ammunition costs, as well as reducing related safety and environmental issues of live-ammunition training (Soetedjo *et al.*, 2011). However, these training simulations have seen rapid development in recent years, 'with simulators evolving from basic shooting systems into more immersive situations' (de Armas *et al.*, 2020: 3495). With law enforcement training, recent research has shown that 'realistic VR-based trainings, either by themselves or in combination with the traditional hands-on training, can be as effective as highly resource-intensive practical training sessions' (Saunders *et al.*, 2019: 1908). Meanwhile, in the nuclear industry, the use of VR simulations has shown potential for developing security strategies, allowing site personnel to train for hostile situations within virtual versions of high-security facilities (da Silva *et al.*, 2015). This becomes even more useful in the case of hypothetical nuclear accidents, whereby VR allows for crisis training without actual exposure to potentially harmful environments (Caracena *et al.*, 2017).

In March 2022, the Russian army began retreating from the positions they had established within the Chernobyl Exclusion Zone in Ukraine as part of their invasion launched earlier that year (Kamenev, 2022). A story spread that within the abandoned Russian encampments were found maps of the region dating from 1984 – *before the Chernobyl disaster* – suggesting a grave lack of preparation for the contemporary terrain and its various irradiated 'hotspots' (from personal communication with the author's Chernobyl tour guide colleagues). Elsewhere in the country, reports confirmed that 'Russian commanders invaded Ukraine, guided by maps from the last century' (S.B.U., 2022). How much more effective those Russian invasion forces might have been then, if only they had spent some time training with the geographically accurate, playable educational software of the *Chernobyl VR Project*. The 1983 film *War Games* explored the thin line between virtual games and technological warfare: it appears now, 40 years later, technology has caught up with the film's predictions. The US Army has even produced its own video games – the *America's Army* series, which debuted in 2002 – which were used as combat training simulators, as well as for screening and recruiting new soldiers from the public player base (Morris, 2022).

This study has shown how heritage and tourism experiences are increasingly adopting the same types of virtual technologies that have been previously used in video games: technologies which also have application in military training simulators, recruitment tools or even as pre-programmable drone flight maps. Therefore, it is inevitable that these three fields – gaming, heritage and security – will continue to converge in the future through their increasing shared use of the same virtual technologies.

Heritage Hacking

In December 2019, more than 3 million players attended a live event promoting the latest *Star Wars* film, which was hosted virtually in the Massively Multiplayer Online (MMO) 2017 game *Fortnite* (Coulson, 2019). This was an unprecedented public relations (PR) move for Disney, who own the film franchise, and it succeeded by repackaging an advertisement as an interactive playable event. For consumers, virtual worlds are beginning to present an appealing alternative to real-world travel and tourism; however, the full potential of this technology is yet to be realised. For instance, some musicians are already giving virtual performances, and at some point, newscasters, politicians and other public figures more used to working with traditional PR approaches will realise that they too can target their audiences inside virtual worlds. To that end, future virtual events might take the form of virtual warzone reporting, immersive crisis coverage, interactive historical tours or virtual political rallies in front of national monuments, and even at those which no longer exist. Such events could be attended, potentially, by far more people than could fit into the same venues in real life.

Virtual heritage experiences currently see nowhere near the level of engagement that virtual games enjoy. However, this is set to change in time. Consider this: the MMO game *Fortnite* reported 400 million active players in 2021 (Garton, 2022). These players are very often young people who have grown up with the reality of socialising in shared virtual worlds. As this younger generation grows into adulthood, the idea of also consuming touristic and heritage experiences in virtual space will be very much normalised. As a result, it is likely that specific virtual places, such as virtual monuments, will begin to embody the same kind of symbolic power and spatial significance that their real-world counterparts already have. Virtual monuments will not be considered a novelty facsimile, but rather they too will begin to 'reflect – and expose for study – social tensions, political realities, and cultural values' (Foote & Azaryahu, 2007: 125). There will even be monuments that exist solely in these virtual worlds.

That said, however, a key difference with these virtual monuments is that they will not always be owned by the state. Monuments (in the real world) are inherently political objects, and as already noted, even the choice of which events do or do not deserve memorialisation is an exercise in ideology. Conversely, the (currently, largely) democratic nature of virtual realms allows a greater freedom for critiquing, challenging or countering the message of monuments – even those which the respective states would rather not discuss. As a case in point, Bulgaria does not list or promote the Buzludzha Memorial House – a controversial site of communist heritage – among its national tourism destinations. Nevertheless, this ruined monument has become a focus of global attention through the online sharing of images, and by 2018, an estimated 26,000 people were visiting the site each year. About half of these people were foreigners and of those, approximately 3500 annual visitors had travelled to Bulgaria for the primary purpose of seeing this monument (Fawcus, 2022). Therefore, the shift from state-offered and state-controlled tourism activities to a virtual world filled with user-created content is likely to mark a fundamental shift in the prominence and accessibility of comparable sites of 'dissonant', 'difficult' or 'unwanted' heritage.

With contested heritage in mind, the political-artistic project NUMENT (with which the author has had some involvement) reflects a similar principle (Nument, 2022). Billing itself as an open-source mapping project for recording and publicising civil unrest, the NUMENT project guides users in placing their own digital monument (a so-called *nument*) as user-created content on Google Maps.

Specifically, these are in places where historic events such as protests or uprisings have gone un-memorialised by the respective state. The project explains:

> In the process of democratising the memory of these events, NUMENT challenges traditional top-down approaches to public memory, and asks: Who has the right to make a monument? (Nument, 2022: online)

The NUMENT project is just a hint of what is to come, as both the production of virtual 'memoryscapes' (Kennedy, 2022), and the performance of virtual counteractions are inevitably set to escalate in step with developing technology. Indeed, just as controversial monuments or sites of difficult heritage in the real world are targets for acts of protest, demonstration or other forms of subversion, when virtual versions of such sites become more available, more visited and more widely accepted as 'authentic' heritage expressions. These will themselves then become targets for new forms of political action by hackers and cyber revolutionaries. Importantly, it should not be assumed that virtual worlds will forever remain as democratic as they are today, as there are already indications of an encroaching power struggle for hegemonic control over virtual social spaces.

The Battle for the Metaverse

At present, the virtual realm is something of the Wild West of yesteryear, which encompassed the geography, history, folklore, culture and associated lawlessness of the America expansion in the 1800s. Thousands of different (and often unregulated) virtual spaces have been created, and explored by millions of global users, from social platforms such as *Second Life* (2003), to massive online games like *World of Warcraft* (2004), *Roblox* (2006) or the world's all-time best-selling game, *Minecraft* (2011). Many such games welcome user-crafted content. For example, *Minecraft*'s world now features dozens of iterations of each of the real world's most famous monuments, and at least three versions of the Buzludzha Memorial House in Bulgaria (Fawcus, 2022). The result of this has been the evolution of oddly democratic, if uneven, virtual social playgrounds. However, there are also dangers to working with unmoderated user-submitted content. The AR world of *Pokémon Go* (2016), for instance, gathered its in-game locations from a database submitted by players of the developer Niantic's previous game (*Ingress*, released in 2012). By uncritically incorporating these maps, the new game made several missteps, including by inviting its users to engage in play at sites such as the United States Holocaust Memorial Museum in Washington, DC (Peterson, 2016) and at the Holodomor Genocide Museum and Monument in Kyiv, Ukraine. The latter eventually put up a sign asking visitors to please refrain from catching virtual monsters during their visit (Richter, 2016).

Currently, these various virtual worlds exist entirely unconnected to one another. Each is separate and distinct, and in terms of authority, most belong to their respective game development companies and are governed according to that company's own in-game laws. However, it is expected that virtual worlds will play a greater role in people's lives in the future – the CEO of tech company NVIDIA predicts that future virtual worlds 'will be photorealistic, obey the laws of physics and be inhabited by human avatars and AI beings' (cited in S.M.U., 2022). Consequently, some companies already anticipate such an outcome and are making serious efforts to stake pre-emptive control over future virtual spaces. For example, Facebook began making overtures into the world of social VR first in 2014, with its purchase of the VR company Oculus for $2 billion (Solomon, 2014), and later, when its rebranded parent company, Meta, launched its own virtual social platform: *Horizon Worlds* (2021). Over the following 12 months a reported figure of almost $2 billion was spent on virtual real estate, in what was described as a *metaverse land grab* (Tidy, 2022). For some years now critics have been warning that 'the end of a free and open web is imminent', because 'Facebook and Google now have direct influence over nearly three quarters of all internet traffic' (Cuthbertson, 2017: online). Even the act of renaming the Facebook company to 'Meta' implies that this organisation intends to secure similar influence within emerging virtual worlds, to the extent of being perceived as synonymous with the very notion of a metaverse (in the same way that Google has with web searches).

In the future, virtual heritage experiences will not exist as standalone experiences offered solely by site managers and accessed discretely through their own websites or software. Rather, companies such as Meta (and others, including those yet to venture into this field), will seek to provide the entire operating frameworks within which countless virtual excursions might be situated and made possible. As companies, rather than governments, begin to dictate the creation of these virtual heritage maps, the selection of sites on offer will increasingly answer to audience demand, rather than to any sense of national ideology or regional pride. As a result, sites of dark tourism, of difficult or contested heritage, taboo monuments, former conflict points and battlefields, even sites not typically offered for touristic consumption in the real world, will inevitably be offered as virtual travel experiences so long as there is a market demand. Within such a framework, ideology will bow to capital. As Mark Fisher (2009: 4) states, 'capitalism subsumes and consumes all of previous history: one effect of its "system of equivalence" which can assign all cultural objects, whether they are religious iconography, pornography, or Das Kapital, a monetary value'.

Virtual maps of real monuments, visited remotely by thousands of users around the world, will also prove to have tremendous value in a world increasingly infatuated with *Big Data* (Mayer-Schönberger & Cukier, 2014). Maps of human behaviour are powerful. In 2022, Amazon purchased iRobot, the company which creates the Roomba intelligent vacuum cleaners. Subsequently, the director of the non-profit digital-rights-advocacy organisation Fight for the Future commented, 'acquiring a company that's essentially built on mapping the inside of people's homes seems like a natural extension of the surveillance reach that Amazon already has' (Tangalakis-Lippert, 2022: online). Such data provides an incredible tool for marketers, but it also has security potential (and perils). Indeed, the company Ring, who produce home surveillance systems and CCTV cameras, in 2022 confirmed that on multiple occasions it had shared footage from customers' homes with law enforcement, without having a warrant to do so (Tangalakis-Lippert, 2022). Therefore, future virtual maps of monuments, as places of 'exposed tensions' and 'history made visible', will become focal points for new conflicts and will prove fertile grounds for collecting data in relation to visitor patterns, behaviours and demographics, particularly from a security and law enforcement perspective. Whoever owns these maps – that is, whichever company wins the race to be seen as the legitimate hosts of the Metaverse – will profit enormously from ensuing data collection. We have grown accustomed to an era in which access to online maps, and the power to create new maps has been democratised. Yet, the advent of innovative technology and the migration to new (virtual) social platforms offers new opportunities to exert control.

A final prediction for the future, is that eventually these virtual worlds will begin to build themselves. Companies such as Meta and Google already own a vast amount of location information, in the form of photographs and geotags uploaded to their websites by users. Just in the last few years we have seen striking advancements in the field of AI-generated art, and at some point, we may see an AI system capable of reading spatial information from photographs. At that point, Meta could take its millions of user-submitted photographs of any one location, viewed from every conceivable angle, and from these have an AI generate a fully detailed and explorable 3D model. Naturally, the military application of such technology would be astounding – AI systems that are able to generate realistic combat simulations based on reconnaissance photography – and whichever company first secures a patent to these tools is going to become difficult to compete with thereafter. More generally, however, once AI-powered virtual worlds are effectively able to build and expand themselves, we are liable to eventually reach a day when the real world starts to feel quite small in comparison.

Conclusion

This chapter set out to explore what the future of digital difficult heritage might look like, with a particular focus on the role that representations of monuments and memorial spaces are set to play in the virtual worlds of our future. The study argued that the fields of heritage, gaming and security already show a great deal of overlap in their application of similar virtual technologies. As a case in point, the same innovative software solution that might be applied to preserve an interactive record of an endangered heritage site, might also (with the addition of weapons, and antagonists) quite easily form the basis of an immersive 3D shooting game; or indeed, a weapons-training simulation for military, security or law enforcement personnel.

This chapter also examined the popularity of MMO games, played by millions worldwide and, consequently, posited that a generation who grew up with the normalisation of such virtual social experiences will also in future find it normal to consume virtual and remote versions of heritage, tourism or museum experiences. However, it was shown that various corporations are presently engaged in a battle for control and dominance within emergent collective virtual worlds – what has been called the 'metaverse'. To that end, the chapter suggested that whichever companies should emerge as the victors will profit enormously from the resultant 'big data' associated with studying the behaviour of millions of virtual visitors at sites of digitised culture and heritage.

Moreover, the chapter predicted a shift in hegemonic and ideological control over memorial spaces, as perceived significance and visitor focus moves from traditional and state-owned physical memorial tourism to a model where increasing numbers of visitors derive similar experiences at corporate-owned virtual versions instead. Places that might once have been considered taboo, or 'difficult' heritage within the gaze of political hegemonies, under a corporate model might instead be managed un-ideologically and purely according to market demand. Though inevitably, such a model would attract criticism – and to this end, the chapter foretold the emergence of digital hackers, and cyber revolutionaries, active at virtual sites of digitised difficult heritage.

8 Language as a Mediator: Commodifying Future Dark Tourism

Marián Alesón-Carbonell

Introduction

Over the last two decades research on dark tourism has flourished. Indeed, this 'specific interest' activity has gained acceptance and recognition as a draw for tourists to places where typical lures of heliocentrism, hedonism or recreation do not characterise the tourist activity. A considerable period has now passed since the publication of the first studies on 'heritage that hurts' (Uzzell & Ballantyne, 1998), 'black spots' (Rojek, 1993), 'infamous sites' (Dann, 1994), 'thanatourism' (Seaton, 1996), 'atrocity tourism' (Ashworth, 2004) and the coinage of the term 'dark tourism' by Foley and Lennon (1996a) and Lennon and Foley (2000). Yet, far from being exhausted, this field of study still engages many interdisciplinary scholars despite criticism about early theoretical tenets, the blurriness of terminology or the feeling that the concept was triggered by spurious fashion. Dark tourism has somehow superseded the early 'theoretical fragility' of the beginnings (Biran & Poria, 2012; Sharpley & Stone, 2009) by developing theories that aim to understand the phenomenon of the attraction of the *dark* more comprehensively.

Some researchers, for instance, have argued that dark tourism cannot be a separate experience from cultural or heritage tourism and that there is no apparent reason to distinguish between these two concepts (Biran & Poria, 2012; Ekin & Akbulut, 2018; Light, 2017b). However, dark tourism has allowed tourism studies to reflect upon the limits of the tourism experience in a different way, including but not limited to studying visitors' emotions (e.g. Uzzell & Ballantyne, 1998: 2), their motivations beyond hedonism (e.g. Sharpley, 2012), by exploring how the media constructs tourism sites in a globalised world (e.g. Andrews, 2019) or how tourism can be a generator of reconciliation and peace (Kim & Prideaux, 2003; Rousvoal, 2020) or reconstruction, particularly, after a

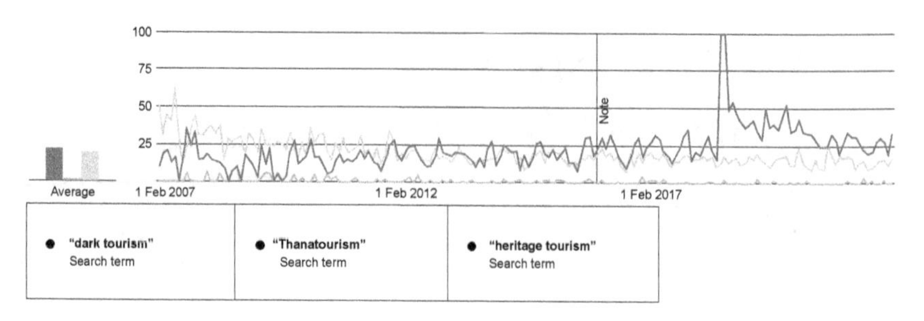

Figure 8.1 Interest over time of selected terms on the internet
Source: Google Trends (2023).

natural disaster or tragic event (e.g. Cai *et al.*, 2022; Stone & Grebenar, 2022). Consequently, 'dark tourism' is regarded as the most accepted definition in the fields of study of the academy, and it is no longer a rare phenomenon (Sharpley, 2005), as the 1,390,000 mentions in Google search currently show (at the time of writing) in comparison to other well-known categories, such as 'special-interest tourism' (122,000 hits), 'thanatourism' (80,800 hits) or 'grief tourism' (13,100 hits). It is also the most accepted term in academia and the media (Ekin & Akbulut, 2018: 79) and, as Figure 8.1 illustrates, one of the most abundant terms in the field as regards internet searches.[1]

This chapter argues that the field of dark tourism has evolved towards a conception that supersedes previous postmodern definitions (Foley & Lennon, 1996a, 1996b). Hence, the subject field has opened the scope of research to other complementary disciplines that can offer additional insights. This is the case of the linguistic approach to dark tourism sites. Language, as a pivotal element in dark tourism promotion, not only creates fascination but also describes striking spectacles, lures tourists and devises commercial pulls that might border somehow irreverence, yet mediates in the understanding of the sacred (Sharpley, 2009a; Stone, 2012a, 2012b; Stone & Sharpley, 2008). More, language within dark tourism helps to memorialise darker sites. Even in the same geography, dark tourism promotes opposing dialectic forces between *dark(er)* and *light(er)* representations, where language becomes either a sanitising instrument in the site's transformation into a touristic product or an inciter of darker representations. Although some research has been conducted on the construction and consumption of dark narratives (cf. Luna-Cortés *et al.*, 2022), few studies have applied linguistic research methods to analyse discursive strategies employed in the language of dark tourism (for example Alesón-Carbonell, 2014; Rousvoal, 2020; Wodak & Richardson, 2009).

The aim of this chapter is to highlight some of the linguistic methodologies that can be applied in the future, especially from the area of corpus linguistics and, subsequently, critically discuss how results yielded from linguistic analyses can contribute to a better understanding of dark tourism studies and practice. The findings of complementary disciplines, rather than adding to the fuzziness of the theory, as maintained by some commentators (for instance, Ashworth & Isaac, 2015; Biran & Poria, 2012; Light, 2017b; Nhlabathi & Maharaj, 2020), may offer a different yet fascinating point of view. To that end, this chapter discusses how diverse disciplinary approaches support a comprehensive vision of dark tourism under a metamodern framework which, in turn, reflects the field's maturity. The chapter also presents linguistic methodologies, pointing out their contribution to aspects such as language intercultural mediation roles within dark international settings, or the language function in the promotion, interpretation and creation of dark sites. Finally, although some limitations are discussed, the chapter concludes how a linguistic approach can contribute to the field's future development.

'New Directions, New Disciplines': Towards a meta-modern understanding of future dark tourism

A key effect of the subject field's maturity has been the agreement on encouraging future studies of dark tourism in different directions (Stone, 2011). On the one hand, current literature points out that dark tourism is a multi-layered, multifaceted phenomenon that is not perceived in the same way by practitioners, local communities or tourism investors, who also respond to diverse agendas and motivations. On the other hand, there is a common agreement on the necessity of opening the scope of research to encompass different cultural perspectives, especially non-Western (Tarasheva, 2011; Tarifa-Fernández *et al.*, 2022), and the vision of other related disciplines and methodologies: for example, language (Lagos *et al.*, 2015), multimodality (e.g. Krisjanous, 2016), statistics and quantitative research (e.g. Cai *et al.*, 2022), psychology (Llorens Simón, 2022; Martini & Buda, 2020), (social-)media studies (e.g. Wight, 2020) and feminism (e.g. Fodor, 2022; Stone & Morton, 2022).

The increased interest for dark tourism (research) is also due to the attraction exerted by liminality. As Ekin and Akbulut (2018: 74) state, the tourist experience 'is not only a combination of economic transactions but also a theoretical composition of historical, natural, and traditional gains', and dark tourism has provided the perfect laboratory to test the limits of this commercialisation and cultural gain in tourism. In the typological framework of dark tourism 'shades' offered by Stone (2006) in his Dark Tourism Spectrum model, researchers can find many cases where processes of commodification and the limits posed by ideological, spiritual, political, cultural or personal stances can be studied. The awareness of how tourism providers refer to education, memorialisation, remembrance or sanitisation practices in the construction of the sites and how visitors are motivated and drawn there, can not only shed light upon dark tourism, but also on other tourism experiences where these opposing forces are not so obvious.

Although dark tourism practitioners do not hold similar motivations, nor do sites draw attention using the same motivational pulls, this myriad of possibilities enriches the research field. Contrary to previous criticism, which pointed out some fuzziness or lack of clarity in the discipline (Tarifa-Fernández *et al.*, 2022), Stone and Grebenar (2022) argue that dark tourism is polysemic in the sense that visitors and sites are understood, experienced and interpreted in diverse ways. Therefore, studying the dark tourism phenomenon from diverse points of view is crucial. In this sense, research is moving away from the typical conceptualisation of dark tourism as a postmodern product. Subsequently, the current dark tourism experience may be considered a colloid – an amalgam – of experiences that defy mainstream Western agendas of race, gender, heroism or consumption.

Thus, dark tourism emerges as places where meaning is continuously contested, reinterpreted, transformed, adapted and retold. This situation does not weaken the theory but adds to the realisation that dark tourism is a product of meta-modernity. Following Vermeulen and Van den Akker (2010: 3):

> ... current modernity can no longer be characterised by either the modern discourse of the universal gaze of the White, Western male or its postmodern deconstruction along the heterogeneous lines of race, gender, class, and locality.

In our meta-modern world, post-modern deconstruction is not enough. It is necessary to give way to the construction of other realities, which include different genders, other preoccupations (for example, climate change, civil rights, minorities or universal accessibility), other nationalities, other races, other religions, other conceptualisation of globalisation or other ways of commemoration and respect. Nevertheless, metamodernity does not depart entirely from the tenets of postmodernity but, rather, focuses on the fragmentation of reality. Interpretation is achieved by adding multiple points of view, whereas experience is an amalgam of different polysemic realities. The challenge of dark tourism research is how to encompass different perspectives and disciplines to construct a sound theory of the dark tourism experience under this new paradigm of metamodernity, exploring the demand (e.g. Willard *et al.*, 2022) and supply-side points of view (e.g. Jordan & Prayag, 2021; Seraphin & Korstanje, 2021). Moreover, advancements related to the analysis of distinct types of dark tourism, numerous ways of experiencing the *dark* and multiple interpretations about the functions of tourism sites add to the metamodernist conviction that reality is an amalgam of different perspectives.

It is here that language and linguistic perspectives are an example of disciplines that can offer new insight as they pursue complementary objectives. Besides, as a fundamental means of human communication, language mediates the whole tourism experience. This mediation is typically performed in three functional stages: firstly, construction of the tourism product before its consumption through promotion; secondly, transmission of the interpretation on-site; and thirdly, maintenance of the site's collective memory in reviews, posts and comments. Language has long been considered a metaphor for tourism, and as Graham Dann claimed in his seminal book, *The Language of Tourism*, 'so pervasive and essential is the language of tourism that, without it, tourism itself would cease to exist' (1996: 249). Thus, studying dark tourism from a linguistic point of view could enrich the field and help understand how tourists engage or are attracted to sites marked by the macabre.

Although the extant literature on dark tourism language is not abundant (Alesón-Carbonell, 2014; Light, 2017b), the interest is increasing. The main reason is twofold. Firstly, some researchers with a linguistic background have started to be attracted to the field as dark tourism language somehow challenges the tenets of the language of tourism. Secondly, researchers have realised that the application of linguistic and discourse analysis methodologies may yield rich interesting results that can complement other widely used methods (Çakar, 2018; Krisjanous, 2016; Lagos *et al.*, 2015; Luna-Cortés *et al.*, 2022; Upton *et al.*, 2018; Wight, 2020). These methodologies can widen our knowledge about linguistic resources available for the construction of dark sites by disclosing the 'content' of discourse, as well as the contextual and genre features that shape narratives. Examples include semiotic analysis (e.g. Akerman, 2016), critical discourse analysis (e.g. Phillips *et al.*, 2021; Rousvoal, 2020; Wight, 2020), corpus linguistics (e.g. Alesón-Carbonell, 2014; Lagos *et al.*, 2015), semantic annotation (e.g. Gavriely-Nuri, 2010), multimodal analysis (Krisjanous, 2016) or multi-dimensional analysis (e.g. Biber, 2019).

A detailed linguistic analysis can also reveal questions related to 'power and ideology', 'control', 'variation', 'manipulation' and 'agency'; those which are not evident on the surface of the narratives. Moreover, technological developments in corpus linguistics can facilitate the analysis of millions of data words (e.g. concordancers, keyword analysers, word sketches, machine translation, semantic annotation or sentiment analysis). These methods minimise the limitation of specific studies that, without these resources, are barely reduced to describe specific cases without the possibility of a broader generalisation of results.

Future Construction of Global Dark Sites through Language

Critical Discourse Analysis (CDA) offers one of the earliest studies, where Siegenthaler (2002) analyses 20 entries from Nagasaki and Hiroshima guidebooks to unveil the 'social control' and the processes of 'sanitisation' and 'normalisation' exerted over tourists in these guides. He argues that the selection of information presented intends to shape identity of these cities and, in turn, shows how the image of both sites has gone through different lines of interpretation. While Hiroshima 'plays a role as the ultimate exemplar ... of the post-war Japanese experience', Nagasaki presents 'a consistent and measured picture of a city drawing strength from its cultural continuities' (Siegenthaler, 2002: 1133). Furthermore, Siegenthaler (2002) elicits some vocabulary choices for Hiroshima – *kenso* (uproarious or noisy) and *seijaku* (silence or quiet) – which represent a process of sanitisation and forced forgetfulness by offering alternative interpretations of the city that obviate its dark past. These examples offer the relevance of vocabulary choice in dark tourism interpretation.

Following this pioneering work on the application of CDA in dark tourism sites, Wodak and Richardson (2009) highlight the relevant role of the 'museums or *lieux de mémoire*' in the construction of hegemonic discourses of identity. She claims the necessity of applying the CDA methodology to understand better the power of language and its role in perpetuating the traumatic past. Additionally, Wodak (2010) reflects upon the 'discursive construction of history' and highlights how distinct types of discourses of past traumatic events are used to create national identities and myths, through which these events are remembered, cleaned, debated, normalised or simply forgotten depending on political and cultural agendas. She goes on to present a framework of analysis for CDA practitioners based on determining the central *topoi* and exploring the linguistic resources of the discursive strategies employed.[2]

The hypothesis that *topoi* (topics) and argumentative strategies are used in dark sites with both informative and persuasive objectives. In doing so, they create a contested dialectic space where raw facts (death, atrocity) overlap with the intended interpretation (commercial, entertaining). Following Hyland (2005), the contestation ends when participants engage with the message and accept the senders' expressed viewpoint (Figure 8.2). Linguistic analysis can help us examine how facts are presented (paying attention to specific linguistic triggers) and how persuasive strategies work to ease the confrontation. In addition, corpora tools can facilitate the comparison of usages in different contexts and sites.

Although the scope of this chapter does not allow for a comprehensive vision of all analytical possibilities, we will examine some examples of fine-grained text analysis.[3] With regards to *topoi*, corpus

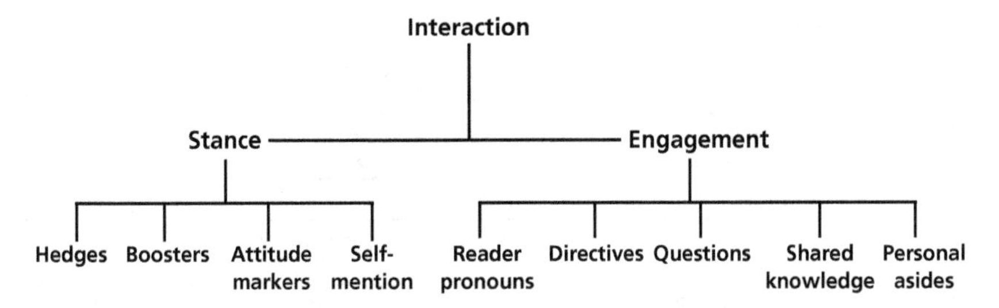

Figure 8.2 Key linguistic resources for interaction
Source: Hyland (2005: 177).

tools are usually employed for keyword extraction and tagging. The difference between these methods and manual tagging is that the selection of words does not depend on the researcher's point of view but on the statistical comparison of frequencies or the comparison with already evaluated ontologies. For example, the analysis of topics in a corpus of 186 WW1 and WW2 dark sites websites (WWcorpus) offers the following results as in Figure 8.3.

If we take a closer look at the word 'remembrance', for example, we can compare its keyness[4] across different reference corpora to contrast the results (i.e. in general English EnTenTen20© and in a subcorpora of recreational texts from EnTenTen20©). The calculations of relative frequency (per million words) reveal that 'remembrance' is a key topic in the WWcorpus (304.82 relative frequencies over 1.16 in the Recreation Subcorpora and 4.61 in the EnTenTen20© general corpus).

		Frequency?	
	Term	Focus	Reference
1	western approach	51	5,004
2	utah beach	43	2,175
3	military camp	49	10,828
4	military vehicle	59	22,838
5	tank museum	30	1,313
6	bloody gulch	27	66
7	first world war	118	155,194
8	itinerary planner	25	357
9	itinerary basket	24	0

Figure 8.3 List of keywords taking EnTenTen20© as a reference corpus with SketchENgine©

Table 8.1 Keyness scores of the lemma 'Remembrance'

Frequencies		**Relative Frequencies (per million words)**		**Keyness Score**
Dark Tourism corpus	*EnTenTen20©* Recreation	Dark Tourism corpus	*EnTenTen20©* Recreation	
44	584	304.82	1.16	141,7
Dark Tourism corpus	*EnTenTen20©* General	Dark Tourism corpus	*EnTenTen20©* General	
44	198,908.00	304.82	4.61	54.5

Source: own source by Sketch Engine@.

These results mean that 'remembrance' in the WWcorpus is statistically more relevant (Table 8.1).

Another interesting tool is the SketchEngine© thesaurus, which creates an automatically generated list of synonyms belonging to the same semantic field. This tool is very versatile as it allows the exploration of specific recurrent topics. For instance, in the WWcorpus, we can look up the lemma 'do' and compare it with the same query in a reference corpus (i.e. a corpus of 100 general dark tourism sites). Figures 8.4 and 8.5 indicate that WW1 and WW2 sites are revealed as sites of 'hope' in contrast with general dark tourism sites where the verb 'know' may imply that the central interpretation is 'education'.

Figure 8.4 Verbs of action in the WWcorpus
Source: Author.

Figure 8.5 Verbs of action in the Dark Sites Corpus
Source: Author.

A careful examination of the data can also help us determine nuances and shades of the dark in these sites' interpretation. An exploratory study carried out in 2014 hints at the possibility of determining at least three different interpretations of WW1 and WW2 promotional advertising (Alesón-Carbonell, 2014). Namely 100% Dark sites (sites on the darkest shade of the cline), Commercialisation Sites (sites on the lighter side) and Contrasting Sites (sites in the middle of the cline which feature both dark and commercial-loaded language). Argumentative strategies are also crucial, as the context of use can affect the final meaning of an utterance. A way of eliciting how a particular topic is constructed in discourse is to determine the syntactic patterns where this topic is used. We can see an example with the query 'death' in the WWCorpus performed with the tool WordSketch© and a comparative search in the 100-Dark-sites corpus (Figure 8.6).

At first sight, we can see how the discursive strategies around the notion of 'death' are more diverse in general dark sites. Conversely, in WW1 and WW2 sites, death experience is either static, with the verb 'to be' expressing a state or is experienced in a receptive way with the verb 'to come'. We commemorate, remember and face 'death' on those sites. In contrast, in general dark sites, the experience with death is richer, and other interesting subtopics emerge, such as the 'good death' or 'to embrace death'. These subtopics can be subsequently analysed in their concordances.

A final reflection about the language of dark tourism incontestably must be directed at its role as a cultural mediator. In global sites, such as WW1 and WW2 sites, where the interpretation is not only directed to the local population, the issue of how we communicate the contents and narratives is fundamental. The perception of the sacred is culturally

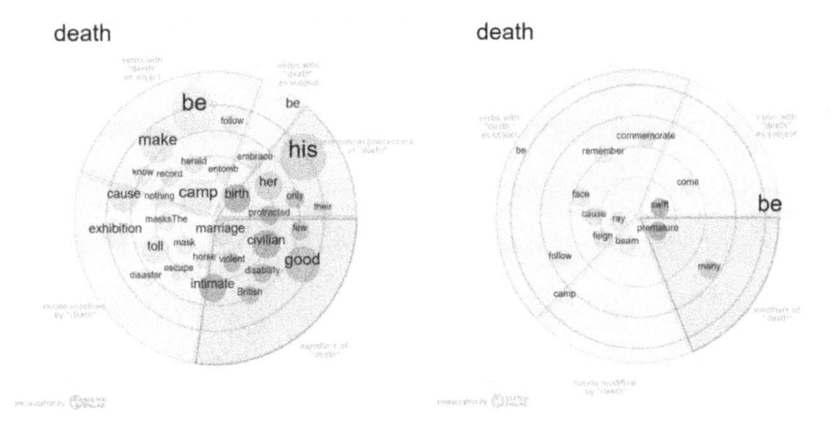

Figure 8.6 Discursive strategies for 'death' in the WWcorpus and Dark Sites Corpus
Source: Author.

bounded, and dark tourism sites, which are interpreted as such by the tourist gaze, may not be understood in the same way by diverse reception cultures (Martini & Buda, 2020). As Hyland (2005: 175) highlights, persuasion and information can only be apprehended by other cultures if language can:

> ... connect with a communal ideology or value system concerning what is taken to be normal, interesting, relevant, novel, useful, good, bad, and so on ... To be persuasive, writers need to connect with this value system, making rhetorical choices which evaluate both their propositions, and their audience.

The problem with language in global sites is that except for guides' oral interpretations (Liljeblad, 2020; Macdonald, 2006), the information received through promotion and on-site is usually only available in English and the mother tongue of the site (Figure 8.7). In addition, translations are usually direct renderings of meaning and contrary to their mission of intercultural mediation, they usually lack an adaptation to the value systems of the recipient culture, as mentioned before (Durán Muñoz, 2010). This situation leads to problematic issues with visitors, not only for what is said, but also for what is over-said or even missed. Some studies have highlighted, for example, problematic receptions of Holocaust sites in Poland by Jews who consider that part of the history has not been told (Lennon & Foley, 1999; Siegenthaler, 2002).

Experts have also highlighted the necessity of applying techniques for quality linguistic mediation, such as glossing (Sumberg, 2004), localisation (Pierini, 2007), languaging (Cappelli, 2013) or transcreation

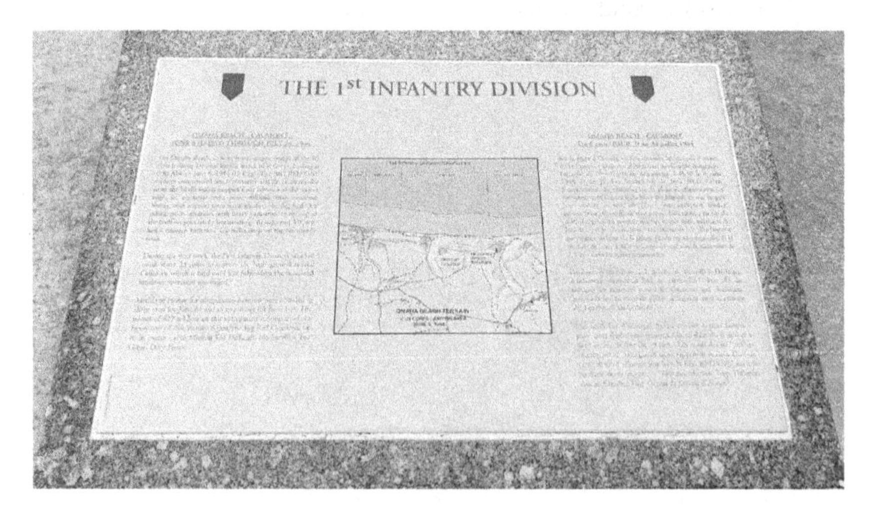

Figure 8.7 Bilingual plaque on Omaha beach
Source: Author.

(Malenkina & Ivanov, 2018). Transcreation is a provocative mediation resource that mixes translation and creation, which is not exempt from criticism for the new meanings added to the original text. An excellent example of transcreation in a tourism brochure has been extracted from the Costa Blanca Official Guide of la Marina-Baixa County. There, the translator adds a dark reference to 'bones' (a metonymy of the town cemetery, which is placed in the castle's gardens), whose mention is absent from the original Spanish text. The translation (below) deviates from the original text, and contrary to what is expected, it completely fulfils the text's marketing function by attracting foreign visitors to a tourist site that may otherwise lack appeal (Costablanca, n.d.):

> Spanish original text: *Castell de Guadalest, es un pueblo de cuento escondido entre montañas. Al acercarte verás que se abre como un desplegable. Sobre la roca, en silencio, reposan las ruinas del castillo almohade de San José.*[5]
>
> English translated text: Tucked away between the mountains, the town of Castell de Guadalest opens up like a picture book as you approach. Up above, the ruins of the Almohad Castle of San José lie silent as old bones upon the rock (my stress).

These adaptations to global audiences require professionally informed translations, which are not so abundant in the market. At sites where cultural and nationalistic identities contest interpretation, this need is urgent. More research and professionals are necessary for the field who can mediate the future interpretation of dark sites to reach a global market. Overall, linguists and language experts have started to realise dark tourism's potential. Even so, being cognizant of the limitations of linguistic studies is essential. Linguistic analyses usually focus on one type of semiotic sign; texts or oral expressions (Wight, 2020). Therefore, these studies should also encompass the critical reflection of language in its broad polysemic context of use.

Conclusion

Language is undoubtedly a powerful tool that not only lures the tourist to the geographies of death but also constructs and maintains dark interpretation of the sites through time. Besides, the role of language in dark tourism is pivotal in all the stages of the journey (Dann, 1996). Therefore, as this chapter proposes, the analysis of dark tourism language is necessary to fully understand the communication process in dark sites and the construction of future dark tourism products.

The problematic realisation of those sites as entertainment attractions or hallowed places of memory is reproduced in the texts (Alesón-Carbonell, 2014). In dark tourism, the hypothesis is that language oscillates between shades of *dark* and *light* because narratives adapt their rhetoric to the commodification process that the interpretation of these sites demand. This variation creates opposing dialectic forces between dark and light representations materialised through language. Moreover, language also becomes the tool of intercultural communication, as translations facilitate dark sites' interpretation to a broader globalised market. How texts maintain the 'collective memory' of the original death, atrocity or disaster that originated the dark experience is still unresolved (Stone & Grebenar, 2022: 469). Transcreation, awareness and professionalisation are needed, apart from further research in these areas from different perspectives and disciplines.

Linguistic perspectives can add value to the study of future dark tourism by complementing and colliding with other approaches in a meta-modern agenda. Language encourages engagement with death and the construction of the dark side of tourism, but questions remain. Although the interest in the linguistic description of dark tourism is just emerging, it already shows an exciting potential for further research. Findings in the area may support previous results and provide additional sound evidence for the new advancements in the field.

Acknowledgements

The author would like to thank Mr Ashley Noad and Mr Manuel Palazón for thoroughly proofreading the paper and for their insightful comments. Special thanks go to Dr Philip Stone for his revision, support and suggestions which have served to highly improve the quality of the definitive version of the chapter.

Notes

(1) The data used for the graph is relative. As the webpage explains as regards the Interest-over-time tool ('Google Trends', 2023): 'Numbers represent search interest relative to the highest point on the chart for the given region and time. A value of 100 is the peak popularity for the term, and a value of 50 means that the term is half as popular. A score of 0 means that there was not enough data for this term'.

(2) The study of *topoi* is remarkably like the methodology of Content Analysis; what differs is the *topoi's* supportive analysis of linguistic features that complements the thematic study of discourse and the degree to which data is subjectively manipulated.

(3) All the examples and graphs have been analysed using the SketchEngine© corpus tool (https://app.sketchengine.eu).

(4) Keyness is a statistical value that calculates the salience of a word in a corpus of texts compared to a reference corpus. The list of keywords from a corpus shows the words that are more frequent in the focus corpus but, at the same time, rare in the reference corpus; thus, highlighting the inherent vocabulary of a set of texts.

(5) Direct translation of the excerpt with no transcreation: 'Castell de Guadalest is a fairy-tale village hidden in the mountains. As you approach it, you will see that it opens like a fold-out. On the rock, in silence, the ruins of the Almohad castle of San José lie'.

9 'McDeath' – A Future of Dark Travel and End of Life Palliative Care

Saffron Dale, Crispin Dale and Neil Robinson

Introduction

The global fast food restaurant chain McDonald's catchy marketing strapline *I'm Lovin' It* is etched into the collective modern psyche. Meanwhile, the slogan of Dignitas (the Swiss-based self-determination and assisted dying organisation) *To Live with Dignity, To Die with Dignity* does not possess the same effect as McDonald's, though this chapter argues that the Dignitas' slogan will be near ubiquitous in the future, as in the case of McDonald's. Since suicide tourism is a growing industry (Yew *et al.*, 2019; Yu *et al.*, 2020a), this chapter argues that Dignitas and other sites offering assisted suicide (abbreviated to 'SOAS' hereafter) are likely to be commercialised and, subsequently, McDonaldised (after Ritzer, 2014). Indeed, this exploratory chapter as a positional study suggests McDonaldisation undermines the ethical theory that supports the existence of SOAS, namely situational ethics. This provocative study concludes that a McDonaldisation of SOAS will change, for some people at least, our future conception *of* dying and our relationship *to* death. Therefore, the aim of the chapter is to offer a challenging, yet inquisitive and sensitive account of what might happen to the future of assisted dying and its problematic aspects of commodification.

This study will refer to the term 'suicide tourism' which emerged in the literature following 'The Suicide Tourist' documentary in 2007 (Zaritsyk, 2007). The term has been used to describe an individual who travels to request an assisted suicide at a particular destination (Haesen, 2018). Normally, the motivation for this travel or 'tourism' is a result of the individual being unable to legally engage in assisted suicide in their place of residence (Kılıçlar *et al.*, 2017). The term has been questioned on ethical grounds, including for its lack of sensitivity (Sperling, 2020). However, a more interesting point of contention is the etymological accuracy of the term (Haesen, 2018). 'Tourism' indicates to a round trip with an expected return date, while the suicidal nature of the event does not allow for actualisation of this return. The classification of an assisted death as 'suicide' can also be questioned (Sperling, 2020). Yet, for the purposes of this research, the phenomenon will be referred to as 'suicide tourism' to correspond to recent literature and since the authors regard the term as neither insensitive nor inaccurate.

This study will also refer to 'assisted death' which can be understood as the act of deliberately assisting another person to kill themselves (NHS, 2020). This differs from the definition of voluntary euthanasia which involves a deliberate act to end a person's life by another, at the request of the person killed (Richards, 2017). Thus, in the former, an individual only prescribes/provides someone the means to die, but they do not actually kill the person. Since SOAS only provides assisted death rather than euthanasia, this chapter will limit itself to reference of the former.

This chapter's use of the 'slippery slope' argument also necessitates clarification. Although legitimacy of the 'slippery slope' argument is contentious as its reference to future developments cannot be empirically sustained, this study assumes there is reason to accept a weaker empirical version of the argument. As defined by Boer, a weaker version proposes that *A* will probably (or possibly) lead to *B* (Boer, 2003). Formalised, this version of the slippery slope argument utilised is:

A) The existence and current operation of SOAS will lead to

B) the McDonaldisation of SOAS

Despite the contentious nature of the slippery slope argument, this chapter will propose there is sufficient empirical evidence to grant B. This chapter will also refer to Ritzer's concept of 'McDonaldisation'. McDonaldisation is defined as the phenomenon in which increasing aspects of society adopt characteristics of the McDonald's fast-food restaurant. The four defining principles of McDonaldisation are efficiency, predictability, calculability and control through the substitution of human for non-human technology (Ritzer, 2014). This chapter will refer to the phenomenon of a McDonaldisation of SOAS as a McDonaldised assisted death – or, in short, for the purpose of this study and without prejudice or pejorative – a 'McDeath'.

With regards to ethical dimensions of a future McDeath, this chapter will refer to Fletcher's consequentialist moral theory 'situational ethics'. Joseph Fletcher founded situational ethics which posits that we should make moral judgements based upon individual circumstances rather than by following normative moral principles (Fletcher, 1966). Fletcher proposes that the only principle we should follow when making moral judgements is *agape*, a biblical term that is rooted in the concept of 'unconditional love'. Thus, Fletcher suggests we should use agape to always do the most loving thing in any situation. This ethical theory opposes Immanuel Kant's deontology which asserts that we should follow prescriptive and universal moral principles when making moral judgements. Fletcher's situational ethics often supports arguments for the legalisation of assisted suicide as it encourages us to *situationally* view individual suffering. Therefore, the right to die is justified in many cases. As opposed to this, Kantian ethics asserts that suicide is the same as murder and is, thus, always morally wrong regardless of the circumstances. Since moral relativism appears to infiltrate modern society, this chapter will explore how an ethical theory that is often used to support the legalisation of SOAS is undermined by the likelihood of a McDeath. This chapter now outlines why the McDonaldisation of SOAS is likely.

Towards a McDonaldisation of SOAS

To suggest that the McDonaldisation of SOAS is undermined by the ethical reasoning that supports it, this chapter argues that a McDonaldisation of SOAS is likely. Herein, 'McDeath' is defined as travelling for the purpose of engaging in a commodified assisted suicide resulting in end of life. In this section, three reasons will be identified as to why McDeath is likely. These include firstly empirical evidence of the growth of SOAS; secondly, an inclination towards moral relativism; and thirdly, a consumer value of SOAS.

Empirical evidence of the growth of SOAS

The McDonaldisation of SOAS is likely since there is both statistical evidence and scholarly support to suggest that suicide tourists are rapidly increasing. While suicide remains a common phenomenon, this study does not focus on suicide-related deaths but, rather, the focus is on the increase in so-called suicide tourism. That said, suicide in international travellers was previously noted to be the fourth most common cause of traveller mortality (MacPherson *et al.*, 2007). Indeed, people travel abroad to die. Yet, this study is interested in sites and organisations that assist travellers to end their lives. Consequently, this chapter takes 'Dignitas' as its primary focus and investigates the growth of Dignitas as a business.

Since Dignitas was founded in 1998, 1000 individuals have travelled there to die, with approximately 935 'suicide tourists' from overseas (Schweye, 2011). Although it is difficult to obtain statistics from Dignitas, figures published in Britain show that the number of assisted-suicide deaths in Switzerland had increased by 700% in 11 years (Ertelt, 2012). Dignitas now reports approximately 75,000 registered members, which demonstrates how support for the organisation has significantly grown since it was first founded. Kılıçlar *et al.* (2017) also report that, between 2008 and 2012, there were 611 cases of non-Swiss citizens travelling for Dignitas' services. Clearly, Dignitas has expanded as a business, both in terms of its customer base and external support.

However, not only does statistical evidence support the growth of SOAS but scholars have noted the expansion of SOAS. Miller and Gonzalez (2013) suggest the growing popularity of suicide tourism has resulted in associated business expansion. Meanwhile, Mondal and Bhowmik (2018: 35) argue that 'suicide tourism has formed a dedicated market for itself'. They go on to assert that, with an annual revenue of 51m generated from assisted suicide on the supply side and, subsequently, an increasing need to live and die with dignity on the demand side, the option to legally end one's life with ease will soon become a tourism-business phenomenon (Mondal & Bhowmik, 2018). To that end, Safyan (2011) recognises that there has been an emergence of death tourism as a new 'industry'. Although SOAS is a growing business phenomenon, it raises profound moral implications, particularly if the concept of a standardised 'McDeath' is to be realised.

Inclination towards moral relativism

Throughout the 19th and 20th centuries, an inclination towards moral relativism has been evidenced. Westacott (online) states moral relativism has become significantly more popular in the last two centuries due to several factors. These include an appreciation for cultural diversity because of anthropological studies, as well as the secularisation of modern (Western) society. Moreover, there has been a critical attitude toward colonialism and scepticism toward moral objectivism given the inability to verify value judgements in the same way as factual claims (Westacott, 2024). Nevertheless, this study focuses on Fletcher's ethical theory of 'situational ethics'. Although research is scarce regarding the influence of situational ethics in everyday moral decision making in contemporary society, it is evident that humans favour the consideration of circumstantial differentiae when making moral evaluations as opposed to normative moral principles (Richardson, 2018). Consequently, the legalisation of assisted suicide in six countries and various US states marks our inclination towards moral relativism (Wong, 2023). Indeed, more governments are willing to take individual circumstances and suffering into consideration when permitting assisted suicide (Downie, 2022). This opposes a more religious, colonial and morally objective society where the very act of suicide, in a UK context, was a crime until 1961. Therefore, this growing inclination toward moral relativism and a 'situational' way of evaluating moral judgements only adds to the likelihood of a McDeath.

Consumer value

A potential McDeath will have significant consumer value. Firstly, as opposed to dark tourism sites such as the London Dungeon visitor attraction, or Berlin's Jewish Museum, SOAS offer a tangible assisted death service that involves no sense of imaginative travel. Secondly, that SOAS may provide the aesthetic of a 'good death' – or where mortality is at least controlled – adds to potential consumer value. To some people, and for palliative care reasons, undergoing an assisted death at a SOAS surrounded by loved ones might offer an attractive alternative to non-assisted suicide. These two reasons for consumer demand fulfil the four types of customer-perceived value commonly discussed in the literature. These include functional, monetary, social and psychological value. For example, the functional value corresponds to the tangible service/solution offered to the consumer, namely the assisted suicide. Whereas the aesthetic of a 'good death' is socially and psychologically valuable, the consumer gets to spend their final end-of-life moments with family and offers an opportunity to die with dignity. All that is left is for future consumers to weigh up the cost of the service relative to the service's perceived worth. Yet, a McDonaldised assisted suicide, offered on a mass scale, may prove inexpensive compared to the care and medical assistance involved in keeping the consumer alive. It is to the potential mass scale and marketing of a so-called McDeath that this chapter now turns.

Marketing 'McDeath'

The question remains of what a future 'McDeath' will look like? Provocatively, will there be golden arches? Will there be a limited menu of suicide methods on a touchscreen kiosk to choose from? Will there be people queueing up in the drive thru, only to come out in a coffin on the other side? Will employers get a bonus for getting the most customers 'in and out' in a day? Emotion aside, there is likely to exist a disparity between diverse types of SOAS. When a product becomes a global business phenomenon, different measures of market perception, quality and prices exist. For example, with food, we have Michelin star restaurants and KFC; with clothes, we have Primark and Tommy Hilfiger; and with future death, we will have luxury assisted-suicide services and McDeath's. For those who can afford it, they can peacefully die at a site like Dignitas which provides them with the time, understanding and accommodation to make a well-informed and comfortable decision. In a McDeath future, mistakes will undoubtedly be made. Customers may be rushed into making decisions, there may be miscommunication or misunderstanding, and limited scope for amendment, all leading to a potentially ill-informed and uncomfortable dying process. Yet, due to effective marketing techniques and a weighing up of the monetary value, a McDeath may be, to some people at least, a better alternative to prolonged suffering.

Thus, based on the marketing techniques already employed by SOAS like Dignitas and Exit International, another Swiss-based organisation that supports assisted dying, the future of a McDeath and how it will attract its customers has already been set in motion. If in the future, many countries legalise assisted dying, it is conceivable that global companies will make death a new business venture. Since assisted death will have an increased demand due to the universality of end-of-life suicide, the success of one SOAS may lead to increased availability and competition of organisations. To create a successful McDeath, neo-liberal marketing techniques will be utilised to attract customers, including a catchy slogan, promoting the aesthetics of a 'good death', creating a sense of novelty as well as comparing alternative options (and suffering).

A catchy marketing 'McDeath' slogan

Some organisations have already begun marketing their assisted suicide packages via the 'right to die' slogan (Yu et al., 2020b). Indeed, the first thing you see on Dignitas' website homepage is *'Dignitas: To Live with Dignity, To Die with Dignity'*. Miller and Gonzalez (2013) assert that assisted suicide organisations emphasise freedom of choice and the right to die with dignity to their clients by packaging the assisted suicide service. Any global business needs a catchy slogan to summarise their business. In this case, Dignitas's current slogan is to get individuals to brand and associate Dignitas with death and dying with dignity (and control over suffering). Just like McDonald's utilised *'I'm Lovin' It'* and Tesco's include *'Every Little Helps'* (a British multinational grocer and retailer) in their advertisements, these slogans instantly come to mind when thinking of the business. Taking the 'right to die' or 'die with dignity' slogan, this can potentially embed the organisation's moral philosophy into the mass market and consumer.

Aesthetic of a good death

It is likely that any future SOAS will utilise the aesthetic of a 'good death' to market its service to the mass market. There are many components to a 'good death' (Kılıçlar *et al.*, 2017). The most obvious one is dying surrounded by family and loved ones, particularly with the full support of family. After conducting interviews with British suicide tourists, Richards (2017) deduced that some chose to travel to Dignitas because of the challenges involved with committing suicide by themselves. For instance, the individual must 'get it right' and there were also concerns expressed about being interrupted, someone finding the body and having to take full responsibility for one's death without emotional support. To that end, one can imagine future television advertisements scenarios: for instance, someone comes home and finds the body of a loved one who has committed suicide. A superimposed voice states 'Dignitas: Die with Dignity' as the screen fades to black!

Richards (2017) also concluded that some travelled to Dignitas due to the aesthetics of how they wanted to die. This often involved a death with dignity. Yet, interestingly, Richards (2017) suggests that death reflects something of an individual's character or the values they have subscribed to in their life. Therefore, the chosen technique reveals something of the identity of a dying individual. This view is supported by Lawton (2000), who argues that during the dying process, the body-as-subject becomes the body-as-object, defined purely in terms of what it cannot do. This body-as-object 'aesthetic' is often the experience associated with a medicalised hospital death. Therefore, any future SOAS can offer a more dignified alternative, allowing individuals to retain a sense of autonomy, control and dignity.

Creating a sense of novelty

Since novelty is a means of demand for dark tourism experiences (Grebenar, 2018), it is likely that novelty will be utilised to attract future suicide tourists. Indeed, if different organisations are competing to gain clientele, they are likely to promote the novelty of travelling to a new place and, more specifically, their place. To most people, the fact that SOAS are in a foreign country where there exists no emotional or civil attachment may attract a certain number of customers (Sperling, 2022). Moreover, the unfamiliar location may make it easier for the customer and their family to accept the nature of an alien event. Furthermore, since assisted suicide is not likely to be legalised everywhere in the future, different countries and cities will compete for 'consumers'. Subsequently, an assisted suicide package in Paris, for example, may offer 'farewell trips' to the Eiffel tower; whereas Dignitas may offer complimentary guided tours around Zurich before 'departing'. Thus, how SOAS will utilise their specific locations as selling points for future marketing remains a distinct possibility.

Additionally, creating a sense of novelty may also be made marketable by promoting travel to a new destination, to an 'afterlife', or by promising a 'new adventure'. There is also a possibility that different suicide techniques may be used and marketed as a way of travelling to a new destination. Philip Nitschke, who has designed several end-of-life machines and founded the organisation Exit International in 1997 (based in Switzerland, where assisted suicide was legalised in 1937) created the 'Sarco' machine. This technology displays an elegant design that is 'intended to suggest a sense of occasion: of travel to a *new destination* [original emphasis] while inducing a peaceful, even euphoric death' (SARCO, 2022). It is evident, therefore, that the ability of end-of-life technology to transport someone to a 'new destination' is already being capitalised. In the future, these limited options are likely to be selected electronically by the customer, prior to arrival, with small amendments charged at an extra cost. In any case, it is likely that the concept of 'novelty' will be utilised by a future McDeath.

Comparing the alternatives

A final way that McDeath will market its services is by comparing what it offers to the morbid alternatives, including suicide alone or the suffering of end-of-life pain. Therefore, SOAS will offer assisted death, located in non-medicalised environments where 'suicide tourists' can be surrounded by their families without constant medical intervention or the attempt to prolong life. Additionally, the experience of a miscalculated or blundered suicide, or having a loved one discover the corpse, might make a McDeath for some people significantly more appealing. Overall, in the future, SOAS may offer different packages to suit diverse needs. Yet, the aesthetic of a controlled, certain and resolute death will be capitalised on by a 'free death market' philosophy. In other words, by adopting contemporary marketing techniques of a McDeath, this exploratory study has set the parameters of a future McDeath based on how it will promote its services. Of course, notwithstanding business ramifications, any future McDeath will have profound societal and ethical implications.

Future Ethical Implications of a 'McDeath'

Since there are many ethical theories and implications that this study could address, this section will limit its attention to Fletcher's situational ethics. As situational ethics is the most common ethical theory invoked to support assisted suicide, this study will argue why a McDeath undermines the situational reasoning that supports its service. Defined earlier in this chapter, situational ethics considers only the context of an act when evaluating it ethically, rather than judging it only according to absolute moral standards. Therefore, this study now addresses each of the four principles of McDonaldisation in turn, namely, efficiency, predictability, calculability and control through the substitution of non-human technology and argue why each one opposes situational ethics.

Efficiency

Placing 'efficiency' and 'assisted death' in the same sentence is morally problematic. On one hand, an efficient death may be what some future consumers require if they are experiencing intolerable pain. However, an *efficient* McDeath will result in consequences that oppose situation ethics when applied to all consumers. For example, the aim of any McDeath employees working under an efficient McDonaldised system will be to process customers 'in and out' as efficiently as possible. To create an efficient system, sacrifices will have to be made. Subsequently, individual character and needs of each case might get overlooked to facilitate the swift assisted suicide of people. This ignores the fundamental idea behind situation ethics that posits that each case is unique and deserves a unique moral judgement.

There may also be cases where an individual changes their mind about which suicide technique they want to use, which family members they want around them, the date they want their death to take place or and even if they want to die at all. In favour of an efficient system, a regulated workforce will prioritise the most efficient means to serve the customer and produce the result – that is, an assisted death. This also might produce an element of inflexibility. For instance, if a consumer puts down a deposit for an assisted death, they may not get the deposit back if they need to change the date or decide not to go through with it. The financial pressure involved in 'backing out' may force consumer to unwillingly go through with the assisted death, adding another morally problematic dimension to a McDeath. Moreover, Ritzer (2014) notes that the prioritisation of efficiency in McDonaldised systems commonly involves a displacement of goals (Ritzer, 2014). The aim of a McDeath will be to operate an efficient system that will make workers lose sight of their goal. In short, to provide customers with a peaceful and dignified death.

Predictability

The most significant way a McDeath opposes situational ethics is due to its adherence to the principle of predictability. Since predictability necessarily involves an element of standardisation, routine and consistency, it completely contrasts an ethical theory that establishes moral judgements upon individual circumstances. Under a McDonaldised system, every McDeath will look the same, with limited scope for individual requests and amendments. For instance, it can be imagined that future SOAS websites might include a limited number of suicide techniques and suicide packages that can be selected from, with little room for adjustment. This mirrors the same limited menu that McDonald's restaurants offer; customers can select 'without mayo' and 'extra ketchup', but even these changes are limited. No customer has a completely individualised experience at McDonald's, and this will be the same with a McDeath.

Calculability

As Ritzer (2014) points out, the dominance of quantifiable measures is the most defining characteristic of a rational society. With the calculability principle, a business's success is measured on the product or service's quantity rather than quality. Therefore, the success of a McDeath will be based on the number of deaths recorded as opposed to the quality of the service offered. As Ritzer notes, McDonald's gloats about 'how many billions of hamburgers it has sold' rather than the 'quality of those burgers' (Ritzer, 2014: 376). Therefore, just as McDonald's employees are trained to process as many customers and orders as fast as possible, McDeath employees will be encouraged to work in the same way. As Ritzer (2014: 376) states 'quality is secondary if indeed there is any concern at all for it'.

Control through non-human technology

Ritzer (1993) predicted the substitution of non-human technology before it had taken full force at McDonald's. Indeed, Ritzer's '*The McDonaldization of Society*' was published in 1993 and McDonald's touchscreen kiosks were first introduced in 2015. As Ritzer predicted, now the McDonald's experience involves even less human interaction. Mirroring this substitution of non-human technology, Philip Nitschke (founder of Exit International) has devised a completely computerised assisted death, involving no human interaction. Here, patients are given intravenous infusion tubes that are connected to a laptop computer. The patient answers three questions that appear on the screen. The final question reads: '*If you press this button, you will receive a lethal injection and die in 15 seconds – Do you wish to proceed?*' If the patient answers all three questions affirmatively, the computer switches on a pre-prepared dose of Nembutal, killing the patient. The computerised system was designed to offer a more intimate, de-medicalised dying experience, involving no interactions with a physician and only that of family.

Of course, there is significant scope for error with such a system. The computerised systems may not work properly and kill someone without having asked the three questions or misinterpret a 'No' for a 'Yes'. Since there may be no human worker present to correct the issue or physically see that the patient has decided to reverse their decision, the individual may be killed against their will. However, it is probable that by the time McDeaths exist in the future, we will be so technologically advanced that errors will be extremely unlikely. Nevertheless, the substitution of non-human technology will mean there is less room for human empathy within the dying process. McDeaths will be so focused on providing an efficient and affordable death that human empathy will be sacrificed.

In the current Dignitas model, patients must meet with a doctor who prescribes the lethal drug and two Dignitas staff members organise the death. Prior to this, there is also extensive correspondence between the patient and organisation, including a thorough examination of the patient's medical records and mental health (Gentleman, 2009).

Yet, if a McDeath exists that promotes an efficient dying process, governed by non-human technology, this level of human empathy and interaction will cease. Meetings may be cut out altogether and instead replaced by online booking systems and online questionnaires that evaluate the individual's suitability to receive an assisted death. If the goal of a McDeath is its profitability, it is also likely that the suitability criteria will be inclusive. For instance, those with non-terminal illnesses or individuals who are severely depressed may fit the eligibility criteria to receive an assisted death. Moreover, due to the potential dominance of non-human technology, there might be no attempt made to offer mentally ill or non-terminally ill customers alternative options.

Other ethical considerations

There is also a further problem that may arise from a future McDeath, particularly likely if there are competitors in a so-called 'mortality market'. It is conceivable that there will be luxury SOAS, offering better accommodation, more personal, individualised and tailored care. On the other hand, there will exist more affordable McDeaths that offer a more efficient but standardised, impersonal and predictable death service. Thus, the poor may suffer the consequences of a McDonaldised death. Given the concerns we explored in this section, it will be the poorest in society that face the potential mistakes and impersonal services offered by a McDeath. Moreover, it is likely that people will be judged on their location of assisted death. Just as we judge someone based on what area they live in, and whether they attended a private or state school (certainly in the UK), individuals may be judged on the service they/a family member uses to die. This is an unavoidable consequence of a 'free death market'.

People may be forced into receiving an assisted death by family members, another conceivable problem. Financial and social strains of keeping a terminally or severely ill family member alive might, for some, become too burdensome, and a McDeath might offer a reasonable solution. Even if it is a requirement that the consumer receiving the assisted death signs off on it, an individual may feel pressured to apply for an assisted death as they do not want to be a burden. It is here that Velleman (1992) argues that having the option of assisted death will make some feel an obligation to be eliminated. Velleman (1992) goes on to argue that having the option to be euthanised can be harmful even if we decide not to exercise it as we can no longer have the status quo (survival) without choosing it. Furthermore, if someone refuses assisted death, others will hold the individual responsible for choosing this situation and may be asked to justify their decision. Thus, if the individual is aware of the financial burden for family members, they may take the option to die. Yet, had an affordable McDeath option not been there, they may have died a natural death. It is this conception of death as an 'option' that raises issues with mortality itself.

'McDeath' and Conceptions of Death

A future McDeath and the rise of suicide tourism will change our relationship with death. This will happen in several ways including the sequestration of death, McDeath as a heterotopia and the illusion of control.

The sequestration of death

There already exists an abstract-present death dichotomy even though death floats in the realm of the hyper-visible (Salem, 1999). Modern society has reduced a confrontation of death in public forums, facilitating an abstraction or 'sequestration of death' (Grebenar, 2018). Grebenar (2018) argues that society has separated death in this way to preserve ontological security (being content with one's identity and being). Consequently, death has become 'taboo', and being faced with death in contemporary society is unnatural and frightening. It could be argued that the legalisation of assisted suicide and having McDeaths as a standard product or service may bring death closer to us with the realities of mortality. Conversely, it is more likely that the reverse will be set into effect. If death occurs in remote McDeath sites, death will once again become an invisible and abstract process. Furthermore, by commercialising death and dying, we turn the dying process into a commodity, further abstracting it and making death an unnatural and de-personalised process. The only difference will be is that death will be controlled by humans in the sense that we can now choose when to die. Yet, this simultaneous need to control and abstract death in a world populated by McDeaths will lead to McDeath organisations being spaces outside the normalcy of places, referred to as a heterotopia.

'McDeath' as a heterotopia

If we abstract death by further removing and commercialising it, death may transform into what Michel Foucault labelled a *heterotopia*. In Foucault's '*Of Other Spaces: Utopias and Heterotopias*', he describes heterotopias as 'counter-sites ... enacted utopia in which real sites ... are simultaneously represented, contested, and inverted' (Foucault,

1984: 3). Although the concept of a heterotopia is contested, it is commonly understood as a space that is 'Other', both mirroring and distorting reality (Faramelli *et al.*, 2020). Since this chapter is interested in death, Foucault provides the example of a cemetery as a heterotopia. Cemeteries are often located in the urban suburbs, constituting the 'other city, where each family possesses its dark resting place'. (Foucault, 1984: 6). Cemeteries glorify the body's remains and uphold the 'cult of the dead' by giving everyone their own little box of 'personal decay' (Foucault, 1984).

Nevertheless, it is Foucault's sixth principle of heterotopia that this study is focused. It is here that Foucault asserts that heterotopias have a function in relation to all the space that remains, this function unfolding between two extreme poles. On the one hand, a heterotopia's function is to create a space of illusion that exposes every real space, all the sites inside of which human life is partitioned, as still more illusory. Yet, on the other hand, their function is to create a space that is 'othered' but ordered and well-arranged as opposed to our chaotic reality. It can be argued that a McDeath lies at both ends of this dichotomy regarding the way it functions. Firstly, a McDeath will create an illusion that we can control death by exposing how chaotic and unpredictable human life and dying a 'natural death' is. A McDeath will also demonstrate how partitioned human life is from death in the same way that cemeteries do, cornered away on the fringes of society. Moreover, a McDeath will create an 'Other' space that allows humans to control their own fates within the constraints of a pre-arranged suicide package, opposing the unexpected and unpredictable way people naturally die.

Therefore, by transforming the dying process into a kind of 'heterotopia', we are dramatically altering our relationship to death. It could be argued that a medicalised hospital death has already 'Othered' death. Yet, it is the element of control and function over death on a mass scale that distinguishes a McDeath from a modern hospitalised death. Furthermore, the commercialisation of death that strengthens the abstract-present death dichotomy provides an 'Otherness' of death that will result from a McDeath.

Illusion of control

The control we have over death, or at least perceptions of mortality, will change our relationship to it. However, it is this 'illusion of control' that will be the most disconcerting consequence of a McDeath. Although it appears to be a choice, to go to a SOAS and choose when, where and how you die, the reality is, this choice will be superficial. It is likely that when SOAS are McDonaldised, several global companies will dominate the 'free death market'. The variables that will inform your 'death decision' are likely to constitute your financial status, convenience and the influences of neoliberal marketing and advertising. In contrast, the current Dignitas model allows patients to have complete control and autonomy over (their) death. In this case, there is no obvious ulterior motive behind the non-profit organisation other than to help individuals die with dignity. Each patient case is treated with care and evaluated on its individual merits. Yet, the likelihood of a McDeath will end an individual's autonomy over death at the hands of global corporations. To that end, the present Dignitas model is the most authentic and ethical SOAS we will get. However, that is dependent on whether certain factors are actualised in the future, including the legalisation of assisted suicide in other parts of the world, as well the privatisation of future SOAS. Death will become an abstract 'Other', a heterotopia and a superficial choice.

Conclusion

This chapter has set out several conceptual parameters that demonstrates a future McDonaldisation of SOAS, giving rise to a potential 'McDeath' phenomenon. The reality and viability of a McDeath becomes probable because future marketing and commodification techniques, based upon practices already being implemented by current SOAS. Having explored what a McDeath will look like, this study examined ethical implications of McDeath, particularly its incompatibility with Fletcher's situational ethics. Indeed, what could be considered a fundamental moral dilemma, a McDeath is likely to alter our relationship to death, making it an abstract and turning SOAS space into a heterotopian place. Ironically, a McDeath will offer an illusion of control, yet we will possess limited control. Suicide tourism is making an industry for itself that is likely to thrive in the future, regardless of its negative ethical implications. A one-way travel excursion to mortality could be the stuff of nightmares, but it also raises the future spectre of the darker side of travel. Notwithstanding inherent ethical debates, the current Dignitas model provides a 'kalthanasia' or 'best death' due to the autonomy and dignity it allows and the non-profit nature of the organisation. Yet, we hope this study acts as a warning before death and the process of dying is embraced by neo-liberal free markets. A medicalised death, controlled by the State, and despite its 'hi-tech bad death' portrayals, may provide a better alternative to the future McDonaldisation of death. Consequently, just as Ritzer (2014) predicted the McDonaldisation of contemporary organisations and society, we hope that any predictions of a commercialised and standardised palliative end-of-life 'McDeath' will not dominate the future of mortality.

10 Enlightening Dark Tourism Horizons in a Post-Apocalyptic Arctic: A Geopoetic Approach

Alix Varnajot

Introduction

In August 2019, anthropologists Cymene Howe and Dominic Boyer (Rice University, USA) organised a commemorative ceremony for the loss of an Icelandic glacier (Árnason & Hafsteinsson, 2020). Located northeast of Reykjavik, the *Ok* glacier (*Okjokull* in Icelandic) was one of many small glaciers found in Iceland. *Ok* formed approximately 700 years ago and in the early 20th century was still about 15 square kilometre in size. However, in September 2014, geologist Oddur Sigurðsson stated on Icelandic national TV that *Ok* could not be considered a glacier anymore because it was no longer meeting the criteria to be regarded as such (Árnason & Hafsteinsson, 2020). While there is no consensus of what minimum size a body of ice should classify as a glacier, it is commonly accepted that below 0.1 square kilometre, a glacier does not have enough mass to move under its own weight (USGS, n.d.). Hence, in August 2019, a 'mock funeral' at *Ok* organised by locals and the two anthropologists, witnessed over 100 attendees, including Iceland's Prime Minister Katrin Jakobsdottir and former United Nations High Commissioner for Human Rights, Mary Robinson (BBC (British Broadcasting Corporation), 2019). A commemorative plaque inscribed with a brief emotive 'letter to the future' was installed on a bare rock where the glacier used to be. The plaque reads in both Icelandic and English:

Ok is the first Icelandic glacier to lose its status as a glacier.
In the next 200 years all our glaciers are expected to follow the same path.
This monument is to acknowledge that we know
what is happening and what needs to be done.
Only you know if we did it.

Okjokull was not the first Icelandic – nor Arctic – glacier to have disappeared due to climate change, but its demise went viral in the global media and, subsequently, clearly epitomises ongoing shrinking of the Arctic cryosphere, that is – glaciers, permafrost, snow, sea, lake and river ice. Moreover, the mock funeral event demonstrates broader narratives of death and ruination associated with climate change and the Anthropocene (Bravo, 2009; Howe, 2022; Sörlin, 2009).

According to Sörlin (2015), the melting of the Arctic cryosphere represents a core event of the Anthropocene, which designates a new epoch in which '[t]he human imprint on the global environment has now become so large and active that it rivals some of the great forces of Nature in its impact on the functioning of the Earth system' (Steffen *et al.*, 2011: 842). Although the Anthropocene was first thought as a geological era, it has now become a bridging concept, encompassing the humanities and social sciences (Gren & Huijbens, 2019). The Anthropocene is often related to anxiety-driven narratives (Buck, 2015), as well as ruination and post-apocalyptic imaginaries (Bennett, 2020; Huijbens, 2021; Varnajot & Saarinen, 2021). In parallel, the melting Arctic cryosphere induced by global climate change has been characterised and defined as a slow-onset disaster (UNDRR, online). Indeed, as *Okjokull* showed, scenes of vanished cryosphere in the Arctic have become sites of dark tourism – that is, visits to sites of death and disasters – highlighting connections between natural disasters and tourism (Rucinska, 2016; Wright & Sharpley, 2018). Consequently, both the 'death' of *Okjokull* from global climate change and its mourning ceremony provide compelling resources for conceptual reflection on these interlocked themes, including the Anthropocene, dark tourism, climate change and more-than-human deaths (Sideris, 2020). Moreover, the recent mock funeral at *Okjokull* introduces reflection upon what may happen to future Arctic tourism and its associated narratives when the cryosphere disappears.

As Varnajot and Saarinen (2021) argued, the future of Arctic tourism is guided by the narratives we – researchers, the tourism industry, media, popular culture – develop today regarding the Arctic, its changing environment and inhabitants. In this context, *geopoetics* provides an innovative tool to better understand the framing of current narratives about the Arctic in relation to dark tourism, but also, more importantly, to cultivate new ones that are grounded in various meanings and viewpoints. Therefore, by examining current narratives on Arctic tourism and climate change estimates in the region, the purpose of this chapter is to critically explore future pathways for Arctic tourism narrative development and associated Arctic tourism experiences in a *cryospheric-less* Circumpolar North. Firstly, the chapter discusses current practices, experiences and narratives of Arctic tourism within the context of climate change and a shrinking cryosphere. The chapter then focuses upon future dark tourism and ruination narratives associated with post-apocalyptic imaginaries and, specifically, the vanishing of the cryosphere as an event of the Anthropocene. Finally, using geopoetics as a conceptual framing device, the chapter offers futuristic insights on alternative Arctic tourism narratives.

Narratives and the State of Arctic Tourism in the Anthropocene

Narratives conceptualisation has been well discussed over the past decades in relation to a narrative turn in social sciences, and literature and history (for example see Goodson & Gill, 2011 and Price, 2010). However, while there is no consensus on the definition of narrative (but see Abbott, 2002; Genette, 1982; or Prince, 1999 for different approaches), most narratives have in common 'material signs, [a] discourse, which convey a certain meaning (or content), [a] story, and fulfil a certain social function' (Ryan, 2007: 24). Ryan (2007) further argues that such a definition implies that narratives should also communicate a meaningful story to an audience. To that end, narratives commonly associated to Arctic tourism communicate specific stories to tourists about the Arctic region. This set of narratives has recently been well studied and conceptualised in tourism by Nordic scholars and has been referred to as 'Arctification' (Bohn & Varnajot, 2021; Carson, 2020; Cooper *et al.*, 2019; Marjavaara *et al.*, 2022; Müller & Viken, 2017; Rantala *et al.*, 2019; Varnajot & Saarinen, 2021, 2022).

Consequently, Arctification can be understood as a social phenomenon resulting in the stereotypical production of cryospheric narratives, images and places in the North as being Arctic (Carson, 2020; Rantala *et al.*, 2019). These narratives feed an imaginary of the Arctic (tourism) associated with white, cold and snowy scenery, and empty of people landscapes (Varnajot & Saarinen, 2022). Moreover, in tourism, Arctification further leads to a standardisation of tourism products and experiences engaging with snow and ice (Saarinen & Varnajot, 2019). As a result, Arctic tourism refers to activities and experiences that are dependent on the presence of cryosphere – for instance, ice-fishing, snowmobiling, reindeer- and dogsledding, visiting or spending a night in an ice castle or enjoying white and snowy vistas in general. Indeed, as Saarinen and Varnajot (2019) suggest, Arctic tourism as we know it today is made by outsiders, for outsiders. Thus, Arctic tourism may be defined as tourism taking place in northern latitudes wherein tourists engage in experiences producing and reproducing cryospheric and winter-based imaginaries. Importantly, however, progressive global climate change is challenging these hegemonic winter-based narratives, as well as safe implementation of the aforementioned cryospheric-based tourist activities. In the context of this chapter, therefore, I argue that this may lead to dark tourism and apocalyptic narratives in the future.

Global climate change impacts all forms of ice within the Arctic (IPCC (Intergovernmental Panel on Climate Change), 2019). In this chapter, I refer to land-based cryosphere, including glaciers, snow and lake and river ice. Although thawing permafrost has been analysed as having tremendous impacts on infrastructures (for example, roads, buildings and pipelines) (Hjort *et al.*, 2018), it does not affect the tourism industry as much as other forms of cryosphere since the permafrost remains out of sight and is not needed to support any nature-based Arctic tourism activity and vista (at least in the short term). Subsequently, the Arctic tourism industry is requiring more artificial snow to preserve Arctification and (expectant) white vistas to maintain satisfactory Arctic tourist experiences (Varnajot & Saarinen, 2022). Additionally, it is worth noting that the lack of snow, frozen lakes and rivers, and of white vistas more generally, affects Arctic aesthetics and, thus the Arctic tourist experience. This may cause poor publicity for destinations but also present challenges in meeting tourists' expectations and satisfaction (Herva *et al.*, 2020; Tervo-Kankare *et al.*, 2013; Varnajot & Saarinen, 2022). The IPCC (2019) also indicates that smaller glaciers with limited ice cover, such as *Okjokúll*, are most vulnerable to global climate change. Indeed, glaciers have become infamous symbols of climate change and the Anthropocene with Carey (2007: 497) even considering them as 'endangered species' and Inkpen (2022: 84) as 'fellow mortals of the present'. Consequently, as glaciers thaw and retreat, they leave behind potential spaces for developing dark tourism places.

Mourning, Morbidity and the Educative: Arctic Ruination and Future Dark Tourism

The idea of dark tourism and ruination narratives are often interconnected (Dobraszczyk, 2010; Sharpley & Wright, 2018; Varnajot & Saarinen, 2022). As recalled by Bennett (2020), in the Anthropocene, the study of ruination is shifting to the deteriorating planet, where nature itself is turning into ruins. This is epitomised by the melting cryosphere and the *Okjokúll* episode as noted earlier. According to DeSilvey and Edensor (2013), 'ruin' refers both to an object and a process. As a process, ruination is embedded on a temporal scale, in-between a functional past and a future that needs to be redefined (Tonnelat, 2008). Within Arctic tourism, the functional past refers to Arctic tourism as we know it today (and as defined previously); while the future to be redefined could be assimilated to the visions of post-Arctic tourism futures (Varnajot & Saarinen, 2021, 2022). Therefore, in terms of Arctic ruination – a vanished glacier such as *Okjokúll* – articulates the vanished or disappearing past with the future.

Conversely, Lucas (2013: 195) makes a distinction between classical and recent ruins whereby 'the classical ruin is an aged ruin, one that has settled into stasis where the actual process of ruination and decay has either already happened or has slowed down so much as to be imperceptible. In contrast, the recent ruin is new, still decaying'. In other words, from a contemporary perspective, aged ruins (for example, an abandoned Greek temple or medieval abbey) have had a slow process of ruination. Meanwhile, modern ruins (for example, a derelict factory) seem to appear suddenly, following an unpredictable disaster or economic decline (DeSilvey & Edensor, 2013; Lucas, 2013; Wilford, 2008). Hence, within this context, climate change and the melting of the Arctic cryosphere can be understood as a slow process of ruination leading to classical ruins. Therefore, classical ruins are incremental and accretive and occur out of sight. Lucas (2013: 194) goes further and describes classical ruins as a form of art, with graceful decay '[evoking] an aesthetic of attraction'. Nevertheless, ruins of the planet tend to resonate with anxiety-driven narratives associated with the Anthropocene (Buck, 2015). These narratives are deterministic, reductionist and speak to a distressing apocalyptic future that is slowly replacing familiar conditions of a world we consider perpetual.

The future of the Arctic: Towards dark tourism?

Dark tourism refers to 'visitations to places where tragedies or historically noteworthy death occurred and that continue to impact our lives' (Tarlow, 2005: 48). Thus, it is linked to tourism and experiences of places associated with death (Stone & Sharpley, 2008; Sharpley & Stone, 2009). Although usually focusing upon human deaths; in the Anthropocene, dark tourism is increasingly encompassing places associated with death of *more-than-human* objects. In other words, the vanishing of *Okjokull* represent scenes of noteworthy death (that is, death of a landscape), where people gather to mourn the lost ice (and its consequences). Moreover, installation of commemorative plaques and the organisation of such 'funerals' for glaciers can be interpreted as collective and public mourning responses to irrevocable changes in the environment (Cunsolo, 2012), but also as dark tourism. Thus, dark tourism can become a potential mediator for people to be able to mourn *more-than-human* objects such as glaciers: just like media news, art or photographs are mediators for some people to mourn victims of wars, natural disasters, poverty or diseases (Reser & Swim, 2011). However, due to the slow yet foreseeable climate change and ruination processes at stake, which have been evidenced by increasingly accurate IPCC Reports, Cunsolo (2012) argues that people can experience anticipatory grieving. In turn, this is because of deterministic and reductionist narratives that, subsequently, lead to dark tourism practices. This anticipatory grieving is based upon previous mourning experiences from other deaths, as well as understanding current and projected climate change societal impacts and environment consequences (Doherty & Clayton, 2011).

When the Arctic is imagined as a white place that is full of ice and snow, the melting of the cryosphere induced by global climate change will lead to increased narratives of ruination and dark tourism practices. It is here where the future apocalyptic and cryospheric-less Arctic will be considered as a field of ruins. This depicts a *dark* post-Arctic tourism destination where 'rivers and lakes that used to freeze remain ice-free all year round ... [and] lands have lost their snowy landscapes, and glaciers have melted or retreated' (Varnajot & Saarinen, 2021: 2). As such, a cryospheric-less Arctic grounded in narratives of ruination can produce visions of an apocalyptic aftermath induced by climate change. Thus, rather than being about the mourning of lost cryosphere, dark tourism in a future Arctic might lean towards more morbid practices, where people gaze at desolated landscapes and where *more-than-human* objects 'have died'. This resonates with Rucinska's (2016) claim that visits to sites of natural disasters can also be understood as dark tourism. Accordingly, there are three types of tourists pursuing visits to sites of natural hazards, including 'those interested in natural hazards themselves; those interested in landscape deformation and experiencing emotions shortly after extreme events – natural disasters – occur; and finally, those interested in historic places long after an extreme event takes place' (Rucinska, 2016: 1385). In a future cryospheric-less Arctic, the second category of tourists highlighted by Rucinska could be understood as those seeking a morbid thrill, which raises broader ethical concerns and moral dilemmas (Light, 2017b; Stone & Sharpley, 2014). It is worth noting, that this practice has already been named, often by the media, as catastrophe tourism, climate change and extinction tourism or climate change voyeurism (Dawson *et al.*, 2011).

Nevertheless, dark tourism is not only about the mourning and the morbid, but can also provide educational experiences (Cohen, 2011; Iliev, 2021; Yan *et al.*, 2016). Indeed, Iliev (2021: 970) argues that a 'number of individuals visit sites of dark tourism ... for education, learning, [and] understanding about what happened at the site'. For example, in future Arctic dark tourism, educational dark tourism could demonstrate through tourist exhibitions 'how the Arctic was before' using virtual reality tools (Varnajot & Saarinen, 2021), but also provide information about what can still be done to safeguard other vulnerable regions across the globe. By developing dark tourism practices such as mock funerals or commemorative events at already vulnerable Arctic destinations, sites of *more-than-human* deaths could help to better understand the global dimension of climate change. Indeed, following Latour's (2014: 1) reflection when he was '[thinking] that it is easy for us to agree that, in modernism, people are not equipped with the mental and emotional repertoire to deal with such a vast scale of events', future Arctic dark tourism could help overcome this challenge. In return, this could lead to people engaging in future dark tourism experiences to adopt more pro-environmental behaviours. It is expected that dark tourism practices will epitomise mourning, morbid and educative motivations among future visitors of the Arctic. That said, how the future Arctic is produced through touristic narratives remains to be seen. It is to this point that I now turn, with a specific focus on geopoetics as a conceptual framing device to create new touristic narratives (for the future Arctic).

Geopoetics and Future Narrative Alternatives

As stated by Magrane (2021: 9), 'everything changing opens up the possibility of re-thinking how individuals, societies, and cultures relate with each other and with the non-humans and materials with whom humans share the planet'. Consequently, climate change may lead to apocalyptic visions for the future of Arctic tourism and associated dark tourism, but may also offer opportunities to redefine, reinvent and reimagine a plurality of Arctic tomorrows and narratives. While science has a limited role in this process; climatologists, glaciologists, biologists and others have a diagnostic role, which is only the first step in understanding climate change. Of course, it is these scientific endeavours that we know how much temperatures have risen and, subsequently, how much the cryosphere has melted. However, science does not indicate the path to follow in this process of narrative reinvention. Therefore, a multidisciplinary social science perspective is necessary in that the arts, literature and other creative work have a critical role in the making of future visions for Arctic tourism, as well as for human–environment relationships. As such, the notion of geopoetics as a conceptual framing device 'focuses on the ways writing-as-making … can help us to diagnose troubled worlds and prefigure new ones' (Cresswell, 2022: 374).

The etymology of the term 'geopoetics' originates from the Greek *geo* for 'earth' and *poetics* for 'making' – as in creating something new into existence that did not exist before (Cresswell, 2022). Geopoetics highlights connections between geography and creative narratives and, subsequently, describes how 'we live on and with the Earth', including the Arctic (Magrane, 2015: 87). Geopoetics is a subfield of *geohumanities* and brings together poetry and critical geography (Magrane, 2021). However, in the context of this chapter, rather than focusing on poems per se, I understand geopoetics as the making of new narratives in the tourism industry. Therefore, geopoetics can take multiple forms that may be specific to tourism, including tourism promotion materials, social media, travel magazines and blogs, as well as collective representations and imaginaries. Geopoetics, as argued by Magrane (2021: 11), 'includes the following characteristics: a critical awareness of the social and cultural constructions of … place, space, landscape, nature, and scale; a reflexive consideration of how places are represented and, in turn, made; [and] an engagement with speculative futures and the world-making possibilities of language'. In practice, 'denominations, definitions, and metaphors are all part of conditioning spatial understanding' (Medby, 2019: 124). As a result, through narrative-making, geopoetics can form the basis of place-making (see Tuan, 1991) and, therefore, have the power to change how the Arctic is produced within future touristic narratives.

Therefore, I argue geopoetics can offer pluralistic avenues for the future of Arctic tourism by developing 'diverse images representing a variety of Arctic meanings' (Rantala *et al.*, 2019: 14). Consequently, this geopoetical diversity can mitigate anxiety-driven ruination narratives and the potential expansion of dark tourism and any morally dubious practices. Nevertheless, my aim here is not to consider dark tourism as a burden or as negative per se. As discussed earlier, dark tourism can provide educative experiences and has become an economic opportunity for many destinations (Kim & Butler, 2015). However, within the context of this chapter, considering a potential cryospheric-less Arctic, the future of tourism as 'dark tourism' sustains ethical issues of framing the Arctic for outsiders, by outsiders. Indeed, this cryospheric-less vision still considers the Arctic through the lens of ice – or indeed, the lack of it. Moreover, future dark tourism associated with a post-apocalyptic narrative of the Arctic is powerful and will oversimplify realities of the region. These include overlooking local communities' perspectives on issues associated with the shrinking of the cryosphere and climate change, because for those living in the region the Arctic is not only about snow and ice (Carey, 2007; Jackson, 2015; Varnajot & Saarinen, 2022).

Hence, geopoetics as a tool used by local communities and tourism entrepreneurs can avoid this future stereotype and can help develop a variety of narratives that are grounded in future Arctic realities, rather than simply thinking, and picturing the Arctic in the future subjunctive (Howe, 2020). Indeed, as recalled by Müller (2015), there are various landscapes, climates, cultures and seasons in the Arctic, which all can become inspirational sources for geopoetics. Indeed, this would mean emancipation of Arctic tourism from stereotypical cryospheric-based representations, including for the mitigation of deterministic and reductionist ruins futures. For instance, this can be achieved by developing narratives grounded in the midnight sun, the *ruska* (a Finnish term that designates the colourful autumn foliage of boreal forests) or the various circumpolar indigenous cultures (Sámi, Inuit, Nenets, Aleut, to name a few). These examples are currently underrepresented in tourism promotional materials and overshadowed by Arctification. Using geopoetics, tourism promotional materials can creatively engage with the reality of the Arctic (Acker, 2021). In turn, this can act as efficient leverage points in changing future Arctic narratives given their significant role in preparing trips and visits. Geopoetics in tourism promotion materials can even become resistance tools against outsiders' dark tourism and post-apocalyptic narratives (Engelmann, 2021; Nassar, 2021). Importantly, this resonates with Cresswell's (2021) call to experiment with language and creative writings and to embrace hybrid texts: in this case, combining geopoetics with tourism promotional materials.

Conclusion

Melting cryosphere has become an infamous symbol for climate change and the Anthropocene, triggering visions of apocalyptic futures (Howe, 2022; Sörlin, 2015; Huijbens, 2021; Varnajot & Saarinen, 2021). In such visions, the Arctic without its cryosphere would turn into a desolated region filled with ruins of the Anthropocene favourable for the development of dark tourism practices. The stories of *Okjokull* and the mock funerals for *more-than-human* cryospheric objects are only foretastes of what may happen in the future if we do not produce other narratives for the Arctic (tourism) that are based upon dynamic realities of the region and grounded in locals' everyday experience of the Arctic. Nevertheless, dark tourism does not have to necessarily be perceived as a negative outcome. Indeed, if well implemented and managed, dark tourism may become an opportunity for education regarding climate change, Arctic geography and anthropogenic-induced impacts on the cryosphere. Dark tourism can therefore, potentially at least, turn visitors of the Arctic into environmental ambassadors. This becomes even more relevant since last-chance tourism's long-terms effects of ambassadorship remain to be confirmed (Hughes, 2013; Miller *et al.*, 2020).

In this context, the role of geopoetics – and art and literature in general – may have a critical role in developing new narratives about the Arctic, but also in making sure that dark tourism does not turn unethical. Geopoetics' strength 'is in the power of noticing' (Cresswell, 2021: 36), and offers meaning making that includes otherwise neglected or forgotten details that were previously dominated by entrenched narratives. However, looking for 'more-than-ice' narratives should not be understood as an underestimation or overlooking continuing impacts the Arctic is currently facing due to climate change. Rather, the use of geopoetics may help us to rethink the Arctic within tourism both ontologically and axiologically. It can also be utilised to better understand geographical intricacies of the environmental, as well as social changes at stake. It is outsiders' imagination – through Arctification – that produces the stereotypical idea of current Arctic tourism. Hence, in the future, the framing of tourism narratives through geopoetics ensures new Arctic imaginations.

11 'Shrines and Rites of Passage': Toward a Future of Dark Tourism Chronicles

Maximiliano E. Korstanje

Introduction

Dark tourism has evolved in recent decades as a global social phenomenon captivating the attention of both scholars and the media alike. As Hooper and Lennon (2016) put it, dark tourism has successfully crystallised as an object of study as well as a category which can be analytically examined, particularly of how societies deal with difficult heritage and the noteworthy dead within visitor economies. For scholars such as Philip Stone, dark tourism is defined as a ritual not only associated with the idea of *thanatopsis* – that is, a contemplation of mortality – but also, an attempt to reconcile one's own life with memorialised death and the fatality of the significant Other dead (Stone, 2012a, 2012b; Stone & Sharpley, 2008). Meanwhile, dark tourism in practice may take on various 'shades of darkness': ranging from darkest to lightest subtypes which, in turn, creates The Dark Tourism Spectrum typological model (Stone, 2006). While the lightest end of the conceptual spectrum model represents visitor sites with a strong entertainment orientation, the darkest sites signal sites of extreme mourning and suffering (Heuermann & Chhabra, 2014; Light, 2017b). Although the academic literature on dark tourism has grown and matured over recent years, and while beyond the scope of this chapter to offer a comprehensive review, dark tourism scholarship can be grouped into three clear areas. Firstly, studies based on thanatological and anthropological aspects of death within contemporary society (for example, see Stone 2011, 2013a; and Sharpley, 2009). Secondly, dark tourism studies with a strict focus in heritage, culture and pilgrimage studies (for example, see Collins-Kreiner, 2016a, 2016b; Isaac & Ashworth, 2011; Olsen & Korstanje, 2019). And finally, the emergence of dark tourism which suggests a new type of neo-colonialism (for example, see Korstanje, 2017; Tzanelli, 2016). Of course, these different schools of thought have inherent strengths and weaknesses, yet dark tourism is something more complex than simply an anthropological issue or simply a touristic experience. In short, dark tourism as subject area should be approached with interdisciplinarity, particularly with broader social scientific studies in death education and cultural heritage discourse (Stone, 2013a).

Dark tourism as a research field of study is based on what Adam Franklin dubbed *tourist-centricity* – which means an obsession for tourists as the only source of valid and reliable information. In other words, tourist-centricity leads professional researchers to ignore the role played by other actors (Franklin, 2007), while at the same time, applied research is limited to conducted questionnaires or interviews excluding other methodologies. Under some research circumstances, tourists that are being researched might be unfamiliar with their inner world and deep-seated emotions or might be scarce with the truth to protect their own interests, feelings or beliefs (Korstanje & Ivanov, 2012; Korstanje & Baker, 2018). Despite this, the inclusion of qualitative research, including analysis of content and ethnographies remains important in future dark tourism studies (Buda & McIntosh, 2013; Korstanje & Baker, 2018; Potts, 2012). These future research approaches should overcome tourist centricity and, subsequently, be post-disciplinary in research orientation (Korstanje, 2017; Skinner, 2016; Stone, 2013a; Tzanelli, 2016). Equally important for the future of dark tourism scholarship is the role played by politics and the construction of shrines within dark tourism destinations, and its influences and consequences thereof (Korstanje & Baker, 2018). Therefore, the purpose of this chapter is to address the politicalisation of dark tourism and examine how the presence of shrines can offer (political) chronicles and narratives for the future. Moreover, the chapter focuses upon anthropological aspects and subsequent icons that offer a semiotic role in the political influence of dark tourism and, specifically, the formation of shrines and monuments that become established within the visitor economy. Thus, drawing upon several original auto-ethnographies, this chapter lays foundations toward a new understanding of dark tourism, as originally associated with thanatology. The chapter argues that future dark tourism will entail a new social rite of passage which is culturally and politically determined. Firstly, however, the chapter offers a review of dark tourism before examining shrines and aspects of politicalisation and the future role of dark tourism.

Dark Tourism: A Background Review

One of the original works dedicated to consumerism of 'dark sites' within the visitor economy can be traced back to Rojek (1993) who coined the term *black spots*. These so-called 'black spots' within an ever-increasing memorialised landscape referred to grave sites and monuments where people of significance were commemorated. Rojek calls attention to the fact that these spaces are memorialised as spaces of contemporary remembrance and visited by increasing numbers of tourists. Consequently, black spots are marked by a clear commoditisation of fatality and death. The classification of these sites encompasses not only spaces of death, but also postmodern places reconstructed through modern audiovisual media and spectacle. While some 'black spots' are designed to remember the significant dead and offer contemplation and even nostalgic discourses, others are oriented to offer (re)presentations of sudden, unexplained or calamitous death (Rojek, 1993). Similarly, Blom (2000, 2007) refers to *morbid tourism* as a new niche of tourism consumption which entails sophisticated commercial activity revolving around mass visitation to sites of accidents, disasters or other noteworthy deaths, including graves of celebrities, battlefields and natural disasters. Meanwhile, Tumarkin (2005) introduces the notion of *traumascape* to denote sites which are historically determined by tragedies or fatal events, but which today are informing our cultural present. Tumarkin (2005) goes on to allude that the articulation of narratives and stories fabricated offers identity to those places shaped by pain, loss and violence. Importantly, however, far from being recreational spaces of consumption, these (dark) sites are strongly conditioned by politics.

Other definitions of dark tourism have been offered by scholars including Strange and Kempa (2003), Biran and Hyde (2013), Light (2017b) and White and Frew (2013). However, while some diversification of what constitutes dark tourism remains (Hooper & Lennon, 2016), including its nature and conceptual parameters, some have applauded the idea of defining dark tourism as a form of heritage (Korstanje, 2017; Light, 2017a; Sather-Wagstaff, 2011), or as a type of sacred pilgrimage (Biran *et al.*, 2011; Hartmann, 2014; Lennon & Foley, 2000). Nonetheless, dark tourism as a practice was widely consolidated in the mid-20th century when technology allowed touristic mass travel to be faster, easier and more accessible and affordable (Seaton & Lennon, 2004). However, Sharpley and Stone (2009) argue that many dark tourism destinations are accidental, or in other words, some sites of dark tourism are not purposedly designed. Although these sites are structured around a set of common values, dark tourism allows for a new reinterpretation of the past, including consequences for consuming certain kinds of dark tourism experiences. It is here that thanatopsis is proposed as a key factor in dark tourism consumption (Stone, 2012a, 2012b; Stone & Sharpley, 2008). Moreover, Seaton (1996) argues that dark tourism is centred on a thanatopic tradition – that is, a private contemplation of death through objects or others – a tradition that emerged in the Middle Ages. Indeed, Stone (2012a) associated with the problems of understanding death in a secularised society as one of the vital forces of dark tourism. Stone (2012a) suggests dark tourism should be understood as a phenomenological experience based upon the urgency for contemplating one's own finitude through significant 'Other' death. This reflexive sentiment has notably gained a considerable position because of the modern contemporary visitors' economy. That said, it is important not to lose sight of dark tourism experiences that are characterised by other factors. On one hand, visitors might be psychologically moved to understand their death in a high-secularised world. On the other hand, dark tourism experiences might mediate as a social filter between the chaos ignited by death and the order of life (Stone, 2012a, 2012b).

Furthermore, Stone (2006) provides a taxonomy to classify dark tourism sites according to a spectrum model which ranges from the lightest to the darkest side. Semantics aside, Stone (2006: 146) defines his Dark Tourism Spectrum model as a conceptual framework which helps to describe the 'multi-hued nature of dark tourism sites'. Within this framework, Stone (2006) located 'seven dark suppliers', each orchestrated according to their intersection with demand. Rather than focusing on demand, the spectrum model delineates the parameters of supply (in which to locate demand factors). Although dark tourism is strictly enrooted in the contemplation of death, dark tourism places evolve over time and chronological distance. Indeed, the chronology and evolution of specific dark tourism formation rests on three key variables. Firstly, immediacy and spontaneity of the dark sensation; secondly, dissociation between purposefully constructed sites and/or accidental sites; and thirdly, the pedagogic nature of dark tourism and politics. In turn, these variables of dark tourism raise profound issues and questions of how to classify such sites, particularly when future dark tourism is viewed under a 'rites of passage' lens.

Dark Tourism as a Rite of Passage

The term *rite of passage* was originally used by anthropologist Arnold van Gennep to symbolise any sociocultural ritual which happens whenever an individual departs an 'in-group' to participate in 'another group' (Van Gennep, 2013). Consequently, the rite of the passage opens perceptual doors to a limonoid state which is temporal for the group. Once *accepted* into the new group, the individual has a new status. That said, rites of passage denote any society has various groupings that, in turn, all form smaller societies. Indeed, Van Gennep (2013) distinguishes two spheres, namely: the sacred and the profane. Social groups move very well in the constellations of sacred spheres. To validate their customs, groups often perform some rites to pass from one group to another. In other words, rites of passage are rituals articulated in a ceremony so that the group (or community) remains united. Examples of these societal and/or religious rites of passage include ceremonies such as baptism, graduations, initiation journeys, weddings, funerals and so forth. Van Gennep (2013) outlines three stages of the rite of passage, which incorporates the separation of the in-group, liminality and re-incorporation. In the first stage, the individual separates from the status and role which signifies a much deeper detachment from the older group. The liminal stage is traversed by a temporal state of transition where the subject lacks status and identity. Within the re-incorporation stage, the individual is finally accepted into the new group while completing the ritual (Van Gennep, 2013). Similar observations by Turner (2020) suggest the liminal stage is based upon a geographical separation that is started with a sacred journey (but not necessarily in all cases). Turner (2020) uses the term pre-liminal phase (separation), liminal phase (transition) and post-liminal phase (incorporation). Transition puts the individual into contest between the two involved groups simply because they are *betwixt* and *between* while moving in a limbo (Turner, 2020).

Scholars have applauded the idea of defining tourism as a rite of passage or pilgrimage (that is, a *journey*). As Graburn (1983, 2004, 2017) has noted, tourism should be understood as a secular ritual oriented to mitigate the social frustrations that transpire during working lives. In this case, tourism is seen as a ritual of reversal where the individual accepts the limonoid risks of abandoning the security of the home. In this respect, the act of travelling is associated not only with the quest for new experiences, but also with new statuses and identities (Graburn, 1983, 2004, 2017). Meanwhile, Cohen (1985) called attention to considering tourism as a rite of play where the quest for novelty is juxtaposed with the need for recreation. Although in dark tourism studies little attention has been paid to the role of rites of passage, some interesting works recently emerged have emphasised the importance of defining dark tourism as a type of sacred pilgrimage (Hartmann *et al.*, 2018; McMorran, 2015; Olsen & Korstanje, 2019). In this vein, Korstanje and Olsen (2019) remind us that dark tourism can be defined as a ritual pilgrimage – or sacred journey – which not only allows society to understand traumatic events but enhances resilience. Drawing upon the work of Philip Stone, Korstanje and Olsen (2019) acknowledge that secularisation has displaced religion from the public realm to the private sphere. As a result, society articulates new mechanisms to deal with contingency and uncertainness. It is here that questions are raised about the nature of dark tourism and its experiences, including existential questions such as what is the purpose of (my) life? What will happen when I die? Is death the end of everything?

Dark tourism engages with a negotiation between the ordinary Self and notions of death through the fatality of the significant Other. Moreover, Sharma (2019) considers dark tourism as a ritual pilgrimage where the spatial manifestations of the sacred emanate. Specifically, Sharma (2019) advocates that the sacred is culturally engulfed through the exercise of power. Within dark tourism, this occurs because dark tourism and politics are inextricably intertwined. Furthermore, this raises the question to what extent is dark tourism interlinked to conflict? Laing and Frost (2016) lament that specialised literature has developed a bad (pejorative) interpretation of what *darkness* is. Indeed, the term *dark* or *darkness* leads us to think of evil, deviance or malfeasance. While life is pondered and valorised in the Western social imaginary, death (or at least dying) is neglected or deemed frightening. Therefore, Laing and Frost (2016) propose a new understanding of dark tourism as the epicentre of *wellness* and the empathy for the 'Other'. Laing and Frost (2016) also argue dark tourism helps not only understand traumatic events but also educate our emotions towards a sense of wellbeing. Indeed, within the context of commemorative events, Laing and Frost (2016) suggest visitors confront ideas of their finitude while maintaining ontological security and overall wellbeing (also see Stone & Sharpley, 2008). Likewise, Collins-Kreiner (2019) argues that new types of tourism market segments associated with the macabre and the horror (that is, dark tourism or post-disaster tourism) has been gradually surfacing since the end of the millennium. Consequently, dark tourism activates new levels of research avenues that focus on broader notions of pilgrimage. To that end, ideas of what pilgrimage is, and the role of contemporary dark tourism has moved scholarship to a new state of rejuvenation. It is here that dark tourism not only educates visitors but also shapes new identities, especially when commemorative shrines and memorials are constructed within visitor economies.

Commemorative Shrines and Memorials: Toward a Future State

Dark tourism shrines, as articulated in Stone's Dark Tourism Spectrum taxonomy (noted earlier) do not always accept or cater to mass tourism, certainly in the initial stages of development. At this stage, tourists are seen as agents who are part of a broader political, (sometimes) corrupt societal system (Korstanje & Baker, 2018; Raine, 2013). However, while some tourism is rejected at shrines, other visitation is welcomed as an opportunity to provide visitors with a message. Therefore, drawing upon ethnographic studies conducted by the author at various dark tourism shrine sites, the remainder of this chapter sets out several principles that can be adopted for the future development and touristic consumption of shrine sites. Notwithstanding inherent limitations with ethnography, including issues of respondents' bias, fabrication and misunderstandings, the research method can offer useful 'rich data'. This is certainly the case for reflexive tourist encounters, such as those found within shrine visitation.

Therefore, to offer some contextualisation, this chapter draws upon a field study conducted by the author in the Sanctuary of Cromañón, Buenos Aires, Argentina. The Sanctuary of Cromañón became a *dark shrine* after 194 people lost their lives and 1492 individuals were injured. The Republica Cromañón (Cro-Magnon Republic), located in Buenos Aires, Argentina, was a venue that host music events. On 30 December 2004, the venue hosted rock band Callejeros, with an audience of 3000 people. During the show, someone in the audience lit a pyrotechnic flare which, subsequently, set fire to the ceiling whereby the resultant combustion took hold, and disaster ensued. The site today is a dark shrine dedicated to the victims and survivors. During a field trip to the site, a young male respondent (approximately 22 years old) informed the author that he had attended the event and was a witness to the tragedy. However, after some careful analysis and reflection, it transpired that the respondent had not in fact attended the event, nor did he witness the tragedy; but rather he had fabricated his story. That said, the stories he reported as evidence were contrasted and incorporated with other (real) evidence to draw a conceptual model to decipher the phenomenon. In short, the ethnographer acts as a drawer, a painter who constructs an approximation to social reality. Hence, in an alliance with other ethnographies conducted by the author on dark shrines such as at Ground Zero in New York, USA, (site of the 9/11 terrorist atrocities), Atocha Monument (a memorial at Atocha railway station in Madrid to commemorate victims of the train bombings on 11 March 2004), ESMA (the former Navy Mechanics School which operated as a clandestine detention, torture and extermination centre during the 1976–1983 Argentine dictatorship), Cromañón provided the author with vital information to plot elementary icons and elements of dark tourism shrines. It is these icons and elements that are proposed to form any future formation of dark shrines, especially those which initially evolve after a tragedy and are organic by default rather than design. These icons are organised as:

(1) sacralisation of victims;
(2) attachment to a foundational narrative;
(3) levels of internal conflict/cohesion; and
(4) the acceptance or rejection of tours.

Sacralisation of victims

The sacralisation of victims should be understood as an anthropological process whereby human groups symbolise character that confronts not only death and dying but also, for some people at least, God. As a direct consequence of disasters, dark shrines are often constructed in the exact or near location where people have died and, in so doing, marks the exact moment of separation between the body and the soul. Within a brief period, these organic sites are furnished with flowers (representing life), personal mementos of victims, privy letters, artwork or photographs dedicated to the victims, as well as candles or other votive trinkets and regalia symbolising triumph of life (light) over death (darkness). Religious relics can also be present in dark shrines. Anthropologically speaking, dark shrines, as well as the sacralisation of the victims, remind us not only how the death suddenly disrupts and interrogates culture, but also the human resistance to acts of corruption, greed or political injustices that might have contributed to the causes of any disaster.

Attachment to a foundational narrative

The sacralisation of victims invariably leads to a second element, based on the need to respond to the question: why? Or, more specifically, why has a particular disaster or tragedy befallen us? These questions invariably require a foundational narrative which helps survivors to deal with their pain and sense of loss of both people and place. Often, creating these narratives, victims are viewed as heroes who have sacrificed their lives for protecting the broader community. However, far from being unilateral or homogenous, diverse groups often struggle to impose and/or control the story narrative and, consequently, political dissonance often sets in. These narratives centre on what ethnographers call a 'scapegoat mechanism' whereby a process of simplification of binary good vs. bad is employed and any malfeasance should be defeated. Often in these circumstances, the figure of rogues is taken on by corrupt politicians, businesspeople or, as in the case of Atocha and Ground Zero, terrorists or the Juntas in the case of ESMA. The foundational narrative occupies a central position in dark shrine formation, but over time, it may lead towards a climate of conflict or social cohesion, among all the sub-groups involved in political narrative settings.

Levels of internal conflict/cohesion

The levels of internal conflict or cohesion are influenced by two key factors. On one hand, the number of resources which are distributed to the subgroups involved in any dark shrine creation. For instance, in Cromañón where financial aid is distributed unevenly by the government, the conflict among groups is stronger than in, say, at the sites of Ground Zero or Atocha. Indeed, a fairer distribution of resources legitimises the local authorities which, in turn, can enhance political cohesion as well as hegemony. Of course, the opposite may be true, where discretionary disbursement of pensions to disaster survivors, for example, introduces contention and resentment. Moreover, in this case, some minorities or subgroups monopolise a whole portion of pensions pushing other collectives to marginal positions. Meanwhile, coherent and reliable information management reduces the risks of internal conflicts against authorities. In the Cromañon case, local authorities (including the rock band musicians themselves) were blamed as the source of failure or corruption that facilitated the disaster, particularly because the venue transgressed many security and safety standards.

Acceptance or rejection of organised tours

The acceptance or rejection of organised tours depends where the dark tourism site is positioned on the Dark Tourism Spectrum taxonomy (Stone, 2006). However, other factors should be considered. Indeed, dark shrines where mass tourism is rejected often develop narratives that are hostile to political corruption. In terms of tragic events, any subsequent tourism is seen as a commercial activity which commoditises survivors' pain. These sites are supported by local donations, but they refuse to accept economic benefits that arise from tourism. This is the case with ESMA and Cromañón, but perhaps not at Ground Zero. In the case ESMA, for survivors, the Juntas violated human rights to smash the opposition of worker union leaders, students and scholars to the liberal economic policies of Martinez de Hoz. For them, the economic factor is demonised as the start of the end. The same applies to Cromañón where local authorities and political leaders are accused of corruption because of bribes and, therefore, appear insensitive to survivors' suffering. Meanwhile, Ground Zero, which welcomes thousands of tourists daily, 9/11 memorials are viewed more as symbols of unity and nationhood. In this regard, therefore, for social imaginary, 9/11 marked a starting point where the US struggled to recover/promote/impose democracy in certain parts of the world. The narrative is not only manipulated by political authorities, but also helps install a sense of nationalism that is stimulated by authorities through a 'heritage that hurts'.

Conclusion

Over recent years, there has been a burgeoning growth of publications in the broad subject field of dark tourism. This new niche has captivated scholars worldwide while interrogating the nature and evolution of postmodern leisure. Furthermore, the specialised literature ranges from those studies which focus on dark tourism as an anthropological attempt to contemplate ones' own finitude through death of the Other (known as the thanatopic tradition), to heritage-based studies which define dark tourism as a sacred pilgrimage. Consequently, we have commented on the strengths and weaknesses of each theory exposing some methodological problems associated with what Franklin (2007) dubbed a 'tourist centricity'. This methodological caveat is in part resolved by Stone (2006) where he proffers a conceptual taxonomy spectrum of dark tourism, ranging from the lightest forms to the darkest form. Stone (2006) illustrates not only how shrine formation gives valid information to analysts respecting the dark allegories, or the influence of political discourses, but he also paved the way for the rise of a dark tourism future as a new emerging conceptual framework.

As Stone (2006) argues, shrine formation (within dark tourism) implies a deep process of politicisation which had remained overlooked by scholars. This happens simply because politics has placed us in a marginal position in the original academic debates concerning dark tourism. As discussed by Stone, while some destinations are fabricated to ensure a pleasurable experience (lightest sphere of the spectrum), others are not willing to welcome organised mass tours (darkest sphere). Undoubtedly, Stone's conceptual model has much to say in the dark tourism future and, of course, this chapter continues the discussion while giving a new fresh insight chiefly based on four main variables. These variables explain in the evolution of time not only the shrine formation but also the roots of Stone's typological spectrum. That said, the theoretical model includes the sacralisation of victims, attachment to a foundational narrative, levels of internal conflict/cohesion and the acceptance or rejection of tours. The sacralisation of victims should be understood as a process that originated from sudden or unexpected traumatic events.

Indeed, there is an anthropological drive that leads humans to rememorise disasters at the site where, in turn, memorialisation finally takes root. Firstly, dark shrines are constructed to remind us not only that (human) corruption might be a key factor behind a disaster, but also how human character successfully recovers from adverse situations. Secondly, a foundational narrative emanates to keep social cohesion while a scapegoat mechanism is activated. Politicians, privileged actors, authorities or even ethnic minorities may be very well blamed for a disaster. Under some conditions, strangers are demonised as the key drivers that accelerated conditions to the catastrophe. Thirdly, the site survives or simply perishes according to the levels of conflict and how open the community is to external actors. The levels of conflicts, or how successful it is, is regulated as well as the internal cohesion are key factors for the dark tourism shrine's future. Finally, acceptance or rejection of organised tours is given by significant political and cultural aspects such as nationalism, corruption, fragmentation or hostility against strangers. For the sake of clarity, this chapter synthesises the fieldworker notes of ethnographies conducted in Cromañón, Ground Zero and ESMA. This chapter has critically discussed to what extent dark tourism is a cultural issue engulfed in politics, and how dark tourism in the future will always be politicised. Indeed, to control portrayals of the tragic past is to control the present, as well as to influence the future. At the same time, the chapter has laid foundations of four dimensions to understand how some dark tourism sites evolve to be tourist-friendly, while others reject organised tours. In addition, this study has identified the icons and elements of dark tourism shrines towards a new understanding of the phenomenon. While the sacralisation of victims speaks to us of the human character which goes through contingency, each site develops its own narrative attachment. At the same time, each site has its types of cohesion and state of conflict to impose or internalise the common narrative. The acceptance-rejection of organised tours is given by cosmologies supported and regulated by authorities. It is this politicisation of disaster and narrative control of past cultural trauma that will continue to influence the future (re)presentation of dark tourism.

12 Survivor Voices and Disaster Education: Future Commemoration and Remembrance at Dark Tourism Sites

Elspeth Frew and Clare Lade

Introduction

Natural disasters such as bushfires and earthquakes can often lead to lives being lost. Close to the place where the natural disaster has occurred, a memorial site may be built soon afterwards to commemorate individuals who have died, and commemorative events may be staged at the site on anniversaries of the tragedy. Doka (2003: 192) suggests that tragedies demand public ritual and memorialisation which can help 'soothe and unify a public coping with tragedy'. This is particularly so while families of victims and the survivors work through the five stages of grief, including denial, anger, bargaining, depression and acceptance (Kübler-Ross, 1970). Museums have gradually shifted their public narratives from being 'disciplinary spaces of academic history' to places of memory, place and community (Andermann & Arnold-de Simine, 2012: 3) and, subsequently, this new museology reflects an increased emphasis on inclusion and diversity (Frew, 2018).

It follows that memorials should reflect needs of the local community who experienced the disaster and provide the means to support these individuals in their grief. The purpose of this chapter, therefore, is to examine how future disaster memorialisation should incorporate commemorative narratives of loss and grief, but also educative narratives including information on avoidance of future disasters. Using a case study approach, the chapter outlines the future of disaster commemoration and remembrance within the context of dark tourism. In so doing, the study suggests future commemorations of disasters and other calamities should be inclusive and community centric for victim and survivor voices to be heard and recalled.

Commemorating Calamities: Towards Disaster Education

When a natural disaster impacts a whole community, the survivors may suffer from post-traumatic stress disorder. Specifically, there can be an increase in the rate of domestic violence, or there may be family breakdowns (Bryant *et al.*, 2021; Rees & Wells, 2020). Some authors suggest that a keen sense of community, a communal identity and a shared account of impacts and traumas can play a critical role in recovery (Chin & Talpelli, 2015; Misra *et al.*, 2017; Richardson & Maninger, 2016). Seizing new opportunities following a disaster can enable survivors to find and/or reshape their voice not only in the sense of self-representation but also to potentially influence recovery outcomes (Few *et al.*, 2021; Zhang, 2016). First-hand accounts given by survivors of a tragic event have been described by Mahn *et al.* (2021: 74) as a 'vernacular memorialisation' which can help convey the personal and emotionally charged memories of the disaster.

In such a way these first-hand accounts by survivors and family members of victims can be impactful at memorial sites and at commemorative events and may help with the grieving process. Atkinson-Phillips (2022: 1) notes that memorial sites not only commemorate the dead, but can also commemorate the experience of the survivors, particularly if the memorial sites become a form of 'symbolic reparation' of trauma. Such examples include the Holocaust and concentration camps; slavery; the Stolen Generations (a period from the early 20th century to the 1970s in Australia where Aboriginal children were removed from their families); or the Irish Potato Famine (also known as the Great Famine, a period of starvation and disease in Ireland from 1845 to 1852, often attributed to British colonial policies). The move towards remembering the lived experience of pain, loss and trauma suggests a 'shift in public memorialization' which can help acknowledge any marginalised communities that their stories have been heard (Atkinson-Phillips, 2022: 13). However, this standardised approach to memorialisation, whereby memorial visitors are moved 'through a narrative arc from trauma to recovery', may create 'neat narratives of *closure* which risks a sentimental approach that potentially silences any survivor expressions of grief and ongoing pain or anger' (Atkinson-Phillips, 2022: 12).

After a tragic occurrence such as a bushfire, diverse types of events can be staged at the site of the disaster such as community information sessions, fundraising events, grieving events, community rebuilding, re-openings, VIP visits or thanksgiving events (Sanders *et al.*, 2015). The inclusion of dignitaries has been shown to be important, with the on-site presence of a Premier, Prime Minister, government Minister or Police Commissioner usually well received from a public perspective (Carayannopoulos, 2017). Commemorative events also have social and political significance, and when they are staged on key anniversaries, they can contribute to place making, destination marketing and community building (Viol *et al.*, 2018). However, there is the danger that such commemorative events may become commercialised or commodified and lose their authentic meaning, particularly if event organisers can see their potential for event tourism (Getz, 2008). The use of Faulkner's (2001) phases of disaster management may help reinforce that a collection of such staged events at a site of natural disaster could be viewed as part of a region's event portfolio, and in the case of damaging bushfires may be designed to support post-disaster recovery (Ziakas & Getz, 2021).

However, in recent years some memorial sites have incorporated educational aspects to inform and enlighten locals, as well as tourists on how to behave in the event of an emergency. Moreover, this reflects the inevitability of devastating natural events and the need to safeguard the greater community from associated avoidable deaths. The expressions of *disaster education*, *disaster risk education* or *disaster prevention education* are used to highlight that education can have a pivotal role in reducing the impact of disasters (Dufty, 2020). Research has shown that when people are shown how to react to disaster situations, this can help them respond promptly and appropriately and, consequently, protect themselves and others during times of emergencies (Shaw *et al.*, 2011). Therefore, if a community is psychologically and physically prepared for natural hazards, then they are more likely to respond appropriately during the next natural emergency (Boylan & Lawrence, 2020). Such a view reinforces a need to incorporate disaster education into natural disaster related memorials and commemorative events. This will raise awareness and understanding of such disasters for future generations, as the following case examples and the remainder of this chapter highlights.

Commemorative Events

A Case Study Approach

- The *Marysville Bushfire Memorial* opened in 2018 and commemorates the bushfire victims who died during the bushfires which burned from 7 February 2009 until 5 March 2009 within the townships of Murrindindi, Narbethong, Granton, Marysville, Buxton and Taggerty in Victoria, Australia (Victoria State Government, 2022). Thirty-nine people were lost in the bushfires, with 34 being residents in the local area (Murrindindi Shire Council, 2022).

- The *Ash Wednesday Bushfire Education Centre and Memorial* is in a former kindergarten in Cockatoo, Victoria, Australia and opened in 2016. It was previously used as a place of sanctuary by residents during a bushfire on 16 February 1983. The centre is now dedicated as a place of learning about events during the devastating bushfires. The memorial in the garden commemorates 47 people who died in the state of Victoria, Australia (Ash Wednesday Bushfire Education Centre, 2021).
- The *Canterbury Earthquake National Memorial* in Christchurch, New Zealand, opened in 2017 and commemorates 185 people who died following the Christchurch earthquake on 22 February 2011. The memorial also recognises the large amount of destruction of the city's infrastructure (Orchiston & Higham, 2014). New Zealand has a history of fatal earthquakes due to its location on the Pacific–Australian tectonic plate interface (Orchiston & Higham, 2014).
- The *Whakaari/White Island Volcanic Eruption Memorial Events* were held in Whakatane, New Zealand, immediately after the tragedy on 9 December 2019. Events were also held on the first and second anniversary of the disaster, commemorating 22 people who died because of the volcano erupting.

The commemorative anniversary events associated with the natural disaster case studies reveal many examples of attendees engaging in symbolic rituals at these events. For example, the 2nd Bushfire Anniversary Memorial Service for the 2009 Victorian bushfires was held in Federation Square, Melbourne, and was organised by staff of the Victorian Bushfires Reconstruction and Recovery Commission with input from Community Recovery Committees and the Bereaved Committee Advisory Group. The 2nd anniversary service paid particular attention to the impact of the disaster on locations, towns and broader communities, and the attendees were encouraged to write messages on blank yellow ribbons of remembrance and attach them to a tree and to light candles (Museums Victoria Collections, 2022). Similarly, for the 10th anniversary of the 2009 Victorian bushfires in 2019 a range of commemorative events were held at various locations across Victoria, including a temporary exhibition staged at the Melbourne Museum which contained photographs, objects and images from Museums Victoria's Victorian Bushfires collection, including stories of community recovery. The temporary exhibition featured a Remembrance Tree for visitors to post their own reflections and leave messages of support (Tout-Smith, 2019).

With an estimated annual visitation of 18,000 tourists, Whakaari/White Island, New Zealand, had been operating as a privately owned tourist island attraction for over 30 years (ABC, 2020; Shrimpton, 2019). Visitors to Whakaari/White Island at the time of the tragedy were passengers of the cruise ship 'Ovation of the Seas' but were unaware that official Level Two warnings were in place, meaning moderate to heightened volcanic unrest (Geonet, 2022). Within hours of the Whakaari/White Island eruption, close family members participated in a M ori spiritual service and blessing, while police and expert rescuers set about retrieving victim bodies from the island. In the hours following the eruption, a makeshift memorial was erected on a temporary fence alongside the waterfront where flowers, letters and poems were left for the victims and their families (Harris, 2019). Such a spontaneous outpouring of emotion in the form of messages and mementos placed close to the tragic site is like the phenomenon of individuals visiting roadside memorials or locally created temporary shrines following an unexpected and/or violent death (Klaassens *et al.*, 2013; MacConville, 2010). On the day of the volcanic eruption, family members of the victims also travelled to within one kilometre of the island and participated in a traditional M ori blessing and spiritual service on board their boat and returned to Whakatane, the closest town to Whakaari/ White Island where they waited in a nearby park, supported by the local community (Harris, 2019). Following the disastrous event, tours to the island were immediately banned. The island is presently closed to tourists with ongoing court cases over responsibility of the disaster continuing (Taylor, 2020).

In 2018, on the first anniversary of the Whakaari/White Island volcano eruption disaster, New Zealand's Prime Minister Jacinda Adern and Governor General Dame Patsy Reddy gathered with over 100 survivors, victims' families, first responders and rescue workers to observe a minute silence at 2.11pm in Whakatane (Taylor, 2020). Prior to this commemoration event, a dawn service consisting of prayers and emotional songs was held at Whakatane Heads, with Whakaari/ White Island in clear view (Taylor, 2020). Expressions of gratitude were conveyed by those survivors and family members (in person or via video recording) to those first responders who had contributed to saving their lives, as well as those involved in the rescue and body retrieval mission in the hours and days following. Family members of the victims read messages of loss, love and grief while survivors spoke of scars and steps in their recovery being constant reminders of their ordeal. The second anniversary of the Whakaari/White Island tragedy in 2019 was more low key, marked by a community memorial gathering in Whakatane where prayers and reflection dedicated to the victims, locals and first responders took place (Rolleston, 2021). Attendee numbers were limited to 100 people due to global pandemic Covid-19 restrictions at the time; however, it is anticipated that in the future there will be a national memorial observation which will provide an opportunity for those overseas people more directly impacted by the eruption to attend and be embraced by the local community (Rolleston, 2021). While an official memorial site is yet to be constructed for the Whakaari/White Island victims, in a sense, the volcanic island itself is considered a memorial site with the remains of two victims unrecovered. In addition, some survivors and victims' families are yet to return to the site to seek some form of closure within their recovery journey (if they so wish). Recognising that victims of this disaster included 20 foreign tourists from Australia, Germany and the USA, as well as New Zealanders (Taylor, 2020), pandemic travel restrictions were in place between 2020 and 2022. Moreover, several survivors are still undergoing treatment for their injuries, and this may have contributed to a delayed formal memorial development.

Similarly, the inaugural Canterbury Earthquake anniversary commemorative event in 2012 was attended by then New Zealand Prime Minister John Key and the Governor General Sir Jerry Mateparae among several other dignitaries. The memorial event was opened by a Māori blessing followed by the national anthem played by the New Zealand Army Band (Australian Geographic, 2012). Speeches emphasised the heavy emotion that the city was feeling because of such loss and devastation, with recognition made to first responders and rescue services. The local mayor spoke of looking towards the future and uniting as a community to recover and rebuild the city. Earthquake victims' names were also read out before a period of two minutes silence was observed (Australian Geographic, 2012). A separate commemoration was held earlier in the day, which focused on the families of the earthquake victims. The ten-year memorial service in 2021 was held at the Canterbury Earthquake National Memorial with Prime Minister Jacinda Ardern delivering a speech and an emotive poem, followed by music played by the New Zealand Army Band. As part of the commemoration event, flowers were displayed in construction cones and attendees participated in the annual River of Flowers by throwing flowers into the Avon and Heathcote rivers. In the lead up to the 10th anniversary commemorative event, some survivors shared their stories via several media platforms; many recalling the day's events and how it had impacted their daily lives in subsequent years. Many expressed their gratitude to their rescuers and reflected upon their changed outlook upon life because of surviving the tragic disaster event. Some survivors noting that they were living each day as if it were their last and recognised increased community cohesiveness because of the disaster. Some survivors have remained in Christchurch to heal as a community, while others have chosen to leave for them to be able to recover mentally from the earthquake (New Zealand Herald, 2021a, 2021b).

At these commemorative events held at Marysville, Christchurch and Whakatane there were a variety of interpretative techniques used, such as symbolism, poetry and first-hand accounts by survivors and family members of the victims. Thus, the portfolio of commemorative events held on the anniversaries of the natural disasters appear to involve and engage the survivors and families of the victims, with the inclusion of first-hand accounts assisting the memories and reflections to be more powerful, emotive and heartfelt. Moreover, there appears to be a difference in the content of first and second anniversaries compared to the 10th anniversary. The first and second anniversaries reflected raw grief and high emotions, while on the 10th anniversary, it was more reflective; acknowledging the passage of time and various stages of grief. However, in each case, survivor contributions were poignant, local, personal and not necessarily designed for consumption by tourists or those not associated with the area. Poetry and flowers were also prominent at each of the commemoration events, with poetry within memorialisation often used to emphasise 'hope and healing' as well as helping to assist people with managing grief and to remember (Luger, 2015: 183).

Memorialisation and Grief Management

At the Marysville Memorial there is little evidence of individual survivor reflections, but more evidence of bold, positive statements about the community. For example, the phrase written in the largest font located on the inscription wall at the Marysville Memorial states: *We must all move forward together but must never forget*. On one of the columns, it also states: *Community: New growth, new hopes, the magic will return again – a community united*, with other words appearing around the site including *renewal, united, remembered, loved, regrowth, regeneration* and *cherished*. Thus, the Marysville Memorial emphasises a need for the community to regenerate to ensure its survival. This may reflect that a considerable amount of time (nine years at the time of writing) had passed between the tragedy and the opening of the Marysville memorial. Indeed, this time may have inadvertently accommodated the physical and emotional recovery of the local community, given the bushfires caused the destruction of 90% of the buildings in the town (Silvester, 2019; Figures 12.1 and 12.2).

The following sentences also appear on the wall of the Marysville Memorials:

> Smoke curls up to mingle with a bleached sky and the fires herald their beginning. The hot wind whips up the flames into frenzy until the earth is blackened, houses are lost and people perish. Whole lives are changed or destroyed, never to be the same again and we grieve for the terrible losses. We reach out to help each other where we can.

This reflects that the local community impacted by the natural disaster is transitioning through various cycles of grief. Indeed, it demonstrates

Figures 12.1 and 12.2 Marysville Memorial
Source: Frew (Author).

that the community is moving to the final stage of acceptance (Kübler-Ross, 1970) of the tragedy over time, reflected in the focus of the memorial being on the future, renewal and regeneration of the community.

Meanwhile, the Canterbury Earthquake National Memorial, Christchurch, was unveiled in 2017 on the 6th anniversary of the earthquake and was created using NZ$10 million from the Government and an additional $1 million from the Mayoral Relief Fund (Killick, 2015). It pays respect to those 185 people who lost their lives in the earthquake and those who were seriously injured and survivors. The memorial also acknowledges the shared trauma and the support received during the response and recovery that followed (Canterbury Earthquake Memorial, 2022). Survivors and families of victims gave feedback on six shortlisted memorial designs from over 330 submissions (Canterbury Earthquake Memorial, 2022). The memorial was carefully designed based upon 'ideas to remember' and included input from survivors as well as victims' family members. Suggestions to incorporate water and greenery to create a peaceful and beautiful space were made, a place to remember and to find peace, and a place of past and future (Canterbury Earthquake Memorial, 2022). The memorial designed by Slovenian architect Grega Vezjak. It consists of two separate areas along either side of the Avon River, including a park on the north bank containing trees, gardens and seating looking out over the river towards the memorial wall situated on the south bank (Canterbury Earthquake Memorial, 2022). Some survivors voiced their concern regarding the appropriateness of the selected memorial being a 3.5 metre wall made of heavy marble, particularly as many victims were crushed by similar heavy objects. However, the memorial was selected as it was considered 'an evocative and powerful expression of loss and remembrance, an elegant and contemporary design that was a strong civic statement' (Canterbury Earthquake Memorial, 2022; Figure 12.3).

The memorial wall lists the 185 victims' names and states:

> We remember those who died, those who were hurt and those who experienced loss. We offer our thanks to those who came for us, to those who risked their lives for ours, and to those who supported us. Together we are stronger.

Any non-perishable mementos such as heartfelt notes and cards which are placed at the memorial following each 22nd February anniversary are collected by the Canterbury Museum. These have been added to the museum's collection and may be displayed in the future to assist in sharing the story of the Canterbury Earthquake (Canterbury Earthquake Memorial, 2022). In November 2022, the authors visited the site (Figure 12.4) and saw a note located below the name of

Figure 12.3 Canterbury Earthquake National Memorial
Source: Frew (Author).

25-year-old Matthew McEachen, signed by his mother, father and sister which said:

> Please don't ask if I am over it yet, I'll never get over it. Please don't tell me he is in a better place. He's not here with us. Please don't say at least he isn't suffering. I haven't come to terms with why he had to suffer at all. Please don't tell me you know how I feel, unless you have lost a child. Please don't ask if I feel better, bereavement isn't a condition that clears up. Please don't tell me we had him for so many years. What year would you choose for your child to die? Please don't tell me God never gives us more than we can bear. Please just say you are sorry. Please just say you remember our child. Please mention our child's name. Please just let me cry.

In the Christchurch memorial example, survivor voices were heard via the feedback on the initial memorial design. In addition, there is evidence of occasional informal responses from families of the victims through deposited notes and cards on site. However, there is no evidence of formal survivor voices included on the memorial wall itself. Instead, the quote provided above simply thanks the first responders and rescuers and recognises the importance of the community coming together to heal. Thus, a criticism of the Marysville and Canterbury Memorial sites may be the lack of strong onsite survivor voices. The encouragement at

McEachen – Aged 25
Please don't ask me if I am over it yet, I'll never get over it
Please don't tell me he is in a better place, He's not here with us
Please don't say at least he isn't suffering
I haven't come to terms with why he had to suffer at all
Please don't tell me you know how I feel, unless you have lost a child
Please don't ask me if I feel better,
Bereavement isn't a condition that clears up
Please don't tell me we had him for so many years
What year would you choose for your child to die?
Please don't tell me God never gives us more than we can bear
Please just say you are sorry,
Please just say you remember our child
Please mention our child's name, Please just let me cry
In loving memory of Matti, who will always be Loved & in our hearts forever
Mum (Jeanette) Dad (Bruce) & Sister (Sarah)

Figure 12.4 Canterbury Earthquake National Memorial
Source: Frew (Author).

these memorials for the survivors, the families of victims and the local surrounding community to move forward together as a community. Indeed, they are encouraged to progress through the grief cycle which may, subsequently, reflect the government and community desire that people have reached the final grief stage of acceptance (Kübler-Ross, 1970). Moreover, it reflects that the community is looking towards the future for the sake of community renewal and regeneration. This may reveal an example of Atkinson-Phillips' (2022) neat narrative of 'closure' where time has passed with the associated hope that the community is recovering. However, the informal responses by some bereaved families may suggest that for some families of victims this is not the necessarily the situation.

Disaster education and disaster preparedness

Prior to the 2009 Victorian bushfires, residents living in communities with bushfire risk were advised by the relevant government authorities such as the Country Fire Authority (CFA) to *prepare, stay and defend or leave early*. In other words, residents were expected to have an awareness of the bushfire related risks to their property and their associated safety and were expected to prepare themselves and their property for the impact of bushfires, taking account of their own circumstances. Since the 2009 bushfires the government advice is similar in terms of resident planning and preparedness, but there is now a strong emphasis on resident self-evacuation (Handmer *et al.*, 2019).

The Ash Wednesday Bushfire Education Centre tells the stories of the eight major fires in Victoria on 16 February 1983 and contains many photos of the struggle by communities and individuals during and after the bushfires. The education centre is in the former kindergarten which was saved from demolition by the community and restored into an education centre to tell the story of the bushfires in the area. The centre has touch screen computers that hold substantial amounts of information, including statistics and photos of the fire affected areas from all over Victoria. A large LCD screen provides continuous video footage of news stories and interviews with those associated with the fires. The building and information contained within, is described as a 'fantastic resource for students doing research into bushfires for school projects' (Ash Wednesday Bushfire Education Centre, 2021). In the garden, the CFA has provided information to assist people in understanding what to do when living or travelling in high fire danger areas. For example, the CFA encourages residents to actively protect themselves and their property by asking and then answering the following question: *How a bushfire can destroy lives?* Answer: *Ember attack, radiant heat, direct flame contact, wind*. Another CFA sign offers suggestions about using non-flammable mulch in the garden to limit the advance of the bushfire towards property and there is information on choosing fire-wise plants including indigenous species, with a link to the CFA website to help people select fire-wise plants for their gardens (Melbourne Playgrounds, 2022).

Conclusion

This chapter discusses how best to commemorate lives lost due to natural disasters in Australia and New Zealand and makes predictions about future memorialisation. There appears to be a trend at natural disaster sites to incorporate educational aspects in the commemoration which raises awareness among visitors on how to behave if the emergency arises again which, in turn, helps protect locals and visitors from avoidable deaths. The inclusion of disaster education at such sites is a trend that is likely to continue as it reflects the inevitability of bushfires in Australia and earthquakes in New Zealand, and the need to educate communities to minimise risk to both residents and visitors to the region.

At the memorial sites, care needs to be taken by event organisers to ensure voices of the survivors who experienced the tragedy first hand and/or who have lost loved ones in the tragedy are included at such events. Consequently, this may help in their gradual emotional and physical recovery. At commemorative events staged on the anniversary of tragic events, the inclusion of survivor voices can be important as it allows the event attendees to hear first-hand accounts from survivors. The inclusion of survivor voices at these commemorative events and their integration into physical memorials can add a level of poignancy to the event/site. This is through recognition of personal losses of family and friends and associated impacts on local community cohesion. It also helps with authenticity as it reflects the thoughts and feelings of the local community rather than visitors. Thus, the portfolio of commemorative events held on the anniversaries of the tragic events appear to involve and engage the survivors and families of the victims, with the inclusion of first-hand accounts assisting the memories and reflections to be more powerful and heartfelt.

The contemporary memorials examined within this chapter were built after a considerable passage of time and appear to focus on moving on from the natural disaster and re-establishing the community, with a recognition of the importance of recovering from the tragedy to ensure the community survives. Allowing the local community's recovery to transition further through the grief cycle over time may be reflected in the more bold, positive statements echoing community growth and unity, with hope and regeneration specifically noted at the Marysville and Christchurch sites. Stories and reflections from survivors can now be seen more frequently as part of the on-site events at contemporary memorials, and this is likely to continue in the future. However, these anniversary events and contemporary memorials are not primarily designed with tourists in mind. Instead, their primarily focus appears to be on the survivors, the family of victims and the recovery of the local community. Further research into the role of survivor voices at the physical memorial and commemorative event is required, and a recognition that when designing such memorials, the grief among survivors and family of victims may not necessarily have been completely resolved.

13 Future of Dark Tourism in Kosovo: From Divisions to Digital Possibilities

Abit Hoxha and Kenneth Andresen

Introduction

Kosovo has received limited attention in the literature when it comes to dark tourism. However, this young nation and the smallest country in the Balkans, with a dramatic and often tragic past of wars and conflicts, has potential for dark tourism development. The purpose of this chapter, therefore, is to highlight dark tourism within Kosovo and, in so doing, examine inherent dissonance in memorialisation at the interface of the visitor economy, as well as outlining potential future interpretations of Kosovo's contested past. In framing dark tourism, Stone (2006: 146) defines it as 'deaths, disasters and atrocities in touristic form are becoming an increasingly pervasive feature within the contemporary tourism landscape, and as such, are ever more providing potential spiritual journeys for the tourist who wishes to gaze upon real and recreated death'. This is an accurate description of travels to locations of past violence throughout Kosovo both for Albanians and Serbs in Kosovo.

Both these ethnic groups are drawn to various places of memory and commemoration which represent conflicting historical events. As Dresler and Fuchs (2020) note regarding sites of dark tourism in the framework of venues for exploration of moral judgements and behaviours, it is obvious that Kosovo is a destination for dark tourism which is manifested either in the form of political tourism or pilgrimage to religious sites. Both these forms of tourism are materialised in various activities at key dark tourism destinations in Kosovo.

Dark Tourism in Kosovo

Kosovo is a recently created country which declared independence from Serbia in 2008, in the aftermath of the Kosovo War in 1998–1999, which led to NATO bombing the former Yugoslavia over a two-month period in 1999. Knowledge about dark tourism in Kosovo is limited and, thus far, has not been studied as an academic discipline but rather a political cause in recent years. That said, Stone and Sharpley (2008: 574) argue that 'despite increasing academic attention paid to dark tourism, understanding of the concept remains limited, particularly from a consumption perspective. That is, the literature focuses primarily on the supply of dark tourism; less attention, however, has been paid to the demand for "dark" touristic experiences'. Visiting sites where violence took place in the near past in Kosovo is part of official history lessons whereby children visit sites as a learning excursion. Thus, this activity is institutionalised, but more as a developed tradition rather than a planned educational strategy. As noted by Sharma 'dark tourism, which deploys taboo subjects and commercially exploits the macabre, has always raised moral conflicts at a collective and individual level while providing new spaces' (2020: 273), whereby these visits often raise questions of exploitative or educational experiences. With some exceptions, most venues of dark tourism lack explanations, information and learning opportunities for visitors in Kosovo. Additionally, most historic sites in Kosovo tell a one-sided story of war, supporting the narratives of one part in the conflict, its victims and dark past. This adds to the arguments of it being a *political pilgrimage* more than a learning experience for visitors.

The destinations of dark tourism in Kosovo have a grim backdrop. During the Kosovo War, according to the Humanitarian Law Centre (HLC), 13,000 people were killed (Domanovic, 2014). In 2014, HLC released a list of people who were killed or went missing during the war, including 8661 Kosovo Albanian civilians, 1797 ethnic Serbs and 447 civilians who were members of other ethnicities such as the Romani people and Bosniaks. The story of war in Kosovo is one of the main fields where dark tourism developed after violence ceased in 1999. In places such as Prekaz in central Kosovo, Racak in eastern Kosovo and Meje in western Kosovo, venues where massacres were committed by Serbian forces are on show. These gravesites have been turned into visiting sites and pilgrimage destinations for millions of visitors every year (Kult Plus, 2018).

Commemoration events offer a unique opportunity to witness the perspective of 'dark tourism' in the framework of a desire to learn about history and to better understand causes of such tragedies, as well as paying respect to victims. Indeed, fascination with the conflicted and dark past is a common theme in all political tourism in Kosovo (Piña, 2021). Public commemorations, including politicians and other public figures, emphasise the call to people to visit these places. It is here that dark tourism in Kosovo offers what Stone (2012a: 1565) calls 'a modern mediating institution which not only provides a physical place to link the living with the dead, but also allows a cognitive space for the Self to construct contemporary ontological meanings of mortality'.

Dark Tourism Sites in Kosovo

Kosovo's political tourism developed after the war. Kosovar Albanians mostly visit sites related to the last war and resistance against Serbian rule over Kosovo, most of them turned into 'pilgrimage places important for the nation' (Di Lellio *et al.*, 2013). Meanwhile, Serbs visit older religious sites that have become more important in lieu of political developments and political venues that have become more religious for the same reasons. These places, either commemorating the Battle of Kosovo in 1389, or Orthodox monasteries, have received a renewed political significance, especially after Kosovo declared independence. In the Serbian political sphere, these places are described as 'threatened' or 'in danger' and calls are frequently made to Serbs to visit these pilgrimage places (Ryassaphore Nun Natalia, n.d.). However, two places are worthy of mention in this chapter, namely the Memorial Complex Adem Jashari, and the Racak Massacre site.

Memorial Complex Adem Jashari

A certain type of tourism has developed in response to violent acts of killing in the Kosovo War where, now, the sacrifices and resistance are *celebritised*. Prekaz i Poshtëm is a village near Skënderaj in central Kosovo. As a stronghold of the Kosovo Liberation Army (KLA) in the 1990s, it has become a symbol of resistance against Serbian rule of Kosovo. Traditionally, venues for visiting Prekaz extend from the early 1900s until the last resistance act of Jashari Family in 1998, where 28 members of this family were killed in their own house resisting a brutal attack from Serbian forces. Elsie (2010) describes Adem Jashari as someone who became a legend with his heroic death. 'With his fierce resistance and dramatic death, Adem Jashari, the *legendary commander* [original emphasis], became a quintessence of the Albanian freedom fighter determined to rid Kosovo of Serb occupation and was hailed as a martyr for the KLA' (Elsie, 2010: 142). Elsie (2010: 142) also offers especially valuable information regarding visits on this site by suggesting that 'what is left of the compound of Jashari family in Prekaz has been preserved as a museum and has become the object of mass pilgrimage in recent years'.

Presently, the Memorial Complex Adem Jashari (Figure 13.1) is extended throughout the village, which includes the original house of the Jashari family, the *kulla* (a distinct Ottoman 'tower' building traditionally designed to symbolise resistance or to offer security), original garden, a small museum/souvenir shop, a former bunker

Figure 13.1 Memorial Complex Adem Jashari in Prekaz
Source: Komuna e Skenderajt (CC BY-NC-ND).

where Jashari used to shelter and the gravesite. This place of collective memory entered governmental plans immediately in 1999 with the idea to preserve and maintain it as a symbol of resistance. In 2015, it was listed on the List of Cultural Heritage sites under temporary protection to preserve it from private and municipal interventions which would be contrary to government plans for this complex (Decision 116/2015). The municipality that Prekaz is part of has constructed an identity of Serbian rule resistance, most notably through venues of collective memory. On the web page of Municipality of Skenderaj (Online), four main 'kulla' are in primary visual presentation, with an emphasis of resistance.

Prekaz and the Memorial Complex Adem Jashari is seen as a site where visitors can learn about the killing of an entire family, except for two survivors, learn the history of the KLA, as well as looking to the future. The tour in the Memorial Complex includes talks about the family, and how some family members who were living in Germany at the time of the massacre are now living near the Memorial Complex. The Parliament of Kosovo declared the area of the Memorial Complex a zone with special interest enforced by law, and where the national guard of the Kosovo Security Forces (KSF) stands indefinitely in honour of the fallen.

Consequently, the Memorial Complex Adem Jashari has become one of the most important venues to visit for the entire Albanian population, inside and outside Kosovo. In 2022, the museum curator, working to exhibit and explain events to visitors, explained that, in the last 23 years of its existence, Memorial Complex Adem Jashari is estimated to have been visited by 12 million visitors according to local media reports of Kult Plus (2018). This has been possible because many people go there annually or during the summer holidays, including organised school visits, joint excursions from unions of teachers and employees, as well as the Albanian diaspora. Prekaz is also referred to as the *Albanian Mekka,* implying that every Albanian should go on a pilgrimage to pay respect to the fallen in resistance against Serbian rule of Kosovo. Thus, this site can be considered a place of pilgrimage with a sacred meaning. To that end, in 2004, the Kosovo Assembly regulated it by law as an 'area with special national interest which has an ontological, anthropological, historical, and cultural significance for Kosovo citizens' (Law No.2004/39).

Moreover, the figure of Adem Jashari has become a mythical figure. Di Lellio and Schwandner-Sievers (2006: 157) suggest that 'the representation of Adem Jashari as the legendary commander began in the immediate aftermath of the event, when he became the rallying point for KLA recruits in Kosovo and abroad'. To date, this narrative of 'Legendary Commander' exists and is used in imagery and memorabilia of the events. Furthermore, Di Lellio and Schwanderner-Sievers (2006: 28) argue that 'the site's appeal to its visitors relies on the fact that it serves as a "frontstage" [after Goffman, 1959] for the expression of Pan Albanian national concerns'. Therefore, the relationship between Memorial Complex Adem Jashari and dark tourism can be explained through framing travel and tourism in association with death, disaster and destruction that has long fascinated people (Piña, 2021). The fact the site commemorates a gruesome event that happened only a few decades ago adds to the notion that tragedy is never far. Indeed, it is not only a place of dark tourism but also a place of recent documentation of war crimes.

The Račak Massacre

Račak is a village in eastern Kosovo. In January 1999, Serbian forces attacked the village and killed 45 Kosovar Albanians. The Kosovo Verification Mission (OSCE) head at the time, Ambassador William Walker, a retired American diplomat, on his visit to Račak, found bodies scattered in a valley near the village where victims had been mutilated. Walker declared this event as 'a crime very much against humanity' and condemned what he labelled 'an unspeakable atrocity' (BBC News Europe, 1999b). US President Bill Clinton condemned it as a massacre and, subsequently, William Walker was declared a *persona non grata* by the Serbian government. This was considered a critical juncture in the Kosovo War, which led to NATO intervention against Yugoslavia. It resulted in a 78-day military air campaign that brought Serbia to the table to sign the Kumanovo Agreement, whereby NATO forces (KFOR) entered Kosovo as peacekeepers (NATO, 1999).

Račak is especially important in Kosovo's past as it marks a turning point in recent history and the site is visited by thousands annually. Mostly, the anniversary is commemorated under the direct patronage of the State institutions. However, Račak is not an ordinary story of war, where the struggle of narrative persists and differs accordingly within various public discourses. Immediately after the massacre and the international media attention it received, the Serbian Government invited an 'independent' forensic commission from Belorussia to join the Yugoslav forensic experts and investigate what has happened in Račak. At the same time, a Finnish team of forensic investigators and forensic anthropologists were investigating. The Belorussian and Yugoslav commission generated a report that all the victims, including a 12-year-old, were separatist guerrillas and not civilians (BBC News Europe, 1999b). The Finnish investigator who led the independent investigation, anthropology expert Dr Helena Ranta, called it a 'crime against humanity', though refusing as a scientist to directly label it a massacre or assign blame to any specific party (Gall, 1999). Later, Slobodan Milosevic (former President of Serbia and Yugoslavia) and his subordinates were accused of war crimes and crimes against humanity including the massacre of Račak (ICTY, 1999).

This event is particularly opposed in Serbian narratives of war in Kosovo as it marks the turning point of the West against Serbia which, subsequently, led to NATO intervention. Serbian President Aleksandar Vucic denied the event, calling it a hoax and fabricated massacre (Isufi, 2019). Several films and documentaries in Serbia were made fuelling conspiracies about the CIA (the American foreign intelligence service) involvement and international plans to blame Serbia for wrongdoings as a trigger for the NATO bombing. RTS, the public television service in Serbia, made a documentary in 2019 called 'Racak, Lies and Truths', where experts discuss how the massacre was fabricated In 1999, The Independent newspaper writes about Račak: 'in Kosovo's capital, Pristina, access to the main forensic laboratory is blocked by armed guards from Serbia's special police. Inside, Serbia is attempting to rewrite history' (Neely, 1999). However, the report of Finnish forensic investigation clearly confirms the violent deaths of civilians, including women and a 12-year-old boy.

Račak is a space of turmoil and, consequently, now a place of dark tourism because the massacre is commemorated in Kosovo annually with statements and commemorative musical pieces (Figure 13.2). It is also used as a launching stage for political speeches and promises to address crimes against humanity, other war crimes and accusations of genocide from Serbia. In 2021, Kosovo officials announced the creation of a War Crimes Research Institute at the commemorative site, despite this institute being created twice before. Moreover, William Walker, the former OSCE ambassador and head of KVM in 1999 in Kosovo, participates in this commemoration almost every year, which has turned him into a 'political celebrity'.

Like the Memorial Complex Adem Jashari, Račak has become a site used for organised and private visits. Schools organise trips with

Figure 13.2 A memorial to the victims of the 1999 massacre in Recak/Račak
Source: *EPA/VALDRIN XHEMAJ* (CC BY-NC-ND).

pupils where the bodies of 45 people are buried. Nearby, a memorial like the Vietnam Veteran's Memorial in Washington DC (USA) exists with names and photographs of the victims and has a permanent ceremonial guard honouring the fallen. Within the Račak Memorial Complex, commemorative events are organised annually whereas, in Prekaz, in the Memorial Complex Adem Jashari, commemorative events take place also sporadically after elections, on the 28 November, the day of the Albanian flag and the birthday of Adem Jashari. Moreover, upon specific votes of the governmental cabinet, the entire cabinet visit to pay respects. Consequently, these places have turned into pilgrimage sites for Kosovars. They have developed educational material and documentation that confirm the events. However, in the Serbian narrative, these places represent something different. There, the events are denied, the victims are questioned and there are conspiracy theories of fake bodies and terrorists. These two extremely important memorial places for Kosovar Albanians are thus attacked a second time, not only physically but also in memory. As a result, this heightens the places' sacredness for the Albanians and to offer quasi-religious–political sites for touristic consumption.

Dark Tourism and Quasi-Religious-Political Sites

The Kosovo population is mainly Albanian (about 95%), and the rest are ethnic minorities, including a Kosovo Serb minority. Kosovo Serbs, besides political and social ties with Serbia, also have a close relationship with the Serbian Orthodox Church, which has many religious sites in Kosovo including the Patriarchy of Peja/Pec, the Visoki Decani Monastery and the Monastery of Gracanica. These religious sites are important to Serbian visitors and tourists in many ways, including for political and religious reasons. In addition to religious sites in Kosovo, Serbian history is tied to Kosovo within a political context. For example, myths connected with the Battle of Kosovo (1389) and commemorating the Gazimestan Tower Monument amalgamate religious, political and historic visits. For the Vidovdan, it has turned into an annual Serb pilgrimage on 28 June with many organised tours from Serbia. The Vidovdan is a Serbian national and religious holiday designated by the Serbian Orthodox Church as a Memorial Day to Saint Prince Lazar and the Serbian holy martyrs who fell during the Battle of Kosovo against the Ottoman Empire.

However, unlike the commemoration places in Prekaz and Račak, as noted earlier, the Gazimestan represents events of hundreds of years ago. This 'chronological distance' augments mythical effects too. The site does not end with historical, religious and political tourism but continues further with the (re)generation of myths for political and religious reasons. The Gazimestan Monument was constructed in 1956 by infamous Serbian prime minister Aleksandar Rankovic, who was known for his anti-Albanian stance and, consequently, this monument is seen by many Albanians in that context as well. Gazimestan Monument is designed to look medieval and old and uses Cyrillic inscriptions to 'curse' those who are not ready to defend Kosovo. This site is also the place where Slobodan Milosevic delivered his infamous speech on the 28 June 1989 in his attempt to use the Battle of Kosovo as a victory against the Ottoman Empire to launch his nationalistic agenda by the 'retelling' of myths and mythmaking. Historic research demonstrates that Balkans forces included Serbs, Albanians, Hungarians and others who organised resistance to the Ottoman Empire and epic songs tell a different story (Di Lellio, 2009). However, this does not stop Gazimestan from being a place of annual pilgrimage, where Serbian youngsters wearing T-shirts with images of Milosevic and Ratko Mladic try to visit the site as if it was a holy place. Additionally, Serbian Orthodox priests and monks join in this pilgrimage, thus turning Gazimestan monument into a religious pilgrimage site for their own interests.

Notwithstanding, this pilgrimage is also politicised. Kosovar police make efforts to prevent hateful expressions and potential eruption of violence by asking visitors to remove T-shirts with Milosevic and Ratko Mladic, yet this is mostly met with resistance (Prishtina Insight, 2022). Potential confrontation with the police is also part of the pilgrimage ritual as most visitors expect this and try to hide T-shirts with these images to smuggle them inside and take 'heroic' selfies from the inside or on top of the Gazimestan monument (Radio Free Europe, 2022). Many of these confrontations are later published on social media as another 'attack' by Albanians and renewed Serbian suffering.

Pilgrimage and dark tourism

While Gazimestan is the epicentre of Serbian (dark tourism) pilgrimage in Kosovo, other religious sites are also part of spiritual pilgrimages that Serbs from Serbia and Kosovo undertake. The 'dark tourism' angle to this is the fact that the travel itself is seen as 'sacrifice' because of the perceived risks that are involved in travelling into and around Albanian populated areas. For instance, travel to the Monastery of Decani, in western Kosovo, involves about two hours of travel in Albanian controlled areas, where even being stopped by the traffic police is seen as attempt to prevent Serbs from holy pilgrimage. Similarly, the Patriarchy of Pec is part of organised and private pilgrimages that Serbs take, especially around religious celebrations. These two sites represent centuries of Christian Orthodox practice in Kosovo. In addition to the religious significance, the sites have become highly politicised by the Serbian Orthodox Church. Therefore, Serbs are called to go there. This requires preparations and is described as 'high risk' travel in the Serbian public sphere. Moreover, as it is often difficult for Serbs to stay in Peja in hotels due to inter-ethnic distrust, visiting the Patriarchy always requires preparation, reservation to sleep over and other travel restrictions.

One of the other destinations for dark tourism in the region is also the site where several youngsters of Serbian ethnicity were shot in Peja, which is often referred to as the Panda Bar Massacre. In 1998, while armed conflicts between KLA (Kosovo Liberation Army) and Serbian forces were erupting throughout Kosovo, a group of armed men entered a coffee shop (Café Panda) in the city of Peja and murdered six Kosovo Serbian boys, wounding 15 others. Presently, it is unclear who committed this terrible crime. Widespread belief is that this crime was done by the Serbian secret service to blame the Albanian side for terrorist acts to erupt violence in Kosovo (Haxhijaj, 2018). The investigation is still ongoing but visits to this site are also part of the routes taken by the Serbian tourists in Kosovo.

Overall, Serbian routes of tourism in Kosovo are devolved in two directions that intertwine. Visits to religious sites, which combine dark tourism elements because of perceived degrees of violence and threats associated with these travels, and political tourism, which is associated with political violence, difficult heritage and death. However, it is worth noting that an increasing trend of narratives on social media is used as a mobilisation tool for such pilgrimage and uses hashtags such as that they will be in Prizren next year. Prizren is known for being an important city in religious terms as it served as a centre of a diocese of the Serbian Orthodox Church.

Dissonance and dark tourism

Contrary to the widespread belief that victims of past conflict and sites are biased, in Kosovo there are instances of Kosovo Albanians, Serbs and other ethnicities that were victims of war (crimes) and violence. These memorials are part of the touristic destination precisely because of controversies that they entail and stories that are generated when such memorials are constructed with the attempt to historic revisionism. For example, a monument in Mitrovica, a city that is still divided into the northern part mainly controlled by Serbs and the southern part mainly controlled by Albanians, was constructed in 2015 in commemoration of victims of a rocket attack in the market square. The victims involved children of Roma ethnicity, but their names were not part of the memorial plaque with engraved names of the Albanian victims. This brought the attention of civil society organisations in Kosovo and, upon public pressure, the names of the Roma children were added to the monument. This has caused controversial dissonance debates and generated visits to the venue due to fascination with the fact of names being added after the monument was inaugurated.

Similarly, a monument was erected in the village of Luzhan, near Podujeva in eastern Kosovo, commemorating the death of Kosovo Albanians on a bus hit by a NATO rocket. Victims of the attack included several Serbian individuals travelling on the same bus during the NATO campaign against the former Yugoslavia, but the commemorative monument includes only names of Albanians. Lack of Serbian names in the memorial caused a flux of Serbian pilgrimages and visits precisely to see the absence of Serbian victims in the memorial. Of course, while dissonance is inherent within memorial messages, in Kosovo and elsewhere, the recent conflicted past and difficult heritage makes for a dark tourism future.

The Future of Dark Tourism in Kosovo

Fascination with difficult (his)stories of the past is very much part of the dark tourism industry and troubled and conflicted pasts are the stuff of dark tourism. The Kosovo War has many gaps in its documentation and narratives are still in the making. War crimes are still under investigation and court-based truths, witnesses accounts and stories told by different sides involved in the conflict are insufficient to establish official histories. As fascination with the past presents an opportunity to create learning tools, the future of dark tourism in Kosovo leans towards digitalisation and digital tools as commemorative spaces. In recent years, digital infrastructures have been designed and built to serve as memory space.

Digital and virtual reality museums

Previous descriptions draw a picture of a highly divided landscape of dark tourism sites in Kosovo, mostly along ethnic lines. These sites represent different things in the Albanian and Serbian collective memory.

Therefore, a question arises as to whether places of commemoration exist that represents less division? To that end, a constructive example is the digital School-House Virtual Museum, known as Hertica Family School House (Tur, 2022), which depicts a private home turned into a school under the parallel system of education in a segregationist policy for education in Kosovo in the 1990s. Indeed, private homes were often turned into schools and pupils attended these schools in improvised classrooms.

This virtual museum is a digital reality construction that enables the viewer to visit inside the house of the Hertica family and is constructed based on real case scenario photographs from the 1990s. The house was attacked and burned in 1999 by Serbian forces and is now under the protection of the Ministry of Culture as a special interest building under the list of protected heritage objects in Prishtina. The museum is a virtual reality exhibition of parallel life in Kosovo organised as a form of non-violent resistance. Such digital tools can be transported and exhibited in different museums, and all that is needed is a computer and VR equipment. Consequently, with this tool, technological ability is presented to bring museums into schools, community centres and even homes for subjects that are difficult or contested to reconstruct or do not exist any longer. This place represents a very vital part of the Kosovar society during the 1980s and 1990s and most Albanians can identify with it. The challenge for future developers, however, is how these virtual spaces can become a place that not merely increases division, but also can draw up a common site and narrative of memory for Kosovo.

Digital tours

Digital tours offer contested and competing memory spaces in Kosovo and, subsequently, is another digital tool that presents an excellent opportunity for the future of dark tourism in Kosovo. A present example is a digital tool (app) being developed by Clio Muse under EU funding through the RePAST project (RePAST, 2023) which stands for *Strengthening European Integration through the Analysis of Conflict Discourses: RePAST – Revisiting the Past, Anticipating the Future.* This digital tour in the capital of Kosovo presents 10 different venues with total of 50 stories. These offer narratives from different sides of the conflict to explain layers of conflict and 'truths' from the troubled past. It is designed to provide a walking tour that visitors will be able to follow through Google Maps. Instructions within the app provide varying perspectives and stories about the dark tourism destination, as selected by the team which constructed the app. According to the developers, 'the tour highlights the country's history, the struggle of the citizens and the atrocities that forced half of the population to abandon the country' (Clio Muse Tours, 2023). The tour is called 'contested and competing memory spaces in Kosovo' and includes the Youth Palace named after two socialist Yugoslav partisan heroes; the NEWBORN monument that marks Kosovo Independence day; the Monument of Heroines which commemorates 20,000 raped women during the war in Kosovo; narratives on the former US Secretary of State Madeleine Albright in respect for her dedication to Kosovo; the Brotherhood and Unity monument representing the former leader of peaceful movement; the medieval national hero Gjergj Kastrioti Skenderbeu; the Serbian Orthodox Church at the University of Prishtina campus as the Milosevic-era church was where conflict foundations were laid by religious leaders, but also Zelko Raznjatevic Arkan, a notorious paramilitary leader accused of war crimes in Bosnia and Hercegovina and Kosovo; and the final destination is the Martyr's Cemetery, which includes graves of partisans from the Second World War and as well as the recent war in a single cemetery.

Towards a digital future for memorial complexes

Kosovo is a young nation with high rate of digitalisation and internet penetration. This digital infrastructure is mostly used for communication and family relationships yet has hardly been developed for education and learning processes. In 2018, 79% of 15-year-olds had difficulty comprehending a text of moderate length and complexity, a much higher proportion than the Western Balkans' average of 54% (OECD, 2020). As a result, critics often point out that that Kosovo institutions are in digital poverty in relation to dealing with its troubled past. With a lack of strategic approach to dealing with the past, and knowledge about the past, fascination with the dark past and violence is not provided by regular channels. Furthermore, interpretation of the past is subject to amplifications and misrepresentation due to the distilled nature of historical narratives. Museums, venues of notable events, memorials, monuments and even grave sites rarely have adequate explanations that serve educative purposes and often are subject to glorified and amplified narratives of the dissonant past.

Digital spaces provide a unique (future) opportunity for political tourism and dark tourism in Kosovo. These infrastructures provide real case scenarios and folds of realities which can lead to multi-interpretations of the past within an inclusive manner. Oral histories in digital space potentially provide accounts of witnesses and varying perspectives of the same story, whereas court documents and official documentation give another layer of reality for visitors. As the Kosovo government has invested in turning these places into pilgrimage sites for many, on the one hand attempting to establish political narratives of the Kosovo Liberation Army, on the other hand, they highlight the victimhood of Kosovars. Moreover, it is much more efficient to create a digital space that will enable access to these sites from across the globe. Although investment in preserving the story and finding truths, finding perpetrators and bringing them to justice has not been a main priority thus far, providing space for layers of truths will have a positive impact on the interpretation of this conflicted history. Instead of decades of grandiose plans with infrastructures and developmental projects built with concrete, digital spaces provide a future possibility to connect youth in an appealing way with mobile devices. After the Kosovo War in 1999, most of the site where massacres and atrocities took place turned into a spectacle and tourist destination for many. So far, it is estimated that 12 million visitors have visited *Memorial Complex Adem Jashari* in Prekaz (Kult Plus, 2018), making it the most visited place in Kosovo. Memorial complexes of the future can take advantage of this interest, although digital possibilities of commemoration and remembrance are still in their infancy.

Conclusion

This chapter has described the current situation for dark tourism in Kosovo, as well as offering a future scenario where digital possibilities will be in the vanguard of dark tourism interpretation. Within Kosovo, the main places of commemoration of violence, war and suffering are places that represent one ethnic side. The memorial complexes in Prekaz and Račak are extremely important for the main populace, the Kosovar Albanians. They are important for the continued learning about Kosovo's troubled past. There is a collective understanding to develop these places. Yet, at the same time, it is a fact that these places are discredited by the other side of the conflict, namely in Serbia. This does not lessen the importance of the memorial places. On the contrary, it shows that such places are important. However, in a multi-ethnic society like Kosovo, it is important to acknowledge that the past is contested, and dissonance is inherent. There is no immediate solution to this and that is not the goal. In Kosovo, places of Orthodox Christian heritage are treated as sacred for the Serbs and, as a result, they are highly politicised. Consequently, there appears to be limited desire to decrease this rhetoric within Serbian society.

Therefore, the challenge for dark tourism in Kosovo seems to be developing places of commemoration that can include a wider recognition of suffering on both sides of the conflict. Indeed, this chapter has offered examples of this whereby places of collective trauma from wars and conflicts will always be divisive and will never be neutral. While attempt at neutrality might dilute the truth, the future of digital technology has potential to engage more people, especially younger generations, but also those across societal divisions. This is crucial in Kosovo as, 25 years after the war, post-war generations are now constructing their own memory narratives of the conflict. Presently, it is a fundamental period for commemoration in Kosovo, but also for learning how mistakes from the past can be prevented in the future. Kosovo needs creativity and political willingness to invest in remembrance and cohesive memorialisation, and future dark tourism that can play a vital role in consuming and co-constructing cultural trauma.

14 Millennials, Transitional Memory and the Future of Holocaust Remembrance

Ann-Kathrin McLean

> The Holocaust was an unprecedented genocide, unprecedented because of its global form – not only Jews of Europe but of the whole world were intended to be annihilated. It was totally unpragmatic, it was purely ideological. It ran counter to the interests of Nazi Germany – economically, politically even militarily. And this is a precedent, it can be repeated, not in exactly the same form, nothing ever is. But in similar forms and it has already been in that form. And so, when we deal with mass atrocity hate crimes today, with genocides today, we need to start from the Holocaust. That is the basic importance of not just remembering but acting in accordance with the history that we are witnesses of. Thank you.
>
> Professor Yehuda Bauer
> Israeli historian and scholar of Holocaust Studies
> Avraham Harman Institute of Contemporary Jewry
> Hebrew University of Jerusalem
> (Source: United Nations, 2022)

Introduction

Learning about and understanding hate crimes of the past is essential to preventing monstrous atrocities such as the Holocaust from ever happening again. The future of the memory of the Holocaust is fragile as generations come and go, and we navigate past cultural trauma. The fallibility of managing, interpreting and mediating dark tourism, of which the Holocaust is (re)presented at many visitor sites, is becoming increasingly relevant. Indeed, as we witness revivals in fascist populism there is a growing disconnect between the past and learnings for a collective and peaceful future (McLean, 2023). As the number of eyewitnesses dwindles, millennials (that is, those born between 1981 and 1996) and other post-war generations rely on fractions of collective and cultural memory that shape a new form of memory of the Holocaust (McLean, 2023). As the anchor vector, (visitor) sites of memory face numerous challenges, including but not limited to their sustainability and place in an ever-growing contentious global environment.

Indeed, since the end of the Second World War, Germany continues to learn how to come to terms with the past and navigate cracks within its (genocidal) memory, culture and identity (Hoerner *et al.*, 2019; McLean, 2023; Salzborn, 2018). Understanding how younger post-war generations, such as millennials, navigate this culture is important as they embody a central narrative – as memory agents – for the future of Germany's identity. A careful investigation of acts of remembrance, forms of embodied commemoration and identification of personal values underscore this discussion. The purpose of this chapter, therefore, is to examine how millennial visitors at the Dachau Concentration Camp Memorial Site in Germany (hereafter referred to as Dachau) learn to explore Self and how the Self contributes to the fabric of an entire generation. In this chapter, I aim to advance our understanding of the relationship between Holocaust remembrance, collective memory and a site of trauma and, subsequently, how this relates to societal pressures to commemorate and remember the past. Based upon sociological grounding and informed by ethnographic research methods, this chapter focuses on human behaviour (Prus, 1996) and experiences shared within a group of millennial visitors at the (Dachau) site (Beim, 2007). This chapter contributes to understanding the future of Holocaust remembrance, specifically regarding the millennial generation, and is ordered as follows:

- Dachau as an anchor of history.
- Dark tourism and memoryscapes.
- Millennials and their social frameworks.
- The zone of transitional memory of the Holocaust for the millennial generation.
- Millennials and the future of Holocaust remembrance.

Dachau – An Anchor of History

The Dachau Memorial Site (approximately 20 km northwest of Munich, Germany) anchors history through artefacts, stories and memorial spaces. The site was a concentration camp that the Nazi regime used to torture, humiliate and destroy prisoners' identities (Eichert, 2019; Hausmair, 2018; McLean, 2023; Sivakumaran, 2007). At the time, minority groups at the camp such as Jews, Sinti and Roma people, homosexuals, as well as political activists, experienced Nazi horrors and its disturbing ideology (McLean, 2023). According to Marcuse (2001: 2), Dachau was 'the flagship concentration camp [that] also served as a *school of violence* [original emphasis] for concentration camp leaders'. Dachau was initially set up for 5000 prisoners (Záme ník, 2003); yet, toward the end of the Holocaust, around 750,000 prisoners suffered inhumane conditions at the camp (McLean, 2023; Záme ník, 2003: 22). Due to the inaccuracy of unreported deaths and mass graves, researchers today estimate that around 41,500 people lost their lives at the camp (Hammermann, 2014; McLean, 2023).

As an anchor vector, the site stands boldly as a reminder of a horrific past. In tandem with intersections of other vectors of memory, such as artefacts or films, as well as interpretive stories shared by guides and eyewitnesses, Dachau influences the zone of transitional memory of the Holocaust (McLean, 2023). The site is a vivid reminder of the implications of genocide, where elements of its narrative continue to shape contemporary discourse in various *lieux de memoire* (*site of memory*) today (Nora, 1989). Traumatic sites such as Dachau are significant spaces to learn about Holocaust remembrance, as we are witnessing a (re)emergence of xenophobia and antisemitism worldwide (Arrocha, 2019; Beller, 2020; Kendi, 2019; Lipstadt, 2019; United States Holocaust Memorial Museum, 2023). Recent examples of this trend include shootings at synagogues (Cogan, 2022), as well as vandalism of properties and harassment of specific groups (Hagen, 2022). Prominent celebrity figures, such as Ye West (formerly known as Kanye West, an American rapper and songwriter), openly share their hatred against other cultures, religions and ethnic groups by wearing clothing with the slogans 'White lives matter' or posting images on social media that show the Star of David (the symbol of both Jewish identity and Judaism) merged with a swastika (an ancient cultural symbol appropriated by the Nazi Party and neo-Nazis) (Cogan, 2022). It is examples like these that leads politicians such as Emmanuel Macron (President of France) to state 'let us open our eyes to the rise of xenophobia and antisemitism, tune our ear to the resurgence of racism. Let us never be fooled by the new clothing adopted by the same ideologies of division' (AP News, 2022: 6). Sites of memory, such as Dachau, are the most salient vector of memory to remind people about the horrors of the past and work against denialism, hate, racism and the (re)emergence of antisemitism (McLean, 2023).

The site, its buildings and its symbols enhance the holistic understanding of the magnitude of the Nazi regime and the implications of their twisted ideological approaches to human society. With each physical movement, a new image enters our consciousness, triggers a reaction and shifts our thinking and reflection. Thus, by visiting sites (through dark tourism) such as Dachau, millennials learn to engage in post-witnessing of the Holocaust and, through their experiences, inform the future of Holocaust remembrance (Walden, 2019).

Dark Tourism and Memoryscapes

Dachau, and its touristic consumption, is an example of what scholars have called *dark tourism* or *thanatourism* (Foley & Lennon, 1996a; Light, 2017b; Seaton, 1996, 1999; Stone, 2006, 2012a, 2012b, 2013a; Stone & Sharpley, 2008). Thanatourism acknowledges how individuals confront themselves with the theme of death (Light, 2017b). According to Seaton (1999), this type of tourism includes travel to sites of trauma, such as Dachau. For the visitor, dark tourism introduces tourists to a liminal experience between personal meaning made and symbolic interactions with the site of trauma (Backstead, 2010 as cited in Pastor & Kent, 2020). Moreover, dark tourism sites can also be identified as memoryscapes (Pastor & Kent, 2020; Sather-Wagstaff, 2011). According to Pastor and Kent (2020), memoryscapes indicate fractures of the past that visibly manifested scars of the physical site. Winter (1998) explained that these scars externalise the trauma of those who lived through the experience – something unimaginable to most of us today (McLean, 2023). Hence, as Bruce (2020: 211) states, the present-day challenge for millennials is to:

> [unpack] ... these silent sentinels, with manicured grounds and mature trees, and more often than not plenty of other tourists, can, by virtue of their failure to optically embody the notion of evil, fail to create that bridge to the past that we seek.

Bridging between the past and present across multiple generations is becoming more demanding as we move away from the actual event. Memoryscapes help identify connections between the past and present. However, learning, analysing and understanding what occurred becomes more difficult due to a growing lack of awareness. Knudsen (2011) identified dark sites as places of difficult heritage, while Keil (2005: 481–482) argued that 'if tourism is a means of reassimilating trauma on the level of the collective, this might be because such activity is a mode of commodification and, ultimately, of reassurance, of normativeness, of value-transformation'. Therefore, visiting memorial sites such as Dachau is significant for visitors to experience and better imagine the difficult heritage related to this place and, subsequently, learn appropriate ways of commemorating the Holocaust in the present. Indeed, the described discomfort between tourist expressions and silent observers at a memorial is echoed in work by Griffiths (2019: 190) who notes, 'when this happens, the risk of dark tourism in its most voyeuristic form appears to increase'. Griffiths (2019) goes on to explain the significance of the tourist gaze (after Urry, 2002) that focuses on making sense of the observed behaviour, specifically at influential sites. Meanwhile, Keil (2005) concurs and adds that the gate is the starting point of mapping out the psychic topography in the visitor's imagination that has been informed through cultural memory.

In terms of my own empirical research at Dachau, in contrast to treating the experience of being at Dachau as merely another item to check off their list of places to visit, participants arrived at the site receptive to discovering the significance of the overarching themes that resemble our collective memory of the Holocaust (McLean, 2023). Participants walked as a group along the 'Path of Remembrance', between the railway station and the memorial site, and this experience emphasised the value of collective acts of remembrance (McLean, 2023; Sierp, 2016). From their non-judgmental conversations of support and compassion for each other, I noted that participants created a safe space to express emotions and vulnerability and air thoughts about personal identity (McLean, 2023). Expressing signs of vulnerability can reduce anxiety and self-consciousness about communicating one's feelings and encourage generative dialogue about sensitive topics (Brown, 2018; Goleman & Boyatzis, 2008). At the core of this experience is the solidarity among a cohort that not only struggles to make sense of the horrors of the Holocaust, but also gives each other hope and strength to be mindful advocates for the future of Holocaust remembrance (Sierp & Wüstenberg, 2015).

Anyone familiar with the history of sacred grounds such as concentration camps, sites of war trauma, cemeteries or battlefield knows they are anything but empty. Despite visually appearing desolate, visiting such a site can be suffocating, as if the wind is carrying the stories of the past and the remaining buildings hold the souls of those who experienced the site first-hand (McLean, 2023). The value of millennials visiting such a site is that they can become part of the contemporary fabric of a new form of memory and remembrance culture at the memorial site (McLean, 2023).

Millennials and their Social Frameworks

Born between 1981 and 1996 (Dimock, 2019), the millennial generation struggles to learn from the last eyewitnesses and is exposed to Holocaust remembrance through cultural memory. Millennials occupy a critical moment in society as future generations as they must rely on how memories of the Holocaust are transferred transgenerationally. To unpack how millennials engage with these various elements of both collective and cultural memory, I address the concept of *social frameworks*, as explained by French sociologist Maurice Halbwachs. Social frameworks impact and inform collective memory, an idea pioneered by Halbwachs in the early 1920s (Erll, 2011a, 2011b; Erll *et al.*,

2008; Godfrey & Lilley, 2009; Halbwachs, 1992). The concept of social frameworks is used as a metaphor for carriers created in society and influence the construction of collective memories (Assmann, 2014; Erll, 2011b; Marcel & Mucchielli, 2008) through shared narratives (Tilmans *et al.*, 2010). Specifically, Halbwachs (1992) explained that frameworks resemble judgments, ideas, families and other constructions (see also Assmann, 2008). These constructions can include heritage, education and interests that inform how millennials contribute to constructing memory at a site of trauma. Memories are, therefore, constantly re-formed and imprinted through dynamic social frames that cross transcultural, transnational and without or uncertain social boundaries (Commane & Potton, 2019; Erll, 2011b; Nikulin, 2017; Olick *et al.*, 2011; Rigney, 2018).

The fluidity of memory suggests that both individual and collective memory are linked together. Specifically, both the 'organic memory of the individual' and 'the creation of shared versions of the past' impact the collective memory (Halbwachs, 1997; as cited in Erll, 2011b: 5). Consequently, Becker (2005: 105) suggests 'that individual memories always crystallize in a social framework and that public events leave a deep imprint on those who live through them, especially young people who are in the process of constructing adult identities'. The construction of Self and identities among the millennial generation is instrumental because it allows researchers to pave the way for tomorrow's memory workers and support the environments they need to thrive.

While only the individual houses their memories, each memory is triggered through engagement with social groups (carriers) that influence how it is recalled and forgotten (Olick, 1999). Olick (1999: 335) emphasised that 'memories, in this sense, are as much the products of the symbols and narratives available publicly—and of the social means for storing and transmitting them—as they are the possessions of individuals'. In its simplest forms, then, social frameworks resemble the following phenomena: firstly, the individual memories that are awakened through the interaction of carriers in society; and secondly, commemorative representations that involve mnemonic traces (Olick, 1999).

A more contemporary phrase for mnemonic traces known in the literature today is prosthetic memory – extending the individual's memory beyond the brain (Olick, 1999). Scholars who evaluate prosthetic memory/culture include Landsberg (1995, 2004) and Lury (1998). More recently, and in tandem with Holocaust and memory studies, Kaminsky (2014), Gabrielian and Hirsch (2018), Souto (2018), as well as Peet (2022) have augmented this discussion. Souto (2018), for example, focused on the experience within museums through prosthetic memory, such as authentic objects, to create a connection between the place and the visitor. Meanwhile, Gabrielian and Hirsch (2018: 114) noted that 'prosthetic landscapes refer to the possibility of landscape's portability and experience from elsewhere via the geospatial web' and, therefore, suggest another perspective of how prosthetic memory can be reviewed. While a detailed discussion on prosthetic memory is beyond the scope of this chapter, its implementation of how it can be used as a carrier to inform the memory of the Holocaust among millennials offers avenues for future research.

However, several scholars have criticised Halbwachs' (1992) social framework theory (Erll, 2011b; Gedi & Elam, 1996; Gensburger, 2016; O'Connor, 2019). For example, Gedi and Elam (1996) argue that Halbwachs was highly vague in defining how social frameworks impact collective memory. Specifically, they noted that the lines between individual and collective memory are blurred (Gedi & Elam, 1996), which in turn, speaks to the dynamic and fluid nature of memory. Indeed, blurred lines between the individual and the group are a vigorously debated narrative within memory studies. For instance, Middleton and Brown (2011) address the struggles with Halbwachs' defining elements of group memory. According to Halbwachs, a collective framework defines the group, which seems challenging to occur given that a selection of individuals comprises the group who all join with individual social frameworks and perspectives (Middleton & Brown, 2011). Moreover, when examining individuals within the group, Halbwachs initially argued that the memory contributed by those with no first-hand experience is close to equal to those who experienced the event first-hand (see Becker, 2005).

Despite the criticisms of Halbwachs' social frameworks theory, the concept has been expanded by other scholars over the years and is now a foundational theoretical narrative within memory studies research (Erll, 2011b; Gensburger, 2016; Godfrey & Lilley, 2009; Olick, 2007; Rothberg, 2009). Discussions on memory work are guided by initial ideas of social frameworks and their dynamic constructions. Millennials have not experienced the Holocaust first hand: they rely on what Halbwachs determines as historical memory based on written resources (Nikulin, 2017). Yet, no matter how you describe the role of the individual in the group, collective memory involves individual bias and lacks completeness (Assmann, 2008). Social frameworks become unstable and unprecedented, making it impossible to extrapolate findings on collective memory across an entire generation. However, we can use these frameworks to describe how millennials who visit the site define the Self through interpretive experiences at Dachau and engage with the generalised Other.

Thus, I employ social frameworks as a synonym for carriers and groups of memory that inform the zone of transitional memory of the Holocaust for millennials. For example, Assmann (2008: 51–52) argued that 'a social frame is an implicit or explicit structure of shared concerns, values, experiences, narratives'. Given Assmann's (2008) definition of a social frame and the discussion of social frameworks above, I claim that, in the context of the millennial visitor at Dachau, social frames include: family, friends, class cohort, political community, colleagues, other millennials – that is, the generalised Other.

For millennials to be successful memory agents, they must engage with these specific carriers and, consequently, inform the zone of transitional memory at Dachau. We can refer to this as *localisation* of memory (Middleton & Brown, 2011: 43) who note:

> When Halbwachs talks of collective memory being 'localized' in place, what he is advocating is not simply that there is a relationship between a sense of place and the contents of memory, but something altogether more robust. Collective memory is possible only when social relationships are slowed down and crystallized around objects.

Millennials are influencing the zone of transitional memory of the Holocaust as they focus on specific stories, objects and spaces at the Dachau site. I argue that the zone of transitional memory is a form of what Hirsch (2008, 2012) termed (post)memory. It is particularly relevant in this case as (post)memory allows millennials to learn about the Holocaust via an intergenerational lens (Henig & Ebbrecht-Hartmann, 2022). Indeed, (post)memory can be explored via extensions of Self (Olick, 1999), such as taking photographs, walking, touching or viewing. For example, Zalewska (2017: 100) argued that media contributions 'become participants in the layered process of collective memory building'. Zalewska (2017) emphasised that younger visitors engage in the act of taking selfies at concentration camp memorial sites, raising attention to new forms of commemorating the Holocaust.

Any form of photography is subject to reactions from others, yet a usual form of behaviour at the site, specifically at the entrance gate (Cole, 2020). Through this form of second person witnessing (Douglas, 2020; McLean, 2023), one can explore culture-specific characteristics that define forms of embodiment specific to commemoration (Young, 1989). The benefit when all generations see the power of photography as *witnessing* enables a united approach towards different forms of commemorating and, as result, allowing these forms to be accepted in society. Achieving this benefit enables individuals to look beyond personal assumptions and beliefs that can hinder the acceptance and inclusion of new ways of learning, analysing, understanding and preventing. Specifically, millennials need to take caution when taking selfies (Douglas, 2020; Zalewska, 2017). While taking selfies is rooted within the central attributes of millennials, at sites of mass atrocity, this behaviour can seem inappropriate (Douglas, 2020) and even disturbing to witness (Margalit, 2014).

It is challenging to pinpoint the exact elements of the social framework for millennials as it is impossible to extrapolate the same frames across an entire generation (McLean, 2023). That said, we can find themes and commonalities where variations can be applied to millennials. Specific to the Holocaust, the social framework of millennials includes kinship (that is, family/heritage), personal artefacts, vectors of memory such as film, media and social communities, other millennials and educational cohorts and peers. The interplay of these various carriers is significant to explore as it allows one to become more aware of how memory is reconstructed, influenced and embedded within the zone of transitional memory of the Holocaust for millennials.

The Zone of Transitional Memory of the Holocaust for Millennials

Memory of the Holocaust for the millennial generation is defined by the zone of transitional memory (McLean, 2023). To that end, while social frameworks are shaped by interactions of carriers in society and commemorative representations, the zone highlights the interplay of these elements. Within the zone of transitional memory, millennials move between features of collective and cultural memory to learn about Holocaust remembrance, understand stories associated with it, as well as analyse how to prevent the spread of hatred against culture, race and diversity. Additionally, the zone shapes how millennials act as memory agents for current and future generations.

To schematically illustrate various features or elements of the zone of transitional memory for millennials, Table 14.1 is adapted from Assmann's (2008) original collective and cultural memory definition. It specifically identifies what lies between collective and cultural memory and thus makes the zone unique in its application for the millennial visitor.

Within the zone, millennials are confronted with tension, like (heritage) force fields (Seaton, 2001, 2009) that act upon them and their behaviour, shaping their attributes in commemorating the Holocaust. These forces influence not only the millennial visitor's reflective experience but also the Self and identity of those who visit the site to learn (McLean, 2023). Consequently, there are two different commemorative learning experiences for millennials – those who visit a site of memory or trauma – and those who do not (McLean, 2023). The zone of transitional memory focuses on the narrative and experience of those who visit.

Table 14.1 Zone of transitional memory for millennial visitors at the Dachau Memorial Site

Collective Memory	Zone of Transitional Memory	Cultural Memory
Biological carriers	Transition between biological & materialistic carriers	Materialistic carriers
Definite (80–100 years)	Localised: Place specific	Indefinite
Intergenerational	Intrapersonal values	Transgenerational
Communicative	Via interaction & interpretation	Symbols & signs
Conversational remembering	More embodied experiences	Monuments, texts, pictures

Source: McLean (2023).

The finite closure to life opens new processes, elements and mechanisms to engage with the past and adaptive understanding of the social construct and meaning of death (Stone, 2018). To ignite new commemorative processes and understanding of the Holocaust, millennials at the memorial site must transition between biological and materialistic carriers (McLean, 2023). Millennials are confronted with recordings of stories shared by survivors but also influenced by imagination triggered through cultural memory. They are also experiencing a sense of place through the aura of the site of Dachau (Seaton, 2009; Stone, 2018). Through this experience, millennials learn more about intrapersonal values and how they shape their reaction and action within society (McLean, 2023). Influencing this new memory, millennials also interpret stories and reflections through interaction with fellow visitors and, specifically, certified tour guides at the site (McLean, 2023). In this way, the zone of transitional memory emphasises the significance of visiting a site of memory through a more embodied form of Holocaust remembrance through walking, singing, touching, listening and curated acts of remembrance (McLean, 2023).

At the heart of the zone of transitional memory is the millennial generation themselves who identify as a force field (McLean, 2023). As time passes across generations, there remains a continuum between silence and noise that includes acts of remembrance and commemoration (Dessingué & Winter, 2016). Dessingué and Winter (2016: 4) also note that 'there is a necessity of considering silence, like remembering and forgetting, as changing and performative elements in the way we reconstruct the past'. There is also a continued push and pull between remembering and forgetting, truth and misinformation, as well as authenticity of the site and curated spaces (McLean, 2023). Understanding the zone is therefore important as it describes how Holocaust remembrance is shaped at the site and how it transforms the way the Holocaust is remembered across generations.

Dachau offers a space for visitors to leave behind the comforts of their familiar ways of thinking, critically evaluate their perspectives and reflect deeply upon implications of their experiences. The concepts of reflexivity, looking-glass Self and the generalised Other helped address personal perspectives and thoughts through observation of behaviour at the site (McLean, 2023). The memorial site awakens awareness of one's values and inspires individuals to reflect on how the physical space influences collective memory of the Holocaust (Dekel, 2011; Narvselius & Fedor, 2021). As a theoretical framework, the zone of transitional memory helps future researchers evaluate how millennials learn about Holocaust remembrance and how they can become more holistic memory workers for others. This new form of memory of the Holocaust advances our collective understanding of how millennials create meaning associated with the past to combat further silencing of stories and experiences that must be aired to minimise forgetting the Holocaust.

Conclusion: Millennials and the Future of Holocaust Remembrance

Educators and researchers are crucial in triggering how millennials exercise leadership in global discourse of antisemitism and human rights and, with this, impact the future of Holocaust remembrance. Their role is to inform and inspire millennials to actively engage with learners who can advance their mental models and perspectives (McLean, 2023). Shaping perspectives and providing educational opportunities for millennials enhances how this generation filters through information on memory politics and contributes to collective memory. Educators must also encourage millennials to engage in profound conversations in which they can be vulnerable to sharing emotions and individual experiences. Such a type of respectful dialogue can be achieved by inviting millennials to the table and making explicit that their voice and contributions to the narrative matter. Indeed, it is evident that involving millennials in an informative approach that encouraged the expression of their viewpoints at all stages of the project is essential.

The work of educators and researchers consists in being involved as truth finders. Through dedication and ongoing curiosity, scholars continue to conduct research and bring forward strong recommendations that speak directly to memory politics in modern society. Through their widespread dissemination of research to academic and non-academic audiences, this collective consciousness about learning from past genocides and atrocities helps younger postwar generations become leaders in human rights and democracy for a peaceful and collective future. Additionally, educators inspire the next generation of researchers to advance further scholarly contributions within the many realms of memory studies. Researchers also enable networks and pathways to academic and applied projects. These networks have grown inclusivity, inviting millennials to embed their voices, even as non-academics. In this way, research can connect with a broader audience and include diverse stakeholder engagement in advancing the truth about the Holocaust and rituals to commemorate it in the future (McLean, 2023).

Revealing the truth is vital to combat negative traits of collective memory of the Holocaust, such as denial and silence. Assisting in expanding the global narrative to dismantle misinformation and foster truth is therefore significant. The zone of transitional memory is one additional theoretical element within memory studies that advances discussions about how to remember the Holocaust moving forward. It also shows how millennials can purposefully and respectfully act as second-person witnesses of the Holocaust in the 21st century, and beyond.

15 Between Revival of Memory and Dark Tourism: The Future of Holocaust-Related Sites in Latvia

Aija van der Steina, Maija Rozite, Inese Runce and Kaspars Strods

Introduction

Holocaust sites, deemed to be the *darkest* on the typological spectrum model of dark tourism (Stone, 2006), only became accessible to the Jewish community and tourists in Eastern Europe and the Baltic States after the fall of the Iron Curtain. Although these sites are not primarily developed as tourism products, their main functions are preservation, commemoration of victims, as well as education of tragic pasts (Stone, 2006). However, developing tourism in various dark heritage sites has become inevitable and self-evident. This is due to the evolution of social awareness in Europe, such as coming to terms with a difficult if not contested past, the trans-nationalisation of Holocaust memory (Assmann, 2010) and liberation from the totalitarian Soviet legacy. Of course, memory is never static, but in Eastern and Central Europe, the process of change has been incredibly challenging for individuals and societies. Erll (2011a, 2011b) emphasises that 'travelling memory' is a manifestation of its logic – it arises and exists in movement. Memory carriers are individuals who share a collective past and practice mnemonic rituals. Travel and migration contribute to the global diffusion of the content, forms and practices of memory, creating the phenomenon of 'trans-culture', even in the field of Holocaust memory and heritage.

Within dark tourism sites, the cultural memory of tourists and local communities and groups, as well as the attitudes and cultural expressions of remembrance that result from it, meet and interact. At Holocaust sites, the homogeneous transnational memory of the Holocaust meets with different constructions of national memory. This is particularly true in Eastern Europe, where for 50 years, until the collapse of the USSR, crimes and sites of mass murder committed by the Nazis and Communists were left forgotten, hidden or forbidden. 'Returning' to Europe, where the Europeanisation of Holocaust memory was already underway, Eastern Europe 'became marked by tangible products of Holocaust memory' (Kucia, 2016: 112) such as memorials, museums and memorial plaques at deportation sites, ghettoes and executions.

Returning to the international scene, Latvia also featured dark heritage tourism where the tragic fate of the local population during two totalitarian regimes merged with the process of memory revival. The co-dependency of overcoming difficult history and dark tourism development has changed the significance of Holocaust sites, both in residents' consciousness as well as tourism managers' attitudes towards their use. This process has not been easy and is still underway. It illuminates the nature of dissonant heritage, including selectively glossed-over aspects, and sites subject to politics and ideology that manifest different interpretations and meanings (Roberts & Stone, 2014). Holocaust heritage evokes an 'active' memory that engages the subject in reflections on contemporary politics and society, forcing visitors to consider the Holocaust through the prism of the present (Wight, 2020). These sites also reveal the readiness of the local community to 'speak' about these places and the tragic historical events associated with them. Differences in perceptions and attitudes of the community towards tragic events may exist in places with a complex heritage and, subsequently, conflicting opinions may arise regarding the use and development of such sites.

Therefore, it is important to understand the functions of these sites in the collective heritage to avoid tensions or even conflicts (Roberts & Stone, 2014). Attitudes towards a place may differ from the perspectives of victims, perpetrators, and bystanders (Tunbridge & Ashworth, 1996). Tension may rise among competing groups that want to use sites for their own narratives (Podoshen, 2017). This is especially relevant in the part of Europe which has been affected by totalitarian regimes. Tourists have their own individual or collective memories, attitudes, expectations and understanding. The role of destination and site managers, therefore, is to address potential tensions between distinct groups through interpretations that consider different audiences and local community perspectives (Ashworth & Hartman, 2005; Light, 2017b). Of note is the dualism in collective European memory, which is dominated by the Western European memory frame of the ultimate evil of Nazism and the Holocaust to the exclusion of Communism and Stalinism (Sierp, 2016).

Thus, the homogeneous transnational Holocaust memory combines the history of European countries and the ethical obligation to remember, commemorate and confront these dark events in the future (Diner, 2007). However, fundamental question arises, including how will we remember, commemorate and confront the Holocaust in the post-witness era? How will future Holocaust memory affect the visitation of Holocaust sites? And what will be the impact and role of Holocaust-related sites in Holocaust memory and remembrance? The purpose of this chapter, therefore, is to examine what the future of Holocaust sites will look like, and how the past will matter in the future, within a context of changing memory culture and tourism. In so doing, and adopting Latvia as a case study, the chapter explores four Holocaust-related sites within the context of integration and narratives of national memory and inclusion in tourism, with future development scenarios outlined. Firstly, we highlight a revival of Holocaust memory in Latvia, and consider a complicated past, a national(ised) present and a potential transcultural future.

Revival of Holocaust Memory in Latvia

Formation of statehood and national memory that started in Latvia in the 1920s–1930s, was interrupted for 50 years by the Second World War and two occupations by totalitarian regimes (Nazi Germany and the former USSR), leaving a negative impact on memory preservation and development. Both ideologies had their own narratives of history, memory and suffering. After Latvia regained its independence and freedom (from the USSR in 1991), a gap emerged in Soviet historiography, knowledge and the polarisation of the memories of distinct groups in society. In turn, this led to an inability to form a dialogue and accept each other's stories, suffering and trauma. Consequently, past civil and international military conflicts as well as ideological clashes have left Latvia with a complex heritage, where one of the central themes is the Holocaust and its memorials. Before the Second World War, 30% of the total population in Latvia were minorities of various ethnic and ethno-religious groups. It was home to more than 93,000 Jews in 1935.

During the Holocaust carried out by Nazi Germany, as well as local collaborators, more than 70,000 Latvian Jews and approximately 20,000 international Jews from across Europe, were killed in Latvia. During the subsequent Soviet occupation after the war, the Holocaust was a taboo topic because it did not fit into the ideological framework dominated by the victim narrative of 'Soviet citizens' (Berzins, 2015: 271). Expressions of diversity were excluded by the communist regime, including within discussions, worldviews, traditions, values, travel experiences and memories. Therefore, Holocaust memory and its commemoration did not find a place in the communist regime's interpretations of history, commemorative culture, urban space, rural landscape, museums, archives or tourism. Notwithstanding, relatives and friends of murdered Jews visited various memorials and organised commemorations despite being outside the official communist remembrance agenda, especially in small towns (Lenskis, 2017: 9–11).

However, with the collapse of the Soviet Union in 1991, attitudes towards the Holocaust changed dramatically and, as a result, gained wider coverage in Latvian society. When the painful process of reviving the 'forbidden' memory of the Holocaust began in Eastern Europe, this phase had already ended in Western Europe. To that end, methodological practices of Western European memory culture studies were used as a model in Eastern European studies without paying attention to sidelining the 'overlap of historical experience with both Nazi and Soviet power' and 'how complicated this is, just structurally' (Snyder, 2015: 33). Indeed, the difficult heritage left by the two totalitarian regimes not only revealed long ignored suffering, but also divided Latvian society into several competing groups vying to prove to each other whose suffering and memorial sites should be highlighted and, thus, remembered. In the Baltic States after 1991, Holocaust memory 'controversies were triggered mostly by outside actors' including 'Western media and political representatives and Holocaust survivor organizations', but the obvious lack of historical knowledge was replaced by reviving old stereotypes (Pettai, 2011: 160).

Development of Holocaust memorials implemented by local Jewish communities took shape gradually, often accompanied with deep political and scholarly debates (Lenskis, 2017). Holocaust memory manifested itself through the institutionalisation of Holocaust memorials, attracting different target audiences, creating new educational programmes and building international cooperation bridges with both State institutions and international organisations. In 1990, Holocaust survivor and historian Margers Vestermanis published an unofficial guidebook *Jewish Riga,* whereby other social and ethnic groups, generations, and communities create their own, but in many respects interconnected memory systems (Erll, 2011a, 2011b). Latvian sociologist Baiba Bela (2016) states that memory contains stories about past events and accumulates knowledge of who we are. It is essential for both individuals and societies to create an understanding of what and how people remember, and how individual memory interacts with the values and perceptions of events that are important for the group to which the person belongs. This links Erll's (2011a) idea that all cultural memory must 'travel', and be kept in motion, to 'stay alive' and to have an impact on both individual minds and social formations. Research on oral history and social memory in Latvia shows that individuals and social groups experience difficulties during encounters with other versions of the past and diverse commemoration practices (Bela, 2016), as Holocaust memory and associated sites move from the past to the future through the present.

Holocaust Sites: From the Past to the Future through the Present

Using several case examples of Holocaust-related sites in Latvia, we imaginatively describe the possible development of dark tourism sites in the future. Using scenario planning principles (Ahmadi *et al.*, 2022; Duinker & Greig, 2007; Page *et al.*, 2010; Yeoman, 2012) the following four steps were used for modelling outcomes: firstly, analysing the existing situation; secondly, identifying the main influencing factors and trends; thirdly, defining problematic issues and; finally, identifying uncertainties. Scenario planning is a useful tool to prepare and/or prevent not only potential threats from the external environment (Seyitoğlu & Costa, 2022), but also identify tension or even conflicts between different stakeholders and their interests in difficult heritage sites.

Overall, 284 different Holocaust-related sites have been identified since 2004 in Latvia and characterised in studies by Meler (2013). These sites include primary and secondary sites associated with death and suffering (Wight, 2006). As historical research and the memorialisation process in Latvia continue, the list continues to grow by hitherto unknown and forgotten places. For an in-depth analysis of the situation, four typologically different sites were chosen and analysed as case studies: (a) a ghetto area and museum, (b) a place of death/murder, (c) a small town with historical Jewish heritage and (d) the site of a former Nazi concentration camp.

The Former Riga Ghetto Territory and the Riga Ghetto and Latvian Holocaust Museum located close to the main tourist area of the city was the first case to be analysed. From 1941 to 1943, around 30,000 Riga Jews and those deported from other European countries were interned in the Riga ghetto. The museum, established in 2010, has now become an important attraction for tourists, receiving 25,644 visitors in 2019, of which 74% were foreign tourists (RGLHM, 2021).

The second case was outside the metropolitan area, the small town of Bauska. The Jewish community played an essential role in its history. In 1941, the Nazis, with the participation of local collaborators, destroyed the local community. A memorial for 'Soviet' victims was built at the scene of the murder in Likverteni forest in 1971. The city museum has an exposition on the history of the Jewish community, and a memorial was created in 2017 on the site of the synagogue that was burnt down. The town's Jewish heritage has recently been included in the list of tourist attractions with the creation of an audio-guided route called *The Story of Jews in Bauska*.

The third case – mass murder sites – Biķernieki and Rumbula are the darkest Holocaust history sites in Latvia. In the winter of 1941, over 25,000 Jews were murdered in two days at Rumbula. Around 35,000 Latvian and foreign Jews were murdered in the Biķernieki forest between 1941 and 1944. In 1964, with the Soviet government's permission, a memorial stone with the inscription *Victims of Fascism* was placed at Rumbula because of a Jewish community's initiative and in 2002, a memorial ensemble was erected. In 2001, a memorial to the victims of the Nazis was established at Biķernieki (Meler, 2013). Foreign traveller reviews on Tripadvisor reveal the importance of these two tragic genocide sites in Holocaust memory, describing them as 'the most moving Holocaust memorial I've seen' or 'moving but poor as an "attraction"'.

The final site chosen is a former concentration camp 'Jungfernhof' which was set up in 1941 in Riga, where German and Austrian Jews were imprisoned, and 800 were subsequently buried. After WWII, Soviet army troops were stationed there. In 2010, the construction of a memorial site was commenced as a private initiative, while simultaneously, the city started the construction of a recreation park. In 2021, the initiators of the memorial project discovered and mapped a mass grave. In the future, they envisage the creation of a memorial while the city is renovating the area with the aim of developing a multifunctional urban recreation area.

The analysis of these four cases is based on primary qualitative and quantitative data obtained by the authors as part of a wider state-funded study on Holocaust-related sites in the context of tourism development and collective memory (see acknowledgements). This included observations of Jewish heritage and Holocaust sites throughout Lativa; surveys of residents, domestic and international tourists; and in-depth interviews with stakeholders such as site managers, destination management organisations' representatives, entrepreneurs, urban planners, tour guides and opinion leaders. Summarising the issues faced, the potential challenges for site development and two areas of tension were clearly outlined. Firstly, the growing tourist interest in dark heritage sites and the external pressure to mark, preserve and make these sites accessible is at odds with the desire (unwillingness and inability to speak) of the local population to remain silent and not to reveal these historical events, which are both unpleasant and tragic. Secondly, considerations of preserving dark heritage to commemorate is at odds with the economic and recreational interests of developers, investors and the local community in place development, underscored by the dilemma of the sustainable coexistence of these contrasting functions. To that end, a scenario revealing future possibilities in the interaction of tourism and memory culture which focuses on tensions that may remain, increase or disappear under the influence of numerous factors has been drawn.

Tourism Interaction and Memory Culture: Towards a Future Outcome

In the future, dark tourism demand will be promoted by the increase in total and European intra-regional tourism flows (Moscardo, 2021; Yeoman, 2012; Yeoman *et al.*, 2013) and the popularity of heritage tourism, including dark tourism (Timothy, 2014). As hedonism continues to drive tourism, a focus on classical heritage will endure. However, dark tourism sites will grow in significance, becoming not just sites of painful suffering for the local nation, but also 'places of pain and shame' (Logan & Reeves, 2008). Genealogical tourism (Timothy, 2014) will encourage visits to sites related to Jewish heritage and the Holocaust, although rising anti-Semitism and Holocaust denial in some places (Podoshen, 2017) could discourage Jewish descendants from visiting these sites. The share of leisure tourists visiting these places will increase, attracting both heritage tourists with a deep interest in history, as well as accidental ones who have different travel motives (Beech, 2000).

Due to the institutionalisation of Holocaust memory and the widespread network of international organisations active in the formation of long-term memory, this European darkest heritage will not be forgotten by the loss of living memories (Kucia, 2016). As Holocaust memory becomes even more trans-European, the size and openness of the memory community will depend on the quality and extension of memory, which will be determined by their future framing 'as a historical trauma, as part of a political agenda, a cosmopolitan reference, a universal norm or a global icon' (Assmann, 2010: 112). In a future transnational memory of the Holocaust, Western tourists will associate these sites with a common European heritage that needs to be preserved and the moral obligation to visit and commemorate the victims. As collective memory is particular and limited and has national and cultural boundaries, visitors from nations untouched by the Holocaust and direct Nazi influence and/or with their own historical trauma that overshadows the memory of the Holocaust, will link visitation to Holocaust sites with educational motives and learning about local heritage (Biran *et al.*, 2011; Isaac & Çakmak, 2014). For the descendants of perpetrators and observers/bystanders (Tunbridge & Ashworth, 1996), these sites could become places to seek explanations for the individual behaviour of ancestors and the role of the nation in tragic events. These darkest sites of dark heritage (after Stone, 2006) are sensitive places of humanity's heritage, where the focus is on education, interpretation and the creation of an environment that allows each visitor, regardless of their national origin, social norms, age, maturity, knowledge of history and attachment to the site, to co-create their unique experience (Magee & Gilmore, 2015).

Future monopolisation of the topic and competition between groups in prioritising their stories of suffering gradually disappears.

Discussions are ongoing, where parties strive to balance contentions regarding place development and the preservation of dark historical heritage. An inclusive culture of memory and heterodox heritage practice (Wells & Lixinski, 2016), together with the willingness, power and legal capacity of the local community to influence decision making, ensures sustainable site development. The ethnocentric approach has changed to a more comprehensive inclusion of the heritage of all minorities, including the Jewish historical heritage and its contemporary manifestations. Open public discussion on the nation's experience, suffering and role during and after WWII, including collaboration, enables the Holocaust in Eastern Europe to no longer be considered damaging to national identity and image (Macdonald, 2015). Dark heritage sites are organically included in the tourism offer based on education, memory, deeply individual experience and self-reflection (Podoshen, 2017: 351).

Recommendations online, digital maps (Haynes & Egan, 2019), and popular culture will stimulate future demand for dark tourism sites traditionally not included in mainstream tourism. The role of popular culture in learning about European historical events which have had an influence on the travel and memory culture of residents will be supplemented by various technological solutions (for instance, augmented and extended reality, or personalised robot guides) (Wenzel, 2013). Digitised testimonies will be used to tell personal stories preserved by Holocaust witnesses for a better understanding of events that took place 100 years ago and more. Notwithstanding, digital Holocaust memory and commemoration will not completely replace the desire to experience a historical site in person (Ebbrecht-Hartmann, 2021). However, while the use of innovative technologies raises concerns about the correct interpretation of memories, so a balance between reality and interpretation must be maintained (Snyder, 2017). Technological solutions for preserving, commemorating and consolidating dark heritage in the collective memory of the future will only be successful in places where high quality, reliable and authentic data on the Holocaust and Nazi crimes are available (Verschure & Wierenga, 2022).

Future interfaces: Commemorative culture, economic development and recreation

Although dark heritage is recognised as an important heritage to be preserved, with significant importance for public education and preservation of memory; in practice, there will be conflicting opinions about its use or development because of competing economic interests and pressure from investors. There is currently more support for urban development than for heritage preservation (Timothy, 2014). Those future dark heritage sites that are close to intense tourist flows and popular tourist attractions will be in a better position to promote the growth of tourism infrastructure and services.

As recreational landscapes in the suburbs will be used more intensively (Majewska *et al.*, 2022), the importance of the suburban green area and its multifunctional use will increase (Kalfas *et al.*, 2022). Pressure will remain from city developers and citizens to use suburban mass murder and concentration camp sites as recreation areas. In places with intensive recreation, which are sanctified and designated (after Foot, 2009, cited in Hartman, 2014: 175), the coexistence of both functions – memory and recreation – will continue. Visitors who are less attached to such sites will evaluate the 'intrusion' of recreational activities into the territory of dark heritage and the ethics of this coexistence more critically (Foley & Lennon, 1996a, 1996b; Smith, 2021). These risks can be mitigated by the implementation of green cemeteries reflecting the symbiosis of death and rest, and as places of reflection, recreation and cultural interaction (Skår *et al.*, 2018). Unexplored or forgotten places of death and tragedy will be rectified (Hartman, 2014) by reducing the recreational load or choosing 'softer' recreation activities, combining memory, education and recreation goals.

Dark heritage will also be preserved and marked in ways that do not require the physical demarcation of sites. Traditional and innovative long term and short term, in person, remote and hybrid interpretation tools will be used: including but not limited to ceremonies, video installations, contemporary art, interactive games, the internet of things, augmented, virtual or immersive reality and healing spaces (ICSC [International Coalition of Sites of Conscience], 2018). Debates will continue around ethical aspects of interpretation as its forms become more individualised using new media. The main challenges for dark sites and destination management will continue to be accurate interpretation, authenticity, and non-commodification (Podoshen, 2017), because failed practices may lead to rejection by tourists (Reynolds, 2016) and exploitation by Holocaust deniers. Destination planning and management professionals will need skills related to the ethical aspects of dark heritage conservation, interpretation and communication with tourists and residents in collaboration with all stakeholders (Ferrer-Roca *et al.*, 2021).

As the role and power of the local community grows, conditions arise in which residents become the initiators of the establishment of memorial institutions. Created in 2012, the Žanis Lipke memorial, dedicated to a rescuer of Jews, serves as an example. The museum has become an interactive, modern, youth-oriented place that talks about what needs to be done to prevent the re-occurrence of such tragic events. It is not only a memorial, educational space and tourist attraction, but also a meeting place for the local community, a centre for personal growth, civic courage and education. Shostak (2017) emphasises Holocaust memorialisation must repurpose not just 'horror' but also 'help' stories. Sites that examine the Holocaust from the survivor and rescuer perspective are growing in popularity, yet risk creating an idealised Holocaust image and the fragmentation of cultural memory. It is here that Wóycicka (2019) describes their emergence as part of the *glocalisation* of memory when, despite shared cosmopolitan memory, Holocaust functions and forms of remembrance differ between countries.

Conclusion

This chapter reveals that dark tourism sites and their future development can be seen in the context of travelling cultural memory when the memory of tourists and residents' travels in time and space. The Holocaust has become a part of global and transnational memory and tourism manifested at national and local levels. Inclusion of Holocaust sites in (dark) tourism prevents forgetting and promotes preservation in both physical places as well as memory space. Alternatively, when the memory of residents and tourists interact, the dissonant nature of these places is reduced, and recollection and remembrance are strengthened. This does not exclude various, different expressions of commemorative culture and interpretation. Indeed, tourists will continue to play a vital role in cross-border travel of memories (inbound and outbound), revival of memories and education.

The dark heritage related to WWII, including the Holocaust in Eastern Europe, is more sensitive because it has long been hidden, suppressed, unknown or interpreted in the interests of totalitarian regimes. Residents or certain groups of society and tourists can perceive and interpret Holocaust-related sites through the prism of different memories. The Western perspective cannot be directly applied to the interpretation of events and Holocaust sites in Eastern Europe because it ignores inherent complexities within the context of overlapping and subsequent political ideologies of two regimes. It should be noted that a local community might comprise a generation raised in the former Soviet Union without comprehensive historical knowledge of the events of WWII in which to base memory, including the forgetting of the Holocaust. Consequently, transnational memory and its existence is only possible within the framework of a knowledgeable and inquisitive society.

There are few studies on residents' attitudes towards dark tourism development which could be given context by the guest–host relationship in these places. It can be emphasised that attention should also be paid to visitors opposing the existing memorial culture – Holocaust deniers, neo-Nazis and neo-Bolsheviks, and other radical extreme groups who are already visitors of such sites today. Therefore, in times of uncertainty, several unpredictable internal and external factors affect the development of dark tourism in one direction or another. Future changes that will affect development include transformations in global political forces, the geopolitical situation in Europe, as well as the change in the role of Eastern Europe because of the Russia–Ukraine war, and the possible change of political forces in a country under the influence of global processes and populism. Global economic crises are also unpredictable, including the energy crisis and its impact on travel. Whatever happens in the future, new conflicts, disasters and pandemics will (sadly) create a 'new' dark heritage (Thomas *et al.*, 2019), which will be more contemporary for the generations that will follow.

Acknowledgements

This chapter is a part of the project *Difficult Heritage: Between the Memorisation and Contemporary Tourism Production and Consumption. The Case of Holocaust Sites in Latvia*, funded by the Latvian Council of Science (Project No. lzp-2019/1-0241).

16 'Mirrors of Society': Cemetery Tourism Futures

Marta Soligo

Introduction

In 1984, with the groundbreaking article – *The Sociology of Tourism* – Erik Cohen argued that, even if research on tourists was varied, it consisted of '*touristological* surveys and analysis that meet the practical needs of governments and the tourist industry' (Cohen, 1984: 376 [original emphasis]). He further noted, even if those data – such as the demographic characteristics of tourists – were important to understand tourism trends, they were of 'rather limited sociological relevance in themselves' (Cohen, 1984: 376). Even if almost 40 years have passed since the publication of Cohen's work, we see that positivistic trends in hospitality and tourism research are often still predominant, with tourism typologies making no exception (Goodson & Phillimore, 2004). However, contemporary trends show that, to better understand the future of the tourism realm, experts should try to interpret travel behaviours with a less rigid approach to tourism typologies (Phillimore & Goodson, 2004).

Therefore, this chapter's purpose focuses on a niche form of (dark) tourism, cemetery tourism, with a specific focus on its future. In particular, the futurologist approach undertaken here centres around tourism typology overlaps. Jahanian (2017: 29) defines futurology as 'a systematic attempt to look at long-term future in the field of science, technology, economy, and society for identifying innovative technologies and strengthening strategic research areas with the greatest economic and social benefits'. However, as Sardar (2010) points out, the future does not generate from a vacuum and is not without context, and this also means showing appreciation for history. Thus, futurology studies should *look ahead* by *looking back* (Sardar, 2010). Consequently, this chapter is rooted in the idea that it is not possible to predict future trends without bringing the past and the present into the picture.

This analysis entails a thorough understanding of current tourism developments. On the one hand, lists of tourism typologies, such as the World Tourism Organization's (UNWTO) – which includes clear definitions of trends such as cultural tourism, rural tourism, urban/city tourism, mountain tourism, wellness tourism and so on – offer a good starting point for the analysis of travellers' motivations and destination branding. On the other hand, recent tendencies in the travel market highlight the need for more flexible perspectives rooted in the perception of place identity from a kaleidoscopic point of view. For instance, it would be inaccurate to make the Trinità dei Monti church in Rome fall under a simple typology of religious tourism, since it falls under the film tourism typology as well, being the location of a memorable scene in the 1953 movie *Roman Holiday*, starring Audrey Hepburn and Gregory Peck (Holdaway & Trentin, 2014). Similarly, it would be imprecise to define the longest continuous section of the Berlin Wall still in existence as a mere historical tourism attraction. That section, in fact, later became the East Side Gallery and hosted some famous murals and graffiti and, subsequently, evolved into an art tourism site (Yan *et al.*, 2019). Analogously, with this chapter I argue that, even if dark tourism plays a key role for cemetery visits, typologies such as cultural tourism and celebrity tourism are acquiring increasing importance.

Moreover, of relevance for this chapter is the field of heritage, especially when examining the cultural and historic fabric of cemeteries (Milligan, 2007). In 2014, the International Council of Museums (ICOM, headquartered in Paris and founded in 1946) promulgated the Siena Charter, advocating for a new perspective that perceives museums as part of their cultural landscapes. With the document, ICOM aimed for a new paradigm that looks beyond museum walls, stressing that cultural institutions cannot be isolated from their own social, historic and natural contexts. Similarly, this chapter aims to explain why it is important to investigate cemeteries within their cultural landscapes. In other words, a futurology-oriented analysis of dark tourism should view cemeteries as key elements of their own cultural fabric. This means that, in the future, dark tourism attractions will be increasingly characterised by motivation overlaps. Therefore, it is necessary to understand how tourists' fascination with death can often blend with their interest in other fields. This study focuses on how eight cemeteries in the US and Italy position themselves as attractions for visitors who are interested not only in death-related elements, but also in celebrity culture, history (heritage), as well as fine arts.

Cemetery Tourism: Current and Future Trends

The phenomenon of cemetery tourism refers to visits to gravesites such as memorial parks, mausoleums and graveyards. Cemetery tourism can be considered as a micro-niche of the dark tourism macro-niche

(Novelli, 2005), which Timothy and Nyaupane (2010: 80) define as the activity of 'encountering death and the macabre at sites such as prisons and death camps'. As Foley and Lennon (1996b) point out, once viewed as places for gravity and reverence, cemeteries today are considered places for leisure as well. This means that graveyards are increasingly welcoming tourists as much as mourners. Meanwhile, Rojek (1993) stresses how modernity erased the differences between sacred and profane, progressively removing the feelings of dignity and solemnity that bourgeois culture historically attached to those places. 'With the rise of mass tourism, the metropolitan cemetery, with its collection of illustrious corpses, became a sight to see just like any other monument' (Rojek, 1993: 141). One of the most insightful examples in this sense is the key role of fandom in the Père-Lachaise Cemetery in Paris that, thanks to its notable burials – such as Oscar Wilde and Jim Morrison – is now one of the city's main attractions (Levitt, 2018).

Thus, a nuanced understanding of cemetery tourism entails a reflection on how scholarship on the broader field of dark tourism often refers to the commodification of death and the sites related to it, which frequently become spectacle-oriented attractions (Stone, 2020b). Critical studies that centre around dark tourism progressively recall the 1970s' notion of the *Society of the Spectacle* proposed by Debord, who 'developed the concept of the *spectacle* to refer to the domination of media images and consumer society over the individual while obscuring the nature and effects of capitalism' (Gotham & Krier, 2008: 157). As Korstanje and George's (2015: 129) analysis of dark tourism-related literature reveals, 'under some conditions these sites are commoditized to sell the other'. Therefore, analysing commodification trends within dark tourism means investigating how death-related locations are increasingly becoming tourist attractions. Recalling Urry's (1990) notion of tourist gaze – which refers to the idea that tourists see and perceive places in a mediatised, non-neutral way – Wright and Sharpley (2018) use the term *disaster tourists' gaze*. Indeed, Wright and Sharpley (2018) propose such a term to describe the high number of visits to the Italian city of L'Aquila briefly after it was affected by a major earthquake, and the consequent disappointment of the local community towards the lack of respect shown by tourists. Similarly, Teeger and Vinitzky-Seroussi's (2007) investigation at the Apartheid Museum in South Africa makes the reader wonder if the presence of simulated experiences that represent *what it must have been like*, might not only increase, but also spectacularise, the distance between visitors and the difficult past they are exploring.

Interesting insights for the study of cemetery tourism come also from those analyses that centre around proximity *to* and fascination *with* death. A key notion here is the idea of connecting death-related attractions to people's contemplation of death, which is defined as the 'thanatoptic tradition' (Seaton, 1996; Stone & Sharpley, 2008). While proposing the term 'thanatourism', Seaton (1996: 240) refers to those travel trends that are purely based on 'fascination with death itself, irrespective of the person or persons involved'. However, Seaton (1996: 240) also highlights that there is a second and less pure form of thanatourism, 'in which the dead are both known to, and valued by, the visitor'. Investigating these themes, Stone (2012b) proposed the term 'mortality capital', which entails tourists' contemplation of others' deaths to achieve a form of capital which they can draw upon to aid their own thanatopsis (Stone, 2012a). Therefore, according to Stone and Sharpley (2008), adopting a thanatological perspective allows researchers to connect dark tourism to relevant topics within the sociology of death, such as the social neutralisation of and social responses to death.

Meanwhile, the perspective proposed by Seaton (1996) helps us better understand how the future of cemetery tourism might look. On the one hand, we find tourists who visit gravesites because they know and value the dead. The success of locations such as the so-called Hollywood memorial parks in Los Angeles – which host several stars' burials – shows that an increasing number of travellers are interested in visiting the gravesites of celebrities (Soligo & Dickens, 2020). Star cemetery visits are often rooted in tourists respecting and admiring the dead. On the other hand, however, there is a rapidly developing trend that entails travellers visiting cemeteries for motivations that go beyond the identity of the corpses (Levitt, 2018). Explaining how dark sites can be both places for suffering and cultural entertainment, Korstanje (2017: 9) mentions Stone's (2006) classification based on a dark tourism spectrum: 'darker and lighter products are differentiated according to the degree of suffering they offer to sightseers'. These kinds of differentiations are key for the understanding of future trajectories of cemetery tourism as a micro-niche of the dark tourism phenomenon, especially when it comes to the role of death. As the remainder of this chapter illustrates, while death remains a central element for cemetery tourism, the *shade* of these attractions can be both dark and light, especially when it comes to including in the palette other tourism typologies, such as celebrity tourism, historical (heritage) tourism and art tourism.

Cemetery Tourism Futures: Towards Empirical Evidence

Adopting a multi-sited mobile ethnography conducted in the US and Italy, eight cemeteries were selected for their increasing popularity among tourists. The study entailed undertaking Kusenbach's (2003) go-along strategy, which centres around the observation of informant spatial practices in situ while accessing their experiences and interpretations at the same time. The investigation also adopted what Büscher and Urry (2009) define as 'shadowing/stalking' and 'walking with' a mobile research method whereby the author followed tourists and guides throughout cemeteries to better understand their relationship and interactions. Textual analysis was also used, focusing on underlying ideological and cultural assumptions of the text and, subsequently, offering results in a strategic selection and presentation of analysed text as evidence for the overall argument (Fürsich, 2009). Included in this study was a variety of written material, such as the official websites of the cemeteries and tourism authorities, tour flyers, as well as social media posts.

Five cemeteries were analysed in the US, four in Los Angeles and one in Las Vegas, in addition to three cemeteries in Italy (Milan, Rimini and the Lecco Province). Key findings emerged, including how cemetery tourism is progressively blending death-related elements with three main realms, namely celebrity tourism, history (heritage) and art tourism.

- Hollywood Forever Cemetery in Los Angeles was founded in 1899 and is part of the US National Register of Historic Places. It is the resting place for a conspicuous number of stars, including Judy Garland and Tyrone Power. The cemetery periodically organises cultural events, such as movie screenings and music concerts.
- Pierce Brothers Westwood Village Memorial Park and Mortuary is in the Westwood area (Los Angeles) and its famous burials include Marilyn Monroe, Bettie Page and Ray Bradbury.
- Forest Lawn Memorial Park in Hollywood offers a unique panoramic view of Hollywood and its hills. Among the notable burials there are Bette Davis and Stan Laurel.
- Forest Lawn Memorial Park in Glendale includes famous internments such as Elizabeth Taylor and Michael Jackson. While visiting the location, tourists can enjoy a breathtaking view of downtown Los Angeles and see some artworks replicas, such as Michelangelo's 'David' statue.
- Woodlawn Cemetery in Las Vegas is the city's oldest memorial park and is listed on the US National Register of Historic Places. It is known for hosting the burials of personalities, from performers to casino managers, who were key in the development of Las Vegas and its tourism.
- Monumental Cemetery in Milan is known for hosting both famous burials – which include the Italian novelist Alessandro Manzoni and Davide Campari, owner of the homonymous drink company – and for the presence of famous artworks.
- Monumental and Civic Rimini Cemetery is known for hosting the tomb of Oscar-winning director Federico Fellini, whose body rests underneath a sculpture by Arnaldo Pomodoro, one of Italy's most important contemporary artists.

- The Pasturo Cemetery in the Lecco Province is becoming a progressively important attraction for the admirers of female poet Antonia Pozzi, whose body was buried there in 1938, at the youthful age of 26 years old.

'Sparkling Stars and Dark Shades': Celebrity Cemetery Tourism

It is easy to imagine why cemeteries might be considered as the quintessential dark tourism attraction, given the presence of the conspicuous number of buried bodies. However, a more thorough analysis reveals the kaleidoscopic nature of *darkness* in those locations. Scholars list aspects such as death, disasters, crime, trauma and suffering among the key features that constitute dark tourism (Lennon, 2017). During my walk-along activities in the eight cemeteries, I noticed that those aspects were particularly relevant in the case of notable internments. Specifically, visitors of celebrity cemeteries in Hollywood often showed interest in the way those stars died, especially if particularly mysterious or macabre. This is the case of actor and director William Desmond Taylor, buried at the Hollywood Forever Cemetery, whose unsolved murder in 1922 still raises a sense of curiosity. Similarly, *Fast and Furious* movie fans paying their respect at Paul Walker's burial site at the Forest Lawn Memorial Park-Hollywood Hills view the visit as an occasion to reflect on the car accident that killed the 40-year-old actor in 2013. Indeed, these kinds of obscure stories are important parts of celebrity cemetery tours and are often used by the guides to capture their audience's attention. Listening to narrations while gasping, tourists ask questions, wanting to learn more about the macabre aspects of those happenings and macabre events.

However, a thorough observation of cemetery tourists' behaviours reveals that their fascination with death and the macabre is not the only element that motivates their visits. When it comes to notable burials, the strong influence of celebrity culture emerges, which refers to the centrality of celebrities today and how the media enhances celebrity presence (Driessens, 2014). Thus, aspects such as fandom and celebrity admiration play fundamental roles in cemetery visits. Consequently, on the homepage of the Hollywood Forever Cemetery's website, the introductory section reads:

> Founded in 1899, the national cemetery is one of the world's most historic places, and the final resting place of hundreds of Hollywood legends, including Judy Garland, Cecil B. DeMille, Rudolph Valentino, Mickey Rooney, Tyrone Power, Douglas Fairbanks, Johnny and Dee Dee Ramone, Valerie Harper, Chris Cornell, and hundreds of others. (Hollywoodforever.com, n.d.)

Analysing celebrity sightings, Ferris (2004) notices that star–fan encounters follow precise patterns, which include intense emotions that range from excitement to disappointment. During an informal conversation with a tour guide during the ethnography, she mentioned that once in front of their favourite artists' graves, people often behave as if they are meeting them in person. As I noticed during my observations, tourists perceive cemetery tours as an occasion to be in physical proximity with (celebrity) corpses. They do so by touching and/or taking selfies with the tombstones, repeatedly revealing intense emotions by smiling or crying.

In their work on celebrity culture, Ferris and Harris (2011: 14) describe an asymmetry between stars and fans, which is rooted in the idea that 'the fan knows far more about the identity of the celebrity than vice versa'. Thus, popular culture scholars argue that the general audience's deep knowledge of famous people's public and private lives leads to fans viewing stars as familiar figures (Penfold-Mounce, 2019). In some cases, those asymmetric relationships reach even more intimate dimensions, such as religion and spirituality. Describing the phenomenon of film-induced tourism, Beeton (2005: 32) explains how, starting from the second half of the 20th century, contemporary society developed a *cult of celebrity*: 'while the growth of mass media was central to the cultivation of celebrity, the worship of movie stars filled a psychological or even spiritual need in a century where religion was declining and heroism was becoming more difficult to identify'.

Among the reasons critical studies scholars mention when describing the commodification of memorial parks is that they lost their sacred aura (Soligo & Dickens, 2020). However, an investigation of celebrity tourism within cemeteries reveals strong similarities with the spiritual realm, recalling Beeton's notion of cult of celebrity. When attending the ceremony that takes place every year at the Pierce Brothers Westwood Village Memorial Park & Mortuary during the day of Marilyn Monroe death's anniversary, organised by the Marilyn Remembered fan club, I immediately noticed the importance of that event for her fans. People travelled from all over the world to celebrate the blonde diva at her burial site, crying and kissing her tombstone. Similarly, when I visited Michael Jackson's burial site at the Forest Lawn Memorial Park-Glendale during his birthday and death anniversary, I noticed many tourists who travelled internationally to pay tribute to the former pop star (Figure 16.1).

While leaving posters and cards in front of the door of the chapel where Michael Jackson is buried, fans showed their love by playing his songs and wearing items, such as glittery gloves and fedoras, who recalled the artist iconic style (Soligo & Dickens, 2020). Several Hollywood professionals I interacted with defined tourists' visits to celebrity-related attractions in Los Angeles as contemporary pilgrimages. Indeed, when observing tourists' behaviours, I noticed conspicuous similarities with the way religiose people act and perform while worshipping saints or other religious figures at their burial sites.

Figure 16.1 Fans' tributes in front of Michael Jackson's burial site
Source: Author (CC BY-ND).

Cemeteries as Mirrors of History and Heritage

Several sociological and anthropological works reveal that cemeteries function as mirrors of communities' past lives and historic eras (Warner, 1959). To promote their 'Tombstone Tales' tour at the Woodlawn Cemetery, the Las Vegas-based association Nevada Preservation states:

> Cemeteries are a site for mourning and remembrance, but are also places of great historic value. Here we uncover insight into the people and practices of our past; where the living gain a better understanding of the lives and deaths of people before them. Discover Nevada history, take advantage of the cooler temperatures and transition into autumn on our Woodlawn Cemetery Walking Tour. (Nevadapreservation.org, n.d.)

Nevada Preservation's tour aims to narrate the history of Las Vegas and Nevada through the lives of the people buried at the Woodlawn Cemetery. The notable internments described by the guides include P.J. Goumond, an important investor for the Las Vegas gambling industry during the 1920s, and Stella Parson, the first African American woman to graduate from college in Nevada. With excitement, visitors declared that the Woodlawn Cemetery walking tour represented a unique way to learn about the people who played important roles for Nevada's social, economic and artistic life.

Similarly, the Monumental Cemetery of Milan, which hosts graves of the city's most famous personalities, such as entrepreneurs, writers and entertainers, is becoming one of the city's most visited attractions. The cemetery itself proposes several guided tours, which are promoted on the official website as: 'Along with the chapels of the great Milanese families, culture and entrepreneurship, there are many illustrious personalities who have linked their names to the political and civil history of Milan and Italy' (as translated by the author) (monumentale.comune.milano.it, n.d.). As I will explain in the next section, Milan's Monumental Cemetery is known for hosting some famous works of art. However, it represents a unique attraction for history fans as well. The guided tour I participated in heavily centred on the cemetery as a mirror of the city's heritage. For example, while in front of the tombstone of the world-famous Italian conductor Arturo Toscanini, visitors learn about Milan's musical scene at the beginning of the 20th century.

Moreover, as in the case of celebrity culture, history-based visits to cemeteries often overlap with dark tourism-related motivations. We find this phenomenon in tourists' curiosity when it comes to tragic or traumatic deaths. This is the case of Renato Briano, now buried at the Monumental Cemetery in Milan, and who was brutally killed in 1983 by the militant left-wing organisation Red Brigades. While expressing interest in Briano's tragic death, tourists attending the tour could learn about one of the most complex moments in Italian contemporary history as well. Similarly, visits to poet Antonia Pozzi's gravesite in Pasturo, a mountain town in Northern Italy, uncover a twofold behaviour. On the one hand, the 26-year-old woman's controversial death – which took place in 1938 – reveals tourists' fascination for some macabre aspects. Indeed, it is common knowledge that Pozzi took her own life by swallowing pills and lying down in the snow. However, immersed in a strictly Catholic context where suicide was heavily condemned, her father declared that Antonia died from pneumonia. On the other hand, visits to Pozzi's grave also represent an opportunity to learn more about her and her (now internationally renowned) poetry and discover other important socio-historical aspects. For example, by becoming familiar with her story, tourists acquire information on the discrimination women had to face when approaching the academic world at the beginning of the 20th century – a prejudiced environment that had a significantly negative impact on the poet's life.

Thus, it is interesting to notice that an increasing number of cemeteries target themselves as historical tourism attractions. My study reveals that several memorial park tours target both locals – who see the visit as an occasion to deepen their knowledge of the people that play important roles for their own cities – and tourists – who, while touring the cemeteries, learn more about the history of the city they are visiting.

Connecting Darkness with Beauty: The Cemetery as an Outdoor Art Museum

Cemeteries as heritage sites cannot underestimate the role of artworks in attracting tourists. Describing the Monumental Cemetery, the official website of Milan's tourism authority states:

> The Monumental Cemetery, more than just a simple cemetery, is an extraordinary outdoor museum. It is as if some of the great sculptors of the 1900s were called together to elaborate and reflect on a particularly demanding theme, to be precise, death … From an architectural perspective, you can catch a glimpse of both Romanic and Gothic traces. Along the principal paths, in order to help visitors, there are some maps that bear the indications of the most interesting monuments and among these the Famedio (Memorial Chapel) is indicated. It is a voluminous construction made of bricks and marble in Neo-medieval style where, amongst other personages, Alessandro Manzoni is buried. (yesmilano.it, n.d.)

Through my observations and textual analysis, it emerged that the notion of the cemetery as an outdoor museum is a recurring theme. My investigation at the Milan Monumental Cemetery revealed that tourists consider artworks that stand on top of burial sites as important as the biographies of the deceased. While attending the guided tour of the Monumental Cemetery, I noticed that the description of the statues and monuments almost prevailed on the narrations related to the notable internments (Figure 16.2). Moreover, it emerged that a conspicuous

Figure 16.2 The Monumental Cemetery of Milan
Source: 3giorniamilano.it (CC BY-SA).

number of visitors were more interested in learning about the artworks rather than about the people buried in the cemetery.

Additionally, the guides' comprehensive knowledge in history of the art created a peculiar experience that connected the darkness of death with the beauty of the artworks. As the website of Milan's tourism authority notes:

> And those who imagine this cemetery as an especially sad place are mistaken. In reality, it presents itself as a pleasant place to visit, filled with inscriptions that invite you to remember those who have gone before, rich with information and accompanied by interesting artistic detail. (yesmilano.it, n.d.)

Thus, as happens in the case of Hollywood memorial parks, tourists are invited to abandon the traditional view of cemeteries as sad places. In this case, the presence of artworks by some of the most famous Italian artists – such as Arnaldo Pomodoro, Lucio Fontana and Giò Ponti – represents a way to pay tribute to the departed. A noteworthy example in this sense is Federico Fellini's tomb in his hometown, Rimini. The Oscar-winning director, his wife actor Giulietta Masina and their prematurely dead child Pierfederico are buried under a sculpture by world-renown artist Arnaldo Pomodoro. The bronze artwork, called *The Big Prow,* represents a ship that symbolises the journey towards the afterlife (Figure 16.3).

The sculpture seems to emerge from the stream of water beneath it, recalling the dreamlike atmosphere of Fellini's movies. The conspicuous number of websites that promote tours of Fellini's locations in Rimini

Figure 16.3 Director Federico Fellini's tomb: *The Big Prow* by Arnaldo Pomodoro
Source: tastebologna.net (n.d.) (CC BY-SA).

list his burial site among the must-see attractions. In doing so, they include an overview of Pomodoro's sculpture, explaining how its artistic features function as a tribute to the director's life and his movies.

Artworks are also a key element of Hollywood memorial parks as well. For example, tourists who visit the Forest Lawn Memorial Park – Glendale can tour the Forest Lawn Museum Galleries, together with replicas of Leonardo's Last Supper in the Great Mausoleum and Michelangelo's sculptures in the *Court of David*:

> Introducing 'Court of David', a new distinction property in Forest Lawn – Glendale. You'll be taken back to Michelangelo's glorious renaissance Italy with marble-facade niches with three notable bas-reliefs of classic Italian artworks. At its center, a marvelous 17-foot bronze replica of the statue of Michelangelo's David gazes back into the park. It's not just a place. It's a destination. (forestlawn.com, n.d.)

As illustrated, the cemetery's website invites visitors to not only enjoy the artwork display, but also to perceive the location – borrowing from the tourism jargon – as a *destination*. Thus, predictions in terms of future trends in dark tourism should consider that the number of cemeteries that brand themselves as artistic attractions is significantly growing. This confirms, once again, the flexible and evolving nature of those sites, which are constantly creating new ways to blend death-related features with elements – such as the beauty of art – that allow them to reach broader targets of tourists.

Conclusion

This study adopted a futurology-based approach that starts from the present. In other words, an in-depth qualitative analysis helped me better understand current trends and future possibilities, with a specific focus on cemeteries as cultural heritage landscapes. I paid particular attention to the directions that cemetery tourism is currently taking to predict forthcoming tendencies. Overall, I have argued that cemetery tourism is increasingly blending death-related motivations with other elements. As my investigation reveals, for a conspicuous number of cemetery tourists, aspects such as celebrity culture, history and art often overlap – if not prevail over – the dark ones. Indeed, as Sallay *et al.* (2022: 4) point out:

> Tourists wander through burial grounds with the aim of discovering the artistic, architectural, historical, and scenic heritage that often abounds in cemeteries. The changing perception of cemeteries from a place for burial towards a cultural heritage space provides several opportunities for tourism. It enables the community to explore the development of products and services that help the destination to gain new income while preserving its heritage.

Stakeholders involved in cemetery tourism are gradually advocating for new perspectives that avoid traditional views of burial sites as sad or frightening locations. We see this trend in guided tours, which not only centre around dark components, such as unsolved murders and tragic deaths, but also around thorough descriptions of artistic details and historic facts. Consequently, cemeteries are arranged along a range of dark and light products and experiences (Stone, 2006). This also entails the overlap of contrasting elements, such as the sadness of death and the beauty of art. Specifically, the future of cemetery tourism is marked by the idea that burial sites are unique witnesses of the surrounding context. It is not a coincidence if both cemetery official websites and other tourism marketing outlets promote burial sites as tools to understand the cultural fabric that surrounds them (Milligan, 2007). According to the tourists I interacted with, cemetery visits helped deepen their knowledge of local cultural heritage and history.

Thus, it is important to gaze at the future from a cultural landscape-based standpoint, which entails looking at burial sites as mirrors of the societies that built them. This means that an analysis of cemetery tourism's future could benefit from sociological and anthropological approaches, as explained by Warner (1959), who investigates how those places work as mirrors of communities' past lives and historic eras. As my study has suggested, the mirror in this sense is twofold. If it is true that cemeteries tell the stories of the host communities, it is equally correct to state that those sites are also tools to understand guest (or tourists)-related trends. This is particularly the case of celebrity culture, whose dominant presence in present-day society is reflected in cemetery visits, which are increasingly rooted in fandom and popular culture. To that end, future studies in dark tourism should focus both on proximity – such as local heritage and the surrounding context – and on contemporary society at large, given significant influences that social changes have on (dark) tourism trends.

17 'Not the Right Sort of Visitors': Future Challenges of Cemetery Tourism

Janine Marriott

Introduction

A historic 19th century cemetery in the UK may not seem the obvious choice of place for people to spend their free time. Yet, there is a long history of travel for leisure or pilgrimage to burial grounds and deathscapes as specific purposeful destinations. From at least the medieval era, pilgrimages to places of interment were an early form of tourism (Seaton, 1996), and burial grounds have been places for visitors to learn from and be inspired by. Long before the academic inclusion of historic cemeteries into the category of dark tourism, these sites in the UK have been spaces with multiple audiences, uses and purposes. Therefore, the aim of my chapter is to outline inherent dilemmas in managing historic cemeteries as a touristic resource, as well as examining future challenges faced by authorities and custodians.

From the beginning of the 19th century historic cemeteries have primarily been places of burial but also places of leisure and tourism (Curl, 1975; Curl, 2004; Seaton, 2002). This is evidenced by several 19th century cemetery guidebooks (Barker, 1869; Clark, 1843; Dolby, 1845; Grinsted, 1857; Justyne, 1865; Manning, 1915; Shaw, 1851) for visitors to these spaces, which demonstrate that visiting a cemetery to see the grave of a famous person was not unusual for a Victorian tourist. As the introduction to the *Last Home of Departed Genius* publication by Grinsted (1867: v) states: 'The passion for visiting burial-places of eminent persons has distinguished all ages'. There are also articles that appeared in 19th century newspapers describing visiting cemeteries for their aesthetic appeal, providing advice on the most beautiful, those with the best views and even some mocking those who chose to visit them for leisure (Mudford, 1841), which shows how widespread the practice was. Among the wealthy, mainly British and European, visiting burial grounds, catacombs and significant burial sites in European cities was an established tradition with a trip to them, seen as a part of the Grand Tour or other leisure trip. Since the 18th century, evidence of visits to deathscapes includes publications of these visits in books and newspapers, and it is clear there is a long history of people visiting and engaging with funerary sites and objects (Seaton, 2002) as well as using them for burial. When defining a 19th century historic cemetery, the categorisation by Rugg (2000) of what makes a cemetery a cemetery is used. However, the background to the development of these historic cemeteries is well outlined by a variety of academics (Brooks, 1989; Curl, 1975; Dunk & Rugg, 1994; Johnson, 2008; Tarlow, 2000; Worpole, 1997, 2003) and is not reiterated here.

Historic Cemeteries: An Overview

Despite the history of historic cemeteries as public places for the living as well as spaces for the dead, Grabalov and Nordh (2021) note that truly little has been done to explore cemeteries as public space, possibly because they challenge the rigid interpretation of public space. In the UK, a variety of reports and articles highlight that cemeteries can and should be retained as public space (The Environment, Transport and Regional Affairs Committee [ETRA], 2001), but there seems to be little appetite at local or national government levels for a joined-up approach around the future of cemetery management or use. Cemeteries can be both an excellent community and visitor space, and Woodthorpe (2011) highlights numerous categories and disciplines that cemeteries may fit into. Woodthorpe goes on to note it is better when researching these sites to not divide cemeteries into separate academic partitions but to see them as multidisciplinary. As such, historic cemeteries are not only a rich and varied source for academic research, but they can also provide a range of experiences for visitors and local communities, and not just those considered to be locations of dark tourism (Sharpley, 2005, 2009a; Sharpley & Stone, 2009). Although for many historic cemeteries their heyday has passed, and attitudes to visiting a cemetery have changed, it is important to state that many are still working burial sites undertaking the disposal of human remains.

However, out of the hundreds of cemeteries created in the 18th and early 19th centuries, a number are closed, almost full or less well used. As Woodthorpe (2011) points out, a lack of national guidance in England around cemeteries means that many local authorities that care for cemeteries have marginalised them. Consequently, these spaces are threatened by this low status, and by the fact that they can be at threat of closure due to lack of burial space. It is also worth noting that many historic cemeteries are also challenging to use and maintain as a burial ground as they are not neatly laid out like modern lawn cemeteries. This means that a Local Authority (LA) may put more resources into modern burial spaces and encourage, or even force, use of the areas and grounds that are easier to maintain, thereby creating a cycle of neglect for older burial grounds and areas within them. Subsequently, people become less inclined to visit and use the space as it is perceived to be neglected, leading LAs to invest less in their maintenance. In the UK almost all cemeteries are now under the control of LA or religious organisations (Rugg, 2020), and very few of these historic landscapes are owned or run by private businesses or trusts (see Marriott, 2023, for a trust list.) Unlike historic cemeteries in most European countries, UK and Irish burial remains are not usually removed after a set number of years for the grave to be reused; even though the grave is leased, it is not reused after the lease expires. This complicated relationship between leases, cemetery authorities, and an expectation of *in perpetuity* burial means they are not often reused. That said, Highgate Cemetery and Camberwell Old Cemetery/Southwark Council in London reuse grave space in a limited way, so even though legal, it can be possible. Rugg (2020: 866) points out that reuse is environmentally and financially logical and suggests 'without an effective grave reuse system, income is likely to decline, and the cemetery becomes a wasting asset'.

Even though there is a potential crisis looming in UK urban areas as burial grounds fill up, there is currently little appetite for grave reuse in England and Wales and it is a delicate, often politically sensitive and time-consuming process. However, when historic cemeteries are threatened with destruction, communities often rally round to save and protect them. Awareness raising activities can include public engagement activities, especially talks, visitor tours and open days which encourage engagement from people who are not family members or friends of the deceased to the site. Few members of the public understand the legalities of grave maintenance (at most UK sites the grave owner, not the cemetery, is liable for maintenance of the grave) and that the lack of budget for site maintenance can cause issues. When public engagement activities are undertaken to raise funds for maintenance and resources, even sometimes staffing, some members of the public do not understand the need for the activities as the budgetary and maintenance issues are poorly communicated by the organisation.

Potentially, the change in status of a number of these historic deathscapes – from burial grounds in use, to rarely used, disused or closed to burial and cremains – can be regarded as either an opportunity or a challenge, depending on how the spaces are managed for the living. These cemeteries can have great opportunities for all types of visitor including mourners, or those seeking solace (Bachelor, 2004), secular pilgrims (Seaton, 2002), nature and science or geography enthusiasts, those interested in cultural heritage including architecture, archaeology and history (Paraskevopoulou, 2019), family history researchers, walkers, general and dark tourists/thanatourists (Seaton & Lennon, 2004) and those seeking a quiet contemplative or reflective space in an heavily urbanised area. With this wide-ranging and varied audience base, an argument can be made for retaining and utilising cemeteries even if they are closed to burials. Interestingly, it is not common for burial authorities to utilise these public landscapes for the local community and even less common for them to employ staff who are directly involved in encouraging use of the landscape for public engagement or public history, or just as a public park. When there are staff employed to engage visitors (and this is currently a small percentage of historic cemeteries in the UK), it is often undertaken by a Charitable Trust (CT) or a *Friends of* group. At the time of writing, the only LA cemeteries that have a staff member devoted to engaging visitors are Brookwood Cemetery in Surrey and Sheffield General Cemetery. Other sites with dedicated staff undertaking this role include Tower Hamlets Cemetery and Abney Park Cemetery (both London), where the staff members are employed by the *Friends of* the cemetery with permission from the LA. Meanwhile, Arnos Vale Cemetery (Bristol), York Cemetery and the famous Highgate Cemetery (London) employ staff through a CT, and Willesden Jewish Cemetery (London) employ staff via the United Synagogue. It is worth noting that Glasnevin Cemetery in Dublin, Ireland is also run by a CT, and although beyond the scope of this chapter, employs a variety of staff to engage visitors and even has a museum and café.

In the UK, however, a variety of the visitor engagement occurring in cemeteries is delivered ad hoc by volunteers who support and are members of the *Friends of* the cemetery. This is undertaken with the permission of the owners but rarely comes with any financial support, with *Friends of* groups fundraising for landscape and building maintenance, site interpretation, tours, talks, as well as memorial and remembrance ceremonies. Indeed, the importance of *Friends of* groups is highlighted by Paraskevopoulou (2016), who explored four historic cemeteries and the role that their Friends groups had in saving and managing the sites.

Cemeteries: Demonstrating Future Value

In my role as a cemetery public engagement manager, I regard cemeteries as important heritage assets that should not be lost, and I explore what value they possess to ensure their protection. To that end, it is necessary to prove cemetery value (beyond the obvious role of interment) to owners and managers as they can be seen as financial liabilities that were once mercantile sites, but now cost more than they make (if anything at all). Moreover, urban expansion can be challenging to cemeteries, as sites can be seen as prime land suitable for expansion;

but if the importance of these spaces is better understood by LAs, then the threat might be lessened.

When considering value of cemeteries as public space it is worth exploring their tangible and intangible opportunities and benefits. This can be undertaken by reviewing cemeteries that are already engaging with visitors and providing resources to local communities and beyond. To have value, it is not necessary for a UK heritage cemetery to have the kudos of a world-famous cemetery such as Père Lachaise Cemetery in Paris or Highgate Cemetery in London. Even the most humble and small historic cemetery has something to offer and can be marketed as a potential visitor location. A number have listed landscape status, listed graves, gates or buildings (Historic England, n.d.), making them important heritage assets. Yet, even without these recognised qualities, cemeteries can still be valuable sources of history and heritage, especially as a resource for family genealogists, war graves enthusiasts or local historians. They are also extremely valuable green spaces (McClymont, 2018), not just for the flora and fauna which are of interest to visitors, but also as part of local green infrastructure including flood defences, soil quality, water and air cleaning, and as a remover of city-wide pollution due to their range of mature trees and greenery. Cemeteries are often situated in urban green spaces and as urban densification envelopes them, provide much needed green space for communities who may not have a garden or local park. Consequently, they can be an attraction for nature-loving tourists or those seeking sightings of specific animals, birds, or flora or fauna. Several cemeteries already highlight their importance as green spaces. For instance, Arnos Vale Cemetery is a designated Special Site of Conservation Interest (SSCI), Tower Hamlets Cemetery (Tower Hamlets Council, 2023) and Bisley Road Cemetery in Stroud (Stroud Town Council, 2020) are included in the local authority green space plans, demonstrating the value placed by the local authority on the sites due to the environmental impact they have on the local area.

Due to these reasons, local communities are very resistant to burial grounds being built on, even if they have no personal link to the people remembered in the cemetery because they are seen as public spaces. Examples of public fighting for these spaces include Highgate Cemetery (Barker & Gay, 1984; Bulmer, 2020) and Arnos Vale Cemetery (Marriott, 2023), which involved court battles, public petitions and direct action. However, there was still reluctance by local authorities to take on financial burdens of the cemetery from the private owners, but ownership solutions were found. With careful research, surveys and local knowledge, a historic cemetery has the potential to be a community and visitor space while maintaining its key role as a burial space and a bereavement place, if organisations and groups caring for them balance the needs of all its users. As McClymont (2018) demonstrates, cemetery functions can conflict, but they usually coexist peacefully. Therefore, from cemeteries that are currently engaging the public, sensitive management, and an understanding of various audiences, as well as the rich natural and heritage resource of the site, allied with individualised approaches, can help secure cemeteries for the living in the future.

Valuable but not valued

Proving value to authorities can be a struggle and needs careful planning. Dunk and Rugg (1994) suggest cemetery managers (usually employed by the LA) do not believe historic cemeteries have anything to offer. A grassroots and organic approach to saving cemeteries often comes from a *Friends of* group or a CT set up by local people working towards highlighting the special nature of their cemetery to protect it or prove its value. However, this needs to be systematically assessed. Its qualities and resources can include designed landscapes, historic built environments, mature but delicate ecosystems (through wildlife surveys), artistic or noteworthy monuments, special memorials, and mausoleums, plus the historical identity of the destination (Seaton, 2002). This detailed analysis can lead to a better understanding of what social, recreational, educational and nature-related events and opportunities can be offered, helping to prove the cemetery is an important asset in a LA portfolio.

An evaluation report by the *Friends of* Tower Hamlets Cemetery Park (2022: 28) in London for funder NLHF on the 'Heritage and Us' project made it clear that taking stock and assessing what is important to visitors has immense value. As such, it can help sites understand what can be done next to engage people in the future. This type of analysis can reveal a community venue for hire, a public engagement site for informal education, a local recreation space like a park, a green ark/nature reserve or just a contemplative or spiritual space. It may seem crass to consider a cemetery as having financial value, but when encouraging investment of money, staff or resources, there needs to be a demonstration of community value and the potential for generating income (separate from interment income) from tours, talks, venue hire, concerts and film screenings. It is vital when identifying value and importance that the needs of all site users are understood, so the next step would be to understand the motivations and needs of visitors and to understand that cemeteries are not just multi-disciplinary but are multi-use.

Future Challenges of Cemetery Tourism: Towards Managing Visitation

Academic research and public consultation demonstrate evidence that historic cemeteries have a diverse range of visitors who often have a strong affection and concern for the welfare of the cemetery. Many of the concerns expressed in consultations and research by Woodthorpe

(2011) and Deering (2010) demonstrate that people wish to protect the site from a variety of real or perceived threats, including destruction by owners or LAs, antisocial and disrespectful behaviour and neglect. In some cases, users form into grassroots *Friends of* groups that work to protect the site, and there are currently over 120 active cemetery *Friends* groups in the UK (private correspondence with the National Federation of Cemetery Friends). There are varying levels of involvement and reasons for protecting the site at various stages in the cemeteries' life, including as a protest or pressure group to prevent destruction (Arnos Vale Cemetery, Bristol), to guard against terminal decline (Abney Park Cemetery, London) or to preserve the site and the wildlife landscape (Tower Hamlets Cemetery, London). Other groups may be determined to keep the cemetery as a working local burial space (York Cemetery, and Highgate Cemetery in London), or to preserve an important piece of local history and public space (Flaybrick Memorial Garden in Liverpool, or Hyde Park Cemetery in Doncaster).

However, not all campaigners and *Friends of* group members have the same goals. Disagreements can occur between those wanting a wildlife-friendly site and those who feel overgrowth and wild plants in and around graves is disrespectful or untidy. Moreover, there are those who feel a cemetery should only be for the bereaved, and that local people with no connection to the site should not use it for recreation, including cycling, dog walking, jogging, lunch breaks or for personal exercise (as seen in Birmingham Cemeteries). A Hackney Council report (2018) (on Abney Park Cemetery, London) concluded that 'regardless of the capacity in which they visit, a large majority of Park users share common ground over wanting to know more about Abney Park and wanting to see more activity on site'. Reagan (2018: 104), in her Abney Park research, highlights that what is appropriate in a cemetery evolves and changes, and shifting cultural attitudes affect this. This shift will undoubtedly continue, so there are many reasons to work to protect and save an historic cemetery. There is a range of different audiences that may use it, and there are also likely to be clashes between users wanting different things. However, this cannot be a reason to not move forward, but friction among visitation users will need management. Indeed, 'the cemetery is no longer a meandering landscape so beautifully illustrated by Laudon; it is a political, contested, and dynamic space accessed by a wide range of people who carry with them varying expectations and demands' (Woodthorpe, 2011: 272).

Therefore, cemeteries are places of contradiction, whereby they are both public and private spaces at the same time and in terms of a public/private dichotomy, Nielsen and Groes (2014: 114) note that cemeteries are:

- a place for grief (private) but also a place for contemplation (public);
- a public place for public engagement activities but with consideration of the suitability of those activities to ensure respect for private grief;

- graves owned by families (private)/space owned by the local community or council (public);
- an eternal place (private)/a place for everyone to utilise (public);
- a place for those with a connection (private) but a place where everyone could connect (public).

It is here that Principle 4 of the Ename Charter (ICOMOS, 2008) offers a good guide when considering how a historic cemetery could be managed for visitors, while carefully considering the bereaved and members of the local community. Moreover, this includes respecting the 'authenticity of cultural heritage sites, by communicating the significance of their historic fabric and cultural values and protecting them from the adverse impact of intrusive interpretive infrastructure, visitor pressure, inaccurate or inappropriate interpretation' (ICOMOS, 2008).

Due to their sacred and spiritual nature it is important that cemeteries are not, and should not become, mass tourism sites (Seaton, 2002). Practically, such sites are unlikely to have suitable resources to accommodate mass tourism due to a lack of car parking capacity and are not always located in accessible spots via public transport. The ecological impact on the site must be also considered, as large numbers of visitors to certain locations could cause wear and tear on paths, impact on delicate ecosystems and cause irreversible damage to cultural heritage. Cemeteries are spiritual and emotional landscapes, and the kind of signage and site interpretation that might be acceptable in a historic house or landscape can be intrusive and jarring (Figure 17.1), especially if certain 'extraordinary' people are highlighted buried within the cemetery, potentially disregarding 'ordinary' loved ones and upsetting families. Mourners may also perceive large groups of tourists as morbid or voyeuristic, so careful consideration of how a site is presented for the tourist or casual visitor will facilitate how people are expected to behave.

It is difficult to discern who is using a historic cemetery because, unlike other heritage sites, they are rarely ticketed or monitored for visitation. Highgate Cemetery is the only site in the UK that charges entry to anyone who is not a relation; so, unless ticketed events occur, then site users are hard to quantify. However, there has been some research that looked at reasons for visiting a site (Dunk & Rugg, 1994; Deering, 2010; Woodthorpe, 2011), and particularly those who might be included on 'A Dark Tourist Spectrum' typology (Raine, 2013). Raine (2013) observed that, at a selection of burial grounds (Bunhill Fields in London, St Margaret's Graveyard in Whitby and Weaste Cemetery in Salford), visitors had diverse range of motivations and can be divided into four main categories, namely Devotion (mourners and pilgrims), Experience (morbidly curious and thrill seekers), Discover (information seekers and hobbyists) and Incidental (sightseers, retreaters and passive

Figure 17.1 Temporary signage at Highgate Cemetery, London
Source: Author.

recreationists). This research shows that mourners are certainly not the only site users, but they are important users. To support the management of visitors after assessing the resources and prominent features of a cemetery, consultation with current and future audiences should be undertaken. In 2018, for example, Hackney Borough Council undertook a public consultation on Abney Park Cemetery (Hackney Council, 2018), and in 2022 the *Friends of* Tower Hamlets Cemetery Park undertook a consultation with users. Both consultations revealed the importance of these sites to the local community, highlighting people wanted them to be more useful and user friendly with amenities such as benches, signage, toilets and a café, while not spoiling the unique aura of these sites and being mindful of their special nature.

Attracting visitors to cemeteries

When considering the attributes of UK historic cemeteries for leisure and tourism, it is unlikely that most will have a grave of a famous/infamous person that people will want to visit. The UK exception to this is Highgate Cemetery that contains the grave of German philosopher Karl Marx, which has proved a definite tourist attraction. When attracting visitors, the lack of a famous grave does not mean that there are not specific graves in cemeteries that are not a visitor location. Indeed, many visitors to historic cemeteries are choosing to visit the sites specifically because of their cultural, historic, natural or landscape significance, and this could be described as secular pilgrimage. It is worth noting that many cemeteries will have notable people that may be the pilgrimage focus of visitors who may have religious or cultural connections. In Arnos Vale Cemetery, for instance, the grave of important Hindu religious thinker Rajah Ram Mohan Roy is a well-visited focal point, and in Abney Park Cemetery the grave of the founder of the Salvation Army, William Booth, is regularly sought out. A different kind of secular pilgrimage often comes from literature, with fans of J.R.R. Tolkien leaving tokens such as pens or polyhedral dice on his grave at Wolvercote Cemetery in Oxford. Meanwhile, Willesden Jewish Cemetery in London holds the remains of ground-breaking scientist Rosalind Franklin and Chief Rabbi Israel Brodie, and people come to visit these graves to place a stone to show respect. These types of seekers are niche and looking for specific graves, so unless there are resources to help them engage more with the site then their visit will be brief.

Another audience that might visit are those regarded as 'dark tourists', although most visitors to historic cemeteries do not attend for a spooky or morbid experiences, especially as there are no human remains on show. Cemeteries are not sites of 'spectacular death' (Jacobson, 2016; Stone, 2018: 1020), so these tourists are more *thanatourists* seeking an encounter with the person in the grave than for any thrill-seeking reason. Visitors do not see themselves as engaging with dark tourism or dark heritage and do not see anything macabre or gruesome in their visit. As Light (2017b) explains, visitors may not even be consciously seeking an encounter with death at all. If they are, then they may be looking for a *memento mori* moment, or a place to be contemplative of mortality (Stone & Sharpley, 2008). As Stone (2012b) suggests, cemeteries are perfect places where the dead act as 'guardians of the living'. However, regardless of the motivations to visit cemeteries, barriers to visiting and engaging fully with the site must be considered and where possible addressed.

Barriers to visiting cemeteries

Having explored the reason and motivations of visitors, it is important to consider why people may not visit cemeteries. Many *Friends of* groups were set up because the neglect and perceived lack of action by owners prompted them to improve sites, campaign for better landscape and grave management, and even to take or share ownership (examples include York Cemetery, Abney Park Cemetery and Arnos Vale Cemetery). An unkempt or obviously neglected site can feel dangerous to potential visitors and can promote strong feelings. Uncared-for buildings, monuments and landscape can lead to the cemetery being perceived as an unsafe space. As people visit family graves less than they used to, mature plants and trees that were often planted over a hundred years ago need careful maintenance if they are to be safe for visitors. However, Dunk and Rugg (1994) note that cemetery managers are resistant to ecological management. There is also an issue with families no longer visiting their family graves due to infirmity, death or just because they have moved away and no longer tend or maintain plots, adding to the picture of decay.

These factors can create a cycle of neglect and people feel less able to visit due to antisocial behaviour (Deering, 2010: 88), vandalism, or 'purple recreation' (that is, those partaking in deviant activities) (Deering, 2012) which occurs more often at a neglected site. Even when cemetery *Friends of* groups try to improve neglected grounds, they can meet with resistance from LAs that run cemeteries, both modern and 19th century. LAs often apply blanket rules about grave maintenance, plants and other activities that prevent volunteers from undertaking site improvements. A tidy, safe feeling landscape with clear litter bins and frequently updated signage is valuable in discouraging perceived antisocial behaviour, demonstrating that the site is managed and open to visitors (Figure 17.2).

People may also be unwilling to visit a historic cemetery if they perceive it to be a place which should only be visited if there is a family

Figure 17.2 Visitors relaxing in the landscape at Arnos Vale Cemetery
Source: Author.

connection and, therefore, require permission to enter. The walled and contained nature (Rugg, 2000) of historic cemeteries also adds to this perception of a private space. Potential visitors may also consider the cemetery to be irrelevant if it is not their history, culture, faith group or community remembered on site. Although many cemeteries in the UK are not specific to one faith group, belief system or social group, the community using it 150 years ago is not always the community around it now. Proving relevance is key to ensuring that visitors feel welcome. When interpretation and public engagement is undertaken it must be broad ranging and inclusive to ensure that the stories of the wealthy, white, straight, and male are not the only ones told. Indeed, intersectionality, sensitivity and care (Stone & Morton, 2022) are vital to welcoming visitors to site. Examples of intersectionality include the LGBTQ+ 'Queerly Departed' tour hosted regularly at Brompton Cemetery in London led by public historian and professional guide Sheldon K. Goodman and museum professional Sacha Coward, and the 'Wonderful Women' tour developed by volunteers and staff at Arnos Vale Cemetery. There is much more that can be undertaken in this area as this kind of research is more challenging because histories are more hidden. Moreover, there are some cemeteries that are managed by specific faith groups or military organisations and the rules and expectations in these spaces can be different. Consequently, some may not be suitable as public visitor spaces. However, one notable exception is Willesden Jewish Cemetery in London which, in 2015 after receiving a Heritage Lottery Fund grant, set out to turn this working (but almost full) cemetery into a welcoming visitor space (Abrahms, 2022) while honouring Jewish customs and traditions, and telling the story of Jewish burial and remembrance.

Like many other historic landscapes there are many ways to encourage visitors to come to site, and some of these management tools are active while others are passive (Deering, 2010, 2012). Active management includes welcoming signage, which is more important for a cemetery than other sites as people may be unsure if they are allowed on site, but it must be subtle and respectful. It is also important to have some signage in the landscape, either permanent or temporary, to indicate facilities like toilets and water points, where to get a map or relevant leaflet, rules of behaviour, and opening and closing times. This may seem obvious for any historic site, but when audiences have not been catered for in the past, these necessities may not have been considered, especially by volunteer-led *Friends of* groups who know the site well but are not heritage professionals with an understanding of visitor engagement requirements. The use of the internet has also changed the way cemeteries welcome visitors. Some historic cemeteries have social media accounts or websites managed by *Friends* groups, or public engagement staff (but rarely LA bereavement services staff).

These online resources help people to feel welcome and to plan their visit, and will advertise events such as talks, tours, concerts, films, theatre performances, and open days. Some historic cemeteries go further to make visitors welcome with exhibitions, a reception area, staff or volunteers greeting people, and even a café (for example, Arnos Vale Cemetery [Bristol], Brompton Cemetery [London], Abney Park Cemetery [London], Glasnevin Cemetery [Dublin] and the City of London Cemetery and Crematorium who are building a café), making the venue more like a heritage attraction experience.

Conclusion

Cemeteries do not have to be closed to burial to be useful for a range of audiences. Being a visitor space can save and protect them and raise awareness of usefulness. If using Stone's 'Dark Tourism Spectrum' typology (Stone, 2006), then cemetery visitation is 'grey' tourism rather than truly 'dark' tourism. In other words, no one died on site and the space is not necessarily morbid, but they must be treated with the same sensitivities that would be applied to other dark tourism sites due to their spiritual nature (Bachelor, 2004). The liminality of cemeteries can help them be viewed as a special experience or a bordered retreat. It is vital that audiences understand they are welcome but are also clear about what is acceptable, as they are still places of the dead and places reflecting human mortality. Protecting these spaces now, by welcoming in visitors, will mean they exist as resources for the future, either as a vital urban green space, a source of culture and heritage or even renewed in the future as a place for burying and scattering human remains as rules and expectations change.

Cemeteries are places of the dead, and even though the remains are hidden they can still have a vital role in 'mediating relationships of mortality' (Drvenkar *et al.*, 2015). The European Cemeteries Route, a cultural route certified by the Council of Europe, declares cemeteries are 'an essential part of our civilization' and they demonstrate both tangible and intangible heritage. Saving them and engaging visitors can have a positive benefit to people and the local economy, so they should be protected for everyone and for the future.

18 'Into the horrors of the gloomy jail': Towards a Future of UK Prison Tourism and Penal Architecture

Allan Brodie

Into the horrors of the gloomy jail?

Unpity'd, and unheard, where misery moans;
Where sickness pines; where thirst and hunger burn,
And poor misfortune feels the lash of vice.

Introduction

James Thomson wrote these lines in 1726, a decade before he ended up in prison for debt (Thomson, 1726; James Thomson, *Oxford Dictionary of National Biography*, 2008). He had experienced the inside of a prison, if not yet as a prisoner, then perhaps as an intrigued visitor. Each year hundreds of thousands of people visit sites with connections to imprisonment. The most popular in the UK is the Tower of London (ALVA, 2023), a place of imprisonment for 800 years, but there are historic castles across the country that have served as prisons. There are also several former purpose-built prison buildings that closed during the past 200 years and have been converted into museums. They offer a wide range of experiences from former staff showing visitors around their old workplace to long-gone institutions serving as a space to explore everything from local history and agricultural machinery to ghoulish exhibits and tales of gory executions. Imprisonment in Britain can be told as a series of reforming ideas, their achievements and failures most clearly expressed in successive generations of buildings. For instance, John Howard's revelations about the state for England's prisons prompted a wave of new prison buildings to replace unsuitable structures. Since the mid-19th century, a series of reforms and changes in the size of the prison population have led to further prison closures. While many of these institutions have disappeared, others have found new lives, sometimes as museums and visitor attractions.

Since the mid-20th century, successive British governments have shared an ambition to replace an ageing building stock with new prisons. This was in part driven by a desire to improve prison conditions, but there was a strong financial motive to replace expensive, small, urban prisons with new large purpose-built facilities on brownfield sites, releasing the historic locations for lucrative development. The inexorable rise in the prison population in the late 20th century thwarted most of these attempts, but more stable numbers led to 19 prisons closing during the 2010s and almost half of these were historic sites. At present, there is a glut of historic prisons in search of a future. Therefore, the purpose of this chapter is to highlight futures for these prisons by examining the history of prison closures in England and, subsequently, the uses that the buildings and sites have enjoyed or endured. Moreover, the chapter asks what factors might determine their future and just how many prison museums can one country sustain? Thus, to address this, it is necessary to examine the history of prison tourism, contrasting inquisitive and investigative tourism, the pleasure seekers with the more positive, educative side of tourism.

Prison Closures in Great Britain

The first concerted round of prison closures was the largest. It resulted from John Howard's survey of England's prisons that transformed the way that people were detained in prison. His findings, first published in 1777 in *The State of the Prisons*, documented insecure, badly maintained buildings overseen by staff reliant on levying fees from prisoners for their livelihood (Howard, 1777). Prisoners were held in filthy, disease-ridden conditions, sometimes in pits or cellars, chained unless they paid to be released from their fetters. Another problem was ease of access: people could pay gaolers to look at prisoners and there was little separation of inmates by gender, potentially leading to spectacles to amuse or concern visitors. Moreover, purpose-built structures were rare. The key characteristic for a prison at this date was that it was secure and, therefore, most were in castles or as part of a civic building, such as a town hall. There were a small number of purpose-built prisons. For example, at Ripon (North Yorkshire) the House of Correction was housed in a substantial 17th century building beside the county gaol, while in York the county gaol of 1701–1705 also survives – both are now museums (Brodie *et al.*, 2002: 17, 20). Some of the oldest, smaller, purpose-built prisons became local museums, such as the 13th century prison at Ely, the 14th century prison at Hexham or the mid-18th century Old Gaol at Buckingham. The most comprehensive reconstruction programme was undertaken in Gloucestershire, where Sir George Onesiphorus Paul transformed his county's prisons after Howard published a damning description of them (Howard, 1777: 343–352; Whiting, 1975). The County Gaol, along with the County Bridewell and the Debtor's Prison, was housed in Gloucester Castle. There were four other small prisons in a poor state of repair. In their place, four new bridewells prisons were built by 1791 at Lawford's Gate in Bristol, Horsley, Littledean and Northleach, along with a new county gaol in Gloucester (Whiting, 1979: 11). The prison at Lawford's Gate had become a House of Remand by the 1860s under police control rather than being a prison (Lawford's Gate Prison History, 2023; Lawford's Gate GRO Catalogue, n.d.). It was demolished in 1926 and the site became housing in the 1930s. Horsley Gaol near Stroud also became a house of remand and was believed to have been demolished in the 1880s (Horsley Prison History, 2023). A house later used as a nursing home, Horsley Priory, replaced the gaol, but it retains some original fabric and detailing that belonged to the gaol (HEA BF 084675). It was later divided into flats and offices and acted as the offices for a County Council Depot.

Meanwhile, the prison at Northleach became a house of remand in 1857 and the treadmill house was converted into a police station. The cell blocks were demolished in 1936–1937, but the front block, the combined keeper's house and gate was used by the police before becoming home to the Lloyd Baker Rural Life collection of agricultural equipment (Northleach Historic England Listing, 2012; Northleach Prison Website, 2023). Littledean Gaol ceased to be used as a prison in 1854 and became a police station and remand prison (HEA BF 076967). In 1874, the eastern wing of Littledean was converted into a court room. When it was visited by the author in 1987, the courthouse furniture had been removed and the space was filled with the computers of Ecclesiastical Insurance who had recently acquired the site (Littledean Gaol Ecclesiastical Insurance, 2012: 72). The west wing retained its cells, which were ingeniously used to store the company's records. Littledean Gaol was sold in 2003 and was refurbished by its new owners partly as a family home and to house the 'Crime Through Time Museum' (Littledean Gaol Ecclesiastical Insurance, 2012: 97).

By the early 19th century, some of the new prisons were increasing in size and complexity. Daniel Asher Alexander's Maidstone Prison (1810–1822) provided day rooms on the ground floor with 452-night cells on the first and second floors, which were arranged to accommodate twenty-seven classes of inmates separately (Chalkin, 1984: 2; Evans, 1982: 269). The reforming principles of Howard combined with the new emphasis on classifying inmates continued the process of rendering old prisons redundant. However, by the 1830s, the British government was looking to the USA in search of a new direction in prison management

(Brodie *et al.*, 2002: 85–7). The result was the separate system, designed to prevent communication between prisoners, therefore limiting so-called contamination of first or minor offenders by habitual criminals. Inmates would sleep and work alone in their larger cell and separation was extended to the chapel and exercise yards, creating a solitude designed to induce reflection (Brodie *et al.*, 2002: 90ff). A programme of reconstruction and adaptation of existing prisons began in the 1840s and at many existing prisons new wings were also added. The large prison at Gloucester had some of its small cells enlarged, but to cater for more prisoners a new wing was added in 1844 (HEA BF 088880). There was also an urgent need for new purpose-built facilities. The large, radial prison at Pentonville, opened in 1842, established a model for new prisons and wings that would be followed across the country (Brodie *et al.*, 2002: 93–105).

The new system prompted the continuing closure of many smaller prisons, even ones that had only been built during the previous 50 years, as was the case in Gloucestershire. The 1865 Prison Act abolished 13 borough gaols and one liberty prison, and several other municipal gaols closed (RIP, 34 (N): 6; RIP 37 (N): vi; RIP, 39 (S): vii). Several county gaols and houses of correction closed between 1842 and 1877. Fisherton Anger, near Salisbury, closed in 1870 but its central block survived as a private residence and later as a military headquarters (Fisherton Anger VCH Online, 2019). The site succumbed in the later 20th century to road construction. Abingdon's gaol suffered a different fate: demolition was deemed to be too expensive by the local authority and therefore it served as a grain store, then a leisure centre and now offers luxury hospitality provision in the form of the Old Gaol Serviced Apartments (Abingdon Gaol, 2016; Abingdon Gaol Apartments, 2023).

The most profound change in prison administration resulted from the 1877 Prison Act, leading to the centralising and rationalising of the patchwork of locally run prisons. They were brought under the control of the newly established Prison Commission, which would be responsible for all local prisons in England and Wales. Its first action was to take over any prisons that it deemed suitable; those considered unfit were closed. Of the 113 English and Welsh prisons in operation on 1 April 1878, 45 had closed by the end of August (RPC, 1878: 6, 7, 20–26, 33–35). It was again predominantly smaller borough and town prisons that closed, though 11 county prisons also ceased operation. The House of Correction at Folkingham in Lincolnshire closed in 1878, as did the Lincoln Castle County gaol. The inmates were accommodated in the new prison in Lincoln that had opened in 1872 (RPC, 1878: 1, 22). At Folkingham, the buildings within the perimeter were converted into ten dwellings, which were demolished in 1955 with the main gatehouse now being used as a holiday property (Folkingham Landmark Trust, 2023). The prison within the castle at Lincoln was initially unused until the county's archives decided to move into the gaol in 1948 (*The Times*, 18 December 1948: 5); it is now a museum (Lincoln Castle Museum, 2024).

Prison closures continued after 1878 due to a drop in the prison population, with a further 14 closing between 1879 and 1894 (Brodie *et al.*, 2002: 145–147). The most celebrated loss was Newgate in London, which closed in 1882, except for detaining prisoners being tried at the adjacent Central Criminal Court (RPC, 1881–2: 3). The demolition of the prison began in August 1902 and the new courthouse opened in February 1907 (HEA BF 093775). By 1895, there were only 50 local prisons in England and a further seven in Wales (RPC, 1894–5: app.17, 56). The daily average population of local prisons dropped from 20,833 in 1878 to 13,604 in 1895. Meanwhile, convict prisons, created to deal with people being transported to Australia, were run nationally and separately from local prisons. From 1857, they were increasingly used to hold inmates enduring penal servitude, who would have previously been transported (RDCP, 1890–1: v–vi). Convict numbers also fell during the late 19th century, so that by 1898, 2826 were imprisoned. Between 1882 and 1906, 12 convict prisons closed, including Millbank in London, which is now the site of Tate Britain (RPC, 1890–1: 8–9). By 1922, the four remaining convict prisons of Dartmoor, Liverpool, Maidstone and Parkhurst contained 2392 cells (RPC, 1922–3: 75–77).

In the early 20th century, the closure of further local prisons would be a direct consequence of the continuing declining prison population, with the daily average number of local prisoners falling from 14,352 in 1913 to 7,938 in 1929. Between 1914 and 1922, 24 English and Welsh local prisons closed, of which nine subsequently re-opened when prisoner numbers began to rise from 1940 onwards. A further round of closures was made in 1922 for reasons of national economy and between 1925 and 1931, another seven prisons closed (Brodie *et al.*, 2002: 170–172). By the end of 1931, there were only 24 local prisons in England and two in Wales (RPC, 1930: 60; RPC, 1931: app.4). Of the 14 prisons that were closed permanently between 1914 and 1931, eight were conveyed to the local council and six were sold privately (Record of Settlements, nos. 7, 10, 11, 12, 14, 21, 22, 26, 37, 39, 42, 49, 52, 54, 55). Eight of the 14 prisons had been demolished by 1957, while the remaining 6 survived, at least in part (Prisons Relinquished by Prison Commissioners). Derbyshire County Council declined to buy the former county gaol and it was sold in 1929, becoming a greyhound stadium, which was later redeveloped for housing. At York, the County Gaol closed in 1932 (Record of Settlements, no. 56). The female prison was bought by the corporation to house John Lamplugh Kirk's collection of bygones, opening as the York Castle Museum on 23 April 1938; the adjacent debtor's prison became part of the museum in 1952 (York Castle Museum Wikipedia, 2023). However, the main York prison building of 1849 was demolished only to make way for a car park (Tomlinson, 1975: 595).

Between the wars, the prison population remained stable at around 10,000 per year, but from 1940 onwards it rose continually reaching 30,000 by 1962 and peaking at over 85,000 in the mid-2010s. In 2022, the prison population of England and Wales stood at around 81,000 (Prison Population Figures Howard League, 2022). Instead of closures, former military sites and country houses were pressed into use after 1945. A few closed prisons were reactivated, namely Canterbury, Northallerton and Reading which reopened in 1946, followed in 1948 by Portsmouth, Preston and Shepton Mallet in 1966 (RPC, 1945: 85; RPC, 1948: 66). All these prisons closed in 2013/14 apart from Preston. By the early 1960s, a concerted programme of prison building was underway, providing 17 New Wave prisons. This was intended to replace outdated Victorian prisons, but this objective was defeated by the inexorable rise of the prison population. There were occasional closures before the 2010s when continued use was no longer viable. For instance, in 1996, HMP Oxford closed. This 18th and 19th century prison shared its site with the remains of the medieval castle. After a brief period when it was used as a film location, it became a Malmaison Hotel. Part of the site, particularly the remains of the medieval castle and some of the 18th century prison, has opened as a museum where visitors conduct prison tourism as they are shown around by costumed tour guides (Oxford Prison Tourism, 2023).

British Prison Tourism: A Brief History

By the 18th century, a growing number of people were travelling around Britain on holiday. A number of these tourists left behind travel journals that reveals interest in the wonders of nature, historic sites and grand houses. Bishop Richard Pococke was a regular visitor to such locations in the mid-18th century, but like many other diarists of the period, he also had an appetite for examining aspects of contemporary life, including early manifestations of the Industrial Revolution (Pococke, 1888-9: I, 16, 105, 110–111; II, 114, 116). Pococke also visited the Battle of Culloden site as well as active military sites, such as Fort Cumberland near Portsmouth, and Dover Castle where he saw French prisoners of war during the 1750s (Pococke, 1887: 104–108; Pococke 1888-9: II, 114, 93). In 1815, Thomas Lott enjoyed a visit to Deal Castle in Kent, an artillery fort constructed by King Henry VIII (Grandfield, 1989: 78), while 16-year-old Charles Powell was interested in Martello towers on the Kent Coast in 1823. Powell also looked at steamships at Ramsgate, vessels at the cutting edge of technology at the time (Hull, 1966: 111–113). Meanwhile, Daniel Benham in 1829 visited Margate's new gas works and made several visits to the Royal Sea Bathing Infirmary (Whyman, 1980: 197, 191, 200, 207, 211). Prisons might also be on the holiday agenda. Charles Powell visited the new Maidstone Gaol in Kent recounting how they 'walked to the New Jail a fine stone building – went into the wards and chapel – saw the prisoners spinning, weaving, making mats, string, ropes, etc., then we came into dinner' (Hull, 1966: 110). At the end of his day's visit, he concluded that 'the Jail a large, strong, melancholy and clean place of punishment' (Hull, 1966: 110).

Touring prisons was a regular part of London life. In 1714, John Macky visited Bridewell and noted that 'Many a pretty Girl is brought into it with their fine Cloaths, but for all that is forc'd to receive Correction here for Night-Walking; of which Sort of Cattel this City abounds more than any City in the World' (Macky, 1714: 195). Gaolers made a living by levying fees from prisoners, and some supplemented their income by charging visitors to wander around their prison. William Pitt, the keeper of Newgate prison in London, made more than £3000 from people wanting to see imprisoned Jacobites, while visitors to see the notorious highwayman Jack Shephard (often referred to as 'Honest Jack') paid £200 in 1716 (McConville, 1981: 71). On 3 May 1763, James Boswell visited Newgate simply out of curiosity (Pottle, 1950: 250–251) and William Hogarth (the English artist, pictorial satirist, and social critic) was clearly a visitor to the Fleet Debtor's Prison and Bedlam (London), depicting the interiors of both in *The Rake's Progress*. Hogarth also painted Moll Hackabout, a prostitute imprisoned in Bridewell prison (London) in *A Harlot's Progress*. Hogarth's 1731 painting of A Scene from *The Beggar's Opera* illustrates highwayman Captain Macheath chained in Newgate Prison, a fictional character in John Gay's *The Beggar's Opera* (1728).

The life of prisoners could amuse visitors, but their deaths were also part of the Georgian entertainment landscape (Seaton & Dann, 2018). Executions at Tyburn, for instance, were often riotous and in 1783 the new prison at Newgate became the site for London's public executions. County gaols across Britain were also sites of public executions. At Gloucester, these took place at the gate of the new prison built in the 1780s. The body of the hanged prisoner dropped through a trapdoor to dangle inside the gateway, an arrangement reproduced when a new gate was added in 1826 once the site had been enlarged (Neild, 1812: 245; HEA BF 088880). These early visitors to prisons were in search of amusement, enjoying the darkest of the dark tourism spectrum (after Stone, 2006), but there was a more positive side to early prison tourism, (indeed, if that term can be used). In addition to the inquisitive tourism of thrill-seekers, there was the investigative tourism of people who wanted to witness conditions to affect change. To that end, Dr Thomas Bray published *An Essay Towards ye Reformation of Newgate and Other Prisons in and about London* in 1702 (Hinde, 1951: 21–26). He condemned the conditions in Newgate and advocated many reforms that would eventually be enacted decades later. After his election as High

Sheriff of Bedfordshire in 1773, John Howard set off around England, and later Europe, to record conditions in prisons (Ramsay, 1977: 4). In Paris, Howard visited several prisons without incident, but his visit to the Bastille proved to be difficult. After knocking on the door, he was allowed to enter, and he looked around the building exterior:

> But whilst I was contemplating this gloomy mansion, an officer came out of the Castle much surprised, and I was forced to retreat through the mute guard, and thus regained that freedom, which for one locked up within those walls it is next to impossible to obtain. (Howard, 1777: 93)

The relaxed attitude to visiting prisons became more difficult as the 19th century progressed, though it did not cease entirely. Jane Austen visited Canterbury prison in November 1813 with her brother Edward, as he was a visiting magistrate (Jane Austen Letter, 2011). Charles Dickens describes his visit to Newgate in 1836, describing it as a 'gloomy depository of the guilt and misery of London' (Dickens, 1987: 201). From the 1860s onwards, executions were held behind prison walls. Consequently, public gratification had to be achieved through gruesome accounts in newspapers, tales of suffering in prison, and in the 20th century, film, and television depictions of the tough life inside. The growing number of closed prisons during the 19th and 20th centuries, regardless of their reuse, has allowed people to make some connection with the penal architectural and the prison experience. This might be by staying in a former prison converted to a hotel (for example at the Malmaison Hotel in Oxford, the Bodmin Jail Hotel in Cornwall, or the Bridewell Hotel in Liverpool); by using an archive; or visiting a gym in a converted gaol (for example, at the former Northallerton prison in County Durham). Sometimes, working prisons or at least part of them, allow public access as part of heritage events and open days. In September 2022, HMP Hull offered the public a chance to see an exhibition including historical photos and artefacts but emphasised that admission does not include a tour of the actual prison itself (HMP Hull Open Day, 2022). Meanwhile, HMP Grendon Underwood in Buckinghamshire actively invites visitors to 'social afternoons' (of which the author has participated in) where members of the public can meet inmates as part of their rehabilitation programme (Hodgkinson & Urquhart, 2019: 43).

The most potent interaction via the buildings might be through their reuse as museums. There is no definitive list of prison museums in the world and looking around the globe they range from small local sites to large headline ones as different as Alcatraz, Robben Island and various sites of the Holocaust (Ashworth & Tunbridge, 2019; Strange & Kempa, 2003). These are self-evidently now prison museums, but some sites raise the puzzling question of what is a prison museum? For example, The Clink in Southwark, London, a place name that has become a synonym for imprisonment, is thought to be a prison museum but this is a contemporary visitor attraction on a site that was a gaol from the 12th century until 1780. With the historic building of the Clink prison having long succumbed to pressures of redevelopment, Welch (2015) points out that visitors learn and reflect upon the darker aspects of punishment. The Clink is also reminiscent of the lighter fun factory experience of visitor attractions such as the London Dungeon (after Stone, 2006; also, Welch, 2015: 1–4).

There are many old prisons that have been converted into museums devoted to local history and other subjects, with their former function being very much a secondary part of the visitor experience. Examples include Northleach (a former prison in the Cotswolds which closed in 1857) with its collection of agricultural machinery, and York Castle Gaol where a visit is dominated by recreated rooms and a reconstructed street from the past. However, other former gaols are devoted largely, or solely, to telling the story of crime and punishment. Lincoln Castle Gaol is focused on the prison experience, while the new Bodmin Jail combines the story of the prison with tales of local crimes (Bodmin Jail Visit, 2023). The Bodmin Jail Attraction also incorporates the 'Dark Walk' experience, featuring the latest technology and theatrical performances that allow visitors to immerse themselves in the life (and death) of prisoners. Meanwhile, the National Justice Museum (formerly known as the Galleries of Justice) in Nottingham involves visitors partly self-guiding around the site and its many exhibits, including Britain's last working gallows (last used in 1961) and kept in full working order until 1992. Visitors to the National Justice Museum are also greeted by costumed interpreters who perform roles of courtroom and prison staff (Hodgkinson & Urquhart, 2019: 46–47). A humorous performance regularly takes place in the courtyard in which an unsuspecting visitor is selected for hanging but is given an obligatory stay of execution at the last moment. After the performance, and more ominously, there is an opportunity to 'stand in the shoes' of a convict who is about to be hanged. Littledean Gaol in Gloucestershire is now the home of the 'Crime though Time Collection', but also has diverse (and unrelated) displays on provocative subjects as the Iranian Embassy Siege, Celebrity Sleaze & Scandal, the Nazis and the Ku Klux Klan (Littledean Jail, 2022). Many prison museums also pride themselves with being haunted and offer paranormal visits designed to capture some of the apparent supernatural atmosphere of the places. For example, ghost tours are held at Shrewsbury Prison, which boasts the title of being the second most haunted jail in the world, without stating which is the most haunted jail!

Whatever approach is taken by curators to entertaining customers, conveying information and delivering messages, the building will be central to a prison museum. Visitors will be experiencing a penal architecture that they are, hopefully, unfamiliar with, but they will also be due to making the connection between the building and its occupants. Within an international context, Robben Island in South Africa is renowned as a World Heritage Site, less for its architecture than its most celebrate occupant, Nelson Mandela (Robben Island World Heritage Inscription, 2023; Strange & Kempa, 2003). Meanwhile, Alcatraz in San Francisco, USA, is famed as 'The Rock', gaining its Hollywoodised celebrity from its perceived toughness, its geographical location and its inmates, including Al Capone and Robert Franklin Stroud, often referred to as 'The Birdman of Alcatraz' (Strange & Kempa, 2003). None of Britain's current existing prison museums are set in prison buildings that have such prominent figures for neoliberal marketing. Notorious criminals may have graced some of their cells but would be unlikely to attract many paying customers through the doors. Importantly, there is also little in Britain's prison museum stock that might be felt to be highly contested or particularly dark. Britain has no equivalent of the concentration camps/ prisons of the Holocaust, or Japanese occupation, or the Killing Fields sites such as at Tuol Sleng in Cambodia. However, the prison museums of Ireland and Northern Ireland, such as HMP Crumlin Road in Belfast or Kilmainham Gaol in Dublin, raise questions regarding the independence of the island of Ireland, the Troubles, and the future of the island itself. Crumlin Road Gaol, a direct copy of HMP Pentonville in London, closed in 1996 (Crumlin Road Prison, 1999). Now a museum, it offers visitors everything from the 'Gaol Experience' to live music events and can also be used as a conference and wedding venue (Crumlin Road Prison Visit, 2023). Walking tours and an excursion in a Black taxicab allow visitors to see the gaol in the context of some key sites of The Troubles. Meanwhile, Kilmainham between 1916 and 1922 held many imprisoned Irish nationalists following the Easter Rising of 1916 and a number were executed there (Barton & Brown, 2015: 244). The last inmates at Kilmainham had left by 1924 and the building was officially closed in 1929. In 1938, it held an open day and later reopened as one of the earliest prison museums in 1971, after briefly being used as a film location replicating Wormwood Scrubs in the 1969 *The Italian Job* movie.

The Future of British Closed Prisons

The earlier review of past prison closures suggests several futures for former prison sites, and several factors that will influence their future. One option for closed prisons was simply to reopen them after many years of being mothballed. Other sites have found new uses that allowed substantial parts of the historic prison architecture to survive. The prison at Lincoln Castle still exists as it was used by the county as an archive and a similar future led to the survival of Ruthin Gaol in Denbighshire, which ceased to be a prison in 1916. The local County Council bought the buildings in 1926 and used them for offices, storing county archives, and as the town library (Ruthin Gaol History, 2010). In 2004, the Gaol was extensively renovated and reopened as a museum (Ruthin Gaol Museum, 2023). At Scarborough, the Borough Gaol of 1866 closed in 1878 and part of the prison, its perimeter wall including the gate have survived, as it was used as a council depot. The small gaol at Horsley in Gloucestershire survived at least in part due to it also being a council depot. Abingdon Gaol in Oxfordshire has survived unexpectedly as part of the town's leisure centre before becoming serviced apartments. However, local authority intervention does not always guarantee the substantial survival of prison buildings. Carmarthenshire Council bought the prison site in the town in 1924, demolished the Georgian and Victorian prison buildings and built a new County Hall that was completed after the Second World War (Carmarthen County Hall, 2023; HEA BF 093951). In contrast, the buildings of HMP Oxford have survived due to its recent closure (1996) and its suitable location in a popular tourist destination for a rapid conversion into a hotel and visitor attraction (Oxford Malmaison Hotel, 2023). However, Bodmin Gaol in Cornwall closed in 1927 and was sold two years later (HEA BF 090945). By the late 20th century, part of the site was used as a builder's yard while the remainder of the untouched, but decaying buildings were open to the public. In 2015, a businessperson took over the site, achieving his 'vision of turning this historical landmark into a world class tourist attraction and hotel' (Bodmin Jail, 2023).

At many closed prison sites, the most common features that survive are the perimeter walls, which would be costly to remove, and any buildings that can easily be converted into domestic accommodation. The Georgian prison at Bury St Edmunds closed in 1878, with the site being sold in 1881. By 1883, the only substantial buildings surviving were the central governor's house and the entrance complex (HEA BF 093774). Gatehouses have survived more often because they were more adaptable than cell blocks. As was mentioned above, the entrance to Folkingham House of Correction in Lincolnshire has become holiday accommodation while the gate of Monmouth Gaol in South Wales has been converted into two private dwellings. Part of St Albans prison enjoyed a period of celebrity after its closure. Its gate became the entrance to the fictional HMP Slade during the opening sequence to the 1970s British television comedy series 'Porridge'. Another factor may be stigma: until recently people may have been reluctant to stay, or live in a former cell block, but for some people the perceived darkness of staying or residing in a former site of incarceration is now a virtue. The early conversions of old prison buildings into domestic accommodation were not works aimed at prestigious occupants. However, the prison hotels at Oxford and Bodmin are aimed at the upper end of the hotel market, and as will be discussed later, the recent purchase of several closed prison sites by City and Country for prestigious heritage (re)developments suggests that prison sites are now felt suitable for expensive investment.

In contrast, many historic prisons that have closed have been demolished and their sites redeveloped with little or no recognition of their previous function. William Blackburn's prison at Liverpool (completed in the early 1790s), was demolished when the current HMP Liverpool at Walton opened in 1855. The site is now occupied by a car park and railway line, though the road name Great Howard Street provides a hint of its former existence (HEA BF 093742). The nearby prison at Kirkdale had closed by 1894 and the site was sold to Liverpool Corporation (RPC, 1895: 11). The prison was demolished soon after, and its site is now used as the Kirkdale Recreation Ground (HEA BF 093834). At Salford, the last reminder of the prison of 1790 is the street name New Bailey Street. These prisons closed due to more appropriate, and more up-to-date, accommodation being provided nearby, and their sites were cleared due to rapid urban expansion. Similar pressures apply in smaller settlements. The county gaol at Devizes in Wiltshire closed in 1921 and it was demolished in 1927. It is now the site of a mid-20th century housing development (HEA BF 093720). Wiltshire's other county gaol at Fisherton Anger now largely lies beneath modern roads.

There are several factors that seem to contribute to determining the future of a prison site. As already discussed, a site owned by, or sold to, a local authority may potentially enjoy a different future to one that passes into private hands. This factor needs to be considered alongside the commercial opportunity of the site, which is often determined by the prison's location. Firstly, while there will be a significant market for hotel rooms in a converted prison in a popular tourist destination such as Oxford, for example, this is unlikely to be a solution for reusing a prison building in most provincial UK towns and cities. Another factor regarding location is where a prison is situated within a settlement. When prisons were being rebuilt, decisions were made whether to stay in the traditional central location, often within an historic castle or move to a new site at the edge of the settlement (Brodie, 2019). Due to rapid population growth in the late 18th and 19th centuries, a new site is likely to be closer to the historic town centre if the prison moved in the 1780s, than if a new location was selected in the mid-19th century. A central site is likely to be more conducive for reuse as a dark tourism destination, as this is where visitors to a settlement will focus their attention while enjoying the historic settlement and its other attractions. New prisons in the mid-19th century were often built in areas where other forms of unpleasant activity were concentrated. Towns were becoming larger and more complex, with often a peripheral area where industrial sites, a hospital, a workhouse, a gas works, and later sewage treatment facilities might be concentrated. For instance, the 1852 Ordnance Survey map shows Leeds Borough Gaol standing in fields hemmed in by railway lines on two sides (Yorkshire Sheet 218, 1852 Ordnance Survey map). Other industrial ventures and a gasworks was present, but during the second half of the 19th century, they were joined by ironworks, forges, mills, a larger gasworks and the cemetery (Yorkshire Sheet CCXVIII.NW, 1894 Ordnance Survey map). Of course, this would be an ideal location for a new prison, but this might not be today a popular area for a visitor attraction or a high-value commercial or housing development.

The decision making of two centuries ago regarding location has contributed to determining the future of prison sites in another way. Remaining on the historic castle means that the potential for creating visitor attractions is enhanced compared to reusing prison buildings on new greenfield sites in the mid-19th century. It is also likely to restrict in some ways the future use of a closed prison as historic sites will enjoy a greater degree of heritage protection than a new, purpose-built Victorian prison. According to UK heritage protection regulations, a castle site may be a Grade I listed building, whereas a purpose-built prison would normally contain Grade II structures and, therefore, provide more opportunities for change. Moreover, there is also likely to be greater pressure from local people concerning the future of a prominent central site than one in a more distant suburban location. With these factors in mind, it is worth examining recently closed prison sites to assess their potential for survival and their potential reuse for (dark) tourism purposes or otherwise.

Closed Prison Futures: Dark Tourism and Beyond

HMP Blundeston in Suffolk was the future once. Opened in 1963, it marked the start of a programme to improve English prisons (Brodie *et al.*, 2002: 195ff). However, in September 2013, the Ministry of Justice announced that HMP Blundeston would close by March 2014 (BBC (British Broadcasting Corporation) News Blundeston closure, 2013). It was sold in January 2016 for £3 million and the first part of the site has been redeveloped as 38 four-bedroom houses of 10 designs, each named after a Suffolk village. There is no mention that this was the site of a former prison (Blundeston Badger Homes, 2023).

During the 2010s, 19 prisons closed, and almost half of these were historic prisons. Having reviewed the fate of previous closed prisons in this chapter, the question that arises is what is likely to be the future for these sites and, particularly, the historic ones? One option was to reopen old prisons as the inmate population rose. This is unlikely to happen to any recent closures; but two sites have been closed recently and demolished to make way for new prisons. In Northamptonshire, HMP Wellingborough has been redeveloped as HMP Five Wells, while in Leicestershire, HMYOI & RC Glen Parva is making way for the new HMP Fosse. These are ideal reuses as they are brownfield sites and perform the same original function. It also further cements the current government's policy of shifting control from HM Prison Service to the private sector. The same has already happened in the recent past. For instance, Pucklechurch Remand Centre in South Gloucestershire closed in February 1996 and was redeveloped as HMP Ashfield, initially for young offenders but it is now an adult male sex offenders' prison. Similarly, Lowdham Grange in Nottinghamshire, the first open borstal institution (a former youth detention centre) in England when it opened in 1930, closed in February 1996, but it retained its name when the new prison opened in February 1998.

HMP Blundeston, like Devizes, Liverpool and Salford prisons, is being redeveloped with little or no mention of its earlier function. The main imperative here is to maximise the value of the real estate and, subsequently, a housing development often proves to be the most lucrative. HMP Latchmere House in Richmond-upon-Thames, the former interrogation Camp 020 during the Second World War, closed in 2011. The historic house was converted into apartments while new homes were built around it. HMP Bullwood Hall, a former women's prison, and young offenders' institution with no historic prison buildings on the site, closed in 2014 and has also been replaced by housing. Likewise, HMP Blantyre House in Kent, a former resettlement prison for men, which closed in January 2016, has been left without a certain future, though its rural location may mean it has a potential future as a housing development. Meanwhile, HMP Holloway in London, rebuilt in the 1970s, closed in July 2016. Peabody, one of the oldest and largest not-for-profit housing associations in the UK, bought the site in March 2019 and plan to create almost a thousand new homes, including 60% of the new stock as affordable housing. The £400m redevelopment scheme includes 15 high rise tower blocks up to 14 storeys tall, a type of development that might be appropriate in a dense urban area. However, this redevelopment has attracted some concern from the local community and, particularly, the height of some of the proposed tower blocks which breaches the council's planning guidelines (HMP Holloway Site Development, 2023).

The presence of historic prison structures can potentially add further complications for the reuse of sites. For example, on the outskirts of Newport on the Isle of Wight, HMP Camp Hill's proximity to the two remaining units of the current HMP Isle of Wight makes transforming it into a much-needed housing development challenging, and the government has struggled to persuade the local council to take the site. In this case, another complicating factor is the presence of three listed buildings. However, this should not be a significant hindrance as the gatehouse, administration block, and chapel appear to be eminently reusable and would add character to any redevelopment. Similarly, HMP Brockhill in Worcestershire closed in 2011 and although its 1960s buildings are not listed, it faces comparable limitations on redevelopment due to its proximity to other remaining part of the nearby HMP Hewell complex.

The listing of buildings (a UK legal protection for architecture of special interest or historic importance) should not be an impediment to considered reuse. At HMYOI Northallerton in North Yorkshire, two historic buildings have been listed at the heart of the prison site, but these have proved to be adaptable; the former female wing has become C4DI Northallerton, a digital technology centre. The remainder of the site with new buildings and car parking is a retail and leisure destination called Treadmills, an acknowledgement rather than a denial of the site's history. HMP Kingston at Portsmouth, which closed in 2013, is being converted into 84 flats and duplexes. The development is called The Old Portsmouth Gaol and the retention of so much of the historic prison means that the developer is using its history as a positive marketing tool.

HMP Ashwell closed in 2011 and Rutland County Council acquired the site to establish the Oakham Enterprise Park. The prison buildings have been retained thus far and are currently used for Airsoft events (a team-based shooting game using spherical plastic projectiles fired from low-power airguns), as well as ghost hunts and sleepovers. This is a rural site and there is not yet the need to replace the buildings with potentially more lucrative uses. The buildings at HMP Ashwell are enjoying what may be a transitional use before a more permanent future emerges. The same is happening with several recently closed historic prisons. Some are being used as film locations, or for the exploration of the paranormal. HMP Oxford led the way, its main Victorian wing appearing in many television programmes and films before it was converted into a hotel. HMP Shrewsbury has appeared in three major British television soap operas, while HMP Canterbury was used to depict the wings of HMP Belmarsh (in London) in the 2019 film *Avengement*, despite over a century separating the construction of the two prisons. The most remarkable use of a prison as a film location was in the 2019 film *The Informer*. A British-made film set partly in an American prison; the filmmakers produced a three-dimensional depiction of HMP Gloucester for the location shot on the banks of a river in New York. Thereafter, many of the scenes are recognisably set in parts of the distinctive British prison.

Some recently closed prison sites are also being marketed as visitor attractions, pending their longer-term future being realised. City and Country, a private sector company which specialises in heritage (re)developments in Great Britain, purchased HMP Dorchester (in Dorset), HMP Gloucester, and HMP Shepton Mallet (in Somerset) after they closed in 2013. They will be converted into homes, but until this process begins in earnest the sites are welcoming visitors. It is unclear whether there will be any future development of museology at these sites, or any significant marking of the site(s) as former prisons. Yet, converting prison wings into domestic accommodation is challenging if the character of the building is to be retained and, therefore, alternatives to housing may prove to be easier to achieve. As noted earlier, HMP Oxford's Victorian wing has become a hotel, as has part of Bodmin Jail, a route followed at a few places around the world, including in Helsinki, Stockholm and Boston (USA). A slight variation on this future had been planned at Canterbury. The site of the prison was bought by Canterbury Christ Church University to convert into student accommodation, though this has not yet proved to be financially viable.

While the prisons at Dorchester, Gloucester and Shepton Mallet were rapidly acquired for residential development, there were problems with the disposal of HMP Shrewsbury. After it closed in 2013, it was bought by a developer to convert into flats and student accommodation, but due to concerns regarding traffic, the outline proposal was refused. Instead, it has been turned into a visitor attraction with more than just the chance to visit the prison. On offer are opportunities to try to escape in what is described as 'The World's Most Interactive Prison' (Shrewsbury Prison Visit, 2023). Meanwhile, the future of HMP Reading in Berkshire is still uncertain. It has been used as an arts venue and a campaign is currently supported by the local MPs and several celebrities for this to be its long-term future. The reason for this is that Oscar Wilde once graced cell C.3.3. for part of his incarceration from 1895 to 1897.

One recently closed prison that is gradually morphing into a permanent visitor attraction is Lancaster Castle, its important medieval and penal heritage meaning that other developments are unlikely to be permitted. A Grade I listed building, meaning that it is 'of exceptional special interest', it was built on the site of a Roman fort and retains the 12th century keep and an array of medieval structures. Its prison architecture dates from the late 18th century to the mid-19th century and includes the female penitentiary (1818–1821), designed by J.M. Gandy. The half-rotunda is the closest prison block in design in Britain to Jeremy Bentham's proposed Panopticon (HEA BF 093737). Attached to the prison is the Shire Hall of 1798, which is still in use as a Crown Court. Following the Prison's closure, parts of the castle became available to visitors (Lancaster Castle, 2023) and since June 2022, one of the prison wings has been home to the Lancashire Police Museum (Lancaster Police Museum, 2023).

Conclusion

England and Wales currently have 121 prisons open (England and Wales Prisons, 2023); Scotland has 17 (Scottish Prisons, 2023) and Northern Ireland has three (Northern Ireland Prisons, 2023). Of the prisons in England and Wales, 29 are on historic sites, with the vast majority of these being on potentially valuable urban sites. Any of these historic prison sites have the potential to be housing developments working with the historic fabric of the prisons. All but five are comprehensively listed or have listed buildings, though any new development proposal after a site closes is likely to lead to a reconsideration of the level and extent of statutory protection to provide clarity for any developer. There are a further ten prison sites with historic buildings, including a former education establishment, a Victorian fortification, an orphanage, a site with four early 20th century aircraft hangars and country houses. These are all in rural settings and have little pedigree as a prison so are unlikely to be suitable to become a 'prison museum' or a visitor attraction. If these close, it is most likely that they will become sites for new housing if any development is viable within the location.

As recent closures have demonstrated, historic prison sites can be adapted for a variety of new functions, though this may take several years to realise. Prior to this, closed prison sites may enjoy a temporary life as a visitor attraction, but that potential substantial number calls into question the quantity and quality of so-called prison experiences. More realistically, any future historic prison closures may only be marked by some limited reminder of their function, such as modest displays or recognition through the name of new developments, if penal pasts remain potential marketing tools. However, there seem to be two important exceptions to this future. Northern Ireland's most notorious prison during The Troubles (a period of violent sectarian conflict from the late 1960s to 1998) was HMP Maze (on the outskirts of Lisburn), and the site of the H-Blocks used to house paramilitary prisoners. Following its closure in 2000, the intention was for the site to include a museum, a multi-purpose sports stadium, and an office, hotel, and leisure village. There was also a plan to develop a peace centre at the site, but these have not yet come to fruition (Maze Long Kesh Timeline, 2020).

HMP Dartmoor in Devon also presents a particular problem for the future. The intention was to close the prison in 2023 and the Prison Service gave its ten-year notice to the Duchy of Cornwall. As part of the closure plan, Historic England revised its listing of the buildings on the site to provide clarity for future development, leading to 15 separate listed building descriptions. The same exercise also explored ideas for the future of the prison buildings once it was to be returned to the Duchy. A key problem facing the site is location. It is situated near Princetown with a population of only 1500 people, and within the Dartmoor National Park. Any high-value housing development would be at odds with the existing, inexpensive housing market, whereas if the prison were located near a large urban centre, this might be more viable. Exclusive reuse as a museum is obvious but impractical as the likely visitor numbers would be insufficient to maintain so many large buildings. Moreover, there is already a popular small museum across the road from the prison and tourists have been visiting the area since the 19th century. Some use as a hostel or hotel might also be an option but this might be only one of several functions in the reuse of the site. Although its closure has been postponed, it is likely to be considered again in the future.

The range of content in prison museums ranges from the humorous to the darkest exhibits and testimonies often focus on suffering and death. Each museum takes a different approach to curating visitor information and any underlying messages. This will involve the display of evocative artefacts: for instance, the National Justice Museum in Nottingham has housed the collection from the former HM Prison Service Museum since 2005 and therefore has a wealth of authentic items to exhibit. The use of accounts to explain the prison experience is a key element of most prison museums. This can be delivered by display panels, in spoken words, via performers, or through films and projections. An interesting variation on this was introduced at the Port Arthur Historic Site in Australia where visitors are given a card about an individual convict's life in prison to focus on as they walk around (Maxwell-Stewart, 2013: 27–28). With modern technology, it may be possible to offer a more immersive and personalised experience. As noted earlier, the new museum at Bodmin Jail uses innovative technology in what is described as a 'brand new £8.5 million immersive visitor attraction' that includes a new 'Dark Walk' experience (Bodmin Jail Visit, 2023). Projections bring to life offenders from the past but other forms of modern technology may play a role in other museums. It may be possible to use augmented reality to place visitors in the footsteps of former staff and prisoners, a technique that has already been used for walks around several UK towns and cities (Unboxed Story Trails, 2022). Nonetheless, existing prison museums offer several types of visitor experience from the informed and considered, to the ghoulish, and even bizarre. They are now a small, but notable part of the UK museum landscape and visiting these sites of pained penal lives is now often taken for granted. In conclusion, this poem (below) written in biro ink on a cell wall at HMP Garth in Lancashire was left as a message for the next cell occupant (HEA photograph AA97/07373). However, replace the exclamation marks with question marks, and it might serve as a commentary on the ethics of prison tourism and its future:

I was ere

Now I'm not.

Now you're here

Sick or What!!

Abbreviations

HEA BF	Historic England Archive Building File
HMP	His Majesty's Prisons
HMYOI	His Majesty's Young Offender Institution
RC	Remand Centre
RDCP	Reports of the Directors of Convict Prisons
RIP	Reports of the Inspectors of Prisons
RPC	Report of the Work of the Prison Commission
VCH	Victoria County History
34(N)	34th Report of the Northern District, PP, 1871 (C.259), XXIX
37(N)	37th Report of the Northern District, PP, 1873 (C.811), XXXII
39(S)	39th Report of the Southern District, PP, 1875 (C.1261), XXXVII

19 'Finding a Light in Dark Places': Lighter Dark Tourism Futures

Brianna Wyatt

'Happiness can be found even in the darkest of times, when one only remembers to turn on the light'. Professor Albus Dumbledore (Master of the Elder Wand & Headmaster of Hogwarts, from the *Harry Potter and the Prisoner of Azkaban* film, 2004).

Introduction

Over the past 25 years or so, dark tourism in practice has become a dominant force within the broader visitor economy. Across global tourism, events and hospitality industries, sites *of* death, or sites *associated with* suffering or the seemingly macabre (Stone, 2006) are now offered not only at in situ and purpose-built visitor attractions, but also through mobile and temporary pop-up experiences. These include music, cultural and community festivals and events, as well as restaurants and places of accommodation that are either dark themed or are conversions of former dark places. The business of dark tourism is booming. Given that development of dark tourism is based upon notions of postmodern commodified death and touristic consumption (Foley & Lennon, 1997), the rise of dark tourism and proliferation of dark experiences are a direct result of growing societal interests in staged themes and recreated scenes of death and the macabre. Whether it be morbid curiosity, a desire to engage with death in a safe space or to reflect and contemplate about death and past suffering (Light & Ivanova, 2021), societal interests and motivations to engage with dark themes and experiences has grown out of the enduring commodification of death and the macabre (Stone, 2012a).

Death as spectatorship has permeated society for centuries. For example, ancient Roman audiences flocked to the Roman Coliseum to watch gladiators fight to their death (Stone & Sharpley, 2008), or sat on the banks of Lake Fucinus to watch *naumachiae* – mock naval battles in which participants were expected to kill each other or drown (Dunkle, 2014). In the 17th century, death became a commodity as ticket sales increased for curious onlookers when waxworks of the dead became prominent exhibitions at London's Bartholomew Fair (Owens, 2012). This was further popularised in the late 18th and early 19th century by Madame Tussaud's Chamber of Horrors in which death, or at least the portrayal of death, became part of a mercantile system (Owens, 2012). Throughout the 20th and 21st centuries, treatments of death and the macabre have been influenced by the development of technology and the media. This has not only helped to desensitise society to grisly images (Hodgkinson, 2015; Pimentel-Biscaia & Marques, 2022), but has also fuelled society's uncanny fascination with death. Thus, capitalising on society's 'thank God, that's not me' mentality (Dann, 1998) and the commercial benefits of (re)packaged representations of death, dark tourism has developed into an industry of commerce and spectacle for camera-wielding tourists (Stone, 2020b; Tarlow, 2005).

Given the global proliferation of dark tourism experiences, scholars have since established criteria and classifications by which different experiences can be identified and understood. Stone's (2006) 'Dark Tourism Spectrum' taxonomy is the most referenced framework to date. Drawing upon earlier works of Dann (1998) and Sharpley (2005), who both proposed dark tourism experiences differ in terms of content, purpose, and visitor motivations, Stone's (2006) Dark Tourism Spectrum model brought forward considerations for interpretation and the way in which dark tourism experiences are created – or rather – commercialised. It is within this conceptual framing that current understanding of between dark and light experiences has been based and, more importantly, for the purpose of this chapter, an understanding of how dark and light visitor experiences are distinct with reference to commercialism. Although the business of both dark and light dark tourism commodify death into visitor attractions that profit from ticket and retail sales, lighter attractions have a higher tourism infrastructure and are specifically commercially driven (Stone, 2006). Juxtaposed to darker attractions (for instance, *Auschwitz-Birkenau Memorial and Museum*) that are more serious in nature, so-called lighter attractions are typically more fun centric. These distinctions are observed in the attractions' interpretation – including the visitor experience and its design. Dark attractions tend to offer commemorative experiences with spaces for learning and reflection, whereas lighter attractions generally offer *edutainment* experiences through the blurring of education and entertainment and the use of innovative and engaging methods (for example, special effects, augmented/virtual reality technology, sensory stimulation, re-enactment, co-creation and amusement/thrill rides (Wright, 2021; Wyatt *et al.*, 2021, 2023). However, binaries within this dark–light framing extends to commercial activities that underpin visitor attraction operations, as lighter attractions typically have a greater sense of play in their marketing, retail and customer interactions than darker attractions.

Dark tourism has had a profound effect on the wider tourism industry, particularly since many dark tourism sites and attractions are now semiotic markers for destinations (including the *9/11 Memorial* for New York, the *Catacombs* for Paris and the *Anne Frank House Museum* for Amsterdam). However, due to developments in mass (social) media and technology, visitors are motivated to seek out increasingly immersive and interactive experiences (Alabau-Montoya & Ruiz-Molina, 2020; Neuhofer & Buhalis, 2014). Indeed, dark(er) attractions are beginning to utilise more fully commercial tactics traditionally used by lighter attractions to remain relevant and effectively respond to current demands. With this in mind, and a focus upon commodification futures, the aim of this chapter is to critically explore the commercialism of lighter dark tourism. In so doing, the study ascertains how lighter dark tourism is driving the dark tourism sector into the future. This is particularly so as more attractions are adopting commercial methods to meet evolving expectations and demands of current and future visitors. This chapter is framed by futures thinking and, subsequently, adopts Inayatullah's (2008) Six Pillars framework to establish strategic foresight and deepen futures thinking in relation to lighter dark tourism. The Six Pillars refers to *time*, *anticipation*, *timing*, *deepening*, *alternatives* and *transformations*. It is to each of these Six Pillars within the confines of dark tourism futures that this study now turns. Consequently, the chapter sets out conceptual parameters of examining the future of dark tourism, particularly those visitor attractions and experiences located at the lighter end of the Dark Tourism Spectrum.

Mapping the Future of Lighter Dark Tourism: Towards a Six Pillar Framework

As the first pillar of the Six Pillars framework, mapping is concerned with *time* – that is the past, present, and future. This establishes a historical timeline that can help to create a framework from which to move into the future (Inayatullah, 2008). Within this triangulation of time, the future pulls the present forward, which is simultaneously pushed forward by current trends and drivers. These can be weighed down by issues of the past, which can act as barriers to possibilities for the future (Inayatullah, 2013). Adopting this principle, this study offers a triangulation of time by addressing the past, present and future of lighter dark tourism.

Lighter dark tourism – the past

The most prominent lighter dark tourism attraction, if following the criteria of the Dark Tourism Spectrum typology (Stone, 2006), is arguably the London Dungeon visitor attraction. Opened in 1974, the attraction was originally a wax exhibition of horrifying history, comprising themed tableaux under the Tooley Street arches of London Bridge railway station in Southwark (Mortlock, 2019). The London Dungeon attraction was inspired by the lack of education and insight at its competitor *Madame Tussaud's Chamber of Horrors* and, similarly, the lack of aesthetic realism in exhibitions at the *Tower of London* (Alston, 2016). In the original Dungeon experience, visitors were led through a series of grisly themed exhibitions that included animatronics and actors (Alston, 2016). While this 'museum' sought to teach visitors about dark history, its use of animatronics and actors was Disneyfied, and thus created a greater entertainment value than many of its dark themed competitors. This blurring of education with entertainment – or edutainment – sparked public interest. Indeed, an increase of visitation in the 1990s with a greater use of innovative interpretation methods and higher commercialism saw the London Dungeon welcome 527,000 visitors in 1993, growing to 700,000 visitors by 1997. As Evans *et al.* (1999) notes, this was a respectable number given the attraction was contending against other major Southwark attractions, such as the *Tower of London* and the *British Museum*. However, when compared to, for example, London's *Clink Museum* (another lighter dark tourism attraction nearby), which drew in 20,000 visitors in 1995 (Evans *et al.*, 1999), the London Dungeon attraction was doing something different.

Despite public interest in the London Dungeon, critics labelled it as frivolous, inauthentic and inconsequential with little educational value and directed towards children (Ivanova & Light, 2018; Seaton & Lennon, 2004). Numerous reasons for this initial response include society, more generally, may have been uncomfortable with live performances of past horrors and tragic events – as was the case with the 1994 protests of slave auction re-enactments at Colonial Williamsburg (USA) (Carson, 1998; Jones, 1994). Conversely, while live performances were an issue for negative responses, the *Salem Witch Dungeon* since 1974 has successfully used live actors to re-enact the 1692 Salem Witch Trials, of which 19 people were executed by hanging. Moreover, a potential reason for negative reviews of the initial London Dungeon might have been the overt display of gore. Even so, the *Museo Della Tortura* in Siena, Italy, has been displaying instruments of torture and the death penalty since 1966. Likewise, negative responses of the early London Dungeon visitor attraction might be attributed to the commercialised merchandise visitors could purchase in the Dungeon gift shop. Yet, comparable products (for example, key chains, t-shirts, plush toys or books) are also offered at other dark locations, such as *Alcatraz*, *Robben Island* and even at the *Oklahoma City Bombing Memorial and Museum*. Yet, at these sites, mercantile mementos are considered 'dignified' and focused on 'recovery' or contributing to the local community (Clark, 2009; Strange & Kempa, 2003).

Therefore, given that the Dungeon experiences are no different from their darker counter parts in terms of commodification – that is, gory displays or gift shops (Stone & Grebenar, 2022), a potential reason for why the London Dungeon became the vilified attraction of the emergent dark tourism industry was specifically its entertainment value and fun-centric agenda. Moreover, the current ownership of the London Dungeon attraction is theme park operator Merlin Entertainments plc, the second largest theme park operator in the world (after Disney): a company that has expanded the Dungeon experience internationally, including in Amsterdam, Hamburg, Edinburgh, York, Blackpool and Shanghai.

Lighter dark tourism – the present (and the lightening of dark tourism)

Throughout the mid-to-late noughties and into the present, the Dungeon visitor attraction has developed into a global brand, inspiring other attractions to blur education with entertainment and capitalise on dark history. For instance, visitor attractions such as the *Dunbrody Famine Ship* in Ireland and the *National Justice Museum* in Nottingham (UK) now use re-enactment to retell tragic (hi)stories; while others, such as *The Real Mary King's Close* in Edinburgh adopt the *Horrible Histories* style of storytelling (part of the Horrible Histories franchise in the UK) with the use of smell pods to emit scents of vomit or damp to help create authentic experiences of medieval life with the Plague (Wyatt, 2019). Adapting lighter dark tourism to a mobile platform has also become a recent popular trend. For example, Dublin's *Gravedigger Ghost Bus* tour offers theatre on wheels. In a fully equipped double decker bus that has been redesigned to resemble a crypt (lower deck) and a coffin (upper deck); visitors laugh their way around infamous places in Dublin as they learn about the plague and other supernatural stories from committed guide-actors (Wyatt, 2019). Moreover, some attractions, including *The Real Mary King's Close* in Edinburgh, are now offering virtual experiences, pre-recorded and/or live-streamed, as well as AR (Augmented Reality) guidebooks via QR codes. Moving beyond the virtual-scape, some locations, such as the *Conner Prairie Living History Museum* (Indiana, USA) and the *Battle of Bannockburn Memorial and Museum* (Stirling, Scotland) are taking immersion a step further with co-created experiences where visitors can assume the role of a character and, subsequently, re-enact the history which they are learning.

Recognising commercial benefits of virtual tourism, particularly in the wake of the global pandemic COVID-19, the traditionally viewed 'darker' attractions have become inspired by what has been happening at the lighter end of the Dark Tourism Spectrum classification (Stone, 2006). Sites such as the *Auschwitz-Birkenau Memorial and Museum* (where the epitome of the Holocaust is represented in former Nazi occupied Poland) now offers a 360 virtual reality (VR) experience using over 200 high-quality panoramic photographs of the original site and buildings (Auschwitz-Birkenau, 2022). This VR visitor experience is supported with historical descriptions, witness accounts, archival documents, and other photographs, including artworks created by the prisoners, and objects related to the history of the camp (Auschwitz-Birkenau, 2022). Additionally, KZ-Gedenkstätte (a former Nazi concentration camp near Hamburg which imprisoned political prisoners) now uses augmented reality (AR) in *The Liberated* virtual tour by overlaying authentic historical images onto current-day images to help visitors to experience what happened on the day the camp was liberated by British Allied troops in May 1945. Moving beyond the virtual-scape and using immersive technologies within lighter dark tourism, the *Oklahoma City Bombing Memorial and Museum* now uses sensory stimulation technologies with authentic emergency dispatch recordings to simulate tragic events of the domestic terrorist truck bombing on 19 April, 1995 of the Alfred P. Murrah Federal Building in which 168 people perished. Consequently, visitors are provided with an immersive experience of the terrorism attack and its aftermath. Similarly, the *Titanic Experience* in Belfast now offers a ride that takes visitors through staged scenes of the ship's development until its fateful sinking on its maiden voyage in 1912.

These examples not only demonstrate lighter dark tourism's influence and how dark(er) attractions are starting to adopt more visitor attractive interpretations, but they help to reinforce the significance of what lighter dark tourism has been doing for years. That is, utilising technology to blur entertainment with education to create unique and memorable experiences. Therefore, the growth of dark tourism attractions that have started using these tactics once found only at sites at the lighter end of the Dark Tourism Spectrum model has been in response to rising expectations of commercialised experiences – specifically, the offering of cafes, gift shops and an increased use of technology that enhances the overall visitor experience (Krisjanous & Carruthers, 2018; Poade, 2017). This has been further influenced by the increasing influence of digital and mass media (Perry, 2020). As such, there is an increasing understanding that visitors now largely expect their experiences of 'most' dark tourism attractions to be more engaging, immersive, simulated, co-created, and/or participatory (Alabau-Montoya & Ruiz-Molina, 2020; Light & Ivanova, 2021). (The term 'most' is applied as more research is required for confirmation.) That said, however, this is important to consider when discussing the future of dark tourism and the commodification of death and the macabre, because the critical profiling in early dark tourism scholarship that established binaries from which the *dark* became separated from the *light* has been recently challenged from perspectives of visitors.

Of course, lighter dark tourism attractions use entertainment and a *Horrible Histories* style interpretation that is clearly inspired by Disneyfied theming and imagineering. However, recent research has demonstrated how these experiences offer meaningful edutainment through simulated and immersive realism that creates space for not just enjoyment, but also learning, reflection and contemplation about the realities of mortality (Alabau-Montoya & Ruiz-Molina, 2020; Light & Ivanova, 2021; Wyatt *et al.*, 2021). Indeed, Light and Ivanova (2021) drawing upon the mortality mediation concept outlined by Stone and Sharpley (2008) and Stone (2012a, 2012b), have demonstrated visitors to lighter dark tourism sites such as the Dungeon attractions, are able to recognise the fun-centric nature but also the tragic (hi)stories are about real people from the past. This not only makes them more appreciative of their own life, but also mediates the present and reminds them of how life was harsh for those who lived and suffered in the past (Light & Ivanova, 2021). This reinforces Bowman and Pezzullo's (2010) earlier arguments that visitors do not necessarily ascribe dark tourism experiences as being either *dark* or *light,* semantically at least. Rather, it has been an academic exercise to prescribe binaries (for instance, education vs. entertaining; authentic vs. inauthentic) and to set conceptual rules and expectations for what is acceptable for a site to be considered 'dark' or otherwise. Therefore, the acceptance (and now expectation) of edutainment interpretation within dark tourism among visitors allows for more innovative possibilities in the future.

Lighter dark tourism – the future

The growth of lighter dark tourism has helped costume, prop, and set-design companies in the creative industries to flourish, such as *Aroma Prime* – a bespoke aroma design service in Rochdale, England – which has become a leading supplier of scents for themed visitor attractions and parks. With smells such as 'rotting flesh' and 'vomit', creative companies such as *Aroma Prime* help to enhance the sensorial visitor experience. It is likely that the creative industries will continue to thrive as lighter dark tourism attractions continue to adapt to changes in visitor demand. Specifically, technology and innovative design companies will most certainly benefit in the future from the continued growth of the lighter dark tourism industry. It is also likely that darker tourism attractions will continue to adopt techniques of lighter attractions, thus softening the dark(est)-light(er) binaries over time (after Stone, 2006).

Moreover, the increased use (and future development of) 3D projections and handheld AR and VR experiences are being observed in a wide range of both lighter and darker visitor experiences. Therefore, it is likely that wearable technologies could be used in the immediate future, particularly in lighter experiences, to further immerse visitors in their experiences and give visitors more ownership over how they experience difficult heritage, tragic history, as well as future scenarios (Wright, 2018, 2021). Additionally, internet-driven and virtual experiences will certainly be likely in the future, particularly if the wider dark tourism industry continues to capitalise on society's acceptance of online experiences. Indeed, some lighter experiences, such as the *Lizzie Borden House* (the notorious site of unsolved murders in 1892 in Fall River, MA, USA), are already starting to benefit from live streaming. The next step will therefore likely be remote dark tourism, particularly given the success *Visit Faroe Islands* had with this innovation during the COVID-19 lockdowns (Leotta, 2022). Such innovations will create greater opportunities for unbodied travel experiences, allowing people to escape their reality and imaginatively travel somewhere new (Zerva, 2021). Consequently, it will also help to induce greater (dark) tourism interests and create future 'bucket-list' travel motivations (Leotta, 2022).

Lighter dark tourism has been a neglected and misunderstood area of dark tourism (Stone, 2009; Ivanova & Light, 2018; Wyatt *et al.*, 2021). Yet, lighter dark tourism neoliberal market tactics have become mercantile drivers for the future of dark tourism. With increasing demand for more engaging and immersive experiences, a corresponding accrual of innovation in commercial and interpretation activities will result (Inayatullah, 2013). In turn, there is likely to be greater rationality concerning lighter dark tourism attractions, as well as the use of edutainment inspired interpretation in even the *darkest* of places.

Anticipating Lighter Dark Tourism Futures

The second pillar of the Six Pillars framework refers to *anticipation* which can help to identify where new innovations will start and how consequences of today might impact the long-term future (Inayatullah, 2008). Considering the triangulation of time and dark tourism futures, as previously discussed, one of two future scenarios might be likely:

> *Scenario 1*. The dark(est)-light(est) binaries will continue to shrink, and scholars will become more like minded with visitors and view the blurring of education with entertainment to create meaningful edutainment.
>
> *Scenario 2*. The binaries will remain, but as technology continues to advance, darker attractions will apply a more conservative approach with the use of technological developments. For example, photo overlays and 360° VR experiences, while lighter attractions will capitalize on wearable technologies, advanced simulation rides, or location-based gameplay experiences akin to *Star Wars: Secrets of the Empire* (US).

With both scenarios, dark tourism in general is likely to be commercially driven, with all attractions providing a café, restaurant, or other refreshment facilities, as well as gift shops and/or visitor centres with merchandise. Considering the technologies that currently exist, either scenario is possible. However, a recent content review of TripAdvisor posts for Dungeon experiences, for example, illustrated mixed responses in that not all visitors appreciate satire and mocking attitudes of actors, while others complain the acting, technologies and/or rides are mundane. Therefore, Scenario 2 is much more likely in the immediate future, as lighter dark tourism attractions will elevate their experiences with more advanced technologies to meet future visitor expectations.

Nonetheless, newer technologies, such as artificial intelligence and remote tourism, will become a growing trend, as noted earlier. Moreover, given the emergence of dark themed hospitality experiences, such as the *Karosta Prison Hotel* in Latvia or *The Coffin Club* in the USA, there is potential for more 'dark' themed guest experiences. Indeed, with increasing expectations of unique and memorable experiences allied with new immersion and simulation technologies, it is entirely possible that the Dungeon experience capitalises upon a Dungeon inspired hotel or resort akin to the *Star Wars: Galactic Starcruiser* hotel experience at the Walt Disney World Resort (FL, USA). Yet, it is noted that these *anticipations* are constrained to current understandings of sociocultural trends. As Light and Ivanova (2021) and Qian *et al.* (2022) have both noted, Western societies are more inclined to participate in the spectacularisation of death because they are culturally removed from the realities of it (also see Stone, 2020). That said, however, mass media – specifically film and television – has started to influence a wider spectrum of visitors to seek out dark tourism experiences (Qian *et al.*, 2022).

Timing the Future of Lighter Dark Tourism

The third pillar of the Six Pillars framework refers to *timing*. In other words, timing in terms of futurology is the search for grand patterns of history and the identification of models for change (Inayatullah, 2008). In turn, this offers better understanding of the shape of time and possibilities of long-term change (Inayatullah, 2013). Considering the changes that have occurred throughout the history of lighter dark tourism, as mapped out earlier in Pillar One and taking into consideration the anticipations set out in Pillar Two, it is likely lighter dark tourism will be influenced by a time of 'new futures' driven by a creative minority. According to Inayatullah (2013), this creative minority will challenge traditionalist ideas and innovate socially, culturally, technologically, and even politically. Many lighter attractions are already doing this to a certain extent, which has influenced some dark attractions, as noted earlier. However, it is likely that as the creative industries continue to grow and commercial endeavours expand, innovative determination and greater rationality will unhinge existing dark tourism power structures that continue to look down on lighter dark tourism activities. Consequently, greater sustainability is created among lighter dark tourism attractions within the wider dark tourism sector.

Deepening the Future of Lighter Dark Tourism

When applied through a causal layer analysis, or rather, an unpacking of what the future might look like at distinct levels or 'depths', *deepening* the future is the fourth pillar of the Six Pillars framework (Inayatullah, 2013). The levels included within this pillar are focused on day-to-day issues, systemic issues, worldviews and myths or metaphors. Collectively, these levels examine what is occurring internally within dark tourism practice and scholarship and, subsequently, evaluate how this is influencing and being influenced by what is happening externally within the wider tourism industry. While beyond the scope of this chapter, these influences include global issues at the social, cultural, economic and political level. Importantly, however, for lighter dark tourism scholarship to move forward, there must be an increased discussion and critical conversation between dark tourism scholars and industry practitioners about the dark–light binaries established nearly 20 years ago. Consequently, it remains to be seen whether such conceptual prescriptions are required in the future given the contemporary commercialisation being observed at even the darkest of dark tourism sites.

Creating Alternatives for the Future of Lighter Dark Tourism

The fifth pillar, creating *alternatives*, is based on scenario planning (Inayatullah, 2013). While the previous pillars help scan visitor experiences of lighter dark tourism, Pillar Five can be considered the risk assessment for futures thinking. Regarding lighter dark tourism futures, the worst possible scenario would be a status quo or decline in technology and technological advancement. Unrealistic as this is, it would cause most 'lighter' attractions to revert to static exhibitions and at best, animatronics, found in the original London Dungeon visitor attraction. Of course, tour guides and re-enactments would still be possible, but the lack of, for example, lighting and sound effects, would drastically change most experiences. In fact, this would render lighter attractions to be much less 'light' when compared to what darker attractions are now doing.

Indeed, VR and AR experiences would certainly restrict the level of immersion visitors could experience, and the loss of, for example, YouTube, would cause many attractions to lose a substantial number of unbodied visitors. Another highly unlikely scenario that could create an alternative future would be if society decided to live simplistically to encourage sustainable living to better combat climate change. This would certainly influence commercialisation as gift shops and the sale of merchandise would be rendered useless, or rather, unsustainable. Since many attractions are sustained by their retail sales, this would certainly impact the scope of dark tourism. To that end, Inayatullah (2008) proposes several different models for addressing negative alternatives, all of which share features of the traditional SWOT analysis found in marketing discourse.

Transforming the Future of Dark Tourism

The sixth and final pillar – *transformation* – focuses on the most preferred outcome of Pillar Five's scenario planning analysis (Inayatullah, 2013). The preferred future is based on creative visualisation and taking the necessary steps to ensure positive futures (Inayatullah, 2008). While this appears straightforward, lighter dark tourism is reliant upon demand forces that, in turn, are influenced by economic, political and sociocultural factors. Therefore, the ability to purposefully move lighter dark tourism into a specific future is almost impossible. However, based on current societal trends and issues, and an understanding of the historical timeline of lighter dark tourism's past, it is most likely that the future of lighter dark tourism will continue to capitalise upon advanced technologies and society's morbid fascinations (Urquhart, 2022; Wight, 2020).

Additionally, dark(er) tourism attractions will continue to be 'lightened' by the commercial and interpretation techniques often found within lighter dark tourism attractions. While the dark–light binaries do appear to be currently diluting, the anticipated technologies of the future will surely reaffirm some of the traditional prescriptions that have set darker attractions as 'elite' and lighter attractions as 'popular' (Seaton & Lennon, 2004). While a conceptual distinction between the dark and light in dark tourism might always remain, there is no denying that light has been shed in some of the darkest of places, and thus lighter dark tourism will continue to shine its way into the future.

Conclusion

There has been a proliferation of lighter dark tourism experiences and, subsequently, an increasing use of advanced technologies and simulation effect. These include but are not limited to environment manipulation, sensory stimulation, and co-creative re-enactment within darker experiences (Wright, 2021; Wyatt *et al.*, 2021, 2023). Specifically, these innovations extend Neuhofer and Buhalis' (2014) proposal of an Experience Economy 3.0, whereby a sustained public preference for technologically enhanced visitor experiences is reflected. This chapter has discussed such enhanced experiences through interpretation techniques found in lighter dark tourism and how this effort has influenced dark(er) experiences. In doing so, this chapter has highlighted the contributions of lighter dark tourism to the enhancement of dark(er) visitor experiences. While traditional interpretation methods, such as text panels and artefact visual displays add value to dark(er) tourism experiences, this chapter has demonstrated the value of lighter interpretation techniques (i.e. edutainment) for creating meaningful and engaged learning experiences. By using Inayatullah's (2008) Six Pillars framework to establish a historical timeline of lighter dark tourism developments, this chapter has demonstrated the influence lighter dark tourism has had on the wider dark tourism experience-scape.

Considering the public's growing preference for technologically enhanced and hyper-real experiences (Alabau-Montoya & Ruiz-Molina, 2020; Light & Ivanova, 2021; Qian *et al.*, 2022), the inclusion of these 'lighter' experiences across the full Dark Tourism Spectrum taxonomy (Stone, 2006) provides opportunities for greater visitor engagement motivations and, consequently, deeper learning experiences. Therefore, future research should explore dark(er) experiences through a 'lighter' lens, explore their use of edutainment techniques for enhanced visitor experiences, and critically assess how and what visitors are learning within these spaces when compared to traditionally static and less technologically enhanced experiences. This will help to extend knowledge and understanding, as well as to help soften the dark(est)–light(er) binaries that have long directed and often separated dark tourism scholars. Importantly, this will prompt greater dialogue between scholars about the benefits of blurring dark and light experience qualities, while at the same time encouraging practitioners to learn from each other to enhance their future visitor experiences.

20 Future of Dark Tourism Festivals: Technology and the Tourist Experience

Luisa Golz and Tony Johnston

Fear isn't so difficult to understand. After all, weren't we all frightened as children? Nothing has changed since Little Red Riding Hood faced the big bad wolf. What frightens us today is exactly the same sort of thing that frightened us yesterday. It's just a different wolf. This fright complex is rooted in every individual.
Alfred Hitchcock, 1972

Introduction

Death, disaster and 'darkness' sell. Indeed, in an age of consumption, we love to be scared. Some people simply just *cannot* get enough of fear. Consider the multitude of death, disaster and darkness consumption opportunities on offer today. We, the consumers, can purchase books about death (for example murder mystery novels), music with dark themes (for instance, death metal), video games showcasing violence (consider first person shooter platforms), movies with graphic death (think on almost any Quentin Tarantino film), reality and fictional television series posited as 'must-watch' entertainment (such as Netflix's *Squid Game*), games and toys to ease the younger consumer into the arena (for example, toy guns), among many other products and experience associated with darkness.

Within a touristic context, this form of dark consumption includes visitation to tourism sites which have a strong association with death and disaster and, as pertinent to this research, attending festivals with dark and death related themes (Dobscha, 2016; Light, 2017a; Seaton, 1996; Sharpley, 2005; Stone, 2012a). Death has become an inescapable product in today's visitor economy (Dobscha, 2016; Stone, 2012b) with dark tourism festival products evident worldwide, for all ages and all tastes, genders, and consumer backgrounds, ranging from religious and spiritual festivals to those centred-on identity and subcultures, the arts and culture events, alongside re-enactment performances (Table 20.1).

Table 20.1 A sample of dark tourism festivals as of 2022

Location	Festival Name	
Dublin, Ireland	The Bram Stoker Festival (This festival is a celebration of the life of Bram Stoker, author of Dracula, with light shows, tours, talks and readings).	October
Whitby, United Kingdom	Whitby Goth Weekend (a gothic themed festival with emphasis on music and identity and strong references to Stoker's Dracula)	Easter and October
Navan, Ireland	Púca Festival (púca is the Irish for ghost and this festival has an emphasis on storytelling and expressions of culture related to Irish mythology)	October
Salem, USA	Haunted Happenings (This is one of the world's largest Hallowe'en festivals with strong emphasis on costumes, fireworks, art, culture)	October
Derry, Northern Ireland	Derry Hallowe'en (Similar to Salem, the Derry event is also a large festival, with many indoor and outdoor events over the Hallowe'en period)	October
Mexico City, Mexico	Dia de Muertos (an international religious event but this is the largest)	November
Ghost Festival, SE Asia	A festival held across South-East Asia on which day the dead are believed to visit the living.	15th night of the 7th month

In this chapter, therefore, we explore the future of dark tourism festivals, discussing some implications of (future) technology for the tourist experience. While festivals come and go, and themes evolve, the fundamentals have not changed significantly over the centuries. Most festivals will involve firstly, physically present attendees; secondly, people who join to celebrate a performance, as well as art, food and drink or some other form of cultural heritage and; thirdly, have specific location attributes. These basic ingredients have remained static for some time. However, it is all change. Rapid technological advancements mean today's festivals are heavily exposed to macro forces that are quickly reconfiguring promotion, spatial organisation, and the visitor experience. The potential for change soon is immense. Dark tourism festivals are especially likely to experience momentous change as technology has strong potential to affect emotions through providing embodied experiences, and particularly through impacting upon dystopian and liminal sensations (Wright, 2020).

Through analysing product development trends and consumer behaviour, our chapter will explore the potential for technology to reconfigure dark festival experiences. This area of study remains unexplored thus far. We suggest the development of virtual, but embodied, tourism experiences through the application of Augmented Reality (AR), Virtual Reality (VR) and modern technologies will play a significant role in framing future tourist experiences. The current and potential application of technologies in other areas of tourism will be analysed in this chapter to establish future scenarios for dark tourism festivals.

Dark Tourism Festivals and Technology: Towards a Future

Dark tourism festivals facilitate interactions between society and death, frequently framed through an entertainment lens (Dunkley, 2017; Penfold-Mounce, 2016). Such festivals offer the visitor an experience which can be dystopian and liminal, and often mediated through co-creation with festival organisers (Light, 2009; Pimentel Biscaia & Marques, 2022; Podoshen *et al.*, 2015; Sharpley, 2005). Festival stakeholders are motivated by opportunities to develop niche tourism products and shoulder-season events, which attract high-spend tourists (BBC [British Broadcasting Corporation], 2021). Participants, on the other hand, have a desire to be taken outside of their familiar surroundings in a liminal space which facilitates contemplation of death or the macabre (Bristow, 2020; Light, 2009).

Rapid technological advancements in the early 21st century, followed by the onset of the Covid-19 pandemic in early 2020, have caused an imaginative rethink for festival organisers on how to plan and deliver festivals and engage with audiences. Technological advancements utilised more broadly in the tourism and leisure industry include the use of virtual reality (VR), augmented reality (AR), holograms, 5-dimensional cinema experiences, sensory experiences and biomechanics. A non-dark example could be the fully immersive digital experience documenting the UK rock band *The Who*, launched in 2022 in Hastings, utilising 'next generation XR technology' to tell the story of the band's early days (MWRF, 2022). A specific dark tourism example of how AR has been successfully used, is the Spike Island Prison in County Cork, Ireland (Rountree, 2022). It is here that augmented reality on mobile phones is used to animate the museum's environs and former prison conditions. Similarly, the proposed and actual use of drones to represent the complete architecture of ruins offer a mechanism to alter the physical reality of a location using technology (Orlean, 2021).

Tourism scholars began to discuss the emergence of VR experiences in tourism during the mid-1990s (Williams & Hobson, 1995). A shift from theoretical discussions of the use of VR to practical uses in tourism was noted and a wide variety of impacts on the tourism industry were predicted. Discussions and predictions have continued, including the notion of virtual realms and travel to dark sites within contexts of film, literature, the internet, as well as in online games (Mcdaniel, 2018). Tourists can now (virtually) travel to sites of death and disaster while imagining that they are in a different place 'without actually being in that place' (Mcdaniel, 2018: 3). Moreover, modern technologies facilitate access to areas of natural disaster and war, giving the new 'dark tourist' the opportunity to visit virtual traumascapes (Korstanje & George, 2017).

Technology used as part of the dark tourism experience has potential to educate as well as immerse the tourist and, subsequently, create an entirely different level of experience. Dark tourism scholars have analysed how digital media can be used to provide more engaging dark tourism experiences. For instance, using a three-tiered approach, the application of social media, mobile and blogging as part of dark tourism experiences has been analysed by Bolan and Simone-Charteris (2018). Moreover, immersive technologies such as virtual reality have the potential to bring macabre stories and dark histories to life and may replace more traditional forms of interpretation. Additionally, several dark tourism sites are now available to visit virtually, such as the infamous prison island of Alcatraz or the crematoria of Auschwitz extermination camp (Strange & Kempa, 2003). Yet, it has also been highlighted that experiences of virtual dark tourism environments were 'scarce' (Bolan & Simone-Charteris, 2018). This represents a gap in the research, especially when analysing the potential of virtual environments at dark tourism festivals.

Potential negative impacts of the use of technology at dark tourism sites have also been discussed, for example the 'selfie phenomenon' (Podoshen *et al.*, 2018). Fisher and Bolter (2018) propose a framework for ethically sound dark tourism augmented reality experiences to avoid the 'kitschification' of dark sites (Fisher & Bolter, 2018; Stone & Grebenar, 2022). In recent years, it has been proposed that the use of VR in cultural and heritage tourism has had several positive impacts, yet it has also affected the perceived authenticity of tourism experiences (Shehade & Stylianou-Lambert, 2020). Applied to dark tourism experiences, Wang *et al.* (2021) specifically recommend the use of VR technology, creating potentially more authentic experiences and even inspiring awe. The use of dark themed songs in conjunction with augmented reality experiences has also been discussed and suggestions have been made how virtual dark tourism environments should be designed (Handayani & Korstanje, 2020). Yet there is currently no research that examines how newer technologies can find utilisation at festivals with dark and Gothic themes.

Apart from audio sound, visual lighting has also been found to affect the experience at dark tourism sites. By adjusting the brightness, or indeed the darkness of visual material, the sensory stimulation changes and this affects the psychological experience as well as behaviour (Lv *et al.*, 2022). This can also be observed at dark tourism festivals where many events are deliberately staged in the hours of darkness and 'dark aesthetics' play a significant role (Podoshen *et al.*, 2015). Indeed, the use of costumes, photography, and creativity are an intricate part of dark tourism festivals (Golz, 2021). The participants become part of the creation of a performance and absorb the experience. In early festival research, this is examined and described as festival participants 'become living signs of themselves' in that participants embody and perform meaning, thus distributing their own powerful messages (Kirshenblatt-Gimblett, 1984). In dark tourism research, performance has been analysed by reviewing questions about ritual, play, identity, everyday life and embodiment at the nexus of tourism and death (Bowman & Peluzzo, 2009). This act of performance has been increasingly mentioned when analysing concepts of embodiment, as a means of absorbing experience (Skinner, 2016). This is central to the tourist's experience, as outlined by McEvoy (2014) in the context of tourists partaking in ghost tourism activities, including ghost tours.

Movement such as walking can also be seen as a catalyst for embodiment within dark tourism experiences, as it is a more open and immersive experience than simply driving through an area. Through purposeful movement, for example, by following a tour guide at a tour of the Falls Road in Belfast, Northern Ireland, tourists consume The Troubles in an embodied manner (Skinner, 2016). This behaviour can also be observed at the Whitby Goth Weekend, where participants walk the streets of the town and take over the streetscapes of Whitby (Hodkinson, 2002). At this dark tourism festival embodiment is especially evident. The festival participants of the Whitby Goth Weekend dress up in elaborate outfits and become the main attraction of the event as others attend to simply gaze (Hodkinson, 2002). This process can also be observed at other festivals too, including for example at the Redhead Days festival in the Netherlands, where people with red hair are the focus of the event (Simons, 2020).

Dark tourism festivals can offer experiences that are liminal, embodied and at times even dystopian. Yet what does the future hold for these festivals and how are advances in technology likely to affect the festival participant's experience? The remainder of this chapter explores the future of dark tourism festivals, which is achieved through two objectives; namely exploring the embodiment of virtual reality dark experiences and predicting future trends based on such. And, secondly, discussing consumer predictions for technological impacts upon dark tourism festivals. In so doing, the study adopts a focus group approach and, subsequently, empirically reports how research participants 'experience' a virtual reality dark tourism site.

Dark Tourism Virtual Experiences: Towards Empirical Evidence

This study adopts an interpretive approach, utilising a qualitative and inductive methodology to explore the richness of the topic at hand. The main research method included use of a focus group to collect primary data, which was supplemented by a comprehensive literature review. Focus group participants were recruited from postgraduate students in a university in Ireland. All participants were in a single faculty, including four different nationalities represented in the study, with four male students and one female student.

To stimulate discussion all participants were given the opportunity to test a dark experience on a virtual reality headset, namely Meta's *Oculus Quest*. To facilitate this, each participant was brought individually into a university meeting room along with both researchers. Participants were asked if they had used a VR headset before, which none had. As it can take a few minutes to become comfortable with the technology (e.g. with vision, adjusting head strap and setting boundaries) each user was given the headset to use for a few minutes to become familiar. This commenced with using the application '*Wander,*' which is based on '*Google Maps*' and gave participants the opportunity to become familiar and comfortable using the headset. Each participant then used the headset to try the chosen experience and were given around 30 minutes to sample and explore each experience (Table 20.2). The headset was cleaned thoroughly with disinfectant wipes between each user. On completion of the VR experience each participant was asked to return to the meeting room when everyone was ready that afternoon for the focus group. The focus group lasted for 45 minutes.

The focus group was transcribed, and discussion was coded and mapped against two thematic areas: Embodiment of Dark Tourism, and Future Scenarios and New Technology. Initially discussion centred around the physical senses. The participants of the dark tourism VR experience described their experience as 'unique' and some commented that they felt as if they were really in the place that is portrayed during the experience. Some commented on what they saw and praised the quality of the graphics, mentioning how 'realistic' they were. Others commented on the audio experience, for example while visiting the Anne Frank House: 'you could hear the rain outside on the roof and that was emotional'. It was agreed that overall, audio aspects enhanced the experience, as for example one VR experience also included being spoken to directly. The guide in the Iraq 'Home After War' experience touched some of the participants' emotions and this experience was described as impactful and personal.

Emotions described ranged from curiosity, amazement to fear, panic, and in one case also boredom. One participant mentioned that they were 'feeling small' and 'vulnerable', which gives an insight into the importance of the scale used in VR experiences. Specific fears were also mentioned by some participants, including the sound of a bomb exploding was described as frightening. Meanwhile, standing on a high roof caused one participant to experience fear of heights, again feeling quite vulnerable. Participants' comments show that strong emotions can be elicited during a dark tourism VR experience, with some participants even claimed to have an 'out of body' experience. Others were acutely aware of their actual surroundings for most of the experience and knew that 'this is not real'. One distinct negative was described during the experience by some participants, that being the lack of being able to feel

Table 20.2 Key VR experience information

Number	Title of VR Experience Chosen by Participant	Full Description of the Application from the Occulus Quest Website	Type
1	Anne Frank House VR, (Occulus, 2022a)	In 1942, during the Second World War, Anne Frank, a thirteen-year-old Jewish girl and her family were forced to go into hiding to escape persecution from the Nazis. For more than two years, the Franks and 4 others would live in the 'Secret Annex' of an old office building in Amsterdam, sharing the burden of living in hiding in confined quarters with the constant threat of discovery. The award-winning Anne Frank House VR offers a unique and emotional insight into these two years. Experience the world-famous Secret Annex in a never before seen way. Travel back to the years of the Second World War and wander through the rooms of the Annex that housed the group of 8 Jewish people as they hid from the Nazis. Immerse yourself in Anne's thoughts as you traverse each faithfully recreated room, thanks to the power of VR, and find out what happened to the Annex' brave inhabitants.	Room space application where the user can 'move' around the room by walking in their own space.
2	Home After War, (Occulus, 2022b)	'Home After War' is a room-scale, interactive virtual reality experience that takes you to Fallujah, a city that was, until recently, under Islamic State (IS) control. The war against IS has ended but the city is still unsafe. There's one looming fear for returning refugees – booby trapped homes and improvised explosive devices (IEDs) in the neighbourhoods. Ahmaied Hamad Khalaf and his family returned home after the fighting subsided. Explore Ahmaied's home by either walking physically or teleporting in the space as he tells you his story about returning to a home that might be booby trapped. Witness life outside the four walls of his house through 360° videos embedded in the space. Hear Ahmaied speak of his loss, and his hopes. Learn what it's like to fear the home you once loved.	Room space application where the user can 'move' around the room by walking in their own space.
3	Jurassic World, (Occulus, 2022c)	Jurassic World: Apatosaurus The Jurassic World: Apatosaurus VR Experience allows the viewer for the first time to see what it feels like to be in the presence and close proximity of a living dinosaur and to experience a sense of connection with it - with the mixture of awe, striking beauty and danger that this implies. Jurassic World: BLUE Dinosaurs have overtaken the turbulent Isla Nublar, but the threat of a natural disaster erupting looms eerily over the island. Follow Blue, a highly intelligent Velociraptor, on her quest for survival, using VR to experience her extraordinary sensorial abilities and awareness as she scours for food and water, searches for signs of life, and fights against some of the island's most threatening predators.	3D video content. Each video clip is several minutes in length.
4	National Geographic Visit the Okavango Delta in 360°, (National Geographic, 2022)	Glide through the waterways of Botswana's Okavango Delta and come face to face with its wildlife in this immersive 360 experience. Through Okavango Eternal, work is underway to help protect the source waters of this one-of-a-kind region, and support tourism that benefits local communities.	3D video content. 4 minutes.

Table 20.3 A sample of participant experiences and predictions for future

Senses and emotions	Current situation	Future possibilities
Sight and sound	'Now the equipment is a little bit heavy. In my case it was nice because I went to Jurassic Park and I saw the dinosaurs which is something you can't see in the real life. It was very nice because it really is like you are there.' 'I felt impressed by the explosion of the volcano. It was moving.' 'I had the same with the explosion. Suddenly there was a bomb ... I was like what's happening?'	'The equipment will improve as well I believe. I believe they will make it lighter. So probably you won't feel it so much ... you will feel more like you are in touch with what you are seeing.' 'Well the technology keeps advancing all the time so I assume there will be much better graphics at some stage. So it will look more realistic. As well as other participants mentioned, we already have some effects that were very good but I assume this will be advanced as well ... so that it feels more like a real thing.'
Smell and touch	'If I go to a festival I would really like to interact with people, really interact with things, have the smells ... have the complete experience. This for now can't give you the complete experience. It would give you some parts but I would miss the rest.' 'If there is a wave, you can feel some water splashed on your face. Probably not something you can do at home right now, but who knows in the future? I mean who thought ten years ago that we'd have VR experiences where you feel like you are really there.'	'New technology emerges and it moves constantly, we don't know what's going to happen. But it's not too far-fetched to think that they will come up with something that will stimulate parts of your brain, as if something is touching you somewhere.' 'Yes, the scale was impressive. And you really wanted to touch the animals and see how it felt. So yes, it moved our emotions even if it was in a different way doing different experiences. But the curiosity and the amazement ...'
Fear	'And then fear came with the bomb for sure. And then the moment on the roof, I felt like I have nothing under my feet. I have a fear of heights, I was panicking there. I tried to make myself realise that this is not real but it felt so real.'	'So at festivals it could be the same. For example Dracula as a holograph walking around. So I think this would be a way of improving the experience and it would appeal to your feelings in a better way. It would be more emotional I'd say like this.'
Sensory Engagement and physical environment	'The more your senses are engaged with it, the more you are glued to the experience and it becomes more enjoyable. And the more you forget about the place you are actually in. It will depend on the quality of the video that is used by the festival organisers, so it is all about the creativity as well.'	'You can stay at home or put on some goggles and go virtually to the festival. With the VR we can also connect with each other. We can all stay at home and have our own hologram or whatever ... maybe that wouldn't be as bad. But again I would miss going away, I wouldn't just want to log off ... I want to keep listening to people, I want to listen to sounds but I also need to move.'
Emotional connection	'I was in the house in Iraq where the father guided me through his house, he had lost two sons and it felt like he was directly talking to me. I could see him all the time and I was glued to him. It looked so realistic and felt very personal. It was impactful as it lasted a good few minutes.'	I think VR from a festival perspective can work as a marketing tool. It will never replace a festival, at least from my perspective. But if I go to a dark tourism festival, let's say something related to Dracula. ... If I am already there and I can add something else to my experience, rather than have some people or posters or haunted houses... but sometimes I think if you can add something extra I think that VR would be nice.

and touch their surroundings enforced the feeling that the experience was not completely realistic.

Within the context of emotional engagement, and particularly notions around darkness and fear, participants noted the potential for technology to impact on the configuration of festivals. Participants thought the use of holograms could be beneficial at festivals. For example, a hologram of Dracula at a gothic themed festival may engage in storytelling, frights and scares, or more simply to provide general festival information such as practical information, including facilities and navigation, or ordering food and drink. Other comments noted the intersection between technology and dark tourism festivals, including social interaction, promotion possibilities and access. Lack of social interaction via a virtual environment was cited as an issue but one which is almost inevitable that technology will overcome soon, much in the way social media has reduced physical interaction and has partly replaced it with online interaction. More positively towards near term future technological impact on dark tourism festivals, participants offered the view that virtual reality was likely to add value to both promotion and the tourist experience. Taster experiences to lure visitors to physically visit a (dark) festival are likely to become common, utilising virtual reality to engage with the sensations and emotions documented in Table 20.3. Access was also noted as an area where VR can add value, notably in relation to time or financial constraints: '... if I don't have the time to travel but I have two to three hours free at home ... it would be interesting'.

Conclusion

The future for dark tourism festivals offers many intersection points between technology and festival promotion, spatial organisation and visitor experiences. Enhanced stimulation of the senses through technology will occur, for example through use of virtual and augmented reality technology to stimulate warmth, sight, sound and touch. Complex emotions, as for example described by this study, fear or the feeling of insecurity can be emulated by such technologies and this opens a realm of different opportunities for new dark tourism festival experiences.

At the more extreme end of these technological possibilities complex ethical issues will arise and these will require further interrogation. For instance, future studies may address research questions, including but not limited to, could future dark tourism festivals offer a visitor experience hologram encounter with the dead? Could auxiliary elements be incorporated in the experience, such as the use of fake (or real) blood to heighten scary and frightful encounters? Or to contemplate another problematic scenario: could the festivities utilise technology to recreate loved ones who would walk among us again as holograms? Indeed, further possibilities exist through use of embodied technological experience. Could technology in future simulate extreme pain or even death-like experiences for the visitor? Technologically advanced liminal or even dystopian spaces need to be managed and controlled to enhance and regulate these types of experiences. Further research will need to consider the role of festival managers and organisers who will be tasked with orchestrating these new experiences.

Finally, experiences such as psychological tricks of the mind, simulated time travel, déjà vu or out of body experiences are certainly likely to exist and a multidisciplinary research exploration will be required to negotiate the associated issues. Moreover, combining virtual reality with hypnosis opens complex possibilities concerning psychogeography and liminality. Indeed, implications for future dark tourism and the use of VR are fraught with moral complexities, as well as technological quandaries. Further research will inevitably develop these debates in future dark tourism scholarship as technology continues to advance.

21 Future Dystopian Attractions: Benign Masochism in Dark Tourism

Robert S. Bristow, Alina Gross and Ian Jenkins

Human misery and murder – so long as they were fake – were intriguing, and we, as a group, could glimpse the, from the safety of a show.
(Kullstroem, 2017: 263)

Introduction

Ancient Roman gladiatorial games may be one of the first practices of dark tourism where the spectator sought not only a death experience but one for entertainment (Stone, 2006). Thus, the birth of fright tourism emerged when the visitor desired some pleasurable opportunity at a dark event and not one simply seeking a pilgrimage or educational prospect. Today, fright attractions are big business. In the US alone, the autumn Halloween season accounts for US$10 billion (National Retail Federation, 2022). That interest is expected to continue in a society that will survive the current global COVID-19 pandemic (at the time of writing). This voyeuristic audience is drawn to a fictional future of death and suffering, while insisting on a sanitised experience. Even during the pandemic period, Halloween seasons have remained interest in these attractions, albeit one with face medical masks and social distancing. Beyond Halloween, that interest is found throughout the world. For example, the Japanese culture has a strong fascination with ghost themed fright attractions despite a real and horrific history.

The future of dark tourism destinations will still appeal to those seeking solace or to embrace our horrid history. Yet, these histories may yield unpleasant memories that have a long-lasting fate. For fright tourism, these settings that are sometime called 'dark fun factories' (after Stone, 2006) which are frequently fictionalised accounts of the past, present or future (Powell & Iankova, 2016; Stone, 2009). Indeed, a fun-centric setting is central in fright attractions (Bristow & Newman, 2005; Kendrick, 1991; Wyatt *et al.*, 2023), whereby settings are guided by industry gatekeepers who manipulate history into a tourist product for mass touristic consumption (Bristow, 2020; Tzanelli, 2016). Therefore, the purpose of this chapter, is to anticipate the potential future of fright tourism based upon a macabre interest in death, yet one disinfected from reality to escape the realism of death and suffering today. Consequently, we offer a brief history of the interest in fright attractions and link both the aversion to risk as well as the appeal of risky venues in present-day society. We also explore a global industry where several cultural milieus are discovered in our case study approach to understand the desirability of various fright attractions. This offers examples of the global prospect of citizens that desire a safe, sanitary, yet frightfully fun situation that we suspect will continue in a world that faces death and suffering on a regular basis. We offer several suggestions for the future tourism industry to incorporate the morbid desire of fright tourists.

'Fright Tourism': A Brief History

Throughout history, people have long been drawn to war zones and other sites of conflict. In many cases these may be historical pilgrimages yielding some liminal transformation entwined to the events of death (Ashworth & Hartmann, 2005; Collins-Kreiner, 2016a, 2016b; Hartmann, 2014; Lennon & Foley, 2000; Seaton, 1996). Today, these travels are known to contribute to thanatourism (Seaton, 1996) or dark tourism (Foley & Lennon, 1996a, 1996b). Moreover, recent dark tourism scholarship has explored sites of the Holocaust (Pastor & Kent, 2020; Reynolds, 2016), slavery heritage (Miles, 2015; Nelson, 2020), disasters (Chen & Xu, 2021; Martini & Buda, 2020), cremation celebrations (Sharma, 2020; Sharma & Rickly, 2019), genocide (Isaac & Çakmak, 2016; Tan, 2019) and so-called 'dark fun factories' (Powell & Iankova, 2016; Stone, 2010). These latter examples can also reflect the interest in 'lighter' dark tourism opportunities – that is, the breadth of dark tourism visitor attractions and sites that are delineated by Stone's (2006) Dark Tourism Spectrum taxonomy. It is here that on one end of this conceptual typology we find sites *of* death, while at other end of the typology are sites *associated with* death (Stone, 2006). For some dark tourism sites, authentic experiences are more relevant while this is not the case for the lighter end of the Spectrum model. Accordingly, while both concerned with death and are visitor 'attractions', one cannot compare, say Auschwitz-Birkenau Memorial and Museum in Poland (darker) to that of Madame Tussauds (lighter) in Sydney, Australia.

However, as a typological subset of dark tourism, fright tourism tends to be found in inauthentic settings, where the visitor attraction is for fun and entertainment (Bristow & Jenkins, 2020). The destination and/or attraction/site may have a dark history, such as Salem, Massachusetts, and its associated Witch Trials of 1692 (Weir, 2012), or the history of Vlad Țepeș in present-day Romania that was exploited in Bram Stoker's Dracula (Busby, 2022; Light, 2007, 2016). Indeed, throughout history, individuals have sought the bizarre and unusual. For instance, the Grand Guignol (*Le Théâtre du Grand-Guignol*) met the demand for live action theatrical productions featuring horror entertainment in Paris (Hand & Wilson, 2000). Shows began in 1897 and lasted until 1962, presenting gory effects to an audience. Modern day fright attractions reached a global market about the same time as horror films became widely available to a population seeking surreal experiences of motion pictures. Beginning in the early part of the last century, several German-produced films introduced horror for terror entertainment (Tamborini & Weaver, 1996). These included *Das Cabinet des Dr. Caligari* (1919) and *Nosferatu* (1921). Shortly later, *Topper* (1937) introduced movie fans to the themes of fun and fright, highlighting a connection that had been growing for centuries.

These examples offer evidence that audiences are drawn to a macabre fantasy world that are found in fright attractions that, in turn, may yield some edutainment (Wyatt *et al.*, 2020). Like bygone visitors of yesteryear seeking gladiatorial spectacles or watching medieval public hangings, there will always be a market for people seeking a dark setting, yet one that is safe, socially sanctioned and temporal. Consequently, this introduces the theoretical basis of risk in tourism, something management (the producer) wants to reduce while the visitor (the consumer) seeks to achieve.

Risk (in Tourism)

Life without risk would not be life. From the moment we are born we face a life of risk and if we have managed to reach adulthood, we could be a good manager of risk. This can be reflected in the way that insurance companies work and the assessment of the probability of harm or damage occurring. Subsequently, the higher the risk the less likely you are to be insured or the costs of the premium becomes prohibitive. Risk can be likelihood of harm, which exists in many different physical and mental forms. However, in many ways risk offers a certain exultation of spirit to life and offers 'joie de vivre' in many of life's experiences (Jenkins, 2019). Indeed, some people who have had life threatening experiences and survived have said that they have never felt more alive after that event (Jenkins, 2019; Piekarz *et al.*, 2015). However, this offers something of a paradox in contemporary society. On the one hand, the emergence of a postmodern society has ensured the diminution of actual risk. For many people disease, accidents and other mortal perils have been diminished by technology and scientific knowledge, to the extent that witnessing or experiencing the death of others is now an uncommon phenomenon compared to some centuries ago (Pierkarz *et al.*, 2015). Yet, on the other hand, a cosseted postmodern society has a counter effect in terms of risk, because as risks have diminished there seems to have been a resurgence of the need for consumers to experience risk, or rather managed/perceived risks. Therefore, risk is an inherent human need to make humans feel alive but one which seems played out by the boom in leisure and tourism activities that have an inherent risk factor.

However, risk is not a singular concept but can be divided into objective risk and subjective risk. It is here, at this intersection between objectivity and subjectivity, that can be found the development of some dystopian attractions (Jenkins, 2019; Piekarz *et al.*, 2015). Dystopian tourist attractions can be defined as: an attraction that provokes a disturbing emotional response to the tourism experience, challenging the individual's morality and moral compass and their cultural social perception of reality, by considering uncomfortable and disturbing reposes to the visitor's experience of the attraction. This definition can be seen as an embellishment of number of authors, but in particular Podoshen *et al.* (2015) and Pimentel-Biscaia and Marques (2022). Objective risk is the statistical likelihood of a consumer facing harm from an activity or action (Piekarz *et al.*, 2015). For example, those of flying compared to driving a car, and an adumbration that driving is more dangerous than flying. Whereas subjective risk is the perceived likelihood of harm that might happen if an action of activity is undertaken (Piekarz *et al.*, 2015). This is obviously a consequence quite different from the actual harm or negative outcome that is most likely to occur.

Adventure tourism can be considered an exemplar of this need for experiencing risk which, as a leisure activity, has developed exponentially over the past 50 years or so (Baral *et al.*, 2004; Jenkins, 2019). It is now a key component in many tourist destination offerings and even in cruise ship packages. The many types of adventure experience provide exactly what can be found in dystopian tourist experiences – that is, of an adrenaline rush. This is reflective of primal instincts of how to react to potential danger within the subject risk found in a particular activity (Jenkins, 2019). Consequently, confronting fears and experiencing fear in controlled environments seems to fulfil the missing element of risk, now distilled out of the Western postmodern consumer society. Adventure then can be seen, vicariously, as another form of risk experience and varies both in objective and subjective risks. Thus, risk experience is very much related to personality types and how the subjective risk is perceived (Reisinger & Mavondo, 2005).

Dystopian attractions reflect a form of adventure which are not necessarily physical but more of a psychological risk and related to the perceived primal fears of humans. The need to be frightened is primordial and has evolved with us as Homo Sapiens. It may well be genetically written into our DNA, such as fear of snakes, spiders, heights, water and so on; although all hazards have the potential to create acute injury, if dealt with in an inappropriate way. It is here that much of the futuristic and dystopian tourist attractions are focused upon imagined fears, even though they may relate to actual or imagined physical harm (Wright, 2018). However, experiencing physical harm is not what future tourist will experience: it is the imaginary harm and the tourist's empathy with the received harmful experiences of others. It is others who have had this fear, but the tourist seems able to place themselves into the shoes of those who had experienced harm and the objective risk of this situation. To that end, immersive experiences are a prime motivation in many tourism products (Beck *et al.*, 2019; Bec *et al.*, 2019).

That said, most leisure establishments are aware of the need to ensure safety and reduce the likelihood of injury to their clients. For instance, Disney has prioritised ensuring customer safety and its variety of attractions (Disney World, 2022; WDW, 2022). These include adrenaline rides and adventure sites that have shown that the objective risk of harm is low, even though the tourist is expecting to face fear and thrills. This might appear incongruous when given the previous discussion on associations between risk and fear. However, the heightened awareness of risk and the need for safety seems to have emerged during the late 1980s and 1990s, when there was a perceived rise in the number customers being injured at leisure and tourist sites. This was first initiated in the US and then became more prevalent in Europe (Jenkins, 2019; Piekarz *et al.*, 2015). It seems evident that if companies have customer injuries and deaths then not only does the reputation of the company suffer but many become financially unviable and must close. As noted earlier, many of the dystopian attractions have little objective risk of harm but are there to evoke fearful experiences. Therefore, it is assumed that the consumer realises that the actual objective risk is extremely small (Karl *et al.*, 2020) and that psychological fear is what is expected at these attractions. Therefore, a disassociation between fear and objective risk at these attractions is evident. There is also evidence to show customers understand enjoyment can be had because the likelihood of harm is small, so the fear experience is not the same real exposure to a life threating or harmful circumstance (Bristow, 2020; Where the Road Forks, 2023).

The safety management of these attractions follow codes of practice like all types of public attractions. Therefore, risk assessments and common hazards are identified such as routes around the attraction are free from hazards. Consideration is also given to surfaces and walls, including fire hazards and adhering to a country's health and safety legislation. Another part of the risk assessment should be given to the psychological risks that customers might have, although this is a blurred area as fear related to psychological pain is itself part of the package. Moreover, the focus should be on the longevity of effects of the experience. Attractions usually have age limits, reflecting younger customers' notions of fear (Kerr *et al.*, 2023). For example, it is recommended that children under the age of 14 should not visit Auschwitz-Birkenau (Auschwitz Tours, 2022).

That said, there is evidence to suggest that objective risk does occur and there have been deaths attributed to these attractions ranging from accidental deaths, PTSD, and heart attacks all attributed to the notion of experiencing fear attractions in safe spaces (BBC [British Broadcasting Corporation], 2017a, 2017b; NBC Universal, 2014). Collectively, risks in tourism are a common theme in the literature. For adventure tourists, rock climbing, white-water paddling and surfing are illustrations of physically demanding activities that require levels of skill to reduce the risk (Jenkins, 2019). Yet, other risks may be of a psychological nature when tourists seek opportunities for macabre or dangerous experiences in war zones, pandemics or extreme poverty and crime (Pelton, 2001). Fuelled by popular media, including Pelton's (2001) work, there is a strange attraction for thrilling actions (Anderson *et al.*, 2020; Baral *et al.*, 2004; Clasen, 2017; Currie, 1997; Kendrick, 1991). Indeed, Pelton (2001) created a global industry of visiting dangerous places where war, corruption and other threats were expected, whereby his tours are not for the inexperienced or bashful. Ghoulish titillation is a phrase offered by Wilson (2004: 169) and it is the attraction to risky endeavours that is especially sought (Hajibaba *et al.*, 2015). Thus, management has the challenging balance act in the future to push risk to the limits while at the same time minimise it (Piekarz *et al.*, 2015).

Benign Masochism

The question remains, what is the attraction to risk? Rozin *et al.* (2013) introduced a fascination with pain through examples of food and diet. In these cases, spicy food, despite the potential pain and discomfort, was found to be an attractive choice for individuals. However, the draw toward pleasure and pain is nothing new. Building upon this theme, Klein (2014) argued that the masochism seeking experience can offer some pleasure beyond tasting spicy food and included deep tissue massages, getting tattoos, and running endurance races. Klein (2014: 54–55) even suggests 'by separating out sensations (even pain) from qualities of painfulness and pleasantness, however, we find that there is nothing in the structure of either of those qualities that excludes the other'.

Meanwhile, Helm (2002) offers a theoretical perspective that linked the two concepts (of pleasure and pain) noting the natural attraction to elements that pleasure us, while for many there is repulsion away from un-pleasurable events. Within tourism research, DeVisser-Amundson *et al.* (2016) suggest there is a category of tourist that seeks to experience activities outside their normal comfort zone. Indeed, a comfort zone is often highlighted in dark tourism attractions where an audience is motivated toward the site for aspects of fun (Ashworth & Isaac, 2015; Hoffner & Levine, 2005). Additional research linking pain with tourism offers an introduction to *Benign Masochism* for pleasurable tourism (Nørfelt *et al.*, 2022). These authors report how stimulation felt during a tourist exchange can add to the experience and, consequently, adds to the literature on pain and pleasure. Notwithstanding, if management can ensure a safe experience, fright attractions can yield a satisfactory opportunity in our urban centre and contribute to its future revitalisation (Bristow & Jenkins, 2020).

However, challenges exist to overcome enough of the risks for tourists to visit areas believed to be too unsafe. Yet risk varies and as we have seen, some risks are physical while others are psychological, and each are perceived differently by the tourist. For these reasons, we now turn to explore how a region's cultural, geopolitical and religious influences drive a desire for fright attractions, something we expect to continue in the future.

Fright Attractions: A Case Study Approach

In the following case studies, an examination of a region's cultural, geopolitical and/or religious guidance are shown to sway the citizens to seek and participate in fright attractions; a gentler, yet still a horrific experience for fun and entertainment. It is for these reasons the broad history of Halloween continues to contribute to celebrations around the globe (Linton, 1951). The case studies include Japan, Mexico and Romania as examples yielding a different impact on fright attractions.

Japan

When examining prominent themes of horror and tourism in Japan, those relating to Feudal Japan such as warlords, warfare and suicide are significant. The other prominent theme in Japan's horror history relates to nuclear attacks and radiation. The most famous example of Japan's horror attractions and media would be Godzilla, who has been prominent in the monster movie genre for 70 years or so and has appeared in films, shows, books, comics, video games and other popular cultural depictions. While Godzilla itself may be fictional, the concept of Godzilla was heavily influenced by Japan's dark past (Balmain, 2008).

Indeed, Godzilla as a reptilian monster is awakened/empowered by nuclear radiation and was conceptualised in response to the 1945 nuclear bombings of Hiroshima and Nagasaki by the USA. There is widespread agreement that Godzilla – the enormous, destructive, prehistoric monster – is a metaphor for nuclear weapons (Low, 1993). Nuclear fear and perceptions, coupled with the history of Japanese involvement in radiological technologies, have been used as a basis for analysing these films in the context of Japanese history, as well as the film's impact on public perceptions of radiation (Crowder *et al.*, 2016).

Japanese haunted attractions are not influenced by only warfare, but also by its historic system of feudal governance and living. For example, one of Japan's more recent haunted attractions has been located at the *Fuji-Q Highland* amusement park in Yamanashi Prefecture within the foothills of Mount Fuji. It has been designed based on a backstory involving the Japanese feudal lord Takeda Shingen (Varley, 2000). The narrative of one of the amusement park rides tells of an abandoned mine dug out by greedy robbers who attempted to pilfer great wealth and treasures left behind by Takeda Shingen. Also known as the 'Tiger of Kai', Shingen was a powerful *daimyo* (a Japanese magnate or feudal lord) with exceptional military prestige in the late Sengoku period of the 16th century. Unexplained, gruesome deaths suddenly befell the robbers, which led to the mine being sealed up to protect the locals (Ruide, 2019).

There is also notable cultural tolerance for suicide in Japan, and in certain Japanese contexts suicide has been classified as a morally correct action. The country's more tolerant attitude towards suicide may stem from the historical significance of suicide in the Japanese military. The most significant example of this stems from feudal Japan where honourable suicide was committed among Samurai as a justified response towards inevitable defeat in battle and was also performed to restore honour to a warriors' family. Daiba Haunted School is an attraction in Odaiba designed to look like an abandoned and blighted school accompanying a storyline that involves making one's way inside with a torch to save the souls of teachers and students who committed suicide many years ago (*Time Out*, 2022). While this storyline's suicides are, of course, of a different nature than the feudal Japan example, there still may be some cultural influence towards such themes.

Mexico

Mexico's cultural approach to horror is influenced by the country's unique perspective on the topic of death, and this influences their dark tourism attractions (Speakman, 2019). Certainly, nothing can demonstrate this as well as Mexico's *Dia de Los Muertos* (Day of the Dead), an annual holiday traditionally celebrated on the 1st and 2nd November which commemorates the return to earth of one's deceased loved ones. The roots of this dark culture stem from the Aztec people over 1000 years ago in what has now become central Mexico (Roman, 2020). During that period, Aztecs used skulls to commemorate the dead and symbolic skulls remain an integral part of this tradition. Along with skulls, the other horror related images, symbols and the supernatural are important in Mexican culture, such as an extensive belief in ghosts. This stems originally from millennium ago when the Aztecs had belief in the soul going on to one of three places: *Tlalocan*, a paradise for those who drowned; *Mictlan*, for the souls of people who died from other causes (Kondori, 2005); and the *Sun*, for warriors and women who the Aztecs believed became hummingbirds. The Aztecs also believed that the *Cihuateto*, spirits of women who died in childbirth (Schwartz, 2018), would return on specified days hoping to take children they had not been able to have themselves.

Moreover, Mexican, and other Latin American influences of indigenous religion, Catholicism and European witchcraft, termed *Brujeria* as a form of sorcery (Herrera-Sobek, 2012; Lewis, 2003), have shaped Mexican culture in many ways, and certainly has made an impact on the country's fright tourism. For example, the city of Catemaco in the state of Veracruz, is an internationally recognised hub for witchcraft and magic. In March each year, the city has its annual witchcraft festival (Festival of Magical Rites, Ceremonies and Handcrafts) and attracts approximately 5000 visitors from around the world (Vina, 2023). From the 1970s, tourism has increased because of the fame of Gonzalo Aguirre, a famous Head Sorcerer (or *Brujo Mayor*) who lived in Catemaco and attracted politicians, entertainers and others who had him perform rituals (McKinley, 2008). Sorcery continues to be an important part of the tourism there, with many practitioners having calling cards and websites.

Romania

Romania's connections to horror most notably stem from the gothic horror novel, *Dracula*, by Bram Stoker and published in 1897. While Stoker was himself Irish, some aspects of the Dracula character were inspired by the infamous Wallachian *Prince Vlad the Impaler* (also known as Vlad III) who ruled Wallachia, a historical and geographical region of present-day Romania, from 1456 to 1462 (Kaplan, 2012). Dracula has become a household name, appearing frequently in shows, movies, media, and other mediums in popular culture. Stoker's work also spawned so-called Dracula Tourism in Romania, which involves travelling to Dracula related sites in the country, as well as sites related to Dracula's real (that is, the historical Vlad III) or fictional travels (Light, 2007). Such sites include the *Dracula Museum* in Bucharest, *Castle Bran* in Transylvania (invariably marketed as *'Dracula's Castle'*), Sighişoara (a UNESCO Heritage site and one of the few medieval fortified towns in Europe that is still inhabited) and the village of Piatra Fantanele (which is home to *Hotel Dracula*, inaugurated in 1983 in the style of a medieval castle). However, making Dracula Tourism more complicated is the fact that, despite the economic advantages, government leaders view tourism like this as promoting false (or at least fictionalised) images of Romania, rather than real (if not authentic) Romanian culture and history (Bristow & Newman, 2005; Light, 2007, 2016, 2017a), and consequently restricted any Dracula theme parks from 2007 to 2026 being initiated.

Conclusion

This chapter has briefly outlined three global examples that are anticipated to contribute to the future demand of fright tourism. This is based on the understanding of fright tourists, their demand for safe and scary opportunities, while mitigating inherent risks found when travelling. In these cases, the basis of this future demand is founded upon the cultural, geopolitical and/or religious backgrounds of citizens living in Japan, Mexico and Romania. Certainly, other cultural realms exist in the growing field of fright tourism. However, our exploratory examination cannot and does not examine the variety of cultural influences on risk (Karl *et al.*, 2020); yet, in the infancy of fright tourism scholarship, we commence the scholarly debate for further scrutiny, research and interrogation.

We have provided a preliminary examination into the future of fright attractions and our efforts are not meant to be exhaustive. Nevertheless, this chapter does document a framework in which to locate fright tourism and reconnoitre future research avenues. Folklore in Japan, for instance, yields an understanding of the importance of legends in a communal dialogue. Moreover, outside global influences have impacted Japan where the end of the World War II forced citizens to accept a major intrusion into their lives; one that subsequently prompted the growth of Godzilla. This may have also prompted the inclusive nature of an island nation dictating a strict protocol in daily living. Japanese would then obviously seek chances to 'let loose', countering the norms of societal behaviour. Then there are the religious overtones of *Día de Muertos* or *Día de los Muertos* (Day of the Dead) originating in Mexico at the beginning of November. While a celebration of loved one's death, exotic costumes with skulls is all too like many fright attractions and, consequently, has become Westernised as a festival.

Finally, as an exemplar of fright attractions, Romania's history is fraught with internal and external conflicts. Gothic mysteries of the late 19th century were exploited by Irish author Bram Stoker who penned Dracula. Through a rich narrative using letters, diary entries and other communications, Stoker's fictional account had enough truth, albeit little, to make the story plausible. Later adaptions in film promoted the story of vampires and other blood sucking creations to draw a global audience. Today, tourists visit the region for both the myth and the reality (Bristow & Newman, 2005).

With the breadth and depth of these cultural identities, we suspect a long-standing desire of future fright attractions. These will be sanitised for broad appeal, yet still gruesome enough to appeal to those seeking a dark experience. The world will continue to have enough dark events including, at the time of writing, the COVID-19 global pandemic and Russia's war in Ukraine, as well as other natural and human induced disasters that citizens will seek a diversion. To that end, it is this diversion that will mitigate risk so fright tourism and the *dark fun factories* around the globe will meet that demand.

22 Future Directions in Death Studies and Dark Tourism

Michael Brennan

Introduction

Since the emergence of academic interest in dark tourism in the mid-1990s (Foley & Lennon, 1996a; Lennon & Foley, 2000), scholars in the field have been engaged in various debates. These include discussions about the personal motivations driving interest in dark tourism (Iliev, 2021; Yuill, 2003), the provenance of dark tourism both in concept and practice (Seaton, 1996; Stone, 2005, 2013a), degrees and the 'conceptual shading' of dark tourism (Miles, 2002; Stone, 2006), and whether there are 'dark' elements to be found in all aspects of tourism more generally (Tunbridge & Ashworth, 2017). Additionally, there has been debates about supply-side and business issues of promoting tourism that can be seen as 'dark' (Seaton & Lennon, 2004). These debates extend to 'thanatopsis' and 'mortality salience' (Seaton, 1996), especially the opportunity that dark tourism may provide for grieving personal losses and for reflecting upon one's own mortality. Work at the intersection of thanatology and dark tourism has indicated that sites of dark tourism may provide a mediating link between the living and the dead (Stone, 2012a, 2012b; Walter, 2009), a vehicle for confronting death in modern society (Stone & Sharply, 2008) and an opportunity for grieving losses (un)related to the deaths encountered (Darlington, 2014).

Recent commentary on public grieving following the death of the British monarch HM Queen Elizabeth II, has illustrated how *deathways* surrounding public mourning – that is, laying flowers at major tourist landmarks, signing public books of condolence, queuing for hours to file past the monarch while lying in state or public participation in funeral events – can themselves be understood as containing elements of tourism that are 'dark'. In short, stirring up personal losses triggered by the death of a 'distant' Other. Curiously, tourist grievers waiting in line to view HM Queen Elizabeth's coffin in Westminster Hall during September

2022 had to file past the Covid-19 memorial wall on the bank of the river Thames, reminding us that there has yet to be a national commemorative public event or permanent memorial to the 200,000 deaths in the UK resulting from the coronavirus pandemic (Stone, 2020a). Consequently, grief is often vicarious, with various losses routinely inserted one within the other.

Death and loss of various kinds, whether individual or collective, following personal tragedy or public disaster, often involves looking back (in reminiscence) as well as looking ahead to life without the deceased and those we have lost. Death, and the bereavement it entails, is often a catastrophic and traumatic event involving major psycho-social transition. Like other turning points and historical moments involving transformation and change, death and loss prompt 'futures thinking' involving contemplation on what possibilities may lie ahead for us. The turn of the century, end of the Second World War in Europe, and the information technology revolution of the 1970s, for instance, each prompted waves of speculation and 'futurology'. So too have the recent coronavirus global pandemic, Britain's withdrawal from the European Union and climate emergency that threatens us with planetary extinction. Thus, the uncertainty that confronts us in the third decade of the 21st century provides further opportunities for reflection and looking forward. Transformations in death mentalities (Jacobsen, 2016; Stone, 2018, 2020b), recent shifts in the scholarly study of death (Walter, 2020) and the challenges presented by the pursuit of social and climate justice provide further opportunities to consider the intersections and synergies between dark tourism and thanatology. Therefore, the purpose of my chapter is to critically explore these potential synergies. Firstly, however, I begin by situating my discussion within a discourse of 'futurology' and the inherent risks involved.

Sociology, Thanatology and Futurology

My own discipline of sociology has an ambivalent relationship with the future. The classical European tradition was profoundly future facing. Marx's historical materialism and Comte's 'law of three stages' serve as cases in point; each envisioning an optimistic, evolutionary, and progressive view of the future. In Marx's case, this vision was marked by the twin demise of capitalism and inevitable victory of the industrial proletariat on the road to scientific socialism. For Comte, it was by the constructive alignment between forms of knowledge and the social organisation of society, culminating in the positivist-industrial stage. The ambitious, and at times grandiloquent, claims of European sociologists from the classical era has led to accusations of hubris and, worse still – more recently – to claims of Eurocentrism. The tendency to generate universal 'laws' of social development from the position of the global North, in ways that neglect local differences in regions of the global South, has led to accusations of the colonisation of knowledge analogous to the colonisation of people and land (Meghji, 2021; Woodman & Threadgold, 2021).

Like early sociology, the 'futures field' is a 'quintessentially modern project' that, more specifically, uses social forecasting to offer rational planning (Westwood, 2000). At the same time, while early European sociology was future oriented, current sociology is often accused of being backward looking in its refusal to give-up on its founding European thinkers, a reflection of social scientific knowledge as cumulative rather than marked by a series of paradigmatic revolutions (Kuhn, 2012 [1962]). Another accusation levelled against sociology is that it is 'present-centred' (Elias, 1997), neglecting the role of the past in shaping the present and future. Much of contemporary sociology has retreated from attempts at anticipating the future. In part, this is because apparent failures of Marxist analysis in forecasting the demise of capitalism signals an inability to 'get the future right' (Urry, 2016: 5); but also, perhaps because of the pejorative associations between social planning and engineering designs on society (Turner, 1998). With notable exceptions (for example, Bell, 1973; and Toffler, 1970), sociology's hiatus from the futures field has led to a vacuum that has been filled by other organisations (for instance, Rand Corporation – a non-partisan American global policy think-tank and research institute), or in which 'futures thinking' has been pushed to the margins as an academic sub-specialism (but see, Yeoman & McMahon-Beattie, 2020).

Such marginalisation has led to calls from some quarters for the mainstreaming of 'futures thinking' within sociology (Urry, 2016). Not least because futurology is profoundly social: both in anticipating future consequences of social action, as well as directing our attention to the implications of present social behaviour. Fundamental changes in lifestyle needed to slow the effects of climate change are illustrative of this. In truth, 'futures thinking' is an implicit feature of all modern societies, be it in terms of household budgeting, or wider projections and modelling used by governments or businesses and other organisations. Modelling potential futures and outcomes – probable, plausible and preferable – is something most of us in the UK became acutely aware of from government briefings during the coronavirus pandemic (2020/21), with projections and scenarios involving vaccinations, hospital beds and deaths that might ensue from the pandemic.

This kind of 'futures literacy' and planning, helping organisations to anticipate and manage potential risks, threats and opportunities will be recognisable to anyone who has ever undertaken a SWOT analysis aimed at identifying potential strengths, weaknesses, opportunities and threats. The calculus of 'futures thinking' extends too beyond, but also in ways connected with 'wicked' postmodern challenges (Miller, 2011), including tourism analyses projecting future trends, threats and untapped potential of new markets and destinations. The misfortune of disasters that some communities suffer may also provide new opportunities for disaster tourism, including Covid-19 tourism-memorialisation as an outlet for touristic adventure or an opportunity for therapeutic healing (Cai *et al.*, 2022; Jorden, 2021; Stone, 2020a).

Despite a profound need for 'futures thinking', there are notable absences of 'futures literacy' in large swathes of human life. For instance, plans for social care, an ageing population and end-of-life are all areas currently neglected in government policy and individual preparations in the UK. Recent research from the Marie Curie foundation and Cardiff University has indicated that over half of people surveyed agreed that, as a society, we still do not talk about death enough (Marie Curie, 2021). Nearly 90% of respondents said they had not heard of the term 'advance directive' describing the written documentation for expressing a person's healthcare wishes should they be unable to communicate them. Meanwhile, more than half of the people surveyed in the last years of their life said they did not know where to find information about making advance care plans. These are prominent issues, both for the individual and for wider society. Government policy is crucial here not just in planning necessary infrastructure and funding for an ageing population with healthcare needs and co-morbidities, but also in helping to set the agenda, shape conversation and influence individual decision making and future planning.

Thanatology Today

Thanatology, the specialist academic study of death, dying and bereavement is an amorphous and multidisciplinary field. The term itself, derived from Greek mythology (where Thanatos was the personification of death), has been unevenly applied. It has been embraced more enthusiastically in the US, where the academic study of death was first formalised in university courses and professional accreditation beginning in the 1970s. This is far less so in the UK, where the nomenclature 'death studies' has been used to describe the academic study of death, dying and bereavement. In the US, the subject field has been dominated by psychologists, while in the UK by sociologists and social scientists. These different paths of development have also progressed on different timescales. In the US, most of thanatology's growth occurred in the 1970s, alongside a perceptible shift in death mentalities, in which social movements advocating a 'good death' first emerged (Lofland, 1978; see also Smith, 2019; Troyer, 2019), and books on death and mortality achieved both critical mass and folkloric status within American public consciousness (for example, Ernest Becker, [1973], who was awarded the Pulitzer Prize for general non-fiction; and

Elisabeth Kübler-Ross, [1970], who was named as one the '100 Most Important Thinkers' of the 20th century). In the UK, the specialist academic study of death emerged later in the 1990s, and at the same time (although in ways unrelated), as the academic study of dark tourism (Foley & Lennon, 1996a; Seaton, 1996).

Despite attempts to restore sociology to the centre of thanatology in the USA (Cox & Thompson, 2021; Thompson *et al.*, 2016) from where it has been displaced by psychology, other differences with death studies as practised in the UK persist. Chief among these differences is the 'humanistic' versus 'critical' strain within USA thanatology and UK death studies. In the USA, thanatology has been taught as death education, with a view to better preparing people for facing death and, consequently, learning to appreciate life. However, in the UK, academics in death studies have often taken a more critical stance towards end-of-life care policy, funeral provision and bereavement services in ways characteristic of a sociological perspective (for example, Borgstrom & Walter, 2015; Walter, 2017a, 2017b). Sociological critics have warned against the insularity of a USA-led thanatology, namely of a 'thanatological ghetto' that speaks only to itself but not beyond its own sub-disciplinary community of academics and practitioners (Walter, 1993: 289; see also Jacobsen, 2022; Walter, 2008).[1]

Since I first entered the field of *death studies* at the end of 1990s, the network of academics, researchers and practitioners has grown tremendously. This growth has occurred in parallel to the burgeoning revival of interest in death and dying outside of the academy. In the networks of interest in mortality (online and in-person – at conferences and colloquia) there is now considerable crossover between academics, practitioners, activists and the morbidly curious; so much so that lines between these divides have become increasingly blurred. The Order of the Good Death (2023), for example, comprises activists and academics advocating not only for 'death positivity' and more open conversations about the end of life, but also argues against the disempowerment, environmental destruction and financial exploitation wrought by the modern funeral industry. Such advocacy is fused with a concern for social justice and the need to redress patterned inequities in access to end-of-life care and inequalities in how, when, and where particular social groups die.

Radical currents within the field of thanatology are helping to re-shape its focus and constitution. Walter's (1993) call for the integration of death studies within the core concerns of more general sociology is increasingly being actioned in recent activity in the field. A focus on inequality, social divisions, power, politics and the State, for example, has been an explicit concern of research activity, networks and conferences in recent years, including the themed annual conference hosted by the Centre for Death and Society (CDAS) at the University of

Bath, UK. This has included a focus on death technologies of power and control, death-focused activism, economics of death and poverty and deaths that result from state-sanctioned violence and killing, or because of negligence and neglect by state providers of care. These developments extend to a renewed focus on the need to decolonise bereavement studies in ways that move beyond straightforward issues of equality, diversity and inclusion (Hamilton *et al.*, 2022).

These currents can also be seen in discussions around social death, necro-politics, and a renewed focus on the nexus between race and death. The notion of 'social death' implies that some individuals and social groups are treated less fairly than others: as if they are already dead (even before biological death) in ways likely to hasten possibility of their actual death. Stripping individuals and groups of the essential characteristics of what it means to be human, effectively assigning them 'non-person' status, and reducing them to 'bare life' (Agamben, 1998), clears a pathway to their physical extermination. The 'natal alienation' (Patterson, 1982) of slavery, by which Black people were denied and separated from their ancestral ties, and the attempted erasure of the (collective) memory of an ethnic/racial group as a defining characteristic of genocide (Card, 2010), are both manifestations of social death.

Necro-politics extends this by making death a vehicle by which power – as biopolitics (Foucault, 1981, 2007) – is exercised over bodies and populations as the ultimate expression of sovereignty (Mbembe, 2003). A focus on the brutalisation of populations, especially in the global South, and threat of violence and death as part of the contemporary global polity helps relocate the study of death (Alphin & Debrix, 2020; Truscello, 2020). This is particularly so within the orbit of racial political hegemony whereby whole populations are Othered and oppressed. Death is not the 'great leveller' once assumed in thanatology. Moreover, the 'American way' of death, and its attendant denial, is unrepresentative of all American social groups' experiences, which has been a major focus of the Collective for Radical Death Studies (2023). Importantly, increased impetus by emerging global social movements like 'Black Lives Matter' (following the 2020 murder of George Floyd in Minneapolis, USA), research and scholarship in thanatology highlighting the significance but subsequent silencing of Black academic voices on the specificity and proximity to death of Black people's experiences has gained significant traction in recent years (Amanik & Fletcher, 2020; Puri, 2021).

Therefore, these developments raise significant questions, not simply for thanatology (and the ways in which it must change to help de-centre Whiteness as its default position), but also for studies of dark tourism and the implications for supply-side organisation and marketing of dark tourist destinations, not least sites of 'difficult heritage'.

Thanatological and Dark Tourism Futures

Decolonising society

A long-standing assumption underlying much commercial tourism, especially overseas travel by tourists from the global North to destinations in the global South, is that it is rooted in a colonial mindset that essentialises and Orientalises people and places as exotic and Other (Causevic, 2019; Chetty, 2011; Putcha, 2020). This is part of the *tourist gaze*, which is constructed through difference and in relation to its opposite (Urry, 1990). In this instance, such contrast is constructed not just between tourist and non-tourist, or between leisure and opposition to regulated paid work, but between East and West and is sustained, mediated, and reproduced in the cultural imaginary through discursive representation (Said, 1978).

The destructive and exploitative nature of mass tourism as a legacy of colonialism has been well documented and has been taken up in recent years in debates about the intersectional possibilities heralded by dark tourism analysis, heritage management, and postcolonial studies (Carrigan, 2015).[2] In the UK, memorial and heritage tourism that confronts Britain's imperial past has developed in recent years, including in places like Liverpool's slavery museum in the city's Albert Docks, although hidden away on the third floor of the euphemistically named 'Maritime Museum'. Learning through an immersive – and deeply disturbing – exhibition about the Middle Passage experiences of slaves as they were transported in brutalising conditions from Africa to the Americas is a 'dark tourist' experience that many day-trippers to Liverpool will have encountered, incidentally as they toured the Albert Docks (see Rice, 2003, 2009; Wood, 2000).[3] These are not necessarily seasoned dark tourists seeking out grisly and macabre experiences, but often inadvertent and accidental dark tourists whose travel takes them into unexpected territory. Nevertheless, it provides a potential didactic opportunity for education, to learn about the history of racism and, in this instance, about the experience of Black Scousers, in ways that may be transformative and have long-lasting impact upon visitors. Similar opportunities for dark tourism embedded within wider non-dark touristic experiences of museums can also be found in places such as Bristol's *M-Shed Museum*. Here, in another English maritime city with links to the transatlantic slave trade, lies the statue of slave trader, Edward Colston, a name with long associations to the city, including its hospitals and schools. Since it was toppled by protesters in the wake of Black Lives Matter demonstrations, Colston's graffitied statue has provided a focal point in a carefully curated exhibition that invites dialogue about empire, race and the place of statues and buildings that celebrate the lives of people with associations to the slave trade (Bristol Museums, 2023; Morris, 2021).

Consequently, we see the interplay between tourism, museum/exhibition visits, and elements which are 'dark'. The dark tourist, like the public mourner (Walter, 1999: 35), may not necessarily be deliberately seeking out a 'dark' experience but may inadvertently find themselves caught up in a prevailing exhibition or event as a visitor or more general tourist. Such instances nevertheless provide opportunities for education and self-exploration, whether in terms of issues like race, racism and decolonisation, death education or mortality salience: all in ways that may contribute to wider public conversation and debate. New directions in tourism, which also contains elements that are 'dark', and which attempt to resist the 'colonising' tendencies of mass commercial tourism, are also beginning to emerge. This 'solidarity' (or 'justice') tourism positions itself in opposition to tourism that is socially and environmentally destructive, instead providing organised cultural exchanges between tourists and residents that serve as an educational, political or social activist function. For example, cultural exchange trips to post-Apartheid South Africa or to Israeli occupied parts of the West Bank, may inevitably involve elements that are 'dark'. Indeed, such as a visit to the Apartheid Museum in Johannesburg or opportunities to learn directly from Palestinians about the experience of daily life under military occupation may invoke a sense of 'darkness'. However, such tourism is often explicitly couched in anti- or decolonial terms (Aikau & Gonzalez, 2019; Kelly, 2016; Larson, 2022) in ways intended to invite critical conversations about environmental costs of tourism, food insecurity, or climate change (such as in places like Hawaii).

When disaster tourism and commemoration is examined, it is not difficult to discern that the focus of Western/dominant media reporting of tragedies has prioritised Western lives, while neglecting deaths occurring in the global South. This extends to analysis of non-Western lives, and the ways in which they are framed in media reporting, as less deserving of grief than White/Western lives (Butler, 2009). In this context, solidarity tourism can be seen as an attempt to right this wrong; simultaneously offering opportunities for education and activism to those who visit, and support to the marginalised and oppressed social groups who are its focus. Moreover, studies of dark tourism, as Walter (2008) notes, have been the preserve of UK-based academics, with most attention focused on sites within Europe, USA and Australia (Light, 2017b). Much less attention has been given to sites in the developing world (Friedrich & Johnson, 2013; Levey, 2014), although that is beginning to change (see Carrigan, 2015). The very orientation of Western ways of thinking and seeing may also implicitly underpin much of dark tourist academic interest. In this way, as Light (2017b) notes, not only are dark tourist concepts grounded in 'Western' ways of thinking about the living and the dead but have also in some instances been used uncritically in non-Western contexts in ways that fail to recognise or acknowledge that, in other parts of the world, relationships between societies and their dead may take very different forms (see also Carrigan, 2015; Cohen, 2018). The ongoing challenge for future dark tourism scholarship and research is the imperative to adopt approaches to death and bereavement that are both sensitive to, and appreciative of, non-Western, indigenous concepts and knowledge.

Decarbonising society

Modern societies, in which tourism has developed as a commercially driven industry and pursuit, are high carbon systems that contribute to global warming, climate change and the potentially calamitous consequences for life on earth as we know it. The geological era dominated by the deleterious human impact upon the earth's geology and ecosystems has become known as the 'anthropocene' (a term coined in 2000 to describe this new geological era). As a product of modernity, my own discipline of sociology has been late to the issue of climate change, until recently providing a critique of the social and economic organisation of society, while neglecting damaging effects of high carbon systems upon which modern societies have depended. That, however, has begun to change, with attention in sociology shifting to the social implications and effects of climate change, not least its uneven impact upon populations of the global South. It is here in particular, in places like Bangladesh, where countries and emerging economies which have contributed *least* to climate change will be affected *most* by the impact of drought, flooding, and rising sea levels.

Climate change, and the devastating impact it threatens to unleash on society (including greater political instability, increasing likelihood of famine, war and mass migration as populations flee affected areas) has for decades been part of 'futures thinking' and planning. Climate scientists and organisations such as the Intergovernmental Panel on Climate Change (IPCC) have been at the forefront of such planning. Yet, as Urry (2010, 2011) points out, climate change is not purely a scientific problem demanding a 'science first' approach, but is also a sociological problem, as human actions and behaviour have been complicit in the damaging effects upon the environment produced in highly carbonised modern societies. Therefore, any attempt to reverse or slow the impact of climate change will involve a necessary shift in human behaviour. In other words, in better understanding not only how, societies are organised socially but also, crucially, how they can be reorganised in ways that are carbon neutral.

One potential future outcome of efforts needed to reduce carbon emissions and slow climate change involves a potentially less mobile future, in ways that will impact overseas travel and tourism by limiting carbon-based travel, especially by jet aircraft. The coronavirus pandemic has illustrated how, when faced with the existential threat posed by contagion, governments, but also individuals themselves, imposed curbs on international travel (Garaus & Hudáková, 2022; Neuburger & Egger, 2021). Arresting climate change, as Urry (2010) has argued, requires universal system change and not simply that of individual behaviour; for systems presuppose ingrained patterns of social life in which individual action is embedded. Here, then, Urry's call for the involvement of sociologists and social scientists in debates around climate change as part of 'futures thinking' can be extended to scholars and industry insiders in tourism (including those whose principal focus is dark tourism) in re-envisioning a future that is less harmful to the planet. This may include examining the possibilities for virtual dark tourism, as discussed elsewhere in this book.

Existential consequences for humanity of climate change have been harnessed by environmental campaign groups like Extinction Rebellion, whose discourse and symbolism induces mortality salience, death anxiety, and grief as aspects of Western death mentalities (Walter, 2022). This, as Walter argues, effectively redirects attention away from individual deaths and towards species extinction. In so doing, it helps contribute to the further de-sequestration of death in (post-)modern Western societies. Simultaneously, there is potential future dark tourism interest – as climate change tourism – in the devastating effects of climate change. As a variation in dark tourism, this interest may now extend beyond interest in human-to-human suffering to include human-to-nature degradation caused by wildfires and floods resulting from climate change (Mahoney, 2020). It may also include touristic interest in sites that have borne witness to the widespread loss of human life resulting from climate change in ways that are clearly 'dark' (and may invoke planetary or species-wide mortality salience). Indeed, there is already evidence to indicate a growing market in climate change tourism. For instance, in the opening of Arctic and Antarctic regions to tourism (Leane, 2022; Mahoney, 2020), in organised visits to melting glaciers and icebergs off the coast of Newfoundland and Labrador (Lam & Tegelberg, 2020) and to low-lying Pacific islands likely to disappear in the future due to rising sea levels (Farbotko, 2010). Therefore, as a sub-set of wider commercial tourism, much dark tourism is clearly a contributor to climate change, which is also generating dark tourism interest in environmental and human suffering that are among its effects. A most pressing concern therefore as part of 'futures thinking' needs to be the search for more *sustainable* forms of dark tourism.

Conclusion: Linking Death Studies and Dark Tourism

Presently, we live in a resource rich era in which information abounds. This abundance of information extends to the wealth of resources providing guidance and support on death, dying and bereavement. This is freely available online, and access to which only a few decades earlier would have been unthinkable. Such resources include formally authorised resources provided online by organisations specialising in bereavement support and care, such as Cruse Bereavement Care, Marie Curie or Macmillan Cancer Support. Allied to this are web-based resources provided by university research centres specialising in death, dying and bereavement, such as CDAS as noted earlier, or degree programmes in thanatology, such as those offered at King's University College, Ontario in Canada. Some of these resources exist at the intersection of research and practice, illustrating the cross-over and blurring between these two domains.

Both mainstream and social media also provide an abundance of resources about issues surrounding death, dying, and bereavement. Television, and especially radio programmes in the UK, now routinely feature documentaries about death, dying and bereavement (for example, the BBC (British Broadcasting Corporation) Radio 4 series hosted by Joan Bakewell in 2020, '*We Need to Talk About Death*'). These often involve experts in thanatology and can be seen as providing an easily accessible informal resource for the public who are not necessarily searching for such information. To this extent, such resources can be considered as contributing to a wider climate of thinking about death and dying that is (un)unconsciously imbibed by the listening/viewing public audience in ways that may contribute to a change in death mentalities and *deathways* surrounding death, dying and bereavement.

Social media and the abundance of more 'niche' resources also mean that for people seeking out information on a particular topic (including resources on death, dying, and bereavement), there is now a limitless supply of relevant and useful information and support. The Death Studies podcast (www.thedeathstudiespodcast.com/) is but the latest resource that brings specialist viewpoints and perspectives of thanatologists to a broader, albeit 'narrowcast' public audience. As part of our global commons in the 21st century, these resources rely upon knowledge and information generated in modern society by academics and practitioners, and are part of what Giddens (1987, 1990, 1991, 1992) calls 'institutional reflexivity'. That is to say, the ways in which expert or professional knowledge (in the form of manuals, guides, self-help surveys or therapeutic works) do not simply provide a description of reality but help to constitute that very reality. This is especially when the knowledge they produce is not only imbibed but acted upon by the public (and other professionals) as recipients of it.

At the same time, and while resources on death and dying have expanded, we also now live in an age of 'experiential poverty' (Woodthorpe, 2018) in which many people's first encounter with a close personal bereavement has been delayed until their third or fourth decade by extended life expectancy. In this respect, if people today cannot experience 'reality' directly, including that of death and bereavement, they can at least do so indirectly, as 'pseudo-events' (Boorstin, 1964; also Cohen, 1988), through the mediated experiences of dark tourism provided in museums, exhibitions, and galleries. It is here, then, at the intersection of thanatology and dark tourism that opportunities to respond to such experiential poverty present themselves.

In one key respect, this can be understood as a design issue, and a service-design issue at that. It requires us to consider how we can bring experts and specialists together from different but complementary fields, alongside the users of services, to engineer solutions to problems or inadequacies in how things currently work. In design terms, this is 'citizen-centric' work that involves working backwards, consulting first with service users to ascertain their needs to arrive at a design solution that helps meet them. A particular case in point is provided by the ground-breaking work of the Design for Dying project led by designers from the Royal College of Art (RCA) and their involvement in helping to reimagine the spatial possibilities of the Royal Trinity Hospice in Clapham, South London (Razavi, 2016). Crucially, this service-led design resulted in a design outcome for the hospice that sought to foster an emphasis on life and living (rather than a focus of death and dying) in ways that also simultaneously attempted to counter social exclusion and fading as experiences common to hospice care for those at the end of life.

In the context of dark tourism, such service design requires enlisting the collaborative and interdisciplinary efforts of specialists in and across allied fields – of thanatology, dark tourism, museum and memory studies, bereavement care, etc. – in the service of enhancing user experiences of dark tourist spaces and sites. One such need of users/visitors to dark tourism spaces and sites may be for further information and support following a tourist experience that evokes an emotional response and/or triggers the necessity for working through grief and personal losses (un)related to the site of death and disaster/difficult heritage. This of course presupposes the need for much more 'demand-side' research that tells us more about the motivations and needs of visitors to dark tourist attractions – an imperative and absence identified in the academic literature on dark tourism (Sharpley & Stone, 2009).

Nevertheless, such design could include the greater use of technology that utilises QR codes and augmented reality to enhance and support the visitor experience by linking to resources provided by the caring professions, research centres and third sector organisations as part of our global commons. This kind of technology has already been deployed for more than a decade or so in traditional physical memorials and graveyards to enhance information and help provide an enduring memory of the deceased in ways that illustrate how 'the future is already here' (Gibson, cited in Urry, 2016: 17; also see Kneese, 2014). Unlocking potential synergies between thanatology and dark tourism also needs to be understood as part of a wider on-going project to engage public conversations about grief and loss. This includes engaging in work that helps normalise our reactions to grief, and the meanings attached to various kinds of losses (including non-death losses): especially in the context of a public setting such as a museum or exhibition that contains 'dark' elements. Part of this may involve re-imagining loss and grief in ways that link not only to greater 'mortality salience' but which help precipitate conversations about, as well as action on, important considerations around end-of-life planning and care. Such re-imagining may also involve rethinking how we conceive of and deliver emotional support and care that utilises a 'compassionate communities' approach in which we are all empowered to provide support to those in our community who may need it (Aoun *et al.*, 2018; Kellehear, 2005).

As Giddens has argued, modern institutions and the knowledge and information they generate, are central to the ways in which modern societies (and the individuals that comprise them) improve themselves. Tourism, as Urry (1990) has argued, is also a quintessential product of modernity, as are the knowledge-producing institutions that inform and analyse it. Considering this (and my preceding discussion), and to paraphrase Giddens (1987), to confront the future with any degree of confidence, we must be reflexively capable of modifying our institutions in the face of accelerated social change. This involves continuing to close the gap between death studies and dark tourism, including incorporating new developments within each, to address the issues with which self and society are confronted in the 21st century.

Notes

(1) These observations also stem, in part, from my own experience of teaching in the USA at a state university in the Midwest in the late 2000s and early 2010s, where I served as director of the Center for Death Education and Bioethics (at the University of Wisconsin-La Crosse). While digitisation of academic journals in recent years has helped facilitate the increased porousness of all subject areas and (sub-)disciplines (including thanatology), allowing academics from outside the field to write within it (e.g. Fletcher & McGowan, 2020), the institutional coherence of thanatology in the USA is maintained through organisations like ADEC (Association for Death Education and Counseling), who licence practitioners through accreditation programmes (Fellow in Thanatology) and thereby serve as gatekeepers of authorised knowledge to the field.

(2) These debates extend to the problematic nature of tourism in the global South, including slum and disaster tourism as corollaries of dark tourism, the extent to which the West's role in generating conflicts and disasters in the global South is publicly acknowledged, as well as to debates around 'dissonant heritage' (Tunbridge & Ashworth, 1996) in which public memory about past events may be both contested and traumatic.

(3) Each offer contrasting perspectives on the International Slavery Museum and its representation of slavery and the slave experience: one as a welcome public intervention against a backdrop of cultural amnesia and silence about Britain's role in the international slave trade (Rice, 2009); the other as both a troubling attempt to simulate memory of the Middle Passage in ways that may 'do more harm than good', and a problematic venture more generally, given the alleged lack of public consultation of black Liverpudlians in planning of the museum (Wood, 2000: 300).

Afterword: Back to the Dark Tourism Future

Philip R. Stone

The past is made of facts... I guess the future is just hope
Isaac Marion

In the end, the Grim Reaper will visit us all. Yet, as we live our lives certain of our own eventual demise, those who passed before us in accidental, violent or calamitous circumstances, often warn us of our mistakes and misfortunes. It is here that memorialisation of the significant dead is played out at the interface of global visitor economies. In turn, dark tourism displays our untimely dead and often tell tales of dissonance, contested heritage and political remembrance. Sites of agony and anguish that make the 'stuff' of dark tourism today will be like the sites of dark tourism tomorrow. We will continue to live in a dominion of the dead where the deceased offer authorship to the living. The spectre of those who have tragically died will persist to haunt our collective imaginations, dominate our memorial landscapes and forever act as *memento mori*. As such, our significant dead will inhabit memorialised afterlives to admonish counsel, offer us guidance and caution us against our excesses. Back to the dark tourism future will be very much like that of the present. It will remain full of political and managerial quandaries, ladened with ethical conundrums and contested in what is (re)presented (or not) for mass touristic consumption. Of course, death and cultural trauma will endure at the crux of dark tourism; but how dark tourism is interpreted and experienced within future visitor economies will change and vary enormously.

This book has drawn upon an international authorship where each chapter has laid out a particular dark tourism future, or what the future may hold for specific dark tourism practice. Many of the chapters have looked at the past to gaze towards the future and, in so doing, offered us astute observations about impending and eventual dark tourism development. However, the aim of this Afterword is not to summarise each contributing chapter – that was undertaken in the

Preface – but rather to offer a brief critique of some key insights this book has purported. In turn, I want to be critical in what going back to the future in dark tourism entails and what awaits you when you arrive. To that end, three fundamental themes emerge from the diverse array of issues this book has addressed. Firstly, *technology* through constant transformations and augmentation will continue to play a decisive role in the interpretation and commercialisation of dark tourism. Secondly, the *visitor experience* of those who consume dark tourism will become increasingly immersive and, consequently, break ethical boundaries and push further the emotional envelope. Finally, *thanatological issues* will dominate cross-cultural aspects of remembering our significant Other dead. As such, the politics of remembrance of cultural trauma will prevail and become ever more entrenched.

Future Technology

Undoubtedly, technological advancement will underpin future dark tourism development. Even if the idea of the *Vertopia*, as outlined in Chapter 1, does not fully materialise, future technology will still attempt to fuse reality with hyperrealism. As a result, the interconnectedness of interpretation offered by technology will exponentially increase our exposure to tragedy, where the traumatic dead will compete for memorial space in a saturated dark tourism marketplace. Moreover, implications of commercialisation of difficult heritage, fuelled by granular shifts in the speed and scale of technology, will push dark tourism interpretive innovation to the edge. This will not be a sudden process, but a creeping evolution that is organic, sequential and progressive (that is possibly measured by the decade). Indeed, the robotic development that introduces the 'robo-revolution' in Chapter 4, may gradually occur as we might transgress toward post-humanity in a far future, or at least have dual entity systems of biological and 'living-machine' existence in a trans-human world. Dark tourism in this case will be shaped by the dominant stakeholders in such a nightmarish world, in which robots and humans clash and, subsequently, create new 'black spots' upon a futuristic landscape. Such conflict might also be witnessed in new 'monument wars' as highlighted in Chapter 7. It is here where virtual battles for memorials may create the possibility of virtual dark tourism sites, and where boundaries of reality and hyperreality collide in new dark touristic digital spaces.

In this book, we have outlined various present and future scenarios where advances in AI (Artificial Intelligence), machine learning, robotics and other technologies are defining a new digital era that is opening the doors to new innovations. Yet, many of the technologies are hitherto to be created. It is here that our future(s) is imagined, often by looking back, whereby futurology is governed by plurality of perils and possibilities. Indeed, future dark tourism technology will (re)shape multiple versions of cultural trauma and, as a result, control narratives of difficult heritage(s) both from the painful past, but also from calamities yet to come.

Future Visitor Experiences

A future visitor to dark tourism sites may be accompanied by the virtual dead. In other words, augmented and virtual reality technology will close the boundaries between this world and the next so much that the significant dead will in effect be provided with a virtual afterlife. Indeed, in the continuation of the Bucket List into the Afterlist (as outlined in Chapter 3), the deceased are offered an opportunity to complete things left unfinished in life. Or, at least, the Afterlist has the potential to continue a dead person's consciousness within the digital world (as is the case for the *Vertopia* in Chapter 1) and, in doing so, becomes a machine that learns human behaviour and emotion. It is this emotion and affect that will drive the experience of future dark tourism encounters. With ever-increasing immersive participation, the involvement of visitors in future (re)created dark tourism tragedies will mean a familiarity and intimacy that has been hitherto unseen.

However, increased technological immersion within future dark tourism storytelling will open new ethical dilemmas. For example, in Chapter 5, the impacts of VR upon dark tourism experiences are highlighted; yet these raise fundamental moral questions. The sense of horror and revulsion of future cultural trauma might mean that the dead (and their technological reincarnations) are brought too close for touristic gazing. For instance, at Auschwitz-Birkenau, the epitome site of the Holocaust, visitors of the future may 'meet' the Holocaust dead as they are resurrected through augmented reality or new *Vertopian* technology (after Chapter 1). In turn, the complete immersive visitor experience will allow us to wander in the mansions of the dead and accompany tragic souls to their execution. Of course, achieving the balance between exploiting technology for curatorship and interpretation, while driving visitor footfall in a world of mercantile memorialisation, will be challenging. Nevertheless, ethical codes will be continually influx as moral boundaries are collectively redrawn as effervescent visitor experiences will shape emotive encounters. Moreover, with a polarisation between secularism and religiosity across the world, cross-cultural divisions will open as future societies grapple with how to deal with their significant dead. This will become even more problematic as dark tourism sites will become empty meeting grounds for those who have passed before us, yet immersive visitor experiences will blur the lines between reality (us) and hyperreality (them).

Future Thanatology and our 'Significant Other Dead'

Our significant Other dead are those who have died in tragic or extraordinary circumstances and, subsequently, hold collective relevance to us. The global dark tourism landscape is littered with the significant dead; forewarning us of our failures and faults, as well as our delinquency and delusions. As such, dark tourism offers a thanatological lens upon society and how we culturally treat our important dead. In the future, fundamental interrelationships of the thanatological condition of society will shine light on emerging divisions of entrenched secularisation and dominant religiosity. As the world moves both away from *and* toward sacred canopies that offer religious guidance, our significant dead will be left to the secular devices of dark tourism. In turn, the line between commemoration and commercialisation will be increasingly blurred, so much so that the dead will not only be guardians of the living but will also be a *living*. Through enhanced technological visitor experiences, the dark tourism dead will become products of a mercantile memorial system that uses cultural trauma as trade. The increased retailing of the dead will espouse new death mentalities as the significant dead truly become spectacular in a society of the spectacle.

Even so, with a new death spectacularisation, dark tourism can also bring us a sense of compassion and communitas, as the significant dead offer us insight into our own mortality saliency (as noted in Chapter 22). However, in a future society where death and dying in the ordinary biological sense has undergone wholesale commercialisation and capitalisation, the cheapening and chaining of 'assisted dying' becomes the ultimate dark tourism product. In this bleak future, as outlined in Chapter 9, dying in a highly modernised world might lead to a standard and predictable 'McDeath'. It is here that people will travel (and pay) to die and, consequently, meet the Grim Reaper on their own terms. In this future, deep modernisation of secular global communities will bring material affluence but also spiritual alienation. Moreover, extreme wealth as well as extreme poverty will result in highly psychologically alienated and capitalised societies that lack government but rely on big tech and corporations. The 'McDeath' will be the result of such a society, where death is not only commercialised but valued as a commodity. In this case, it is your responsibility, as reader of this book, to ensure that such a future never occurs.

Concluding Thoughts

Over the past two decades or so, dark tourism as an interdisciplinary brand of scholarly study has shined light on the social reality of our significant dead. Dark tourism tells us stories of tragedy and disaster, issues of commercialisation and ethical consumption, as well as sociocultural responses to heritage, memorialisation and political aspects of remembering (and forgetting). Entrenched within visitor economies, dark tourism is now internationally recognised as travel to sites of death and cultural trauma, as well as the visitor experience of such places. Dark tourism remains a provocative and emotive area of studying the commodification of death and our 'heritage that hurts'. Yet, it is also an enlightening field of research where academic scrutiny and media showcasing of commodified death reveals inherent traits of society and culture.

In many ways, dark tourism shows us the failure of our actions. Whether this is through visiting former sites of war or conflict, human induced calamities, natural disasters, group committed atrocities, individual crimes or any other tragic circumstances in which people untimely die. The practice of remembering events that haunt our imaginations means a process of memorialisation imbued with political strife, cultural dissonance and design struggles. Consequently, there is a failure of modern memorialisation that lies at the heart of contemporary dark tourism. Instead of warning us of our past fights and misfortunes, and the reasons for such conflict, crime or calamity, dark tourism has largely been drawn into a commercial tourism sector that values economic footfall and monetary spend. In other ways, many dark tourism memorial sites are too abstract in their design with postmodern minimalism and plurality in narrative and educative messaging. Dreams of the future are quashed in the nightmares of the past and, consequently, dark tourism fails to narrate to the masses *darkness* that once was and what might be. Therefore, immersive dark tourism experiences, emotive by default and design, and driven by enhanced future technology may alleviate such memorial failures. Dark tourism of the future should serve us warnings from the past and deliver us messages of hope and encouragement from our mistakes. Our significant dead should speak to us through touristic narratives that offer enlightenment in a world that will spin ever faster with technological developments. However, despite the best efforts of this book, we can never know the future. Instead, we offer a book full of critical thoughts that will provoke you to consider and ponder what future dark tourism will entail. Ultimately, futurologists can only be proven right or wrong in time. To that end, it remains to be seen if this book has foreseen the darker side of travel and whether voices of our future dead speak to us through dark tourism.

References

3 giorni a milano (n.d.) The monumental cemetery. See https://3giorniamilano.it/en/what-to-see-and-do/milan-monumental-cemetery (accessed November 2022).

Abbott, H.P. (2002) *The Cambridge Introduction to Narrative*. Cambridge University Press.

Abbott, R. (2020) *The Reasonable Robot: Artificial Intelligence and the Law*. Cambridge University Press.

Abingdon Gaol (2016) Old gaol, bridge street. See https://www.abingdon.gov.uk/abingdon_buildings/old-gaol (accessed April 2023).

Abingdon Gaol Apartments (2023) Old gaol serviced apartments. See https://www.hotels.uk.com/uk/oxfordshire/hotels-in-abingdon/old-gaol-serviced-apartments.ox14-3hn (accessed April 2023).

Abrahms, H. (2022) Willesden Jewish cemetery: Honouring the invisible in the city of the dead. *The London Gardener* 26, 29–41.

Acker, M. (2021) Gesturing toward the common and the desperation: Climate geopoetics' potential. *Dialogues in Human Geography* 11 (1), 23–26.

Adachi, R., Cramer, E.M. and Song, H. (2022) Using virtual reality for tourism marketing: A mediating role of self-presence. *The Social Science Journal* 56 (4), 657–670.

Agamben, G. (1998) *Homo Sacer: Sovereign Power and Bare Life*. Stanford University Press.

Ahmadi K.R., Biabani, H. and Baneshi, E. (2022) Scenarios for the future of tourism in Iran (case study: Hormozgan province). *Journal of Policy Research in Tourism, Leisure and Events* 14 (2), 183–199.

Aiello, D., Fai, S. and Santagati, C. (2019) Virtual museums as a means for promotion and enhancement of cultural heritage. *International Archives of the Photogrammetry, Remote Sensing and Spatial Information Sciences* XLII-2/W15, 33–40.

Aikau, H. and Gonzalez, V. (2019) *Detours: A Decolonial Guide to Hawaii*. Duke University Press.

Akerman, J.R. (2016) Mapping, battlefield guidebooks, and remembering the great war. In E. Liebenberg, I.J. Demhardt and S. Vervust (eds) *History of Military Cartography* (pp. 159–177). Springer.

Alabau-Montoya J. and Ruiz-Molina, M.E. (2020) Enhancing visitor experience with war heritage tourism through information and communication technologies: Evidence from Spanish Civil War museums and sites. *Journal of Heritage Tourism* 15 (5), 500–510.

Aleson-Carbonell, M. (2014) Conflict and Language variation in WWI and II dark sites: An exploratory study. In F. Poppi and J. Schmied (eds) *Tracking Language Change in Specialised and Professional Genres* (160–187). Officina Edizioni.

Alexander, N. (2021) Obsolescence, forgotten: "survivor holograms", virtual reality, and the future of Holocaust commemoration. *Cinergie – Il cinema e le altre arti* 19, 57–68.

Aljazeera (2020) Mother 'reunites' with dead daughter in virtual reality. See https://www.aljazeera.com/news/2020/2/14/mother-reunites-with-dead-daughter-in-virtual-reality (accessed October 2022).

Allen, R. (1992) Memorial geography: Reflections upon a useful strategy for teaching middle school geography students. *Journal of the Middle States Council for the Social Studies* 13, 10–18.

Alphin, C. and Debrix, N. (2020) *Necrogeopolitics: On Death and Death-Making in International Relations*. Routledge.

Alston, A. (2016) *Beyond Immersive Theatre: Aesthetics, Politics and Productive Participation*. Palgrave Macmillan.

ALVA (2023) *Association of Leading Visitor Attractions visitor figures 2022*. See https://www.alva.org.uk/details.cfm?p=617 (accessed April 2023).

Amanik, A. and Fletcher, K. (2020) *Till Death Do Us Part: American Ethnic Cemeteries as Borders Uncrossed*. University of Mississippi Press.

Ana, C.C., Mendes, J., Oom do Valle, P. and Scott, N. (2018) Co-creation of tourist experiences: a literature review. *Current Issues in Tourism* 21 (4), 369–400.

Andermann, J. and Arnold-de Simine, S. (2012) Introduction memory, community and the new museum. *Theory, Culture and Society* 29 (1), 3–13.

Andersen, M.M., Schjoedt, U., Price, H., Rosas, F.E., Scrivner, C. and Clasen, M. (2022) Playing with fear: A field study in recreational horror. *Psychological Science* 31 (12), 1497–1510.

Anderton, K. (2020) Real growth in virtual reality gaming (infographic). See https://www.forbes.com/sites/kevinanderton/2020/10/31/real-growth-in-virtual-reality-gaming-infographic/?sh=5373b78f7e13 (accessed October 2022).

Andrews, M. (2019) Commemorating the First World War in Britain: A cultural legacy of media remembrance. *Journal of War and Culture Studies* 12 (3), 295–313.

Andriotis, K. (2010) Heterotopic erotic oases–the public nude beach experience. *Annals of Tourism Research* 37 (4), 1076–1096.

Angel, L. (2019) *How to Build a Conscious Machine*. Routledge.

Anne Frank House (n.d.) Renewed VR tour of Anne Frank's secret annex. See https://www.annefrank.org/en/about-us/news-and-press/news/2019/7/4/renewed-vr-tour-anne-franks-secret-annex/ (accessed February 2022).

Ansell-Pearson, K. (1997) *Viroid Life. Perspectives on Nietzsche and the Transhuman Condition,* Routledge.

Anthis, J.R. and Paez, E. (2021) Moral circle expansion: A promising strategy to impact the far future. *Futures* 130. See https://doi.org/10.1016/j.futures.2021.102756.

Anthony, T. (2021) *9/11: As the decades pass, the act of remembering evolves*. See https://apnews.com/article/sept-11-anniversary-act-of-remembering-a79312b0979fefee70af5d27f5324c1b (accessed January 2022).

Aoun, S.M., Breen, L.J., White, I., Rumbold, B. and Kellehear, A. (2018) What sources of bereavement support are perceived helpful by bereaved people and why? Empirical evidence for the compassionate communities approach. *Palliative Medicine* 32 (8), 1378–1388.

AP News (2022) 'Let's open our eyes' to rising xenophobia, Macron warns. See https://apnews.com/article/europe-france-race-and-ethnicity-racial-injustice-macron-f119c8167fcdab4322d23695cc8d65c2 (accessed January 2023)

Ariès, P. (1974) *Western Attitudes Toward Death: From the Middle Ages to the Present*. John Hopkins University Press.

Ariès, P. (1981) *The Hour of Our Death* (trans: Weaver, H.). Oxford University Press.

Armitt, L. and Brewster, S. (2021) *Gothic Travel Through Haunted Landscapes: Climates of Fear*. Anthem Press.

Árnason, A. and Hafsteinsson, S.B. (2020) A funeral for a glacier: Mourning the more-than-human at the edge of modernity. *Thanatos* 9 (2), 42–71.

Arnold, M., Gibbs, M., Kohn, T., Meese, J. and Nansen, B. (2018) *Death and Digital Media*. Routledge.

Arrocha, W. (2019) Combating xenophobia and hate through compassionate migration: The present struggle of irregular migrants escaping fear and extreme poverty. *Crime, Law and Social Change* 71 (3), 245–260.

Ash Wednesday Bushfire Education Centre (2021) Ash Wednesday Bushfire Education Centre. See https://awbec.webs.com/ (accessed December 2021).
Ashworth, G.J. (2004) Tourism and the heritage of atrocity: Managing the heritage of South African apartheid for entertainment. In T.V. Singh (ed.) *New Horizons in Tourism: Strange Experiences and Stranger Practices* (pp. 95–108). CABI Publishing.
Ashworth, G. and Hartmann, R. (2005) *The Management of Horror and Human Tragedy. Horror and Human Tragedy Revisited: The Management of Sites of Atrocities for Tourism.* Cognizant Communication Corporation.
Ashworth, G.J. and Isaac, R.K. (2015) Have we illuminated the dark? Shifting perspectives on 'dark' tourism. *Tourism Recreation Research* 40 (3), 316–325.
Ashworth, G.J. and Tunbridge, J.E. (2019) Death camp tourism: Interpretation and management. In G. Hooper and J.J. Lennon (eds) *Dark Tourism Practice and Interpretation* (pp. 69–72). Routledge.
Assmann, A. (2008) Transformations between history and memory. *Social Research* 75 (1), 49–72.
Assmann, A. (2010) The Holocaust — a global memory? Extensions and limits of a new memory community. In A. Assmann and S. Conrad (eds) *Memory in a Global Age. Palgrave Macmillan Memory Studies* (pp. 97–117). Palgrave Macmillan.
Assmann, A. (2014) *Der lange Schatten der Vergangenheit.* C.H. Beck.
Atkinson-Phillips, A. (2022) Remembering experience: Public memorials are not just about the dead anymore. *Memory Studies* 15 (5), 947–962.
Auschwitz-Birkenau State Museum (2022) Virtual tour. See https://panorama.auschwitz.org/ (accessed August 2022).
Auschwitz Tours (2022) Plan a visit to the Auschwitz Concentration Camp. See https://www.theauschwitztours.com/visiting-auschwitz. (accessed September 2022).
Auschwitz V.R. (n.d.) Auschwitz-Birkenau historical VR reconstruction. See https://auschwitzvr.pl/en/ (accessed November 2022).
Australian Broadcasting Corporation (ABC) (2020) Trapped in the volcano, four corners. See https://www.youtube.com/watch?v=fndcCyYzXKg (accessed November 2022).
Australian Geographic (2012) Christchurch earthquake remembered one year on - Australian Geographic. See https://www.australiangeographic.com.au/news/2012/02/christchurch-earthquake-remembered-one-year-on/#:~:text=ON%20THE%20ANNIVERSARY%20OF%20the%20earthquake%20that%20devastated,quake%2C%20which%20struck%20at%2012.51pm%20last%20February%2022 (accessed October 2022).
AZ Quotes (2023) Robin Sharma. See https://www.azquotes.com/quote/1460582 (accessed May 2023).
Bachelor, P. (2004) *Sorrow and Solace: The Social World of the Cemetery.* Routledge.
Baer, L.D. and Ravneberg, B. (2008) The outside and inside in Norwegian and English prisons. *Geografiska Annaler, Series B Human Geography* 90 (2), 205–216.
Ball, M. (2020) The Metaverse: What it is, where to find it, and who will build it. MatthewBall.vc, 13 January. See https://www.matthewball.vc/all/themetaverse (accessed January 2023).
Ball, M. (2022) *The Metaverse. And How it Will Revolutionize Everything.* New York: Liveright Publishing.
Balmain, C. (2008) *Introduction to Japanese Horror Film.* Edinburgh University Press.
Baral A., Baral S. and Morgan N. (2004) Marketing Nepal in an uncertain climate: Confronting perceptions of risk and insecurity. *Journal of Vacation Marketing* 10 (2), 186–192.
Barker, F. and Gay, J. (1984) *Highgate Cemetery: Victorian Valhalla.* John Murray Publishers.
Barker, T.B. (1869) *Abney Park Cemetery: A Complete Descriptive Guide to Every Part of this Beautiful Depository of the Dead.* Houlston and Wright.
Barrett, P. (2006) White thumbs, black bodies: Race, violence, and neoliberal fantasies in grand theft auto: San Andreas. *The Review of Education, Pedagogy, and Cultural Studies* 28 (1), 95–119.

Barton, A. and Brown, A. (2012) Dark tourism and the modern prison. *Prison Service Journal* 199, 44–49.

Barton, A. and Brown, A. (2015) Show me the prison! The development of prison tourism in the UK. *Crime, Media, Culture* 11 (3), 237–258.

Bassett, D.J. (2018) Digital afterlives: From social media platforms to thanabots and beyond. In C. Tandy and M. Perry (eds) *Death and Anti-Death, Volume 16: 200 Years After Frankenstein* (pp. 27–38). Ria University Press.

Baum, S.D., Armstrong, S., Ekenstedt, T., Häggström, O., Hanson, R., Kuhlemann, K., Maas, M.M., Miller, J.D., Salmela, M., Sandberg, A., Sotala, K., Torres, P., Turchin, A. and Yampolskiy, R.V. (2019) Long-term trajectories of human civilization. *Foresight* 21 (1), 53–83.

BBC (2006) Robots could demand legal rights. See http://news.bbc.co.uk/1/hi/technology/6200005.stm (accessed May 2023).

BBC News Blundeston closure (2013) Prisons to close in England as super-prison site revealed. See https://www.bbc.co.uk/news/uk-23958223 (accessed August 2022).

BBC (2017a) Russia warns Poland not to touch Soviet WW2 memorials. See https://www.bbc.com/news/world-europe-40775355 (accessed January 2022).

BBC (2017b) Hong Kong: Man dies at haunted house attraction. See https://www.bbc.co.uk/news/world-asia-41300031 (accessed April 2022).

BBC (2019) Climate change: Iceland holds funeral for melted glacier. See https://www.bbc.co.uk/newsround/49405023 (accessed March 2023).

BBC (2021) Whitby Goth Weekend celebrates Halloween return. See https://www.bbc.com/news/uk-england-york-north-yorkshire-59082186 (accessed November 2022).

BBC News Europe (1999a) Nato crisis talks on massacre. See http://news.bbc.co.uk/1/hi/world/europe/256453.stm (accessed February 2023).

BBC News Europe (1999b) Pathologist: "No Kosovo massacre". See http://news.bbc.co.uk/2/hi/europe/258529.stm (accessed February 2023).

Bearak, B. (2001) Over world protests, Taliban are destroying ancient Buddhas. *The New York Times*. See https://www.nytimes.com/2001/03/04/world/over-world-protests-taliban-are-destroying-ancient-buddhas.html (accessed November 2022).

Bec, A., Moyle, B., Timms, K., Schaffer, V., Skavronskaya, L. and Little, C. (2019) Management of immersive heritage tourism experiences: A conceptual model. *Tourism Management* 72, 117–120.

Beck, J, Rainoldi, M. and Egger, R. (2019) Virtual reality in tourism: A state-of-the-art review. *Tourism Review* 74 (3), 586–612.

Becker, A. (2005) Memory gaps: Maurice Halbwachs, memory and the great war. *Journal of European Studies* 35 (1), 102–113.

Becker, E. (1973) *The Denial of Death*. The Free Press.

Beech, J. (2000) The enigma of holocaust sites as tourist attractions-the case of Buchenwald. *Managing Leisure* 5 (1), 29–41.

Beeton, S. (2005) *Film-Induced Tourism* (1st edn). Channel View Publications.

Beim, A. (2007) The cognitive aspects of collective memory. *Symbolic Interaction* 30 (1), 7–26.

Bela, B. (2016) Complexities of memory travel. The Latvian case. In K. Jõesalu and A. Kannike (eds) *Cultural Patterns and Life Stories* (pp. 211–212). Tallinn University Press.

Bell, D. (1973) *The Coming of Post-Industrial Society: A Venture in Social Forecasting*. Basic Books.

Bell, M.W. (2008) Towards a definition of "virtual worlds". *Journal of Virtual Worlds Research* 1 (1).

Beller, J. (2020) Xenophobia trends in Germany: Increasing negative attitude towards foreigners in younger birth cohorts. *The Social Science Journal*, 1–7.

Bennett, B. and Daly, A. (2020) Recognising rights for robots: Can we? Will we? Should we? *L. Innovation Tech* 12 (1), 60–80.

Bennett, M.M. (2020) Ruins of the Anthropocene: The aesthetics of arctic climate change. *Annals of the American Association of Geographers* 111 (3), 921–931.

Bergan, B. (2021) The scientific reason we're awful to human-like robots. See https://interestingengineering.com/innovation/scientific-reason-awful-to-human-like-robots (accessed May 2023).

Bergman, B. (2022) I watched Meta's controversial 'Surviving 9/11' and found it stomach churning. But it's not what people think it is. Insider. See https://www.businessinsider.com/i-watched-metas-surviving-911-at-sxsw-and-found-it-stomach-churning-2022-3 (accessed April 2022).

Berzins, D. (2015) Communication and ethics of social memory: Discourses of the holocaust in Latvia (1945-2014). Unpublished PhD Thesis, University of Latvia.

Bhabha, H.K. (1994) *The Location of Culture*. Routledge.

Biber, D. (2019) Multidimensional analysis: A historical synopsis. In T.B. Sardinha and M.V. Pinto (eds) *Multi-dimensional Analysis: Research Methods and Current Issues* (pp.11–26). Bloomsbury Academic.

Biran, A. and Buda, D.M. (2018) Unravelling fear of death motives in dark tourism. In P.R. Stone, R. Hartman, T. Seaton R. Sharpley and L.White (eds) *The Palgrave Handbook of Dark Tourism Studies* (pp. 515–532). Palgrave Macmillan.

Biran, A. and Poria, Y. (2012) Reconceptualising dark tourism. In R. Sharpley and P.R. Stone (eds) *Contemporary Tourist Experience: Concepts and Consequences* (pp. 59–70). Routledge.

Biran, A. and Hyde, K.F. (2013) New perspectives on dark tourism. *International Journal of Culture, Tourism and Hospitality Research* 7 (3), 191–198.

Biran, A., Poria, Y. and Oren, G. (2011) Sought experiences at (dark) heritage sites. *Annals of Tourism Research* 38 (3), 820–841.

Bird, G., Westcott, M. and Thiesen, N. (2018) Marketing dark heritage: Building brands, myth-making and social marketing. In P.R. Stone, R. Hartmann, T. Seaton, R. Sharpley and L. White (eds) *The Palgrave Handbook of Dark Tourism Studies* (pp. 645–665). Palgrave Macmillan.

Blom, T. (2000) Morbid tourism-a postmodern market niche with an example from Althorp. *Norsk Geografisk Tidsskrift* 54 (1), 29–36.

Blom, T. (2007) Morbid tourism: The case of Diana, Princess of Wales and Althorp House. In P. Long and N.J. Palmer (eds) *Royal Tourism: Excursions Around Monarchy* (pp. 142–158). Channel View Publications.

Blundeston Badger Homes (2023) Blundeston. See https://www.badgerbuilding.co.uk/lakeside-blundeston-suffolk/ (accessed April 2023).

Bodmin Jail (2023) Redeveloping Bodmin jail. See https://www.bodminjail.org/discover/about-bodmin-jail/redeveloping-bodmin-jail/ (accessed April 2023).

Bodmin Jail Visit (2023) Heritage tours. See https://www.bodminjail.org/ (accessed April 2023).

Boellstorff, T. (2013) Placing the virtual body: Avatar, Chora, Cypherg. In F.E. Mascia-Lees (ed.) *A Companion to the Anthropology of the Body and Embodiment* (pp. 504–520). Wiley-Blackwell.

Boer, T.A. (2003) After the slippery slope: Dutch experiences on regulating active euthanasia. *Journal of the Society of Christian Ethics* 23 (2), 225–242.

Bogner, A., Littig, B. and Menz, W. (2009) Introduction: Expert interviews – An introduction to a new methodological debate. In A. Bogner, B. Littig and W. Menz (eds) *Interviewing Experts: Research Methods Series* (pp. 1–13). Palgrave Macmillan.

Bohil, C., Owen, C.B., Jeong, E.J. and Alicea, B. (2009) Virtual reality and presence. In W.F. Eadie (ed.) *21st Century Communication: A Reference Handbook* (pp. 22–55). Sage.

Bohn, D. and Varnajot, A. (2021) A geopolitical outlook on Arctification in Northern Europe: Insights from tourism, regional branding and higher education institutions. In L. Heininen, H. Exner-Pirot and J. Barnes (eds) *Arctic Yearbook 2021: Defining and Mapping Sovereignties, Policies and Perceptions* (pp. 279–292). Arctic Portal.

Bojic, L. (2022) Metaverse through the prism of power and addiction: What will happen when the virtual world becomes more attractive than reality? *European Journal of Tourism Futures* 10 (22), 1–24.

Bolan, P. and Simone-Charteris, M. (2018) 'Shining a digital light on the dark': Harnessing online media to improve the dark tourism experience. In P.R. Stone, R. Hartmann, T. Seaton, R. Sharpley and L. White (eds) *The Palgrave Handbook of Dark Tourism Studies* (pp. 727–746). Palgrave MacMillan.

Bolas, M. (2019) Foreword. In W.R. Sherman and A.B. Craig (eds) *Understanding Virtual Reality: Interface, Application, and Design* (pp. xvii–xix). Morgan Kaufmann.

Boorstin, D. (1964) *The Image: A Guide to Pseudo-Events in America*. Harper.

Borgstrom, E. and Walter, T. (2015) Choice and compassion at the end of life: A critical analysis of recent English policy discourse. *Social Science and Medicine* 136–137, 99–105.

Bostrom, N. (2003) Astronomical waste: The opportunity cost of delayed technological development. *Utilitas* 15 (3), 308–314.

Bostrom, N. (2005) A history of transhumanist thought. *Journal of Evolution and Technology* 14 (1), 1–25.

Bowman, M.S. and Pezzullo, P.C. (2009) What's so 'dark' about 'dark tourism'?: Death, tours, and performance. *Tourist Studies* 9 (3), 187–202.

Boylan, J.L. and Lawrence, C. (2020) The development and validation of the bushfire psychological preparedness scale. *International Journal of Disaster Risk Reduction* 47. See 101530 https://doi.org/10.1016/j.ijdrr.2020.101530.

Bravo, M.T. (2009) Voices from the sea ice: The reception of climate impact narratives. *Journal of Historical Geography* 35 (2), 256–278.

Bristol Museums (2023) The Colston statue: What next? See https://exhibitions.bristolmuseums.org.uk/the-colston-statue/ (accessed Mar 2023).

Bristow, R.S. (2020) Communitas in fright tourism. *Tourism Geographies* 22 (2), 319–337.

Bristow, R.S. and Jenkins, I. (2020) Geography of fear: Fright tourism contributing to urban revitalization. *Journal of Policy Research in Tourism, Leisure and Events* 12 (2), 262–275.

Bristow, R.S. and Newman, M. (2005) Myth vs. fact: An exploration of fright tourism. In K. Bricker (ed.) *Proceedings of the 2004 Northeastern Recreation Research Symposium. Gen. Tech. Rep. NE-326* (pp. 215–221). US Department of Agriculture, Forest Service, Northeastern Research Station.

Brodie, A. (2019) The Castle or the Green Field: Dilemmas and solutions in English prison planning, 1780-1850. *Prison Service Journal* 246, 4–9.

Brodie, A., Croom, J. and Davies, J.O. (2002) *English Prisons*. English Heritage.

Brooks, C. (1989) *Mortal Remains: The History and Present State of the Victorian and Edwardian Cemetery*. Wheaton published in association with the Victorian Society.

Brown, A. and Waterhouse-Watson, D. (2014) The future of the past: Digital media in Holocaust museums. *Holocaust Studies* 20 (3), 1–32.

Brown, B. (2018) *Dare to Lead: Brave Work. Tough Conversations. Whole Hearts*. Random House.

Brown, J. (2013) Dark tourism shops: Selling 'dark' and 'difficult' products. *International Journal of Culture, Tourism and Hospitality Research* 7 (3), 272–280.

Brubaker, J.R., Hayes, G.R. and Dourish, P. (2013) Beyond the grave: Facebook as a site for the expansion of death and mourning. *The Information Society* 29 (3), 152–163.

Bruce, G. (2020) Trace and aura at sites of former Nazi concentration camps. In M. Gloe and A. Ballis (eds) *Holocaust Education Revisited* (pp. 203–218). Springer.

Bryant, R.A., Gibbs, L., Colin Gallagher, H., Pattison, P., Lusher, D., MacDougall, C., Harms, L., Block, K., Ireton, G., Richardson, J. and Forbes, D. (2021) The dynamic course of psychological outcomes following the Victorian Black Saturday bushfires. *Australian and New Zealand Journal of Psychiatry* 55 (7), 666–677.

Bryn Mawr Film Institute (2022) Movies help generate empathy. See https://brynmawrfilm.org/press/empathy-is-the-first-step/ (accessed April 2022).

Buck, H.J. (2015) On the possibilities of a charming Anthropocene. *Annals of the Association of American Geographers* 105 (2), 369–377.

Buda, D.M. and McIntosh, A.J. (2013) Dark tourism and voyeurism: Tourist arrested for "spying" in Iran. *International Journal of Culture, Tourism and Hospitality Research* 7 (3), 214–226.

Buhalis, D. and Karatay, N. (2022) Mixed reality (MR) for generation Z in cultural heritage tourism towards metaverse. In J.L. Stienmetz, B.F. Rosell and D. Massimo (eds) *Information and Communication Technologies in Tourism 2022* (pp. 16–27). Springer International Publishing.

Buhalis, D., Lin, M. and Leung, D. (2023) Metaverse as a driver for hospitality customer experience and value co-creation: implications for hotel and tourism management and marketing. *International Journal of Contemporary Hospitality Management*. See https://doi.org/10.1108/IJCHM-05-2022-0631 (accessed January 2023).

Bulmer, J. (2020) *Highgate Cemetery: Saved by its Friends. A Souvernir Guide*. Jigsaw Design and Publishing.

Burton, N.R., Hitchen, M.E. and Bryan P.G. (1999) Virtual Stonehenge: A fall from disgrace? In L. Dingwall, S. Exon, V. Gaffney, S. Laflin and M. van Leusen (eds) *Archaeology in the Age of the Internet. CAA97. Computer Applications and Quantitative Methods in Archaeology. Proceedings of the 25th Anniversary Conference, University of Birmingham, April 1997* (BAR International Series 750, CD-ROM). Archaeopress. See https://core.ac.uk/download/pdf/158279488.pdf.

Busby, G. (2022) Dracula tourism. In D. Buhalis (ed.) *Encyclopedia of Tourism Management and Marketing* (pp. 1005–1007). Edward Elgar Publishing.

Büscher, M. and Urry, J. (2009) Mobile methods and the empirical. *European Journal of Social Theory* 12 (1), 99–116.

Butler, J. (2009) *Frames of War. When is Life Grievable?* Verso.

Campa, R. (2019) Nietzsche and transhumanism: A meta-analytical perspective. *Studia Humana* 8 (4), 10–26.

Cai, Y., Li, G., Lui, C. and Wen, L. (2022) Post-pandemic dark tourism in former Epicenters. *Tourism Economics* 28 (1), 175–199.

Çakar, K. (2018) Experiences of visitors to Gallipoli, a nostalgia-themed dark tourism destination: An insight from TripAdvisor. *International Journal of Tourism Cities* 4 (1), 98–109.

Canterbury Earthquake Memorial (2022) Oi Manawa Canterbury earthquake national memorial. See https://www.canterburyearthquakememorial.co.nz/ (accessed November 2022).

Cantor, M. (2019) Facebook could have 4.9bn dead users by 2100, study finds. See https://www.theguardian.com/technology/2019/apr/29/facebook-dead-users-2100-oxford#:~:text=If%20Facebook%20continues%20to%20grow,a%20study%20by%20Oxford%20researchers (accessed August 2022).

Cappelli, G. (2013) Travelling words: Languaging in English tourism discourse. In A. Yarrington, S. Villani and J. Kelly (eds) *Travels and Translations* (pp. 353–374). Rodopi.

Caracena, T.M., Vidal, E.V., Gonçalves, J.G.M. and Peerani, P. (2017) A KD-trees based method for fast radiation source representation for virtual reality dosimetry applications in nuclear safeguards and security. *Progress in Nuclear Energy* 95, 78–83.

Carayannopoulos, G. (2017) *Disaster Management in Australia: Government Coordination in a Time of Crisis*. Taylor and Francis.

Card, C. (2010) *Confronting Evil: Terrorism, Torture, Genocide*. Cambridge University Press.

Carey, M. (2007) The history of ice: How glaciers became an endangered species. *Environmental History* 12 (3), 497–527.

Carmarthen County Hall (2023) Full report for listed buildings. See https://cadwpublic-api.azurewebsites.net/reports/listedbuilding/FullReport?lang=andid=82151 (accessed April 2023).

Carrigan, A. (2015) Dark tourism and postcolonial studies: Critical intersections, *Postcolonial Studies* 17 (3), 236–250.
Carroll, B. and Landry, K. (2010) Logging on and let-ting out: Using online social networks to grieve and to mourn. *Bulletin of Science, Technology and Society* 30 (5), 309–315.
Carson, C. (1998) Colonial Williamsburg and the practice of interpretive planning in American history museums. *The Public Historian* 20 (3), 11–51.
Carson, D. (2020) Urban tourism in the Arctic: A framework for comparison. In D.K. Müller, D.A. Carson, S. de la Barre, B. Granås, G.Þ. Jóhannesson, G. Øyen, O. Rantala, J. Saarinen, T. Salmela, K. Tervo-Kankare and J. Welling (eds) *Arctic Tourism in Times of Changes: Dimensions of Urban Tourism* (pp. 6–17). Nordic Council of Ministers.
Causevic, S. and Neal, M. (2019) The exotic veil: Managing tourist perceptions of national history and statehood in Oman. *Tourist Management* 71, 504–517.
Chalkin, C.W. (1984) *New Maidstone Gaol Order Book, 1805-1823.* Kent Records.
Chalmers, D.J. (2022) *Reality + Virtual Worlds and the Problems of Philosophy.* Allen Lane.
Chen, S. and Xu, H. (2021) The moral gaze in commercialized dark tourism. *Current Issues in Tourism* 24 (15), 2167–2186.
Chernobyl VR Project (2016) Chernobyl Vr Project – Pre-order now! See https://www.thefarm51.com/eng/chernobyl-vr-project-pre-order-now/ (accessed November 2022).
Chetty, D. (2011) The exotic 'Orient' in gender and tourism. In F. Morady and I. Şiriner, (eds) *Globalisation, Religion and Development* (pp. 62–84). IJOPECm.
Chin, N.P. and Talpelli, M. (2015) 'You always have to struggle, so you don't have to struggle': Community trauma recovery after a landslide. *Journal of Loss and Trauma* 20 (4), 306–316.
Cimitero Monumentale Milano (n.d.) *Visita il monumentale.* See https://monumentale.comune.milano.it/index.php/visita-il-monumentale (accessed November 2022).
Cioppa, T.M., Lucas, T.W. and Sanchez, S.M. (2004) Military applications of agent-based simulations. In *Proceedings of the 2004 winter simulation conference, 2004* 1, 165–174. Presented at the 2004 winter simulation conference. IEEE.
Clark, B. (1843) *Handbook for Visitors to Kensal Green Cemetery.* Joseph Masters.
Clark, L.B. (2009) Coming to terms with trauma tourism. *Performance Paradigm* 5 (2), 162–184.
Clasen, M. (2017) *Why Horror Seduces.* Oxford University Press.
Cline, E. (2011) *Ready Player One*Broadway Publishers.
Clio Muse Tours (2023) Contested and competing memory spaces in Kosovo: Self-Guided Audio Tour. See https://cliomusetours.com/tours/contested-and-competing-memory-spaces-in-kosovo/ (accessed June 2023).
Cogan, M. (2022) Antisemitism isn't new. So why did 2022 feel different? This year, hatred against Jews got much harder to ignore. See https://www.vox.com/culture/23519717/antisemitism-hatred-jews-violence (accessed December 2022).
Cohen, E. (1984) The sociology of tourism: Approaches, issues and findings. *Annual Review of Sociology* 10 (1), 373–392.
Cohen, E. (1985) Tourism as play. *Religion* 15 (3), 291–304.
Cohen, E. (1988) Traditions in the qualitative sociology of tourism. *Annals of Tourism Research* 15 (1), 29–46.
Cohen, E.H. (2011) Educational dark tourism at an in populo site: The Holocaust Museum in Jerusalem. *Annals of Tourism Research* 38 (1), 193–209.
Cohen, E. (2018) Thanatourism: A comparative approach. In P.R. Stone, R. Hartmann, T. Seaton, R. Sharpley and L. White (eds) *The Palgrave Handbook of Dark Tourism* (pp. 157–171). Palgrave.
Cole, T. (2020) Photographing survival: Survivor photographs of, and at, Auschwitz. In V. Aarons and P. Lassner (eds) *The Palgrave Handbook of Holocaust Literature and Culture* (pp. 633–648). Springer Nature.
Collective for Radical Death Studies (2023) Death work as synonymous with anti-racism work. See https://radicaldeathstudies.com (accessed Mar 2023).

Collins-Kreiner, N. (2016) The lifecycle of concepts: the case of 'Pilgrimage Tourism'. *Tourism Geographies* 18 (3), 322–334.
Collins-Kreiner, N. (2016) Dark tourism as/is pilgrimage. *Current Issues in Tourism* 19 (12), 1185–1189.
Collins-Kreiner, N. (2019) Pilgrimage tourism-past, present and future rejuvenation: A perspective article. *Tourism Review* 75 (1), 145–148.
Colombi, F. (2023) What is the difference between robots, bots and chatbots? See https://blog.decographic.net/what-is-the-difference-between-robots-bots-and-chatbots#:~:text=A%20bot%20is%20essentially%20a,sometimes%20a%20combination%20of%20both. (accessed May 2023).
Commane, G. and Potton, R. (2019) Instagram and Auschwitz: A critical assessment of the impact social media has on Holocaust representation. *Holocaust Studies* 25 (1–2), 158–181.
Condon, S. (2022) Amazon's Alexa reads a story in the voice of a child's deceased grandma. See https://www.zdnet.com/article/amazon-demos-alexa-reading-a-bedtime-story-in-the-voice-of-a-boys-deceased-grandma/ (accessed September 2022).
Cooper, E.A., Spinei, M. and Varnajot, A. (2019) Countering 'arctification': Dawson city's 'sourtoe cocktail'. *Journal of Tourism Futures* 6 (1), 70–82.
Costablanca (n.d.) La Marina Baixa. See http://www.costablanca.org/Esp/Costa_Blanca_ahora/guias_gratuitas/Guias/cb_la_marina_baixa.pdf (accessed May 2023).
Coulson, J. (2019) More than 3.1 million people watched Fortnite's Star Wars event live. *The Gamer*, See https://www.thegamer.com/fortnite-star-wars-event-live-million-viewers (accessed November 2022).
Council of Europe (n.d.) The European cemeteries routes. See https://www.coe.int/en/web/cultural-routes/the-european-cemeteries-route (accessed June 2023).
Cox, G. and Thompson, N. (2021) *Death and Dying: Sociological Perspectives*. Routledge.
Cresswell, T. (2015) *Place: An Introduction*. Wiley Blackwell.
Cresswell, T. (2021) Beyond geopoetics: For hybrid texts. *Dialogues in Human Geography* 11 (1), 36–39.
Cresswell, T. (2022) Writing (new) worlds: Poetry and place in a time of emergency. *Geografiska Annaler: Series B, Human Geography* 104 (4), 374–389.
Crew, B. (2018) This is what humans will look like in 1,000 years. See https://www.sciencealert.com/watch-this-is-what-humans-will-look-like-in-1-000-years (accessed May 2023).
Crowder, R.J., Chhem, R.K. and Aziz, A.Z. (2016) Godzilla mon amour: The origins and legacy of nuclear fear in Japan. In J. Shigemura and R. Chhem (eds) *Mental Health and Social Issues Following a Nuclear Accident* (pp. 3–14). Springer.
Crumlin Road Prison (1999) Historic building details. See https://apps.communities-ni.gov.uk/Buildings/buildview.aspx?id=4124andjs=false (accessed April 2023).
Crumlin Road Prison Visit (2023) Welcome to the Crumlin road gaol. See https://www.crumlinroadgaol.com/ (accessed April 2023).
Cunsolo, A.W. (2012) Climate change as the work of mourning. *Ethics and the Environment* 17 (2), 137–164.
Curl, J.S. (1975) The architecture and planning of the nineteenth-century cemetery. *Garden History* 3 (3), 13–41.
Curl, J.S. (2004) *The Victorian Celebration of Death*. Sutton Publishing Ltd.
Currie, R.R. (1997) A pleasure-tourism behaviors framework. *Annals of Tourism Research* 24 (4), 884–897.
Cuthbert, O. (2022) Basic drones and VR tech help recreate sites destroyed by Daesh in Iraq. See https://wired.me/culture/art-jameel-daesh-iraq-sites (accessed November 2022).
Cuthbertson, A. (2017) Who controls the internet? Facebook and Google dominance could cause the "death of the web. See https://www.newsweek.com/facebook-google-internet-traffic-net-neutrality-monopoly-699286 (accessed November 2022).

da Silva, M.H., do Espírito Santo, A.C., Marins, E.R., de Siqueira, A.P., Mol, D.M. and de Abreu Mol, A.C. (2015) Using virtual reality to support the physical security of nuclear facilities. *Progress in Nuclear Energy* 78, 19–24.

Daley S. (2022) Robotics technology. See https://builtin.com/robotics (accessed May 2023).

Dalton, D. (2015) *Dark Tourism and Crime*. Routledge.

Daniela, L. (2020) Preface: Why do we need new ways to teach? Virtual reality perspective. In L. Daniela (ed.) *New Perspectives on Virtual and Augmented Reality: Finding New Ways to Teach in a Transformed Learning Environment* (pp. xiii–xvi). Routledge.

Dann, G.M.S. (1994) 'There is no business like old business': Tourism, the nostalgia industry of the future. In W. Theobald (ed.) *Global Tourism* (pp. 29–43). Butterworth-Heinemann.

Dann, G.M.S. (1996) *The Language of Tourism a Sociolinguistic Perspective*. CAB International.

Dann, G. (1998) *The Dark Side of Tourism. Aix-en-Provence:* International Center for Research and Studies in Tourism.

Darlington, C. (2014) Dark tourism: A school visit to Flanders. *Bereavement Care* 33 (2), 44–47.

Davies, C. (2021)Virtual reality tourism ready for takeoff as travellers remain grounded. See https://www.theguardian.com/technology/2021/feb/06/virtual-reality-tourism-ready-for-takeoff-as-travellers-remain-grounded (accessed January 2022).

Dawes, J. (2021) An autonomous robot may have already killed people – here's how the weapons could be more destabilizing than nukes. See https://theconversation.com/an-autonomous-robot-may-have-already-killed-people-heres-how-the-weapons-could-be-more-destabilizing-than-nukes-168049 (accessed May 2023).

Dawson, J., Johnston, M.J., Stewart, E.J., Lemieux, C.J., Lemelin, R.H., Maher, P.T. and Grimwood, B.S.R. (2011) Ethical considerations of last chance tourism. *Journal of Ecotourism* 10 (3), 250–265.

Day, M. (2022) Eastern Europe takes out anger of Ukraine invasion on symbols of Soviet occupation. See https://www.telegraph.co.uk/world-news/2022/05/28/eastern-europe-takes-symbols-soviet-occupation-stand-ukraine (accessed April 2023).

de Armas, C., Tori, R. and Netto, A.V. (2020) Use of virtual reality simulators for training programs in the areas of security and defense: a systematic review. *Multimedia Tools and Applications* 79, 495–3515.

Debord, G. (1967/1994) *The Society of the Spectacle*. Zone Books.

Debusmann, B. (2020) Coronavirus: Is virtual reality tourism about to take off? See https://www.bbc.com/news/business-54658147 (accessed January 2022).

Deering, A. (2010) From anti-social behaviour to x-rated: Exploring social diversity and conflict in the cemetery. In A. Maddrell and J.D. Sidaway (eds) *Deathscapes: Spaces for Death, Dying, Mourning and Remembrance*. Routledge.

Deering, A. (2012) Over their dead bodies: A study of leisure and spatiality in cemeteries. Unpublished PhD thesis, University of Brighton.

Dehaene, M. and De Cauter, L. (2008a) *Heterotopia and the City*. Routledge.

Dehaene, M. and De Cauter, L. (2008b) The space of play: Towards a general theory of heterotopia. In M. Dehaene and L. De Cauter (eds) *Heterotopia and the City* (pp. 88–101). Routledge.

Dekel, I. (2011) Mediated space, mediated memory: New archives at the holocaust memorial in Berlin. In N. Neiger, O. Meyers and E. Zandberg (eds) *On Media Memory, London: Palgrave Macmillan Memory Studies* (pp. 265–277). Palgrave Macmillan.

Deleuze, G. and Guattari, F. (1983) *Anti-Oedipus: Capitalism and Schizophrenia*. University of Minnesota Press.

Desbois, P. (2008) *The Holocaust by Bullets: A Priest's Journey to Uncover the Truth Behind the Murder of 1.5 Million Jews*. Palgrave Macmillan.

DeSilvey, C. and Edensor, T. (2013) Reckoning with ruins. *Progress in Human Geography* 37 (4), 465–485.

Dessingué, A. and Winter, J.M. (2016) Introduction: Remembering, forgetting and silence. In A. Dessingué and J. Winter (eds) *Beyond Memory: Silence and the Aesthetics of Remembrance* (pp. 1–12). Routledge.

DeVisser-Amundson A, De Korte, A. and Williams, S. (2016) “Chill or thrill”: the impact of the “polarity paradox” on hospitality and tourism. *Journal of Tourism Futures* 2 (1), 71–78.

Dickens, C. (1987) *Sketches by Boz*. Oxford University Press.

Digital-immortality-now.com (2022) Digital immortality now – Mission. See http://digital-immortality-now.com/Mission (accessed September 2022).

Di Lellio, A. (2009) *The Battle of Kosovo. An Albanian Epic*. I. B. Tauris.

Di Lellio, A. and Schwandner-Sievers, S. (2006) Sacred journey to a nation: The construction of a shrine in postwar Kosovo. *Journeys* 7 (1), 27–49.

Di Lellio, A. Kompleksiteti i përkujtimoreve të luftës në Kosovë. (2013) Kosovo 2.0. See https://kosovotwopointzero.com/the-complexity-of-kosovos-war-memorials/ (accessed February 2023).

Dimock, M. (2019) Defining generations: Where millennials end and generation Z begins. See https://www.pewresearch.org/short-reads/2019/01/17/where-millennials-end-and-generation-z-begins/ (accessed April 2023).

Diner, D. (2007) *Gegenläufige Gedächtnisse. Über Geltung und Wirkung des Holocaust, Toldot* 7. Vandenhoeck and Ruprecht.

Disney World (2022) Disney World reopening and updated experiences. See https://www.disneyworld.co.uk/experience-updates/ Resort (accessed September 2022).

DMP Co., Ltd. | Miyagi/Sendai. (n.d.) Dark tourism. See http://www.dmp.co.jp/dark-tourism-sendai/ (accessed September 2022).

Dobraszczyk, P. (2010) Petrified ruin: Chernobyl, Pripyat and the death of the city. *City* 14 (4), 371–389.

Dobscha, S. (2016) *Death in a Consumer Culture*. Routledge.

Doherty, T. and Clayton, S. (2011) The psychological impacts of global climate change. *American Psychologist* 6 (4), 265–76.

Doka, K.J. (2003) Memorialization, ritual and public tragedy. In M. Lattanzi-Licht and K.J. Doka (eds) *Living with Grief. Coping with Public Tragedy* (pp. 179–189). Hospice Foundation of America.

Dolby, T. (1845) *Memorials of the Highgate Cemetery, With Illustrations; and an Introductory Essay on Epitaphs and Gravestone Poetry*. Joseph Masters.

Domanovic, M. (2014) List of Kosovo War victims published. *Balkan Insight*. See https://balkaninsight.com/2014/12/10/kosovo-war-victims-list-published/ (accessed February 2023).

Douglas, K. (2020) Youth, trauma and memorialisation: The selfie as witnessing. *Memory Studies* 13 (4), 384–399.

Dove-Viebhan, A. (2007) Embodying hybridity, (en)gendering community: Captain Janeway and the enactment of a feminist heterotopia on Star Trek Voyager. *Women's Studies* 36 (8), 597–618.

Downie, J. (2022) November. From prohibition to permission: The winding road of medical assistance in dying in Canada. In Hec Forum (ed.) (pp. 1–34). Springer.

Doyle, A. (1926) *The History of Spiritualism*. Cassell and Company.

Dreimane, L.F. (2020) Virtual reality learning experience evaluation tool for instructional designers and educators. In L. Daniela (ed.) *New Perspectives on Virtual and Augmented Reality. Finding New Ways to Teach in a Transformed Learning Environment* (pp. 3–21). Routledge.

Dresler, E. and Fuchs, J. (2020) Constructing the moral geographies of educational dark tourism. *Journal of Marketing Management* 37 (5-6), 548–568.

Driessens, O. (2014) Theorizing celebrity cultures: Thickenings of media cultures and the role of cultural (working) memory. *Communications* 39 (2).

Drvenkar, N., Banožic, M. and Živic, D. (2015) Development of memorial tourism as a new concept – Possibilities and restrictions. *Tourism and Hospitality Management* 21 (1), 63–77.

Dufty, N. (2020) *Disaster Education, Communication and Engagement*. Wiley.

Duinker, P.N. and Greig, L.A. (2007) Scenario analysis in environmental impact assessment: Improving explorations of the future. *Environmental impact assessment review* 27 (3), 206–219.

Dunk, J. and Rugg, J. (1994) *The Management of Old Cemetery Land*. Shaw and Sons.

Dunkle, R. (2014) Overview of Roman spectacle. In P. Christesen and D.G. Kyle (eds) *A Companion to Sport and Spectacle in Greek and Roman Antiquity* (pp. 381–394). John Wiley and Sons, Inc.

Dunkley, R. (2015) Beyond temporal reflections in thanatourism research. *Annals of Tourism Research* 52, 177–179.

Dunkley, R. (2017) A light in dark places? Analysing the impact of dark tourism experiences on everyday life. In G. Hooper and J. Lennon (eds) *Dark Tourism: Practice and Interpretation* (pp. 108–120). Routledge.

Durán Muñoz, I. (2010) El español y su dimensión mediadora en el ámbito turístico. In L. González and P. Hernúñez (eds) *Actas del IV Congreso «El Español, Lengua de Traducción»: El español, lengua de traducción para la cooperación y el diálogo* (pp. 347–358). EsLetra.

Dwivedi, Y.K., Hughes, L.,Wang, Y., Alalwan, A.A., Ahn, S.J., Balakrishnana, J., Barta, S., Belk, R., Buhalis, D., Dutot, V., Felix, R., Fillieri, R., Flavian, C., Gustafsson, A., Hinsch, C., Hollensen, S., Jain, V., Kim,J., Krishen, A.S., Lartey. S., Pandey, N., Ribeiro-Navarrete, S., Raman, R., Rauschnabel, P.A., Sharma, A., Sigala, M., Veloutsou, C. and Wirtz, J. (2022) Metaverse marketing: How the metaverse will shape the future of consumer research and practice. *Psychology and Marketing* 40, 750–776.

Eaton, M.A. (2015) "Give us a sign of your presence": Paranormal investigation as a spiritual practice. *Sociology of Religion* 76 (4), 389–412.

Eaton, M.A. (2020) *Sensing Spirits: Paranormal Investigation and the Social Construction of Ghosts*. Routledge.

Ebbrecht-Hartmann, T. (2021) Commemorating from a distance: the digital transformation of Holocaust memory in times of COVID-19. *Media, Culture and Society* 43 (6), 1095–1112.

Eichert, D. (2019) "Homosexualization" revisited: An audience-focused theorization of wartime male sexual violence. *International Feminist Journal of Politics* 21 (3), 409–433.

Ekin, Y. and Akbulut, O. (2018) Battlefield Tourism: An examination of events held by European institutions and their websites related to battlefields. *International Journal of Contemporary Economics and Administrative Sciences* 8 (1), 73–123.

Elias, N. (1997) Towards a theory of social processes: A translation. *The British Journal of Sociology* 48 (3), 355–383.

ELIXIR AI. (2022) ELIXIR AI. See https://www.elixirforever.com/ (accessed September 2022).

Elsie, R. (2010) *Historical Dictionary of Kosovo*. Scarecrow Press.

Emanuel, P., Walper, S., DiEuliis, D., Klein, N., Petro, J.B. and Giordano, J. (2019) *Cyborg Soldier 2050: Human/Machine Fusion and the Implications for the Future of the DOD*. CCDC.

En Vols (2022) Two artists restore iconic historical monuments using only drones. See https://www.en-vols.com/en/inspirations-en/historical-monuments-drones-art (accessed November 2022).

Engelmann, S. (2021) Geopoetics: On organising, mourning, and the incalculable. *Dialogues in Human Geography* 11 (1), 31–35.

England and Wales Prisons (2023) Collection, prisons in England and Wales. See https://www.gov.uk/government/collections/prisons-in-england-and-wales (accessed April 2023).

Erll, A. (2011a) *Memory in Culture*. Palgrave Macmillan.
Erll, A. (2011b) Travelling memory. *Parallax* 17 (4), 4–18.
Erll, A., Nünning A. and Young, S.B. (2008) *Cultural Memory Studies: An International and Interdisciplinary Handbook*. Walter de Gruyter.
Ernst, J. (1991) Land for the living? The land use and conservation of urban cemeteries and churchyards. *Local Government Policy Making* 17 (4), 14–22.
Ertelt, S. (2012) Switzerland: Assisted suicide deaths up 700% in 11 years. See www.lifenews.com/2012/03/29/switzerland-assisted-suicide-deaths-up-700-in-11-years (accessed November 22).
Eternime (2022) Who wants to live forever? See https://eternime.breezy.hr/ (accessed September 2022).
European Commission (2018) Situation of young people in the European Union. See https://op.europa.eu/en/publication-detail/-publication/b6985c0c-743f-11e8-9483-01aa75ed71a1 (accessed November 2022).
European Parliament Committee on Legal Affairs (2017) Report with recommendations to the commission on civil law rules on robotics (No. 2015/2103(INL), See https://www.europarl.europa.eu/doceo/document/A-8-2017-0005_EN.html (accessed May 2023).
Evangelho, J. (2016) With "Chernobyl VR," The Farm 51 is building the history book of the future. See https://www.forbes.com/sites/jasonevangelho/2016/06/20/with-chernobyl-vr-the-farm-51-is- building-the-history-book-of-the-future (accessed January 2022).
Evans, R. (1982) The *Fabrication of Virtue*. Cambridge University Press.
Evans, G., Shaw, S., White, J. and Bohrer, J. (1999) Jubilee Line extension impact study: Visitor activity scoping report. See https://citeseerx.ist.psu.edu/viewdoc/download?doi=10.1.1.470.6380andrep=rep1andtype=pdf (accessed August 2022).
Fake a Vacation (n.d.) You could be here. See https://www.fakeavacation.com/ (accessed October 2022).
Faramelli, A., Hancock, D.W. and White, R.G. (2020) *Spaces of Crisis and Critique: Heterotopias Beyond Foucault*. Bloomsbury Publishing.
Farbotko, C. (2010) Wishful sinking: Disappearing islands, climate refugees and cosmopolitan experimentation. *Asia Pacific Viewpoint* 51 (1), 47–60.
Fassi, F., Mandelli, A., Teruggi, S., Rechichi, F., Fiorillo, F. and Achille, C. (2016) *VR for Cultural Heritage A VR-WEB-BIM for the Future Maintenance of Milan's Cathedral*. Springer International Publishing Switzerland.
Faulkner, B. (2001) Towards a framework for tourism disaster management. *Tourism Management* 22, 135–147.
Fawcus, R. (2022) The Buzludzha Memorial House and the precarious fate of communist monuments in post-communist space. Unpublished PhD thesis, University of Central Lancashire. See https://clok.uclan.ac.uk/45604
Feingold, L. (2017) Newseum guests can walk through streets of Berlin during Cold War with UMD team's help. *The Diamondback*. See https://dbknews.com/2017/09/27/virtual-reality-berlin-wall-newseum (accessed January 2022).
Ferguson, R. (2012) Death of an avatar: Implications of presence for learners and educators in virtual worlds. *Journal of Gaming and Virtual Worlds* 4 (2), 137–152.
Ferrer-Roca, N., Weston, R., Guia, J., Mihalic, T., Blasco, D., Prats, L., Lawler, M. and Jarratt, D. (2021) Back to the future: Challenges of European tourism of tomorrow. *Journal of Tourism Futures* 7 (2), 184–191.
Ferris, K. (2004) Seeing and being seen. *Journal of Contemporary Ethnography* 33 (3), 236–264.
Ferris, K. and Harris, S.R. (2011) *Stargazing: Celebrity, Fame, and Social Interaction*. Routledge.
Few, R., Marsh, H., Jain, G., Singh, C. and Tebboth, M.G.L. (2021) Representing recovery: How the construction and contestation of needs and priorities can shape long-term outcomes for disaster-affected people. *Progress in Development Studies* 21 (1), 7–25.

Fisher, E. (2010) Contemporary technology discourse and the legitimation of capitalism. *European Journal of Social Theory* 13 (2), 229–252.

Fisher, M. (2009) *Capitalist Realism: Is There No Alternative?* Zero Books.

Fisher, M. (2011) The truth about iconic 2003 Saddam statue-toppling. See https://www.theatlantic.com/international/archive/2011/01/the-truth-about-iconic-2003-saddam-statue-toppling/342802 (accessed January 2022).

Fisher, J.A. and Bolter, J.D. (2018) Ethical considerations for AR experiences at dark tourism sites. In 2018 IEEE International Symposium on Mixed and Augmented Reality Adjunct (ISMAR-Adjunct) In *2018 IEEE International Symposium on Mixed and Augmented Reality Adjunct (ISMAR-Adjunct)* (pp. 365-369). IEEE.

Fisherton Anger VCH Online (2019) Fisherton anger. See https://www.british-history.ac.uk/vch/wilts/vol6/pp180-194 (accessed April 2023).

Fletcher, J. (1966) *Situation Ethics: The New Morality*. SCM Press.

Fletcher, S. and McGowan, W. (2020) The state of the UK funeral industry. *Critical Social Policy* 41 (2), 249–269.

Fodor, G. (2022) Female representations and presences in Romanian First World War commemorative art. *Territorial Identity and Development* 7 (2), 29–53.

Foley, M. and Lennon, J.J. (1996a) Editorial: Heart of darkness. *International Journal of Heritage Studies* 2 (4), 198–211.

Foley, M. and Lennon, J.J. (1996b) JFK and dark tourism: A fascination with assassination. *International Journal of Heritage Studies* 2 (4), 198–211.

Foley, M. and Lennon, J.J. (1997) Dark tourism: An ethical dilemma. In M. Foley, J. Lennon and G. Maxwell (eds) *Hospitality, Tourism and Leisure Management* (pp. 153–164). Cassell.

Folkingham Landmark Trust (2023) The house of correction. See https://www.landmarktrust.org.uk/search-and-book/properties/house-of-correction-8655/#Overview (accessed April 2023).

Foote, K.E. and Azaryahu, M. (2007) Toward a geography of memory: Geographical dimensions of public memory and commemoration. *Journal of Political and Military Sociology, Summer 2007* 35 (1), 125–144.

Forest Lawn (2021) Court of David, Forest Lawn. See https://forestlawn.com/videos/court-of-david-english/ (accessed November 2022).

Forrest, A. and Devlin, K. (2023) AI could 'kill many humans' within two years, warns Sunak adviser. See https://www.independent.co.uk/news/uk/politics/ai-artificial-intelligence-kill-humans-sunak-b2352099.html (accessed June 2023).

Foucault, M. ((1966) 1970) *The Order of Things*. Tavistock.

Foucault, M. ((1967) 1984) Des espaces autres. Une conférence inédite de Michel Foucault. *Architecture, Mouvement, Continuite* 5, 46–49.

Foucault, M. (1981) *The History of Sexuality, Volume 1: An Introduction*. Penguin.

Foucault, M. (2007) *Security, Territory, Population: Lectures at the College de France, 1977-78*. Palgrave.

Foucault, M. (2008) Of other spaces (L. De Cauter and M. Dehaene, Trans.). In M. Dehaene and L. De Cauter (eds) *Heterotopia and the City: Public Space in a Postcivil Society* (pp. 13–29). Routledge.

Franck, K. and Stevens, Q. (2015) *Memorials as Spaces of Engagement: Design, Use and Meaning*. Routledge.

Franklin, A. (2007) The problem with tourism theory. In I. Altejvic, A. Pritchard and N. Morgan (eds) *The Critical Turn in Tourism Studies: Innovative Research Methodologies* (pp. 131–148). Elsevier.

Frew, E. (2018) Exhibiting death and disaster: Museological perspectives. In P.R. Stone, R. Hartmann, T. Seaton, R. Sharpley and L. White (eds) *The Palgrave Handbook of Dark Tourism Studies* (pp. 693–706). Palgrave Macmillan.

Friedrich, M. and Johnson, T. (2013) Beauty versus tragedy: Thanatourism and the memorialisation of the 1994 Rwandan genocide. *Journal of Tourism and Cultural Change* 11 (4), 302–320.

Friends of Tower Hamlets Cemetery Park (2022) *Heritage and Us: Unlocking the Hidden Heritage of Tower Hamlets Cemetery Park for the Wider Community*. Report to funder.

Fürsich, E. (2009) In defense of textual analysis. *Journalism Studies* 10 (2), 238–252.

Gabrielian, A. and Hirsch, A.B. (2018) Prosthetic landscapes: Place and placelessness in the digitization of memorials. *Journal of Historic Preservation, History, Theory, and Criticism* 15 (2), 113–131.

Gall, C. (1999) Serbs' killing of 40 Albanians ruled a crime against humanity. *The New York Times*. See https://www.nytimes.com/1999/03/18/world/serbs-killing-of-40-albanians-ruled-a-crime-against-humanity.html (accessed February 2023).

Garaus, M. and Hudáková, M. (2022) The impact of the COVID-19 pandemic on tourists' air travel intentions: The role of perceived health risk and trust in the airline. *Journal of Air Transport Management* 103, 102249.

García-Ramírez, G.M. (2016) Victim, P Victim, Perpetrator and Bystander P or and Bystander Perspectiv erspectives: Vatiations in atiations in Language Usage, Empathy and Violence Sensitivity, *Open Access Dissertations. Paper 489*.

Garton, A. (2022) How many people play Fortnite? Player count in 2022 *Dexerto*. See https://www.dexerto.com/fortnite/how-many-people-play-fortnite-player-count-1666278 (accessed November 2022).

Gavriely-Nuri, D. (2010) The idiosyncratic language of Israeli 'peace': A cultural approach to Critical Discourse Analysis (CCDA) *Discourse and Society* 21 (5), 565–585.

Gedi, N. and Elam, Y. (1996) Collective memory—what is it? *History and Memory* 8 (1), 30–50.

Gellers, J.C. (2020) *Rights for Robots: Artificial Intelligence, Animal and Environmental Law*. Routledge.

Genette, G. (1982) *Figures of Literary Discourse*. Columbia University Press.

Gensburger, S. (2016) Halbwachs' studies in collective memory: A founding text for contemporary 'memory studies'? *Journal of Classical Sociology* 16 (4), 396–413.

Gentleman, A. (2009) Inside the Dignitas house See https://www.theguardian.com/society/2009/nov/18/assisted-suicide-dignitas-house (accessed November 22).

Geonet (2022) Volcano – Whakaari/White Island, alert level. See https://www.geonet.org.nz/volcano/whiteisland (accessed November 2022).

Georgieva, M. (2017) 'The Berlin Wall VR experience', Digital bodies. See https://www.digitalbodies.net/vr-experience/the-berlin-wall- vr-experience (accessed January 2022).

Getz, D. (2008) Event tourism: Definition, evolution and research. *Tourism Management* 29, 403–428.

Gibbons, S. (2018) Empathy mapping: The first step in design thinking. *Nielsen Norman Group*, See https://www.nngroup.com/articles/empathy-mapping/ (accessed February 2022).

Gibson, M. (2007) Death and mourning in technologically mediated culture. *Health Sociology Review* 16 (5), 415–424.

Giddens, A. (1987) *Social Theory and Modern Sociology*. Polity.

Giddens, A. (1990) *The Consequences of Modernity*. Polity.

Giddens, A. (1991) *Modernity and Self-Identity: Self and Society in the Late Modern Age*. Polity.

Giddens, A. (1992) *The Transformation of Intimacy: Sexuality, Love and Eroticism in Modern Societies*. Polity.

Girvan, C. (2018) What is a virtual world? Definition and classification. *Education Tech Research Dev* 66, 1087–1100.

GlobalNews. (2020) Virtual reality "reunites" mother with dead daughter in South Korean doc. See https://www.youtube.com/watch?v=0p8HZVCZSkc (accessed October 2022).

Godfrey, R. and Lilley, S. (2009) Visual consumption, collective memory and the representation of war. *Consumption Markets and Culture* 12 (4), 275–300.

Goffman, E. (1959) *The Presentation of Self in Everyday Life*. Doubleday.

Goffman, E. (1971) *Relations in Public*. Anchor Books.
Goffman, E. (1974) *Frame Analysis: An Essay on the Organization of Experience*. Harper and Row.
Goldfield, A. (2021) Five human species you may not know about. See https://www.sapiens.org/archaeology/ancient-human-species/ (accessed May 2023).
Goleman, D. and Boyatzis, R. (2008) Social intelligence and the biology of leadership. *Harvard Business Review* 86 (9), 74–81.
Golz, L. (2021) The show must go on(line) - Social media marketing during a pandemic: the case of two Dracula themed dark tourism festivals. *Journal of Dracula Studies* 23, 76–107.
Golz, L. (2022) Co-creation of experiences at dark tourism festivals. *International Conference on Tourism Research* (pp. 584–587).
González-Tennant, E. (2013) New heritage and dark tourism: A mixed methods approach to social justice in Rosewood, Florida. *Heritage and Society* 6 (1), 62–88.
Goodson, I.F. and Gill, S.R. (2011) The narrative turn in social research. *Counterpoints* 386, 17–33.
Goodson, L. and Phillimore, J. (2004) The inquiry paradigm in qualitative tourism research. In J. Phillimore and L. Goodson (eds) *Qualitative Research in Tourism: Ontologies, Epistemologies and Methodologies* (pp. 30–45). Routledge.
Google Trends (2023) Goggle trends. See https://trends.google.com/ (accessed January 2023).
Gordon, J. (2003) Hybridity, heterotopia and mateship in China Miéville's 'Perdido Street station'. *Science Fiction Studies* 30 (3), 456–476.
Goslin, M. and Morie, J.F. (1996) *Virtopia*: Emotional experiences in virtual environments. *LEONARDO* 29 (2), 95–100.
Gotham, K.F. and Krier, D.A. (2008) From the culture industry to the Society of the Spectacle: Critical Theory and the situationist international. *Current Perspectives in Social Theory* 25, 155–192.
Grabalov, P. and Nordh, H. (2021) The future of urban cemeteries as public spaces – insights from Oslo and Copenhagen. *Planning Theory and Practice* 23 (1), 81–98.
Graburn, N.H. (1983) The anthropology of tourism. *Annals of Tourism Tesearch* 10 (1), 9–33.
Graburn, N.H. (2004) Secular ritual: A general theory of tourism. In S. Gmelch and A. Kaul (eds) *Tourists and Tourism: A Reader* (pp. 23–34). Waveland Press.
Graburn, N. (2017) Key figure of mobility: The tourist. *Social Anthropology* 25 (1), 83–96.
Grandfield, Y. (1989) The holiday diary of Thomas Lott: 12-22 July, 1815. *Archaeologia Cantiana* 107, 63–82.
Granic, I., Lobel, A. and Engels, R.C.M.E. (2014) The benefits of playing video games. *American Psychologist* 69 (1), 66–78.
Grau, O. (2003) *Virtual Art: From Illusion to Immersion*. MIT Press.
Grbin, M. (2015) Foucault and space. Социолошки преглед XLIX (3), 305–312.
Greater London Authority. (2016) The London plan 2016. See https://www.london.gov.uk/programmes-strategies/planning/london-plan/past-versions-and-alterations-london-plan/london-plan-2016/london-plan-2016-pdf (accessed November 2022).
Grebenar, A. (2018) The commodification of dark tourism: Conceptualising the visitor experience. Unpublished PhD thesis, University of Central Lancashire. See https://clok.uclan.ac.uk/23361/?template=default_internal (accessed March 2023).
Gren, M. and Huijbens, E.H. (2019) Tourism geography in and of the Anthropocene. In D.K. Müller (ed.) *A Research Agenda for Tourism Geographies* (pp. 117–127). Edward Edgar Publishing.
Griffiths, C. (2019) Encountering Auschwitz: Touring the Auschwitz-Birkenau state museum. *Holocaust Studies* 25 (1–2), 182–200.
Grinsted, T.P. (1857a) *Norwood Cemetery: A Descriptive Sketch*. G. Hill.
Grinsted, T.P. (1857b) *Last Home of Departed Genius: With Biographical Sketches of Poets, Painters, and Players*. G Routledge and Sons.

Guarrasi, V. (2001) Paradoxes of modern and postmodern geography: Heterotopia of landscape and cartographic logic. In C. Minca (ed.) *Postmodern Geography* (pp. 226–237). Blackwell.
Gunkel, D.J. (2018) *Robot Rights*. The MIT Press.
Gupta, N. and Mangla, R. (2020) *Artificial Intelligence Basics*. Mercury Learning and Information.
Guttentag, D.A. (2010) Virtual reality: Applications and implications for tourism. *Tourism Management* 31 (5), 637–651.
Hackney Council (2018) Abney park user survey report: Consultation report, Hackney Council. See https://consultation.hackney.gov.uk/leisure-parks-green-spaces/abney-park-improvements/results/abneyparkusersurveyreport.pdf (accessed September 2022).
Haesen, S. (2018) How people travelling abroad to die came to be called "death tourists", and why they shouldn't. *Journal of Social Work in End of Life and Palliative Care* 14 (4), 244–247.
Hagen, L. (2022) Antisemitism is on the rise and it's not just about Ye. *NPR*. See https://www.npr.org/2022/11/30/1139971241/anti-semitism-is-on-the-rise-and-not-just-among-high-profile-figures (accessed December 2022).
Hajibaba, H., Gretzel, U., Leisch, F. and Dolnicar, S. (2015) Crisis-resistant tourists. *Annals of Tourism Research* 53, 46–60.
Halbwachs, M. (1992) *On Collective Memory*. University of Chicago Press.
Hallevy, G. (2013) *When Robots Kill. Artificial Intelligence Under Criminal Law*. Northeastern University Press.
Hallqvist, J. (2018) Negotiating humanity: Anthropomorphic robots in the Swedish television series Real Humans. *Science Fiction Film and Television* 11 (3), 449–467.
Hamilton, S., Golding, B. and Ribbens McCarthy, J. (2022) Do we need to decolonise bereavement studies? *Bereavement: Journal of Grief and Responses to Death* 1, 1–7.
Hammermann, G. (2014) Was können Gedenkstätten leisten: Chancen und Grenzen von Gedenkstättenbesuchen. In H. Roth (ed.) *Was hat der Holocaust mit mir zu tun? 37 Antworten* (pp. 206–211). Pantheon Verlag.
Hand, R.J and Wilson, M. (2000) The Grand-Guignol: Aspects of theory and practice. *Theatre Research International* 25 (3), 266–275.
Handmer, J., Van der Merwe, M. and O'Neill, S. (2019) The risk of dying in bushfires: A comparative analysis of fatalities and survivors. *Progress in Disaster Science* 1, 1–9.
Hanson Robotics (2018) Sophia. See https://www.hansonrobotics.com/sophia/ (accessed May 2023).
Harari, Y.N. (2015) *Homo Deus: A Brief History of Tomorrow*. Penguin.
Harris, J. and Anthis, J.R. (2021) The moral consideration of artificial entities: A literature review. See http://arxiv.org/abs/2102.04215 (accessed May 2023).
Harris, R. (2019) Inside the daring mission to recover the dead from White Island. See, https://www.smh.com.au/world/oceania/inside-the-daring-mission-to-recover-the-dead-from-white-island-20191213-p53jqt.html (accessed November 2022).
Harrison, M. (2023) AI tasked with destroying humanity now trying new tactic. See https://futurism.com/ai-destroying-humanity-new-tactic (accessed May 2023).
Hartmann, R. (2014) Dark tourism, thanatourism, and dissonance in heritage tourism management: New directions in contemporary tourism research. *Journal of Heritage Tourism* 9 (2), 166–182.
Hartmann, R. (2018) Tourism to memorial sites of the Holocaust. In P.R. Stone, R. Hartmann, T. Seaton, R. Sharpley and L. White (eds) *The Palgrave Handbook of Dark Tourism Studies* (pp. 469–507). Palgrave Macmillan.
Hartmann, R., Lennon, J., Reynolds, D.P., Rice, A., Rosenbaum, A.T. and Stone, P.R. (2018) The history of dark tourism. *Journal of Tourism History* 10 (3), 269–295.
Harvey, D. (2000a) *Spaces of Hope*. Edinburgh University Press.
Harvey, D. (2000b) Cosmopolitanism and the banality of geographical evils. *Public Culture* 12 (2), 529–564.

Harvey, D. (2007) The Kantian roots of Foucault's dilemma. In J.W. Crampton and S. Elden (eds) *Space, Knowledge, and Power* (pp. 41–47). Ashgate.

Harvey, D. (2009) *Cosmopolitanism and the Geographies of Freedom*. Columbia University Press.

Hassapopoulou, M. (2018) Playing with history: Collective memory, national trauma and dark tourism in virtual reality docugames. *New Review of Film and Television Studies* 16 (4), 365–392.

Hausmair, B. (2018) Identity destruction or survival in small things? Rethinking prisoner tags from the Mauthausen concentration camp. *International Journal of Historical Archaeology* 22 (3), 472–491.

Haxhijaj, S. (2018) *Balkan Insight*. See https://balkaninsight.com/author/serbeze-hadiaj/?lang=sr (accessed March 2024).

Haxhiaj, F.R., Serbeze. (2018) Kosovo's Panda Café massacre mystery unsolved 20 years on. *Balkan Insight*. See https://balkaninsight.com/2018/12/14/kosovo-s-panda-caf%C3%A9-massacre-mystery-unsolved-20-years-on-12-13-2018/ (accessed July 2023).

Haynes, N.C. and Egan, D. (2019) The implications of 'miniatourism' for urban tourism destination futures–from micropubs to microbars. *Journal of Tourism Futures* 7 (2), 226–231.

Hellsten, S.K. (2012) The meaning of life during a transition from modernity to transhumanism and posthumanity. *Journal of Anthropology* 1, 1–8.

Helm, B.W. (2002) Felt evaluations: A theory of pleasure and pain. *American Philosophical Quarterly* 39 (1), 13–30.

Henig, L. and Ebbrecht-Hartmann, T. (2022) Witnessing Eva stories: Media witnessing and self-inscription in social media memory. *New Media and Society* 1, 202–226.

Herrera-Sobek, M. (2012) *Celebrating Latino Folklore: An Encyclopedia of Cultural Traditions*. ABC-CLIO.

Herrman, J. and Browning, K. Are we in the metaverse yet? *The New York Times*, 29 Oct. See https://www.nytimes.com/2021/07/10/style/metaverse-virtual-worlds.html (accessed January 2023).

Herva, V.-P., Varnajot, A. and Pashkevich, A. (2020) Bad Santa: cultural heritage, mystification of the Arctic, and tourism as an extractive industry. *The Polar Journal* 10 (2), 375–396.

Hess, A. (2007) In digital remembrance: Vernacular memory and the rhetorical construction of web memorials. *Media, Culture and Society* 29 (5), 812–830.

Hetherington, K. (1997) *The Badlands of Modernity: Heterotopia and Social Ordering*. Routledge.

Heuermann, K. and Chhabra, D. (2014) The darker side of dark tourism: An authenticity perspective. *Tourism Analysis* 19 (2), 213–225.

Hinde, R.S.E. (1951) *The British Penal System*. Gerald Duckworth and Co Ltd.

Hintz, C. (2020) Chernobyl, Centralia, Paris Catacombs and more strange places you can explore virtually. *Cult of Weird*, See https://www.cultofweird.com/travel/10-strange-places-you-can-explore-virtually (accessed January 2022).

Hirsch, M. (2008) The generation of postmemory. *Poetics Today* 29 (1), 103–128.

Hirsch, M. (2012) *The Generation of Postmemory: Writing and Visual Culture after the Holocaust*. Columbia University Press.

Historic England (n.d.) The National Heritage List for England (NHLE) search engine. See https://historicengland.org.uk/listing/the-list/ (accessed November 2022).

Hitchcock, A. (1972) *Masters of Cinema* (Interview) 1972.

Hjort, J., Karjalainen, O., Aalto, J., Westermann, S., Romanovsky, V.E., Nelson, F.E., Etzelmüller, B. and Luoto, M. (2018) Degrading permafrost puts Arctic infrastructure at risk by mid-century. *Nature Communications* 9 (1), 1–9.

Hjorth, D. (2005) Organizational entrepreneurship. *Journal of Management Inquiry* 14 (4), 386–398.

HMP Holloway Site Development (2023) Council defers decision on AHMM's controversial Holloway Prison plans. See https://www.architectsjournal.co.uk/news/ahmm-holloway-prison-plans-deferred (accessed April 2023).

HMP Hull Open Day (2022) H.M. Prison Hull. See https://www.heritageopendays.org.uk/visiting/event/within-these-walls-an-exhibition-illustrating-the-history-of-h.m.-prison-hu (accessed August 2022).

Hodalska, M. (2017) Selfies at horror sites: dark tourism, ghoulish souvenirs and digital narcissism. *Zeszyty Prasoznawcze* 60 (2), 405–423.

Hodgkinson, S. (2015) Rethinking Holocaust representation: Reflections on Rex Bloomstein's KZ. *The Howard Journal of Criminal Justice* 54 (5), 451–468.

Hodgkinson, S. and Urquhart, D. (2019) Prison tourism - Exploring the spectacle of punishment in the UK. In G. Hooper and J.J. Lennon (eds) *Dark Tourism Practice and Interpretation* (pp. 40–54). Routledge.

Hodkinson, P. (2002) *Goth. Identity, Style and Subculture.* Berg Publishers.

Hoerner, J.M., Jaax, A. and Rodon, T. (2019) The long-term impact of the location of concentration camps on radical-right voting in Germany. *Research and Politics* 6 (4), 1–8.

Hoffner, C.A. and Levine, K.J. (2005) Enjoyment of mediated fright and violence: A meta-analysis. *Media Psychology* 7 (2), 207–237.

Holdaway, D. and Trentin, F. (2014) Roman fever: Anarchiving Eternal Rome, from roman holiday to petrolio. *Journal of Romance Studies* 14 (3).

Hollensen, S., Kotler, P. and Opresnik, M.O. (2023) Metaverse: the new marketing universe. *Journal of Business Strategy* 44 (3), 119–125.

Hollywood Forever (2021) Hollywood Forever Cemetery: Funeral and cremation services in Hollywood. See https://hollywoodforever.com/ (accessed November 2022).

Hon, A. (2016) VR will break museums. *Medium.* See https://medium.com/@adrianhon/vr-will-break-museums-794bfaa78ce4 (accessed January 2022).

Hooper, G. and Lennon, J. (2016) *Dark Tourism.* Routledge.

Horsley Prison History (2023) Horsley House of Correction. See https://www.prisonhistory.org/prison/horsley-house-of-correction/ (accessed April 2023).

Hoskins, A. (2003) Signs of the Holocaust: Exhibiting memory in a mediated age. *Media, Culture and Society* 25 (1), 7–22.

Howard, J. (1777) *The State of the Prisons in England and Wales.* Warrington.

Howe, C. (2020) Melt in the future subjunctive. In O. Angé and D. Berliner (eds) *Ecological Nostalgias: Memory, Affect and Creativity in Times of Ecological Upheavals* (pp. 166–177). Berghahn Books.

Howe, C. (2022) To melt away: Abstractive sensations in ice. In A. Mason (ed.) *Arctic Abstractive Industry: Assembling the Valuable and Vulnerable North* (pp. 27–44). Berghahn Books.

Hughes, K. (2013) Measuring the impact of viewing wildlife: Do positive intentions equate to long-term changes in conservation behaviour? *Journal of Sustainable Tourism* 21 (1), 42–59.

Huijbens, E.H. (2021) The emerging earths of climatic emergencies: On the island geography of life in modernity's ruins. *Geografiska Annaler: Series B, Human Geography* 103 (2), 88–102.

Hull, F. (1966) A Kentish holiday, 1823. *Archaeologia Cantiana* 81, 109–117, 111–113.

Hurtado, J.H. (2023) Towards a postmortal society of virtualised ancestors? The Virtual Deceased Person and the preservation of the social bond. *Mortality* 28 (1), 90–105.

Huspi Projects Portfolio (2022) Chornobyl mobile AR app. See https://huspi.com/portfolio/chorno byl -app-ar-mobile-app/ (accessed October 2022).

Hyland, K. (2005) Stance and engagement: A model of interaction in academic discourse. *Discourse Studies* 7 (2), 173–192.

ICOM (2014) *The Siena Charter.* rep. Siena, Italy: ICOM, pp. 1–5.

ICOMOS (2008) The ICOMOS Charter for the Interpretation and Presentation of Cultural Heritage Sites (Ename Charter). See https://www.icomos.org/en/resources/charters-and-texts (accessed June 2023).

ICTY (Online) (1999) United Nations International Criminal Tribunal for the former Yugoslavia. See www.icty.org (accessed March 2024).

Ide, A. (2015) ICT and dark tourism. See http://agrilife.org/ertr/files/2015/02/SP04_MktSession_Ide.pdf (accessed October 2022).

Iliev, D. (2021) Consumption, motivation and experience in dark tourism: A conceptual and critical analysis. *Tourism Geographies* 23 (5-6), 963–984.

Inayatullah, S. (2008) Six pillars: Futures thinking for transforming. *Foresight* 10 (1), 4–21.

Inayatullah, S. (2013) Futures studies: Theories and methods. In R.F. Al-Rodhan (ed.) *There's a Future: Visions for a Better World* (pp. 37–66). BBVA.

Inkpen, D. (2022) Ever higher: The mountain cryosphere. In K. Dodds and S. Sörlin (eds) *Ice Humanities: Living, Working and Thinking in a Melting World* (pp. 72–88). Manchester University Press.

International Coalition of Sites of Conscience (ICSC) (2018) Interpretation of sites of memory. See www.sitesofconscience.org/interpretation-of-sites-of-memory/ (accessed September 2022).

Invernizzi-Accetti, C. (2017) A small Italian town can teach the world how to defuse controversial monuments. See https://www.theguardian.com/commentisfree/2017/dec/06/bolzano-italian-town-defuse- controversial-monuments (accessed January 2022).

IPCC (2019) *IPCC Special Report on the Ocean and Cryosphere in a Changing Climate.* Cambridge University Press.

Ironside, R. (2018) The allure of dark tourism: Legend tripping and ghost seeking in dark places. In D.D. Waskul and M. Eaton (eds) *The Supernatural in Society, Culture and History* (pp. 95–115). Temple University Press.

Isaac, R.K. and Ashworth, G.J. (2011) Moving from pilgrimage to "dark" tourism: Leveraging tourism in Palestine. *Tourism Culture and Communication* 11 (3), 149–164.

Isaac, R.K. and Çakmak, E. (2014) Understanding visitor's motivation at sites of death and disaster: The case of former transit camp Westerbork, the Netherlands. *Current Issues in Tourism* 17 (2), 164–179.

Isaac, R.K. and Çakmak, E. (2016) Understanding the motivations and emotions of visitors at Tuol Sleng Genocide Prison Museum (S-21) in Phnom Penh, Cambodia. *International Journal of Tourism Cities* 2 (3), 232–247.

Isufi, P. (2019) Serbian President accused of spreading hate by denying massacre. *Balkan Insight*. See https://balkaninsight.com/2019/12/06/serbian-president-accused-of-spreading-hate-by-denying-massacre/ (accessed February 2023).

Ivanova, P. and Light, D. (2018) 'It's not that we like death or anything': Exploring the motivations and experiences of visitors to a lighter dark tourism attraction. *Journal of Heritage Tourism* 13 (4), 356–369.

Jackson, M. (2015) Glaciers and climate change: Narratives of ruined futures. *Wiley Interdisciplinary Reviews: Climate Change* 6 (5), 479–492.

Jacobs, K. (2004) Pornography in small places and other spaces. *Cultural Studies* 18, 67–83.

Jacobsen, M.H. (2016) 'Spectacular death' – proposing a new fifth phase to Philippe Ariès's admirable history of death'. *Humanities* 5 (19), 1–20.

Jacobson, M.H. (2018) *The Age of Spectacular Death*. Routledge.

Jacobsen, M.H. (2022) Contemplating a career in death and dying – An interview with Tony Walter. *Mortality* 27 (2), 228–253.

Jahanian, M. (2017) Futures studies of tourism with a spirituality perspective. *International Journal of Tourism and Spirituality* 42 (1), 24–39.

James Thomson, Oxford Dictionary of National Biography (2008) Thomson, James. See https://doi.org/10.1093/ref:odnb/27306 (accessed April 2023).

Jane Austen Letter (2011) My dearest Cassandra. See https://pemberley.com/janeinfo/brablt12.html#letter69 (accessed April 2023).

Jarratt, D., Phelan, C., Wain, J. and Dale, S. (2018) Developing a sense of place toolkit: Identifying destination uniqueness. *Tourism and Hospitality Research* 19 (4), 408–421.

Jenkins, I. (2019) *Adventure Tourism and Outdoor Activities Management: A 21st Century Toolkit*. CABI.

Johnson, P. (2008) The modern cemetery: A design for life. *Social and Cultural Geography* 9 (7), 777–790.

Johnson, P. (2013) The geographies of Heterotopia. *Geography Compass* 7 (11), 790–803.

Jones, T. (1994) Living history or undying racism? Colonial Williamsburg 'slave auction' draws protest, support. See https://www.washingtonpost.com/archive/politics/1994/10/11/living-history-or-undying-racism-colonial-williamsburg-slave-auction-draws-protest-support/5a6ec396-e6f8-4a71-a185-8ece86afa166/ (accessed March 2023).

Jordan, E.J. and Prayag, G. (2021) Residents' cognitive appraisals, emotions, and coping strategies at local dark tourism sites. *Journal of Travel Research* 61 (4), 887–902.

Jordan, J.M. (2016) *Robots*. The MIP Press Essential Knowledge Series.

Jorden, R. (2021) How long before Covid tours become part of the dark tourism trend? *Skift*. See https://skift.com/2021/09/15/how-long-before-covid-tours-become-part-of-the-dark-tourism-trend/ (accessed March 2023).

Joyce, P (2003) *The Rule of Freedom*. Verso.

Justyne, W. (1865) *Guide to Highgate Cemetery*. Moore.

Kalfas, D., Chatzitheodoridis, F., Loizou, E. and Melfou, K. (2022) Willingness to pay for urban and suburban green. *Sustainability* 14 (4), 23–32.

Kamenev, M. (2022) How Russia took over Chernobyl. *Open Democracy*, See https://www.opendemocracy.net/en/odr/chernobyl-russian-occupation-nuclear-radiation-effects (accessed April 2023).

Kaminsky, A. (2014) Memory, postmemory, prosthetic memory: Reflections on the Holocaust and the dirty war in Argentine narrative. See https://conservancy.umn.edu/bitstream/handle/11299/184474/hiol_14_06_kaminsky_memory_postmemory_prosthetic_memory.pdf?sequence=1andisAllowed=y (accessed December 2022).

Kansteiner, W. (2017) Transnational Holocaust memory, digital culture and the end of reception studies. In T.S. Andersen and B. Törnquist-Plewa (eds) *The Twentieth Century in European Memory: Transcultural Mediation and Reception* (pp. 305–344). Brill.

Kaplan, A. (2012) *Dracula: The Life of Vlad the Impaler*. The Rosen Publishing Group, Inc.

Kaplan, J. (2015) *Humans Need Not Apply*. Yale University Press.

Karl, M., Muskat, B. and Ritchie, B.W. (2020) Which travel risks are more salient for destination choice? An examination of the tourist's decision-making process. *Journal of Destination Marketing and Management* 18, 100–487.

Kaul, A. and Skinner, J. (2018) *Leisure and Death*. University Press of Colorado.

Keil, C. (2005) Sightseeing in the mansions of the dead. *Social and Cultural Geography* 6 (4), 479–494.

Kellehear, A. (2005) *Compassionate Cities: Public Health and End-of-Life Care*. Routledge.

Kelly, J. (2016) Asymmetrical itineraries: Militarism, tourism and solidarity on occupied Palestine. *American Quarterly* 68 (3), 723–745.

Kendi, I.X. (2019) *How to be an Antiracist*. One World.

Kendrick, W.M. (1991) *The Thrill of Fear: 250 Years of Scary Entertainment*. Grove Weidenfeld.

Kennedy, T.M. (2022) Mapping "memoryscapes": Reconfiguring the theoretical terrain of rhetoric and memory. *Journal of Advanced Composition* 33 (3/4), 763–781.

Kern, K. (2008) Heterotopia of the theme park street. In M. Dehaene and L. De Cauter (eds) *Heterotopia and the City* (pp. 104–116). Routledge.

Kerr, M.M., Stone, P.R. and Price, R.H. (2023) *Children, Young People and Dark Tourism*. Routledge.

Kılıçlar, A., Küçükergin, F.N., Kurt, S., Adıgüzel, B., Özkan, B. and Aktuna, H. (2017) One way ticket-route to death: How right is to promote as a commercial initiative? *Journal of Business Research-Türk* 84–105.

Killick, D. (2015) Do we need to spend $11m on a memorial? See https://www.stuff.co.nz/the-press/opinion/66921130/do-we-need-to-spend-11m-on-a-memorial (accessed November 2022).

Kim, S. and Butler, G. (2015) Local community perspectives towards dark tourism development: The case of Snowtown, South Australia. *Journal of Tourism and Cultural Change* 13 (1), 78–89.

Kim, S.S. and Prideaux, B. (2003) Tourism, peace, politics and ideology: Impacts of the Mt. Gumgang tour project in the Korean Peninsula. *Tourism Management* 24 (6), 675–685.

King, B. (2017) *Augmented-Artırılmış Gerçeklik*. Mediacat Publishing.

Kirshenblatt-Gimblett, B. (1984) *Destination Culture: Tourism, Museums and Heritage*. University of California Press.

Klaassens, M., Groote, P.D. and Vanclay, F.M. (2013) Expressions of private mourning in public space: The evolving structure of spontaneous and permanent roadside memorials in the Netherlands. *Death Studies* 37 (2), 145–171.

Klastrup, L. (2006) Death Matters: Understanding Gameworld Experiences. ACE '06, Proceedings of the 2006 ACM SIGCHI *International Conference on Advances in Computer Entertainment Technology*, June, pp.29-es. See https://dl.acm.org/doi/10.1145/1178823.1178859 (accessed February 2023).

Klein, C. (2014) The penumbral theory of masochistic pleasure. *Review of Philosophy and Psychology* 5 (1), 41–55.

Kneese, T. (2014) QR codes for the dead: Graveyards are becoming smart places, but will today's technology last for eternity? *The Atlantic*. See https://www.theatlantic.com/technology/archive/2014/05/qr-codes-for-the-dead/370901/ (accessed March 2023).

Knudsen, T.B. (2011) Thanatourism: Witnessing difficult pasts. *Tourist Studies* 11 (1), 55–72.

Kondori, M. (2005) Aztecs' heavens and hells. *Journal of the Humanities* 14 (50), 135–142.

Koohang, A. *et al.* (2023) Shaping the metaverse into reality: Multidisciplinary perspectives on opportunities, challenges and future research. *Journal of Computer Information Systems*. See https://www.academia.edu/94457087 (accessed January 2023).

Korstanje, M.E. (2017) *The Rise of Thana-capitalism and Tourism*. Routledge.

Korstanje, M.E. and Baker, D. (2018) Politics of dark tourism: The case of Cromanon and ESMA, Buenos Aires, Argentina. In P.R. Stone, R. Hartmann, T. Seaton, R. Sharpley and L. White (eds) *The Palgrave Handbook of Dark Tourism Studies* (pp. 533–552). Palgrave Macmillan.

Korstanje, M.E. and George, B. (2015) Dark tourism: Revisiting some philosophical issues. *e-Review of Tourism Research* 12 (1/2), 127–137.

Korstanje, M. and George, B. (2017) Virtual traumascapes and exploring the roots of dark tourism. *IGI Global (Advances in Hospitality, Tourism and the Services Industry* (pp. 2475–6547).

Korstanje, M.E. and Handayani, B. (2020) Virtual dark tourism: The role of sound branding and augmented reality for death sites. In G. Pavlidis (ed.) *Applying Innovative Technologies in Heritage Science* (pp. 231–249). IGI Global.

Korstanje, M.E. and Ivanov, S.H. (2012) Tourism as a form of new psychological resilience: The inception of dark tourism. *CULTUr-revista de Cultura e Turismo* 6 (4), 56–71.

Korstanje, M.E and Olsen, D. (2019) Negotiating the intersection between dark tourism and pilgrimage. In D. Olsen and M. Korstanje (eds) *Dark Tourism and Pilgrimage* (pp. 1–15). CABI.

Kounavis, C.D., Kasimati, A.E. and Zamani, E.D. (2012) Enhancing the tourism experience through mobile augmented reality: Challenges and prospects. *International Journal of Engineering Business Management* 4, 1–6.

Kraken (2023) What is Decentraland? The beginner's guide. *Kraken*, See https://www.kraken.com/en-gb/learn/what-is-decentraland-mana (accessed January 2023).
Krisjanous, J. (2016) An exploratory multimodal discourse analysis of dark tourism websites: Communicating issues around contested sites. *Journal of Destination Marketing and Management* 5 (4), 341–350.
Krisjanous, J. and Carruthers, J. (2018) Walking on the light side: Investigating the world of ghost tour operators and entrepreneurial marketing. *Qualitative Market Research: An International Journal* 21 (2), 232–252.
Kübler-Ross, E. (1970) *On Death and Dying*. Macmillan.
Kucia, M. (2016) The Europeanization of Holocaust memory and Eastern Europe. *East European Politics and Societies* 30 (01), 97–119.
Kuhn, T. (2012/1962) *The Structure of Scientific Revolutions, 50th Anniversary Edition*. University of Chicago Press.
Kullstroem, C. (2017) *Drawn to the Dark: Exploration in Scare Tourism Around the World*. Pelican.
Kult Plus (2018) Kompleksi "Adem Jashari" me mbi 12 milion vizitorë. *KultPlus*. See https://www.kultplus.com/trashegimia/35820/ (accessed February 2023).
Kusenbach, M. (2003) Street phenomenology: The go-along as ethnographic research tool. *Ethnography* 4 (3), 455–485.
Lagos, E., Harris, A. and Sigala, M. (2015) Emotional language for image formation and market segmentation in dark tourism destinations: Findings from tour operators' websites promoting Gallipoli. *Tourismos* 10 (2), 153–170.
Laing, J. and Frost, W. (2016) In dark tourism and dark events: A journey to positive resolution and well-being. In S. Filep, J. Laing and M. Csikszentmihalyi (eds) *Positive Tourism* (pp. 82–99). Routledge.
Lam, A. and Tegelberg, M. (2020) Dark tourism in iceberg alley: The hidden ecological costs of consuming iceberg deaths. In A. Lam and M. Tegelberg (eds) *Criminal Anthroposcenes: Media and Crime in the Vanishing Arctic* (pp. 145–187). Palgrave.
Lancaster Castle (2023) This is Lancaster castle. See https://www.lancastercastle.com/ (accessed April 2023).
Lancashire Police Museum (2023) Welcome To Lancashire Police Museum. See https://www.lancashirepolicemuseum.co.uk/ (accessed April 2023).
Landsberg, A. (1995) Prosthetic memory: Total recall and blade runner. *Body and Society* 1 (3–4), 175–189.
Landsberg, A. (2004) *Prosthetic Memory: The Transformation of American Remembrance in the Age of Mass Culture*. Columbia University Press.
Larson, Z. (2022) Tourism gets a refresh in the hands of activists seeking to decolonize the industry. Smithsonian Magazine. See https://www.smithsonianmag.com/travel/tourism-gets-refresh-in-hands-activists-seeking-to-decolonize-industry-180979739/ (accessed March 2023).
Latour, B. (2014) Agency at the time of the anthropocene. *New Literary History* 45 (1), 1–18.
Lawford's Gate GRO Catalogue (n.d.) County gaol and houses of correction. See https://catalogue.gloucestershire.gov.uk/records/Q/8 (accessed April 2023).
Lawford's Gate Prison History (2023) Lawford's Gate house of correction. See https://www.prisonhistory.org/prison/lawfords-gate-house-of-correction/ (accessed April 2023).
Lawton, J. (2000) *The Dying Process*. Routledge.
Leane, E. (2022) Cryonnarratives for warming times: Icebergs as planetary travellers. In K. Dodds and S. Sorlin (eds) *Ice Humanities: Living, Working and Thinking in a Melting World* (pp. 250–265). Manchester University Press.
Lefebvre, H. (1991) *The Production of Space*. Blackwell.
Lehrer, E., Milton, C.E. and Patterson, M.E. (2011) *Curating Difficult Knowledge: Violent Pasts in Public Places*. Palgrave Macmillan UK.
Lellio, A.D. and Schwandner-Sievers, S. (2006) The legendary commander: The construction of an Albanian master-narrative in post-war Kosovo. *Nations and Nationalism* 12 (3), 513–529.

Lennon, J. (2017) Dark tourism. *Oxford Research Encyclopedia of Criminology and Criminal Justice* 1–41.

Lennon, J. and Foley, M. (1999) Interpretation of the unimaginable: The U.S. Holocaust Memorial Museum, Washington, D.C. and 'dark tourism.' *Journal of Travel Research* 38 (1), 46–50.

Lennon, J. and Foley, M. (2000) *Dark Tourism: The Attraction of Death and Disaster.* Continuum.

Lennon, J.J. and Tiberghien, G. (2020) Kazakhstan Gulag heritage: Dark tourism and selective interpretation. *International Journal of Tourism Research* 22 (3), 364–374.

Lenskis, I. (2017) *Holocaust Commemoration in Latvia in the Course of Time 1945–2015.* Museum 'Jews in Latvia'.

Leotta, A. (2022) Virtual tourism in the age of COVID-19: A case study of the Faroe Islands' 'remote tourism' campaign. In D. Bonelli and A. Leotta (eds) *Audiovisual Tourism Promotion: A Critical Overview* (pp. 107–125). Palgrave Macmillan.

LETA (2022) Landscape preparations start in Riga to commence Soviet Victory Monument's removal. *Baltic News Network.* See https://bnn-news.com/landscape-preparations-start-in-riga-to-commence-soviet-victory-monuments-removal-237407 (accessed November 2022).

Levey, C.L. (2014) The Navy Mechanics School (ESMA) and the politics of trauma tourism in Argentina. In B. Sion (ed.) *Death Tourism: Disaster Sites as Recreational Landscape.* Seagull.

Levitt, L. (2018) Fandom and its afterlife. In C. Lundberg and V. Ziakas (eds) *The Routledge Handbook of Popular Culture and Tourism* (pp. 196–200). Routledge.

Lew, A.A. (2017) Tourism planning and place making: Place-making or placemaking? *Tourism Geographies* 19 (3), 448–466.

Lewis, L.A. (2003) *Hall of Mirrors: Power, Witchcraft, and Caste in Colonial Mexico.* Duke University Press.

LifeNaut (2022) Welcome to LifeNaut.com. See https://www.lifenaut.com/ (accessed September 2022).

Liff, S. (2003) Shaping e-access in the cybercafé: Networks, boundaries and heterotopian innovation. *New Media and Society* 5 (3), 13–334.

Light, D. (2007) Dracula tourism in Romania: Cultural identity and the state. *Annals of Tourism Research* 34 (3), 746–765.

Light, D. (2009) Performing Transylvania: Tourism, fantasy and play in a liminal place. *Tourist Studies* 9 (3), 240–258.

Light, D. (2016) *The Dracula Dilemma: Tourism, Identity and the State in Romania.* Routledge.

Light, D. (2017a) The undead and dark tourism: Dracula tourism in Romania. In G. Hooper and J.J. Lennon (eds) *Dark Tourism: Practice and Interpretation* (pp. 121–133). Routledge.

Light, D. (2017b) Progress in dark tourism and thanatourism research: An uneasy relationship with heritage tourism. *Tourism Management* 61, 275–301.

Light, D. and Ivanova, P. (2021) Thanatopsis and mortality mediation within "lightest" dark tourism. *Tourism Review* 77 (2), 622–635.

Liljeblad, J. (2020) Tour guides and the transnational promotion of human rights: Agency, structure and norm translators in responsible travel. *Tourist Studies* 20 (3), 314–335.

Linaza, M.T., Gutierrez, A. and García, A. (2013) Pervasive augmented reality games to experience tourism destinations. In Z. Xiang and I. Tussyadiah (eds) *Information and Communication Technologies in Tourism 2014: Proceedings of the International Conference* (pp. 497–509). Springer International Publishing.

Lincoln Castle Museum (2023) Visiting the Victorian prison at Lincoln Castle. See https://www.lincolncastle.com/content/victorian-prison (accessed April 2023).

Lincoln Castle Museum (2024) Welcome to Lincoln Castle. See https://www.lincolncastle.com/ (accessed March 2024).

Linkman, A. (2011) *Photography and Death*. Reaktion Books.

Linton, R. (1951) Halloween. *Scientific American* 185 (4), 62–67.

Lipstadt, D.E. (2019) *Antisemitism: Here and Now*. Scribe Publications.

Lischer, S.K. (2019) Narrating atrocity: Genocide memorials, dark tourism, and the politics of memory. *Review of International Studies* 45 (5), 805–827.

Littledean Gaol (2022) Littledean jail unlocked. See https://www.littledeanjail.com/ (accessed August 2022).

Littledean Gaol Ecclesiastical Insurance (2012) Littledean gaol. See https://www.ecclesiastical.com/documents/125-anniversary.pdf 72 (accessed April 2023).

Llorens Simón, E.M. (2022) On empathy in online tourism experience. High-frequency adjective patterns in English and Spanish promotional language. *Elua* (38), 301–323.

Lofland, L. (1978) *The Craft of Dying. The Modern Face of Death*. Sage.

Logan, W. and Reeves, K. (2008) Introduction: Remembering places of pain and shame. In W. Logan and K. Reeves (eds) *Places of Pain and Shame* (pp. 15–28). Routledge.

Lord, B. (2006) Foucault's museum: Difference, representation and genealogy. *Museum and Society* 4 (1), 11–14.

Low, M. (1993) The birth of Godzilla: Nuclear fear and the ideology of Japan as victim. *Japanese Studies* 13 (2), 48–58.

Lucas, G. (2013) Ruins. In P. Graves-Brown, R. Harrison and A. Piccini (eds) *The Oxford Handbook of the Archeology of the Contemporary World* (pp. 192–203). Oxford University Press.

Luger, M. (2015) Poetry as monument: Jenny Holzer and the memorial poems of 9/11. *Memory Studies* 8 (2), 183–196.

Luna-Cortés, G., López-Bonilla, L.M. and López-Bonilla, J.M. (2022) The consumption of dark narratives: A systematic review and research agenda. *Journal of Business Research* 145 (June 2022), 524–534.

Lury, C. (1998) *Prosthetic Culture: Photography, Memory and Identity*. Routledge.

Lv, X. *et al.* (2022) Exploring visual embodiment effect in dark tourism: The influence of visual darkness on dark experience. *Tourism Management* 89, 104438.

MacCannell, D. (1976) *The Tourist: A New Theory of the Leisure Class*. University of California Press.

MacConville, U. (2010) Roadside memorials: Making grief visible. *Bereavement Care* 29 (3), 34–36.

Macdonald, S. (2006) Mediating heritage: Tour guides at the former Nazi Party Rally Grounds, Nuremberg. *Tourist Studies* 6 (2), 119–138.

Macdonald, S. (2009) *Difficult Heritage: Negotiating the Nazi past in Nuremberg and Beyond*. Routledge.

Macdonald, S. (2015) Is 'difficult heritage still 'difficult'? Why public acknowledgement of past perpetration may no longer be so unsettling to collective identities. *Museum International* 67 (1-4), 6–22.

MacDonald, G. and Alsford, S. (1997) Conclusion: Toward the meta-museum. In K. Jones-Garmil (ed.) *The Wired Museum - Emerging Technology and Changing Paradigms* (pp. 267–278). American Association of Museums.

Macky, J. (1714) *A Journey Through England*. Caldecott, 1, 195.

MacPherson, D., Gushulak, B. and Sandhu, J. (2007) Death and international travel – the Canadian experience: 1996 to 2004. *Travel Med* 14, 77–84.

Magee, R. and Gilmore, A. (2015) Heritage site management: From dark tourism to transformative service experience? *The Service Industries Journal* 35 (15-16), 898–917.

Magrane, E. (2015) Situating geopoetics. *GeoHumanities* 1 (1), 86–102.

Magrane, E. (2021) Climate geopoetics (the earth is a composted poem). *Dialogues in Human Geography* 11 (1), 8–22.

Mahn, C., Scarles, C., Edwards, J. and Tribe, J. (2021) Personalising disaster: Community storytelling and sharing in New Orleans post-Katrina tourism. *Tourist Studies* 21 (2), 156–177.

Mahoney, P. (2020) Behold, the horror of man: Dark tourism in the anthropocene. *Journal of Tourism and Leisure Studies* 5 (2), 1–18.

Majewska, A., Denis, M., Krzysztofik, S. and Cysek-Pawlak, M.M. (2022) The development of small towns and towns of well-being: Current trends, 30 years after the change in the political system, based on the Warsaw suburban area. *Land Use Policy* 115 (19), 1–12.

Malenkina, N. and Ivanov, S. (2018) A linguistic analysis of the official tourism websites of the seventeen Spanish Autonomous Communities. *Journal of Destination Marketing and Management* 9, 204–233,

Mamak, K. (2021) Whether to save a robot or a human: On the ethical and legal limits of protections for robots. *Frontiers in Robotics and AI* 8, 1–10.

Mamedov, M. (2016) Post Soviet monuments war. *Russia Direct*. See http://www.russia-direct.org/opinion/post-soviet-monuments-war (accessed November 2017).

Mandelartz, P. (2016) Goth tourism: Sun, sea, sex and dark leisure? Insights into the tourist identity of the Gothic Culture. In T. Johnston and P. Mandelartz (eds) *Thanatourism: Case Studies in Travel to the Dark Side* (pp. 61–84). Goodfellow.

Manning, E.H. (1915) *Handbook of the Birmingham General Cemetery; Together with Biographical Notes on those Interred Therein*. Hudson and Son.

Marasco, A., Buonincontri, P., Van Niekerk, M., Orlowski, M. and Okumus, F. (2018) Exploring the role of next-generation virtual technologies in destination marketing. *Journal of Destination Marketing and Management* 9, 138–148.

Marcel, J-C. and Mucchielli, L. (2008) Maurice Halbwachs's memoire collective. In A. Erll, A. Nünning and S.B. Young (eds) *Cultural Memory Studies, An International and Interdisciplinary Handbook* (pp. 141–149). Walter de Gruyter.

Marcuse, H. (2001) *Legacies of Dachau: The Uses and Abuses of a Concentration Camp, 1933 – 2001*. Cambridge University Press.

Margalit, R. (2014) Should Auschwitz be a site for selfies? *The New Yorker*. See https://www.newyorker.com/culture/culture-desk/should-auschwitz-be-a-site-for-selfies (accessed December 2022).

Marie Curie (2021) Palliative care research centre, division of population medicine Cardiff. See https://www.marie curie.org.uk (accessed March 2023).

Marjavaara, R., Nilsson, R.O. and Müller, D.K. (2022) The Arctification of northern tourism: A longitudinal geographical analysis of firm names in Sweden. *Polar Geography* 45 (2), 119–136.

Marr, B. (2023) Should we stop developing AI for the good of humanity? See https://www.forbes.com/sites/bernardmarr/2023/05/03/should-we-stop-developing-ai-for-the-good-of-humanity/ (accessed May 2023).

Marriott, J. (2023) Talking about the D word: Public engagement. In T. Biers and K.S. Clary (eds) *The Routledge Handbook of Museums, Heritage, and Death* (pp. 607–621). Routledge International Handbooks.

Martini, A. and Buda, D.M. (2020) Dark tourism and affect: Framing places of death and disaster. *Current Issues in Tourism* 23 (6), 679–692.

Mather, M. (2022) Killer robots have been approved to fight crime. What are the legal, ethical concerns? See https://www.law.virginia.edu/news/202212/killer-robots-have-been-approved-fight-crime-what-are-legal-ethical-concerns (accessed May 2023).

Maurer, K. and Rostbøll, C.F. (2020) Demoxie: Reflections on digital democracy in Dave Eggers' novel The Circle. *First Monday* 25 (5). https://doi.org/10.5210/fm.v25i5.10650.

Maxwell-Stewart, H (2013) 'The lottery of life': Convict tourism at Port Arthur historic site, Australia. *Prison Service Journal* 210, 24–28.

Mayer-Schönberger, V. and Cukier, K. (2014) *Big Data: A Revolution That Will Transform How We Live, Work, and Think*. Harper Business.

Maze Long Kesh Timeline (2020) Site history, maze long kesh timeline. See http://mazelongkesh.com/site-history/ (accessed April 2023).

Mažeikienė, N. (2021) Introduction. Nuclear tourism as an emerging area of learning about nuclear energy. In N. Mažeikienė (ed.) *Learning the Nuclear: Educational Tourism in (Post) Industrial Sites* (pp. 11–18). Peter-Lang.

Mbembe, A. (2003) Necropolitics. *Public Culture* 15 (1), 11–40.

McClymont, K. (2018) 'They have different ways of doing things': Cemeteries, diversity and local place attachment. *Journal of Intercultural Studies* 39 (3), 267–285.

McConville, S. (1981) *A History of English Prison Administration*. Routledge and Kegan Paul.

Mcdaniel, K.N. (2018) *Virtual Dark Tourism, Ghost Roads*. Palgrave, MacMillan.

McEvoy, E. (2014) Gothic tourism. In G. Byron and D. Townshend (eds) *The Gothic World* (pp. 476–486). Routledge.

McKenzie, B. (2018) 'Death as a commodity': The retailing of dark tourism. In P.R. Stone, R. Hartmann, T. Seaton, R. Sharpley and L. White (eds) *The Palgrave Handbook of Dark Tourism Studies* (pp. 667–691). Palgrave Macmillan.

Mckie, R. (2018) No death and an enhanced life: Is the future transhuman? See https://www.theguardian.com/technology/2018/may/06/no-death-and-an-enhanced-life-is-the-future-transhuman (accessed May 2023).

McKinley Jr., J.C. (2008) Travelers in search of Mexico's magic find town of witches and warlocks. *The New York Times*, 28 March.

McLean, A. (2023) Millennials as second-person witnesses of the Holocaust: A case study on the Dachau concentration camp memorial site. Unpublished PhD thesis, Royal Roads University.

McLeod, K. (2016) Living in the immaterial world: Holograms and spirituality in recent popular music. *Popular Music and Society* 39 (5), 501–515.

McMorran, C. (2015) Between fan pilgrimage and dark tourism: Competing agendas in overseas field learning. *Journal of Geography in Higher Education* 39 (4), 568–583.

McNally, P. and Inayatullah, S. (1988) The rights of robots: Technology, culture and law in the 21st century. *Futures* 20 (2), 119–136.

McNamee, M. and Edwards, S. (2006) Transhumanism, medical technology and slippery slopes. *Journal of Medical Ethics* 32 (9), 513–518.

McNamee, S. (2000) Foucault's heterotopia and children's everyday lives. *Childhood* 7 (4), 479–492.

Medby, I.A. (2019) Language-games, geography, and making sense of the Arctic. *Geoforum* 107, 124–133.

Meerzon, Y. (2007) The ideal city: Heterotopia or panopticon? On Joseph Brodsky's play marbles and its fictional spaces. *Modern Drama* 50 (2), 184–209.

Meese, J., Nansen, B., Kohn, T., Arnold M. and Gibbs, M. (2015) Posthumous personhood and the affordances of digital media. *Mortality* 20 (4), 408–420.

Meghji, A. (2021) *Decolonizing Sociology*. Polity Press.

Melbourne Playgrounds (2022) Ash Wednesday Bushfire Education Centre (Cockatoo). See https://www.melbourneplaygrounds.com.au/ash-wednesday-bushfire-education-centre-cockatoo (accessed November 2022).

Meler, M. (2013) *Jewish Latvia: Sites to Remember.* Association of Latvian and Estonian Jews in Israel.

Mellor, P.A. and Shilling, C. (1993) Modernity, self-identity and the sequestration of death. *Sociology* 27 (3), 411–431. https://doi.org/10.1177/0038038593027003005.

Merkx, C. and Nawijn, J. (2021) Virtual reality tourism experiences: Addiction and isolation. *Tourism Management* 87, 1–4.

Microsoft Asia News Center (2017) AI in Japan: Boy bot's big honor. See https://news.microsoft.com/apac/2017/11/20/ai-japan-boy-bots-big-honor/ (accessed May 2023).

Middleton, D. and Brown, S.D. (2011) Memory and space in the work of Maurice Halbwachs. In P. Meusburger, M. Heffernan and E. Wunder (eds) *Cultural Memories* (pp. 29–49). Springer.

Miles, T. (2015) *Tales from the Haunted South: Dark Tourism and Memories of Slavery From the Civil War Era*. UNC Press Books.

Miles, W. (2002) Auschwitz: Museum interpretation and darker tourism. *Annals of Tourism Research* 29 (4), 1175–1178.
Miller, D.S. and Gonzalez, C. (2013) When death is the destination: The business of death tourism – despite legal and social implications. *International Journal Of Culture, Tourism And Hospitality Research* 7 (3), 293–306.
Miller, L.B., Hallo, J.C., Dvorak, R.G., Fefer, J.P., Peterson, B.A. and Brownlee, M.T. (2020) On the edge of the world: Examining pro-environmental outcomes of last chance tourism in Kaktovik, Alaska. *Journal of Sustainable Tourism* 28 (11), 1703–1722.
Miller, R. (2011) Futures literacy—Embracing complexity and using the future. *Ethos* 10, 23–28.
Milligan, C.A. (2018) Virtually historical: Performing dark tourism through alternate history games. In K. McDaniel (ed.) *Virtual Dark Tourism* (pp. 265–285). Palgrave Macmillan.
Milligan, M.J. (2007) Buildings as history: The place of collective memory in the study of Historic Preservation. *Symbolic Interaction* 30 (1), 105–123.
Milgram, P. and Kishino, F. (1994) A taxonomy of mixed reality visual displays. *IEICE Transactions on Information Systems* 77 (12), 1321–1329.
Milgram, P., Takemura, H., Utsumi, A. and Kishino, F. (1995) Augmented reality: A class of displays on the reality-virtuality continuum. In H. Das (ed.) *Telemanipulator and Telepresence Technologies* (pp. 282–292). Spie.
Misra, S., Goswami, R., Mondal, T. and Jana, R. (2017) Social networks in the context of community response to disaster: Study of a cyclone-affected community in Coastal West Bengal, India. *International Journal of Disaster Risk Reduction* 22, 281–296.
Mitchell, L.M., Stephenson, P.H., Cadell, S. and Macdonald, M.E. (2012) Death and grief on-line: Virtual memorialization and changing concepts of childhood death and parental bereavement on the Internet. *Health Sociology Review* 21 (4), 413–431.
Mizokami, K. (2019) The U.S. army expects to field cyborg soldiers by 2050. See https://www.popularmechanics.com/military/research/a29963287/us-army-cyborgs/ (accessed May 2023).
Mondal, A.P. and Bhowmik, P. (2018) Physician assisted suicide tourism – a future global business phenomenon. *The Business and Management Review* 10 (1), 35–43.
Morie, J.F. (2007) Meaning and emplacement in expressive immersive virtual environments. Unpublished PhD Thesis, University of East London.
Morris, C. (2022) After 20 years, the U.S. Army is shutting down its recruitment video game, "America's Army". *Fast Company*. See https://www.fastcompany.com/90720653/after-20-years-the-u-s-army-is-shutting-down-its-recruitment-video-game-americas-army (accessed November 2022).
Morris, S. (2020) Druids prepare for virtual solstice as Stonehenge asks people to stay away. See https://www.theguardian.com/uk- news/2020/jun/19/druids-prepare-for-virtual-solstice-as-stonehenge-asks-people-to-stay- away-coronavirus (accessed January 2022).
Morris, S. (2021) Statue of slave trader Edward Colston to go on display in Bristol museum. *Guardian*. See https://www.theguardian.com/uk-news/2021/may/28/statue-of-slave-trader-edward-colston-to-go-on-display-in-bristol-museum (accessed March 2023).
Morton, E. (2016) Bulgaria bans public display of communist symbols. See https://www.calvertjournal.com/news/show/7304/bulgaria-bans-public-display-of-communist-symbols (accessed January 2022).
Morten, R., Stone, P.R. and Jarratt, D. (2018) Dark tourism as psychogeography: An initial exploration. In P.R. Stone, R. Hartmann, T. Seaton, R. Sharpley and L. White (eds) *The Palgrave Handbook of Dark Tourism Studies* (pp. 227–255). Palgrave Macmillan.
Mortlock, J. (2019) Braving the London Dungeon. Love pop ups London. See https://lovepopupslondon.com/2019/08/05/braving-the-london-dungeon/ (accessed April 2023).
Moscardo, G. (2021) The story turn in tourism: Forces and futures. *Journal of Tourism Futures* 7 (2), 168–173.

Motalebi, N. (2017) The ephemeral dream space: (Re)Activating an evocative architecture through computational devices and bodily interaction. Unpublished MSc thesis, Graduate School of Arts and Architecture, Pennsylvania State University, USA.

Mudford, W. (1841) Cemeteries and churchyards- A visit to Kensal Green. *Bentley's Miscellany 1837-1868* 9, 92–97.

Müller, D.K. (2015) Issues in Arctic tourism. In B. Evengård, J. Nymand Larsen and Ø. Paasche (eds) *The New Arctic* (pp. 147–158). Springer.

Müller, D.K. and Viken, A. (2017) Toward a de-essentializing of indigenous tourism? In A. Viken and D.K. Müller (eds) *Tourism and Indigeneity in the Arctic* (pp. 281–289). Channel View Publications.

Municipality of Skenderaj (Online) (n.d.) Mission & vision. See www.kk.rks-gov.nett/skenderaj/ (accessed March 2024).

Muresan, A. and Pohl. H. (2019) *Chats with Bots: Balancing Imitation and Engagement.* Extended Abstracts of the 2019 CHI Conference on Human Factors in Computing Systems, pp. 1–6.

Murrindindi Shire Council (2022) Marysville bushfire memorial infosheet. See https://www.murrindindi.vic.gov.au/files/assets/public/documents/other/marysville-bushfire-memorial-infosheet.pdf (accessed November 2022).

Museum Revolution (n.d.) Newseum will virtually send visitors to Berlin Wall during Cold War. See https://museumrevolution.com/newseum-will- virtually-send-visitors-berlin-wall-cold-war (accessed January 2022).

Museums Victoria Collections (2022) Collections. See https://collections.museumsvictoria.com.au/items/1807372 (accessed October 2022).

MWRF (2022) The Who Exhibition an immersive journey. See https://rnrwof.co.uk/ (accessed October 2022).

Narvselius, E. and Fedor, J. (2021) *Diversity in the East-Central European Borderlands: Memories, Cityscapes, People.* Ibidem-Verlag.

Nassar, A. (2021) Geopoetics: Storytelling against mastery. *Dialogues in Human Geography* 11 (1), 27–30.

National Geographic (2022) Visit the Okavango Delta in 360°. See https://www.youtube.com/watch?v=BZy1XUTCiL4 (accessed October 2022).

National Retail Federation (2022) Halloween data center. See https://nrf.com/insights/holiday-and-seasonal-trends/halloween/halloween-data-center (accessed September 2022).

NATO (1999) NATO and Kosovo: Military technical agreement—9 June. See https://www.nato.int/kosovo/docu/a990609a.htm (accessed December 2022).

NBC Universal (2014) 16:30 Scared to death? Teen has fatal heart attack at Ohio haunted house. Seehttps://www.nbcnews.com/news/us-news/scared-death-teen-has-fatal-heart-attack-ohio-haunted-house-n230811 (accessed April 2022).

Neely, B. (1999) Serbs rewrite history of Racak massacre. *The Independent.* See https://www.independent.co.uk/news/serbs-rewrite-history-of-racak-massacre-1075680.html (accessed March 2024).

Neiger, M. (2020) Theorizing media memory: Six elements defining the role of the media in shaping collective memory in the digital age. *Sociology Compass* 14 (5).

Neild, J. (1812) State of the prisons in England, Scotland and Wales. *The National Archives.* See https://archive.org/details/stateofprisonsin00neil (accessed March 2024).

Nelson, V. (2020) Liminality and difficult heritage in tourism. *Tourism Geographies* 22 (2), 298–318.

Neuberger, L. and Egger, R. (2021) Travel risk perception and travel behaviour during the COVID-19 pandemic 2020: A case study of the DACH region. *Current Issues in Tourism* 24 (7), 1003–1016.

Neuburger, L., Beck, J. and Egger, R. (2018) The 'Phygital' tourist experience: The use of augmented and virtual reality in destination marketing. In M.A. Camilleri (ed.) *Tourism Planning and Destination Marketing* (pp. 183–202). Emerald Publishing.

Neuhofer, B. and Buhalis, D. (2012) Understanding and managing technology-enabled enhanced tourist experiences. Paper presented at the 2nd Conference on Hospitality and Tourism Marketing and Management (Corfu, 31 May–3 June).

Neuhofer, B. and Buhalis, D. (2014) Technology enhanced tourism experience. Digital tourism think tank: Technical report. See https://www.researchgate.net/publication/272566581-Technology_enhanced_tourism_experience#fullTextFileContent (accessed October 2022).

Neuhofer, B., Buhalis, D. and Ladkin, A. (2012) Conceptualising technology enhanced destination experiences. *Journal of Destination Marketing and Management* 1 (1–2), 36–46.

Nevada Preservation (n.d.) Tombstone tales. See https://nevadapreservation.org/wp-content/uploads/2019/08/WoodlawnTour_2019_FINAL.pdf (accessed November 2022).

New Zealand Herald (2021a) Christchurch earthquake survivors share their powerful stories 10 years on. See https://www.nzherald.co.nz/nz/christchurch-earthquake-survivors-share-their-powerful-stories-10-years-on/3BRLXYTF22G6WCVBKZSKA5RCPI/ (accessed November 2022).

New Zealand Herald (2021b) Christchurch quake 10th anniversary: Memorial service run-down released. See https://www.nzherald.co.nz/nz/christchurch-quake-10th-anniversary-memorial-service-run-down-released/RXU46257YP56V6ULAGVAXW2MYQ/ (accessed November 2022).

Nhlabathi, S.S. and Maharaj, B. (2020) The dark tourism discipline: A creative brand in a competitive academic environment? *Current Issues in Tourism* 23 (19), 2428–2439.

NHS (2020, July 28) Euthanasia and assisted suicide. See https://www.nhs.uk/conditions/euthanasia-and-assisted-suicide/ (accessed November 22).

Niebyl, D. (2016) 'Kamenska', Spomenik database. See https://www.spomenikdatabase.org/kamenska (accessed January 2022).

Nielsen, A.P. and Groes, L. (2014) Ethnography inside the walls: Studying the contested space of the cemetery. Ethnographic Praxis in Industry Conference Proceedings, EPIC 2014, Paper Session 2: Place and the City, pp.108–118.

Nikulin, D. (2017) Maurice Halbwachs. In S. Bernecker and K. Michaelian (eds) *The Routledge Handbook of Philosophy of Memory* (pp. 528–536). Routledge.

Nobody's Listening (n.d.) Virtual reality. See https://www.nobodys-listening.com/virtualreality (accessed April 2023).

Nora, P. (1989) Between memory and history: les lieux de mémoire. *Representations* 26 (26), 7–24.

Nørfelt, A, Kock, F., Karpen, I.O. and Josiassen, A. (2022) Pleasure through pain: An empirical examination of benign masochism in tourism. *Journal of Travel Research* 62 (2), 448–468.

Northern Ireland Prisons (2023) Prison estate. See https://www.justice-ni.gov.uk/topics/prisons/prison-estate (accessed April 2023).

Northleach Historic England Listing (2012) The Old Prison, formerly Northleach House Of Correction. See https://historicengland.org.uk/listing/the-list/list-entry/1090470?section=official-list-entry (accessed April 2023).

Northleach Prison Website (2023) Explore. See https://www.theoldprison.co.uk/ (accessed April 2023).

Novelli, M. (2005) *Niche Tourism: Contemporary Issues, Trends and Cases*. Routledge.

Nument (2022) Nument website. See https://nument.xyz. (accessed November 2022).

Occulus (2022a) Anne Frank House VR. See https://www.oculus.com/experiences/go/1596151970428159/ (accessed October 2022).

Occulus (2022b) Home after war. See https://www.oculus.com/experiences/quest/2900834523285203/ (accessed October 2022).

Occulus (2022c) Jurrassic world. See https://www.oculus.com/experiences/quest/2557465320986444/ (accessed October 2022).

O'Connor, P. (2019) The unanchored past: Three modes of collective memory. *Memory Studies* 15 (4), 634–649.

OECD (2020) Education in the Western Balkans: Findings from PISA, PISA, OECD Publishing, Paris. See https://doi.org/10.1787/764847ff-en (accessed July 2023).

Olick, J.K. (1999) Collective memory: The two cultures. *Sociological Theory* 17 (3), 333–348.

Olick, J.K. (2007) *The Politics of Regret: On Collective Memory and Historical Responsibility*. Routledge.

Olick, J.K., Vinitzky-Seroussi, V. and Levy, D. (2011) *The Collective Memory Reader*. Oxford University Press.

Olsen, D.H. and Korstanje, M.E. (2019) *Dark Tourism and Pilgrimage*. CABI.

Olsson, T. and Salo, M. (2011) Online user survey on current mobile augmented reality applications. Paper presented at the 10th IEEE International Symposium on Mixed and Augmented Reality-ISMAR (Basel, 26–29 October).

Orchiston, C. and Higham, J.E.S. (2014) Knowledge management and tourism recovery (de)marketing: The Christchurch earthquakes 2010–2011. *Current Issues in Tourism* 19 (1), 64–84.

Order of the Good Death (2023) Welcome to the future of death. See www.orderofthegooddeath.com (accessed March 2023).

Orlean, S. (2021) Zooming in on Petra. See https://www.smithsonianmag.com/history/petra-jordan-drone-3d-scan-digital-modeling-180970310/ (accessed October 2022).

Ostrow, A. (2011) After your final status update. See https://www.ted.com/talks/adam_ostrow_after_your_final_status_update/transcript?language=en (accessed February 2023).

Owens, M.E. (2012) John Webster, Tussaud Laureate: The waxworks in The Duchess of Malfi. *ELH* 79 (4), 851–877.

Oxford Malmaison Hotel (2023) Oxford, Better than your average prison. See https://www.malmaison.com/locations/oxford/?gclid=Cj0KCQjwla-hBhD7ARIsAM9tQKsC-dGK-xZDOIZSOQSQGSRAFNWyPF0R1GWEgFKclwkW1ZgYTcVPatYaAtFdEALw_wcB (accessed April 2023).

Oxford Prison Tourism (2023) Victorian murder mystery and dinner. See https://www.oxfordcastleandprison.co.uk/ (accessed April 2023).

Page, S.J., Yeoman, I., Connell, J. and Greenwood, C. (2010) Scenario planning as a tool to understand uncertainty in tourism: The example of transport and tourism in Scotland in 2025. *Current Issues in Tourism* 13 (2), 99–137.

Paliewicz, N.S. and Hasian, M. (2017) Popular memory at Ground Zero: A heterotopology of the National September 11 Memorial and Museum. *Popular Communication* 15 (1), 19–36.

Paraskevopoulou, I. (2016) Historic cemeteries: Saved and managed by their friends. Unpublished MA thesis, University of York.

Paraskevopoulou, I. (2019) The cultural heritage of cemeteries. In E. Georgitsoyanni (ed.) *Ancient Greek Art and European Funerary Art* (pp. 257–276). Cambridge Scholars Publishing.

Pastor, D. and Kent, A.J. (2020) Transformative landscapes: Liminality and visitors' emotional experiences at German memorial sites. *Tourism Geographies* 22 (2), 250–272.

Patterson, O. (1982) *Slavery and Social Death: A Comparative Study*. Harvard University Press.

Peet, G. (2022) Remembering the Holocaust: The evolution of memory on a divided continent. Unpublished PhD thesis, The University of North Carolina.

Pelau, C., Dabija, D-C. and Ene, I. (2021) What makes an AI device human-like? The role of interaction quality, empathy and perceived psychological anthropomorphic characteristics in the acceptance of artificial intelligence in the service industry. *Computers in Human Behaviour* 122, 1–9.

Pelton, R.Y. (2001) *The Adventurist: My Life in Dangerous Places*. Crown.

Penfold-Mounce, R. (2016) Corpses, popular culture and forensic science: Public obsession with death. *Mortality* 21 (1), 19–35.

Penfold-Mounce, R. (2019) Celebrity deaths and the thanatological imagination. In A. Teodorescu and M.H. Jacobsen (eds) *Death in Contemporary Popular Culture* (pp. 51–64). Routledge.

Percoco, J. (1998) *A Passion for the Past: Creative Teaching of U.S. History*. Heinemann.

Perry, R.E. (2020) The Holocaust is present: Reenacting the Holocaust, then and now. Holocaust studies. *A Journal of Culture and History* 26 (2), 152–180.

Petersen, S. (2007) The ethics of robot servitude. *Journal of Experimental and Theoretical Artificial Intelligence* 19 (1), 43–54.

Peterson, A. (2016) *Holocaust* Museum to visitors: Please stop catching Pokémon here. *The Washington Post*. See https://www.washingtonpost.com/news/the-switch/wp/2016/07/12/holocaust-museum-to-visitors-please-stop-catching-pokemon-here (accessed November 2022).

Pettai, E.C. (2011) Establishing 'Holocaust memory' – A comparison of Estonia and Latvia. In O. Rathkolb and I. Sooman (eds) *Historical Memory Culture in the Enlarged Baltic Sea Region and its Symptoms Today* (pp. 159–173). University of Vienna Press.

Phillimore, J. and Goodson, L. (2004) Progress in qualitative research in tourism. In J. Phillmore and L. Goodson (eds) *Qualitative Research in Tourism: Ontologies, Epistemologies and Methodologies* (pp. 3–29). Routledge.

Phillips, T., Taylor, J., Narain, E. and Chandler, P. (2021) Selling authentic happiness: Indigenous wellbeing and romanticised inequality in tourism advertising. *Annals of Tourism Research* 87, 1–13.

Phipps, P. (1999) Tourists, terrorists, death and value. In R. Kaur and J. Hutnyk (eds) *Travel Worlds: Journeys in Contemporary Cultural Politics* (pp. 74–93). Zed Books.

Piekarz, M., Jenkins, I. and Mills, P. (2015) *Risk and Safety Management in the Leisure, Events, Tourism and Sports Industries*. CABI.

Pierini, P. (2007) Quality in web translation: An investigation into UK and Italian tourism web sites. *The Journal of Specialised Translation* 8, 85–103.

Pimentel-Biscaia, M.S. and Marques, L. (2022) Dystopian dark tourism: Affective experiences in Dismaland. *Tourism Geographies* 24 (2–3), 306–325.

Piña, U. (2021) Digital resources: Dark tourism in Latin America. *Oxford Research Encyclopedia of Latin American History*. See https://doi.org/10.1093/acrefore/9780199366439.013.919 (accessed December 2022).

PlayStation (2017) Chernobyl VR Project – release trailer | PS VR. YouTube. See https://www.youtube.com/watch?v=U00WaZ_cbqo (accessed October 2022).

Poade, D.M. (2017) The business of dark tourism: The management of dark tourism visitor sites and attractions with special reference to innovation. Published PhD thesis, University of Exeter.

Pococke, R. (1887) *Tours in Scotland 1747, 1750 and 1760*. Scottish Historical Society.

Pococke, R. (1888–9) *The Travels Through England of Dr Richard Pococke*. 2 volumes, Camden Society.

Podoshen, J.S. (2017) Trajectories in Holocaust tourism. *Journal of Heritage Tourism* 12 (4), 347–364.

Podoshen, J.S., Venkatesh, V., Wallin, J., Andrzejewski, S.A. and Jin, Z. (2015) Dystopian dark tourism: An exploratory examination. *Tourism Management* 51 (12), 316–328.

Podoshen, J.S., Grace Y., Andrzejewski, S.A., Wallin, J. and Venkatesh, V. (2018) Dark tourism, abjection and blood: A festival context. *Tourism Management* 64, 346–356.

Possamai, A. and Lee, M. (2011) Hyper-real religions: Fear, anxiety and Late-Modern Religious Innovation. *Journal of Sociology* 47 (3), 227–242.

Pottle, F.A. (1950) *Boswell's London Journal 1762-3*. William Heinemann.

Potts, T.J. (2012) 'Dark tourism' and the 'kitschification' of 9/11. *Tourist Studies* 12 (3), 232–249.

Powell, R. and Iankova, K. (2016) Dark London: Dimensions and characteristics of dark tourism supply in the UK capital. *Anatolia* 27 (3), 339–351.

Prahm, C., Bressler, M., Eckstein, K., Kuzuoka, H., Daigeler, A. and Kolbenschlag, J. (2022) Developing a wearable Augmented Reality for treating phantom limb pain using the Microsoft Hololens 2. Paper presented at the Augmented Humans International Conference (Kashiwa, 13–15 March).

Price, P. L. (2010) Cultural geography and the stories we tell ourselves. *Cultural Geographies* 17 (2), 203–210.

Prince G. (1999) *A Dictionary of Narratology*. University of Nebraska Press.

Prishtina Insight (2022) Kosovo police crack down on vidovdan provocations. June 29. See https://prishtinainsight.com/kosovo-police-crack-down-on-vidovdan-provocations/ (accessed June 2023).

Prison Population Figures Howard League (2022) Less crime, safer communities, fewer people in prison. See https://howardleague.org/prisons-information/prison-watch (accessed August 2022).

Prisons Relinquished (n.d.) Prison Commissioners, manuscript formerly in the Prison Service Library, London: Abell House.

Pristina, U.S.E. (2022) Ambassador Jeffrey Hovenier's remarks at the Recak/Racak massacre commemoration. U.S. embassy in Kosovo. See https://xk.usembassy.gov/recak150122/ (accessed December 2022).

Prus, R.C. (1996) *Symbolic Interaction and Ethnographic Research: Intersubjectivity and the Study of Human Lived Experience*. State University of New York Press.

Puri, J. (2021) The forgotten lives of sociology of death: Remembering Du Bois, MArtineau and Wells. *The American Sociologist* 52 (3), 638–655.

Putcha, R. (2020) After *Eat, Pray, Love*: Tourism, Orientalism, and cartographies of salvation. *Tourist Studies* 20 (4), 450–466.

Qian, L., Zheng, C., Wang, J., Pérez Sánchez, M.d.l.Á, Parra López, E. and Li, H. (2022) Dark tourism destinations: The relationships between tourists' on-site experience, destination image and behavioural intention. *Tourism Review* 77 (2), 607–621.

Radio Free Europe (2022) Dozens injured as Serbs, Kosovo police clash. 28 June. See https://www.rferl.org/a/24629223.html (accessed July 2023).

Raine, R. (2013) A dark tourism spectrum. *International Journal of Culture, Tourism and Hospitality Work* 7, 242–256.

Ramsay, M. (1977) John Howard and the discovery of the prison. *The Howard Journal of Penology and Crime Prevention* 16 (2), 1–16.

Rantala, O., de la Barre, S., Granås, B., Jóhannesson, G.Þ., Müller, D.K., Saarinen, J., Tervo-Kankare, K., Maher, P.T. and Niskala, M. (2019) *Arctic Tourism in Times of Change: Seasonality*. Nordic Council of Ministers.

Rasinger, J., Fuchs, M., Beer, T. and Höpken, W. (2009) Building a mobile tourist guide based on tourists' on-site information needs. *Tourism Analysis* 14 (4), 483–502.

Razavi, L. (2016) Royal College of Art students collaborate with London hospice to 're-style' the experience of death. *The Independent*. See https://www.independent.co.uk/life-style/health-and-families/features/royal-college-of-art-students-collaborate-with-london-hospice-to-restyle-the-experience-of-death-a6879861.html (accessed March 2023).

Reagan, R. (2018) Abney rambles: Performing heritage as an audio walking practice in Abney Park Cemetery. Unpublished PhD thesis, University of London.

Record of Settlements (n.d.) Record of Settlements with County and Borough Prison Authorities in 1878, manuscript formerly in Prison Service Headquarters Library, London: Abell House.

Rees, S. and Wells, R. (2020) Bushfires, COVID-19 and the urgent need for an Australian Task Force on gender, mental health and disaster. *Australian and New Zealand Journal of Psychiatry* 54 (11), 1135–1136.

Reese, J. (2018) *The End of Animal Farming*. Beacon Press.

Reisinger, Y. and Mavondo, F. (2005) Travel anxiety and intentions to travel internationally: Implications of travel risk perception. *Journal of Travel Research* 43 (3), 212–225.

Relph, E. (1976) *Place and Placelessness*. Pion Limited.

RePast (2023) Revisiting the past, anticipating the future. See https://www.repast.eu/ (accessed June 2023).

Reser, J.P. and Swim. J.K. (2011) Adapting to and coping with the threat and impacts of climate change. *American Psychologist* 66 (4), 277–289.

Retro Futuro (2022a) Excursions with augmented reality (VR/AR) in Pompeii. See https://pompeii.refutur.com/en (accessed November 2022).

Retro Futuro (2022b) Schedule and prices.Excursions with augmented reality (VR/AR) in Pompeii. See https://pompeii.refutur.com/en/#excursions (accessed November 2022).

Reynolds, D. (2016) Consumers or witnesses? Holocaust tourists and the problem of authenticity. *Journal of Consumer Culture* 16 (2), 334–353.

Rice, A. (2003) *Radical Narratives of the Black Atlantic*. Continuum.

Rice, A. (2009) Museums, Memorials and plantation houses in the Black Atlantic: Slavery and the development of dark tourism. In R. Sharpley and P.R. Stone (eds) (2009) *The Darker Side of Travel: The Theory and Practice of Dark Tourism* (pp. 224–246). Channel View Publications.

Richards, N. (2017) Assisted suicide as a remedy for suffering? The end-of-life preferences of British "suicide tourists". *Medical Anthropology* 36 (4), 348–362.

Richardson, B.K. and Maninger, L. (2016) We were all in the same boat: An exploratory study of communal coping in disaster recovery. *Southern Communication Journal* 81 (2), 107–122.

Richardson, H.S. (2018, August 27) Moral reasoning. See https://plato.stanford.edu/entries/reasoning-moral/#SituMoraReas (accessed November 22).

Richter, D. (2016) Hunting for Pokémon in the Chernobyl Exclusion Zone. *Ex Utopia*. See https://www.exutopia.com/hunting-for-pokemon-in-the-chernobyl-exclusion-zone (accessed November 2022).

Riga Ghetto and Holocaust Museum in Latvia (RGLHM) (2021) Visitor statistics 2010 – 2020 (unpublished data).

Rigney, A. (2018) Remembrance as remaking: Memories of the nation revisited. *Nations and Nationalism* 24 (2), 240–257.

Ritzer, G. (1993) *The McDonalization of Society*. Sage Publications.

Ritzer, G. (2014) *The McDonaldization of Society* (8th edn). Sage Publications.

Robben Island World Heritage Inscription (2023) Robben Island. See https://whc.unesco.org/en/list/916 (accessed April 2023).

Roberts, C. and Stone, P.R. (2014) Dark tourism and dark heritage: Emergent themes, issues and consequences. In I. Convery, G. Corsane and P. Davies (eds) *Displaced Heritage: Responses to Disaster, Trauma and Loss* (pp. 9–18). Boydell Press.

Robertson, J. (2014) Human rights versus robot rights: Forecasts from Japan. *Critical Asian Studies* 46 (4), 571–598.

Robins, K. and Webster, F. (2020) The long history of the information revolution. In R. Blom, E. Karvonen, H. Melin, K. Nordenstreng, E. Puoskari, F. Webster (eds) *The Information Society Reader* (pp. 62–80). Routledge.

Rofe, M.W. (2013) Considering the limits of rural place making opportunities: Rural dystopias and dark tourism. *Landscape Research* 38 (2), 262–272.

Rogers, S. (2020) How virtual reality could help the travel and tourism industry in the aftermath of the Coronavirus outbreak. *Forbes*. See https://www.forbes.com/sites/solrogers/2020/03/18/virtual-reality-and-tourism-whats-already-happening-is-it-the-future (accessed January 2022).

Rojek, C. (1993) *Ways of Escape: Modern Transformations in Leisure and Travel*. Palgrave Macmillan.

Rolleston, T. (2021) Whakaari/White Island eruption: Victims remembered with karakia from Ngāti Awa. See Whakaari https://www.rnz.co.nz/news/Whakaari-White-Island/457571/whakaari-white-island-eruption-victims-remembered-with-karakia-from-ngati-awa (accessed November 2022).

Roman, I. (2020) Day of the dead: How ancient traditions grew into a global holiday. See https://www.history.com/news/day-dead-dia-de-muertos-origins (accessed April 2022).

Roman, M., Kosiński, R., Bhatta, K., Niedziółka, A. and Krasnodębski, A. (2022) Virtual and space tourism as new trends in travelling at the time of the COVID-19 pandemic. *Sustainability* 14 (2), 2–26.

Rotenberg, R. (1995) *Landscape and Power in Vienna*. Johns Hopkins University Press.

Rothberg, M. (2009) *Multidirectional Memory: Remembering the Holocaust in the Age of Decolonization*. Stanford University Press.

Rountree, S. (2022) VR experience at Cork's Spike Island is Ireland's largest augmented reality adventure. See https://www.corkbeo.ie/culture/vr-experience-corks-spike-island-24826757 (accessed October 2022).

Rousseaux, F. and Thouvenin, I. (2009) Exploring informed virtual sites through Michel Foucault's heterotopias. *International Journal of Humanities and Arts Computing* 3 (1–2), 175–191.

Rousvoal, N. (2020) Commemorating Britishness during the centennial of the First World War: A comparative analysis of political commemorative speeches in Northern Ireland and in Scotland. *European Journal of English Studies* 24 (2), 115–129.

Rozin, P., Guillot, L., Fincher, K., Rozin, A. and Tsukayama, E. (2013) Glad to be sad and other examples of benign masochism. *Judgment and Decision Making* 8 (4), 439.

RPC (1878) Report of the work of the Prison Commission. *The National Archives*. See https://discovery.nationalarchives.gov.uk/details/r/C11497 (accessed March 2024).

Rucinska, D. (2016) Natural disaster tourism as a type of dark tourism. *International Journal of Humanities and Social Sciences* 10 (5), 1458–1462.

Rugg, J. (2000) Defining the place of burial: what makes a cemetery a cemetery? *Mortality* 5, 259–275.

Rugg, J. (2020) Social justice and cemetery systems. *Death Studies* 46 (4), 861–874.

Ruide, K. (2019) Japanese amusement park's new horror attraction involves handcuffing visitors in the dark. See https://soranews24.com/2019/03/25/japanese-amusement-parks-new-horror-attraction-involves-handcuffing-visitors-in-the-dark/ (accessed April 2022).

Rutherford, J. (1990) The third space. Interview with Homi Bhabha. In J. Rutherford (ed.) *Identity, Community, Culture, Difference* (pp. 207–221). Lawrence and Wishart.

Ruthin Gaol History (2010) A history of Ruthin Gaol. See http://news.bbc.co.uk/local/northeastwales/hi/people_and_places/history/newsid_8555000/8555937.stm (accessed April 2023).

Ruthin Gaol Museum (2023) Ruthin Gaol. See https://www.denbighshire.gov.uk/en/leisure-and-tourism/museums-and-historic-houses/ruthin-gaol.aspx (accessed April 2023).

Ryan, J. (2018) VR tour of Hiroshima bombing created by Japanese students. *CNET*. See https://www.cnet.com/culture/vr-tour-of-hiroshima-atomic-bombing-created-by-japanese-students-virtual-reality/ (accessed October 2022).

Ryan, M. (2007) Toward a definition of narrative. In D. Herman (ed.) *Cambridge Companion to Narrative* (pp. 22–35). Cambridge University Press.

Ryassaphore Nun Natalia (Online) (n.d.) Orthodox Christianity. See www.orthochristian.com (accessed March 2024).

Saarinen, J. and Varnajot, A. (2019) The Arctic in tourism: Complementing and contesting perspectives on tourism in the Arctic. *Polar Geography* 42 (2), 109–124.

Safyan, A. (2011) A call for international regulation of the thriving industry of death tourism. *Loyola of Los Angeles International and Comprehensive Law Review* 33, 287–319.

Said, E. (1978) *Orientalism: Western Conceptions of the Orient*. Penguin.

Saldanha, A. (2008) Heterotopia and structuralism. *Environment and Planning A* 40 (9), 2080–2096.

Salem, T. (1999) Physician-assisted suicide promoting autonomy or medicalizing suicide? *The Hastings Center Report* 29 (3), 30–36.

Sallay, Á., Mikházi, Z., Tar, I.G. and Takács, K. (2022) Cemeteries as a part of green infrastructure and tourism. *Sustainability* 14 (5), 2918.

Salzborn, S. (2018) Antisemitism in the "Alternative for Germany" party. *German Politics and Society* 36 (3), 74–93.

Samuel, S. (2019) Humans keep directing abuse - even racism - at robots. See https://www.vox.com/future-perfect/2019/8/2/20746236/ai-robot-empathy-ethics-racism-gender-bias (accessed May 2023).

Sanders, D., Laing, J. and Frost, W. (2015) Exploring the role and importance of post-disaster events in rural communities. *Journal of Rural Studies* 41, 82–94.

Santo, D.E. and Hunter, J. (2021) *Mattering the Invisible: Technologies, Bodies, and the Realm of the Spectral*. Berghahn Books.

SARCO (2022) Concept: Where art meets its end. See https://www.exitinternational.net/sarco/concept/ (accessed November 22).

Sardar, Z. (2010) The namesake: Futures; futures studies; futurology; futuristic; foresight—what's in a name? *Futures* 42 (3), 177–184.

Sather-Wagstaff, J. (2011) *Heritage that Hurts: Tourists in the Memoryscapes of September 11*. Left Coast Press.

Saunders, J., Davey, S., Bayerl, P.S. and Lohrmann, P. (2019) Validating virtual reality as an effective training medium in the security domain. *2019 IEEE Conference on Virtual Reality and 3D User Interfaces (VR)* pp. 1908–1911.

Savin-Baden, M. (2019) Postdigital afterlife? *Postdigital Science and Education* 1 (2), 303–306.

Savin-Baden, M. (2022) *AI for Death and Dying*. Taylor and Francis.

S.B.U. (2022) SBU vstanovyla, shcho rosiys'ki komandyry vtorhlysya v Ukrayinu, keruyuchys' kartamy z mynuloho stolittya (The SBU established that Russian commanders invaded Ukraine, guided by maps from the last century). *Security Service of Ukraine*. See https://ssu.gov.ua/novyny/sbu-vstanovyla-shcho-rosiiski-komandyry-vtorhlasia-v-ukrainu-keruiuchys-kartamy-z-mynuloho-stolittia (accessed April 2023).

Schroeder, R. (2008) Defining virtual worlds and virtual environments. *Journal of Virtual Worlds Research* 1 (1).

Schwartz, D.A. (2018) Aztec pregnancy: Archaeological and cultural foundations for motherhood and childbearing in Ancient Mesoamerica. In D. Schwartz (ed.) *Maternal Death and Pregnancy-Related Morbidity Among Indigenous Women of Mexico and Central America. Global Maternal and Child Health* (pp. 11–33). Springer.

Schweye, C. (2011) Europe's suicide tourism. See www.cafebabel.co.uk/article/ 34386/assisted-suicide-tourism (accessed November 22).

Scottish Prisons (2023) Prisons. See https://www.sps.gov.uk/Corporate/Prisons/Prisons.aspx (accessed April 2023).

Seaton, A.V. (1996) Guided by the dark: From thanatopsis to thanatourism. *International Journal of Heritage Studies* 2 (4), 234–244.

Seaton, A.V. (1999) War and thanatourism: Waterloo 1815–1914. *Annals of Tourism Research* 26 (1), 130–158.

Seaton, A.V. (2001) Sources of slavery-destinations of slavery: The silences and disclosures of slavery heritage in the UK and US. *International Journal of Hospitality and Tourism Administration* 2 (3-4), 107–129.

Seaton, A.V. (2002) Thanatourism's final frontiers? Visits to cemeteries, churchyards and funerary sites as sacred and secular pilgrimage. *Tourism Recreation Research* 27 (2), 73–82.

Seaton, T. (A.V) (2009) Purposeful otherness: Approaches to the management of thanatourism. In R. Sharpley and P.R. Stone (eds) *The Darker Side of Travel: The Theory and Practice of Dark Tourism* (pp. 75–108). Channel View Publications.

Seaton, T (A.V) (2018) Encountering engineered and orchestrated remembrance: A situational model of dark tourism and its history. In P.R. Stone *et al.* (eds) *Palgrave Handbook of Dark Tourism Studies* (pp. 9–31). Palgrave.

Seaton, T (A.V) and Dann, G.M.S. (2009) Crime, punishment and dark tourism: The carnivalesque spectacles of the English judicial system. In P.R. Stone, R. Hartmann, T. Seaton, R. Sharpley and L. White (eds) *The Palgrave Handbook of Dark Tourism Studies* (pp. 33–76). Palgrave Macmillan.

Seaton, T (A.V) and Dann, M.S.G (2018) Crime, punishment, and dark tourism: The carnivalesque spectacles of the English judicial system. In P.R. Stone *et al.* (eds) *Palgrave Handbook of Dark Tourism Studies* (pp. 33–76). Palgrave.

Seaton, A.V. and Lennon, J. (2004) Thanatourism in the early 21st century: Moral panics, ulterior motives and alterior desires. In T. Singh (ed.) *New Horizons in Tourism: Strange Experiences and Stranger Practices* (pp. 63–82). CABI Publishing.

Seger, C.A. (1994) Implicit learning. *Psychological Bulletin* 115 (2), 163–196.

Seraphin, H. and Korstanje, M.E. (2021) Dark tourism tribes: Social capital as a variable. In C. Pforr, R. Dowling and M. Volgger (eds) *Consumer Tribes in Tourism: Contemporary Perspectives on Special-Interest Tourism* (pp. 83–99). Springer.

Serbia, R. (n.d.) Račak—Laži i istine. Radio televizija Srbije. See http://www.rts.rs/page/tv/sr/story/22/rts-svet/3767003/racak---lazi-i-istine.html (accessed February 2023).

Seyitoğlu, F. and Costa, C. (2022) A systematic review of scenario planning studies in tourism and hospitality research. *Journal of Policy Research in Tourism Leisure and Events* 1–18.

Shackley, M. (2002) Space, sanctity and service; the English Cathedral as heterotopia. *International Journal of Tourism Research* 4 (5), 345–352.

Sharma, N. (2019) Interpreting the sacred in dark tourism. In D. Olsen and M. Korstanje (eds) *Dark Tourism and Pilgrimage* (pp. 25–37). CABI.

Sharma, N. (2020) Dark tourism and moral disengagement in liminal spaces. *Tourism Geographies* 22 (2), 273–297.

Sharma, N. and Rickly, J. (2019) 'The smell of death and the smell of life': Authenticity, anxiety and perceptions of death at Varanasi's cremation grounds. *Journal of Heritage Tourism* 14 (5–6), 466–477.

Sharma, R. (2021) *If I Had a Time Machine, Chapter 1.* Cited in Lohrmann, D. and Tan, S. *Cyber Mayday and the Day After.* Wiley.

Sharpley, R. (2005) Travels to the edge of darkness; Towards a typology of "dark tourism". In M. Aicken, S. Page and C. Ryan (eds) *Taking Tourism to the Limits: Issues, Concepts and Managerial Perspectives* (pp. 215–226). Elsevier.

Sharpley, R. (2009a) Shedding light on dark tourism. In R. Sharpley and P.R. Stone (eds) *The Darker Side of Travel: The Theory and Practice of Dark Tourism* (pp. 3–22). Channel View Publications.

Sharpley, R. (2009b) Dark tourism and political ideology: Towards a governance model. In R. Sharpley and P.R. Stone (eds) *The Darker Side of Travel: The Theory and Practice of Dark Tourism* (pp. 145–163). Channel View Publications.

Sharpley, R. (2012) Towards an understanding of 'genocide tourism' An analysis of visitors' accounts of their experience of recent genocide sites. In R. Sharpley and P.R. Stone (eds) *Contemporary Tourist Experience: Concepts and Consequences* (pp. 95–109). Routledge.

Sharpley, R. and Stone, P.R. (2009) *The Darker Side of Travel: The Theory and Practice of Dark Tourism. Aspects of Tourism.* Channel View Publications.

Sharpley, R. and Wright, D. (2018) Disasters and disaster tourism: The role of the media. In P.R. Stone, R. Hartmann, T. Seaton, R. Sharpley and L. White (eds) *The Palgrave Handbook of Dark Tourism Studies* (pp. 335–354). Palgrave MacMillan.

Shaw, J.F. (1851) *The Christian Visitor's Handbook to London: Comprising a Guide to All the Objects of Interest in the Metropolis, Together With a List of Churches and Chapels, With the Ministers and Times of Service.* Partridge and Oakey.

Shaw, R., Takeuchi, Y., Ru Gwee, Q. and Shiwaku, K. (2011) Chapter 1 Disaster education: An introduction. In R. Shaw, K. Shiwaku and Y. Takeuchi (eds) *Disaster Education* (pp. 1–22). Emerald Group Publishing.

Shehade, M. and Stylianou-Lambert, T. (2020) Revisiting authenticity in the age of the digital transformation of cultural tourism. In V. Katsoni and T. Spyriadis (eds) *Cultural and Tourism Innovation in the Digital Era* (pp. 3–16). Springer International Publishing.

Sherman, W.R. and Craig, A.B. (2019) *Understanding Virtual Reality: Interface, Application and Design.* Morgan Kaufmann.

Shneier, M. and Bostelman, R. (2015) *Literature review of mobile robots for manufacturing* (No. NIST IR 8022) (p. NIST IR 8022) National Institute of Standards and Technology.

Shostak, A.B. (2017) *Stealth Altruism: Forbidden Care as Jewish Resistance in the Holocaust*. Routledge.

Shrewsbury Prison Visit (2023) An immersive dark tourism attraction. See https://www.shrewsburyprison.com/ (accessed April 2023).

Shrimpton, W. (2019) White Island's long history of unrest hasn't stopped tourism. *Newshub*. See https://www.newshub.co.nz/home/new-zealand/2019/12/white-island-s-long-history-of-unrest-hasn-t-stopped-tourism.html (accessed April 2022).

Sideris, L.H. (2020) Grave reminders: Grief and vulnerability in the Anthropocene. *Religions* 11 (6), 293.

Siegenthaler, P. (2002) Hiroshima and Nagasaki in Japanese guidebooks. *Annals of Tourism Research* 29 (4), 1111–1137.

Sierp, A. (2016) Drawing lessons from the past: Mapping change in Central and South-Eastern Europe. *East European Politics and Societies* 30 (01), 3–9.

Sierp, A. and Wüstenberg, J. (2015) Linking the local and the transnational: Rethinking memory politics in Europe. *Journal of Contemporary European Studies* 23 (3), 321–329.

Silvester, J. (2019) Insight: Unlikely survivor flies from ashes. *The Age*, 2 February 2019, p. 34.

Simon, M. (2017) HardWIRED: So, what is a robot really? See https://www.wired.com/video/watch/hardwired-so-what-is-a-robot-really (accessed May 2023).

Simons, I. (2020) Changing identities through collective performance at events: The case of the Redhead Days. *Leisure Studies* 39 (4), 568–584.

Sivakumaran, S. (2007) Sexual violence against men in armed conflict. *European Journal of International Law* 18 (2), 253–276.

Skår, M. and Nordh, H. and Swensen, G. (2018) Green urban cemeteries: More than just parks. *Journal of Urbanism: International Research on Placemaking and Urban Sustainability* 11 (3), 362–382.

Skinner, J. (2016) Walking the Falls: Dark tourism and the significance of movement on the political tour of West Belfast. *Tourist Studies* 16 (1), 23–39.

Slater, M. (2017) Implicit learning through embodiment in immersive virtual reality. In D. Liu, C. Dede, R. Huang and J. Richards (eds) *Virtual, Augmented, and Mixed Realities in Education: Smart Computing and Intelligence* (pp. 19–33). Springer.

Slater, M. (2018) Immersion and the illusion of presence in virtual reality. *British Journal of Psychology* 109, 431–433.

Smith, J.K. (2021) *Robotic Persons: Our Future with Social Robots*. Westbow Press.

Smith, L. (2006) *Uses of Heritage*. Routledge.

Smith, L. (2021) *Emotional Heritage: Visitor Engagement at Museums and Heritage Sites*. Routledge.

Smith, R. (2019) The struggle to create a new craft of dying—what is medicine's role? *BMJ Opinion*. See https://blogs.bmj.com/bmj/2019/12/18/richard-smith-the-struggle-to-create-a-new-craft-of-dying-what-is-medicines-role/ (accesse March 2023).

Smith, S.F. (2014) Virtual cloning: Transformation or imitation – Reforming the Saderup Court's transformative use test for rights of publicity. *California Legal History* 9, 339–382.

S.M.U. (2022, 29 April) Meta and the metaverse. *Perspectives@SMU*, Institutional Knowledge at Singapore Management University. See https://cmp.smu.edu.sg/article/meta-and-metaverse (accessed November 2022).

Snyder, T. (2015) European mass killing and European commemoration. In V. Tismaneanu and B.C Iacob (eds) *Remembrance, History and Justice. Coming to Terms with Traumatic Pasts in Democratic Societies* (pp. 23–43). Central European University Press.

Snyder, T. (2017) *On Tyranny. Twenty Lessons from the Twentieth Century*. The Bodley Head.

Soetedjo, A., Nurcahyo, E. and Nakhoda, Y.I. (2011) Development of a cost-effective shooting simulator using laser pointer. *Proceedings of the 2011 International Conference on Electrical Engineering and Informatics*, pp. 1–5.

Sofka, C. (2010) History and healing: Museums as healing spaces. *The International Journal of the Inclusive Museum* 2 (4), 79–90.

Soja, E. (1989) *Postmodern Geographies: The Reassertion of Space in Critical Social Theory*. Verso.

Soja, E. (1995) Heterotopologies: A remembrance of other spaces in the Citadel-LA. In S. Watson and K. Gibson (eds) *Postmodern Cities and Spaces* (pp. 13–34). Blackwell.

Soja, E. (1996) *Thirdspace: Journeys to Los Angeles and Other Real-and-Imagined Places*. Blackwell.

Soligo, M. and Dickens, D.R. (2020) Rest in fame: Celebrity tourism in Hollywood cemeteries. *Tourism Culture and Communication* 20 (2), 141–150.

Solomon, B. (2014) Facebook buys Oculus, virtual reality gaming startup, for $2 billion. See https://www.forbes.com/sites/briansolomon/2014/03/25/facebook-buys-oculus-virtual-reality-gaming-startup-for-2-billion (accessed November 2022).

Solomon, S., Greenberg, J. and Pyszczynski, T. (2015) *The Worm at the Core: On the Role of Death in Life*. Penguin Books.

Sorgner, S. and Nietzsche, L. (2009) The overhuman, and transhumanism. *Journal of Evolution and Technology* 20 (1), 29–42.

Sörlin, S. (2009) Narratives and counter-narratives of climate change: North Atlantic glaciology and meteorology, c. 1930–1955. *Journal of Historical Geography* 35 (2), 237–255.

Sörlin, S. (2015) Cryo-history: Narratives of ice and the emerging Arctic humanities. In B. Evengård, J. Nymand Larsen and Ø. Paasche (eds) *The New Arctic* (pp. 327–339). Springer.

Souto, A. (2018) Experiencing memory museums in Berlin. The Otto Weidt Workshop for the Blind Museum and the Jewish Museum Berlin. *Museum and Society* 16 (1), 1–27.

Speakman, M. (2019) Dark tourism consumption in Mexico City: A new perspective of the thanatological experience. *Journal of Tourism Analysis: Revista de Analisis Turistico* 26 (2), 152–168.

Sperling, D. (2020) *Suicide Tourism*. Wiley.

Sperling, D. (2022) Travelling to die: Views, attitudes and end-of-life preferences of Israelis considering receiving aid-in-dying in Switzerland. *Medical Ethics* 23 (1), 1–18.

Spokes, M., Denham, J. and Lehmann, B. (2018) *Death, Memorialisation and Seviant Spaces*. Emerald Publishing.

Staiff, R. (2014) *Re-Imaging Heritage Interpretation: Enhancing the Past Future*. Ashgate Publishing Limited.

Steam (2018) Titanic VR. See https://store.steampowered.com/app/741430/Titanic_VR/ (accessed October 2022).

Steffen, W., Grinevald, J., Crutzen, P. and McNeill, J. (2011) The anthropocene: Conceptual and historical perspectives. *Philosophical Transactions of the Royal Society A* 369, 842–867.

Stephenson, N. (1992) *Snow Crash*. Spectra Publishing.

Stevens, Q., Franck, K.A. and Fazakerley, R. (2012) Counter-monuments: The anti-monumental and the dialogic. *The Journal of Architecture* 17 (6), 951–972.

Stone, P.R. (2005) Dark tourism: An old concept in a new world. *Tourism: The Tourism Society* IV (25), 20.

Stone, P.R. (2006) A dark tourism spectrum: Towards a typology of death and macabre related tourist sites, attractions and exhibitions. *Tourism: An Interdisciplinary International Journal* 52 (2), 145–160.

Stone, P.R. (2009a) Making absent death present: Consuming dark tourism in contemporary society. In R. Sharpley and P.R. Stone (eds) *The Darker Side of Travel: The Theory and Practice of Dark Tourism* (pp. 23–38). Channel View Publications.

Stone, P.R. (2009b) 'It's a bloody guide': Fun, fear and a lighter side of dark tourism at The Dungeon visitor attractions, UK. In R. Sharpley and P.R. Stone (eds) *The Darker Side of Travel: The Theory and Practice of Dark Tourism* (pp. 167–185). Channel View Publications.

Stone, P.R. (2010) Death, dying and dark tourism in contemporary society: A theoretical and empirical analysis. Unpublished PhD thesis, See University of Central Lancashire, Preston, UK.

Stone, P.R. (2011) Dark tourism: Towards a new post-disciplinary research agenda. *International Journal Tourism Anthropology* 14 (34), 318–332.

Stone, P.R. (2012a) Dark tourism and significant other death: Towards a Model of Mortality Mediation. *Annals of Tourism Research* 39 (3),1565–1587.

Stone, P.R. (2012b) Dark tourism as 'mortality capital': The case of Ground Zero and the Significant Other Dead. In R. Sharpley and P.R. Stone (eds) *Contemporary Tourist Experience: Concepts and Consequences* (pp. 71–94). Routledge.

Stone, P.R. (2013a) Dark tourism scholarship: A critical review. *International Journal of Culture, Tourism and Hospitality Research* 7 (3), 307–318.

Stone, P.R. (2013b) Dark tourism, heterotopias and post-apocalyptic places: The case of Chernobyl. In E. Frew and L. White (eds) *Dark Tourism and Place Identity: Managing and Interpreting Dark Places* (pp. 79–93). Routledge.

Stone, P.R. (2013c) Book review: Necromantism – travelling to meet the dead, 1750-1860. *Journal of Heritage Tourism* 8 (2), 1–3.

Stone, P.R. (2018) Dark tourism in an age of 'spectacular death'. In P.R. Stone, R. Hartmann, T. Seaton, R.A. Sharpley and L. White (eds) *The Palgrave Handbook of Dark Tourism Studies* (pp. 189–210). Palgrave Macmillan.

Stone, P.R. (2019) 'Following in the footsteps': Dark tourism as metempsychotic pilgrimage. In D.H. Olsen and M. Korstanje (eds) *Dark Tourism and Pilgrimage.* CABI Religious Tourism and Pilgrimage Series. CABI.

Stone, P.R (2020a) Dark tourism sites will heal us from the trauma of coronavirus. *The Conversation.* See https://theconversation.com/dark-tourism-memorial-sites-will-help-us-heal-from-the-trauma-of-coronavirus-139164 (accessed March 2023).

Stone, P.R. (2020b) Dark tourism and 'spectacular death': Towards a conceptual framework. *Annals of Tourism Research* 83. https://doi.org/10.1016/j.annals.2019.102826 (accessed February 2023).

Stone, P.R and Grebenar, A. (2022) 'Making tragic places': Dark tourism and the commodification of atrocity. *Journal of Tourism and Cultural Change* 20 (4), 457–474.

Stone, P.R. and Morton, C. (2022) Portrayal of the female dead in dark tourism. *Annals of Tourism Research* 97, 1–14.

Stone, P.R. and Sharpley, R. (2008) Consuming dark tourism: A thanatological perspective. *Annals of Tourism Research* 35, 574–595.

Stone, P.R. and Sharpley, R. (2014) Deviance, dark tourism and 'dark leisure': Towards a (re)configuration of morality and the taboo in secular society. In S. Elkington and S. Gammon (eds) *Contemporary Perspectives in Leisure: Meanings, Motives and Lifelong Learning* (pp. 54–64). Routledge.

Stone, P.R. and Stewart, H. (forthcoming) 'Haunted happenings and the urban supernatural': Dark events and placemaking in Salem, USA. *Revenant Journal,* 'Supernatural Cities' Special Issue. http://www.revenantjournal.com/

Stone, R. and Ojika, T. (2000) Virtual heritage: What next? *IEEE Multimedia* 7 (2), 73–74.

Strange, C. and Kempa, M. (2003) Shades of dark tourism: Alcatraz and Robben Island. *Annals of Tourism Research* 30 (2), 386–405.

Strick, K. (2023) Is the AI apocalypse actually coming? What life could look like if robots take over. See https://www.standard.co.uk/insider/ai-apocalypse-life-robots-take-over-elon-musk-chatgpt-b1078423.html (accessed June 2023).

Stroud Town Council (2020) Bisley Road Cemetery, Stroud Local Nature Reserve Management Plan 2020–2024. See https://www.stroudtown.gov.uk/uploads/bisley-road-cemetery-management-plan-final-2020-01-22.pdf?v=1584448045 (accessed November 2022).

Stylianou-Lambert, T., Bounia, A. and Heraclidou, A. (2022) *Emerging Technologies and Museums: Mediating Difficult Heritage*. Berghahn Books.

Sumberg, C. (2004) Brand leadership at stake: Selling France to British tourists. *Translator* 10 (2), 329–353.

Sumiala, J. (2022) *Mediated Death*. Polity Press.

Sweeting, J. (2019) Authenticity: Depicting the past in historical videogames. In M. Punt (ed.) *Transtechnology Research Reader 2018* (pp. 62–83). Transtechnology Research at University of Plymouth.

Taft, I. (2016) Police use of robot to kill Dallas suspect unprecedented, experts say. See https://www.texastribune.org/2016/07/08/use-robot-kill-dallas-suspect-first-experts-say/ (accessed May 2023).

Takahashi, K., Inomo, H., Shiraki, W., Isouchi, C. and Takahashi, M. (2017) Experience-based training in earthquake evacuation for school teachers. *Journal of Disaster Research* 12 (4), 782–791.

Tamborini, R. and Weaver, J. (1996) Frightening entertainment: A historical perspective of fictional horror. In R. Tamborini and J. Weaver (eds) *Horror Films: Current Research on Audience Preferences and Reactions* (pp. 1–13). Routledge.

Tan, G.A. (2019) The convergence of dark tourism and pilgrimage tourism: The case of Phnom Sampeau, Cambodia. In D. Olsen and M. Korstanje (eds) *Dark Tourism and Pilgrimage* (pp. 38–47). CABI.

Tangalakis-Lippert, K. (2022) Amazon bought the company that makes the Roomba … See https://www.businessinsider.com/amazon-roomba-vacuums-most-dangerous-threatening-acquisition-in-company-history-2022-8 (accessed November 2022).

Tanner, J.C. (2017) Hiroshima plans Ar app showing before/after images of atomic bombing. See https://disruptive.asia/hiroshima-augmented-reality-app/ (accessed September 2022).

Tarasheva, E. (2011) The place of Eastern European researchers in international discourse: Critical discourse analysis applied to corpora from specialised journals. *Discourse and Society* 22 (2), 190–208.

Targo (n.d.) Surviving 9/11 - 27 hours under the rubble, See https://www.targostories.com/surviving-911 (accessed March 2022).

Tarlow, P. (2005) Dark tourism: The appealing dark side of tourism and more. In M. Novelli (ed.) *Niche Tourism: Contemporary Issues, Trends and Cases* (pp. 47–58). Elsevier.

Tarlow, S. (2000) Landscapes of memory: The nineteenth century garden cemetery. *European Journal of Archaeology* 3, 217–238.

Tarifa-Fernández, J., Carmona-Moreno, E. and Sánchez-Fernández, R. (2022) An attempt to clarify what deserves to remain dark: A long look back. *Tourism and Hospitality Research* 23 (4), 517–532.

Taste Bologna (no date) Following Fellini: An itinerary in Rimini. See https://www.tastebologna.net/blog/fellini-rimini (accessed November 2022).

Taylor, P. (2020) White Island volcano anniversary: Ardern leads nation in mourning tourists who died. See https://www.theguardian.com/world/2020/dec/09/white-island-volcano-anniversary-ardern-leads-nation-in-mourning-tourists-who-died (accessed October 2022).

Teeger, C. and Vinitzky-Seroussi, V. (2007) Controlling for consensus: Commemorating apartheid in South Africa. *Symbolic Interaction* 30 (1), 57–78.

Terstappen, G.C. and Reggiani, A. (2001) In silico research in drug discovery. *Trends in Pharmacological Sciences* 22 (1), 23–26.

Tervo-Kankare, K., Hall, C.M. and Saarinen, J. (2013) Christmas tourists' perceptions to climate change in Rovaniemi, Finland. *Tourism Geographies* 15 (2), 292–317.

The Dalí (n.d.) 'The Dalí' website. See https://thedali.org (accessed January 2022).

The Environment, Transport and Regional Affairs Committee (2001) Eight Report: Cemeteries, (HC) London: The Stationary Office. See, https://publications.parliament.uk/pa/cm200001/cmselect/cmenvtra/91/9106.htm (accessed May 2023).

The Independent (1999) Serbs rewrite history of Racak massacre. See https://www.independent.co.uk/news/serbs-rewrite-history-of-racak-massacre-1075680.html (accessed June 2023).

The wind won- 360 degrees in Auschwitz. (2022) A virtual-reality tour of the Auschwitz-Birkenau camp. See https://jvr360.co.il/en (accessed September 2022).

Thomas, S.E., Herva, V.P., Seitsonen, O. and Koskinen-Koivisto, E. (2019) Dark heritage. In C. Smith (ed.) *Encyclopedia of Global Archaeology.* https://doi.org/10.1007/978-3-319-51726-1_3197-1.

Thompson, D. (1965) Can a machine be conscious? *The British Journal for the Philosophy of Science* 16 (61), 33–43.

Thompson, N., Allan, J., Caverhill, P., Cox, G., Davies, B., Doka, K., Granek, L., Harris, D., Ho, A., Klass, D., Small, N. and Wittkowski, J. (2016) The case for a sociology of death, dying and bereavement. *Death Studies* 40 (3), 172–181.

Thomson, J. (1726) *Winter A Poem*. Dublin.

Tidy, J. (2022) Billions being spent in metaverse land grab. See https://www.bbc.com/news/technology-63488059 (accessed November 2022).

Tilmans, K., Vree, F.v. and Winter, J.M. (2010) *Performing the Past: Memory, History, and Identity in Modern Europe.* Amsterdam University Press.

Time Magazine. (2018) Japanese students recreated Hiroshima bombing in virtual reality. See https://www.youtube.com/watch?v=RfXULE7UtpA (accessed November 2022).

Time Out (2022) Daiba haunted school. See https://www.timeout.com/tokyo/things-to-do/daiba-haunted-school (accessed July 2022).

Timothy, D.J. (2014) Contemporary cultural heritage and tourism: Development issues and emerging trends. *Public Archaeology* 13 (1–3), 30–47.

Timothy, D.J. and Nyaupane, G.P. (2010) *Cultural Heritage and Tourism in the Developing World: A Regional Perspective.* Routledge.

Toffler, A. (1970) *Future Shock*. Bantam Books.

tom Dieck, M.C. and Jung, T.H. (2017) Value of augmented reality at cultural heritage sites: A stakeholder approach. *Journal of Destination Marketing and Management* 6 (2), 110–117.

Tomlinson, H.M. (1975) Victorian prisons: Administration and architecture, 1835-77. Unpublished PhD thesis, University of London.

Tonnelat, S. (2008) 'Out of frame': The (in)visible life of urban interstice. *Ethnography* 9 (3), 291–324.

Toussaint S. and Decrop, A. (2013) The Père-Lachaise Cemtery: Between dark tourism and heterotopic consumption. In L. White and E. Frew (eds) *Dark Tourism and Place Identity: Managing and Interpreting Dark Places* (pp. 13–27). Routledge.

Tout-Smith, D. (2019) From the heart: Remembering the 2009 Victorian bushfires in museums Victoria collections. See https://collections.museumsvictoria.com.au/articles/16631 (accessed October 2022).

Tower Hamlets Council (2023) Tower Hamlets Cemetery Park and Ackroyd Drive GreenLink Nature Reserve. See https://www.towerhamlets.gov.uk/lgnl/leisure_and_culture/parks_and_open_spaces/cemetery_park.aspx (accessed November 2022).

Towers-Clark, C. (2018) Cyborgs are here and you'd better get used to it. See https://www.forbes.com/sites/charlestowersclark/2018/10/01/cyborgs-are-here-and-youd-better-get-used-to-it/ (accessed May 2023).

Troyer, J. (2019) Introduction. In L. Lofland (ed.)*The Craft of Dying. The Modern Face of Death. 40th Anniversary Edition*. MIT Press.

Truscello, M. (2020) *Infrastructural Brutalism: Art and the Necropolitics of Infrastructure.* MIT Press.
Tsunami AR, Japan. (n.d.) Ishinomaki future support. See http://ishinomakisupport.com/category/memory cat/ (accessed June 2022).
Tuan, Y.F. (1977) *Space and Place: The Perspective of Experience.* University of Minnesota Press.
Tuan, Y.F. (1991) Language and the making of place: A narrative-descriptive approach. *Annals of the Association of American Geographers* 81 (4), 684–696.
Tucci, L. (2022) What is the metaverse? *Tech Target*, 18 Nov. See https://www.techtarget.com/whatis/feature/The-metaverse-explained-Everything-you-need-to-know (accessed January 2023).
Tumarkin, M.M. (2005) *Traumascapes: The Power and Fate of Places Transformed by Tragedy.* Melbourne Univ. Publishing.
Tunbridge, J. and Ashworth, G. (1996) *Dissonant Heritage: The Management of the Past as a Resource in Conflict.* Wiley.
Tunbridge, J. and Ashworth, G. (2017) Is all tourism dark? In G. Hopper and J. Lennon (eds) *Dark Tourism: Practice and Interpretation* (pp. 12–25). Routledge.
Tur, A.R. (2022) The Kosovar school that has become an icon of resistance against Serbia. *Ara in English.* See https://en.ara.cat/culture/the-kosovar-school-that-has-become-an-icon-of-resistance-against-serbia_1_4488145.html (accessed July 2023).
Turner, J.H. (1998) Must sociological theory and practice be so far apart? A polemical answer. *Sociological Perspectives* 41 (2), 243–258.
Turner, J. (2018) *Robot Rules: Regulating Artificial Intelligence.* Palgrave Macmillan.
Turner, V.W. (2020) *Schism and Continuity in an African Society: A Study of Ndembu Village Life.* Routledge.
Tussyadiah, I.P. and Fesenmaier, D.R. (2009) Mediating tourist experiences: Access to places via shared videos. *Annals of Tourism Research* 36 (1), 24–40.
Tzanelli, R. (2016) *Thanatourism and Cinematic Representations of Risk: Screening the End of Tourism.* Routledge.
Unboxed Story Trails (2022) Unboxed story trails. See https://unboxed2022.uk/storytrails (accessed August 2022).
UNDRR (Online) United Nations Office for Disaster Risk Reduction, www.undrr.org (accessed: 26 March 2024).
United Nations (1999) President Milosevic and four other senior fry officials indicted for murder, persecution and deportation in Kosovo. *International Criminal Tribunal for the former Yugoslavia.* See https://www.icty.org/sid/7765 (accessed February 2023).
United Nations (2022) UN remembers 'unprecedented horror and calculated cruelty' of the Holocaust. *UN News.* See https://news.un.org/en/story/2022/01/1110712 (accessed March 2024).
United Nations Office for Disaster Risk Reduction (n.d.) Disaster. See https://www.undrr.org/terminology/disaster (accessed October 2022).
United States Holocaust Memorial Museum (2023) Antisemitism today. See www.ushmm.org/antisemitism/what-is-antisemitism/antisemitism-today (accessed December 2022).
Upton, A., Schänzel, H. and Lück, M. (2018) Reflections of battlefield tourist experiences associated with Vietnam War sites: An analysis of travel blogs. *Journal of Heritage Tourism* 13 (3), 197–210.
Urquhart, D. (2022) Understanding the attraction: Prison tourism and the public gaze. *The British Journal of Criminology* 62 (6), 1359–1379.
Urry, J. (1990) *The Tourist Gaze: Leisure and Travel in Contemporary Societies.* Sage.
Urry, J. (2002) *The Tourist Gaze* (2nd edn). Sage.
Urry, J. (2010) Sociology facing climate change. *Sociological Research Online* 15 (3), 145–147.
Urry, J. (2011) *Climate Change and Society.* Polity.
Urry, J. (2016) *What is the Future?* Polity.

Urry, J. and Larsen, J. (2011) *The Tourist Gaze* (3rd edn). Sage Publishing.
USGS (n.d.) Is there a size criterion for a glacier? See: https://www.usgs.gov/faqs/there-size-criterion-glacier?qt-news_science_products=0 (accessed October 2022).
Uzzell, D.L. and Ballantyne, R. (1998a) Interpreting our heritage: A theoretical interpretation. In D.L. Uzzell and R. Ballantyne (eds) *Contemporary Issues in Heritage and Environmental Interpretation: Problems and Prospects* (pp. 1–11). The Stationery Office.
Uzzell, D. and Ballantyne, R. (1998b) Heritage that hurts: Interpretation in a post-modern world. In D. Uzzell and R. Ballantyne (eds) *Contemporary Issues in Heritage and Environmental Interpretation: Problems and Prospects* (pp. 152–171). The Stationery Office.
Van Gennep, A. (2013) *The Rites of Passage*. Routledge.
van Wynsberghe, A. (2013) Designing robots for care: Care centered value-sensitive design. *Science and Engineering Ethics* 19 (2), 407–433.
Varley, P. (2000) *Japanese Culture*. University of Hawaii Press.
Varnajot, A. and Saarinen, J. (2021) 'After glaciers?' Towards post-Arctic tourism. *Annals of Tourism Research* 91. 103205. https://doi.org/10.1016/j.annals.2021.103205
Varnajot, A. and Saarinen, J. (2022) Emerging post-Arctic tourism in the age of Anthropocene: Case Finnish Lapland. *Scandinavian Journal of Hospitality and Tourism* 22 (4–5), 357–371.
Velleman, D.J. (1992) Against the right to die. *The Journal of Medicine and Philosophy* 17, 665–681.
Vermeulen, T. and van den Akker, R. (2010) Notes on metamodernism. *Journal of Aesthetics and Culture* 2 (1), 1–14.
Verschure, P.F. and Wierenga, S. (2022) Future memory: A digital humanities approach for the preservation and presentation of the history of the Holocaust and Nazi crimes. *Holocaust Studies* 28 (3), 331–357.
Victoria State Government (2022) 2009 Victorian bushfire memorials, regional development Victoria. See https://www.rdv.vic.gov.au/resources/2009-bushfire-memorials (accessed October 2022).
Vina, D.A. (2023) Inside the black mass of Mexican sorcerer Enrique Marthen. *El El País*. See https://english.elpais.com/international/2023-03-06/inside-the-black-mass-of-mexican-sorcerer-enrique-marthen.html (accessed April 2023).
Viol, M., Todd, L., Theodoraki, E. and Anastasiadou, C. (2018) The role of iconic-historic commemorative events in event tourism: Insights from the 20th and 25th anniversaries of the fall of the Berlin Wall. *Tourism Management* 69, 246–262.
Virtual reality Alcatraz escape (2021) Real life experience by nipsapp gaming. *Nipsapp*. See https://nipsapp.com/virtual-reality-alcatraz-escape-multiplayer (accessed October 2022).
Virtual tour – Auschwitz. Auschwitz. (n.d.) Panaroma Auschwitz-Birkenau. See https://panorama.auschwitz.org/tour1,en.html (accessed September 2022).
Virtual tour of Auschwitz (2022) The Holocaust history – A people's and survivor history. See https://remember.org/auschwitz (accessed September 2022).
Virtual visit. Catacombes (n.d.) A virtual visit of the Catacombs of Paris. See https://www.catacombes.paris.fr/en/virtual-visit (accessed October 2022).
Walden, V. (2019) What is 'virtual Holocaust memory'? *Memory Studies* 15, 621–633.
Walden, V.G. (2022a) What is "virtual Holocaust memory"? *Memory Studies* 15 (4), 621–633.
Walden, V.G. (2022b) Understanding Holocaust memory and education in the digital age: Before and after Covid-19. *Holocaust Studies* 28 (3), 257–278.
Walter, T. (1993) Sociologists never die. British sociology and death. In D. Clark (ed.) *Sociology of Death: Theory, Culture, Practice* (pp. 264–295). Blackwell.
Walter, T. (1999) The questions people asked. In T. Walter (ed.) *The Mourning for Diana*. Berg.
Walter, T. (2008) The sociology of death. *Sociology Compass* 2 (1), 317–336.

Walter, T. (2009) Dark tourism: Mediating between the dead and the living. In R. Sharpley and P.R. Stone (eds) *The Darker Side of Travel: The Theory and Practice of Dark Tourism* (pp. 39–55). Channel View Publications.

Walter, T. (2015) New mourners, old mourners: Online memorial culture as a chapter in the history of mourning. *New Review of Hypermedia and Multimedia* 21 (1–2), 10–24.

Walter, T. (2017a) Bodies and ceremonies: Is the UK funeral industry still fit for purpose? *Mortality* 22 (3), 194–208.

Walter, T. (2017b) *What Death Means Now: Thinking Critically About Dying and Grieving.* Policy Press.

Walter, T. (2020) *Death in the Modern World.* Sage Publications.

Walter, T. (2022) 'Heading for extinction': How the climate and ecological emergency reframes mortality. *Mortality.* https://doi.org/10.1080/13576275.2022.2072718.

Wang, E., Shen, C., Zheng, J., Wu, D. and Cao, N. (2021) The antecedents and consequences of awe in dark tourism. *Current Issues in Tourism* 24 (8), 1169–1183.

Wang, W., Chen, S. and Xu, H. (2019) Resident attitudes towards dark tourism, a perspective of place-based identity motives. *Current Issues in Tourism* 22 (13), 1601–1616.

Warner, W.L. (1959) *The Living and the Dead: A Study of the Symbolic Life of Americans.* Yale University Press.

Waters, S. and Russell, W.B. (2012) Monuments all over the world: Using historical monuments to teach cultural geography. *Social Studies Research and Practice* 7 (2), 33–46.

WDW Travels (2022) How safe Are Disney World rides really? See https://wdwtravels.com/disney-world-tips/how-safe-are-disney-world-rides-really/ 1/17 (accessed September 2022).

Weber, M. (1946) Science as a vocation. In A.I. Tauber (ed.) *Science and the Quest for Reality* (pp. 382–394). Palgrave Macmillan.

Weir, R.E. (2012) Bewitched and bewildered: Salem witches, empty factories, and tourist dollars. *Historical Journal of Massachusetts* 40 (1/2), 178–211.

Welch, M. (2015) *Escape to Prison: Penal Tourism and the Pull of Punishment.* University of California Press.

Wells, J.C. and Lixinski, L. (2016) Heritage values and legal rules: Identification and treatment of the historic environment via an adaptive regulatory framework (part 1). *Journal of Cultural Heritage Management and Sustainable Development* 6 (3), 345–364.

Wenzel, J. (2013) Virtual reality applications for the tourism industry: Opportunities for the European tourism industry? In A. Postma, I. Yeoman and J. Oskam (eds) *The Future of European Tourism* (pp. 271–289). Stenden University of Applied Sciences.

West, K. (2000) Memorial awareness board memoranda to the select committee on environment (CEM 57). See https://publications.parliament.uk/pa/cm200001/cmselect/cmenvtra/91/91m63.htm (accessed June 2023).

Westacott, E. (2024) Moral relativism. See https://iep.utm.edu/moral-re/#SH1b (accessed November 22).

Westover, P. (2012) *Necromanticism: Travelling to Meet the Dead, 1750 – 1860.* Palgrave Macmillan.

Westreich, S. (2020) How many dead people are on Facebook? See https://medium.com/swlh/how-many-dead-people-are-on-facebook-aa296fea4676 (accessed August 2022).

Westwood, S. (2000) Rebranding Britain: Sociology, futures and futurology. *Sociology* 34 (1), 185–202.

Where The Road Forks (2023) Dark tourism ethics and criticisms. See https://wheretheroadforks.com/dark-tourism-ethics-and-criticisms/#:~:text=Many%20dark%20tourism%20sites%20see,perfectly%20safe%20form%20of%20tourism (accessed April 2023).

White, L. and Frew, E. (2013) *Dark Tourism and Place Identity: Managing and Interpreting Dark Places.* Routledge.

Whitehead, C., Schofield, T. and Bozoglu, G. (2021) *Plural Heritages and Community Co-production: Designing, Walking and Remembering.* Routledge.

Whiting, J.R.S. (1975) *Prison Reform in Gloucestershire 1776-1820.* Phillimore.

Whiting, J.R.S. (1979) *A House of Correction*. Alan Sutton.

Whyman, J. (1980) A three-week holiday in Ramsgate during July and August 1829. *Archaeologia Cantiana* 96, 185–225.

Wight, A.C. (2006) Philosophical and methodological praxes in dark tourism: Controversy, contention and the evolving paradigm. *Journal of Vacation Marketing* 12 (2), 119–129.

Wight, A.C. (2020) Visitor perceptions of European Holocaust Heritage: A social media analysis. *Tourism Management* 81, 104–142.

Wilford, A. (2015) Celebrity 'Tourists' and the terrible spectacle of re-territorializing trauma in Chechnya's post-urbacide city. *American Society of Theatre Research*, November 5–8, Portland, Oregon. http://eprints.chi.ac.uk/id/eprint/2047/ (accessed July 2021).

Wilford, J. (2008) Out of rubble: Natural disaster and the materiality of the house. *Environment and Planning D: Society and Space* 26 (4), 647–662.

Willard, P., Frew, E. and Lade, C. (2022) Culloden Battlefield: The visitor experience in the context of the experience economy model. *International Journal of Heritage Studies* 28 (2), 252–273.

Williams, A. and Merton, M. (2009) Adolescents' online networking following the death of a peer. *Journal of Adolescent Research* 24 (1), 67–90.

Williams, P. (2011) Memorial museums and the objectification of suffering. In J. Marstine (ed.) *The Routledge Companion to Museum Ethics: Redefining Ethics for the Twenty-First-Century Museum* (pp. 220–235). Routledge.

Williams, P. and Hobson, J.P. (1995) Virtual reality and tourism: Fact or fantasy? *Tourism Management* 16 (6), 423–427.

Wilson, J.Z. (2004) Dark tourism and the celebrity prisoner: Front and back regions in representations of an Australian historical prison. *Journal of Australian Studies* 28 (82), 1–13.

Wilson, J.Z. (2008) *Prison: Cultural Memory and Dark Tourism*. Peter Lang.

Winter, J. (1998) *Sites of Memory, Sites of Mourning: The Great War in European Cultural History*. Cambridge University Press.

Wodak, R. (2010) The discursive construction of history. Brief considerations. *Mots* (94), 57–65.

Wodak, R. and Richardson, J. E. (2009) On the politics of remembering (or not). *Critical Discourse Studies* 6 (4), 231–235.

Wong, D.B. (2023) *Moral Relativism and Pluralism. Elements in Ethics*. Cambridge University Press.

Wood, A. (2022) Summary of Michel Foucault's 'Of other spaces'. *Comm149F: Rhetoric and Public Life,* See https://www.sjsu.edu/faculty/wooda/149F/149-Foucault.html (accessed December 2022).

Wood, M. (2000) *Blind Memory: Visual Representations of Slavery in England and America, 1780-1865*. Routledge.

Woodman, D. and Threadgold, S. (2021) *This is Sociology: A Short Introduction*. Sage.

Woodthorpe, K. (2011) Sustaining the contemporary cemetery: Implementing policy alongside conflicting perspectives and purpose. *Mortality* 16, 259–276.

Woodthorpe, K. (2018) From Prince Charles and his mother down, why Britain finds it hard to talk about death. See https://theconversation.com/from-prince-charles-and-his-mother-down-why-britain-finds-it-hard-to-talk-about-death-107155 (accessed March 2023).

Worpole, K. (1997) *The Cemetery in the City: Report for the Gulbenkian Foundation*. Comedia.

Worpole, K. (2003) *Last Landscapes: The Architecture of the Cemetery in the West*. Reaktion Books.

Wóycicka, Z. (2019) Global patterns, local interpretations: New Polish museums dedicated to the rescue of Jews during the Holocaust. *Holocaust Studies* 25 (3), 248–272.

Wright, D.W.M. (2016) Hunting humans: A future for tourism in 2200. *Futures* 78/79, 34–46.

Wright, D.W.M. (2018) Terror park: A future theme park in 2100. *Futures* 96, 1–22.

Wright, D.W.M. (2020) Immersive dark tourism experiences. In M.H. Jacobsen (ed.) *The Age of Spectacular Death*. Routledge.

Wright, D.W.M. (2021) Immersive dark tourism experiences: Storytelling at dark tourism attractions in 'the immersive death'. In M.H. Jacobsen (ed.) *The Age of Spectacular Death* (pp. 89–109). Routledge.

Wright, D.W.M. and Sharpley, R. (2018) Local community perceptions of disaster tourism: The case of L'Aquila, Italy. *Current Issues in Tourism* 21 (14), 1569–1585.

Wright, D.W.M. and Zascerinska, S. (2023) Becoming immortal: Future wellness and medical tourism markets. *Journal of Tourism Futures* 9 (2), 168–195. https://doi.org/10.1108/JTF-05-2021-0119

Wyatt, B. (2019) Influences on interpretation: A critical evaluation of the influences on the design and management of interpretation at lighter dark visitor attractions. Unpublished PhD thesis, Edinburgh Napier University.

Wyatt, B., Leask, A. and Barron, P. (2021) Designing dark tourism experiences: An exploration of edutainment interpretation at lighter dark visitor attractions. *Journal of Heritage Tourism* 16 (4), 433–449.

Wyatt, B., Leask, A. and Barron, P. (2023) Re-enactment in lighter dark tourism: An exploration of re-enactor tour guides and their perspectives on creating visitor experiences. *Journal of Travel Research* 63 (2), 496–516. https://doi.org/10.1177/00472875221151074.

Yan, L., Xu B., Sun, Z. and Xu, Y. (2019) Street art as alternative attractions: A case of the East Side Gallery. *Tourism Management Perspectives* 29, 76–85.

Yan, B.J., Zhang, J., Zhang, H.L., Lu, S.J. and Guo, Y.R. (2016) Investigating the motivation–experience relationship in a dark tourism space: A case study of the Beichuan earthquake relics. China. *Tourism Management* 53, 108–121.

Yeoman, I. (2008) *Tomorrow's Tourist*. Elsevier.

Yeoman, I. (2012) *2050 – Tomorrow's Tourism*. Channel View Publications.

Yeoman, I. and McMahon-Beattie, U. (2020) *The Future Past of Tourism: Historical Perspectives and Future Evolutions*. Channel View Publications.

Yeoman, I., Postma, A. and Oskam, J. (2013) Introduction. In A. Postma, I. Yeoman and J. Oskam (eds) *The Future of European Tourism* (pp. 24–34). Stenden University of Applied Sciences.

Yes Milano (no date) Monumental cemetery. See https://www.yesmilano.it/en/see-and-do/venues/monumental-cemetery (accessed November 2022).

Yew Jun, G. Flaherty, G.T. and Hallahan, B. (2019) Final journeys: Exploring the realities of suicide tourism. *International Society of Travel Medicine* 1–3.

York Castle Museum Wikipedia (2023) York Castle. See https://en.wikipedia.org/wiki/York_Castle_Museum (accessed April 2023).

Yoshida, K., Bui, H.T. and Lee, T.J. (2016) Does tourism illuminate the darkness of Hiroshima and Nagasaki? *Journal of Destination Marketing and Management* 5 (4), 333–340.

Young, C. and Light, D. (2016) Interrogating spaces of and for the dead as 'alternative spaces': Cemeteries, corpses and site of dark tourism. *International Review of Social Research* 6 (2), 61–72.

Young, J.E. (1989) After the Holocaust: National attitudes to Jews: the texture of memory: Holocaust memorials and meaning. *Holocaust and Genocide Studies* 4 (1), 63–76.

Young, J.E., Hawkins, R., Sharlin, E. and Igarashi, T. (2009) Toward acceptable domestic robots: Applying insights from social psychology. *International Journal of Social Robotics* 1 (1), 95–108.

Yorkshire Sheet 218. (n.d.) 1852 Ordnance Survey map. See https://maps.nls.uk/view/102344959 (accessed April 2023).

Yorkshire Sheet CCXVIII.NW. (n.d) 1894 Ordnance Survey map. See https://maps.nls.uk/view/100947074 (accessed April 2023).

Yu C.E., Wen J., Meng F. (2020a) Defining physician-assisted suicide tourism and travel. *Journal of Hospitality and Tourism Research* 44 (4), 694–703.

Yu, C.E., Wen, J. and Yang, S. (2020b) Viewpoint of suicide travel: An exploratory study on YouTube comments. *Tourism Management Perspectives* 34, 1–8.

Yuen, E.K. (2013) Treatment of social anxiety disorder using online virtual environments in Second Life. *Behaviour Therapy* 44 (1), 51–61.

Yuill, S. (2003) Dark tourism: Understanding visitor motivation at sites of death and disaster. Unpublished MSc thesis, Texas A & M University.

Yung, R. and Khoo-Lattimore, C. (2019) New realities: A systematic literature review on virtual reality and augmented reality in tourism research. *Current Issues in Tourism* 22 (17), 2056–2081.

Zalewska, M. (2017) Selfies from Auschwitz: Rethinking the relationship between spaces of memory and places of commemoration in the digital age. *Studies in Russian, Eurasian and Central European New Media* 18, 95–116.

Zámečník, S. (2003) *That was Dachau: 1933-1945*. Le cherche midi.

Zaritsyk, J. (2007) The Suicide Tourist. CTV and Point Grey Pictures Inc., Public Broadcasting.

Zascerinska, S. (2022) Kicking the bucket or living life to the full? Socio-psychological motivations for compiling a bucket list. Unpublished PhD thesis, University of Central Lancashire.

Zascerinska, S., Sharpley, R. and Wright, D. (2022) Living life or denying death? Towards an understanding of the bucket list. *Tourism Recreation Research*. https://doi.org/10.1080/02508281.2021.2015673.

Zerva, K. (2021) Dark tourism on Netflix: From place to person-dependent. *Tourism Management Perspectives* 38, 100–823.

Zhang Q. (2016) Disaster response and recovery: Aid and social change. *Annals of Anthropological Practice* 40 (1), 86–97.

Ziakas, V. and Getz, D. (2021) Event portfolio management: An emerging transdisciplinary field of theory and praxis. *Tourism Management* 83. https://doi.org/10.1016/j.tourman.2020.104233.

Index

afterlife xix, xx, 1, 9, 27, 44, 45, 48, 49, 121, 208, 292
Albania xxi, xxv, 162–5, 168–72, 174
Aldous Huxley 14
Angkor Wat 92
Anne Frank 79, 81, 83, 87, 245, 260–1
  Secret Annex 79, 81, 87, 261
Antarctic xxi, 285
Antonia Pozzi 203, 206
Apartheid Musuem, South Africa 200
Arctic xv, xxi, 130–7, 285
  Anthropocene xv, xxi, 130–3, 137, 284
Argentina xii, 144
Arnaldo Pomodoro 202, 208
Arnos Vale Cemetery, Bristol, UK xiii, 214–15, 217, 220–3
Arthur Conan Doyle 40–1
Atocha Monument 144
atrocity xxi, 59–60, 66, 81, 103, 108, 114, 166, 176, 183
Australia x, xii, 150–2, 154, 160–1, 228, 241, 266, 283

Baltic States xiv, 187, 190
Bangladesh 284
Berlin, Germany 93–4, 119, 199
Bisley Road Cemetery, Stroud, UK 215
bucket list xvi, xx, 38–9, 41, 44–8, 250, 292
  Afterlist xx, 38–9, 44–8, 292
Buenos Aires 144
Bulgaria x, 91–2, 95, 98–9
Buzludzha Memorial House, Bulgaria x, 95, 98–9

Camberwell Old Cemetery, London 213
Canterbury Earthquake National Memorial 152, 154, 157–9
capitalism xii, 100, 200, 277–8
cemeteries xii, xxii, 71,127, 180, 195, 199–223
  art 95, 101, 133, 137, 195, 199, 201–2, 206, 208–10, 256, 287
  artwork 145, 208–9
  burial grounds xxii, 209, 211–13, 215, 218
  'friends of' 214, 216–17, 219–22
  gravesites 163, 199, 201
  graveyards 199–200, 287
  mausoleums 199, 216
  memorial parks 199, 201, 204, 208–9
  Pere-Lachaise 16, 200
  public engagement xiii, 213–14, 216–17, 222
  sculpture 94, 202, 208–9
Centre for Death & Society (CDAS), University of Bath 280
Chernobyl 15–16, 30, 62, 68–9, 71, 75, 92–4, 97
Christchurch, New Zealand 152, 154, 157–8, 161
chronological distance 11, 36, 141, 169
climate change xv, 106, 130–7, 253, 278, 283–5
  Environment xiii, xv, xix, 19–20, 22, 25, 27, 29–30, 32, 37, 54, 63, 74, 79, 82, 84–5, 130,133–5, 177, 191, 193, 206, 212, 253, 262–3, 284
  Environmental xv, xviii–xix, xxi, 16, 70, 96, 135, 137, 215, 280, 283, 285
commemoration xix, xxi, xxiv, 17, 27, 29, 34–5, 106,149, 153–5, 161–3, 167, 169, 171–2, 174–5, 177, 183, 185, 187, 189, 191, 194, 283, 293
commercialism xix, xxiv, 244–6
  business xii–xiii, xv, xxiii, 2, 73, 75, 117–20, 122, 243–4, 265, 276
  commodifica tion xii, xix, xxi, 12, 37, 67, 105, 114–15, 128, 179, 195, 200, 204, 243, 245, 247–8, 294
  corporate 14, 102
  Google 92, 98, 100–1, 104, 114, 172, 260

management ix–x, xii, xv–xvi, xix, xxii, 17, 39, 47, 146, 151, 155, 192, 195, 212, 216–17, 219–22, 226, 267, 269–71, 282
marketing xi, xiii, xv, xxiii, 12, 21, 61–2, 74, 113, 115, 119–22, 128, 151, 210, 233, 238, 240, , 245, 253, 262, 281
Meta 73, 81, 88, 100–1
selling 35, 99, 121
souvenirs 35
Communism 188
community xxi, 17, 35, 71, 74, 142, 145, 147, 149–55, 157–61, 172, 183, 187–8, 191–6, 200, 209, 212, 214–16, 218–19, 222, 237, 243, 246, 280, 288
control xx, 14, 23–6, 30, 54, 56–9, 90, 96, 99–102, 107–8, 116, 120–2, 124, 126–8, 145, 148, 213, 226–7, 236, 261, 281, 292
COVID-19 xiii, 21, 34, 77, 82, 92, 153, 247, 250, 257, 265, 275, 277, 279
culture xi, xiii, 11, 14–15, 18, 22, 26–7, 33, 36, 53, 99, 102, 112, 130, 138, 145, 172, 177, 180–1, 184, 189–90, 192–4, 196, 199–200, 203–4, 206, 209–10, 222–3, 255–6, 265, 273–4, 294
collective memory xxii, 107, 114, 165, 171, 177, 180–86, 192–4, 281
cultural memory 177, 180, 184–5, 187, 190, 196
Necromantic 11
social frameworks 177, 180–2, 184

Dallas, USA 56
Dark Fun Factories 265–6, 275
dark tourism ix–xxv, 11–17, 23–4, 26–7, 30, 33–8, 44, 46–7, 51, 59–62, 66–8, 70–9, 81, 84, 89–90, 100, 103–8, 110–14, 119, 121, 129–44, 146–9, 162–4, 166–8, 170–9, 187–8, 191, 193–4, 196–201, 203, 206, 209–12, 220, 223, 230, 235–6, 243–60, 262–6, 271–2, 276–7, 280–5, 287–8, 290–4
communities xiii, 34, 65, 105, 136, 150, 152, 160–1, 184, 187, 190, 205, 210, 212–13, 215, 261, 279, 288, 293
consumption xviii, xx–xxi, xiii, 11, 13, 15–17, 24, 33, 35–6, 39, 47, 66, 89, 100, 104, 106–7, 140, 143, 155, 163, 168, 179, 197, 243, 255, 266, 290, 293
Dark Tourism Spectrum 105, 138, 141, 143, 146, 201, 223, 230, 244–5, 247–8, 254, 266
darker xxi, xxiii, 67–8, 70–2, 75, 92, 104, 128, 201, 232, 244–5, 247, 249–50, 252–3, 266, 294
deathscape(s) 33, 36–7
disaster xviii, xxi, 15–16, 66–70, 72, 74, 76, 97, 104, 114, 130, 133, 144–55, 160–1, 166, 200, 255, 257, 261, 277, 279, 283, 287–8, 293
economic xiv, xviii, 14, 21, 64, 73, 105, 133, 136, 146, 192, 194, 197–8, 205, 252–3, 274, 284, 294
environment xiii, xv, xix, 19–20, 22, 25, 27, 29–30, 32, 37, 54, 63, 74, 79, 82, 84–5, 130, 133–5, 177, 191, 193, 206, 212, 253, 262–3, 284
landscape(s) xiii, xxi–xxii, 4, 25, 34, 37, 45, 55, 59, 92, 133, 136, 140, 162, 171, 190, 210, 214–15, 217–18, 220–2, 230, 241, 291, 293
lighter xxiii, 111, 201, 232, 243–54, 262, 266
mediated experiences 287
memoryscapes 99, 177, 179
peace 103, 157, 240
placemaking 11–13, 17, 19–20, 22–3
politics xix, 13, 139–41, 143, 147, 186, 188, 280–1, 291
production xi, xviii, 13, 18, 25, 71, 89, 99, 131, 197
shrines xxi, 91, 138–9, 143–8, 153
social xi–xiv, xviii–xxiii, 6, 9, 14–15, 17, 22, 24–7, 31, 33–5, 38–9, 41–4, 46, 51–3, 57, 65–6, 69, 75–6, 78, 82, 91–2, 98–102, 105, 108, 119, 125, 130–1, 135, 137–9, 141–7, 151, 168–70, 177–8, 180–5, 187, 190, 193, 198–9, 201–2, 205, 210, 216, 222, 230–1, 245, 252, 258, 263, 268, 277–81, 283–8, 293
strategies 67, 73–4, 78, 96, 104, 108, 111
technological xi–xii, xviii–xx, xxiv, 10, 12, 14, 19, 22–4, 27, 31, 36, 42, 51, 53–4, 59, 61, 64–7, 75, 77, 87, 90, 94, 97, 107, 172, 194, 250, 252, 256–7, 259, 263–4, 291–4
thanatourism xii, 103–4, 179, 201, 266
Day of the Dead 272, 274
death ix–x, xviii, xx–xxi, xxiii–xxv, 1, 9–11, 16, 23, 27–34, 36–7, 39–48, 57, 60, 62, 66–7, 70–6, 78, 108, 111, 113–16, 118–28, 130, 133, 138–46, 153, 162, 164, 166, 170–1, 179, 185, 191, 195, 199–204, 206–10, 220–1,

221, 232, 241, 243–4, 246, 248, 251, 255, 257, 259, 264–6, 268, 272, 274, 276–7, 279–81, 283–8, 290, 293–4
dead xvii–xx, xxii–xxv, 1, 3–4, 8, 10–12, 15–16, 23–5, 27, 31, 33–4, 36–42, 44–5, 47–9, 61, 73, 127, 138, 140, 150, 164, 201, 208, 212, 220, 223, 244, 256, 263, 272–4, 276, 281, 283–4, 290–4
death anxiety 47, 285
death studies xxiii, 276, 279–81, 285–6, 288
deceased xx, xxii, 1–2, 10, 27, 30–1, 34, 37–42, 44–8, 207, 213, 272, 277, 288, 290, 292
dying ix, xxi, 41, 115, 119–21, 124–8, 143–4, 279–80, 286–7, 293
fatality xviii, 11, 70–1, 138, 140, 142
grief xix, xxi, 27, 29–32, 35, 38, 41–2, 72, 104, 149–50, 153, 155, 159, 161, 217, 277, 283, 285, 287–8
immortality xx, 10, 23, 36, 41, 43–4, 46, 48–9, 58
living xvi, xix–xx, xxii, xxiv–xxv, 1–2, 11, 22, 27, 30–3, 36–7, 39–42, 44–51, 79, 93, 136, 154, 160, 164–5, 193, 205, 212–13, 216, 220, 230, 247, 253, 256, 258, 261, 272, 274, 276, 283, 287, 290–1, 293
mentalities xxiii, 23, 277, 279, 285–6, 293
mortality xviii–xix, xxi, 1, 22–3, 117, 119, 125–8, 138, 164, 201, 220, 223, 249, 279–80, 293
mortality salience xxiii, 276, 283, 285, 288
sequestration of death 126, 285
spectacular death 46–8, 220
thanatoptic 201
transhuman(ism) 50–1, 56, 59
Virtual Afterlife xix, 27–37, 292
decolonisation 283
design xv, 20, 70, 72, 94, 121, 144, 157–8, 239, 244, 249, 287, 294
development(s) ix–xii, xiv–xv, xxii, 34–5, 40–4, 52, 54, 57–8, 64, 82, 92–3, 95–6, 100, 105, 130, 137, 143, 154, 162, 188–92, 194, 196–7, 202, 209, 212, 225, 235–8, 240, 243–4, 248–9, 256, 268, 277, 279, 290–1
Dracula 256, 262–3, 267, 273–4
dystopian futures xxiii, 14, 31, 265

earthquake 72, 152, 154, 157–9, 200
Edinburgh 247
education ix, xi, xiv, xxi, 17, 36–7, 59, 78–9, 82, 85–6, 106, 110, 134, 137, 139, 149–52, 160–1, 172–3, 181, 187, 193–6, 216, 240, 244, 246–50, 280, 282–3, 288
disaster xviii, xxi, 15–16, 66–70, 72, 74, 76, 97, 104, 114, 130, 133, 143–55, 160–1, 166, 200, 255, 257, 261, 277, 279, 283, 287–8, 293
focus group 82, 259–60
history ix–x, xiv–xv, xxi–xxii, xiv, 17–18, 33, 37, 40, 50, 52, 55–7, 60, 62, 66–8, 73, 84–5, 91, 93–5, 99–101, 108, 112, 131, 149, 152, 163, 165–7, 169, 172, 174, 176–7, 180, 188–93, 198–9, 202, 205–6, 208–12, 214–15, 217, 222, 224–6, 229, 232, 234, 238, 246–8, 250–1, 265–7, 271–2, 274, 282
learning x, xxiii, 45, 77–9, 82–3, 85, 88–9, 134, 152, 163, 171, 173–6, 179, 183–4, 186, 193–4, 208, 244, 247, 249, 254, 280, 282, 291
memory x, xiii, xix, xxi–xxii, 10, 16–17, 25, 41, 48, 72, 78–9, 83, 85, 87, 95, 99, 107, 113–14, 149, 162, 165, 168, 171–3, 175–8, 180–96, 281, 287–9
young people xiv, 81, 98, 181
Edward Soja 18
Eiffel Tower 38, 48, 121
emotion 9, 22, 61, 119, 153–4, 292
affect 57, 61, 82, 111, 132, 189, 196–7, 217, 230, 256, 258–9, 292
emotional 12, 20, 25, 28, 32, 66–7, 74–5, 77, 81, 87, 89, 121, 134, 153, 155, 161, 218, 260–3, 268, 287–8, 291
England x, xiv–xv, 8, 212–13, 215, 225–9, 231, 237, 239–40, 249
entertainment 25, 47, 53, 113, 138, 201, 230, 244, 246–50, 255, 257, 265, 267, 271
Erving Goffman 12, 25
ESMA 144–7
ethics xix, 34, 46, 74, 115–18, 122–3, 128, 195, 241
ethical xxi, xxiii, 24, 34, 37, 48, 67, 73–4, 79, 88, 115–18, 122–3, 125, 128, 134, 136, 189, 195, 263, 290–3
moral(s) xviii, 14, 34, 37, 55, 7480, 116–18, 120,122–3, 128, 134, 162–3, 193, 264, 268, 292
moral relativism 117–18

morality xix, 34, 268
situational ethics 115–18, 122–3, 128
ethnography 143, 201, 204
events xiii, xv, xviii, xxi, 17, 25, 29, 31, 33, 35–7, 57, 68, 71, 74–6, 79, 85, 87, 89, 91–2, 97–9, 108, 134, 140, 142–4, 146–7, 149–52, 154–5, 161–3, 165–6, 168–9, 173, 181, 188–90, 192–6, 202–3, 216, 218, 223, 231, 233, 238, 243, 246, 248, 255–8, 266, 271, 275–6, 287–8, 294
execution(s) 4, 9, 72, 232, 292
exhibition xv, 1, 7, 9–10, 25, 36, 82, 85, 88, 152,172, 231,, 246, 282–3, 288
exhibit 96, 165, 241

fear 3, 6–8, 14, 255, 260–3, 268–70, 272
festival(s) 34, 80, 255–9, 262–4, 273–4
Flaybrick Memorial Garden, Liverpool, UK 217
fright ix, xii, xxiii, 255, 265–7, 271, 273–5
funerals 133–4, 137, 142
future xii, xv, xvii–xxv, 1, 5, 7, 10–14, 19–20, 22–7, 30–1, 36–7, 39, 42–52, 54–5, 57–68, 70–8, 80–2, 85, 88–91, 93, 97, 100–5, 108, 113–16, 119–26,128–37, 139, 141, 143–4, 147–9, 151, 153–4, 157, 159, 161–2, 165, 171, 180, 182, 184–7, 189, 191–4, 196–201, 209–12, 214, 216, 219, 223–5, 233, 235–41, 245, 249–57, 259–60, 262–6, 269–71, 274–9, 284–5, 288, 290
futures x, xii–xiii, xv–xix, xxi–xxiii, 2, 11, 27, 132, 136–7, 198, 201, 225, 233, 236, 243, 245, 250–3, 277–9, 282, 284–5
futures thinking xviii, xxiii, 245, 252, 277–9, 284–5
futurology xv, xvii–xviii, xx, xxii–xxiii, 10, 12, 23, 26, 50, 60, 198–9, 209, 251, 277–8, 291
planning xi, xiii, 28, 65–6, 160, 191
scenario(s) xix–xxi, 12, 24–8, 31–2, 39, 48, 172,174, 1912, 250–3, 263

genocide 59–60, 78–9, 99, 167, 176, 178, 192, 266, 281
geopoetics xxi, 130–1, 135–7
George Orwell 14, 24
Germany xi, 92, 94 ,154, 165, 176–7, 189
Ghosts xxiii, 10, 20, 33,41, 273
haunt 10–11, 13, 33, 290, 294
spiritualism 40
Gio Ponti 208
Global South 278, 281–4, 288
Godzilla 271–2, 274
gothic 207, 256, 258, 263, 273–4
Great Britain 225, 238
grief tourism 104
grieving 30–2, 35, 40, 42–3, 133, 150, 276
mourning 35, 42, 48, 130, 132–5, 138, 205, 276
Grim Reaper 1, 10, 23, 290, 293
Ground Zero 16–17, 79, 144–7
9/11 16, 79, 85, 87–8, 144, 146, 245
New York 16, 27–8, 32, 144, 238, 245

Halloween 265, 271
Henri Lefebvre 13
heritage x–xi, xiii–xv, xviii–xx, xxii, xxiv, xxv, 11–12, 17, 24, 26, 37, 59–60, 62, 67, 74, 77–90, 92, 94–104, 138–40, 146,165, 170–1, 174, 179, 181, 184, 187–97, 199, 201–2, 205–7, 209–10, 213–16, 218, 220, 222–3, 231, 233–4, 236, 238–9, 250, 256, 258, 266, 274, 281–2, 287–8, 290–1, 294
dark heritage xiii, xv, xx, 74, 77–9, 81–3, 85–9, 187–8, 192–7, 220
difficult heritage x–xi,xiv–xv, xviii–xx, xxiv, 11, 17, 62, 78, 81–2, 89–90, 96, 99, 102, 138, 170–1, 179, 190–1, 197, 250, 281, 287, 291–2
dissonant heritage xix, 78, 188, 288
penal heritage xix, xxii, 12, 24, 26, 239
virtual heritage 79, 98, 100
Highgate Cemetery, London 213–15, 217–19
Hiroshima, Japan 68–9, 108, 272
Hollywood 201–4, 208–9
Holocaust xiii–xv, xxii, 35–7, 68, 77–80, 82, 84–5, 88, 99, 112, 150, 176–97, 231, 233, 247, 266, 292
Antisemitism xxii, 178, 186
Auschwitz-Birkenau 16, 62, 68, 244, 247–8, 266, 270, 292
Collective memory xxii, 17, 107, 114, 165, 171, 177, 180–6, 192–4, 281
Dachau Concentration Camp xxii, 35, 177
Illinois Holocaust Museum & Education Centre 36–7
Nazi/Nazi party/Nazism 16, 80, 176–8, 188–91, 193–4, 247–8
Remembrance xiii, xix, xxi–xxii, 17, 48, 59, 106, 109–10, 140, 149, 152, 157, 174–80, 184–6, 188–90, 196, 205, 214, 222, 290–1

Transitional memory xiii, xxii, 176–8, 182–6
US Holocaust Memorial Museum 68, 99, 178
hope ix, 91, 94, 110, 128, 155, 159, 161, 180, 290, 294
Horrible Histories 247, 249
horror 143, 195, 267, 271–3, 292
Hyde Park Cemetery, Doncaster, UK 217
hyperreality x, xix, 1, 10, 20, 291–2

Iceland xi, 129
information xvi, xxi, xxiv, 19, 34–5, 37, 42–3, 56, 62, 64–6, 69, 73–4, 76, 101, 108, 112, 134, 139, 144, 146–7, 149–50, 160, 163–4, 186, 206, 208, 218, 232, 241, 261, 263, 277, 279, 285–8
Information Revolution xxiv, 19, 64
International Council of Museum (ICOM) xiv
Irish Potato Famine (Great Famine) 150
Iron Curtain 187
Italy xiv, xxii, 68–9, 94, 199, 201–2, 206, 209, 246

Japan xxiii, 38, 55
Jim Morrison xvii, 200

Karl Marx 220
KFC 119
Killing Fields, Cambodia 71–2, 233
Kitschification 258
Kosovan War 162–4, 166, 171, 174
Kosovo xxi, 162–75

Las Vegas xiv, 202, 205
Latvia xiii–xv, xx, xxii, 77, 79–80, 88–9, 92, 95, 187–92, 251
legal 30, 55–6, 194, 213, 238
legalisation 117–18, 126, 128
Lewis Henry Younge 14
liminality 105, 142, 223, 264
linguistics xx, 105, 107
interpretation x, xiii, xv, xix–xx, 19, 37, 77–8, 85, 88–9, 105–8, 110–11, 113–14, 143, 173–4, 184, 193–6, 212, 214, 218, 222, 244, 246, 249–50, 253–4, 258, 291–2
language ix, xx, 58, 80, 103–5, 107–8, 111–14, 136–7
Los Angeles 201–2, 204
Lucio Fontana 208

macabre xviii, xxiii–xxiv, 36, 41, 47, 71, 107, 143, 163, 200, 203, 206, 220, 243–4, 248, 257–8, 266–7, 270, 282
Madame Tussauds 266
Madrid 144
management ix–x, xii, xv–xvi, xix, xxii, 17, 39, 47, 146, , 151, 155, 192, 195, 212, 216–17, 219–22, 226, 267, 269–71, 282
masochism xxiii, 265, 270–1
Maurice Halbwachs 180
media ix, xi, xiv, xix, 9, 17, 20, 24–5, 27, 30–1, 33, 36, 38–44, 53, 57, 65, 69–70, 78, 83–6, 89, 91, 103–5, 130, 133–5, 138, 140, 154, 165, 167, 169–70, 178, 183–4, 190, 195, 200, 202–4, 222, 244–5, 248, 251, 258, 263, 270–1, 273, 283, 286, 294
mediating xx, xxii, 39, 78, 90, 163, 176, 223, 276
Memorial Complex Adem Jashari, Prekaz 164–8, 174
memorials ix, 34–5, 42, 60, 85, 143, 146, 149, 151, 153, 155, 159, 161, 171, , 173, 188–90, 216, 287, 291
exhibition(s) xv, 1, 7, 9–10, 25, 36, 82, 85, 88, 152,172, 231, 246, 282–3, 288
memorialisation x, xi, xix–xxii, 12–13, 31, 35, 41, 48, 59, 90, 94, 98, 106, 147, 149–51, 155, 161–2, 175, 191, 195, 279, 290, 292, 294
monument(s) xx, 90–2, 94–5, 98–9, 129, 144, 169, 171, 173, 200, 291
monument maps xx, 90
museum(s) xiv, 16–17, 36–7, 68, 77, 79–81, 86–8, 92–3, 96, 99, 102, 119, 152, 157, 164–5, 172, 178, 191, 195,199–200, , 207, 209, 214, 222, 226, 228–9, 231–4, 239–41, 244, 246–8, 266, 273, 282–3, 287–9
visitor attraction(s) 9, 96, 119, 232, 234, 236, 239–41, 244, 246–7, 252, 266
memory xxii, 107, 114, 165, 171, 177, 180–86, 192–4, 281
Mexico xxiii, 256, 271–4
Michel Foucault 13, 126
dystopia 11, 14, 58
dystopian futures 31
Foucauldian xix, 11–13, 25
heterotopia 11, 14–19, 22–3, 126–8
heterotopology 15, 18, 22
utopia xvii, 11, 13–14, 17, 25, 126
Vertopia/Vertopian xix, 1–2, 4–5, 7, 9–10, 12, 19, 22–6, 291–2

Milan 202, 206–7
millennials xiii, xxii, 176–86
Mother Teresa xxv
motivations xvi, 103, 105–6, 135, 199, 201, 206, 209, 216, 218, 220, 243–4, 250, 254, 276, 287
museology xxi, 78, 149, 238

narrative(s) xxi, 42, 50, 53, 60, 74, 86, 94, 96, 104, 107, 111, 114, 130–7, 139–40, 144–50, 159, 163, 166–8, 170–3, 175, 177–8, 181–2, 184, 186, 188–9, 272, 274, 292, 294
NATO 163, 166–7, 171
necro-politics 281
Netflix 77
New Zealand 152, 154, 160–1

Oculus Quest 82, 260
Oscar Wilde 200, 239
Ottoman Empire 169

pain xviii, xxiii, 6, 51, 59, 72, 75, 122–3, 140, 145–6, 150, 193, 264, 270–1
pandemic 34, 77, 82, 92–3, 153, 247, 257, 265, 275, 277–8, 284
past x, xvii–xxiv, 2, 5, 8, 10, 17,19, 25–6, 37, 39–40, 51, 54, 59–60, 62, 68, 70, 78–9, 83–6, 91–2, 94, 108, 131–2, 140, 148, 157, 162–3, 166, 170–81, 185–7, 189–91, 198, 200, 205, 210, 222, 224, 232–3, 237, 241, 243, 245–6, 249, 253, 266, 268, 271, 276–8, 282, 288, 290, 292–4
penal architecture xxii, 224, 232
  gaol xv, 225–8, 230–5, 238
  HMP (His Majesty's Prisons) 229, 231, 231, 233–42
  historic x, xiii, xxii, 37, 71, 79, 81, 85, 99, 134, 163, 169, 171, 199, 202–3, 205, 210–26, 229, 232–3, 235–42, 272
  prisoners 177–8, 225, 227–30, 232, 240–1, 248
Philip Stone 114, 138, 142
photography 40–1, 61, 101, 183, 258
  photo(s) 38–9, 41–2, 45–6, 93, 160, 231, 250
  post-mortem 36, 40
  selfie 35, 38, 48, 258
  video(s) 34, 38–40, 42–5, 58, 61, 70, 83, 97, 153, 160, 195, 255, 261–2, 271
pilgrimage xxiv, 138, 140, 142–3, 146, 162–4, 166, 168–70, 173, 211, 220, 265
pilgrims 213, 218
Pitt Rivers Museum 92
Pompeii 68–70
postmodern/post-modern xx, 33, 104, 106, 140, 146, 243, 267–8, 278, 294
  meta-modern xx, 105–6, 114
  modernity 77, 106, 200, 284, 288
present x, xvii, xix, xxii, xxv, 5, 8, 11, 14, 20–2, 25–7, 29, 36–7, 39–44, 50, 54–5, 57–8, 62, 72, 74, 78, 88–9, 94, 97, 99, 108, 124, 126–8, 132, 140, 145, 148, 172, 179, 188–9, 191, 198, 209–10, 225, 235, 245, 247, 249, 256, 266–7, 273, 278, 287, 290–1
Primark 119
Pripyat, Ukraine 69, 71, 75, 92–3
prison(s) x, xxii, 5, 17, 68, 200, 224–43, 251, 257–8

Račak Memorial Complex 168
race xx, 6, 55, 101, 106, 184, 281–3
racism 178, 282–3
Ray Bradbury 202
reality xi–xii, xvii, xix–xx, xxiii, 1, 5, 12, 16–17, 20, 22–5, 29–34, 36, 44, 50, 52, 54, 60–3, 65–78, 81–6, 88, 92, 96, 98, 106–7, 127–8, 134, 136, 144, 171–3, 194–5, 208, 241, 244, 247–8, 250, 255–61, 263–4, 266, 268, 275, 286–7, 291–3
re-enactment(s) 244, 246–7, 252–3, 255
regeneration 155, 157, 159, 161
religious x, xiv, xxi, xxiii, 14, 33–4, 36, 100, 118, 142, 145, 162, 164, 168–70, 173, 199, 204, 213, 220, 255–6, 271, 274, 293
remembrance xiii, xix, xxi–xxii, 17, 48, 59, 106, 109–10, 140, 149, 152, 157, 174–80, 184–6, 188–90, 196, 205, 214, 222, 290–1
Renato Briano 206
research ix–xvi, xx, xxiv, 21, 43, 53, 57–8, 60, 62, 73, 77, 81–2, 84, 86–7, 89, 95–6, 103–6, 113–14, 116, 118, 139, 143, 151, 160–1, 167, 169, 177, 180, 182, 186, 190–1, 198, 202, 212, 215–19, 222, 248–9, 254–5, 258–9, 263–4, 271, 274, 278–81, 284, 286–7, 294
  methodology 79–80, 108, 114, 259
Riga Ghetto and Latvian Holocaust Museum 191
Rimini 202, 208
Rio de Janeiro, Brazil 62
risk xii, xxiii, 32, 151, 160–1, 170, 179, 196, 252, 266–71, 274–5

rite of passage xxi, 139, 141–2
Roman Empire xviii
Romania xxiii, 267, 271, 273–4

Sacred xx, xxii, 12, 16, 35, 104, 111, 140–3, 146, 166, 174, 180, 200, 204, 218, 293
Salem, MA, USA 17, 126, 246, 256, 267
  Witch trials 17, 246, 267
Salvador Dali Museum 93
San Francisco, USA 56, 233
Sanctuary of Cromanon 144
Sao Paulo, Brazil 62
science fiction (Sci-Fi) 17, 50, 53, 55–6, 60
Scotland xii, xiv, 45, 239, 247
secular(ised) xix, xxiv, 12, 33, 118, 141–2, 213, 220, 292–3
Serbia 162–74
Serbian Orthodox Church 168–70, 173
shrine xxi, 91, 138–9, 143–8, 153
signage 218–19, 221–2
Sir Thomas More 13
Snow Crash 21, 32
social xi–xiv, xviii–xxiii, 6, 9, 14–15, 17, 22, 24–7, 31, 33–5, 38–9, 41–4, 46, 51–3, 57, 65–6, 69, 75–6, 78, 82, 91–2, 98–102, 105, 108, 119, 125, 130–1, 135, 137–9, 141–7, 151, 168–70, 177–8, 180–5, 187, 190, 193, 198–9, 201–2, 205, 210, 216, 222, 230–1, 245, 252, 258, 263, 268, 277–81, 283–8, 293
social media xix, 9, 24, 27, 31, 38–9, 41–4, 57, 65, 105, 135, 169–70, 178, 202, 222, 245, 258, 263, 286
  Facebook 31, 38–9, 42, 44, 72, 100
  Instagram 41
  Twitter (now X) 41
  YouTube 42, 252
society x, xiii, xx, xxii–xxiv, 5–6, 11–15, 17, 19, 22, 24–5, 27, 33, 36–7, 44, 47–8, 50–7, 60, 90–1, 116–18, 124–8, 138, 141–2, 171–2, 174, 178, 180–1, 183–6, 188–90, 196, 198, 200, 204, 210, 243–4, 246, 253, 257, 265–8, 276–80, 282, 284, 286, 288, 293–4
sociology ix, xiii–xv, 23, 198, 201, 277–8, 280, 284
Soviet Union/USSR 15, 69, 188–9, 190, 196
Spain ix
spiritual 5, 12, 27, 33–4, 36, 41, 76, 105, 153, 162, 170, 204, 216, 218, 223, 255, 293
Stalinism 188
Stella Parson 205
suffering xxiii, xxv, 29, 36, 51, 59–60, 66, 72, 75–6, 79, 89, 117–18, 120, 122, 138, 146, 158, 169, 174, 189–91, 193–4, 201, 203, 231, 241, 243, 265–6, 285
suicide xxi, 115–23, 126–8, 206, 271–2
  Dignitas 115, 117–21, 125, 128
  Euthanasia xxi, 116
  'McDeath' xxi, 115, 117–20, 122, 126, 128, 293
  McDonaldisation xxi, 115–17, 122, 128
  Palliative care xxi, 115, 119
surrealism 20, 24
survivor(s) xxi, 36–7, 40, 69, 71–2, 79–80, 85, 144–6, 149–50, 153–5, 157–9, 161, 165, 185, 190, 196

technology/technologies x–xii, xvi, xix–xx, xxiii, 11, 12, 13, 16, 19–22, 25, 27, 29, 31, 33–4, 39–46, 48–53, 56, 58, 60–80, 83, 85–8, 90, 92–7, 99, 101–2, 116, 121–2, 124–5, 140, 174, 194, 198, 229, 232, 238, 241, 244–5, 248–53, 255–64, 268, 272, 277, 281, 287, 291–2, 294
  3D cameras 92
  androids 54
  Artificial intelligence (AI) xxiv, 27, 42, 50, 61
  augmented Reality (AR) 61–3, 68, 72, 92, 248, 256–7
  avatar 1–4, 7, 9–10, 20–2, 43
  big data xix, 27, 31, 101–2
  bots 43, 53–4
  chatbots 53
  ChatGPT xxiv, 57–8
  computers 43, 45, 52, 54, 58, 160, 226
  cyborgs 50–2, 56, 59–60
  digital x–xi, xix–xxi, xxiv, 1, 5, 10, 12, 21, 23–4, 27, 31, 34, 36, 38–9, 41, 43–9, 53, 60, 63, 74, 77–8, 81, 84, 86–7, 90, 94, 98, 101–2, 162, 171–4, 194, 238, 248, 257–8, 291–2
  hologram 3, 34, 262–3
  humanoid 52, 54
  hybrid 137, 195
  hyperreality x,xix, 1, 10, 20, 291–2
  machine(s) xx, xxiv, 21, 45, 52–6, 58–9, 85, 107, 121, 291–2
  machine learning 45, 291
  metaverse 2, 4, 9, 20–2, 32, 67–8, 73, 76, 99–102
  Microsoft 21, 55, 58, 63
  mixed realities (MR) xx, 44
  non-human 50, 116, 122, 124–5, 135
  photogrammetry 92–3
  QR codes 247, 287

robotic xx, 46, 50–1, 53–5, 60, 291
robots xx, 43, 50–7, 59–60, 291
simulations 54, 72, 96, 101
thanatechnology xx, 48–9
virtual xi, xix–xx, 1, 2, 10–12, 19–37, 44–6, 61–72, 74–5 77–84, 86, 88, 90, 92–102, 134, 171–2, 195, 244, 247–8, 250, 256–64, 285, 291–2
virtual reality (VR) 30, 61–3, 71, 77, 92, 248, 256–7
virtual world xix, 1, 2, 11, 19–23, 26, 33–4, 37, 63, 96–102

Tesco 120
thanatology 139, 276–7, 279–81, 286–8, 293
thanatopsis 138, 140, 201, 276
The Ash Wednesday Bushfire Education Centre & Memorial 152, 160
The London Dungeon 119, 232, 246–7
The Matrix 22
The Six Pillars Framework 245, 250–2
The Troubles 233, 240, 259
time xvii–xviii, xxi, xxiii–xxiv, 1, 5, 8, 10, 15–16, 18, 20–1, 23, 25, 28, 32–6, 38–40, 43, 56, 58, 60, 67, 69–70, 72, 75, 86, 91–9, 104, 113–14, 119, 124, 139, 147, 152–3, 155, 157, 159, 161, 165–8, 174, 177, 185, 196, 214, 229, 245, 250–1, 254, 261–5, 275, 294
Tommy Hilfiger 119
tourism ix–xxv, 1, 11–17, 23–7, 30, 33–8, 44, 46–8, 51, 59–63, 65–8, 70–81, 85, 89–90, 92, 98, 100, 102–21, 126, 128–44, 146–51, 162–80, 187–220, 223–5, 229–31, 235–6, 241–77, 279–88, 290–4
tourist x, xiv, xviii, xx–xxv, 10–12, 15–17, 24–5, 37, 48, 62, 64–6, 70–2, 74–5, 86, 103, 105, 112–13, 115, 131–2, 134, 139, 143, 147–8, 152, 162, 174, 179, 191–2, 194–5, 198, 200, 211, 218, 220, 234–5, 255–7, 263, 266, 268–9, 271, 276, 281–3, 287
AR 61–5, 67–70, 72–5, 92–3, 96, 99, 247–9, 252, 256–7
Behaviour xii, xix, 3, 15, 35, 37, 45, 74, 54, 56–8, 101–2, 177, 180, 183–5, 193, 206, 217, 221–2, 256, 258–9, 274, 278, 284–5, 292
cultural trauma xxi, xxv, 17, 148, 175–6, 290–4
dark tourists 71–2, 75, 214, 220, 282
embodiment 17, 19–20, 22–4, 46, 183, 259–60
emotional 12, 20, 25, 28, 32, 66–7, 74–5, 77, 81, 87, 89, 121, 134, 153, 155, 161, 218, 260–3, 268, 287–8, 291
experience x–xii, xv, xviii, xxiii, 11, 13, 16, 18, 20, 22, 25, 27, 29–31, 33, 36–7, 61–82, 84–6, 88–9, 92–6, 103, 105–8, 111, 114, 121–4, 132–3, 137, 139, 141, 147, 150, 163, 179–82, 184–5, 190–1, 193–4, 208, 218, 223, 231–3, 241, 244, 246–52, 254–65, 268–71, 275, 282–3, 287–9, 291–2, 294
immersive xix–xx, 9, 20, 22–3, 27, 29–31, 35–6, 44, 65, 67, 75, 78, 83–6, 88–9, 92–3, 96–7, 102, 195, 241, 245, 248–50, 257–9, 261, 269, 282, 291–2, 294
MR 61–4, 67–8, 75
performance 12–13, 24, 26, 99, 232, 256, 258–9
thanatourists 214, 220
tourist gaze 11, 112, 179, 200, 282
tragedy xviii, xxiii, xxv, 66, 70–2, 79, 144–5, 149, 152–3, 155, 157, 161, 166, 195, 277, 291, 293
visitor xiii, xv, xviii–xix, xxi–xxiv, 9, 11, 21, 25–6, 37, 61, 65, 75, 77–8, 85, 88, 90, 95–6, 101–2, 119, 138–9, 143, 162, 176–7, 179, 181–2, 184, 193, 201, 212–15, 218, 220, 222–5, 229–30, 22–30, 232, 234, 236, 238–41, 243–9, 251–2, 254–7, 263–7, 283, 287, 290–4
VR xx, 30, 44, 54, 61–4, 67–72, 74–5, 77–89, 92–4, 96–7, 100, 172, 248–50, 252, 256–8, 260–4, 292
tours xi, xviii, 33, 61, 66, 68–70, 92, 98, 121, 144, 146–8, 153, 169, 172–3, 203–4, 206, 208, 210, 213–14, 216, 223, 232–3, 256, 259, 270
Tower Hamlets Cemetery, London 214–17, 219
tragedy xviii, xxiii, xxv, 66, 70–2, 79, 144–5, 149, 152–3, 155, 157, 161, 166, 195, 277, 291, 293
tragedies xviii, 133, 140, 149, 163, 283, 292

UK ix–xi, xiii–xvi, xxii, 25, 40, 55, 58, 92, 118, 125, 211–15, 217–19, 222, 224, 235–8, 241, 247, 257, 277–83, 286

USA ix, xi, xiv, xxii, 17, 36, 56–8, 68–9, 73, 129, 144, 154, 168, 226, 233, 239, 246–7, 250–1, 256, 272, 280–1, 283, 288
UNWTO 199

victim(s) xx, 8, 35, 59–60, 74, 76, 133, 144–5, 147–51, 153–5, 157–61, 163, 166–8, 170–1, 187–9, 191–3
Vietnam Veteran's Memorial, Washington, DC 168
violence xii, xxiv–xxv, 25, 36, 40, 140, 150, 162–3, 169–71, 173–4, 178, 255, 281
visitor attractions 25, 225, 232, 236, 238, 243–5, 247, 249, 266
visitor economies xv, xviii, xxi, xxiii–xxiv, 11, 21, 26, 90, 138, 143, 290, 294

Wales 213, 227–9, 234, 239
war ix, xi–xii, xv, xx, 16, 50, 54–5, 57, 59, 80–1, 91–2, 97, 162–4, 166–7, 171, 173–5, 177, 180, 189, 197, 215, 219, 257, 261, 266, 270, 275, 284, 294
  battle 56, 60, 99, 102, 164, 169, 229, 247, 272
  conflict xi, xix, xxi, 31, 55, 57, 59, 92, 96, 100, 143–5, 147–8, 163, 170–5, 215, 240, 266, 291, 294
  crimes 6, 9, 166–7, 171, 173, 176, 188, 194, 232, 294
  terrorism xii–xiii, 248
  World War II/Second World War/ WWII xv, 16, 80, 86, 173–4, 177, 189, 192, 194, 196, 234, 237, 261, 277
West/Western xii, 33, 47, 105–6, 118, 143, 163, 167, 178, 190, 193, 196, 226, 251, 268, 282–3, 285
Whakaari/White Island 152–4

Yehuda Bauer 176
York Cemetery, UK 214, 217, 220

Žanis Lipke Memorial (ZLM), Lativa xiv, xx, 77, 79–80, 84, 86, 88, 195
Zeppelin Museum 92

Printed in the USA
CPSIA information can be obtained
at www.ICGtesting.com
JSHW010739170824
68284JS00003B/20

9 781845 418977